Critical CALL

Proceedings of the 2015 EUROCALL Conference, Padova, Italy

Edited by Francesca Helm, Linda Bradley,
Marta Guarda, and Sylvie Thouësny

Published by Research-publishing.net, not-for-profit association
Dublin, Ireland; Voillans, France, info@research-publishing.net

© 2015 by Research-publishing.net (collective work)
Each author retains their own copyright

Critical CALL
Proceedings of the 2015 EUROCALL Conference, Padova, Italy
Edited by Francesca Helm, Linda Bradley, Marta Guarda, and Sylvie Thouësny

Rights: All articles in this collection are published under the Attribution-NonCommercial -NoDerivatives 4.0 International (CC BY-NC-ND 4.0) licence. Under this licence, the contents are freely available online (as PDF files) for anybody to read, download, copy, and redistribute provided that the author(s), editorial team, and publisher are properly cited. Commercial use and derivative works are, however, not permitted.

Disclaimer: Research-publishing.net does not take any responsibility for the content of the pages written by the authors of this book. The authors have recognised that the work described was not published before, or that it is not under consideration for publication elsewhere. While the information in this book are believed to be true and accurate on the date of its going to press, neither the editorial team, nor the publisher can accept any legal responsibility for any errors or omissions that may be made. The publisher makes no warranty, expressed or implied, with respect to the material contained herein. While Research-publishing.net is committed to publishing works of integrity, the words are the authors' alone.

Trademark notice: product or corporate names may be trademarks or registered trademarks, and are used only for identification and explanation without intent to infringe.

Copyrighted material: every effort has been made by the editorial team to trace copyright holders and to obtain their permission for the use of copyrighted material in this book. In the event of errors or omissions, please notify the publisher of any corrections that will need to be incorporated in future editions of this book.

Typeset by Research-publishing.net
Cover design by © Giuliano Bocchi
Photos on Cover by © Raphaël Savina (raphael@savina.net)
Fonts used are licensed under a SIL Open Font License

ISBN13: 978-1-908416-28-5 (Paperback - Print on demand, black and white)
Print on demand technology is a high-quality, innovative and ecological printing method; with which the book is never 'out of stock' or 'out of print'.

ISBN13: 978-1-908416-29-2 (Ebook, PDF, colour)
ISBN13: 978-1-908416-30-8 (Ebook, EPUB, colour)

Legal deposit, Ireland: The National Library of Ireland, The Library of Trinity College, The Library of the University of Limerick, The Library of Dublin City University, The Library of NUI Cork, The Library of NUI Maynooth, The Library of University College Dublin, The Library of NUI Galway.

Legal deposit, United Kingdom: The British Library.
British Library Cataloguing-in-Publication Data.
A cataloguing record for this book is available from the British Library.

Legal deposit, France: Bibliothèque Nationale de France - Dépôt légal: décembre 2015.

Table of contents

xiii Critical CALL

xv Conference committees

1 The effect of iPad assisted language learning on developing EFL students' autonomous language learning
Haifa Albadry

9 Social media as an alternative to Moodle in EFL teaching practice forums
Christopher Allen

16 Towards a learner need-oriented second language collocation writing assistant
Margarita Alonso Ramos, Roberto Carlini, Joan Codina-Filbà, Ana Orol, Orsolya Vincze, and Leo Wanner

24 Un test senza stress: un supporto per orientarsi nell'italiano
Marina Artese

30 Vocabulary acquisition in L2: does CALL really help?
Irina Averianova

36 State of the art of language learning design using mobile technology: sample apps and some critical reflection
Elena Bárcena, Timothy Read, Joshua Underwood, Hiroyuki Obari, Diana Cojocnean, Toshiko Koyama, Antonio Pareja-Lora, Cristina Calle, Lourdes Pomposo, Noa Talaván, José Ávila-Cabrera, Ana Ibañez, Anna Vermeulen, María Jordano, Jorge Arús-Hita, Pilar Rodríguez, María Dolores Castrillo, Andras Kétyi, Jaime Selwood, Mark Gaved, and Agnes Kukulska-Hulme

44 The alignment of CMC language learning methodologies with the Bridge21 model of 21C learning
Ciarán Bauer, Ann Devitt, and Brendan Tangney

Table of contents

51 Mobile apps to support and assess foreign language learning
Anke Berns, Manuel Palomo-Duarte, Juan Manuel Dodero, Juan Miguel Ruiz-Ladrón, and Andrea Calderón Márquez

57 Dialogue-based CALL: an overview of existing research
Serge Bibauw, Thomas François, and Piet Desmet

65 Applied linguistics project: student-led computer assisted research in high school EAL / EAP
Róbert Bohát, Beata Rödlingová, and Nina Horáková

71 Corpus of High School Academic Texts (COHAT): data-driven, computer assisted discovery in learning academic English
Róbert Bohát, Beata Rödlingová, and Nina Horáková

77 Using mobile devices and the Adobe Connect web conferencing tool in the assessment of EFL student teacher performance
Maria del Carmen Bolona Lopez, Margarita Elizabeth Ortiz, and Christopher Allen

84 From research to research synthesis in CALL
Alex Boulton

91 Language learning beyond Japanese university classrooms: video interviewing for study abroad
John Brine, Emiko Kaneko, Younghyon Heo, Alexander Vazhenin, and Gordon Bateson

97 Tablets in English class: students' activities surrounding online dictionary work
Leona Bunting

102 Set super-chicken to 3! Student and teacher perceptions of Spaceteam ESL
Walcir Cardoso, Jennica Grimshaw, and David Waddington

108 Evaluating text-to-speech synthesizers
Walcir Cardoso, George Smith, and Cesar Garcia Fuentes

114 Collecting, analysing and using longitudinal learner data for language teaching: the case of LONGDALE-IT
Erik Castello

120	How can we use corpus wordlists for language learning? Interfaces between computer corpora and expert intervention *Yu-Hua Chen and Radovan Bruncak*
125	Corpus-supported academic writing: how can technology help? *Madalina Chitez, Christian Rapp, and Otto Kruse*
133	Exploring collaborative writing in wikis: a genre-based approach *Francesca Coccetta*
138	Activities and reflection for influencing beliefs about learning with smartphones *Robert Cochrane*
144	High school students' use of digital tools for learning English vocabulary in an EFL context *Diana Cojocnean*
150	Design and empirical evaluation of controlled L2 practice through mini-games—moving beyond drill-and-kill? *Frederik Cornillie and Piet Desmet*
158	Training ELF teachers to create a blended learning environment: encouraging CMS adoption and implementation *Travis Cote and Brett Milliner*
164	Il Vivit: vivi l'italiano. Un portale per la diffusione della lingua e cultura italiana nel mondo *Elena Maria Duso e Giovanni Cordoni*
170	What do students learn by playing an online simulation game? *Stephan J. Franciosi and Jeffrey Mehring*
177	Gli apprendenti di italiano L2 all'università e le loro abitudini tecnologiche *Ivana Fratter e Micol Altinier*
181	L'evoluzione del test di piazzamento per i corsi di Italiano L2 al Centro Linguistico dell'Università di Padova: utilità e criticità delle TIC *Ivana Fratter, Luisa Marigo, e Luigi Pescina*

186 Developing and evaluating a multimodal course format: Danish for knowledge workers – labour market-related Danish
Karen-Margrete Frederiksen and Katja Årosin Laursen

192 Tracking student retention in open online language courses
Kolbrún Friðriksdóttir and Birna Arnbjörnsdóttir

198 Implementing verbal and non-verbal activities in an intercultural collaboration project for English education
Kiyomi Fujii and Maki Hirotani

204 Graded lexicons: new resources for educational purposes and much more
Núria Gala, Mokhtar B. Billami, Thomas François, and Delphine Bernhard

210 Podcast-mediated language learning: levels of podcast integration and developing vocabulary knowledge
Mahboubeh Gholami and Mojtaba Mohammadi

215 Toward implementing computer-assisted foreign language assessment in the official Spanish University Entrance Examination
Ana Gimeno Sanz and Ana Sevilla Pavón

221 Open online language courses: the multi-level model of the Spanish N(ottingham)OOC
Cecilia Goria and Manuel Lagares

228 Improving summarizing skills with TED talks: an account of a teaching lesson using explicit instruction
Shin'ichi Hashimoto, Eri Fukuda, and Hironobu Okazaki

235 The integration of a three-year-long intercultural collaborative project into a foreign language classroom for the development of intercultural competence
Maki Hirotani and Kiyomi Fujii

243 Selective teaching of L2 pronunciation
Olaf Husby, Jacques Koreman, Violeta Martínez-Paricio, Jardar E. Abrahamsen, Egil Albertsen, Keivan Hedayatfar, and Øyvind Bech

249 VISP 2.0: methodological considerations for the design and implementation of an audio-description based app to improve oral skills
Ana Ibáñez Moreno and Anna Vermeulen

254 The effects of video SCMC on English proficiency, speaking performance and willingness to communicate
Atsushi Iino and Yukiko Yabuta

261 An EFL flipped learning course design: utilizing students' mobile online devices
Yasushige Ishikawa, Reiko Akahane-Yamada, Craig Smith, Mutsumi Kondo, Yasushi Tsubota, and Masatake Dantsuji

268 Integrating telecollaboration for intercultural language acquisition at secondary education: lessons learned
Kristi Jauregi

274 Cross-cultural discussions in a 3D virtual environment and their affordances for learners' motivation and foreign language discussion skills
Kristi Jauregi, Leena Kuure, Pim Bastian, Dennis Reinhardt, and Tuomo Koivisto

281 Testing an online English course: lessons learned from an analysis of post-course proficiency change scores
Rebecca Y. Jee

288 An investigation of a multimedia language lab project in Turkish state universities
Yasin Karatay

294 Combining online and hybrid teaching environments in German courses
Lucrecia Keim

301 Future language teachers learning to become CALL designers – methodological perspectives in studying complexity
Tiina Keisanen and Leena Kuure

306 Practical evaluation of a mobile language learning tool in higher education
András Kétyi

312	The provision of feedback types to EFL learners in synchronous voice computer mediated communication *Chao-Jung Ko*
318	The word frequency effect on second language vocabulary learning *Cesar Koirala*
324	Experimental analyses of the factors affecting the gradience in sentence difficulty judgments *Cesar Koirala and Rebecca Y. Jee*
330	GenieTutor: a computer assisted second-language learning system based on semantic and grammar correctness evaluations *Oh-Woog Kwon, Kiyoung Lee, Young-Kil Kim, and Yunkeun Lee*
336	EFL students' perceptions of corpus-tools as writing references *Shu-Li Lai*
342	Developing and piloting an app for managing self-directed language learning: an action research approach *Elizabeth Lammons, Yuko Momata, Jo Mynard, Junko Noguchi, and Satoko Watkins*
348	Assessing the impact of computer-based formative evaluations in a course of English as a foreign language for undergraduate kinesiology students in Chile *Santos Lazzeri, Ximena Cabezas, Luis Ojeda, and Francisca Leiva*
355	Automated formative evaluations for reading comprehension in an English as a foreign language course: benefits on performance, user satisfaction, and monitoring of higher education students in Chile *Santos Lazzeri, Ximena Cabezas, Luis Ojeda, and Francisca Leiva*
362	A hybrid approach for correcting grammatical errors *Kiyoung Lee, Oh-Woog Kwon, Young-Kil Kim, and Yunkeun Lee*
368	Mi.L.A: multilingual and multifaceted mobile interactive applications for children with autism *Fernando Loizides, Iosif Kartapanis, Francesca Sella, and Salomi Papadima-Sophocleous*

375	AWE-based corrective feedback on developing EFL learners' writing skill *Zhihong Lu, Xiaowei Li, and Zhenxiao Li*
381	The flip side of flipped language teaching *Paul A. Lyddon*
386	Layers of CALL hegemonies: an Iranian experience *S. Susan Marandi, Khadijeh Karimi Alavijeh, and Fatemeh Nami*
392	Integrating CALL into an Iranian EAP course: constraints and affordances *Parisa Mehran and Mehrasa Alizadeh*
397	Exploring the interaction between learners and tools in e-learning environments *Serpil Meri*
404	One year of extensive reading on mobile devices: engagement and impressions *Brett Milliner and Travis Cote*
410	Errors in automatic speech recognition versus difficulties in second language listening *Maryam Sadat Mirzaei, Kourosh Meshgi, Yuya Akita, and Tatsuya Kawahara*
416	Pedagogical values of mobile-assisted task-based activities to enhance speaking skill *Mojtaba Mohammadi and Nastaran Safdari*
421	Using language corpora to develop a virtual resource center for business English *Thi Phuong Le Ngo*
427	The TATL framework for CALL development *Neasa Ní Chiaráin and Ailbhe Ní Chasaide*
433	Successful EFL teaching using mobile technologies in a flipped classroom *Hiroyuki Obari and Stephen Lambacher*

Table of contents

439   TLC Pack unpacked
Margret Oberhofer and Jozef Colpaert

444   Dynamic lesson planning in EFL reading classes through a new e-learning system
Takeshi Okada and Yasunobu Sakamoto

450   Learning about language learning on a MOOC: how Massive, Open, Online and "Course"?
Marina Orsini-Jones, Laura Pibworth-Dolinski, Mike Cribb, Billy Brick, Zoe Gazeley-Eke, Hannah Leinster, and Elwyn Lloyd

458   Instructors' attitudes towards CALL and MALL in L2 classrooms
James W. Pagel, Stephen Lambacher, and David W. Reedy

464   A critical analysis of learner participation in virtual worlds: how can virtual worlds inform our pedagogy?
Luisa Panichi

470   The FARE software
Adriana Pitarello

475   Learners' perceptions of online elements in a beginners' language blended course – implications for CALL design
Hélène Pulker and Elodie Vialleton

480   A TELL English course to meet the needs of a multilevel BA in ELT group: what was wrong?
María del Carmen Reyes Fierro and Natanael Delgado Alvarado

486   Implementing an online vocabulary training program
Charles E. Robertson

490   La sfida dell'ambiente Web 2.0 nella didattica delle lingue minori
Edit Rózsavölgyi

495   Is mobile-assisted language learning really useful? An examination of recall automatization and learner autonomy
Takeshi Sato, Fumiko Murase, and Tyler Burden

502   Creativity and collaboration: using CALL to facilitate international collaboration for online journalism at a Model United Nations event
Mark D. Sheehan, Todd Thorpe, and Robert Dunn

507   Feedback on feedback – does it work?
Oranna Speicher and Sascha Stollhans

512   A comparative study of the effect of CALL on gifted and non-gifted adolescents' English proficiency
Sophie Tai and Hao-Jan Chen

518   Are teachers test-oriented? A comparative corpus-based analysis of the English entrance exam and junior high school English textbooks
Sophie Tai and Hao-Jan Chen

523   Use of mobile testing system PeLe for developing language skills
Svetlana Titova

529   Mandarin students' perceptions of multimodal interaction in a web conferencing environment: a satisfaction survey
Jun-Jie Tseng

536   Computer-mediated synchronous and asynchronous corrective feedback provided by trainee teachers to learners of French: a preliminary study
Julie Vidal and Sylvie Thouësny

543   Examining and supporting online writing – a qualitative pre-study for an analytic learning environment
Ikumi Waragai, Tatsuy Ohta, Marco Raindl, Shuichi Kurabayashi, Yasushi Kiyoki, and Hideyuki Tokuda

549   CALL and less commonly taught languages: challenges and opportunities
Monica Ward

553   I'm a useful NLP tool – get me out of here
Monica Ward

558   Learners' agency in a Facebook-mediated community
Greg Chung-Hsien Wu and Yu-Chuan Joni Chao

564 Exploring mobile apps for English language teaching and learning
Bin Zou and Jiaying Li

569 The use of monolingual mobile dictionaries in the context of reading by intermediate Cantonese EFL learners in Hong Kong
Di Zou, Haoran Xie, and Fu Lee Wang

575 Author index

Critical CALL

The 22nd EUROCALL conference was held at the University of Padova from the 26th to the 29th of August 2015, the first time that EUROCALL has been held in Italy. The event was organized in collaboration with the University Language Centre and the support of the Department of Political Science, Law and International Studies. Over 300 delegates attended the conference and travelled from over 37 different countries to be with us.

The theme of the conference this year was Critical CALL, drawing inspiration from the work carried out in the broader field of Critical Applied Linguistics. The term 'critical' has many possible interpretations, and as Pennycook (2001)[1] outlines, has many concerns. It was from these that we decided on the conference theme, in particular the notion that we should question the assumptions that lie at the basis of our praxis, ideas that have become 'naturalized' and are not called into question. Another concern of Critical Applied Linguistics is the relationship between the macro and the micro, an engagement with issues of power and inequality and an understanding of how our classrooms and conversations are related to broader social, cultural and political relations.

Over 200 presentations were delivered in 68 different sessions, both in English and Italian, on topics related specifically to the theme and also more general CALL topics. 94 of these were submitted as extended papers and appear in this volume of proceedings.

Our keynote speakers, who came from both within and outside the sphere of CALL, contributed greatly to fostering a greater understanding of how we might conceptualize critical CALL, that is, critical approaches to the practice of and research on technology in foreign language education. A critical approach does not offer solutions, but it entails constant questioning of our assumptions, and this is precisely what our keynotes did.

The Graham Davies keynote speaker, Robert O'Dowd, offered a critical review of telecollaborative exchange in foreign language education. He asked questions about the effectiveness of telecollaboration in contributing to the goals of Foreign

---

1 Pennycook, A. (2001). *Critical applied linguistics: a critical introduction*. New York: Routledge.

Language Education, the adequacy of our practices to meet the needs and challenges of our time, such as social justice and multiethnic dialogue, and the adequacy of the constructs on which we have based our practice.

Sian Bayne took us through some of the trends and trajectories of digital education in the last decade and some of its perceived promises and threats. In particular she looked at plagiarism detection and 'regimes of knowledge', active algorithms and the bias in the aggregation of posts in a MOOC, and finally the notion of automated teaching with Teacherbots. She argued that by shifting from the question of 'what works?' in digital education to 'what do we want digital education to do?', we can keep our educational practice fresh, critical and challenging.

Lynn Mario T. Menezes de Souza called our attention to the situatedness of digital technology, which is not simply transferable and context-independent. He highlighted the need to situate technical innovation within a social and political context as he offered us a critical look at current digital media in education. Most importantly, he reminded us that technology is foundational in 'making humanity human', something we should not lose sight of as we reflect on our roles as teachers in an increasingly inhumane world.

Recordings of these keynote addresses, as well as the full program and session abstracts may be found at the conference website: www.eurocall2015.it.

We thank all of the participants of the EUROCALL 2015 conference, and the contributors to these proceedings which reflect the enormous variety of topics which were addressed at this exciting event and the quality of the presentations. We hope you enjoy reading the proceedings as much as we, the editors, have in the preparation of this volume.

Buona lettura!
Francesca Helm
Conference chair of EUROCALL2015

Conference committees

The 2015 EUROCALL Conference on *Critical CALL* was held at the University of Padova in Italy from the 26th to the 29th August 2015. The event was organized in collaboration with the University Language Centre and the support of the Department of Political Science, Law and International Studies.

Programme committee

Programme chairs
- Peppi Taalas (chair), *University of Jyvaskylä, Finland*
- John Gillespie (co-chair), *University of Ulster, United Kingdom*

Committee members
- Katherine Ackerley, *University of Padova, Italy*
- Christine Appel, *Universitat Oberta de Catalunya, Spain*
- David Barr, *University of Ulster, UK*
- Becky Bergman, *Chalmers University of Technology, Sweden*
- Alex Boulton, *Université 2, Nancy, France*
- Claire Bradin Siskin, *Consultant, United States*
- Thierry Chanier, *Université Blaise Pascal, France*
- Suzanne Cloke, *University of Padova, Italy*
- Jozef Colpaert, *University of Antwerp, Belgium*
- Piet Desmet, *KU Leuven, Belgium*
- Melinda Dooly, *Universitat Autònoma de Barcelona, Spain*
- Ivana Fratter, *University of Padua, Italy*
- Ana Gimeno, *Universidad Politecnica de Valencia, Spain*
- Muriel Grosbois, *Université de Paris 4, France*
- Nicolas Guichon, *Université de Lyon 2, France*
- Regine Hampel, *The Open University, UK*
- Mirjam Hauck, *The Open University, UK*
- Phil Hubbard, *Stanford University, USA*
- Juha Jalkanen, *University of Jyväskylä, Finland*
- Leena Kuure, *University of Oulu, Finland*
- Mike Levy, *The University of Queensland, Australia*
- Luisa Marigo, *Centro Linguistico, Italy*
- Vera Menezes, *Universidade Federal de Minas Gerais, Brazil*

- Liam Murray, *University of Limerick, Ireland*
- Susanna Nocchi, *Dublin Institute of Technology, Ireland*
- Robert O'Dowd, *Universidad de León, Spain*
- Sue K. Otto, *University of Iowa, USA*
- Luisa Panichi, *University of Pisa, Italy*
- Salomi Papadima-Sophocleous, *Cyprus University of Technology, Cyprus*
- Hans Paulussen, *University of Leuven, Belgium*
- Pascual Pérez-Paredes, *Universidad de Murcia, Spain*
- Mathias Schulze, *University of Waterloo, Canada*
- Oranna Speicher, *University of Nottingham, UK*
- Glenn Stockwell, *Waseda University, Japan*
- Maija Tammelin, *Independent Consultant, Finland*
- Sylvie Thouësny, *Research-publishing.net, Ireland*
- Cornelia Tschichold, *Swansea University, UK*

Local organising committee

- Francesca Helm (Chair), *University of Padova, Italy*
- Katherine Ackerley, *University of Padova, Italy*
- Daniela Brioschi, *Sistema Congressi, Padova, Italy*
- Caroline Clark, *University of Padova, Italy*
- Suzanne Cloke, *University of Padova, Italy*
- Fiona Dalziel, *University of Padova, Italy*
- Marta Guarda, *University of Padova, Italy*
- Sarah Guth, *University of Padova, Italy*

EUROCALL Executive committee 2014/2015

President and vice-president
- Françoise Blin, President, *Dublin City University, Ireland*
- Peppi Taalas, Vice-President, *University of Jyväskylä, Finland*

Members, elected and co-opted officers
- Kent Andersen, *Syddansk Erhvervsskole, Denmark*
- Alex Boulton, *University of Lorraine, France*
- Mirjam Hauck, *Open University, UK*
- Francesca Helm, *University of Padova, Italy*
- Sake Jager, *University of Groningen, the Netherlands*
- Salomi Papadima-Sophocleous, *Cyprus University of Technology, Cyprus*
- Oranna Speicher, *University of Nottingham, UK*

Appointed officers
- John Gillespie, Treasurer, *University of Ulster, Coleraine, Northern Ireland*
- Toni Patton, Secretary, *University of Ulster, Coleraine, Northern Ireland*

The effect of iPad assisted language learning on developing EFL students' autonomous language learning

Haifa Albadry[1]

Abstract. This paper will present the experience of using iPads with a group of 21 students in a Saudi university over a period of one semester. The purpose of this ongoing study is to explore how students learn to collaborate and interact in English by participating in a teacher-designed English as a Foreign Language (EFL) course. The course aimed at teaching students to work together by using a wide range of activities supported by the use of iPad devices. Data were gathered through a questionnaire, focus group interviews and learners' diaries. The findings indicate that the use of the iPad when integrated carefully into a language course, and with the teacher's instruction, can have positive effects on students' motivation and learning. There is evidence that this form of learning provides students with opportunities to collaborate with their peers, develop relationships and build bonds. Based on these findings, there seem to be clear benefits of integrating mobile devices into language courses.

Keywords: iPad, mobile assisted language learning, collaboration, motivation, learner autonomy.

1. Introduction

The expansion in mobile computing technology has increased its potential benefits as tools to assist learning, and a new form of learning has consequently developed, based on the concept of learners' mobility. Hulme and Shield (2008) defined Mobile Learning (ML) as "learning mediated via handheld devices and potentially

---

1. Newcastle University, Newcastle upon Tyne, UK; h.f.albadry@newcastle.ac.uk

How to cite this article: Albadry, H. (2015). The effect of iPad assisted language learning on developing EFL students' autonomous language learning. In F. Helm, L. Bradley, M. Guarda, & S. Thouësny (Eds), *Critical CALL – Proceedings of the 2015 EUROCALL Conference, Padova, Italy* (pp. 1-8). Dublin: Research-publishing.net. http://dx.doi.org/10.14705/rpnet.2015.000302

available anytime, anywhere. Such learning may be formal or informal" (p. 273). According to this definition, ML has four essential characteristics, which have to be considered when implementing it in teaching and learning contexts: Firstly, learning is ubiquitous; due to the mobility of these handheld devices, learners have the ability to move physically and virtually between multiple contexts and content (Kinash & Brand, 2012). Secondly, learning is not restricted to face-to face-interaction but rather it can also provide learners with opportunities for asynchronous and synchronous interaction (Hall & Smith, 2011). Thirdly, ML defies the three principles of conventional instruction, namely the fixed time, location and pace, as learning can become a continuous and spontaneous process (Hall & Smith, 2011).

ML differs significantly from the typical use of technology provided by occasional visits to computer labs or the supplement of desktop computers in the classroom, in its portability, durability, affordability and personalised nature. Compared to fixed desktops, mobile devices allow for "face-to-face collaboration" which positively affects students' interaction (Meurant, 2010). In addition, these handheld tools do not require fixed arrangement, which computer labs do, in order to incorporate technology into the classroom. Therefore, the range of activities which usually occur in the English for Foreign Learners' (EFL) classroom can easily be altered i.e. students can work individually, in pairs, groups or as a class (Meurant, 2010). There is therefore a growing interest in investigating the attitudes of learners and teachers towards this form of learning, as well as the learning outcomes and the everyday practicalities of incorporating the use of such technology into a language course.

Recently, many instructors and researchers have joined the experience of ML (Li & Li, 2011). Various studies, as a consequence, have been conducted to assess the effectiveness of ML at enhancing collaboration and interaction (Alvarez, Brown, & Nussbaum, 2011; Bowman & Benson, 2009); student engagement (Dualde, Buendia, & Cano, 2010); fostering self-study and self-regulated learning and improving creativity and critical thinking skills (Cavus & Usunboylu, 2009); and raising students' motivation (Rau, Gao, & Wub, 2008). However, other studies have suggested that the ambitious aims of ML are falling short due to the limitations of the mobile devices being used, i.e. smart phones, iPods, laptops, netbooks and PDAs (Wang & Wang, 2009).

This situation has started to change with the emergence of a recent advance in mobile technology, the iPad, which has the potential to provide easy access to efficient pedagogy (Manuguerra & Petocz, 2011). The iPad has a large multi-touch display screen (7.7 inch) which resembles the size of a textbook. According to Henderson and Yeow (2012), such features maximise students' learning experience as they feel more involved, motivated and engaged. Other unique characteristics include its lightweight, long battery life (about ten hours), built-in microphone and camera, built-in App Store which enables learners to access a wide range of educational applications and a page layout which can be altered from portrait to landscape. In addition, the iPad has a streamlined design with no peripheral attachments, such as cabling, mouse or keyboard; and no distracting buttons having just a virtual on-screen keyboard and a single control button. In fact, the highly usable and simple platform of the iPad reduces the learning curve that typically occurs when using technology (Demski, 2011).The combinations of these features makes such devices stand out amongst previous generations of mobile technology due to their unique design which combines laptop functionality with smartphone portability (Murphy, 2011).

This ongoing study proposes to introduce mobile language learning in a Saudi context where classrooms are dominated by teacher-centred instruction, which has deprived students of opportunities to engage in an active learning. Rather, many learners tend to participate in an educational system that focuses on fulfilling the requirements of the course in an artificial environment. In such an approach, learners expect their teacher to impart knowledge to them, which has reduced them to passive recipients and demotivated learners. Therefore, the rationale of this project stems from the writer's assumption that using an iPad device or any similar technology could enhance EFL learning by offering unlimited opportunities to facilitate and enrich language learning. It also seeks to shift the current conventional teacher-centred classroom to a more dynamic one by involving students in an active and independent approach to learning. However, this is to be achieved not by leaving students to themselves but by guiding and giving them a reason to work as an active agent and to take responsibility of their own learning.

The study was guided by the main research question: Can a teacher-guided EFL course, delivered via the iPad device, enhance learners' autonomous language learning?

2. Methods

2.1. Participants

Participants were a group of 21 female students majoring in Computer Sciences at the College of Community in Qatif, Dammam University, Saudi Arabia. Their ages ranged from 19 to 24 years. Students were classified by the coordinator of the English department and by their teacher as at a beginner level in English, based on their first semester exam. Their educational background in learning English varied from six years to 12 years.

2.2. Data collection

In order to provide a holistic investigation of the issues raised in this study, a mixed methods case study research design was adopted, in which a combination of various data collection instruments were used: a) SILL Questionnaires (Strategy Inventory for Language Learning, adopted from Oxford, 1990) which was administered to the students at three separate time points (prior to the study, after 12 weeks, and six months after the end of the study); b) focus group interviews, twenty-one students were divided into three groups of seven each (the interviews were audiotaped to ensure accurate transcription and were performed in Arabic); and c) students' diaries which were submitted weekly subject to students' agreement. By the end of the course, there were 70 entries ranging from four pages to five lines.

2.3. Data analysis

The data obtained from the questionnaires were analysed statistically through SPSS software (Statistical Package for Social Sciences). In regards to the data obtained from learners' diaries and focus group interviews, an inductive thematic analysis was carried out based on Braun and Clarke's (2006) six-phase approach.

2.4. Materials

The project was self-funded, thus, 21 iPads along with the preloaded applications, the ibooks (electronic version of Q Skills for Success Listening and Speaking Book provided by Oxford University Press), the iTune U course management system that was used in the project to supplement the course materials, and the online tracker software were purchased at the researcher's personal expense.

3. Results and discussion

From the data analysis, the potential of the iPad device and the mobile-assisted language learning approach appear to have enhanced some forms of learner autonomy, such as collaborating with others, motivation, and change of attitude as can be seen in the following sections.

3.1. Collaboration

One of the advantages of the iPad-assisted language learning course was that it facilitates the collaborative learning. By using the different applications such as Voice thread and Ask3, students were able to participate more in group work activities. Such Apps have facilitated 'anytime' or 'non-real-time' communication either among students or with the teacher.

> "There are some programmes on the iPad which have made it possible to connect with my classmates outside of class; especially 'Fuze' programme which I began using in class to complete homework tasks and for speaking practice".

It seems that the new learning environment allowed students to form emotional bonds and build bridges with other members of their class, who they previously did not have the chance to get to know. Such optimal conditions, created by the course (which was carefully designed by the researcher to blend the different applications provided via the iPads with the English syllabus) were especially relevant in a situation where face to face interaction was not typically possible.

> "I like the collaborative task of working in a group because it has helped build my communication with my classmates; some of whom I had limited communication with in class only. But now I can communicate with them".

In addition, some reluctant students reported that seeing others' posted answers motivated them to improve their performance and complete the task. The availability of their peers' assignments worked as a model, on which slow students were able to base their own work. Such peer teaching and learning would not have been possible without the affordances provided by the iPad device and the new learning approach.

3.2. Motivation: results from questionnaires

In the SILL questionnaire, learners were asked how using their iPads could impact their engagement with, attitude to, and motivation toward English language learning inside and outside the classroom. Learners indicated their attitude on a five-point Likert scale. Frequencies and percentiles were calculated for eight items specifically designed to elicit learners' responses in relation to their attitude and motivation toward learning English. In this study, the Friedman test was used to determine if there were any differences in students' responses to the SILL questionnaire relevant to their motivation and attitude toward English learning.

Table 1. Results of Friedman test

N	Chi-Square	df	Asymp. Sig.
21	13.488	2	.001

The application of the Friedman test indicated that there was a significant change ($p=.001$) in the students' response in terms of their attitude and motivation towards English language learning over the three time points (Table 1).

The iPad-assisted language course appeared to be highly motivating for students. Several students reported their attempts to improve their English skills. They were motivated enough to do extra work on their own either by seeking opportunities to practise English language, or by interacting with other language users. Most comments showed that they had found the course to be fun, novel, and challenging.

> "This type of programme has made studying more enjoyable and a person can develop herself just by learning to use it in a way they didn't know before".

The majority of students were fond of the new teaching method to the extent that they hoped it would be extended for a longer period.

> "Overall, the course has been enjoyable and beneficial but it is not enough and I wish it was longer".

In addition, evidence from students' interviews provided additional insights into their experience and behaviour after the integration of the iPad device into the course. Indeed, a broadly positive picture emerged in which a remarkable shift from being passive learners to active learners has been shown. Many students emphasised that the iPad-assisted language learning course offered them something different from what they used to have before. For example, one student expressed her enthusiasm to attend the English class which reflects change in her motivation and behaviour after the course.

> "I started to try more, I love trying to work through with the VoiceThred app. for example, I loved working on the topic and discussing it with my friends… because the iPad made it easier for me to communicate. I mean

...mm I felt that studying became exciting and not boring like before, now I like collaborating and communicating".

Overall, comments from students indicate that the majority of students experienced a shift in their behaviour after the intervention. They started to appreciate the new learning experience, which opens the door for new ways of learning and improving their English.

4. Conclusions

The preliminary results of the study suggest considerable potential for the iPad to facilitate students' collaboration as it enabled peer-to-peer interaction, and as a means to increase students' engagement and motivation to learn the target language. Further analysis of the data is expected to offer new insights into the how iPad technology or similar devices can be incorporated into a course, and to help educational institutions and EFL teachers how such devices can facilitate students' collaborative learning and motivation beyond the classroom. Overall, this study demonstrates the potential of mobile-devices in enriching the EFL experience through enabling opportunities that cannot be found in traditional classroom environments.

References

Alvarez, C., Brown, C., & Nussbaum, M. (2011). Comparative study of netbooks and tablet PCs for fostering face-to-face collaborative learning. *Computers in Human Behaviour*, 27(2), 834-844. doi:10.1016/j.chb.2010.11.008

Bowman, D., & Benson, L. (2009). Effectiveness of shared tablet Pc use on facilitating student interactions. *Proceedings of the 2009 American Society for Engineering Education Annual Conference & Exposition.*

Braun, V., & Clarke, V. (2006) Using thematic analysis in psychology. *Qualitative Research in Psychology, 3,* 77-101.

Cavus, N., & Usunboylu, H. (2009). Improving critical thinking skills in mobile learning. *Procedia - Social and Behavioural Sciences, 1*(1), 434-438. doi:10.1016/j.sbspro.2009.01.078

Demski, J. (2011). ELL to go. *The Journal, 38*(5), 28-32.

Dualde, J., Buendia, F., & Cano, J. (2010). On the design of interactive classroom environments based on the tablet PC technology. *Frontiers in Education Conference (FIE) 2010 IEEE.* Washington. doi:10.1109/FIE.2010.5673355

Hall, O. P., & Smith, D. M. (2011). Assessing the role of mobile learning systems in graduate management education. In K. Reggie, J. Fong, L.-F. Kwok, & J. Lam (Eds.), *Hybrid learning* (pp. 279-288). Heidelberg: Springer Berlin.

Henderson, S., & Yeow, J. (2012). iPad in education: a case study of iPad adoption and use in primary school. *Proceedings the 45th Hawaii International Conference on System Sciences.*

Hulme, A., & Shield, L. (2008). An overview of mobile assisted language learning: from content delivery to supported collaboration and interaction. *ReCALL, 20*(3), 271-289.

Kinash, S., & Brand, J. (2012). Challenging mobile learning discourse through research: student perceptions of Blackboard mobile learn and iPads. *Australian Journal of Educational Technology, 28*(4), 639-655.

Li, Y., & Li, J. (2011). Learning on the move: a case study of mobile learning assisted English reading instruction in Chinese tertiary education. *The 6th International Conference on Computer Science 7 Education*. Singapore: IEEE. doi:10.1109/iccse.2011.6028799

Manuguerra, M., & Petocz, P. (2011). Promoting student engagement by integrating new technology into tertiary education: the role of the iPad. *Asian Social Science, 7*(11), 61-65. doi:10.5539/ass.v7n11p61

Meurant, R. (2010). The iPad and EFL digital literacy. *Communications in Computer and Information Science, 123*, 224-234. doi:10.1007/978-3-642-17641-8_27

Murphy, G. (2011). Post-PC devices: a summary of early iPad technology adoption in tertiary environments. *e-Journal of Business Education & Scholarship of Teaching, 5*(1),18-32.

Oxford, R. (1990). *Language learning strategies: what every teacher should know*. New York: Newbury House.

Rau, P.-L. P., Gao, Q., & Wub, L.-M. (2008). Using mobile communication technology in high school education: motivation, pressure, and learning performance. *Computers and Education, 50*, 1-22. doi:10.1016/j.compedu.2006.03.008

Wang, Y., & Wang, H. (2009). Investigating the determinants and age and gender differences in the acceptance of mobile learning. *British Journal of Educational Technology, 40*(1), 92-118. doi:10.1111/j.1467-8535.2007.00809.x

Social media as an alternative to Moodle in EFL teaching practice forums

Christopher Allen[1]

Abstract. This paper reports on the preferences among a group of pre-service English as a Foreign Language (EFL) teacher trainees for social media rather than *Moodle*, an institutional Virtual Learning Environment (VLE), as a forum for support during a recent five week teaching practice in southern Sweden. The teacher trainees responded to a questionnaire relating to preferences for their own *Facebook* group as opposed to the *Moodle* forum set up specifically by the course tutor for the purpose of sharing observations and discussing lesson planning, aspects of reflective practice and resources while on teaching practice. Their reflections shed interesting light on the importance of student EFL teacher ownership and 'student centricity' in the learning space. These concepts emerge from a consideration of the learning space at the intersection of pedagogical, technological and content knowledge and the nature of forum discussions when faced with the alternative between social media and institutionalized learning platforms under the direction of teacher trainers and course managers.

Keywords: teaching practice, online forums, VLE, social media.

1. Introduction

1.1. General

In recent years, VLEs or Learning Management Systems (LMSs) such as *Moodle*, *It's Learning* and *Blackboard* have become ubiquitous in higher education. However it is not always the case that institutionally-administered learning platforms can satisfy both the pedagogical and administrative demands of students especially in the collaborative era entailed by Web 2.0 (Weller, 2007a). This point is especially

---

1. Linnaeus University, Kalmar, Sweden; christopher.allen@lnu.se

How to cite this article: Allen, C. (2015). Social media as an alternative to Moodle in EFL teaching practice forums. In F. Helm, L. Bradley, M. Guarda, & S. Thouësny (Eds), *Critical CALL – Proceedings of the 2015 EUROCALL Conference, Padova, Italy* (pp. 9-15). Dublin: Research-publishing.net. http://dx.doi.org/10.14705/rpnet.2015.000303

pertinent with regards to vocationally-orientated degree programmes involving periods of professional practice away from the campus environment of the training institution.

A period of teaching practice or practicum is an integral part of EFL teaching training courses all over the world, forming an essential component of international courses in teacher certification such as the *CELTA*, *DELTA* and *TKT* administered by Cambridge ESOL as well as programmes leading to qualified teacher status in the state systems of many countries. This paper looks at the role of social media and VLEs such as *Moodle* in providing support and fostering a sense of community among pre-service teacher trainees.

1.2. VLEs in higher education

Despite their widespread popularity in universities and schools, VLEs have been criticized as being mere embodiments of a traditional, institutionalized pedagogy based on a teacher-centred classroom model (Weller, 2006, 2007b). More recently in the light of social media however, critical voices have been raised about VLEs as purveyors of static, unimaginative content, leaving students to go elsewhere to do their learning (Weller, 2006, 2007a). Another important criticism is that behind the institutionalized walls of the VLE, students cannot easily share learning experiences with outsiders.

The use of VLEs has not of course been restricted to purely academic degree programmes and modules. Vocationally-orientated programmes such as teacher training and nursing have also made increasing use of VLEs such as *Moodle* to provide pre-course tasks, course materials and assignments, videos and information about post-course job opportunities. It is suggested here that VLEs can play an important part in the development of a form of transient 'community of practice' in Lave and Wenger's (1991) terms or learning space while students are away from the host institution engaged in professional training.

1.3. Moodle forums

Although the current generation of VLEs typically incorporate a variety of tools and functions for teacher-student and student-student communication, the main function in focus in this article is the *forum function*. VLE forums provide the opportunity for students to participate in online discussions under the direction of the tutors, to initiate discussions themselves or alternatively to respond to postings from their fellow student teachers.

1.4. Facebook and other social media forums

While many university and teacher training college programmes increasingly rely on institutional VLE forums for the delivery of course content, student teachers are perhaps more likely to regularly access the online forums of social media such as *Facebook* and other virtual communities outside of their formal education. With the massive impact of smartphone and 4G technology permitting 'on the fly' postings via social media apps, this trend in the digital behaviour of many young people has become increasingly well-established.

2. Method

The ten student teachers (seven women, three men) who responded to the questionnaire in this study were aged between 20 and 27 and in their fourth term of studying English language didactics. An integral part of the teacher training programme in English is the use of *Moodle* as a VLE (Figure 1).

Figure 1. Screenshot from the *Moodle* forum set up for the student group for their teaching practice period (in Swedish, *verksamhetsförlagd utbildning* or *VFU*)

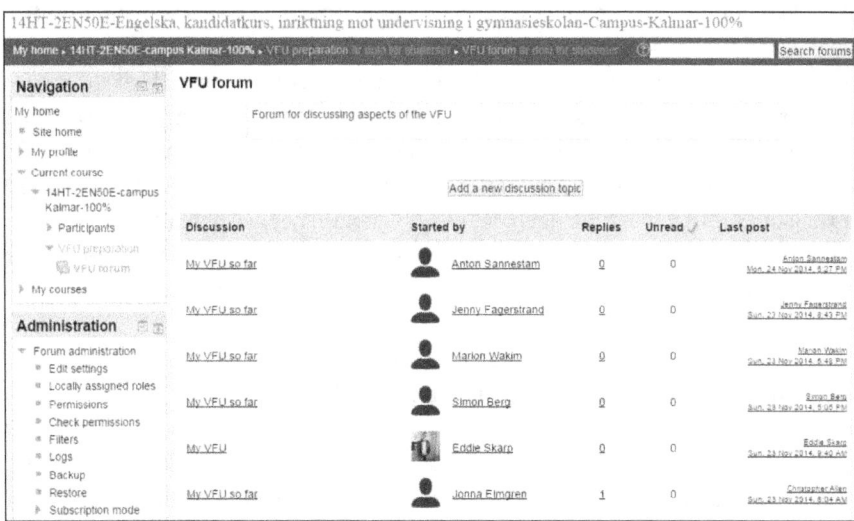

The questionnaire was distributed via the *Moodle* platform and was made up of three parts. *Part A* (3 questions) asked about general ICT skills among the teachers and use of social media and VLEs in their previous studies at upper secondary school level. *Part B* (8 questions) focused more specifically on the importance of internet forums within the teaching practice, while finally *Part C* (8 questions) invited a more detailed comparison between social media (e.g. *Facebook*) and *Moodle* as a forum for reflection and support during the five weeks of teaching practice.

3. Results

3.1. Part A: previous experience of social media and VLEs in educational contexts

All of the respondents rated their knowledge of ICT skills and resources relatively highly, with an average score of 6.7 on the scale of 1 (beginner) and 10 (expert). In Prensky's (2001) terms, respondents were all digital natives, making extensive use of social media with extensive personal learning environments both in private and as part of their studies.

3.2. Part B: online forums for teaching practice support

The results from *Part B* of the survey confirmed the general picture of the importance given to online forums among teacher trainees. These results are summarized in Table 1 below. Ratings of importance were given on the scale of 7 (very important) to 1 (not important); the circle • indicated a mean scoring for each of the forum usage areas. Thus for question (1), the use of forums for exchanging lesson plan tips, the average score among the respondents was 5.9 out of 7. The results indicated the greatest importance attached to exchanging teaching resource tips as well as posing questions to the tutor about language (grammar, lexis, phonology etc) or use of literature in the classroom. Interestingly, forums were seen as less important for reflecting on lesson planning goals and achievement and classroom management.

3.3. Part C: comparison between social media and *Moodle* for teaching practice support

In the final part of the questionnaire, student teachers were asked to compare social media and *Moodle* as a VLE in terms of the usage areas outlined above. The results across these areas of usage confirmed the preference (with one significant exception) for forums within social media such as *Facebook* or *Edmodo* rather than the institutional *Moodle*. These results are shown below in Figure 2. The one significant departure from this overall finding was question 7, the use of the forum for the discussion of administrative problems during the teaching practice period.

Table 1. Average ratings for the importance of usage domains in online forums among student teachers on teaching practice

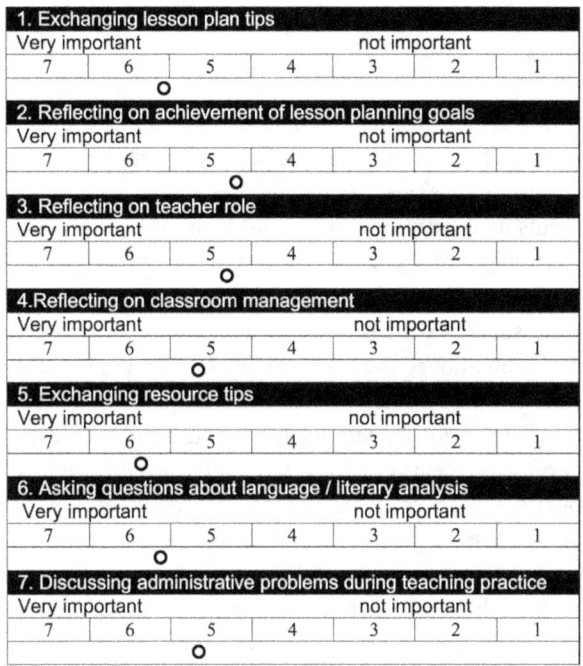

Figure 2. A comparison between social media and *Moodle* as forums for teaching practice

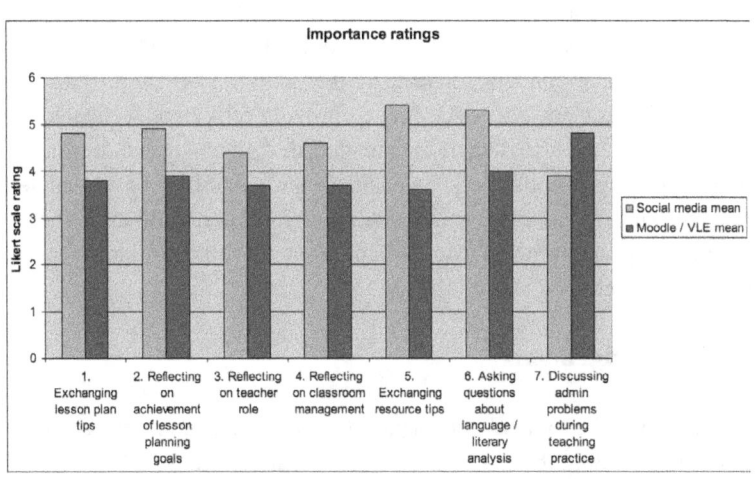

Here there was a clear preference for the use of *Moodle* when bringing up problems such as how many hours should be taught by the teacher, communication with school supervisors, etc.

4. Discussion

A number of factors regarding the preference for social media emerged in the final open question. A significant factor was the presence or absence of the course tutor in the online forum discussions. The closed *Facebook* group was preferred by a number of students as it permitted the 'ventilation' of both positive and negative aspects of the teaching practice and the course in general without the presence of the tutor. In addition, students mentioned familiarity with the *Facebook* interface from their private spheres which they saw as being more user-friendly than the VLE. Students also mentioned the ease with which they could submit and reply to postings via mobile devices, while *Moodle* was frequently seen in terms of more intermittent access via stationary computers.Moodle forums were increasingly seen by the majority of respondents as an institutionally 'owned' platform belonging to their professional development while *Facebook* seamlessly integrates with their 'private' sphere of personal learning environment. *Facebook* in this respect was seen as more 'student-centric'. Nevertheless, some critical voices were raised towards the use of social media as a teaching practice discussion medium; several respondents pointed to the tendency for discussion threads to be 'swamped' by irrelevant postings with little connection to the practice period in school.

5. Conclusions

There is a clear preference for social media rather than an institutional VLE as a forum for the discussion of teaching practice questions with the exception of purely administrative matters relating to the school internship. This state of affairs is problematic for tutors wishing to provide formative feedback over the duration of the practice period. It is intended that future research arising from this conference paper could seek to evaluate the suitability of virtual learning environments such as *Edmodo*, which attempt to incorporate the user-friendliness and integration possibilities of social media in a more institutionally-controlled learning environment.

6. Acknowledgements

The author would like to thank the Department of Language, Linnaeus University for support in attending the EUROCALL 2015 conference.

References

Lave, J., & Wenger, E. (1991). Situated learning: legitimate peripheral participation. New York: Cambridge University Press.

Prensky, M. (2001). Digital natives, digital immigrants part 1. *On the Horizon, 9*(5), 1-6. doi:10.1108/10748120110424816

Weller, M. (2006). VLE 2.0 and future directions in learning environments. In R. Philip, A Voerman, & J. Dalziel (Eds.), *Proceedings of the First International LAMS Conference 2006: Designing the Future of Learning, 6-8 December 2006* (pp. 99-106). Sydney: LAMS Foundation. Retrieved from http://lamsfoundation.org/lams2006/papers.htm

Weller, M. (2007a). *Virtual learning environments: using, choosing and developing your VLE.* Routledge.

Weller, M. (2007b, November 11). The VLE/LMS is dead. *The Ed Techie.* Retrieved from http://nogoodreason.typepad.co.uk/no_good_reason/2007/11/the-vlelms-is-d.html

Towards a learner need-oriented second language collocation writing assistant

Margarita Alonso Ramos[1], Roberto Carlini[2], Joan Codina-Filbà[3], Ana Orol[4], Orsolya Vincze[5], and Leo Wanner[6]

Abstract. The importance of collocations, i.e. idiosyncratic binary word co-occurrences in the context of second language learning has been repeatedly emphasized by scholars working in the field. Some went even so far as to argue that "vocabulary learning is collocation learning" (Hausmann, 1984, p. 395). Empirical studies confirm this argumentation. They show that the "collocation density" in learner corpora is nearly the same as in native corpora, i.e. that the use of collocations by learners is as common as it is by native speakers. At the same time, they also find that the collocation error rate in learner corpora is about 32% (compared to about 3% by native speakers). A CALL-based collocation writing aid could help learners to better master collocations. However, surprisingly little work has been done so far on collocation learning assistants. We propose a collocation writing assistant for American English learners of Spanish which may be used as checker of both isolated collocations and collocations in texts. In addition, it offers the possibility to actively explore and administer collocation resources.

Keywords: second language learning, writing assistant, collocations, miscollocation correction.

---

1. Universidade da Coruña, Spain; lxalonso@udc.es
2. Universitat Pompeu Fabra, Spain; roberto.carlini@upf.edu
3. Universitat Pompeu Fabra, Spain; joan.codina@upf.edu
4. Universidade da Coruña, Spain; ana.orol.gonzalez@udc.es
5. Universidade da Coruña, Spain; ovincze@udc.es
6. ICREA and Universitat Pompeu Fabra, Spain; leo.wanner@upf.edu

How to cite this article: Alonso Ramos, M., Carlini, R., Codina-Filbà, J., Orol, A., Vincze, O., & Wanner, L. (2015). Towards a learner need-oriented second language collocation writing assistant. In F. Helm, L. Bradley, M. Guarda, & S. Thouësny (Eds), *Critical CALL – Proceedings of the 2015 EUROCALL Conference, Padova, Italy* (pp. 16-23). Dublin: Research-publishing.net. http://dx.doi.org/10.14705/rpnet.2015.000304

1. Introduction

The importance of collocations, i.e. idiosyncratic binary word co-occurrences of the type "*hold* [a] *lecture*", "*give* [a] *hint*", "*pass exam*", "*blue skies*", "*overwhelming success*", etc. in the context of second language learning is well known (Granger, 1998; Lewis, 2000; Nesselhauf, 2005). Hausmann (1984) went so far as to argue that "vocabulary learning *IS* collocation learning" (p. 395, our emphasis). Empirical studies confirm this argumentation. According to a study by Orol and Alonso Ramos (2013), the "collocation density" in learner corpora is nearly the same as in native corpora, i.e. the use of collocations by learners is as common as it is by native speakers.

At the same time, the study finds that the collocation error rate in learner corpora is 32% (compared to 3% in native corpora). A CALL-based collocation writing assistant could help learners to better master collocations. However, surprisingly few works address CALL-oriented collocation learning assistants. Most of the existing assistants are limited to the assessment of the correctness of isolated collocations, lists of collocations extracted from a corpus with one of the elements of an assumed miscollocation, and examples of the use of a specific collocation. None of them target the identification and correction of miscollocations in the writings of language learners (as, e.g. spell and grammar checkers do), and none of them follow the active learning paradigm that assigns the learner an active role during learning. We aim to advance the state of the art in this area.

In what follows, we present the HARenES[7] collocation writing assistant, designed to support American English learners of Spanish. The assistant can be used as checker of both isolated collocations and collocations in texts. In addition, it also offers the possibility to actively administer personal collocation resources (e.g. collocation dictionaries, lists of collocations grouped in accordance with specific user criteria, etc).

In Section 2, we first clarify the notion of collocation that underlies the design of the HARenES assistant and then discuss the needs of a learner. Section 3 describes HARenES' functionality at its current state of development. In Section 4, some conclusions are drawn and possible extensions and ameliorations of HARenES are outlined.

---

7. "HARenES" stands for the title of the corresponding research project *Herramienta de ayuda a la redacción en español: procesamiento de colocaciones* 'Support tool for writing in Spanish: Processing of collocations'.

2. What can a learner expect from a collocation-oriented writing assistant?

Given that "collocation" is an ambiguous term in lexicography and computational linguistics, it seems appropriate to offer an exact definition of its use in the given context.

2.1. On the notion of collocation

The term "collocation" as introduced by Firth (1957), and cast into a definition by Halliday (1961), encompasses the statistical distribution of lexical items in context: lexical items that form high probability associations are considered collocations. However, in contemporary lexicography and lexicology, an interpretation that stresses the idiosyncratic nature of collocations prevails. According to Cowie (1994), Hausmann (1984), Mel'čuk (1995) and others, a collocation is a binary idiosyncratic co-occurrence of lexical items between which a direct syntactic dependency holds and where the occurrence of one of the items (the 'base') is subject of free choice by the speaker, while the occurrence of the other item (the 'collocate') is restricted by the base. Thus, in the case of *take [a] walk*, *walk* is the base and *take* is the collocate, in the case of *high speed*, *speed* is the base and *high* the collocate. It is this notion of "collocation" that we find reflected in general collocation dictionaries and that we follow in the design of the HARenES collocation writing assistant.

2.2. Collocations in the context of language learning

As already pointed out above, numerous studies in the context of second language (L2) acquisition demonstrate that collocations in L2 pose a great challenge to any language learner: the fact that they are idiosyncratic implies that, in general[8], they cannot be learned by analogy (as grammatical constructions can be). Native speakers can use their intuition, but learners must learn an overwhelming share of them by heart. Most often, a miscollocation by a learner is a calque from L1 (as, e.g. Sp. **tomar [un] paseo*, lit. 'take [a] walk' instead of *dar [un] paseo* 'give a walk'), an incorrect construction by analogy (as, e.g. **dar [un] camino* (as *dar [un] paseo*), lit. 'give [a] path' instead of *tomar [un] camino* 'take [a] path'), or an

---

8. This does not mean that there are absolutely no regularities between collocations (Mel'cuk & Wanner, 1996); for instance, we "give" a "presentation", as we do in the case of "lecture", "talk", etc.: *give [a] presentation*, *give [a] lecture*, *give [a] talk*, *give [an] outline*, ... However, these regularities are, as a rule, subtle and to a large extent unpredictable.

incorrect construction used to avoid a mistrusted literal translation from L1 (as, e.g. *hacer [una] charla*, lit. 'make a talk', instead of *dar [una] charla*, lit. 'give a talk').

To address these problems, a CALL application should allow the learner to at least:

- verify whether a specific word co-occurrence is a correct collocation in L2 and if it is not, provide alternative suggestions;

- solicit examples of the use of a given collocation in context, i.e. sample sentences in which the collocation occurs;

- explore the collocation space of L2, e.g. which other collocates a given base occurs with and how prominent these collocates are; which other bases share the same collocate(s) as a given base; etc.;

- request the verification / correction of collocations in a given writing;

- administer personal collocation repositories such as collocation dictionaries, created and maintained for better memorization or other purposes.

The HARenES collocation writing assistant attempts to account for these needs.

3. HARenES collocation writing assistant

The on-line HARenES collocation writing assistant has been designed to support second language learners in their needs of the kind sketched above. From the linguistic perspective, these needs can be grouped around isolated collocations, collocations in texts and personalized collocation repositories. In the outline of the webpage of the assistant, the offered functions have been clustered into "collocation checker", "collocation search engine", and "personal collocation dictionary". Figure 1 shows the main page of the HARenES assistant.

In what follows, the three functional modules are presented in separate subsections.

3.1. Treating isolated collocations in HARenES

The basic functionality of the HARenES assistant with respect to isolated collocations concerns the validation of a given word co-occurrence; cf. the corresponding part of the main page in Figure 1. If the co-occurrence is a valid

Figure 1. Main page of the web-based HARenES collocation writing assistant

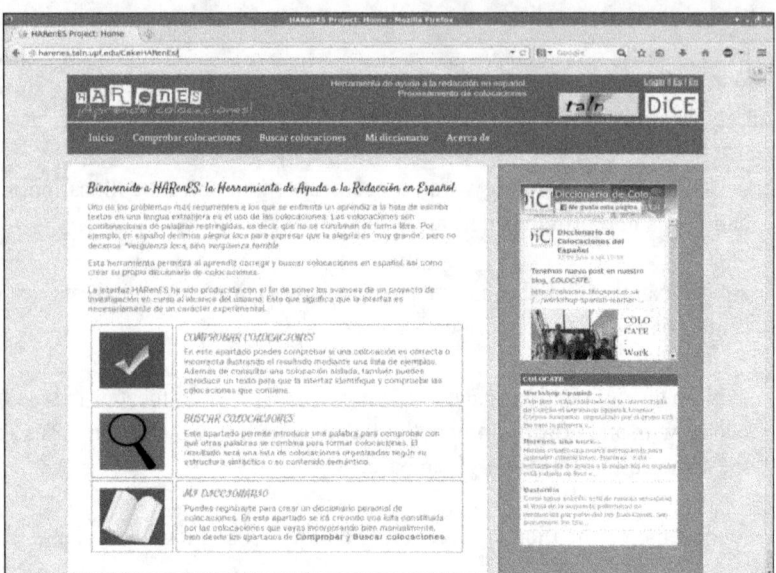

collocation in Spanish, it is flagged in green. If it is considered incorrect, alternative suggestions are proposed; see Carlini, Codina-Filbà, & Wanner (2014) for the collocation validation metrics and the metrics used to select and order alternative suggestions retrieved from a reference corpus. The left snapshot in Figure 2 illustrates this feature. The user may also solicit the illustration of the use of a given collocation in context. To support this feature, HARenES displays some sample sentences (the user decides how many they want to see) in which this collocation occurs from the reference corpus.

Figure 2. Validation of a word co-occurrence and exploration of the collocation space

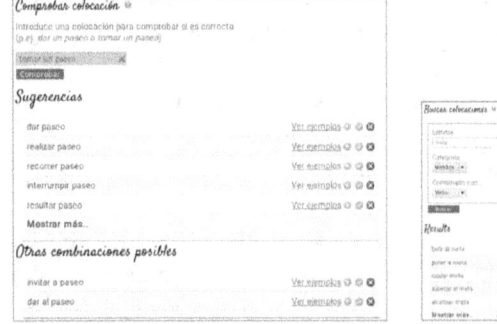
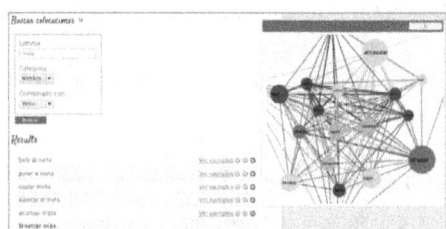

An additional innovative feature of the HARenES writing assistant is that it uses Visual Analytics (VA) techniques to facilitate interactive exploration of the collocation space (Carlini, Codina-Filbà, & Wanner, 2015). Optimal collocation learning is active learning, and active learning is closely related to exploration. For instance, the user may want to explore all collocations of a given base and their intensity of use, contrast the collocation spaces of two different bases, or see the bases of a given collocate lexeme. The right snapshot in Figure 2 shows an example of the use of VA in HARenES.

3.2. Validation of collocations in the writings of learners

An important feature of any advanced learner supporting assistant is that it is able to analyze the learners' writings and correct them with respect to the targeted phenomena. For HARenES, these phenomena are collocations; see Figure 3. The collocation in green (*dar un paseo* 'take a walk') has been detected as correct. Two collocations in red have been detected as erroneous (*recibir sol, lit. 'receive sun' and *entregar comida*, lit. 'deliver food'). When the user passes with the mouse over a miscollocation, one or several correction suggestions are displayed.

Figure 3. Correction of collocations in learner writings

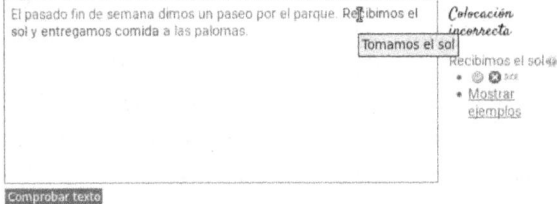

3.3. Maintenance of personal collocation resources

Any learner who actively learns a language compiles lists of collocations that appear especially important, or difficult to them, writes down examples, takes notes, etc. To account for this need, HARenES offers the possibility to actively administer personal collocation resources such as collocation dictionaries (to store collocations, miscollocations and their corrections, examples of collocation use, personal notes on individual (mis)collocations, etc.), lists of collocations grouped in accordance with specific user criteria, etc. Internally, the organization of the database of these personalized collocation repositories is identical to that of the Spanish collocation dictionary DiCE (Alonso Ramos, Nishikawa,

& Vincze, 2010) – which facilitates the import of collocations and example sentences from there. See Figure 4 for an example of a fragment of a personal collocation dictionary.

Figure 4. Maintenance of personal collocation repositories of the learner

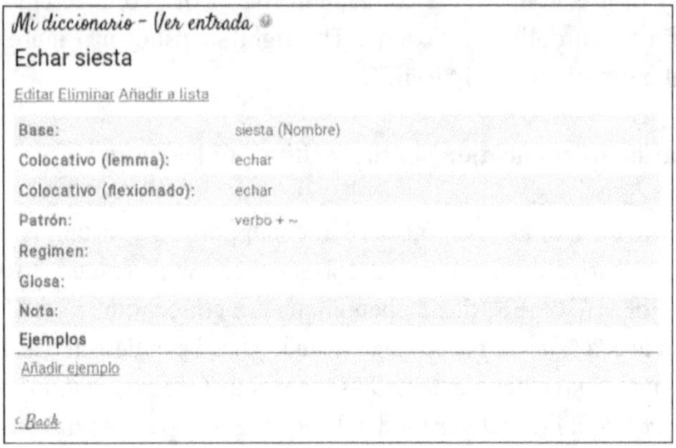

4. Conclusions

We presented the collocation writing assistant HARenES, which supports a language learner by a verification of isolated collocations and collocations in text, provision of correction suggestions for miscollocations, illustration of the use of collocations in context, interactive exploration of collocation spaces and maintenance of personalized collocation repositories.

Some of the features of the current HARenES assistant are about to be further improved. For instance, the ordering of the correction suggestions is still not optimal and the design of the VA module still needs to undergo a revision by a professional interaction designer. Furthermore, the assistant should be further extended by some central features, such as grouping of collocations with respect to a semantic typology and classification of miscollocations encountered in the learner's writing.

5. Acknowledgements

The presented work has been partially funded by the Spanish Ministry of Economy and Competitiveness (MINECO) under the contract numbers FFI2011-30219-C02-01/02.

References

Alonso Ramos, M., Nishikawa, A., & Vincze, O. (2010). DiCE in the web: an online Spanish collocation dictionary. In S. Granger & M. Paquot (Eds.), *eLexicograpy in the 21st century: new challenges, new applications. Proceedings of eLex 2009, Cahiers du Cental 7* (pp. 369-374). Louvain-la-Neuve: Presses universitaires de Louvain.

Carlini, R., Codina-Filbà, J., & Wanner, L. (2014). Improving collocation correction by ranking suggestions using linguistic knowledge. *Proceedings of the 3rd Workshop on NLP for computer-assisted language learning, Uppsala, Sweden.*

Carlini, R., Codina-Filbà, J., & Wanner, L. (2015). Improving the use of electronic collocation resources by visual analytics techniques. *Proceedings of the eLex 2015 Conference.* Herstmonceux Castle.

Cowie, A. (1994). Phraseology. In R. Asher & J. Simpson (Eds.), *The Encyclopedia of language and linguistics, Vol. 6* (pp. 3168-3171). Oxford: Pergamon.

Firth, J. (1957). Modes of meaning. In J. Firth (Ed.), *Papers in linguistics, 1934–1951* (pp. 190-215). Oxford: Oxford University Press.

Granger, S. (1998). Prefabricated patterns in advanced EFL writing: collocations and formulae. In A. Cowie (Ed.), *Phraseology: theory, analysis and applications* (pp. 145-160). Oxford: Oxford University Press.

Halliday, M. A. K. (1961). Categories of the theory of grammar. *Word, 17*, 241-292.

Hausmann, F.-J. (1984). Wortschatzlernen ist Kollokationslernen. Zum Lehren und Lernen französischer Wortwendungen. *Praxis des neusprachlichen Unterrichts, 31*(1), 395-406.

Lewis, M. (2000). *Teaching collocation. Further developments in the lexical approach.* London: LTP.

Mel'čuk, I. (1995). Phrasemes in language and phraseology in linguistics. In M. Everaert, E.-J. van der Linden, A. Schenk, & R. Schreuder (Eds.), *Idioms: structural and psychological perspectives* (pp. 167-232). Hillsdale: Lawrence Erlbaum Associates.

Mel'cuk, I. A., & Wanner, L. (1996). Lexical functions and lexical inheritance for emotion lexemes in German. In L. Wanner (Ed.), *Lexical functions in lexicography and natural language processing* (pp. 209-278). Amsterdam: Benjamins Academic Publishers.

Nesselhauf, N. (2005). *Collocations in a learner corpus.* Amsterdam: Benjamins Academic Publishers. doi:10.1075/scl.14

Orol, A., & Alonso Ramos, M. (2013). A comparative study of collocations in a native corpus and a learner corpus of Spanish. *Procedia–Social and Behavioural Sciences, 96*, 563-570.

Un test senza stress: un supporto per orientarsi nell'italiano

Marina Artese[1]

Abstract. Con l'obiettivo di offrire uno strumento di libero accesso ai potenziali studenti internazionali che vogliono mettere alla prova la loro conoscenza della lingua, ma al tempo stesso motivarli a studiarla ulteriormente, il Centro Linguistico d'Ateneo (CLA) dell'Università di Bologna ha implementato un test per orientare i candidati nella loro competenza linguistico-culturale dell'italiano e per stimolarli a eventuali approfondimenti prima del loro arrivo in Italia nel caso non raggiungessero il livello A1 finale. Al fine di delineare l'approccio metodologico applicato al test, in questo articolo verrà presentata l'analisi didattologica che ha portato alla progettazione e costruzione del test e conseguentemente alla definizione del contenuto degli item.

Parole chiave: testing, approccio sociolinguistico interazionale, narrativa, progettazione.

1. Introduzione

Un "test d'orientamento" è uno strumento che aiuta il discente a posizionarsi nel suo processo d'apprendimento della lingua e aiuta l'istituzione a raccogliere dati sui bisogni dei discenti. Rientra tra i test diagnostici come il test di piazzamento, ma differisce da quest'ultimo soprattutto per l'impatto che ha sulla carriera dello studente.

In questa breve analisi, vedremo come gli obiettivi istituzionali – valutazione del livello linguistico dei potenziali studenti internazionali, motivazione allo studio della lingua prima dell'arrivo in Italia e presentazione dell'istituzione e della città – abbiano portato alle decisioni metodologiche adottate nel test d'orientamento

---

1. Università di Bologna, Italia; marina.artese@unibo.it

How to cite this article: Artese, M. (2015). Un test senza stress: un supporto per orientarsi nell'italiano. In F. Helm, L. Bradley, M. Guarda, & S. Thouësny (Eds), *Critical CALL – Proceedings of the 2015 EUROCALL Conference, Padova, Italy* (pp. 24-29). Dublin: Research-publishing.net. http://dx.doi.org/10.14705/rpnet.2015.000305

sviluppato all'interno del progetto d'Ateneo Almaitaliano dal CLA dell'Università di Bologna, determinandone l'impianto (Figura 1).

Figura 1. Pagina iniziale del test d'orientameno sviluppato all'interno del progetto Almaitaliano[2]

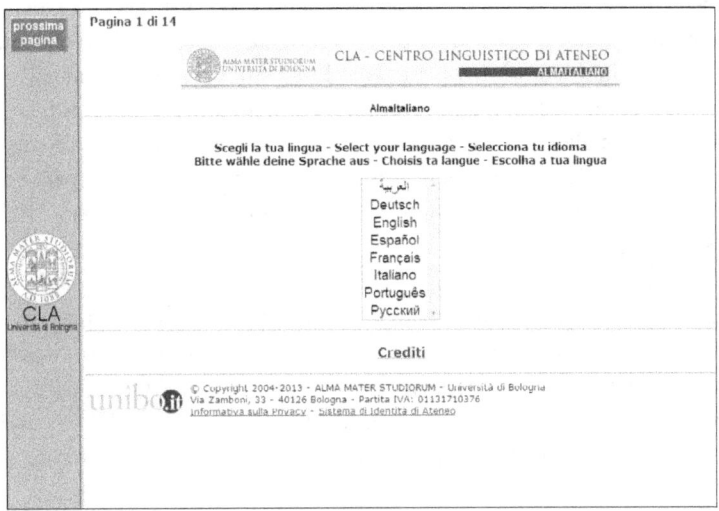

Innanzitutto, verrà descritto lo stile adottato nel test, verrà dispiegata e motivata la costruzione narrativa e la sua finalità e, infine, verranno evidenziate le scelte di carattere politico e valoriale.

2. Metodo

2.1. Stili, strategie e narrativa

Dalla letteratura sul testing e sulla didattica della lingua si è attinto per la determinazione degli obiettivi da valutare nella competenza dell'italiano (Spinelli & Parizzi, 2010), mentre per quel che riguarda l'obiettivo di presentazione del Sé istituzionale da coniugare con la metodologia del testing, si è attinto allo studio dottorale sulla costruzione dell'identità interazionale nella comunicazione didattica (Artese, 2013), in particolare ci si è riferiti alla descrizione degli *stili di comunicazione* ivi distinti in teatrale e interculturale all'interno della classe, informale e burocratico nell'interazione con l'istituzione. Per ridurre la distanza

---

2. http://testing.cliro.unibo.it/perception5/open.php?device=html4&GROUP=demo&NAME=93.66.243.205-113305&SESSION=4366545630601626

sociale e gerarchica tra gli attori coinvolti (studente, insegnante/progettista del test, e istituzione), in questo test è stato accordato un maggior spazio ai primi tre, mentre un ruolo limitato è stato dato allo stile burocratico.

Gli stili di comunicazione sono determinati dall'adozione di *strategie* linguistiche ed extra-linguistiche che a loro volta presentano e co-costruiscono l'identità dei partecipanti all'interazione. In sostanza, lo stile interazionale presenta reciprocamente l'identità degli interlocutori. La *narrazione* è una strategia interazionale (Ciliberti, 2007, p. 74) che è presente in tutti i contesti della comunicazione quotidiana, anche in quello istituzionale. Essa è il racconto di eventi esperienziali e attrae e mantiene l'attenzione degli ascoltatori con strategie di coinvolgimento (per esempio: ripetizione, dettagli) che consentono al pubblico di costruire il senso della storia (Tannen, 2007, pp. 32-42).

L'approccio sociolinguistico interazionale di questo test (somministrato via web) si concretizza nel racconto che si dipana negli item proposti e che narra l'esperienza personale dello studente protagonista della storia. Per facilitare l'appropriazione della modalità esperienziale, nelle consegne iniziali il candidato è invitato a immedesimarsi, impersonando il protagonista, come in un gioco di ruolo.

Per la costruzione dell'intero test sono state identificate le azioni che si compiono dal momento in cui si arriva in città alle prime relazioni amicali. Il percorso del test è incorniciato dal racconto del personaggio fittizio Pierre Dupont, uno studente canadese, che deve affrontare piccole difficoltà legate ad azioni quotidiane: comprendere il nome della fermata del bus per poter scendere nel luogo corretto, chiedere indicazioni stradali, il permesso di soggiorno e così via; gli item del test quindi si susseguono costruendo una storia in cui il personaggio si muove superando ostacoli e prove.

Consapevoli che le scelte metodologiche hanno anche ricadute politiche e valoriali, si è ipotizzato che questo approccio riduca le distanze tra gli attori e conseguentemente la quantità di stress a cui è sottoposto il candidato studente durante il test. L'intenzione valoriale dell'istituzione è orientata all'affiliazione dello studente, offrendo informazioni concrete sulla quotidianità dei primi giorni all'estero, presentate in uno stile informale e ludico (teatrale).

2.2. L'identità istituzionale

Le azioni organizzate in una narrazione presentano caratteristiche che possono essere elaborate tematicamente solo all'interno di un'etica (Ricoeur, 2005, pp. 201-204). L'etica, dal canto suo, dà forma all'agire umano secondo ciò che riteniamo designare il nostro Sé: le nostre azioni disvelano il nostro Sé. Quindi se la narrazione come evento comunicativo identifica il Sé degli interagenti, allora anche l'istituzione disvelerà la propria *identità* nel corso dell'interazione tra lo studente e il test.

3. Discussione

Oltre a motivare allo studio della lingua, il test vuole incuriosire, motivare alla conoscenza della città e della sua università attraverso una scelta di immagini del territorio vere e variegate. Foto, registrazioni audio e video, autentici o rimodulati per adeguarli al livello linguistico, sono scelti per la loro capacità evocativa, perché fanno percepire l'identità di un luogo che non si conosce e di cui si vorrebbe sapere il più possibile per poter prendere una decisione ponderata prima di intraprendere il viaggio.

Le azioni rivelatrici di identità istituzionale sono ravvisabili innanzitutto nell'offerta di uno strumento di rilevazione della competenza liberamente accessibile sul proprio sito, ma anche attraverso le scelte metodologiche che hanno portato alla costruzione del test: per quanto apparentemente banali, le situazioni presentate costituiscono momenti emotivamente densi per lo studente che realmente soggiorna in una sede universitaria straniera, esse sono la narrazione di un'esperienza. La focalizzazione sull'esperienza sposta la tensione emotiva provocata dall'esecuzione del test alle novità di un posto sconosciuto e, in modo indiretto, alle difficoltà che competenze linguistiche insufficienti possono causare. Ma affinché un'esperienza possa dirsi tale, deve essere memorabile. Ciò che rende memorabile un'esperienza è il coinvolgimento emotivo che vi si esperisce, l'empatia che prova chi esegue il test verso il protagonista: a tal fine, la trama, emozionante in sé, contiene anche un item specifico sull'emozione.

L'aspetto esperienziale è anche dato dalla preponderanza di attività di ascolto che non solo cerca di sopperire alla carenza tecnica della valutazione della produzione orale online, ma soprattutto presenta il mondo nella sua oralità. L'innesto del linguaggio visivo sul testo orale, inoltre, rimanda alla complessità del reale ed evoca nello studente esperienze vissute nel suo mondo, ma dislocate spazialmente in un altro, a Bologna, in un tempo non ancora vissuto, il soggiorno all'estero che forse farà. Il rimando alla conoscenza del mondo è una costante; inoltre, l'andirivieni tra vissuto e potenziale vita futura, applicando le strategie di coinvolgimento della ripetizione (di eventi già vissuti) e di dettagli culturalmente dislocati, attiva confronti di tipo interculturale.

I dati sulla ricezione del test sono stati raccolti durante il pilotaggio, nel quale sono stati coinvolti 9 studenti e 5 insegnanti. Dal questionario compilato dagli studenti dopo la somministrazione della versione pilota, il livello di utilità è risultato molto positivo; uno studente, spontaneamente, ha commentato la costruzione del test affermando che è utile perché ci si ritrova esattamente nelle situazioni reali, è quindi utile per avere informazioni e sentirsi un po' meno spaesati all'arrivo.

Oggi, dopo due anni online, il test riceve molti più accessi sia perché viene data regolarmente l'informazione dall'istituzione, sia per il passaparola, sia per la diffusione del tag nei motori di ricerca.

4. Conclusioni

In conclusione, al candidato viene proposta una varietà di situazioni concrete: con le competenze minime richieste (A1 finale), dovrà districarsi tra le "avventure quotidiane" del vivere in un paese straniero e sconosciuto.

La struttura di questo test intende superare lo stile burocratico che caratterizza le comunicazioni istituzionali di questo tipo e cerca di "far vivere" un'esperienza grazie ad una narrazione, il cui protagonista è il candidato. Questa impostazione risponde a due fondamentali esigenze istituzionali: da una parte cercare di motivare i potenziali studenti stranieri ad arrivare nella sede prescelta con un bagaglio linguistico-culturale superiore al livello A1 e, dall'altra, permettere all'istituzione e al territorio cittadino di farsi conoscere.

Attraverso il coinvolgimento, i discenti sono motivati all'apprendimento e sono incoraggiati a partecipare alle attività comunicative in lingua seconda. Inoltre, la narrazione getta le basi per istituire una relazione sociale tra studente e istituzione, in cui l'istituzione disvela anche "un'intenzione valoriale che fa sì che la comunicazione non sia più caratterizzata dalla quotidianità, ma dalla qualità dell'esperienza [...] in una relazione interculturale" (Artese, 2013, p. 259). Il messaggio istituzionale coincide, appunto, con la sua intenzione valoriale: offrire un'esperienza sociale in una relazione interculturale anche durante il momento del test.

5. Ringraziamenti

Un particolare ringraziamento alla co-autrice del test per la progettazione e realizzazione Luisa Bavieri, collega del CLA di Bologna, a Vanio Preti, tecnico informatico della sede di Forlì, che è sempre venuto incontro alle nostre richieste.

Un grazie anche a tutti coloro che con competenza e solerzia ne hanno reso possibile la pubblicazione.

Riferimenti bibliografici

Artese, M. (2013). *Interazioni e identità nella classe d'italiano lingua seconda all'università*. Tesi dottorale XXIV ciclo, Università di Macerata.

Ciliberti, A. (A cura di). (2007). *La costruzione interazionale dell'identità*. Milano: Franco Angeli.

Ricoeur, P. (2005). *Sé come un altro* (4a ristampa). Milano: Jaca Book.

Spinelli, B., & Parizzi, F. (2010). *Profilo della lingua italiana. Livelli di riferimento del QCERT A1, A2, B1, B2*. Milano: La Nuova Italia.

Tannen, D. (2007). *Talking voices. Repetition, dialogue, and imagery in conversational discourse*. New York: Cambridge University Press. doi:10.1017/CBO9780511618987

Vocabulary acquisition in L2: does CALL really help?

Irina Averianova[1]

Abstract. Language competence in various communicative activities in L2 largely depends on the learners' size of vocabulary. The target vocabulary of adult L2 learners should be between 2,000 high frequency words (a critical threshold) and 10,000 word families (for comprehension of university texts). For a TOEIC test, the threshold is estimated to be 3,000 - 4,000 words. The average English vocabulary size of most Japanese university students is significantly beyond these thresholds. Since incidental learning of English vocabulary in Japan is impossible due to the low exposure to the target language, vocabulary should be acquired through intentional learning. This paper reports on the outcomes of two different approaches to intentional vocabulary learning experienced in one Japanese university: using a Web-based vocabulary-learning tool *Word Engine* and non-electronic techniques of rote learning and memorization. During the period when independent vocabulary acquisition with *Word Engine* was included in course requirements, research revealed a significant improvement in mean scores in standardized TOEIC tests and course examinations for students of the equivalent cohorts, i.e. the same year of study and similar curriculum level and content, as well as general student satisfaction with the program and increased motivation towards independent deliberate vocabulary learning.

Keywords: intentional vocabulary acquisition, TOEIC, web-based vocabulary learning system, *Word Engine*.

1. Introduction

Language competence in L2 largely depends on the learners' size of vocabulary, and research has conclusively established the implicit relationship between

---

[1]. Nagoya University of Commerce and Business (NUCB), Japan; averianova@nucba.ac.jp

How to cite this article: Averianova, I. (2015). Vocabulary acquisition in L2: does CALL really help?. In F. Helm, L. Bradley, M. Guarda, & S. Thouësny (Eds), *Critical CALL – Proceedings of the 2015 EUROCALL Conference, Padova, Italy* (pp. 30-35). Dublin: Research-publishing.net. http://dx.doi.org/10.14705/rpnet.2015.000306

vocabulary knowledge and other aspects of linguistic ability (Folse, 2004; Meara, 2002). The target vocabulary of L2 learners is estimated to be over 2,000 high frequency words, a critical threshold (Nation, 2008). In a TOEIC test, the most highly regarded independent means of English proficiency evaluation in corporate Japan, the lexical threshold is crucial, and research shows that a learner would need to know between 3,000 to 4,000 words to understand a current test (Kiyomi & Oghigian, 2009).

With most Japanese business university students involved in this study, there is a huge discrepancy between their average English vocabulary size (700-1500 headwords) and the threshold vocabulary necessary for adequate functioning on various tasks in English and achieving high TOEIC scores. Realizing that vocabulary size plays a significant role in TOEIC performance, two different approaches to boosting vocabulary learning were undertaken: non-electronic techniques of rote learning and memorization and implementation of a Web-based vocabulary-learning program *Word Engine*. The paper reports on the results of these methods by comparing standardized TOEIC test scores and *Intermediate Business English* final test scores for corresponding cohorts of students who used the online program for vocabulary acquisition and those who did not.

2. Method

Lexical research distinguishes between two main approaches to vocabulary learning in L2: explicit, or intentional, learning, when the focus is on the words to be learnt, and implicit, or incidental, when vocabulary learning occurs unconsciously through the other primary objective, such as reading comprehension or learning from context (Schmidt, 1994). Incidental vocabulary acquisition has proved effective for advanced L2 learners (Nagy, 1997) and only after repeated exposure (Waring & Takaki, 2003), e.g. extensive reading or listening. Since these conditions do not apply to our study population due to Japanese students' limited contact with English and insufficient lexicon for contextual deduction, vocabulary should be acquired mostly through intentional learning. A number of studies have recently addressed this problem (Folse, 2004; Nation, 2001) and various suggestions have been made as to the methods and practices to help students acquire more vocabulary both within the limited time in formal educational settings and through individual independent study.

At the time of the study, the university employed English language instructors with adequate educational background (PhD, mostly, or MA in Linguistics or TESOL) and sufficient teaching experience. So, it is assumed that, consistent with their experience and objectives, teachers utilized various non-electronic methods of explicit vocabulary teaching. Teaching materials display activities related to the involvement-load hypothesis (Laufer & Hulstijn, 2001), such as making sentences, filling-in blanks, after-reading activities, words reviews, as well as integrated and isolated form-focused instruction (reading with marginal glosses, reading with a dictionary at one's disposal, etc.), and many other strategies aimed at maximizing vocabulary learning and retention.

However, instructors teaching TOEIC preparation courses recognized a vocabulary deficit as one of the main reasons preventing students from increasing their test scores, and after some research on possible ways to boost vocabulary, it was decided to implement a vocabulary-learning program based on *Word Engine* (Agawa, Black, & Herriman, 2011). In 2009, the university acquired a discount access to the *Lexxica* site, and launched the on-line program *Vocabulary for TOEIC*, which incorporated several principles of high-speed effective rote learning. These included testing the learner's vocabulary ability and customizing the target vocabulary, which is to be learned through the use of flash cards and spaced repetition. Two years later, the *Business Vocabulary* program was introduced, with both core courses, *English for Testing* and *Intermediate Business English*, making independent vocabulary acquisition with *Word Engine* their course requirements. Students were asked to access the site in their spare time with their individual access codes several times each week, in conformity with the concept of spaced learning. Their progress was monitored by using the *Word Engine* "V-Admin" feature to export and store weekly reports with the following data: name, ID-number, course, coverage, location of words in process, total learned words, total time on-line and average time on task per access.

3. Discussion

The first experience of using *Word Engine* at the university was evaluated by correlation of the study population scores in the TOEIC examination in December 2009 (prior to the study period) and in June 2010 (following the 8-week "*Word Engine*" period) with the *Word Engine* data on students' progress in terms of individual word coverage, depth of word recycling and time-on-task. Comparison of the mean scores in December and June TOEIC tests taken at the end of the 1st year and the middle of the 2nd year by student cohorts in the English language program yielded the most statistically significant results. The participants in the study showed a total mean-score improvement of 55 points, which, compared to the average 26.9 points improvement of the equivalent cohort of the previous 11 years, is double the norm (Agawa, Black, & Herriman, 2011).

Two consecutive years of running the program (2010 and 2011) showed a noticeable increase in average TOEIC scores over the previous 5-year (2003-2008) average of 401 for all English department test-takers, with December 2011 TOEIC average being the highest (Table 1).

Table 1. TOEIC scores (test average scores and divergence from the pre-study average)

Test Date	Dec 2008	June 2009	Dec 2009	June 2010	Dec 2010	June 2011	Dec 2011	June 2012	Dec 2012	June 2013	Dec 2013	June 2014	Dec 2014	June 2015
Score	419	411	373	423	438	423	463	432	432	404	422	417	427	391
Div	+18	+10	-28	+22	+37	+22	+62	+31	+31	+3	+21	+16	+26	-10

This rise corresponds with the introduction of the second *Word Engine* program, *Business English*, parallel to the *TOEIC* one. Also, in December 2011, the TOEIC test-takers comprised three cohorts of students (2009, 2010 and 2011 entrants) who had had an experience of using *Word Engine* for independent study. These findings are reported in a study (Averianova, 2012) which addressed the influence of using the program on the dynamics of scores in the final tests of *Intermediate Business English*, a core course that integrated *Word Engine*. The average scores in the final exam of the year, when *Word Engine* was administered for *English for Testing* (2010), and the following year, when the on-line *Business English* program was introduced (2011), were significantly higher than the equivalent tests of the previous or subsequent years (Table 2).

Table 2. Mean scores in *Intermediate Business English* final test

Year	2008	2009	2010	2011	2012
Mean Score	67/110	65/110	73/110	80/110	69/110

Besides the objective factors measured by the formal test results, the subjective factors of student motivation and satisfaction with the program were also explored. All opinion surveys indicated a generally favourable response to using the system. The most relevant findings are presented in Table 3 for the percentages of answers "Agree" and "Strongly Agree" on the selected questions.

These numbers indicate broadly positive student perceptions of *Word Engine* as helping their language acquisition, with the lowest figures being in the "liking" category, which is not surprising since students in general are not enthusiastic about homework, which is "the sore thumb of tertiary education in Japan" (Takemoto,

2004). However, a much higher proportion of those who would like to continue using the program evinces their appreciation of its utility.

Table 3. *Word Engine* opinion survey

Year Question	2009	2010	2011
Word Engine helps me with English	84	82	79
Word Engine helps me with TOEIC	75	76	70
Word Engine helps me with Business English	n/a	n/a	67
Word Engine is a good way to study vocabulary	73	71	62
I like *Word Engine*	60	58	49
I would like to use *Word Engine* again next semester	n/a	69	65

4. Conclusion

Research findings on student achievement in standardized TOEIC tests and *Business English* course tests have shown considerable improvement over the three-year period, when the on-line vocabulary building program *Word Engine* was included in the corresponding course requirements. The study also demonstrated a generally positive attitude of students towards the program as well as their notable motivation for independent structured vocabulary learning. However, in 2012, the university administration inexplicably terminated the official use of *Word Engine,* which coincided with a certain decline in the scores on all comparative tests.

This is not to say that *Word Engine* is a panacea for vocabulary deficiency, and there are certain limitations of this study, such as fluctuating levels of L2 competence in different cohorts, variability of teaching styles and qualifications, changing course loads over the years, and others. Also, further research is needed to better explore the correlation between TOEIC scores and some independent variables of the program, namely "time-on-task" or "word coverage." However, it is still possible to conclude that structured and controlled intentional vocabulary acquisition with CALL tools, such as *Word Engine,* is a powerful asset in L2 learning.

References

Agawa, G., Black, G., & Herriman, M. (2011). Effects of web-based vocabulary training for TOEIC. In A. Stewart (Ed.), *JALT2010 Conference Proceedings* (pp.160-167). Tokyo: JALT.

Averianova, I. (2012). Autonomy and assessment in L2 vocabulary acquisition: effects of the Web-based programme. *5th Independent Learning Association Conference 2012. Abstracts.* Wellington, New Zealand.

Folse, K. (2004). *Vocabulary myths: applying second language research to classroom teaching.* Ann Arbor: University of Michigan Press.

Kiyomi, C., & Oghigian, K. (2009). How many words do you need to know to understand TOEIC, TOEFL & EIKEN? An examination of text coverage and high frequency vocabulary. *The Journal of Asia TEFL, 6,* 121-148.

Laufer, B., & Hulstijn, J. H. (2001). Incidental vocabulary acquisition in a second language: the construct of task-induced involvement. *Applied Linguistics, 22,* 1-26. doi:10.1093/applin/22.1.1

Meara, P. (2002). The rediscovery of vocabulary. *Second Language Research, 18*(4), 393-407. doi:10.1191/0267658302sr211xx

Nagy, W. E. (1997). On the role of context in first and second language acquisition. In N. Schmitt & N. McCarthy (Eds.), *Vocabulary: Description, acquisition, and pedagogy* (pp. 64-83). Cambridge: Cambridge University Press.

Nation, I. S. P. (2001). *Learning vocabulary in another language.* Cambridge: Cambridge University Press. doi:10.1017/CBO9781139524759

Nation, I. S. P. (2008). *Teaching vocabulary. Strategies and techniques.* Boston, USA: Heinle, Cengage Learning.

Schmidt, R. (1994). Deconstructing consciousness in search of useful definitions for applied linguistics. Consciousness in Second Language Learning. *AILA Review, 11,* 11-26.

Takemoto, T. (2004) Homework. *Eigodaigaku. University Level English Education on the Internet.* Retrieved from http://www.nihonbunka.com/eigodaigaku/archives/en/000151.html

Waring, R., & Takaki, M. (2003). At what rate do learners learn and retain new vocabulary from reading a graded reader? *Reading in a Foreign Language, 15,* 130-163.

State of the art of language learning design using mobile technology: sample apps and some critical reflection

Elena Bárcena[1], Timothy Read[1], Joshua Underwood[2], Hiroyuki Obari[3], Diana Cojocnean[4], Toshiko Koyama[5], Antonio Pareja-Lora[6], Cristina Calle[7], Lourdes Pomposo[7], Noa Talaván[1], José Ávila-Cabrera[1], Ana Ibañez[1], Anna Vermeulen[8], María Jordano[1], Jorge Arús-Hita[6], Pilar Rodríguez[1], María Dolores Castrillo[1], Andras Kétyi[9], Jaime Selwood[10], Mark Gaved[11], and Agnes Kukulska-Hulme[11]

Abstract. In this paper, experiences from different research groups illustrate the state-of-the-art of Mobile Assisted Language Learning (henceforth, MALL) in formal and non-formal education. These research samples represent recent and on-going progress made in the field of MALL at an international level and offer encouragement for practitioners who are trying to incorporate these approaches into mainline second language teaching. Furthermore, researchers interested in the field

---

1. UNED, Spain; mbarcena@flog.uned.es; tread@lsi.uned.es; ntalavan@flog.uned.es; javila@flog.uned.es; aibanez@flog.uned.es; mjordano@flog.uned.es; prodriquez@flog.uned.es; mcastrillo@flog.uned.es

2. British Council, Spain; josh.underwood@gmail.com

3. Aoyama Gakuin University, Japan; obari119@gmail.com

4. University of Exeter, UK; diana.cojocnean@gmail.com

5. Osaka Ohtani University, Japan; tokkokoyama@gmail.com

6. UCM, Spain; apareja@sip.ucm.es; jarus@filol.ucm.es

7. Universidad Camilo José Cela, Spain: kriscalle@gmail.com; loupomposo@madrid.uned.es

8. Ghent University, Belgium; anna.vermeulen@ugent.be

9. Budapest Business School, Hungary; ketyi.andras@kkk.bgf.hu

10. Hiroshima University, Japan; jselwood@hiroshima-u.ac.jp

11. The Open University, UK; mark.gaved@open.ac.uk; agnes.kukulska-hulme@open.ac.uk

How to cite this article: Bárcena, E. et al. (2015). State of the art of language learning design using mobile technology: sample apps and some critical reflection. In F. Helm, L. Bradley, M. Guarda, & S. Thouësny (Eds), *Critical CALL – Proceedings of the 2015 EUROCALL Conference, Padova, Italy* (pp. 36-43). Dublin: Research-publishing.net. http://dx.doi.org/10.14705/rpnet.2015.000307

can see that the work presented here exemplifies how fertile it is, which should hopefully serve as motivation to undertake new studies to move the state-of-the-art further on.

Keywords: MALL, apps for smartphones and tablets, lifelong learning, blended learning, autonomous learning, self-regulation, flipped lessons, location-based learning, podcasting, audio description, beacons, Moodle, Busuu, oral comprehension, vocabulary acquisition, business English.

1. Introduction

Eight years after the introduction of the first globally popular smartphone, mobile technology continues to influence how foreign languages are taught and studied. Mobile hand-held devices, namely smartphones and tablets, offer a highly convenient way to integrate digital technology as part of the language-learning process. The huge growth in ownership of such devices amongst the student population means that access to online content, especially through mobile applications (apps), has harnessed their potential for language learning. In 2015, with approximately 1.5 million different apps available to download via app stores such as Google Play and iTunes, institutions, instructors and students have the opportunity to apply new identified forms of MALL that are being discovered in the research community. Hence, in this paper, experiences from different international research groups illustrate the state-of-the-art of MALL in formal and non-formal education.

2. State-of-the-art of MALL in formal and non-formal education

Selwood (2015) has undertaken an analysis of apps that were successful to different extents within the classroom. In addition, a language-learning app designed by the author has given rise to insights into the development and publishing of such tools. Underwood (2014) has integrated language learning design tasks, processes and frameworks in courses for teenage EFL learners and for teacher training (van Lier, 2007). These courses aimed to help participants design their own MALL activities. Analysis of such activities and reflection on the process and outcomes of both kinds of courses suggested some key tensions in MALL. In particular, Underwood (2014) has highlighted participants' varying attitudes to mobile devices for learning (distracter vs. enabler); the need for self-regulation in MALL vs. the use of mobile technology to support self-regulation; and the potential for mobile devices to support regular and repeated fleeting engagement in learning vs. deep immersive learning. These tensions together with reflection on the courses themselves suggested ways in which the design frameworks used could be improved and better integrated with assessment frameworks and activities beyond the time frame and physical location of the course, in order to produce more transferable and durable impacts on participants' learning practices.

In contrast to traditional learning, Obari has claimed the flipped classroom is a unique educational environment which is quickly gaining in popularity among educators worldwide (Obari, Kojima, & Itahashi, 2010; Gualtieri, 2011). In a flipped classroom, students learn the course contents (via online videos, materials, etc.) before coming to class, and spend the bulk of classroom time asking questions and engaging in interactive discussions. An experimental group was exposed to flipped lessons using a variety of materials such as the 'Lecture Ready II' digital text designed for iPad, COOORI e-learning software for learning words and phrases related to the digital text, ATR CALL Brix e-Learning, Newton e-Learning, and TED Talks. An assessment of pre-treatment and post-treatment TOEIC scores and the OPIc computer-based speaking test resulted in a considerable improvement of the flipped classroom group. Post-questionnaires administered to these students indicated that they were more satisfied and motivated by the blended learning environment incorporating MALL.

Cojocnean's work has focused on high school students' use of vocabulary learning strategies in a digital context which had a mixed methodology, including a number of focus group discussions and a post-questionnaire (Palalas, 2011; Pegrum, 2014). The results indicated that most participants had a low usage of digital tools and also moderate attitudes towards the use of MALL and CALL tools in their vocabulary learning. As to students' views on MALL tools, they preferred those that enable incidental vocabulary learning as dedicated apps were not seen to be challenging enough, partially because words appeared out of context. The participants reported that they viewed apps as sources of entertainment rather than learning and that they could not focus on a single activity while using the app. Likewise, the participants explained that in their schools there was not a MALL or CALL culture. Cojocnean concluded that as long as schools do not promote the use of MALL tools in the lessons and teachers do not know exactly how to make use of MALL and CALL in the classroom, there will be fewer chances for students to use mobile technology in their learning outside the classroom.

Koyama's ongoing project aims to explore a dictionary interface while making a comparison of dictionary apps on smartphones and tablets. The project was designed on the basis of the findings of Koyama (2014), which indicates that the participants preferred a physical keyboard equipped with a pocket E-dictionary even though the learning effects seemed to be the same between both dictionaries. The aim of the present study was, therefore, to compare a similar dictionary interface. The participants were university students. In the first session, learners' look-up behavior on a smartphone and tablet apps were compared. They were assigned a word definition and a reading comprehension task with their respective types of dictionary. The time that they needed for the tasks, the number of look-ups, and the quiz scores were verified. In the second session, a recognition test was conducted to investigate how the looked-up words were retained. No differences were found in the time needed and the number of the looked-up words. However, the rate of recognition was higher when they used smartphone-based dictionaries. Additionally, rich feedback was obtained concerning mobile dictionary interface from the participants. Like the participants' feedback in Koyama (2014), all the students insisted that elementary school students should not use smartphones when looking up words. It was inferred, therefore, that mobile dictionaries should be selected according to learners' ages based upon these findings.

The VIOLIN app (VIdeOs for LIsteNing), created by Talaván and Ávila-Cabrera, offers both teachers and students an audiovisual tool for the development of aural skills (Talaván & Ávila-Cabrera, 2015). VIOLIN resorts to the improvement of aural comprehension through audiovisual reception and content-based activities. This app includes a selection of a series of short video clips, based on three features: they are entertaining, self-contained and context-independent. Users can view the video clips, taken from a well-known TV series, independently and every activity is divided into five stages for which users are briefed. Such activities are presented by following four consecutive steps: (1) selective, (2) intensive, (3) global listening, and (4) self-evaluation.

Pareja, Calle and Pomposo produced BusinessApp with both a general and a specific purpose: to help improve its users' oral skills in English and to help them put these oral skills into practice to create and perform effective business presentations (Calle, Pomposo, & Pareja-Lora, 2015; Pareja-Lora, Calle, & Pomposo, 2015). BusinessApp has been developed to be used by professional workers who need to make business presentations in English; and students in general who have to make presentations in any area (and in any language). From a more technical point of view, BusinessApp is a pedagogically and linguistically-based didactic unit previously created by the authors. It contains a series of modules, each one accompanied by examples and exercises which are automatically corrected in order to facilitate autonomous learning.

Ibañez, Vermeulen and Jordano (2015, in press a, in press b) produced VISP (VIdeos for SPeaking), a MALL app that is based on applying audio description (a mode of audio visual translation which consists of orally describing what appears on the screen) to help users practise their speaking abilities. This is especially the case for their lexical and phraseological competences, given the fact that the time audio describers have to narrate what they see on the screen is very limited and they have to use accurate vocabulary in an idiomatic way. This app was tested with several students of English as a foreign language in UNED (Spain) and Ghent University (Belgium). VISP 2.0 has been updated in the light of the relevant data derived from pre and post-questionnaires (included in the app) and the first recordings received from the users, which constitute the essential part of VISP. This app is also framed within the task-based learning and the transferable skills approach, which are considered by the authors to provide adequate and solid methodologies for the development of users' language skills, following the *Common European Framework of References for Languages*.

Arús-Hita and Rodríguez Arancón (2015) have produced the design for a mobile application: Eating out, a Moodle-based EFL self-education digital learning resource. An experiment was carried out with a group of EFL university students at the Universidad Complutense de Madrid (Spain) during a semester, some of them using a PC, others a mobile device. At the end of the semester, a questionnaire was made available to them on Moodle. They answered a number of questions on pedagogical and technical aspects of their experience with Eating out. The contents of the post-questionnaire were based on a quality guide and rubric previously used in our work on the evaluation of EFL apps. The evaluation of Eating out by the students allowed the authors to obtain valuable information that may help to improve this learning resource as well as future apps to be developed. An additional aspect of the post-questionnaire was that the authors could compare the experiences of students working on a computer and a mobile device. They could thus see whether the learning resource was as valid for MALL as it was for CALL, and derive implications as to whether a single resource could be used for both types of teaching.

Bárcena and Read produced the Audio News Trainer for English (ANT), an oral comprehension app developed for the pedagogically guided use of audio news podcasts (Read & Bárcena, in press; Read, Bárcena, & Kukulska-Hulme, in press). Two versions of the app were produced, the difference being the use of social media as a way to motivate students and make them proactive. Research was undertaken with the app to study its motivational properties (and whether news could be an effective domain for listening comprehension training), and whether using the app could modify learning habits and help to establish appropriate metacognitive strategies. Other emergent features of using this app also became apparent as the experiment progressed.

Kétyi (2013) has looked for a language learning strategy involving mobile devices. The main idea was that, if the mobile devices could be integrated in the language teaching practice, students at the Budapest Business School could gain valuable additional learning time outside the classroom and therefore they could improve their language learning accordingly. The mobile language learning app chosen for the project was busuu and the participants were students of four different foreign languages (German, English, Spanish, Italian). It was found that busuu and the similar language learning apps were still new and unknown for the students (only one of them had used busuu before). The use of busuu was straightforward and it worked smoothly on the students' devices. During the study, the research group improved their performance according to the language test results while the control group did not. Analyzing gender data, it was found that female students performed at the post measurement better than male ones. However, according to the students, busuu is not an ultimate language learning tool, since it does not improve every language skill equally. It primarily helps in vocabulary acquisition.

Gaved and Kukulska-Hulme have explored location-triggered mobile language learning accessed through smartphones (Gaved & Peasgood, 2015; Gaved, Greenwood & Peasgood, 2015; Kukulska-Hulme et al., 2015). They have investigated how an emerging technology, Bluetooth beacons, might trigger location-specific learning activities to support informal and incidental learning. On entering an area which has a beacon, a notification (similar to an SMS) is triggered on the learner's phone and invites them to view the learning activity, which can be stored either on a remote website, or locally on the phone to allow access in places without network connectivity. Other location-triggered language learning approaches have been previously tried. However, they have faced the challenges of accuracy, performance indoors as well as outside, or the barrier of explicit and visible interaction with a triggering object in an area. This technology enabled identification of proximity to a place of interest, and yet allowed a user to engage with a learning activity discretely. The authors have also been considering ethical challenges that surround mobile language learning research focusing on location-based activities: investigating issues around tracking of activities, privacy, and participants as co-researchers. They have recently carried out a pilot study with a series of scenarios across Milton Keynes (UK).

3. Conclusion

In summary, the research presented above illustrates recent and ongoing progress made in the field of MALL at international level. This is intended to offer encouragement both for practitioners who are trying to incorporate these techniques into mainline second language teaching and students wishing to make use of this applied technology.

Furthermore, researchers interested in MALL can see that the recent and on-going work presented above exemplify how fertile and promising the field is. This article will hopefully act as a motivation for them to undertake new studies to move the state-of-the-art further on.

References

Arús-Hita, J., & Rodríguez-Arancón, P. (2015) Autonomous learning resources for the teaching of EFL: what learners think, *Encuentro, 23*, 1-15.

Calle, C., Pomposo, L., & Pareja-Lora, A. (2015). BusinessApp: Una aplicación para el aprendizaje del inglés mediante dispositivos móviles en el campo de los negocios. *E-Aesla*, 1. Retrieved from http://cvc.cervantes.es/lengua/eaesla/pdf/01/19.pdf

Gaved, M., Greenwood, R., & Peasgood, A. (2015). Using and appropriating the smart city for community and capacity building amongst migrant language learners. In G. Avram, F. De Cindio & V. Pipek (Eds.), *Proceedings of the 7th International Conference on Communities and Technologies* (pp. 63-72), University of Limerick.

Gaved, M., & Peasgood, A. (2015). Location-based language learning for migrants in a smart city. In *Proceedings of the 15th International Conference on Technology, Policy and Innovation* (ICTPI'15), The Open University.

Gualtieri, M. (2011). Mobile app design best practices: when it comes to designing the mobile user experience (UX), context is kingonline article: Retrieved from http://www.forrester.com/rb/Research/mobile_app_design_best_practices/q/id/59132/t/2

Ibáñez A., Vermeulen, A., & Jordano, M. (2015). Diseño y evaluación de VISP, una aplicación móvil para la práctica de la competencia oral. In A. Pareja-Lora, M.D. Castrillo & M. Jordano (Eds.), *El aprendizaje a distancia de lenguas extranjeras mediante tecnología móvil: del podcasting a los MOOC*. RIED: Revista Iberoamericana de Educación Superior a Distancia.

Ibáñez, A., Vermeulen, A., & Jordano, M. (in press a). Using audio description techniques to improve B1 EFL students' oral competence in MALL: methodological preliminaries. *Proceedings of the 2014 TISLID Conference*, London: Macmillan.

Ibáñez, A., Vermeulen, A., & Jordano, M. (in press b). VISP, an enjoyable app to enhance idiomaticity in English. *Proceedings of the XVIIth International CALL Research Conference: Task Design and CALL,* University Pompeu Fabra.

Kétyi, A. (2013). Using smart phones in language learning – A pilot study to turn CALL into MALL. In L. Bradley & S. Thouësny (Eds.), *20 Years of EUROCALL: learning from the past, looking to the future. Proceedings of the 2013 EUROCALL Conference*, University of Evora, (pp. 129-134). Dublin/Voillans: Research-publishing.net. doi:10.14705/rpnet.2013.000150

Koyama, T. (2014). The impact of smartphone dictionary apps on EFL learning. Poster presented at Eurocall 2014 Conference at the University of Groningen, the Netherlands.

Kukulska-Hulme, A., Gaved, M., Paletta, L., Scanlon, E., Jones, A., & Brasher, A. (2015). Mobile incidental learning to support the inclusion of recent immigrants. *Ubiquitous Learning: an international journal, 7*(2), 9-21.

Lier, L. van. (2007). Action-based teaching, autonomy and identity. *International Journal of Innovation in Language Learning and Teaching, 1*(1), 46-65. doi:10.2167/illt42.0

Obari, H., Kojima, H., & Itahashi, S. (2010). Empowering EFL learners to interact effectively in a blended learning environment. In *Proceedings of World Conference on Educational Multimedia, Hypermedia and Telecommunications 2010* (pp. 3438-3447). Chesapeake, VA: AACE.

Palalas, A. (2011). Mobile-assisted language learning: designing for your students. In S. Thouësny & L. Bradley (Eds.), *Second language teaching and learning with technology: views of emergent researchers* (pp. 71-94). Dublin: Research-publishing.net. doi:10.14705/rpnet.2011.000007

Pareja-Lora, A., Calle, C., & Pomposo, L. (2015). Aprendiendo a hacer presentaciones efectivas en inglés con BusinessApp. *RIED. Revista Iberoamericana de Educación a Distancia (special issue: El aprendizaje de lenguas extranjeras mediante tecnología móvil en el contexto de la educación a distancia y combinada), 18*(3).

Pegrum, M. (2014). *Mobile learning: languages, literacies and cultures.* Basingstoke: Palgrave Macmillan. doi:10.1057/9781137309815

Read, T., & Bárcena, E. (in press). The development of oral comprehension via mobile-based social media and the role of e-leading students. In A. Palalas & M. Ally (Eds.), *The international handbook of mobile-assisted language learning.* Beiing: China University Press.

Read, T., Bárcena, E., & Kukulska-Hulme, A. (in press). Mobile and massive language learning. In E. Martin-Monje, I. Alorza & B. García-Riaza (Eds.), *Technology-enhanced language learning for specialized domains: practical applications and mobility.* London: Routledge.

Selwood, J. (2015). Going paperless in the classroom with mobile devices: pitfalls and benefits. *Hiroshima Studies in Language and Language Education, 18,* 165-177.

Talaván, N., & Ávila-Cabrera, J. J. (2015). Audiovisual reception and MALL: adapting technology to real needs. *Porta Linguarum, 24,* 33-46.

Underwood, J. (2014). Using iPads to help teens design their own activities. In Sake Jager, Linda Bradley, Estelle J. Meima, Sylvie Thouësny (Eds), *CALL Design: Principles and Practice - Proceedings of the 2014 EUROCALL Conference, Groningen, The Netherlands* (pp. 385-390). Dublin Ireland: Research-publishing.net. doi:10.14705/rpnet.2014.000250

The alignment of CMC language learning methodologies with the Bridge21 model of 21C learning

Ciarán Bauer[1], Ann Devitt[2], and Brendan Tangney[3]

Abstract. This paper explores the intersection of learning methodologies to promote the development of 21st century skills with the use of Computer-Mediated Communication (CMC) tools to enhance language learning among adolescent learners. Today, technology offers a greater range of affordances in the teaching and learning of second languages while research shows that student classrooms still continue to concentrate on linguistic competences rather than communicative competences (Gilmore, 2011). The Bridge21 model, which is technology-mediated, team-led and project-based, brings a particular approach to 21st-century learning and is distinguished by the mixture and focus of scaffolding and consistency in the application (Lawlor, Conneely, & Tangney, 2010). An exploratory case study was designed to extend the Bridge21 model to include spatially-separated teams, based in Ireland and Germany, learning together and enhancing the use of oral and aural skills for second language acquisition. Thirty-six students worked on project-based tasks during a six day workshop focused on the usage of authentic materials and CMC tools. The findings suggest that using the Bridge21 learning model succeeded in allowing students to collaborate at a distance and to participate in second language acquisition.

Keywords: 21C learning, CMC, native speakers, collaboration, authentic materials.

---

1. Trinity College Dublin, Ireland; ciaran@bridge21.ie

2. Trinity College Dublin, Ireland; devittan@tcd.ie

3. Trinity College Dublin, Ireland; tangney@tcd.ie

How to cite this article: Bauer, C., Devitt, A., & Tangney, B. (2015). The alignment of CMC language learning methodologies with the Bridge21 model of 21C learning. In F. Helm, L. Bradley, M. Guarda, & S. Thouësny (Eds), *Critical CALL – Proceedings of the 2015 EUROCALL Conference, Padova, Italy* (pp. 44-50). Dublin: Research-publishing.net. http://dx.doi.org/10.14705/rpnet.2015.000308

1. Introduction

This paper explores the intersection of a team based, technology mediated, collaborative model of 21st Century (21C) learning (Bridge21) with a Computer-Mediated Communication approach to second language learning in order to explore the efficacy of the resulting intervention in terms of both language and 21st century skill development.

There is a strong trend in the literature and with policy makers in various jurisdictions to move towards a model of teaching and learning which is labelled 21C. While the concept is not without its critics, in essence, the 21C learning agenda promotes the acquisition of key skills, such as problem solving, collaboration and creativity in addition to mastering curriculum content (Gewertz, 2008; Silva, 2009).

Bridge21 is a particular model of 21C teaching and learning which is being adapted for use in Irish second level schools (Conneely, Lawlor, & Tangney, 2013). The model uses a collaborative learning approach within a social constructivist framework to allow groups of learners, in cooperation with expert mentors, to achieve learning goals through the creation and presentation of shared artefacts.

This study extends the Bridge21 model for use in a distance-based collaborative scenario between German and English language learners. Many of the core principles of the Bridge21 model are mirrored in the affordances of CMC for language learning, in particular the facilitation of student-led activities with a focus on collaborative inquiry and knowledge construction (Kern, Ware, & Warschauer, 2004). Technology is viewed as both a means and an end in the learning process as a key aspect of "everyday dimensions of competent social and professional activity" (Thorne & Black, 2007, p. 149). Chun (2011) provides an excellent overview of the impact of CMC on aspects of language development. This study aims to explore the impact of the collaborative, authentic setting provided by the CMC-mediated Bridge21 model.

2. Method

The project was conducted as an exploratory case study in 2013 over a three week period and involved students located in the Bridge21 learning space in Trinity College Dublin and a post-primary school in Germany. The Irish-based students (n=17) and German-based students (n=20) were divided into four local teams and each team was then paired with a remotely located team. Teams self-organised selecting a team name, lead and assigned roles through the project as per the Bridge21 model. Communication between the spatially separated students took place using Skype and interactions occurred for approximately two hours each day over six days. The objectives of the project were to develop participants' collaborative skills as well as their L2 communicative competence in both written and spoken forms. The projects were structured so as to require local and remote teams to interact in their L2 to co-create some artefacts. Over the two weeks, participants completed four tasks to create multimedia digital artefacts based on information gathered through dialogue (Skype voice and chat functions) with their paired team.

The introductory task involved each team in their L2 creating a "Getting to know you" video of their paired team based on criteria they developed locally during brainstorming. Task 2 involved teams creating an L2 podcast using Audacity based on local radio station themed content with information populated from the spatially-separated team. Task 3 provided an opportunity to reflect on the experience to date. Each team created a website and added materials produced during the workshop. An on-line document was shared between paired teams providing explicit written feedback on their L2, with each native-speaker correcting a non-native speakers' L2 output. The final task involved each team creating a video containing information content researched on-line and outdoors on their local tourist areas. A written blog reflection in their L1 was added to the website by all team participants to complete the project in full.

The data collected included student questionnaires, teacher/mentor interviews and observations, focus group interviews with students and written reflections from task 3. The questionnaires adapted an existing Bridge21 tool focusing on collaborative and creative skills (Lawlor, Conneely, & Tangney, 2010) to include items related to language learning and spatially separated collaboration. The intervention was too short to assess language gains, however the data collection instruments do focus on student attitudes and experience of learning and as Centra and Gaubatz (2005) argue "[w]hen a student rates overall instruction as effective, there is a correspondingly high perception of learning, as well as 'actual' learning as measured by course exams" (p. 19).

This paper reports a synthesis of an Etic Coding and Theming investigation (Creswell, 2002) of the student questionnaires, focus groups and interactions to analyse the students' overall experience, attitudes to teamwork and technology, collaboration at a distance, and communication with native speakers over the internet.

3. Discussion

The process in general was an overwhelming endorsement of the workshops and the methods used for the learning experience with 100% of students rating it "Good" (9) or "Excellent" (23).

Table 1. Themes on the overall experience

Themes on the overall experience	
Social	Fun/Good experience, Working with new people, Made new friends,
Learning	New learning, Friendly atmosphere really helped my learning,
Technology	Using technology, More confident with technology, Trying new technology was good
Collaboration	Working in groups to do the projects, German teams were fun to work with, I have more trust in teamwork now
Language	Improved fluency, Improved my German, Speaking the language, improved my English

As seen in Table 1, the themes emerging from the responses reinforced the positive experience that most of the students shared in the workshops. What is interesting here is that the responses illustrate the integration of language learning with social and collaborative dimensions of the experience:

> "It was a fun experience and has definitely improved my social skills and team skills".

> "I have now more trust in teamwork".

> "I feel over the course of the two weeks I improved on my German and made new friends in both Ireland and Germany".

> "As I could understand the Irish students well, I became better and more secure in my English".

Similarly, in response to the question "Does communicating with native language speakers improve oral fluency?", students responded overwhelmingly positively (30 out of 31 positive responses) and their comments illustrate the integration of language, collaboration, and confidence-building (see Table 2). In terms of the impact of the collaborative, project-based intervention, a review of student output from the digital artefacts showed paired teams sharing information in L2 and creating content. In particular, students felt motivated and supported to complete their tasks:

"When you are being pushed it is easier to learn and be motivated by people around you in a group even more so than the activity itself".

"The other students helped us if we were stuck, we'd ask them and together we made the topics".

Table 2. Language learning with authentic materials

Themes	Codes
Native speakers	Speaking with natives, Local common phrases.
Fluency	Conversation is possible, Improved my fluency, I got to speak a lot, Spontaneous, Hearing pronunciation, Confidence, Improvisation.
Learning	Conversation is possible, Mistakes ok, More understanding, New vocabulary, Will correct you.
Collaborating	Working on projects in German, Peer to peer, Encouragement from others.

The findings suggest that using the Bridge21 learning model afforded students greater opportunities than the regular classroom environment to improve communicative competencies using L2 and authentic materials, e.g. native speakers, music, radio, web content, etc. Students found that communicating with native speakers in an authentic setting, and sharing roles within the group was conducive to language learning and enhanced fluency.

Students reported teams as a very effective way of learning, both locally and remotely, commenting, "It was great to have everybody bringing different skills that enhanced our projects" and "It is a lot easier as part of a team because then you can focus on certain aspects of a project". For example, one Irish-based student noted when speaking to German students, "In the team you have a variety of who you talk to. You're not just talking to the same person over and over again".

4. Conclusions

A review of 21st-century literature shows that we have moved away from an industrial society to an information society (Voogt & Pelgrum, 2005); students need to use skills which promote critical thinking and problem solving and to work in teams with student-directed learning. The students, by using the Bridge21 model, became active learners and embraced a communicative and collaborative setting for language learning. Students commented "It helped me speak more freely in English and I have more trust in teamwork as I improved my vocabulary", and "I was able to speak more characteristically with them", reinforcing the benefits of providing a real-life environment to participate more in the target language.

In respect to language learning, students commented, "If there were words you weren't sure of or how to pronounce them, when hearing the German speakers saying them it helps you learn" and "By native-speaking I obtained an impressive will to speak English". This drive to use authentic materials and not rely on text books mirrored the findings of Gilmore (2007) and the lack of diverse learning methods in the classroom.

5. Acknowledgements

We would like to thank the students who took part in this for all their enthusiasm, dedication, hard work, and also the Bridge21 team and staff of Bischof von Lipp Schule in Mulfingen.

References

Centra, J. A., & Gaubatz, N. B. (2005). Student perceptions of learning and instructional effectiveness in college courses. *ETS Student Instructional Report (SIR)*. Retrieved from https://www.ets.org/Media/Products/perceptions.pdf

Chun, D. M. (2011). Developing intercultural communicative competence through online exchanges. *CALICO Journal, 28*(2), 392-419. doi:10.11139/cj.28.2.392-419

Conneely, C., Lawlor, J., & Tangney, B. (2013). Technology, teamwork and 21st century skills in the Irish classroom. In K. Marshall (Ed.), *Shaping our future: how the lessons of the past can shape educational transformation*. Dublin: Liffey Press.

Creswell, J. W. (2002). *Educational research: planning, conducting, and evaluating quantitative and qualitative research*. Boston: Pearson Edition.

Gewertz, C. (2008). States press ahead on '21 st-century-skills'. *Education Week, 28*(8), 21-23.

Gilmore, A. (2007). Authentic materials and authenticity in foreign language learning. *Language Learning, 40*(2), 97-118. doi:10.1017/s0261444807004144

Gilmore, A. (2011). Japanese learners' communicative competence with authentic materials. *Language Learning, 61*(3), 786-819. doi:10.1111/j.1467-9922.2011.00634.x

Kern, R., Ware, P., & Warschauer, M. (2004). 11. Crossing frontiers: new directions in online pedagogy and research. *Annual Review of Applied Linguistics, 24*, 243-260. doi:10.1017/S0267190504000091

Lawlor, J., Conneely, C., & Tangney, B. (2010). Towards a pragmatic model for group-based, technology-mediated, project-oriented learning–an overview of the B2C model. *Technology Enhanced Learning. Quality of Teaching and Educational Reform*, 602-609. doi:10.1007/978-3-642-13166-0_84

Silva, E. (2009). Measuring skills for 21st-Century Learning. *The Phi Delta Kappan, 90*(9), 630-634.

Thorne, S. L., & Black, R. W. (2007). Language and literacy development in computer-mediated contexts and communities. *Annual Review of Applied Linguistics, 27*, 133-160. doi:10.1017/s0267190508070074

Voogt, J., & Pelgrum, H. (2005). ICT and curriculum change. *Human Technology, 1*(2), 157-175. doi:http://dx.doi.org/10.17011/ht/urn.2005356

Mobile apps to support and assess foreign language learning

Anke Berns[1], Manuel Palomo-Duarte[2], Juan Manuel Dodero[2], Juan Miguel Ruiz-Ladrón[3], and Andrea Calderón Márquez[3]

Abstract. In the last two decades there have been many attempts to integrate all kinds of mobile devices and apps to support formal as well as informal learning processes. However, most of the available apps still support mainly individual learning, using mobile devices to deliver content rather than providing learners with the opportunity to interact with each other. To address this we have designed an app based on a highly interactive, ubiquitous and constructive learning approach. The app is called *Guess it! Language Trainer* and allows learners to share, assess and co-construct their foreign language knowledge. Learning contents are no longer delivered but integrated into versatile tasks. Even though these tasks are being performed individually by each player, the players' interaction with the app performed affects the whole community of learners. The current research paper presents the first results of an ongoing research project using mobile apps to enhance the Foreign Language Learning in a compulsory German language course at a Spanish University. In our paper we will firstly describe a specific app (Guess it! Language Trainer) which has been used to support students' independent language learning outside the classroom. Secondly, we will describe how the app encouraged students to get actively involved in their own learning processes and thirdly, how the teacher can use the information stored in the system to retrace and assess students' language learning.

Keywords: MALL, assessment, foreign language learning, gamified learning.

---

1. University of Cadiz, Spain; anke.berns@uca.es
2. University of Cadiz, Spain; manuel.palomo@uca.es; juanma.dodero@uca.es
3. University of Cadiz, Spain; juanmiguel.ruizladron@alum.uca.es; andrea.calderonmarquez@alum.uca.es

How to cite this article: Berns, A., Palomo-Duarte, M., Dodero, J. M., Ruiz-Ladrón, J. M., & Calderón Márquez, A. (2015). Mobile apps to support and assess foreign language learning. In F. Helm, L. Bradley, M. Guarda, & S. Thouësny (Eds), *Critical CALL – Proceedings of the 2015 EUROCALL Conference, Padova, Italy* (pp. 51-56). Dublin: Research-publishing.net. http://dx.doi.org/10.14705/rpnet.2015.000309

1. Introduction

Despite the enormous efforts foreign language teachers make every day to provide their students with the maximum possible language input, we all know that students rarely get the language input and practice they would need to acquire the competences they are expected to have at the end of the course. Amongst some of the most common reasons are that language courses are often based on an extremely low percentage of classroom teaching, coupled with an extremely high percentage of independent and out-of-class learning. This makes it difficult to provide learners with sufficient language practice within the classroom as well as attend to their individual learning needs. Therefore, many teachers have started integrating blended teaching practices into their course syllabus, thus providing students with additional learning resources and tools to enhance their out-of-class learning. Virtual learning environments such as Social Network Sites, wikis, virtual worlds and others have been popular teaching and learning tools for many years. Some of the reasons for this is that they enable learners and teachers (with access to the internet) to firstly, access much easier learning materials, and secondly, to create highly interactive and collaborative learning environments (Berns & Palomo-Duarte, 2015).

The increasing availability of mobile technologies such as smartphones and tablets which provide access to multimedia resources and tools (audio, video and chat) undoubtedly holds further potential to support students' language learning (Kukulska-Hulme & Shield, 2008; Stockwell & Hubbard, 2013). This, coupled with the fact that mobile data connection has become more affordable, allows for distributed learning anytime and anywhere (Palomo-Duarte, Berns, Dodero, & Cejas, 2014). The purpose of the current project is to explore some of the possibilities of integrating smartphones in blended teaching practices to make independent learning processes both more dynamic and easier to monitor. With this purpose in mind, we have designed an app called *Guess it! Language Trainer*. The app allows learners to acquire new language input as well as to create new language learning contents and share these with other users.

2. Method

2.1. Learning design and architecture

In the following we will offer some insight into the app architecture we designed for the current project and tested with a group of more than 100 students from the University of Cádiz (Spain). The participating students were mainly Spanish native speakers and enrolled in a compulsory German Language course at A1 level from the Common European Framework of References for Languages (CEFR).

The system follows a client-server architecture (see Figure 1), where a server coordinates many smartphones or tablets. The system allows us to identify students' interaction with the app by connecting with the server through the Internet. Furthermore it provides students and teachers with a highly interactive and dynamic learning environment, in which they can access, evaluate and report already existing learning content, consult their learning statistics, etc. (Palomo-Duarte et al., 2014).

Figure 1. System architecture

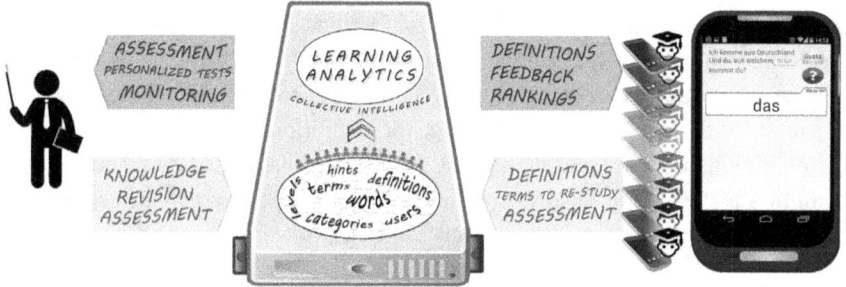

With regard to the game dynamic, players get first the opportunity to play a number of definitions based on the main vocabulary items defined by the CEFR for the A1 level. Vocabulary items have been divided into different categories (freetime, sports, professions, places, etc.) and levels. However, the app can easily be implemented in terms of content, levels, as well as other foreign languages.

In order to play the app, students first have to guess and then assess the definition they have previously been assigned and played, deciding whether the provided definition is correct (in terms of grammar as well as content), precise (understandable or ambiguous), difficult to guess or, even politically incorrect. Once the students have played and assessed a certain number of definitions, they are allowed to create and enter their own definitions. Thus, for every twenty definitions a student has played, the system automatically provides them with a term they are then allowed to create a new definition for. This is then added to the server knowledge base. In this way the knowledge base of our app is constantly being increased and reviewed by the users themselves. As a result of this process, the server will contain different definitions and grades for each of the terms defined. Those definitions that receive higher grades will be displayed more often and vice versa. Nonetheless, all definitions will be displayed (more or less frequently) and constantly be re-assessed by the players. So, if a good definition should unfairly receive some lower grades and hence become scarcely used, it may sooner or later be played again, assessed with a higher grade and become a more "popular" definition. This allows a very dynamic game ecosystem in which students become directly involved in the design process according to their learning preferences and needs (Berns, Palomo-Duarte, Garrido Guerrero, & Páez Piña, 2015).

2.2. Assessing student's foreign language learning

With regard to the assessment of students' foreign language learning, it is worth mentioning that the server programme stores different kinds of data which aim to help teachers evaluate students' learning processes and outcomes. The data which is stored by the server is the following: the definitions available for each term, the definitions each student guessed or failed as well as the assessment of each definition played. Additionally, in order to monitor and assess students' learning processes the course coordinator can access different learning analytics.

As mentioned in Palomo-Duarte et al. (2014), the analytics could provide information on the use each student has made of the app (the number and frequency with which the different levels, words and categories have been played), the number and definitions each player has entered in the app, the evaluation of their definitions (according to the terms that have been guessed and the evaluation their definitions have been given), as well as the evaluation each student gave to the definition entered by other players. Thus, a report of the low-graded definitions can provide insights into the difficulties a particular student (or a group of them) might have regarding the target language. Another report with those definitions that wrongly received high grades can identify those students who are unable to detect mistakes in the target language.

3. Discussion

The results of the game-experience were in general very positive as students increased their vocabulary knowledge in only four weeks (Palomo-Duarte et al., 2014). A comparison between the results from the pre-test and post-test 3 underlines the app's impact on students' vocabulary learning. There is an average of 5,35 points of difference in a range from 0 to 10. Secondly, students reported that by playing and creating definitions themselves they significantly improved their writing skills, getting much more confident in the target language. Only 17 of the 107 students interviewed were not very app acceptant. Some of the reasons for this were the following: students with an iPhone could not install the app on their smartphones, since they were not compatible with the Android operating system the app was designed for. Therefore some students relied on using the devices of other classmates, which allowed them only restricted access to the app. Additionally the version we used in the first year contained several technical mistakes, which sometimes hindered students' learning processes, but which have been adjusted in the more recent version of the app.

4. Conclusions

Language learning in traditional classroom settings has often proved to be lacking in terms of the language practice students need to get the proficiency they are expected to have at the end of the course, especially when the number of students increases. Hence, our proposal focuses on using computer systems to increase students' exposure to the target language providing them with multiple opportunities to obtain as well as to produce new meaningful language input. Unlike virtual worlds, which usually need a powerful server to run and PCs on which to be played, we propose using apps for smartphones (or tablets), since they need a simple server software and light app for widely-spread Android devices. The app we have designed for the present study differs from other already available apps, since it provides learners as well as teachers with new opportunities in terms of learning and assessment.

Even though the designed app needs to be tested with a much larger sample size and for a much longer period, the current experience sheds some light on the possibilities of using mobile apps to facilitate learning as well as assessment processes.

5. Acknowledgements

This work has been funded by the University of Cadiz program for Researching and Innovation in Education (sol-201400047372-tra) as well as by the European Union under the OpenDiscoverySpace (CIP-ICT-PSP-2011-5) and UBIcamp (526843_ LLP-1-2012 Es-Erasmus-ESMO) projects. Many thanks also to all students who participated in the experience and especially to Alberto Cejas Sánchez for the software development.

References

Berns, A., & Palomo-Duarte, M. (2015). Supporting foreign language learning through a gamified app. In. R. Hernández & P. Rankins (Eds.), *Third-level education and second language learning: promoting self-directed learning in new t echnological and educational contexts* (pp. 181-204). Bern: Peter Lang.

Berns, A., Palomo-Duarte, M., Garrido Guerrero, A., & Paez Piña, M. (2015). Learners' expectations and needs: some practical clues for designing foreign language apps. In. J. Colpaert, A. Aerts, M. Oberhofer, & M. Gutiérez-Colón Plana (Eds.), *Task design & CALL proceedings Universitat Rovira i Virgili 6 - 8 July 2015* (pp. 116-123). Antwerpen: Nieuwe Media Dienst.

Kukulska-Hulme, A., & Shield, L. (2008). An overview of mobile assisted language learning: from content delivery to supported collaboration and interaction. *ReCALL, 20*(3), 271-289. doi:10.1017/S0958344008000335

Palomo-Duarte, M., Berns, A., Dodero, J. M., & Cejas, A. (2014). Foreign language learning using a gamificated APP to support peer-assessment. In. F. J. García-Peñalvo (Ed.), *Proceedings TEEM'14. Second international conference on technological ecosystems for enhancing multiculturality, Salamanca, Spain, October 1st - 3rd, 2014* (pp. 381-386). Salamanca: ACM. doi:10.1145/2669711.2669927

Stockwell, G., & Hubbard, P. (2013). Some emerging principles for mobile-assisted language learning. *The International Research Foundation for English Language Education* (pp. 1-15). Retrieved from http://www.tirfonline.org/english-in-the-workforce/mobile-assisted-language-learning/some-emerging-principles-for-mobile-assisted-language-learning/

Dialogue-based CALL: an overview of existing research

Serge Bibauw[1], Thomas François[2], and Piet Desmet[3]

Abstract. Dialogue-based Computer-Assisted Language Learning (CALL) covers applications and systems allowing a learner to practice the target language in a meaning-focused conversational activity with an automated agent. We first present a common definition for dialogue-based CALL, based on three features: dialogue as the activity unit, computer as the interlocutor and negotiation of outcome through open learner production. We then report on a systematic literature review we conducted on the main scientific databases which, after filtering, resulted in 138 relevant papers which were analyzed and coded. Results show a scattered research field, with four different disciplinary approaches. We conclude with observations regarding the remaining challenges and opportunities for Intelligent CALL (ICALL) research.

Keywords: dialogue-based CALL, conversational agent, dialogue system, chatbot, ICALL, literature review.

1. Introduction

Second language acquisition theories have long advocated the need for meaning-focused activities, especially comprehensible interaction (Long, 1996). It has also been amply demonstrated that Synchronous Computer-Mediated Communication (SCMC), notably text-based chat, has a positive effect on the development of L2 proficiency, including speaking proficiency (Lin, 2015). Considering the lack of

---

1. KU Leuven Kulak, iMinds, ITEC; Université catholique de Louvain, IL&C, CENTAL; Universidad Central del Ecuador; serge.bibauw@kuleuven.be
2. Université catholique de Louvain, IL&C, CENTAL; thomas.francois@uclouvain.be
3. KU Leuven Kulak, iMinds, ITEC; piet.desmet@kuleuven.be

How to cite this article: Bibauw, S., François, T., & Desmet, P. (2015). Dialogue-based CALL: an overview of existing research. In F. Helm, L. Bradley, M. Guarda, & S. Thouësny (Eds), *Critical CALL – Proceedings of the 2015 EUROCALL Conference, Padova, Italy* (pp. 57-64). Dublin: Research-publishing.net. http://dx.doi.org/10.14705/rpnet.2015.000310

opportunities for practice with native speakers in most foreign language teaching contexts, there has thus been a steady interest in CALL systems that would allow learners to practice and develop their communicative skills through interactions in natural language with an artificial interlocutor.

Since the first attempts to tackle this problem, numerous researchers have experimented with Natural Language Processing (NLP) techniques to hold conversations with learners. However, research on this matter remains scattered across different disciplines, with only partial mutual awareness of previous works. Previous syntheses have only addressed part of the question, focusing either on speech-based applications (Eskenazi, 2009) or on text-based chatbots (Fryer & Carpenter, 2006), or mentioning it in ICALL in general (Gamper & Knapp, 2002).

The terms used to refer to the systems are not well established either, with important variations and multiple possible keywords. *Dialogue systems*, *conversational agents* and *chatbots* are sometimes differentiated on modal or technical criteria. Klüwer (2011) distinguishes *dialogue systems* from *chatbots* by their "use of more theoretically motivated techniques" (p. 3). Jokinen and McTear (2010) treat *dialogue systems* as necessarily spoken, and *conversational agents* as necessarily embodied, raising issues of multimodality and non-verbal communication; *chatbots* are "conversational systems" (i.e. designed for open-ended small talk) while *dialogue systems* are automatically task-oriented. However, the same authors recognize a growing convergence of all these systems, which blurs the boundaries (Jokinen & McTear, 2010, p. 129). As a result, the three terms are often used interchangeably, in an unspecified usage. Bearing in mind that the challenges for dialogue management and the opportunities for language learning remain essentially equivalent, this is the position we adopted, using *dialogue-based CALL* as an umbrella term.

More importantly, we first propose an operational definition of dialogue-based CALL. This definition served as the main inclusion criteria in the systematic literature review. Analyzing the existing research on the topic, we identified the most important trends and some challenges for future research.

1.1. Towards an operational definition

It is possible to define dialogue-based CALL in a minimal way as (1) **dialogue-based** (2) **interactions with a computer** for language learning purposes. The second element sets us inside *tutorial CALL*, in contrast with computer-mediated communication, where interactions are with other humans *via* a computer. "Dialogue-based" makes the distinction with *item-based* approaches, which have been dominant in autonomous CALL applications. Nevertheless, this definition also applies to any form of interaction that takes the form of a dialogue, such as *branching dialogues* (conversation tree with a limited choice of utterances to select from, often used in adventure games) or systems that do not take into account what the user has previously uttered (certain question-asking systems). It is thus important to state a third characteristic: (3) the interactions must allow a certain **negotiation of outcome** (Young, 1988) through **open learner output**. It is this possibility to negotiate the outcome of the interaction, by uttering a free range of text or speech, that makes it, at the same time, complex to develop, regarding the required natural language processing in the background, and potentially very beneficial for language learning, as it enables the learner to freely build his own meaning.

2. Method

2.1. Collection of a corpus of studies

We performed an extensive search on the leading scientific databases (Web of Science, Scopus, Proquest), using all the possible keywords referring to dialogue systems for language learning, obtaining 604, 494 and 1003 hits respectively (with important overlap). We completed this retrieval process through forward citations and ancestry search from the previous relevant hits. Only peer-reviewed scientific documents (journal papers, conference papers and edited book chapters) and doctoral dissertations were included in our corpus. We then used the above-stated defining features to select papers about dialogue systems only. We discarded papers not directly related to language learning (e.g. only mentioning it as a potential application). At the end of the inclusion/exclusion process, 109 relevant papers remained.

2.2. Analysis

ll remaining papers were manually assessed for system, technological and evaluation aspects, as well as bibliographical information. These characteristics were coded and analyzed mainly in a qualitative manner (see section 4), but also in a quantitative way. The frequencies of all the terms referring to dialogue systems were computed and used as variables in a Principal Component Analysis (PCA). The resulting graph (Figure 2) shows the main variation tendencies, the relationships between terms and the projection of the papers on this variation space.

3. Results

As mentioned above, there is a wide diversity of terms used to refer to dialogue-based CALL. Out of 109 papers, we identified 49 different terms, ranging from *agent-mediated language-learning environment* to *voice-interactive CALL*. Some papers use more general keywords, which tend to conceal the specificity of the system (e.g. *virtual world*, *game*), while others coin their own (28 terms are used once). The most discriminant terms are *intelligent tutoring system*, *chatbot* (or *chatterbot*), *conversational agent*, and *dialogue system*. As shown in Figure 1, *dialogue system* is the most frequent (58 papers mentioned it), probably because it is associated with an important research strand in natural language processing (Jokinen & McTear, 2010). However, what does not appear here is the divergence between papers in the use of certain terms.

Figure 1. Chronological evolution of main key terms used in papers

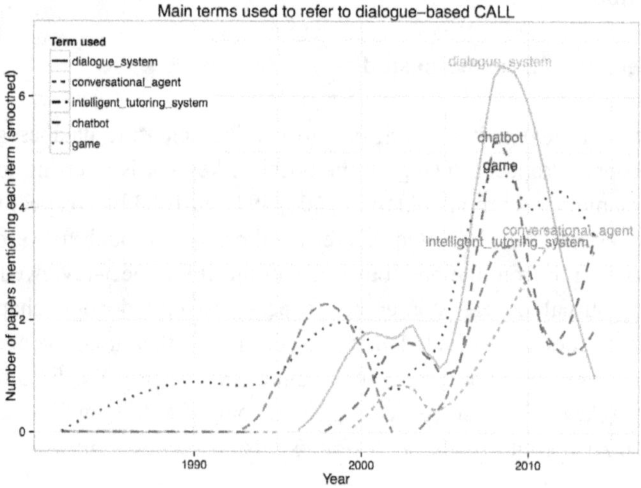

The results from the PCA, presented in Figure 2, help us distinguish different tendencies and clusters among papers. The fact that *chatbot* and *dialogue system* are on opposite sides of the y-axis indicates a negative correlation on the second principal component: papers mentioning one usually do not (or very rarely) mention the other. On the contrary, *conversational agent* is used globally in a similar way as *dialogue system*.

Meanwhile, the first principal component (x-axis) seems to correspond to the importance of the application for language learning: papers on the positive side of the axis tend to be mostly focused on the technological aspects, while those on the left tend to attribute more importance to the analysis of the language learning process. In this sense, the latter commonly use terms like *tutoring systems* and *ICALL*.

Figure 2. Projection of variables (terms frequencies, as lines) and observations (papers) on a bidimensional plot with two principal components (out of 5)

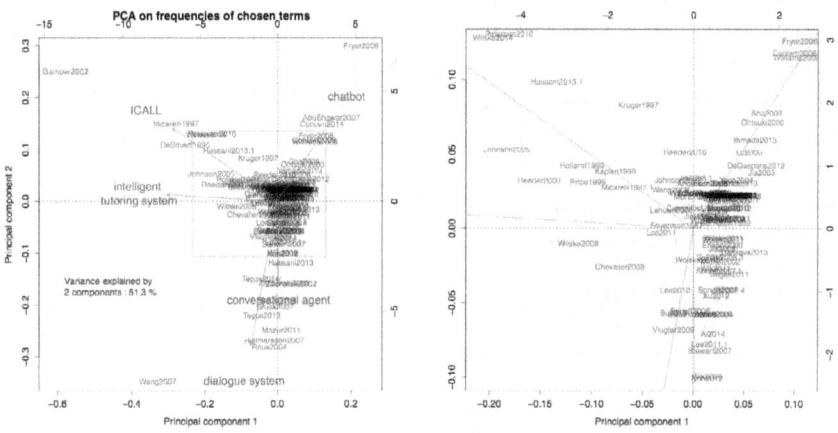

These exploratory analyses show there are different clusters of research on dialogue-based CALL. Through an interpretative and qualitative analysis, we identified four groups of papers, coming from different disciplines. They are presented in Figure 3.

The first group embraces research on Intelligent Tutoring Systems (ITS). ITS existed previously as item-based activities for form-focused practice, but the 1980s and 90s saw many efforts to develop more communicative, dialogue-based activities as part of ITS. Most papers published in this trend show a particular attention to the provision of automated corrective feedback to the learner, but little consideration for dialogue management and natural language generation.

The second group to emerge is related to **games** and **virtual worlds**. Many efforts are contiguous to ITS, with various systems qualifying as both. The gaming side of dialogue systems for language learning has also led to the most important commercial applications (e.g. Johnson, 2007).

The third group encompasses research on (spoken) **dialogue systems** and (embodied) **conversational agents**. It arises mainly from researchers in NLP who decided to apply these techniques to L2 learning (e.g. Morton, Gunson, & Jack, 2012). Here, the focus is predominantly on the technological challenges that such an endeavor poses. It is probably the research area that presents the most significant technological advances and, consequently, it is also the most active.

The last group, focusing on **chatbots**, is the most different. Chatbots, the descendants of ELIZA (Weizenbaum, 1966), are text-based conversational systems. The diffusion of an accessible framework for programming chatbots, AIML, and the popularity of chatbots' competitions, emulating the Turing test, contributed to the creation of countless amateur chatbots. Some research on their application for language learning has been conducted (e.g. Coniam, 2014), but research on this area regularly fails to connect to the parallel work carried out on dialogue systems.

Figure 3. Research on dialogue systems for language learning which appeared in four different disciplines

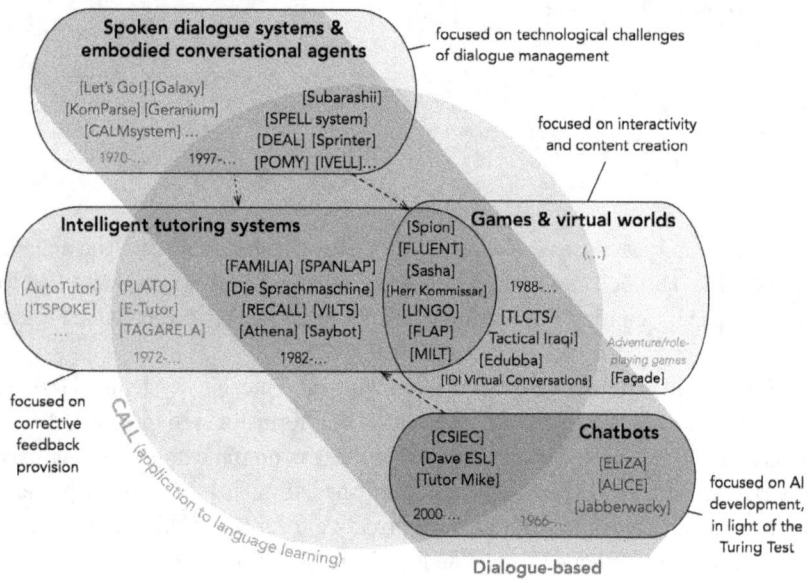

4. Conclusions

We have presented an operational definition of dialogue-based CALL, as dialogue-based interactions with a computer allowing negotiation of outcome through open learner. Such systems have been investigated under various terms and from various perspectives in the past, with complementary interests, bridging CALL, natural language processing, games and artificial intelligence. However, no common framework has been made available, and studies of the effectiveness on L2 learning lack generalizability. Therefore, there is a crucial need for more research and development on this topic.

5. Acknowledgments

This research is supported by *Secretaría de Educación Superior, Ciencia, Tecnología e Innovación* (SENESCYT) from Ecuador, under Doctoral Research Grant 2014-AR2Q7873, and is conducted jointly at KU Leuven Kulak and Université catholique de Louvain in Belgium.

References

Coniam, D. (2014). The linguistic accuracy of chatbots: usability from an ESL perspective. *Text & Talk*, *34*(5), 545-567. doi:10.1515/text-2014-0018

Eskenazi, M. (2009). An overview of spoken language technology for education. *Speech Communication*, *51*(10), 832-844. doi:10.1016/j.specom.2009.04.005

Fryer, L., & Carpenter, R. (2006). Bots as language learning tools. *Language Learning & Technology*, *10*(3), 8-14.

Gamper, J., & Knapp, J. (2002). A review of Intelligent CALL systems. *Computer Assisted Language Learning*, *15*(4), 329-342. doi:10.1076/call.15.4.329.8270

Johnson, W. L. (2007). Serious use of a serious game for language learning. In *Proceedings of the 2007 Conference on Artificial Intelligence in Education: Building Technology Rich Learning Contexts That Work* (pp. 67-74). Amsterdam: IOS Press. Retrieved from http://dl.acm.org/citation.cfm?id=1563601.1563617

Jokinen, K., & McTear, M. F. (2010). *Spoken dialogue systems*. San Rafael, CA: Morgan & Claypool. Retrieved from http://www.morganclaypool.com/doi/abs/10.2200/S00204ED1V01Y200910HLT005

Klüwer, T. (2011). From chatbots to dialog systems. In D. Perez-Marin & I. Pascual-Nieto (Eds.), *Conversational agents and natural language interaction: Techniques and Effective Practices* (pp. 1-22). Hershey, PA, USA: IGI Global. doi:10.4018/978-1-60960-617-6.ch001

Lin, H. (2015). A meta-synthesis of empirical research on the effectiveness of computer-mediated communication (CMC) in SLA. *Language Learning & Technology*, *19*(2), 85-117.

Long, M. H. (1996). The role of the linguistic environment in second language acquisition. In W. C. Ritchie & T. K. Bhatia (Eds.), *Handbook of second language acquisition* (pp. 413-468). San Diego, CA: Academic Press. doi:10.1016/b978-012589042-7/50015-3

Morton, H., Gunson, N., & Jack, M. A. (2012). Interactive language learning through speech-enabled virtual scenarios. *Advances in Human-Computer Interaction*, *2012*, e389523. doi:10.1155/2012/389523

Weizenbaum, J. (1966). ELIZA: a computer program for the study of natural language communication between man and machine. *Communications of the ACM, 9*(1), 36-45. doi:10.1145/365153.365168

Young, R. (1988). Computer-assisted language learning conversations: negotiating an outcome. *CALICO Journal, 5*(3), 65-83.

Applied linguistics project: student-led computer assisted research in high school EAL / EAP

Róbert Bohát[1], Beata Rödlingová[2], and Nina Horáková[3]

Abstract. The Applied Linguistics Project (ALP) started at the International School of Prague (ISP) in 2013. Every year, Grade 9 English as an Additional Language (EAL) students identify an area of learning in need of improvement and design a research method followed by data collection and analysis using basic computer software tools or online corpora. Mimicking authentic research, they write a research paper and present it in front of a panel of experts at Charles University in Prague. The papers are collected in a proceedings book. This research project confirms that high school students – with appropriate scaffolding – are capable of academic research, meta-cognition, and applying data-driven critical thinking to academic language learning with a responsible application of Computer-Assisted Language Learning (CALL).

Keywords: inquiry learning, student-led research, applied linguistics, EAL, English as an additional language.

1. Introduction

For more and more students worldwide, the language of their schooling is not their Mother Tongue (MT). These students learn the new language, as well as in it, through it and about it, facing a double challenge: unlike their native speaker schoolmates who learn unknown concepts through a known language (their MT), EAL students' learning is an equation of two *unknowns* – learning an *unknown*

---

1. International School of Prague, Czech Republic; rbohat@isp.cz
2. International School of Prague, Czech Republic; brodlingova@isp.cz
3. International School of Prague, Czech Republic; nhorakova@isp.cz

How to cite this article: Bohát, R., Rödlingová, B., & Horáková, N. (2015). Applied linguistics project: student-led computer assisted research in high school EAL / EAP. In F. Helm, L. Bradley, M. Guarda, & S. Thouësny (Eds), *Critical CALL – Proceedings of the 2015 EUROCALL Conference, Padova, Italy* (pp. 65-70). Dublin: Research-publishing.net. http://dx.doi.org/10.14705/rpnet.2015.000311

concept in a *partially known* language. Thus, much of their school experience is not based on fully comprehensible input (Krashen, 2003).

Arguing the crucial role of language in learning, Postman (1980) says that "every teacher, regardless of level or subject, must be a language educator" (p. 28). Halliday (1993) adds: "When children learn language... they are learning the foundation of learning itself" (p. 93). In other words, almost all learning is a form of language learning, meaning making through language. As a time-tested biblical proverb says: "Learning comes easily to someone who understands" (Proverbs 14:6 New International Version). Therefore, if students understand better how language works and how their MT and academic language interact, they will be in a position to understand better how learning works – and how to make it easier and more effective. We suggest that a combination of introspection, CALL and a data-driven discovery approach will allow for more engaged, meaningful and efficient learning for all students.

That was the goal of the ALP at the ISP, in which 32 Grade 9 EAL students identified an area where they needed to improve their learning of and through academic English. Each student chose a topic and an appropriate linguistic research method to find out how their learning in academic English works in comparison with learning in their Mother Tongue, how the two languages interact or differ, etc.

The researched topics were: bilingual reading speed and comprehension comparison, basic lexicography, translation, an analysis of academic vocabulary use in context (such as assume, believe, conceive, etc.), or a comparative study of a paremiological minimum (100 most frequently used proverbs) between two languages. Students analyzed their results in a short paper presented at a student linguistic conference held at Charles University in Prague. At the end of the project, the student papers were bound into a proceedings book, in imitation of the real academic research process.

2. Methodologies

2.1. The general pedagogical methodology

Short instructional videos explaining basic data collection and analytical methods were used to train the students in basic applied linguistics methodology ("flipped classroom" approach). A template of the final paper provided a rubric and a list of requirements. For bilingual reading speed and comprehension studies, a minimum of five different texts in each language was required for analysis in bilingual reading speed and comprehension studies. After reading an academic text in MT for at least three minutes, students took a small comprehension test prepared by another speaker of the MT and calculated the reading speed in words or syllables per minute. The same procedure was repeated with texts in English.

The CALL element of the research involved using appropriate software for recording their reading, word count and other quantification tools, as well as data processing in calculating the ratios in words per minute or syllables per minute. They also used graphing software to visualize the results. Another CALL dimension was the use of online corpora, either the parallel multilingual InterCorp by the Institute of the Czech National Corpus or the British National Corpus (BNC).

Corpus based studies produced much larger sets of data, bringing these high school students even closer to authentic academic research. Concordances, collocations, relative frequency and distribution, as well as randomization of large samples were among the most frequently used software tools employed in corpus research. Students conducting these studies also used lexical density, percentages and an analysis of trends to evaluate their results.

3. Discussion

3.1. Data collection, processing and evaluation encouraged through questions

The research paper template is also a springboard for critical thinking in their analysis and interpretation. If a proposal for improved learning is presented, the young researchers need to explain whether there are possible alternative interpretations and their implications for learning strategies or for future research.

Additionally, the conclusion of a student's paper and presentation needs to connect his or her analysis of results to the research question/topic and show how their research answers the question (or not) and why. Further help is provided with questions such as, what are the limitations of your method or results? What counter-arguments can be used against your interpretation? Do the results harmonize with your background research? etc.

As in all academic research, a bibliography has to be included in the paper (MLA style). In the second year of ALP, some of the previous student papers were cited and referenced in new research that expanded on their methodology and findings –

again, imitating the actual research process. In keeping with the concept of additive bilingualism, each paper has an abstract in the student's MT and English.

3.2. Life-long skills and interdisciplinary overlap of ALP

ALP is a multi-modal, meta-cognitive and interdisciplinary discovery learning activity. Students are required to use printed as well as electronic sources to keep their research skills balanced. They also need to combine methodologies of various disciplines: mathematics, language, social studies, and statistics. Interestingly, a Russian student who realized that processing raw data through relative frequency completely changed the seeming implications of the results commented: "This is the first time in my life that I've seen mathematics being useful". A Belgian student's feedback form said: "This project helped me to improve my linguistic skills for both languages [MT and English]... I learned a new study method, now I know what to do if I don't understand a topic at school...". A Japanese native speaker wrote: "Throughout the ALP project, I found out the useful studying techniques which I have been using for four or five months. It is apparent that my grades are ameliorating so much from the first term. I also learned how to write an academic paper". A Czech student who in 2013 conducted a corpus-based study plans to use corpus methods in mass media analysis for his final International Baccalaureate research paper.

4. Conclusions

Students who have done this small-scale linguistic research benefit from the meta-cognitive approach to language learning because it empowers them to become producers of knowledge, not just its passive consumers. The experience of having one's own ideas confirmed or "disproved" by experimental data gave them a deeper understanding of both learning and the limitations of the scientific methodology. Their findings also support the claim that MT inclusion in EAL students' learning makes learning more effective as it removes one of the "unknowns" (i.e. unknown language element) and makes the input more comprehensible. It also demonstrates that high school students are fully capable of academic research, meta-cognition, analysis and critical thinking, with appropriate scaffolding.

An added benefit of working with quantitative data is the valuable practice students received in distinguishing better quality data from lower quality data, and the importance of the sample size. This is indeed a "lifeworthy" skill – the ability to deal with a flood of data, sifting through the information, separating the useful from the useless, and drawing their own conclusions based on (un)observed patterns

(Perkins, 2014). Even students who were less than enthusiastic benefited, as became evident during the feedback collection. One student claimed that he "hasn't learned anything from this project". When asked about the pattern he had mentioned in his presentation, he answered: "Yes, but that was such a small sample!". Thus, this student demonstrated that if nothing else, he learned that small sets of data have limited value when it comes to generalizations and pattern identification – a valuable life skill indeed.

Naturally, there is much room for improving the pedagogical and research value of ALP. For this reason we have also built a specialized Corpus of High School Academic Texts (COHAT – more details in our paper on COHAT, Bohát, Rödlingová, & Horáková, 2015, in this volume). Yet the first two years' worth of preliminary data show that ALP engenders critical thinking and meta-cognition in teenage students, as evidenced by their presentations, papers, and feedback. This harmonizes with Postman's (1980) description of language learning "as a form of metaeducation. That is, one learns a subject and, at the same time, learns what the subject is made of. One learns to talk the subject, but also learns to talk about the talk…" (p. 37). ALP allows the aspiring young researchers to think about their thinking, talk about their talk and learning in their oral presentation to the panel of experts as well as in their papers. This approach has a great potential. "For it is not education to teach students to repeat sentences they do not understand so that they may pass examinations. That is the way of the computer. I prefer the student to be a programmer" (Postman, 1980, p. 37).

5. Acknowledgements

We would like to thank Lawrence Hrubes (ISP EAL department chair), ISP Administration, and Dr Petr Chalupský, Dr Bohuslav Dvořák, and Mgr. Karel Žďárek from Charles University in Prague, Faculty of Education, Department of English Language and Literature for making the ALP possible. Róbert Bohát would like to thank his wife and family for their support without which most of this work could not have been completed.

References

Bohát, R., Rödlingová, B., & Horáková, N. (2015). Corpus of High School Academic Texts (COHAT): data-driven, computer assisted discovery in learning academic English. In F. Helm, L. Bradley, M. Guarda, & S. Thouësny (Eds), *Critical CALL – Proceedings of the 2015 EUROCALL Conference, Padova, Italy* (pp. 71-76). Dublin: Research-publishing.net. doi:10.14705/rpnet.2015.000312

Halliday, M. A. K. (1993). Towards a language-based theory of learning. *Linguistics and Education*, *5*(2), 93-116. doi:10.1016/0898-5898(93)90026-7

Krashen, S. D. (2003). Explorations in language acquisition and use. *The Taipei Lectures*. Portsmouth, NH: Heinemann.

Perkins, D. (2014). *Future wise: educating our children for a changing world*. San Francisco: Jossey-Bass.

Postman, N. (1980). Language education in a knowledge context. *ETC: A Review of General Semantics*, *37*(1), 25-37.

Corpus of High School Academic Texts (COHAT): data-driven, computer assisted discovery in learning academic English

Róbert Bohát[1], Beata Rödlingová[2], and Nina Horáková[3]

Abstract. Corpus of High School Academic Texts (COHAT), currently of 150,000+ words, aims to make academic language instruction a more data-driven and student-centered discovery learning as a special type of Computer-Assisted Language Learning (CALL), emphasizing students' critical thinking and meta-cognition. Since 2013, high school English as an additional language (EAL) students at the International School of Prague (ISP) have worked with corpora to discover the patterns of English in academic contexts. The positive results of their work with corpora inspired the creation of COHAT, providing a high school level bank of exemplary academic English texts by their native and non-native peers. Our focus is on detecting patterns of correct word choice, syntax and style in student writing.

Keywords: corpus linguistics, discovery learning, learner corpus, critical thinking.

1. Introduction

"Language should be studied in actual, attested, authentic instances of use, not as intuitive, invented, isolated sentences" (Stubbs, 1993, p. 2). In order to help high school students benefit from this approach, COHAT was established by the EAL Department at the International School of Prague.

---

1. International School of Prague, Praha, Czech Republic; rbohat@isp.cz
2. International School of Prague, Praha, Czech Republic; brodlingova@isp.cz
3. International School of Prague, Praha, Czech Republic ; nhorakova@isp.cz

How to cite this article: Bohát, R., Rödlingová, B., & Horáková, N. (2015). Corpus of High School Academic Texts (COHAT): data-driven, computer assisted discovery in learning academic English. In F. Helm, L. Bradley, M. Guarda, & S. Thouësny (Eds), *Critical CALL – Proceedings of the 2015 EUROCALL Conference, Padova, Italy* (pp. 71-76). Dublin: Research-publishing.net. http://dx.doi.org/10.14705/rpnet.2015.000312

Since 2013, EAL students at ISP have engaged in a heuristic approach to academic English within the framework of the Applied Linguistics Project (ALP - see our ALP paper in this volume). Students who worked with corpora (InterCorp and BNC) presented their semantic or grammatical discoveries to their classmates, becoming co-teachers in the classroom, which resulted in a lively atmosphere of genuine academic discussion and discovery, confirming the old Latin maxim *Docendo discimus* (By teaching others we learn). The rationale for building a corpus of this type is twofold. First, the existing academic corpora seem to cater predominantly to university level students. Second, most of the high-school learner corpora we found focused on identifying problem areas in non-native speaker texts; the goal of COHAT is to provide high school students with a set of successful academic English texts written by their peers that would focus on detecting patterns of correct word choice, syntax, grammar and style in students' writing. Thus, while recognizing the great value of error detection in learner corpora, we suggest that their value can be enhanced by studying also what the students did well.

2. Method

2.1. Corpus collection and structure

At this first stage, COHAT is relatively small, containing 101 texts with 150,000+ words without annotation, allowing for concordancing, keyword lists, frequency studies, context analysis, and basic collocation studies, using AntConc software (Anthony, 2014). Currently, four discipline-related categories are represented: English and Literature, Social Studies, Maths and Natural Sciences, and Creative Writing (including Speeches & Journalism). Additionally, genres, registers, author's age, gender and mother tongue are recorded in the metadata. The plan is to make it a balanced, representative corpus of student and teacher writing for each high school grade level (i.e. Grade 9, 10, 11, and 12). Following this, grammatical and semantic taggers will be used to annotate the anonymized student texts for further linguistic analysis. As in the university level British Academic Written English (BAWE) Corpus, "only texts that have met departmental requirements for the given level of study" (Alsop & Nesi, 2009, p. 71) were and will continue to be included. The texts are unedited, allowing students to see that some mistakes do not necessarily prevent texts from success.

2.2. COHAT: student discovery in the classroom

How can a learner corpus be used beyond traditional error detection? COHAT and other corpora have been used at ISP also in a constructivist way - as a resource for detecting the patterns of successful language use across genres, subjects, and registers. Students can use either a corpus, or corpus based data sets prepared by teachers, to analyze and generalize their observations about lexis, grammar, or sentence and paragraph structures. Teachers have used the newly built COHAT to create lesson plans for language discovery activities. A few of these lesson plans have been presented at the English Acquisition and Corpora Building 2015 conference in Pardubice, Czech Republic (more information in Bohát, Rödlingová, & Horáková, 2015, this volume). Below we would like to outline a few preliminary results of COHAT analysis as a starting point for developing a wider set of language discovery lesson plans.

One such area of interest is collocations; here the students are encouraged to use the corpus to get to 'know the words by the company they keep', noticing the nuances of meaning emphasized by habitual co-occurrence of words (Firth, 1957). They also help identify idiomatic and fixed expressions. Figure 1 shows the example of the top two collocates of "largely" that tend to have negative connotations in science discourse. Such studies can inform students' word choice with a view to the prevalent collocations and connotations.

Figure 1. 1R collocates of "largely" (by relative frequency)

1R collocates of "largely" (by RF)	
1	disproportional
2	subjective
3	polish
4	through
5	because
6	termed
7	indicates

A grammatical aspect of language can be illustrated by the use of present and past verb tenses in writing about history versus fiction. Figure 2 shows a stronger presence of the present tense of selected verbs in literary analysis and of the past tense in history writing. This is an interesting finding because most teachers emphasize the need to use present tense in fiction and past tense only in discussing historical events. Yet, the COHAT analysis shows past tense verbs in successful literary analysis texts. Thus, a corpus turns out to be – inter alia – also an indicator of whether the teachers' explicit preferences are fully and consistently reflected in exemplary student texts. This may be a good stimulus for student and teacher reflection on the rule.

Figure 2. Present vs. past tenses across genres and subjects

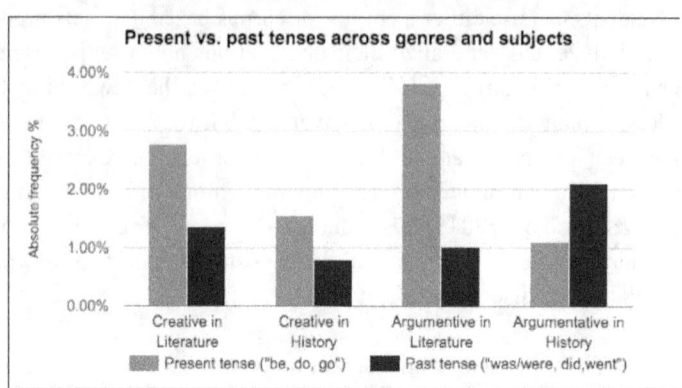

Making texts "flow" is often viewed as an abstract, elusive concept. Figure 3 shows a function based analysis of cohesive devices in COHAT with a 60% prevalence of comparing and contrasting cohesives (transitional words or expressions). Students and teachers can reflect: is this a lack of balance in our students' thinking, using comparative analysis at the expense of cause-and-effect relationships or temporal/purpose expressions? Or is it a symptom of an imbalance in the corpus? Could it indicate the popularity of this genre among the teachers, as these are the text types so frequently provided by our colleagues as exemplary? There could be very good (maybe developmental) reasons for the strong presence of comparative and contrastive texts in earlier years of high school education. Either way, having specific data can help teachers and students think critically about their academic language use and inform future lesson plans.

Figure 3. Cohesives by function

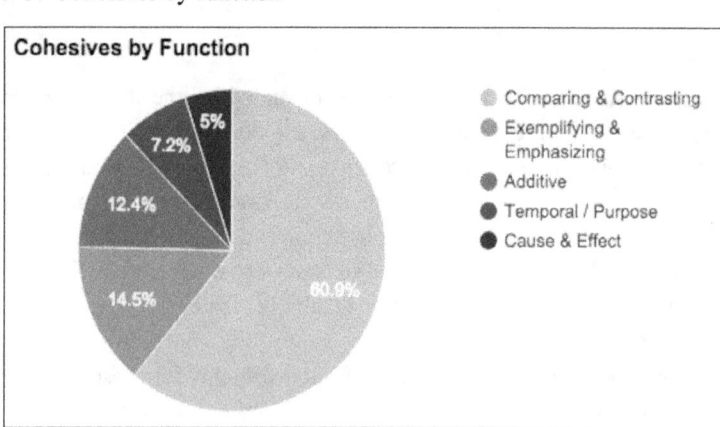

3. Discussion

In terms of language pedagogy, corpora allow for a new application of Wittgenstein's (2001) concept of "language games". Applied to natural language acquisition, the game metaphor presents a challenge: language is a game whose rules are not outlined in a user's manual; the native speaker discovers the rules by observation. In language learning contexts, some of the rules are written down in textbooks, but these are often difficult to understand and internalize. Worse still, thinking about memorized rules of grammar before uttering a sentence typically slows down student communication.

On the other hand, computerized corpora can serve as a playground of sorts for students to observe large quantities of language in use and at least partially make up for the lack of years of constant exposure available to native users. Just as an observer of a chess game played by others can soon start making observations and generalizations about the use of individual pawns, a language learner can observe texts and contexts in a corpus and literally play with the language, similar to what the great 17th-century Czech educator Jan Amos Comenius proposed as Schola ludus – school (learning) by play. This approach resembles natural language acquisition in making learning emerge from meaningful, playful activities.

4. Conclusions

A corpus of exemplary high-school texts going beyond error detection seems to be missing or not readily available. COHAT is designed to serve that purpose and enable students to conduct their own research into the language of academic writing, and with teacher support rediscover 'the rules of the language game' for themselves. Its texts represent an achievable goal for high school students, and the pedagogical approach proposed here encourages inferential, data-driven discovery learning. Additionally, it has proven to be a useful indicator of (dis)harmony between teaching theory and student practice.

A profound definition of learning says that it is "constructing knowledge in collaboration with others", a guided rediscovery of knowledge (Wells, 2001, p. 176). The use of corpora in Academic English classrooms has shown that this rediscovery can be applied to gaining linguistic knowledge, too. It is true that "language looks rather different when you look at a lot of it at once" (Sinclair, 1991, p. 100). High school students of any academic language can benefit from being able to 'look at a lot of language at once' through the lens of a corpus, distinguishing language use by genre, subject or register, for "he who distinguishes well, teaches well", argued Comenius (1948, p. 162). Even better, corpora can be used to help students "distinguish well" through a set of computer assisted game-like learning activities, increasing their engagement by the element of discovery and adventure.

5. Acknowledgements

We would like to thank Lawrence Hrubes (ISP EAL department chair), ISP Administration, as well as doc. Mgr. Václav Cvrček, Ph.D., Mgr. Michal Křen, Ph.D., and Mgr. Lucie Chlumská from the Institute of the Czech National Corpus for their invaluable professional and logistical help. Róbert Bohát would like to thank his wife and family for their support without which most of this work could not have been completed.

References

Alsop, S., & Nesi, H. (2009). Issues in the development of the British Academic Written English (BAWE) corpus. *Corpora, 4*(1), 71-83. doi:10.3366/E1749503209000227

Anthony, L. (2014). AntConc (Version 3.4.3) [Computer Software]. Tokyo, Japan: Waseda University. Retrieved from http://www.laurenceanthony.net/

Bohát, R., Rödlingová, B., & Horáková, N. (2015). Applied linguistics project: student-led computer assisted research in high school EAL / EAP. In F. Helm, L. Bradley, M. Guarda, & S. Thouësny (Eds), *Critical CALL – Proceedings of the 2015 EUROCALL Conference, Padova, Italy* (pp. 65-70). Dublin: Research-publishing. net. doi:10.14705/rpnet.2015.000311

Comenius, J. A. (1948). *Vybrané spisy Jana Amose Komenského. Svazek 1. Praha*. Státní pedagogické nakladatelství.

Firth, J. R. (1957). *Papers in linguistics 1934-51*. Oxford: Oxford University Press.

Sinclair, J. (1991). *Corpus, concordance, collocation*. Oxford: Oxford University Press.

Stubbs, M. (1993). British traditions in text analysis – from Firth to Sinclair. In M. Baker, G. Francis, & E. Tognini-Bonelli (Eds.), *Text and technology: in honour of John Sinclair* (pp. 1-33). Amsterdam: John Benjamins Publishing Co. doi:10.1075/z.64.02stu

Wells, G. (2001). Action, talk, and text: learning and teaching through inquiry. New York: Teachers College Press.

Wittgenstein, L. (2001). Philosophical investigations (3rd ed.). Oxford: Blackwell Publishing Ltd.

Using mobile devices and the Adobe Connect web conferencing tool in the assessment of EFL student teacher performance

Maria del Carmen Bolona Lopez[1], Margarita Elizabeth Ortiz[2], and Christopher Allen[3]

Abstract. This paper describes a project to use mobile devices and video conferencing technology in the assessment of student English as a Foreign Language (EFL) teacher performance on teaching practice in Ecuador. With the increasing availability of mobile devices with video recording facilities, it has become easier for trainers to capture teacher performance on video without recourse to expensive purpose-made video camera equipment and time-consuming editing of video material. Mobile devices and web conferencing tools enable trainers who may be widely separated geographically to share video material of student teacher performance as the basis for the calibration of classroom practice assessment. Ecuadorian EFL teacher trainees on teaching practice were recorded using mobile devices. Videos were then uploaded to a video sharing website and made available to all participating trainers. Using the Cambridge ESOL Teaching Knowledge Test (TKT) score criteria, teacher trainers were asked to rate student performance as captured in the video sequences using the four band rating scale (1-basic; 4-very good). The video material then served as the basis for an online discussion and calibration of student teacher performance using the Adobe Connect web conferencing tool. Trainers were then asked to evaluate the efficacy of mobile device-recorded video material and web conferencing platforms as instruments in the assessment of student teacher performance.

Keywords: teaching practice, mobile phone, Adobe Connect.

---

1. Universidad Casa Grande, Ecuador; mbolona@casagrande.edu.ec
2. Universidad Casa Grande, Ecuador; mortiz@casagrande.edu.ec
3. Linnaeus University, Sweden; christopher.allen@lnu.se

How to cite this article: Bolona Lopez, M. d. C., Ortiz, M. E., & Allen, C. (2015). Using mobile devices and the Adobe Connect web conferencing tool in the assessment of EFL student teacher performance. In F. Helm, L. Bradley, M. Guarda, & S. Thouësny (Eds), *Critical CALL – Proceedings of the 2015 EUROCALL Conference, Padova, Italy* (pp. 77-83). Dublin: Research-publishing.net. http://dx.doi.org/10.14705/rpnet.2015.000313

1. Introduction

1.1. General

Programmes of EFL teacher accreditation have become increasingly international, with standardised assessment forms available for the assessment of student teacher performance for the teaching practice/practicum component. The assessment of classroom performance is complex and involves simultaneous considerations of learning atmosphere, learner interaction and involvement, language and skills focus, classroom management and learner monitoring/feedback. Assessment forms for programmes such as the Cambridge ESOL TKT, CELTA and DELTA offer trainers the advantage of a set of rigorous, internationally-benchmarked criteria, tying lesson planning to the observation and assessment of classroom performance. While language teachers have frequently been seen as technological innovators among their educational peers, the use of technology in the assessment of student teacher performance in the classroom has received less attention in the literature. Modern digital technology in the form of mobile device cameras and video editing enables teacher trainers to capture permanent records of teacher performance for evaluative purposes. These performance records can be compared and evaluated using online forums and video conferencing tools to promote a more objective calibration of teacher trainer assessment.

1.2. Aim

This paper describes the use of a combination of technologies (smartphone, the *Adobe Connect*, video conferencing tool) in the assessment and calibration of classroom pre-service teacher performance in Ecuador. Student teachers engaged in peer-microteaching activities were filmed by their trainers using smartphones, with the video records uploaded to a Moodle forum. Unedited classroom performance captured in the video clips was then assessed amongst the authors using the criteria and 1-4 band assessment rating scale of the TKT. Similarities and discrepancies in ratings were then discussed using the Adobe Connect video conferencing tool.

1.3. Peer-microteaching

McKnight (1980) defines microteaching as "a scaled down realistic classroom training context in which teachers, both experienced and inexperienced, may acquire new teaching skills and refine old ones" (p. 214, quoted in Millis & Smojlowicz, 2006, p. 1). Peer-microteaching enhances the value of the interaction between trainers, student teachers and peers collaborating in reflective teaching training practice. This technique is often used in Teaching English as a Foreign Language (TEFL) accreditation programs to assess student teachers.

Student teachers participated in peer-microteaching lessons videoed on a mobile device for formative assessment purposes. Their "performance skills, cognitive processes and affective learning" in Wallace's (1991, p. 98) terms were determined to assess the extent to which trainees had developed their abilities to design, create, implement and assess a reading lesson according to the TKT assessment form. In this respect, Egbert (2005) points out the relevance of assessment in language teaching and learning when she states that assessment "provides feedback from peers and others; formally, it provides information against a standard regarding how the student is progressing in specific areas" (p. 119).

1.4. Video and mobile phone video use in teacher training

Video can be used to film a teacher's performance "on one or two video cameras, either of the portable kind in an ordinary classroom, or standard cameras in a studio" (Wallace, 1991, p. 101). Cooper, Lavery and Rinvolucri (1991) see this tool as a "supercharged medium of communication and a powerful vehicle of information" (p. 11). Videos preserve a record of teaching performance that can be analyzed and assessed systematically for further applications. Video is therefore a reliable (in testing terms) medium in assessment and feedback procedures that might otherwise be time consuming due to unsystematic data collection and/or a lack of information regarding teaching background and classroom context. In recent years, video recording and editing has become possible via mobile devices. Mobile phone video and sound recording quality have improved rapidly with higher image definition and enhanced sound sensitivity conducive to the recording of complex classroom interactions.

1.5. *Adobe Connect* as a discussion forum

Adobe Connect is a widely used video conferencing tool which has been extensively adopted in higher education. This tool permits informal online meetings, small group collaboration and larger webinars, enabling collaborators to interact with each other using video and sound as well as sharing desktops. For this particular project, the main advantage of *Adobe Connect* is to bring together teacher trainers in Ecuador and Sweden by providing a forum for real-time reflection and discussion of student teacher video performance, as a natural extension to a *Moodle* forum.

2. Method

2.1. Participants

Ten student teachers who were enrolled on a TEFL course offered at an Ecuadorian university participated in this study. The student teachers, aged between 20 and 40 years, were following the second of three modules as part of their programme: teaching reading and writing. All teacher students had Spanish as their L1 although they adopted the policy of using English at all times in the classroom, in line with the principles of communicative language teaching.

2.2. Procedure

Teaching sessions were recorded by one of the authors sitting in a fixed position at the back of the classroom, using a smartphone to record student teachers engaged in microteaching activities. Following each microteaching session, smartphone videos were uploaded to a computer. Feedback was given once all the presentations were finished.

Video materials were then uploaded to *Box,* a secure cloud storage facility. Using *Adobe Connect*, the assessors had several online meetings regarding the scores given to the students. These meetings served as the basis for discussing ratings of student teacher performance as well as evaluating the technology (mobile device, VLE, *Adobe Connect*, etc.) used.

2.3. Recording device

The device used to record students was a smartphone with Android 4.1 as the operating system.

The smartphone had a 3.5 inch display, 320 x 480 pixel resolution, 512 Mb RAM, 5 megapixel camera and a 4 GB storage facility. Video material was saved in the *.mp4* format.

2.4. Evaluation criteria

In order to assess student teacher performance, the Cambridge ESOL TKT rubric was used. The appendix shows the criteria which are divided up into the assessment of the lesson planning (criteria a- e), which match with the assessment of classroom performance (criteria f-j).

3. Results and discussion

The results set out below include the ratings of the three assessors (*T1*, *T2* and *T3* etc) using the TKT band scale (see Table 1). Lesson plan ratings (a-e) are included here for the sake of completeness; the main focus of this paper is the lesson observation criteria (f-j). For each video, the standard deviation (*SD*) or σ of the total scores for each video was calculated, to show the extent or dispersion in ratings between the assessors around the mean rating for each video. The same calculation was performed for each of the *TKT* criteria; σ is listed on the extreme right, indicating the degree of dispersion for ratings of each of these criteria.

Table 1. Comparison of TKT ratings 1-4 of teacher performance between the three assessors

Assessor	Video 1			Video II			Video III			Video IV			Video V			SD
	T1	T2	T3	T1	T2	T3	T1	T2	T3	T1	T2	T3	T1	T2	T3	
TKT criteria																
Lesson plan																
a. Write clear aims	2	0	2	3	1	3	1	4	2	3	1	3	0	0		0 1.95
b. describe lesson components	2	3	2	3	4	3	2	3	2	3	3	2	0	0		0 1.16
c. order stages / components	2	2	2	3	4	4	2	4	2	3	4	3	0	0		0 1.39
d. analyse target language skills	2	3	2	3	4	3	1	4	1	3	4	1	0	3		0 1.39
e. plan use of resources	3	4	3	3	4	3	1	4	2	4	4	3	0	0		0 1.50
Lesson observation																
f. create positive atmosphere	3	4	3	4	4	3	2	4	3	3	4	3	0	3		2 1.07
g. focus on form / skills	2	4	2	3	4	3	1	4	1	3	4	3	0	4		1 1.35
h. classroom management	3	4	3	3	4	3	2	4	2	3	3	3	0	4		1 1.15
i. appropriacy of English usage	3	4	3	3	4	3	2	3	2	4	4	4	0	4		1 1.19
j. monitor learners	2	4	2	4	4	3	2	4	2	3	4	4	0	2		1 1.18
Totals	24	32	24	30	34	29	16	38	19	32	35	28	0	17		6
SD	4.02			2.65			11.93			3.51			8.62			

The results showed the greatest agreement (and smallest *SD*) among the assessors for video II and VI respectively, with relatively wider dispersions in ratings for the remaining videos. One possible explanation here is that the assessors were using the very specific TKT criteria for the first time; these criteria and the Cambridge ESOL reporting forms had yet to be fully integrated into the TEFL programme. Despite these discrepancies, the results indicate the potential for mobile phone video in the assessment of student teachers, provided that a set of benchmarked criteria like the TKT guidelines are adopted at an early stage and firmly anchored in the programme from the start.

The most important finding, however, was the overall positive evaluation of the smartphone as a means of capturing a permanent record of student teacher performance. Compared with purpose-made video cameras, trainers expressed the view that they were more readily familiar with recording and uploading functions of smartphones from everyday use and uploading to social media. Audio and video quality were evaluated as being minimally sufficient for recording the complexities of teacher-learner and learner-learner interactions in the language classroom. Nevertheless, it was agreed that the assessors were too static in their classroom observation points and needed to utilise more fully the mobility of hand-held devices in their recording.

Trainers pointed to the alternative possibility of recording shorter teaching sequences as a showcase of classroom teacher performance (e.g. starting a lesson, transitions between different activities, whole class and group task/pairwork, etc.) in a series of lessons with alternative recording positions and angles. These sequences could then be viewed separately to provide formative feedback throughout the practice or alternatively combined as a single summative assessment. *Adobe Connect* was also seen as a potentially useful medium for the realtime discussion of performance assessment discrepancy. However, bandwidth considerations are an issue here, especially when reviewing teacher performance videos in the sessions using *Adobe Connect*'s screensharing facilities.

4. Conclusion

Overall, this pilot project has indicated the usefulness of the mobile phone/online forum/web conferencing tool combination in the assessment of student teachers on teaching practice. There is considerable potential for this approach in online teacher training programmes involving far-flung student teachers, where trainers may not be able to perform regular classroom observations in person, relying instead on video recording of classroom performance matched with documented lesson planning.

5. Acknowledgements

We would like to thank Universidad Casa Grande, Ecuador and Linnaeus University, Sweden for financial support.

References

Cooper R., Lavery M., & Rinvolucri M. (1991). *Video*. Oxford: Oxford University Press.
Egbert, J. (2005). *CALL essentials, principles and practice in CALL Classrooms*. TESOL Publications.
McKnight, P. C. (1980). Microteaching: development from 1968-1978. *British Journal of Teacher Education, 6*(3), 214-227. doi:10.1080/0260747800060305
Millis, B. J., & Smojlowicz, G. (2006). A microteaching model that maximizes feedback, peer engagement, and teaching enhancement. *The Professional & Organizational Development Network in Higher Education, 18*(6), 1. Retrieved from https://cft.vanderbilt.edu/wp-content/uploads/sites/59/vol18no06_microteaching.htm

Wallace, M. J. (1991). *Training foreign language teachers.* Cambridge. Cambridge University Press.

Appendix TKT lesson planning and observation form

	The lesson plan- the candidate can:	Score
a.	Write detailed, clearly stated and appropriate main aims, subsidiary aims, aims for individual stages in the lesson and personal aims.	
b.	Give adequate details of the different components of a lesson plan such as information about the class; procedures; timing, interaction patterns; anticipated problems with materials, activities and tasks; suggested solutions.	
c.	Give details of stages, activities and tasks which are logically ordered and which are appropriate to the learners and the lesson aims.	
d.	(i) analyse target language, including aspects of form, meaning and phonology; anticipate possible solutions relating to the analysed language; and (ii) identify appropriate strategies to develop the target skills / subskills; anticipate problems and suggest solutions relating to the identified skills.	
e.	Plan the use of appropriate (referenced) materials and / or resources to be used.	

	The lesson - the candidate can:	Score
f.	Create a positive learning atmosphere, ensuring involvement of all the learners.	
g.	(i) focus on language: form, meaning and phonology, and include appropriate practice; and (ii) follow appropriate procedures and use activities to improve learners- skills.	
h.	Set up, manage and time whole-class and individual, pair or group activities, using materials, resources and aids effectively to deliver the planned lesson so that aims are achieved.	
i.	Use English appropriately eg when explaining, instructing, prompting	

From research to research synthesis in CALL

Alex Boulton[1]

Abstract. Any research study can only be fully appreciated once it is situated in relation to existing work. This is no mean feat, however, given the sheer quantity and variety of publications to date. Simply relying on one's background and experience as an expert in the field, coupled with a few internet searches and following up individual references, is likely to lead to a very partial view. This paper argues the need for greater rigour (via meta-analytic and other types of syntheses) to gain a broader, deeper and more balanced understanding of Computer-Assisted Language Learning (CALL).

Keywords: data-driven learning, corpora, research synthesis, meta-analysis.

1. Conducting research

The 'scientific method' has been developed in an attempt to reduce human fallibility in exploring the world around us. However, different researchers clearly go about their work in vastly disparate ways even within a single clearly-defined discipline such as CALL. Many attempts have been made to describe the different practices, one of the most common distinctions being between quantitative and qualitative research. A number of surveys have found the former to be prevalent in international journals in applied linguistics (e.g. Richards, 2009), which may fuel a popular perception that it is more prestigious or even more 'scientific' in some way.

However, there is disagreement about exactly what qualitative and quantitative methods are, and debate about whether there is a clear boundary between them. On the face of it, any set of data is open to some sort of quantification – and indeed needs to be, otherwise it is impossible to know what to make of discussions of a single example, blog extract, or interview response. Is it representative of a

---

1. Atilf, CNRS & Université de Lorraine, France; alex.boulton@univ-lorraine.fr

How to cite this article: Boulton, A. (2015). From research to research synthesis in CALL. In F. Helm, L. Bradley, M. Guarda, & S. Thouësny (Eds), *Critical CALL – Proceedings of the 2015 EUROCALL Conference, Padova, Italy* (pp. 84-90). Dublin: Research-publishing.net. http://dx.doi.org/10.14705/rpnet.2015.000314

more widespread phenomenon, or just an interesting but isolated case? Any data which can be counted but is not (or which stops at the level of raw numbers or percentages), properly invites scepticism from the reader. In the end, the take-home message of many qualitative papers is that the situation is complex (for which the sceptic may read 'vague' and 'subjective'), but that the researchers have found at least some evidence pointing in the right direction (if they are to be believed). Similarly, any overtly quantitative data also needs interpretation for it to make any meaningful contribution. As with qualitative research, it is surprisingly easy to go through the motions and produce poor quantitative studies by simply grinding numbers through an esoteric statistical test chosen for mysterious reasons, leading to a 'voilà' moment of $p<.05$. This is markedly unsatisfactory, and has the opposite defect of qualitative studies in being misleadingly simplistic. While each approach is thus easy to criticise on scientific grounds or personal/cultural preference, it seems likely that the most robust research will derive from truly mixed-methods designs.

2. Reviewing research

The scientific enterprise is incremental and no single study will definitively answer any given issue. The question then is how to gain an accurate overview of research to date where even a small field like CALL sees many hundreds of studies published every year, often with conflicting results. The sheer number of publications means it is always possible to find some evidence that justify almost anything (Hattie, 2009, p. 6); it is therefore essential to find ways to bring greater rigour to research synthesis. Considerable advances have been made in this direction since the publication of the seminal paper by Norris and Ortega in 2000. Today, research synthesis has become almost a field in its own right, with a number of handbooks, recommendations by academic associations and scientific journals, and special issues of prestigious journals or collected volumes. Norris and Ortega's (2010) TimeLine review in *Language Teaching* gives a glimpse of the wealth of work in the area.

Most research synthesis begins with an extensive and principled trawl of the literature related to a clearly defined question, but then can branch in different directions, each with its advantages and disadvantages (see Plonsky, 2014 for an overview). The *narrative synthesis* represents a qualitative approach: it can incorporate any type of study and allows for interpretation and contextualisation by the synthesist, but thereby remains open to charges of subjectivity; and while the picture is carefully nuanced, the final impression may remain correspondingly vague and fuzzy (Han, 2015). Quantitative approaches, on the other hand, attempt to be more objective in their interpretation of the results, but by definition only cater for studies that provide appropriate quantitative data; like primary quantitative studies, meta-analyses tend to leave a single numerical value as the take-home message for the casual reader, which is simplistic and misleading, and does not do justice to the sub-analyses of moderator variables (for other types of synthesis in CALL, see Burston 2013, 2015; Felix 2005, 2008).

3. Meta-analyses in CALL

The principle phases consist in outlining the scope of the topic, collecting and selecting publications, coding and extracting the data for analysis, calculating effect sizes and interpreting them according to various moderator variables – all according to stringent, pre-determined criteria. Though many decisions need to be made, the main constant in most meta-analysis is the calculation of the effect size; most in applied linguistics use Cohen's *d*. This basically compares the difference in means between the control and experimental groups (or pre- and post-tests), while taking into account the variance as given in the pooled standard deviations (Figure 1). Effect size is in many ways more revealing than the more common significance testing; it is recommended if not required by recent APA standards and journals such as *Language Learning*, while some researchers seem to think that *p*-values are at best uninformative and at worst positively harmful, and should be systematically replaced by effect sizes (e.g. Plonsky, 2011). One major advantage of using a standard measure of effect size is that it enables direct comparison of different studies, which is not possible with *p*-values or narrative syntheses.

Figure 1. Formula for Cohen's *d*

$$d = \frac{M_2 - M_1}{\sqrt{\frac{SD_1^2 + SD_2^2}{2}}}$$

As a field, CALL is now sufficiently mature to have given rise to several meta-analyses, some of which are given in Table 1; *k* refers to the number of studies covered in the analysis, and *d* is the effect size itself[2]. The value for *d* needs interpreting (just as do *p*-values, which tend to be set arbitrarily at .05 or .01). For applied linguistics, Oswald and Plonsky (2010) find an average effect size of 0.7,

---

2. Pre/post (within-groups) and control/experimental (between groups) designs are not distinguished in this short paper.

and suggest that 0.4 should be considered small, 1.0 large. The first thing to note from Table 1 is that there are no negative *d*-values in any of the meta-analyses. This is not surprising, since few primary studies set out to discredit an experimental treatment against a control group, and would not expect lower scores in a post-test following treatment. Second, most of the effect sizes are not particularly large, the unweighted mean being just 0.66, with the higher ones mainly derived from smaller samples. Overall, this suggests a medium strength effect of computer-assisted language learning as seen from many different perspectives over many dozens of primary studies involving thousands of learners using a wide variety of tools and techniques. Third, each arrives at a different value; a single meta-analysis does not provide a definitive picture of a field (compare Plonsky and Brown's (2015) discussion of the differing results of 18 meta-analyses of feedback).

Table 1. Meta-analyses in CALL (partly based on Oswald & Plonsky, 2010)

study	year	source	question	k	d
Abraham	2008	Computer Assisted Language Learning	computer-mediated glosses in vocabulary learning	6	1.40
Abraham	2008	Computer Assisted Language Learning	computer-mediated glosses in reading comprehension	11	0.73
Chiu	2013	British Journal of Educational Technology	computer-assisted second language vocabulary instruction	16	0.75
Chiu et al.	2012	British Journal of Educational Technology	digital game-based learning	14	0.53
Cobb & Boulton	2015	Cambridge University Press	data-driven learning	21	1.04
Grgurović et al.	2013	ReCALL	CALL-based language learning	65	0.26
Lin, H.	2014	Language Learning & Technology	CMC and SLA	59	0.44
Lin, H.	2015	ReCALL	CMC in L2 oral proficiency development	25	0.40
Lin, W.C. et al.	2013	Language Learning & Technology	text-based SCMC on SLA	19	0.33
Taylor	2009	CALICO Journal	CALL-based versus paper-based glosses	32	0.49
Yun	2011	Computer Assisted Language Learning	hypertext glosses in vocabulary acquisition	10	0.37
Zhao	2003	CALICO Journal	overall effectiveness of uses of technology in language education	9	1.12

Though as Grgurović, Chapelle, and Shelley (2013) point out, it can be politically useful to be able to quantify the effects of CALL, attempting to account for all the research in a single figure is obviously hugely simplistic. In quantitative research, a major failing in primary studies is that the variation (even if reported in standard deviations) is ironed out in a single overall figure; by definition, a meta-analysis involves far more variation which is also ignored if we only take away a single figure. Fortunately, meta-analysts do not just provide a single overall figure for effect size, they also discuss and interpret it, and in particular conduct analysis of potential moderator variables precisely to see what factors may explain the variation between studies. While it is not possible to go into details here, the reader is strongly encouraged *not* to take away the simple notion that $d=.66$ for CALL (unless it is politically or strategically expedient to justify budgets or investment at a local level, unethical though that may be), but to consult the various meta-analyses listed to see how each explains the variation it uncovers among the primary studies, and to decide whether the variation between the meta-analyses themselves may be attributed to their specific design or research questions. It is also of course important to go to the relevant primary studies, but approaching them after consulting a meta-analysis may help to keep them in perspective.

4. Conclusions

Meta-analysis can be "an immensely valuable scholarly contribution that brings order to confusion, helps set a future research agenda, and at the same time gives the best evidence-based practical advice" (Cumming, 2012, p. 231), but has its limitations and should never be taken as the ultimate answer to a question. What is needed is always more research: more primary studies of different types (where syntheses can help identify areas in need of work), and more syntheses to help make sense of them – again, both qualitative and quantitative.

References

Abraham, L. B. (2008). Computer-mediated glosses in second language reading comprehension and vocabulary learning: a meta-analysis. *Computer Assisted Language Learning, 21*(3), 199-226. doi:10.1080/09588220802090246

Burston, J. (2013). Mobile-assisted language learning: a selected annotated bibliography of implementation studies 1994-2012. *Language Learning & Technology, 17*(3), 157-225.

Burston, J. (2015). Twenty years of MALL project implementation: a meta-analysis of learning outcomes. *ReCALL, 27*(1), 4-20. doi:10.1017/S0958344014000159

Chiu, Y.-H. (2013). Computer-assisted second language vocabulary instruction: a meta-analysis. *British Journal of Educational Technology, 44*(2), E52-E56. doi:10.1111/j.1467-8535.2012.01342.x

Chiu, Y.-H., Kao, C.-W., & Reynolds, B. L. (2012). The relative effectiveness of digital game-based learning types in English as a foreign language setting: a meta-analysis. *British Journal of Educational Technology, 43*(4), E104-E107. doi:10.1111/j.1467-8535.2012.01295.x

Cobb, T., & Boulton, A. (2015). Classroom applications of corpus analysis. In D. Biber & R. Reppen (Eds.), *Cambridge handbook of corpus linguistics* (pp. 478-497). Cambridge: Cambridge University Press. doi:10.1017/CBO9781139764377.027

Cumming, G. (2012). *Understanding the new statistics: effect sizes, confidence intervals, and meta-analysis*. New York: Routledge.

Felix, U. (2005). What do meta-analyses tell us about CALL effectiveness? *ReCALL, 17*(2), 269-288. doi:10.1017/S0958344005000923

Felix, U. (2008). The unreasonable effectiveness of CALL: what have we learned in two decades of research? *ReCALL, 20*(2), 141-161. doi:10.1017/S0958344008000323

Grgurović, M., Chapelle, C. A., & Shelley, M. C. (2013). A meta-analysis of effectiveness studies on computer technology supported language learning. *ReCALL, 25*(2), 165-198. doi:10.1017/S0958344013000013

Han, Z. (2015). Striving for complementarity between narrative and meta-analytic reviews. *Applied Linguistics, 36*(3), 409-415. doi:10.1093/applin/amv026

Hattie, J. (2009). *Visible learning: a synthesis of over 800 meta-analyses relating to achievement*. New York: Routledge.

Lin, H. (2014). Establishing an empirical link between computer-mediated communication (CMC) and SLA: a meta-analysis of the research. *Language Learning & Technology, 18*(3), 120-147.

Lin, H. (2015). Computer-mediated communication (CMC) in L2 oral proficiency development: a meta-analysis. *ReCALL, 27*(3), 261-287. doi:10.1017/S095834401400041X

Lin, W. C., Huang, H. T., & Liou, H. C. (2013). The effects of text-based SCMC on SLA: a meta-analysis. *Language Learning & Technology, 17*(2), 123-142.

Norris, J. M., & Ortega, L. (2000). Effectiveness of L2 instruction: a research synthesis and quantitative meta-analysis. *Language Learning, 50*(3), 417-528. doi:10.1111/0023-8333.00136

Norris, J. M., & Ortega, L. (2010). Research synthesis [Research timeline article.] *Language Teaching, 43*(4), 461-479. doi:10.1017/S0261444810000200

Oswald, F. L., & Plonsky, L. (2010). Meta-analysis in second language research: choices and challenges. *Annual Review of Applied Linguistics, 30*, 85-110. doi:10.1017/S0267190510000115

Plonsky, L. (2011). The effectiveness of second language strategy instruction: a meta-analysis. *Language Learning, 61*(4), 993-1038. doi:10.1111/j.1467-9922.2011.00663.x

Plonsky, L. (2014). Study quality in quantitative L2 research (1990–2010): a methodological synthesis and call for reform. *Modern Language Journal, 98*(1), 450-470. doi:10.1111/j.1540-4781.2014.12058.x

Plonsky, L., & Brown, D. (2015). Domain definition and search techniques in meta-analyses of L2 research (or why 18 meta-analyses of feedback have different results). *Second Language Research, 31*(2), 267-278. doi:10.1177/0267658314536436

Richards, K. (2009). Trends in qualitative research in language teaching since 2000. *Language Teaching, 42*(2), 147-180. doi:10.1017/S0261444808005612

Taylor, A. M. (2009). CALL-based versus paper-based glosses: is there a difference in reading comprehension? *CALICO Journal, 27*(1), 147-160. doi:10.11139/cj.27.1.147-160

Yun, J. (2011). The effects of hypertext glosses on L2 vocabulary acquisition: a meta-analysis. *Computer Assisted Language Learning, 24*(1), 39-58. doi:10.1080/09588221.2010.523285

Zhao, Y. (2003). Recent developments in technology and language learning: a literature review and meta-analysis. *CALICO Journal, 21*(1), 7-27.

Language learning beyond Japanese university classrooms: video interviewing for study abroad

John Brine[1], Emiko Kaneko[2], Younghyon Heo[3], Alexander Vazhenin[4], and Gordon Bateson[5]

Abstract. In 2014, the University of Aizu was accepted for participation in Japan's national TOP Global University (TGU) initiative. In this paper, we describe our use of video interviewing to prepare Japanese students for our Global Experience Gateway study abroad TGU project. Our university specializes in computer science education at undergraduate and graduate levels. Our students are preparing for careers or further research in either software or hardware specializations, and it is expected that English will be required increasingly in computer-related research and business. Within Japanese education, there is a view that the youth are reluctant to speak English (King, 2013), and our students use English infrequently. We have created a study abroad programme, which is intended to motivate students to study more in their regular English language classes to improve language skills and attain higher TOEIC scores. However, improved course grades and test scores do not prepare students with interpersonal communication skills required to function in an English-speaking context. Recent literature on language learning outside of the classroom (Nunan & Richards, 2014) supports our use of video interviewing to prepare students for study abroad. We are teaching Japanese students to conduct and video-record interviews with non-Japanese speakers in preparation for the conversational demands of study abroad. Practice with video equipment, interviewing techniques, simple camera work and editing helps our students to interact with our international

---

1. University of Aizu, Japan; brine@u-aizu.ac.jp
2. University of Aizu, Japan; kaneko@u-aizu.ac.jp
3. University of Aizu, Japan; youngheo@u-aizu.ac.jp
4. University of Aizu, Japan; vazhenin@u-aizu.ac.jp
5. Kochi University of Technology, Japan; bateson.gordon@kochi-tech.ac.jp

How to cite this article: Brine, J., Kaneko, E., Heo, Y., Vazhenin, A., & Bateson, G. (2015). Language learning beyond Japanese university classrooms: video interviewing for study abroad. In F. Helm, L. Bradley, M. Guarda, & S. Thouësny (Eds), *Critical CALL – Proceedings of the 2015 EUROCALL Conference, Padova, Italy* (pp. 91-96). Dublin: Research-publishing.net. http://dx.doi.org/10.14705/rpnet.2015.000315

students and teachers. In this paper we outline the curriculum design, equipment selection, instruction, student project work, and assessment in this course.

Keywords: interviewing, video, study abroad, motivation.

1. Introduction

Within the context of our TGU project, students are being recruited nationally and internationally to enroll in our university to study computer science in English at the undergraduate and graduate levels. While classroom-centered approaches involving teachers and textbooks have been the emphasis in language education in Japan, there is a shift towards more open educational resources.

Nonetheless, students in formal language courses, unless required to do so, are unlikely to make much use of open internet resources. Having operated and taught with a Moodle server since 2004, we have employed open resources and worked to increase student engagement. Recently, we have sought ways to promote student interaction with non-Japanese speakers through authentic language learning activities outside the classroom (Richards, 2015). Our use of digital interviewing provides a communicative context consisting of the introduction, equipment setup, and questions and answers, which provides a scaffold for our Japanese students to conduct interviews with non-Japanese speakers.

2. Course design

In 2014, we began an elective course entitled *Digital Storytelling for Engineering Narratives*. Students were taught to follow a production process (Figure 1) to plan, film, and edit short descriptions and explanations of technical and engineering processes with which they were currently involved.

Figure 1. Video production process

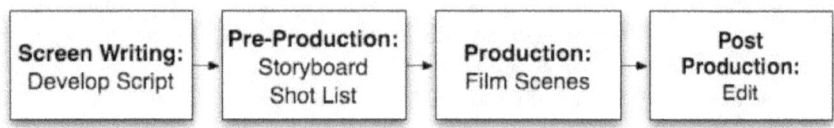

During the first offering of this new experimental course, it became clear that digital storytelling was too open ended for most students. Allowing students to create their own stories was somewhat outside of the experience of most of the students whose previous education had been primarily geared toward succeeding on entrance examinations. They also lacked experience with group project work. Furthermore, the technical content of the course, although not complex, needed more structure. The new structure involved development of three different assignments: 1) *The Door Scene*, 2) demonstration video, and 3) interview video. Each assignment consisted of three phases: pre-production, production, and post-production.

The course required students to create three videos, each of which was no longer than 5 minutes. The first was *The Door Scene* (AFI, 2006, p. 17), a short film about an urgent departure through a door, which was intended to help students learn the basics of storyboarding, camerawork, and acting. The second was a demonstration video to explain a process, such as folding origami paper. Students were expected to improve their skill and to add subtitles. The third was an interview which involved speaking with an international student or professor. Camerawork, subtitling and editing were more demanding for this video. Rubrics were used to evaluate two stages of development for each video: storyboarding and filming.

Our elective classes normally have a maximum of thirty students. The video class was divided into ten groups of three students with each group consisting of a director, actor, and cameraman. Most students now have mobile devices with high-quality video capability. However, ten sets of equipment were prepared (see Appendix 1) with full audio and video capabilities. The equipment was color coded so that students would use the same equipment each time. Each group was awarded a shared grade. Eventually, we intended to have individual members evaluate the performance of their fellow group members and to weigh individual grades accordingly.

In order to design and construct their digital story, students carried out the following steps:

- develop a digital story idea and create an outline;

- write a digital story script;

- create a storyboard;

- design, plan, record, and edit media files;

- produce a digital story in English and publish it online.

Throughout the three assignments students incrementally acquired the skills necessary to reach the ultimate goal of conducting an interview, or structured conversation, with an international student or professor who might or might not know Japanese. Students developed interviews with the support of collections of conversation questions (Internet TESL Journal, n.d.). Interviewees whose first language was Japanese were not selected. During the elective course, we realized that the interview video would be an appropriate exercise for study abroad students with their homestay families, for example. Our interview component in the first course has now become the main assessed activity in our study abroad course.

3. Evaluation

During the elective course called *Digital Storytelling for Engineering Narratives*, we adopted an action research approach during which adjustments to the course were made on a continuous basis according to educational needs.

The second course, entitled *Global Experience Gateway*, ran from October 2014 to March 2015, consisted of pertinent study abroad content, and included the study abroad trip. During the course, students also each completed two required interview videos: one before the study abroad trip and one during. After the course, these two video interview projects were evaluated with an emphasis on specific behavioral criteria in the manner of "can do" assessments.

Rubrics were set up to evaluate student work on two primary tasks. The storyboard criteria included completeness, clarity, camera angles, and scripting. The film production consisted of audio quality, video quality, open-endedness of questions, length of interview, and subtitling. Each step of each video was evaluated in a similar way. The primary goal of the interview videos was to increase student opportunity for authentic conversation around equipment and interview setup, and also during the interviews themselves.

In the second course, individual oral proficiency was also evaluated. Two weeks prior to and at the end of the three week study abroad experience, each student completed the *Oral Proficiency Interview - computer* (OPI-c) test. The OPI-c is a one-hour computerized test of English-usage skills consisting of a series of recorded questions. The evaluations were carried out by American Council on The Teaching of Foreign Languages (ACTFL) evaluators in the United States (Burke, 2015). After only five weeks between two OPIc administrations, 12 out of 18 students increased their level while 6 remained the same (see Table 1).

Table 1. OPI-c scores for 18 study abroad students[1]

	OPIc Same		OPIc Up		
	Female	Male	Female	Male	Row Totals
DNA	1	1	1	0	3
RHIT	0	2	4	3	9
Waikato	1	1	1	3	6
Column Totals	2	4	6	6	18

4. Discussion

Pryde (2015) suggests that students' lack of communication during study abroad may indicate a lack of preparation for conversation (p. 170). Furthermore, Pryde (2015) has found that when students are studying abroad, their homestay hosts tend to dominate conversation (p. 502). Similarly, teachers tend to dominate classroom discourse. Alternatively, conducting interviews provided our students with numerous opportunities to control language in the interactions with English-language speakers. We found that various aspects of video production gave students opportunities to work with the target language, such as 1) preparing the storyboard and script, 2) interacting with interviewee(s) when showing them the interview questions, 3) editing the questions and script, 4) conducting the interview, 5) subtitling the video, and 6) reviewing the subtitles with the interviewee(s). As we develop our courses, we will increase the structure and work on clarifying the evaluative criteria.

5. Conclusions

Our university, and others who have been designated TGU, are attempting to encourage Japanese students to both master technical knowledge and develop the ability to converse in English. In order to improve conversational skills, we have taught students to conduct and video record interviews. The interactional patterns that reinforce student lack of initiation in turn-taking may be changed through digital interviewing by providing students with clear control of the interactional context and by returning the initiation of conversation to the language learners (Lee, 2014).

---

1. Note: DNA refers to Dalian Neusoft Institute and Alpine Electronics, China; RHIT refers to Rose Hulman Institute of Technology, USA; Waikato refers to University of Waikato, New Zealand.

Furthermore, our use of widely available mobile devices with video capacity helps students to gain entry into "legitimate participation" (Darvin & Norton, 2015, p. 50) through an empowering mediating artifact, and thereby bolster confidence.

6. Acknowledgements

We would like to thank the Japan Society for the Promotion of Science for its support.

References

American Film Institute (AFI). (2006). *AFI screen education: the 21st century educator's handbook*. Los Angeles: American Film Institute.

Burke, B. M. (2015). Language proficiency testing for teachers. *The Encyclopedia of Applied Linguistics*. Oxford: Wiley-Blackwell. doi:10.1002/9781405198431.wbeal1468

Darvin, R., & Norton, B. (2015). Identity and a model of investment in applied linguistics. *Annual Review of Applied Linguistics, 35*, 36-56. doi:10.1017/S0267190514000191

Internet TESL Journal. (n.d.). *Conversation questions for the ESL/EFL classroom*. Retrieved from http://iteslj.org/questions/

King, J. (2013). Silence in the second language classrooms of Japanese universities. *Applied Linguistics, 34*(3), 325-343.

Lee, L. (2014). Digital news stories: building language learners' content knowledge and speaking skills. *Foreign Language Annals, 47*(2), 338-356. doi:10.1111/flan.12084

Nunan, D., & Richards, J. C. (Eds.). (2014). *Language learning beyond the classroom*. Routledge.

Pryde, M. (2015). Teaching language learners to elaborate on their responses: a structured, genre-based approach. *Foreign Language Annals, 48*(2), 168-183. doi:10.1111/flan.12135

Richards, J. C. (2015). The changing face of language learning: learning beyond the classroom. *RELC Journal, 46*(1), 5-22. doi:10.1177/0033688214561621

Appendix 1

Apple iPad Mini version 2
iOgrapher Case
Apple Lightning to 30-pin Adapter (0.2 m)
Manfrotto Pixi Mini Tripod
Tascam iXJ2 Preamplifier
Rode Lavalier Microphones
Rode SC3 Adaptors

Tablets in English class: students' activities surrounding online dictionary work

Leona Bunting[1]

Abstract. Tablets have become increasingly popular among young people in Sweden and this rapid increase also resonates in school, especially in classrooms for younger children. The aim of the present study is to analyze and describe how the students deal with the open instructions for a task of using online dictionaries on tablets. Specific focus is on how they act upon the teacher's instruction and how they collaborate with each other and the tablets and whether the teacher contributes to the solving of the task and if so, how. A video-recorded observation of ten minutes in which three students and the teacher interact was chosen for analysis. The recordings were transcribed verbatim and actions described in writing. The students in the sequence went beyond the teacher's instructions of becoming acquainted with online dictionaries and compared variations in search results. Also, the teacher could only see the activities she was directly involved in. Her interaction with the students interrupted and disturbed their focus. To conclude, open instructions demand more of the students and rely heavily on their ability to interpret and understand what is expected in school at the same time as the tablets supported the students' inquisitiveness and power of initiative.

Keywords: mobile assisted language learning, MALL, second language learning, classroom study.

1. Introduction

Tablets have become increasingly popular among young people in Sweden and in 2014, 95% of 9-12-year-olds used tablets for both recreational and school purposes (Alexandersson & Davidsson, 2014; Findahl, 2014). This rapid increase also resonates in school, especially in classrooms for younger children. Tablets are

---

1. University of Gothenburg, Sweden; leona.bunting@ait.gu.se

How to cite this article: Bunting, L. (2015). Tablets in English class: students' activities surrounding online dictionary work. In F. Helm, L. Bradley, M. Guarda, & S. Thouësny (Eds), *Critical CALL – Proceedings of the 2015 EUROCALL Conference, Padova, Italy* (pp. 97-101). Dublin: Research-publishing.net. http://dx.doi.org/10.14705/rpnet.2015.000316

considered to be flexible and user-friendly (Huang, Huang, Huang, & Lin, 2012) as well as relatively cheap and simple to use (Alexandersson & Davidsson, 2014).

Several studies involving tablets regard upper secondary or university students. Some focus on students' perceived use and attitudes to mobile devices (Ott, Haglind, & Lindström, 2014; Pagel & Lambacher, 2014), while others point to their potential for higher education (Kaganer, Giordano, Brion, & Tortoriello, 2013) and particularly for learning English (Huang et al., 2012). A study of 13-14 year-old students in Spain revealed that they began using the tablets spontaneously to support their learning after having been prompted to come up with ideas of how to use them for practising English (Underwood, 2014).

A review of Mobile Assisted Language Learning (MALL) research specifically in the area of second language learning found that most studies have been small-scale, short-term and experimental (Viberg & Grönlund, 2012). While the design of the present study is similar concerning the first two aspects, it differs in the third as it is based on a task initiated by the teacher. It focuses the students' use of tablets during a classroom project in English.

The present study is part of a larger research project in which the relationship is examined between what Swedish pre-teens do with English out of school when they engage in interest-driven activities linked to media and what they do with English in school (Bunting, 2015; Bunting & Lindström, 2013). For this particular study, a classroom project was followed where the students used tablets for exploring online dictionaries. The aim of the present study is to analyze and describe how the students deal with the open instructions of the task. Specific focus is on how they act upon the teacher's instruction and how they collaborate with each other and the tablet. A further interest is whether the teacher contributes to the solving of the task and if so, how. This will be done by scrutinizing a filmed sequence in which three students and their teacher interact.

2. Method

2.1. Gathering data

The present study is an observation study with the researcher as observer as participant (cf. Cohen, Manion & Morrisson, 2011). 28 12 year-old students and their English teacher in a Swedish comprehensive school participated in the study. Permission to video-record the lessons had been obtained from the school, the parents and the students themselves. The teacher informed the parents about the research project and obtained written consent from all of them. The students were asked orally about their willingness to participate. One student declined and is thus not present in the material. The data consists of approximately forty hours of video-recordings from three different cameras; one stationary, one mounted to the teacher's head and one hand-held, operated by the researcher.

The teacher had designed a classroom project in which the students were to work with YouTube on tablets to further their understanding of authentic language, distinguish and learn new vocabulary and finally present their findings orally to their classmates. The whole classroom project, all of which was followed for research purposes, took nine lessons. The work with the online dictionaries assumed one lesson each with two groups. For the present study, a particular sequence was chosen involving three students and the teacher. This sequence lasted ten minutes.

2.2. Analyzing the data

The students engaged in a multitude of activities during the work with the online dictionaries. The sequence with the three students and the teacher that was singled out for closer scrutiny was chosen as it illustrates a learning situation involving a communication breakdown or possibly even a critical incident. The films from the three different cameras concerning this sequence were transcribed verbatim and non-verbal actions were described in writing. All was then merged into one document to obtain a comprehensive view of the material. To strengthen the validity of the analysis, the films and the transcriptions have been used in parallel. To strengthen the reliability of the analytical process, the transcription was studied first by the author and then also by a senior researcher. The data-driven research questions emerged in this process.

3. Discussion

The three students in the chosen sequence went well beyond the instructions given by the teacher of becoming acquainted with online dictionaries and compared variations in search results. The analyzed sequence demonstrates how students can learn together and from each other as they collaboratively work on the task the teacher has given them. Furthermore, the way they interacted with the devices, pointing and writing on each others' tablets, show that the affordances of the tablets also contribute to the learning situation.

The head-mounted camera showed that the teacher could only see the student she was interacting with at any given time; the other activities in the classroom were merely peripheral to her. It thus became impossible for her to see all the activities that went on in the classroom. For example, the teacher did not see that student A and B compared search results for the same word from different online dictionaries, something which she later gave as a task to the whole class. Furthermore, when the teacher asked the group what they were doing and questioned A's choice of word, 'katt' (Swedish for cat), her acting disturbed and interrupted their work. "If you are to use a dictionary, you obviously should look up words you don't know to learn how to use these dictionaries. Right?". She instructed and disciplined at the same time. After the teacher left, A suggested to look up the word 'dagis' (Swedish for kindergarten). He was willing to follow the teacher's instructions to look up something he did not know. B questioned his choice of word and said that they should look up something they needed instead. A interpreted the teacher's instruction verbatim and B interpreted the instruction to contain more than the explicit words. The teacher thus contributed to a shift in focus of the students' work.

Regarding the students' collaboration, it is apparent that B had the preferential right of interpretation while A and C followed his lead. For example, in the aforementioned exchange, B corrected A. Student C sat on his own until he heard A and B laugh. He then moved to sit next to B. A and B both contributed to solving the task while C was peripheral.

4. Conclusions

The filmed sequence of the students and the teacher shows that twelve-year-olds can cope with open instructions, but that such instructions demand more of the students and rely heavily on their ability to interpret and understand what is expected in school. There is thus a risk that open instructions, which leave room for interpretation, are less accessible to students who do not understand the teachers' unvoiced expectations. However, the work with the tablets supported the students' inquisitiveness and power of initiative which are important parts of the learning process.

References

Alexandersson, K., & Davidsson, P. (2014). Eleverna och internet [Students and the internet]. Stockholm: .SE (Stiftelsen för internetinfrastruktur).

Bunting, L., & Lindström, B. (2013). Framing English learning at the intersection of school and out-of-school practices. *Journal of International Scientific Publications: Language, Individual & Society, 7,* part 1, 205-221.

Bunting, L. (2015). Teaching English to boundary crossers - A subject in change. *13th Annual Hawaii Conference on Education, Honolulu, USA, January 5-8, 2015, Proceedings.*

Cohen, L., Manion, L., & Morrison, K. (2011). Research methods in education (7th ed.). London: Routledge.

Findahl, O. (2014). Svenskarna och internet [Swedes and the internet]. Stockholm: .SE (Stiftelsen för internetinfrastruktur).

Huang, Y.-M., Huang, Y.-M., Huang, S.-H. & Lin, Y.-T. (2012). A uniquitous English vocabulary learning system: evidence of active/passive attitudes vs. usefulness/ease-of-use. *Computers & Education, 58,* 273-282. doi:10.1016/j.compedu.2011.08.008

Kaganer, E., Giordano, G.A., Brion, S. & Tortoriello, M. (2013). Media tablets for mobile learning. *Communications of the ACM, 56*(11), 68-75.

Ott, T., Haglind, T., & Lindström, B. (2014) Students' use of mobile phones for school work. In M. Kalz, Y. Bayyurt, & M. Specht (Eds.), *Mobile as mainstream – Towards future challenges in mobile learning; 13th World Conference on Mobile and Contextual Learning, mLearn 2014, Istanbul, Turkey, November 3-5, 2014, Proceedings* (pp. 69-80). doi:10.1007/978-3-319-13416-1_8

Pagel, J. W., & Lambacher S. G. (2014). Patterns and effectiveness of mobile device usage by Japanese undergraduates for L2 acquisition purposes. In S. Jager, L. Bradley, E. J. Meima, & S. Thouësny (Eds.), *CALL Design: Principles and Practice, Proceedings of the 2014 EUROCALL Conference, Groningen, The Netherlands* (pp. 284-289). Dublin Ireland: Research-publishing.net. doi:10.14705/rpnet.2014.000232

Underwood, J. (2014). Using iPads to help teens design their own activities. In S. Jager, L. Bradley, E. J. Meima, & S. Thouësny (Eds.), *CALL Design: Principles and Practice, Proceedings of the 2014 EUROCALL Conference, Groningen, The Netherlands* (pp. 385-390). Dublin Ireland: Research-publishing.net. doi:10.14705/rpnet.2014.000250

Viberg, O., & Grönlund, Å. (2012). Mobile assisted language learning: a literature review. *mLearn, CEUR Workshop Proceedings* (pp. 9-16).

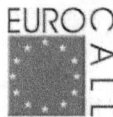 

Set super-chicken to 3! Student and teacher perceptions of Spaceteam ESL

Walcir Cardoso[1], Jennica Grimshaw[2], and David Waddington[3]

Abstract. Digital gaming in education is an area that has been rapidly expanding in popularity and is gradually being applied to second language (L2) contexts (Godwin-Jones, 2014). Mobile gaming in particular offers the benefits of digital gaming while also offering the portability and accessibility of mobile devices (Ogata & Yana, 2003; Stockwell, 2010). This pilot study examines student and teacher perceptions of a mobile team-building game entitled Spaceteam ESL. Although not created as an educational game, Spaceteam ESL allows students to interact in the target L2 (English) while providing a comfortable and enjoyable environment to practice the language. We hypothesize that its regular use may contribute to the development of oral fluency in the target language, as it engages learners in an activity that encourages them to reuse the language that they already know in an automatized (fast) but comprehensible manner. In general, our analyses indicate that users and their instructor perceive Spaceteam ESL positively, as a fun and effective way to practice English.

Keywords: digital gaming in L2 education, MALL, fluency development.

1. Introduction

Although digital gaming was not created for educational purposes, it has great potential for use in second language education (e.g. Chik, 2014; Godwin-Jones, 2014; Kim 2014; Reinders & Wattana, 2014). With the widespread use of mobile devices such as smartphones and tablets, language learners now have in their hands

---

1. Concordia University, Canada; walcir@education.concordia.ca

2. Concordia University, Canada; jennica.grimshaw@gmail.com

3. Concordia University, Canada; dwadding@education.concordia.ca

How to cite this article: Cardoso, W., Grimshaw, J., & Waddington, D. (2015). Set super-chicken to 3! Student and teacher perceptions of Spaceteam ESL. In F. Helm, L. Bradley, M. Guarda, & S. Thouësny (Eds), *Critical CALL – Proceedings of the 2015 EUROCALL Conference, Padova, Italy* (pp. 102-107). Dublin: Research-publishing.net. http://dx.doi.org/10.14705/rpnet.2015.000317

a more accessible alternative to stationary desktop computers, a tool that allows them to learn anytime, anywhere.

According to Nation (2007), the design of any language program or class should include the following four strands: access to meaningful language input, opportunities for meaningful output, a language focus, and opportunities for fluency development. He also recommends that practice should equally target these four strands. However, the last strand, fluency development, is often neglected in the language classroom, "possibly because it does not involve the learning of new language items" (Nation, 2007, p. 8). Fluency development involves making the best use of what is already known (e.g. known vocabulary and pronunciation features) in a fast, automatic, but comprehensive manner. Digital gaming via mobile devices may offer an accessible and time-efficient way for learners to develop fluency.

The current study introduces the mobile game Spaceteam ESL as a classroom tool to promote the development of oral fluency, and examines student and teacher perceptions of the game. Spaceteam ESL is a free digital, interactive team-building game (app) played on mobile devices. It was developed by David Waddington and Walcir Cardoso, based on the original Spaceteam mobile game created by Henry Smith of Sleeping Beast Games. In the adapted version of the game, each team member is presented with a panel of buttons and dials, and a unique set of instructions (see Figure 1). An individual's instructions correspond with those of the team member's panels. The labels for each item on a player's panel are vocabulary combinations randomly generated with a verb + complement (usually adjective + noun or noun + prepositional phrase; e.g. "set super-chicken to 3"). The vocabulary repertoire was taken from the 1,000 most frequently used word list in English, thus allowing learners to practice what they already know, in an automatized but comprehensive manner. As game levels increase, so does the complexity of the vocabulary (word-level frequency and pronunciation difficulty). Players must interact orally with team members to communicate and/or carry out instructions in a limited amount of time to pilot a spaceship. Accordingly, players must be both intelligible and efficient (fast) in speaking so that their teammates can successfully interpret the instructions within the time frame.

As Spaceteam ESL does not explicitly target a specific language feature, the game fulfills another requirement of Nation's (2007) fourth strand of fluency development, as "it does not involve the learning of new language items" (p. 8). Although not created as a pedagogical game, we believe that Spaceteam ESL has the potential to serve as a pedagogical tool for L2 practice in an entertaining and non-threatening manner. We aim to find out whether this hypothesis is correct in this study: What are student and teacher perceptions of Spaceteam ESL?

Figure 1. Spaceteam ESL: the interface

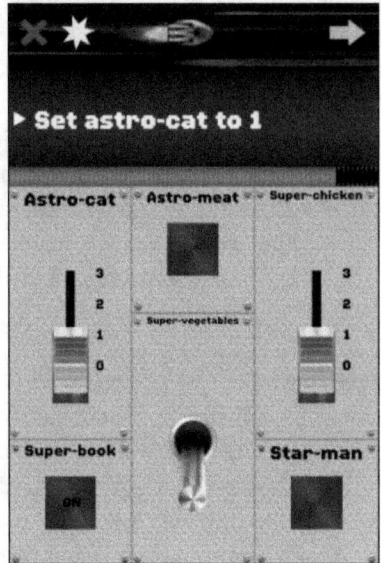

2. Method

2.1. Participants

The participants were ten Chinese students enrolled in an intermediate-level ESL conversation course at a Canadian university. However, due to sporadic attendance rates and participant attrition, only four students were considered.

2.2. Instruments and data collection

A survey was distributed to participants after the final gaming session to obtain reactions to the game. The survey consisted of 15 questions using a 5-point Likert scale ranging from strongly disagree (1) to strongly agree (5). It asked students questions about the impact Spaceteam ESL may have had on their learning experience (e.g. "I felt more comfortable speaking English while playing Spaceteam ESL than I would in front of the teacher"). Open-ended interviews were also conducted in which participants were encouraged to expand on their perceptions of the game. Results collected from an interview with the participants' teacher are also included in this study.

2.3. Procedure

Participants met once a week for a period of four weeks in which they engaged in game-playing for approximately 15-20 minutes. They played Spaceteam ESL in groups of 2-3 players at the beginning of each class as a warm-up activity. Because the study was conducted in early stages of the development of Spaceteam ESL, only the first level of the game was used, the one that contained the 1,000 most frequently used words in English.

3. Results and discussion

The results of the current study are based on an analysis of the oral interviews and the survey results (using descriptive statistics). Due to space constraints, only a set of the responses obtained in the survey and interviews will be reported. In general, participants believed Spaceteam ESL to be a good educational game: they agreed it was a fun way to practice using the target language. However, as only the first level of the game was available at the time when this study took place, the game's target vocabulary and the related pronunciation features became too easy and repetitive for participants after a few sessions. Therefore, some of the participants described Spaceteam ESL as "a good game for beginners".

Two participants and their teacher felt that Spaceteam ESL allowed them to warm-up their oral articulators before the lesson: "my mouth will really open up so we really have a good class after the game". The game also provided participants with the opportunity to self-monitor their pronunciation (e.g. if they observed that no one was following their instructions) and offer peer feedback so that their team could be effective in speaking and listening to commands to succeed in the game.

Survey responses suggest that Spaceteam ESL increases students' motivation to participate in class (Mean: 3.75; SD: 1.25). One participant said that her "mood raised a little bit" during gameplay, and the teacher commented that it generated a positive mood that carried over into the lesson, "creating an overall pleasant atmosphere". The game may have also reduced feelings of nervousness in class: a participant believed that "[Spaceteam ESL] reduced our nervousness ... after playing this game people seem relaxed, at least I felt relaxed, and began to speak in a relaxed way". Participants also expressed that they felt more comfortable using the game in class than other classroom activities (Mean: 4; *SD*: 0.81), and felt more comfortable playing the game than speaking in front of the teacher (Mean: 3.75; *SD*: 1.25).

All participants agreed that Spaceteam ESL helped to increase familiarity between classmates, as the following statements indicate: "[the game] really helped me to know my partner, to know my classmates", "it's kind of a different way to know my classmates, […] it's actually better than just talking". The teacher also mentioned that when addressing each other in class, students had more confidence: "they addressed each other directly rather than through the teacher".

Unfortunately, possibly due to the academic context in which this study was conducted, most participants misinterpreted the purpose of Spaceteam ESL, perceiving it as a pedagogical tool to learn new vocabulary. As discussed earlier, however, one of the purposes of Spaceteam ESL in this study was to promote the development of fluency based on previously acquired language.

4. Conclusions

Based on student and teacher perceptions of the game, Spaceteam ESL has great potential as a tool to help develop oral fluency and pronunciation in the L2 classroom. In addition, it may contribute to some of the important factors that promote L2 learning: it increases learners' (and possibly teachers') motivation, creates a comfortable learning environment, and fosters teamwork and consequently peer-teaching (including peer-feedback). Further research with a larger participant pool and the full version of the game is required for reliable results about the potential benefits of Spaceteam ESL in L2 education.

5. Acknowledgements

We would like to thank the participants and the following individuals for their contribution to this study: Tiago Bione, Nina Padden, George Smith, Henry Smith, Lauren Stratchan, and Stef Rucco. This project was partially funded by the Centre for the Study of Learning and Performance and the Fonds québécois de la recherche sur la société et la culture (ALERT project).

References

Chik, A. (2014). Digital gaming and language learning: autonomy and community. *Language Learning & Technology, 18*(2), 85-100.

Godwin-Jones, R. (2014). Games in language learning: opportunities and challenges. *Language Learning & Technology, 18*(2), 9-19.

Kim, S. H. (2014). Developing autonomous learning for oral proficiency using digital storytelling. *Language Learning & Technology, 18*(2), 20-35.

Nation, P. (2007). The four strands. *Innovation in Language Learning and Teaching, 1*(1), 2-13. doi:10.2167/illt039.0

Ogata, H., & Yano, Y. (2003). How ubiquitous computing can support language learning. *Proceedings of KEST* (pp. 1-6).

Reinders, H., & Wattana, S. (2014). Can I say something? The effects of digital gameplay on willingness to communicate. *Language Learning & Technology, 18*(2), 101-123.

Stockwell, G. (2010). Using mobile phones for vocabulary activities: examining the effect of the platform. *Language Learning & Technology, 14*(2), 95-110.

Evaluating text-to-speech synthesizers

Walcir Cardoso[1], George Smith[2], and Cesar Garcia Fuentes[3]

Abstract. Text-To-Speech (TTS) synthesizers have piqued the interest of researchers for their potential to enhance the L2 acquisition of writing (Kirstein, 2006), vocabulary and reading (Proctor, Dalton, & Grisham, 2007) and pronunciation (Cardoso, Collins, & White, 2012; Soler-Urzua, 2011). Despite their proven effectiveness, there is a need for up-to-date formal evaluations of TTS systems. The present study was an attempt to evaluate the language learning potential of an up-to-date TTS system at two levels: (1) speech quality (comprehensibility, naturalness, accuracy, and intelligibility) and (2) focus on a linguistic form (via a feature identification task). For Task 1, participants listened to and rated human- and TTS-produced stories and sentences on a 6-point scale (1); for Task 2, they listened to 16 human- and TTS-produced sentences to identify the presence of a target feature (English regular past -ed). Results of paired samples t-tests indicated that for speech quality, the human samples earned higher ratings than the TTS samples. For the second task (past -ed perception), the TTS and human-produced samples were equivalent. The discussion of the findings will highlight how TTS can be used to complement and enhance the teaching of L2 pronunciation and other linguistic skills both inside and outside the classroom.

Keywords: computer-assisted language learning, CALL, text-to-speech, technology and language learning.

---

1. Concordia University, Canada; walcir@education.concordia.ca
2. University of Hawaii at Manoa, United States; gfsmith@hawaii.edu
3. Concordia University, Canada; cesgarfu@hotmail.com

How to cite this article: Cardoso, W., Smith, G., & Garcia Fuentes, C. (2015). Evaluating text-to-speech synthesizers. In F. Helm, L. Bradley, M. Guarda, & S. Thouësny (Eds), *Critical CALL – Proceedings of the 2015 EUROCALL Conference, Padova, Italy* (pp. 108-113). Dublin: Research-publishing.net. http://dx.doi.org/10.14705/rpnet.2015.000318

1. Introduction

The provision of target language input of sufficient quality and quantity is an important issue in the field of second language acquisition. Three challenges which exist with this provision are: (1) the need for vast amounts of comprehensible input to develop language competence (Council of Europe, 2001; Krashen, 1985); (2) the need for learner-centered and personalized input (Chapelle, 2001); and (3) the need for exposure to a variety of speech models for robust phonological development (Barcroft & Sommers, 2005).

Traditional face-to-face classroom settings may not be able to meet these criteria due to the inherent restrictions of this teaching context (e.g. teacher-centered, one variety of English used, lack of sustained input practice), especially in foreign-language settings (Cardoso et al., 2012). One remedy to this problem lies in the use of TTS, which can offset some of the limitations of traditional classrooms given that they are highly flexible, learner-centered, and easily accessible. Several studies have attested to the benefits of using TTS for learning writing (Kirstein, 2006), vocabulary and reading (Proctor et al., 2007) and pronunciation (Cardoso et al., 2012; Soler-Urzua, 2011), both in and outside the classroom.

Despite these theoretical and empirical benefits, however, there exist very few formal evaluations of TTS systems, specifically of their potential to promote the ideal conditions under which Second Language Learning (SLA) is thought to occur – a critical stage in the evaluation of Computer-Assisted Language Learning (CALL) applications (Chapelle, 2001; Handley & Hamel, 2005). Those evaluations which do exist have used a wide variety of rating methods, produced mixed results (some demonstrating the adequacy of TTS – Kang, Kashiwagi, Treviranus, & Kaburagi, 2009, some demonstrating inadequacy in some respects – Handley, 2009, Nusbaum, Francis, & Henley, 1995) and date back more than 5 years. The present study was thus an attempt to provide an up-to-date evaluation of a state of the art TTS system concerning its potential to promote ideal SLA processes. The following two evaluation criteria were chosen: (1) the speech quality of the TTS system (input); and (2) the potential for learners to focus on linguistic form in these two types of input. Two research questions were formulated as follows:

- What is the quality of speech produced by TTS systems in comparison with that by humans?

- Can TTS systems provide learners with the opportunity to focus on form?

2. Method

2.1. Participants and design

Fifty-four university-level participants with a variety of L1 backgrounds were recruited at an English-language university in Canada. Two tasks were designed to elicit participants' perceptions of the TTS system: rating speech quality and feature identification. Both tasks had learners listen to speech samples produced by TTS and a human, with the goal being human-TTS equivalency; accordingly, a paired samples design was adopted for the analysis.

2.2. Stimuli and materials

A female speaker of North American English (Julie) in the program NaturalReader 13 (2013) was used as the TTS system, and compared with a native-speaker of the same dialect with similar speech properties. For speech quality, participants listened to two stories and twelve sentences and rated them according to four judgment criteria: comprehensibility, naturalness, pronunciation accuracy, and intelligibility on a 6-point scale. Potential for focus on form was measured by having learners perform an aural feature identification task wherein they judged whether certain sentences contained a target grammar feature (English regular past -ed). Both the stories and sentences were adapted from materials produced by the ALERT research project (Collins et al., 2011). The tasks were performed via Microsoft PowerPoint in a quiet lab at the university, by a trained research assistant.

2.3. Analysis

Data came from the participants' judgments of the stories and sentences that they heard and their accuracy on perceiving past -ed in decontextualized sentences such as "I hated the movie" and "I hate the movie"). The ratings of each participant were tallied, and means were calculated for each story and sentence. Accuracy scores were reported as raw scores, with a maximum of 8 points per speech source (i.e. human or TTS). Main analysis was carried out by means of paired samples t-tests, with an alpha level of .05 used for the determination of statistical significance.

3. Results

Results for the rating task were as follows. For the stories, paired samples t-tests revealed a significant difference in the rating scores on all categories (comprehensibility, $t(54)=-4.77, p<.001$; naturalness, $t(54)=-9.35, p<.001$; accuracy,

$t(54)=-7.32$, $p<.001$; and intelligibility, $t(54)=-6.40$, $p<.001$). Similarly, paired samples t-tests for the sentences also revealed significant differences between the human- and TTS-produced samples for all measures (comprehensibility, $t(54)=-6.13$, $p<.001$; naturalness, $t(54)=-7.63$, $p<.001$; accuracy, $t(54)=-7.34$, $p<.001$; and intelligibility, $t(54)=-6.11$, $p<.001$). For the past -ed identification task, paired samples t-tests revealed no significant differences between the TTS- and human-produced speech samples ($t(54)=-1.93$, $p=.059$). Table 1, Table 2, and Table 3 below show the descriptive statistics according to each task.

Table 1. Descriptive statistics for story rating

	Comprehensibility		Naturalness		Accuracy		Intelligibility	
	Mean	SD	Mean	SD	Mean	SD	Mean	SD
Human	5.66	0.67	5.61	0.68	5.82	0.47	5.54	0.79
TTS	5.14	0.94	3.64	1.63	4.77	1.06	4.50	1.18

Table 2. Descriptive statistics for sentence rating

	Comprehensibility		Naturalness		Accuracy		Intelligibility	
	Mean	SD	Mean	SD	Mean	SD	Mean	SD
Human	5.90	0.29	5.65	0.35	5.74	0.29	5.80	0.38
TTS	5.36	0.69	4.24	1.50	5.35	0.83	4.94	1.01

Table 3. Descriptive statistics for feature identification task

	Mean	SD
Human	6.03	1.38
TTS	5.59	1.12

4. Discussion and conclusions

The present study sought to evaluate the speech quality and potential to focus on linguistic form provided by a state-of-the-art TTS system. First, the results revealed that the samples produced by the TTS system were rated significantly lower than the human-produced samples for all four categories of speech quality (comprehensibility, naturalness, pronunciation accuracy, intelligibility), at both the story and sentence levels. This echoes previous findings that have shown less favorable ratings for TTS-produced speech compared to human speech (e.g. Handley, 2009; Handley & Hamel, 2005; Nusbaum et al., 1995). However, it is important to observe that the mean rating scores assigned to the TTS system for 3 out of the 4 categories (naturalness excluded) were relatively high (4.5-5.3 out of 6). Thus, the speech quality of this particular TTS system can be considered as having achieved the "top rating(s)" needed for advancement to the next stage of evaluation (i.e. the success of activities using TTS) and use in language learning in general (Handley, 2009). The results of the past -ed perception task offer similarly promising results. Statistical equivalency was found for participants' ability to detect the presence of the target feature (past -ed) with high accuracy (~5.5 or 6 out of 8). This indicates that regardless of the source of delivery (human or TTS), participants were equally able to perceive the target form in running speech.

Implications of these results are that modern TTS systems seem to be ready for advancement to further stages of evaluation, but more importantly, for use in language learning activities, particularly as a supplemental source of input which can cater to learners' individual needs and interests. Future research should not only undertake evaluations of TTS' success as a learning tool in classrooms (particularly in English as a foreign language classrooms, where language exposure is limited), but also continue evaluations for a variety of other factors, such as the level of cognitive processing involved in listening to computer-generated speech.

5. Acknowledgements

We would like to thank the participants, Fatma Bouhlal, and Suzanne Ceretta (the human voice) for their invaluable contributions to this project. We would also like to acknowledge the financial support from the Social Sciences and Humanities Research Council of Canada.

References

Barcroft, J., & Sommers, M. S. (2005). Effects of acoustic variability on second language vocabulary learning. *Studies in Second Language Acquisition, 27*, 387-414. doi:10.1017/s0272263105050175

Cardoso, W., Collins, L., & White, J. (2012). Phonological input enhancement via text-to-speech synthesizers: the L2 acquisition of English simple past allomorphy. *Paper presented at the American Association of Applied Linguistics conference, Boston, U.S.A.*

Chapelle, C. A. (2001). Innovative language learning: achieving the vision. *ReCALL, 13*(1), 3-14. doi:10.1017/S0958344001000210

Collins, L., Horst, M., Trofimovich, P., White, J., & Cardoso, W. (2011). Explaining and enhancing efficiency in classroom second language learning. *Research Grant from the Fonds québécois de la recherché sur la société et la Culture (FQRSC), Soutiens aux équipes de recherche.*

Council of Europe (2001). *Common European Framework of Reference for Languages: Learning, teaching, assessment.* Cambridge: Cambridge University Press.

Handley, Z. (2009). Is text-to-speech synthesis ready for use in computer-assisted language learning? *Speech Communication, 51*(10), 906-919. doi:10.1016/j.specom.2008.12.004

Handley, Z., & Hamel, M. J. (2005). Establishing a methodology for benchmarking speech synthesis for computer-assisted language learning (CALL). *Language Learning & Technology, 9*(3), 99-120.

Kang, M., Kashigawi, H., Treviranus, J., & Kaburagi, M. (2009). Synthetic speech in foreign language learning: an evaluation by learners. *International Journal of Speech Technology, 11*(2), 97-106. doi:10.1007/s10772-009-9039-3

Kirstein, M. (2006). *Universalizing universal design: applying text-to-speech technology to English language learners' process writing.* Doctoral dissertation. University of Massachusetts, U.S.A.

Krashen, S. (1985). *The input hypothesis: issues and implications.* New York: Longman.

Nusbaum, H. C., Francis, A. L., & Henly, A. S. (1995). Measuring the naturalness of synthetic speech. *International Journal of Speech Technology, 1*(1), 7-19. doi:10.1007/BF02277176

Proctor, C. P., Dalton, B., & Grisham, D. L. (2007). Scaffolding English language learners and struggling readers in a universal literacy environment with embedded strategy instruction and vocabulary support. *Journal of Literary Research, 39*(1), 71-9.

Soler-Urzua, F. (2011). *The acquisition of English /ɪ/ by Spanish speakers via text-to-speech synthesizers: a quasi-experimental study.* Master's Thesis. Concordia University, Montreal, Canada.

Collecting, analysing and using longitudinal learner data for language teaching: the case of LONGDALE-IT

Erik Castello[1]

Abstract. This study aims to investigate the effectiveness of Data-Driven Learning (DDL) teaching materials based on learner corpus data. The data analysed is made up of texts written by a group of Italian university students and collected as part of the Italian component of the *Longitudinal Database of Learner English* (LONGDALE) project: LONGDALE-IT. All the students participating in the project wrote two texts as a response to the same prompt, one in the first and the other in the second year at university. The data collected in the first year was used to create some DDL materials, which were administered to the students in the second year with the aim of helping them improve on various aspects of their writing, including their use of *it*-extraposition. In this paper, the first-year learner data will be compared to the second-year learner data, and subsequently to a sub-section of the *Louvain Corpus of Native English Essays* (LOCNESS). Quantitative and qualitative findings concerning the use of *it*-extraposition in the learner texts will be discussed, with a view to determining the impact of DDL teaching materials on the learning process.

Keywords: learner corpora, DDL teaching materials, *it*-extraposition constructions, LONGDALE project.

1. Introduction

In the last few decades there has been a burgeoning interest in the use of learner corpora, i.e. electronic collections of authentic, continuous and contextualised foreign or second language texts (Granger, 2009, p. 14), for language learning

---

1. University of Padua, Italy; erik.castello@unipd.it

How to cite this article: Castello, E. (2015). Collecting, analysing and using longitudinal learner data for language teaching: the case of LONGDALE-IT. In F. Helm, L. Bradley, M. Guarda, & S. Thouësny (Eds), *Critical CALL – Proceedings of the 2015 EUROCALL Conference, Padova, Italy* (pp. 114-119). Dublin: Research-publishing.net. http://dx.doi.org/10.14705/rpnet.2015.000319

and teaching. While a large number of learner corpus-based studies have already identified a variety of linguistic features of learner language (e.g. lexical, grammatical, phraseological), more studies are needed on the use of this data to inform pedagogical practice (e.g. Cotos, 2014). In the literature, the term *Data-Driven Learning* (DDL) is used to refer to the use of either native or learner corpora in language learning/teaching (e.g. Chamber, 2010; Gilquin & Granger, 2010), and *Learning-Driven Data* (LDD) is the expression proposed by Seidlhofer (2002) to indicate data collected from specific teaching contexts which are investigated with the aim of "understand[ing] local conditions of relevance" and ultimately devising relevant classroom applications (pp. 213-214). Studies on DDL and LDD have discussed various issues, including how to appropriately combine native and learner data in DDL to fit the local needs, and what the best choice is between autonomous, hands-on, partly serendipitous corpus exploration and the use of paper-based, "hands-off" materials prepared by the teacher (e.g. Boulton, 2012).

This study draws on research conducted on the Italian component of the *Longitudinal Database of Learner English* (LONGDALE), an international project which was launched by the University of Louvain[2], Belgium, in 2008. The aim of the project is to collect a large longitudinal database consisting of data from learners with various mother tongue backgrounds who are followed over a period of at least three years. To date, the project has involved the collection of various data types, including argumentative essays, narratives, and informal interviews. The database also contains comprehensive information about the learners.

This paper aims to explore the effects of DDL teaching materials based on LDD administered to a group of Italian university students over two years. The main focus is on the use of *it*-extraposition in the students' written production collected as part of the Italian component of the LONGDALE project (LONGDALE-IT).

2. Data and method

2.1. The learner population and the data

The data consists in a longitudinal corpus of texts produced by 138 Italian undergraduate students of Linguistic and Cultural Mediation at the University of Padua (Italy), who attended the first-year English language course in 2013-2014 and the second-year course in 2014-2015. At the end of both courses the students were asked to write a text in response to the same prompt, i.e. about their views

---

2. http://www.uclouvain.be/en-cecl-longdale.html

on standard and non-standard English, native-likeness and their expectations for their level of English by the end of the course. The texts, written under no time constraints and of about 450-500 words in length, were gathered through *LimeSurvey*[3]. During the second-year course the learners were exposed to both hands-on and hands-off DDL teaching materials which were based on first-year data and compared to a sub-section of the *Louvain Corpus of Native English Essays* (LOCNESS)[4], a collection of essays written by British and American university students. Not only were the DDL materials used to illustrate and contextualize contrastive lexico-grammatical phenomena, such as the structure of English noun phrases, *it*-extraposition constructions and conjunctive adjuncts, but also to give the students general feedback and to make them think critically about what they had already achieved and what remained to be improved. Generally speaking, as regards productive skills, the target CEFR levels of the first- and second-year courses were B1 and B2 respectively. Table 1 shows quantitative data about the corpora used for the study: the first-year corpus (LONGD_pd1), the second-year corpus (LONGD_pd2), and the LOCNESS sub-corpus.

Table 1. The corpora

	LONGD_pd1	LONGD_pd2	LOCNESS
tokens	43392	64494	35399
types	2324	3307	4547
n. Sentences	1585	2574	1698
words per sentence	27,38	25	20.8
sentences per text (average)	11,4	18,6	21,7
average word number per text	314,4	467,3	453,8
n. of texts	138	138	78

2.2. Methodology for studying *it*-extraposition

The methodology used to conduct the study is Contrastive Interlanguage Analysis (CIA), whereby the learner language represented in *LONGD_pd1* and *LONGD_pd2* "is analyzed in its own right [...] longitudinally" (Granger, 2009, p. 18) and then compared to native data. The aspect that was investigated is the use of *it*-extraposition constructions, that is, clauses containing a formal or anticipatory subject as well as a notional subject, which takes the form of an extraposed embedded clause (Kaltenböck, 2003, p. 236). The types of clauses that can be

---

3. https://www.limesurvey.org/en/
4. http://www.uclouvain.be/en-cecl-locness.html

extraposed are *that*-clauses (e.g. *it could be argued that* …), *wh*-clauses (e.g. *it is debatable whether* …), *to*-clauses (e.g. *it would be interesting to* …), and *for/to*-clauses (e.g. *it is really hard for a learner to achieve them*). By contrast, extraposed *ing*-clauses and noun phrases have a borderline status (Kaltenböck, 2003, p. 247), and are usually not acceptable in formal writing. *It*-extraposition constructions, which function to "depersonalize text and create an impression of […] objectivity", are most common in academic prose, and are syntactically complex, which is why they can present an area of difficulty for L2 writers (Hinkel, 2013, p. 10). Speakers of Italian, in particular, are likely to encounter additional difficulties, in that Italian has no counterpart to *it*-clauses.

The analysis involved the study of all the instances of *it*-extraposition constructions in the corpora, which were retrieved by means of *The Sketch Engine*[5], an online corpus query system. The frequencies of occurrence of various phenomena related to *it*-extraposition were compared using the *Log-Likelihood* statistic (LL)[6], which indicates whether and to what extent differences are statistically significant.

3. Results and discussion

Over the two years, an increase occurred in the overall use of *it*-extraposition constructions (respectively 0.48% and 0.64% of the number of tokens), which is likely to be due to the "awareness raising" effect of the DDL activities administered to the students during the second-year course. It must be pointed out, however, that in both years the students produced more *it*-extraposition constructions than the native speakers (0.25%), which confirms the results of other studies of learner language. Figure 1 represents the distribution of extraposed embedded clauses in the three corpora. The figures are given per total number of *it*-clauses.

As can be seen from Figure 1, in the second year, the learners produced slightly fewer *to*-clauses and opted for more *that*-clauses (LL: +32.59, $p<0.05$), which brings them closer to the native students. It can also be noted that the number of *ing*-clauses decreased over the two years (LL: - 10.54, $p<0.01$), which suggests that most of the learners became aware of the fact that extraposed *ing*-clauses are not appropriate for academic writing. It should then be noticed that in the second year, the learners extraposed a larger number of noun phrases than in the first year (LL: +2.82, $p>0.05$), thus producing more instances of erroneous constructions, such as "**it is necessary a real contact with native-speakers to apply our knowledge*".

---

5. http://www.sketchengine.co.uk

6. http://ucrel.lancs.ac.uk/llwizard.html

Though the DDL materials specifically addressed this aspect, which is notoriously challenging for Italian learners, it clearly remained difficult for the learners, whose production revealed persistent L1 interference. The use of *it*-extraposition in combination with other features of academic English (e.g. passive voice, complex noun phrases, intricate sentences) also proved challenging.

Figure 1. Distribution of extraposed embedded clauses in LONGD_pd1, LONGD_pd2, and in the LOCNESS sub-corpus

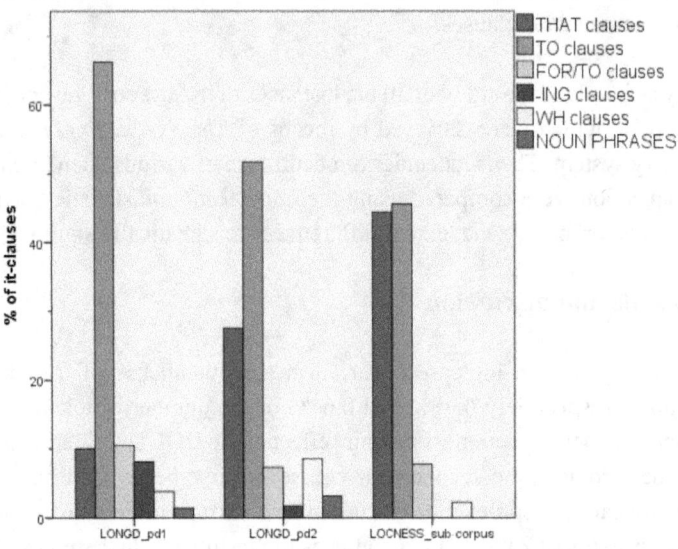

By contrast, other types of mistakes concerning the use of *it*-extraposition decreased significantly over the two years. The decrease in the omission of anticipatory *it* (e.g. "*I think is extremely difficult to be able to talk like a native speaker*"), in particular, was highly significant (LL: -16.27, $p<0.0001$).

4. Conclusions

The main purpose of this study was to test the effectiveness of DDL materials based on LDD data, and ascertain whether a group of Italian university students who were exposed to them improved their use of *it*-extraposition over two years. The results of the analysis have shown that the texts they wrote in the second year are generally more accurate, and suggest that the students' use of *it*-extraposition is evolving towards the native speaker norm. The main exception to this trend is the increase in the number of extraposed noun phrases, which highlights that this is a persistently challenging aspect for Italian learners. The study thus hints that exposing the learners to concordance lines containing their own mistakes and making them reflect on them does not necessarily bring about their complete eradication. This could depend on various factors, including the quality of the DDL materials and the way the students approached them. In order to investigate these aspects further, an analysis could be conducted into the features of the DDL activities, as well as into the students' perception of them. Besides *it*-extraposition, other features of the texts could be investigated, such as the use of the passive voice, the complexity of noun phrases and the intricacy of sentences.

References

Boulton, A. (2012). Hands-on/hands-off: alternative approaches to data-driven learning. In J. Thomas, & A. Boulton (Eds.), *Input, process and product: developments in teaching and language corpora* (pp. 152-168). Brno: Masaryk University Press.

Chambers, A. (2010). What is data-driven learning? In A. O'Keeffe, & M. McCarthy (Eds.), *The Routledge Handbook of Corpus Linguistics* (pp. 345-358). London: Routledge.

Gilquin, G., & Granger, S. (2010). How can data-driven learning be used in language teaching? In A. O'Keeffe, & M. McCarthy (Eds.), *The Routledge Handbook of Corpus Linguistics* (pp. 359-370). London: Routledge, .

Cotos, E. (2014). Enhancing writing pedagogy with learner corpus data. *ReCALL 26*(2), 202-224. doi:10.1017/S0958344014000019

Granger, S. (2009). The contribution of learner corpora to second language acquisition and foreign language teaching: a critical evaluation. In K. Aijmer (Ed.), *Corpora and language teaching* (pp. 13-32). Amsterdam and Philadelphia: John Benjamins. doi:10.1075/scl.33.04gra

Hinkel, E. (2013). Research findings on teaching grammar for academic writing. *English Teaching, 68*(4), 3-22. doi:10.15858/engtea.68.4.201312.3

Kaltenböck, G. (2003). On the syntactic and semantic status of anticipatory *it*. *English Language and Linguistics*, 7(2), 235-255. doi:10.1017/S1360674303001096

Seidlhofer, B. (2002). Pedagogy and local learner corpora: working with learning-driven data. In S. Granger, J. Hung, & S. Petch-Tyson (Eds.), *Computer learner corpora, second language acquisition and foreign language teaching* (pp. 213-234). Amsterdam/Philadelphia: John Benjamins. doi:10.1075/lllt.6.14sei

How can we use corpus wordlists for language learning? Interfaces between computer corpora and expert intervention

Yu-Hua Chen[1] and Radovan Bruncak[2]

Abstract. With the advances in technology, wordlists retrieved from computer corpora have become increasingly popular in recent years. The lexical items in those wordlists are usually selected, according to a set of robust frequency and dispersion criteria, from large corpora of authentic and naturally occurring language. Corpus wordlists are of great value for language learning because words occurring with high frequency are very likely to be encountered in real life. Very little, however, has been reported regarding the applications of corpus wordlists in a Computer Assisted Language Learning (CALL) context. A vocabulary-building app, ColliCrush, is currently being developed on the basis of the Academic Collocation List (Ackermann & Chen, 2013), which consists of 2,468 of the most frequent and pedagogically relevant entries extracted from a 25-million-word academic corpus. Collocation is one of the areas that pose great challenges for second language learners, even at advanced levels. Explicit learning through Mobile Assisted Language Learning (MALL) would therefore contribute to the acquisition of collocation competence outside of the classroom. In this paper, the rationale and design of this project will be described. Future direction for further development will also be discussed.

Keywords: corpus wordlist, vocabulary learning, academic collocation, mobile assisted language learning.

---

1. University of Nottingham Ningbo, China; yu-hua.chen@nottingham.edu.cn
2. QKTech Ltd, London UK; radovan.bruncak@qktech.co

How to cite this article: Chen, Y.-H., & Bruncak, R. (2015). How can we use corpus wordlists for language learning? Interfaces between computer corpora and expert intervention. In F. Helm, L. Bradley, M. Guarda, & S. Thouësny (Eds), *Critical CALL – Proceedings of the 2015 EUROCALL Conference, Padova, Italy* (pp. 120-124). Dublin: Research-publishing.net. http://dx.doi.org/10.14705/rpnet.2015.000320

1. Introduction

Since the publication of the General Service List (West, 1953), a list of the most frequent 2,000 word families in the English language, frequency wordlists have been an area of interest for language teaching and learning. Particularly in recent decades, with the advances in technology, wordlists retrieved from computer corpora have become increasingly popular, e.g. academic wordlists (Coxhead 2000; Gardner & Davies, 2014). The lexical items in those wordlists are often selected with a set of robust frequency and dispersion criteria from large corpora of authentic and naturally occurring language. One obvious advantage for a student seeking to prioritize learning vocabulary items from corpus wordlists is that those lexical items are likely to be encountered in real life as a result of their high frequency. Corpus wordlists can therefore be of great use for vocabulary teaching and learning.

Table 1. Some examples of *make*+noun collocational entries from ACL

1335	make	v	adjustments	n
1336	make	v	arrangements	n
1337	make	v	available	adj
1338	make	v	aware	adj
1339	make	v	contact	n
1340	make (a)	v	contribution	n
1341	make	v	explicit	adj
1342	make	v	policy	n
1343	make	v	provision	n
1344	make	v	visible	adj
1345	make (a)	v	comment	n
1346	make (a)	v	distinction	n
1347	make (a)	v	living	n
1348	make (a)	v	prediction	n
1349	make (a)	v	recommendation	n
1350	make (a)	v	statement	n
1351	make (a)	v	transition	n
1352	make (an)	v	argument	n
1353	make (an)	v	assessment	n
1354	make (an)	v	assumption	n
1355	make (an)	v	impact	n

There are, however, very few applications of corpus wordlists in a CALL context, and we strongly argue that there is a need to develop supporting computer programs based on corpus wordlists as this is one of the most straightforward ways in which corpora can provide readily useable resources for language learning. In this project, a vocabulary-building app called ColliCrush for touch-screen smartphones and tablets is being developed based on the corpus-derived Academic Collocation List (ACL, Ackermann & Chen, 2013). The development of ACL involved computational analysis of an academic corpus of 25 million words and an expert review of a comprehensive data-driven list after taking into account both quantitative and qualitative parameters. The final list consists of 2,468 of the most frequent and pedagogically relevant entries, each annotated with part-of-speech information. See Table 1 for examples of verb+noun collocational entries with one of the delexical verbs *make* that second language students often find challenging and confuse with similar verbs (Altenberg & Granger, 2001).

In the remainder of the paper, first, the theoretical underpinnings of the design of ColliCrush will be summarised from relevant fields. Then, the development of ColliCrush will be described in more detail. This paper will finish with a discussion of future development and a conclusion.

2. Development of ColliCrush

2.1. Design framework

2.1.1. Collocation in language teaching and learning

Collocation is one of the areas that pose great challenges for second language learners, even at advanced levels (e.g. Nesselhauf, 2005). What makes the learning of collocations difficult is that the selection of collocates is often determined by native norms rather than grammatical rules. For example, the verbs *conduct* or *make* have similar meanings. However, only *conduct* collocates with the noun *research*, and this lexical choice is rather arbitrary. For learners whose mother tongue does not distinguish between those verbs (e.g. Mandarin Chinese), trying to remember collocations by rote learning seems to be the best learning strategy. The explicit learning of collocations has, therefore, long been advocated (e.g. Lewis, 1993), and this strongly supports the notion of making collocations the backbone of a vocabulary building app.

It should also be noted that receptive and productive vocabulary knowledge (also known as active and passive vocabulary, see, e.g. Laufer & Paribakht, 1998) is commonly distinguished in vocabulary research. In the context of second language learning, it is very likely that learners do not have difficulty in understanding the collocation *conduct research*, but when they have to produce the verb collocate for *research* in speech or writing, there is a chance that they might choose a wrong collocate, such as *make*. In the design of ColliCrush, therefore, both the recognition and production of collocations will be included in the learning tasks. As vocabulary acquisition is known to be incremental in nature (Schmitt, 2000), repeated encounters with the same collocational items will also be integrated into the design of this app.

2.1.2. Collocation in CALL

Vocabulary is one of the areas that students can easily learn outside of the classroom without formal instruction. As vocabulary acquisition can take place anytime and anywhere, MALL appears to meet the needs of this informal, personal and ubiquitous learning style (Duman, Orhon, & Gedik, 2014). ColliCrush is a language learning application, designed for smartphones and tablets, which will help to raise users' awareness of academic collocations and improve their lexical competence while having some fun along the way. One activity currently being developed is similar to a traditional brick-breaking computer game, where bricks labelled with various verbs, for example, will only be crushed when learners choose the correct verb collocate for a given noun in an item of verb-noun collocation. Otherwise, bricks will continue to pile up to the top until the game is over. Feedback will be provided to learners on such learning and assessment tasks at the end. The design is thus also in line with the increasingly popular trend of Game-Based Learning (GBL) in language education (Reinders, 2012), where learning is considered to be similar to gaming, both consisting of a continuous cycle of error-feedback-reconstruction.

2.2. Future development: collocation in context

For future development, we propose two possible directions to improve ColliCrush or develop similar vocabulary building apps. The first one is to provide more contextual information for individual lexical items, e.g. collocations in use. As mentioned earlier, vocabulary learning is incremental, and vocabulary use in a variety of frequent patterns derived from large corpora will contribute to learners' aggregated lexical and grammatical knowledge. Second, lexical items may be further grouped in terms of functions. For example, students will learn about different functions of academic collocations such as hedging in '*virtually impossible*' or '*relatively few/ little/ rare*'. The integration of functions will raise students' awareness about the broader context of academic English discourse.

3. Conclusion

With the aim of facilitating explicit and effective vocabulary learning, we described the rationale and development of a vocabulary-building app on the basis of a corpus-derived academic collocation list. It is believed that such an app, with the integration of gaming components designed for the MALL environment, will contribute to informal, personal and ubiquitous learning of vocabulary, and hopefully will be more appealing than traditional rote learning for younger generations. Similar vocabulary-building games may also be developed for other corpus vocabulary lists. Information collected from such an online learning platform would in turn contribute to data analytics and be used to determine, for example, the grading of lexical items for the future.

References

Ackermann, K., & Chen, Y. H. (2013). Developing the Academic Collocation List (ACL – A corpus-driven and expert-judged approach. *Journal of English for Academic Purposes, 12*(4), 235-247. doi:10.1016/j.jeap.2013.08.002

Altenberg, B., & Granger, S. (2001). Grammatical and lexical patterning in NS and NNS student writing. *Applied Linguistics, 22*(2), 173-195. doi:10.1093/applin/22.2.173

Coxhead, A. (2000). A new academic word list. *TESOL Quarterly, 34*(2), 213-238. doi:10.2307/3587951

Duman, G., Orhon, G., & Gedik, N. (2014). Research trends in mobile assisted language learning. *ReCALL, 27*(2), 197-216. doi:10.1017/S0958344014000287

Gardner, D., & Davies, M. (2014). A new academic vocabulary list. *Applied Linguistics, 35*(3), 305-327. doi:10.1093/applin/amt015

Laufer, B., & Paribakht, T. S. (1998). The relationship between passive and active vocabularies: effects of language learning context. *Language Learning, 48*(3), 365-391. doi:10.1111/0023-8333.00046

Lewis, M. (1993). *The lexical approach*. Hove: LTP Publications.

Nesselhauf, N. (2005). *Collocations in a learner corpus*. Amsterdam: John Benjamins. doi:10.1075/scl.14

Reinders, H. (Ed.). (2012). *Digital games in language learning and teaching*. Basingstoke: Palgrave Macmillan. doi:10.1057/9781137005267

Schmitt, N. (2000). *Vocabulary in language teaching*. Cambridge: Cambridge University Press.

West, M. (1953). *A general service list of English words*. London: Longman.

Corpus-supported academic writing: how can technology help?

Madalina Chitez[1], Christian Rapp[2], and Otto Kruse[3]

Abstract. Phraseology has long been used in L2 teaching of academic writing, and corpus linguistics has played a major role in the compilation and assessment of academic phrases. However, there are only a few interactive academic writing tools in which corpus methodology is implemented in a real-time design to support formulation processes. In this paper, we describe several corpus-related methods that we have developed and implemented as part of an interactive thesis-writing tool, *Thesis Writer*, designed and constructed jointly by the Language Competence Centre and the Center for Innovative Teaching and Learning of the Zurich University of Applied Sciences in Switzerland. *Thesis Writer* (TW) hosts several linguistic-support tools and is designed in its first pilot version to support thesis writing in economics with the help of two self-compiled corpora in English and German. Students can access the corpora directly via the IMS Open Corpus Workbench or via a pre-selected collection of central rhetorical elements through the phrase book. Several search options and tutorials have been tested and included into the TW platform: the corpus simple search tool, the corpus syntactic search tool, and the academic phrasebook. In the case of the latter, a new methodology led to the identification of lists of phrases distributed in research-cycle sections of the thesis.

Keywords: academic writing, corpus linguistics, language instruction, thesis writing, educational platform, collocation, academic phrases, academic phrasebank, L2 German, L2 English.

---

1. Zurich University of Applied Sciences, Switzerland; madalina.chitez@zhaw.ch
2. Zurich University of Applied Sciences, Switzerland; christian.rapp@zhaw.ch
3. Zurich University of Applied Sciences, Switzerland; otto.kruse@zhaw.ch

How to cite this article: Chitez, M., Rapp, C., & Kruse, O. (2015). Corpus-supported academic writing: how can technology help? In F. Helm, L. Bradley, M. Guarda, & S. Thouësny (Eds), *Critical CALL – Proceedings of the 2015 EUROCALL Conference, Padova, Italy* (pp. 125-132). Dublin: Research-publishing.net. http://dx.doi.org/10.14705/rpnet.2015.000321

1. Introduction

Since the 1970s, when the teaching of writing began to shift from a text-oriented to a process-centered approach, writing instruction has largely abstained from a direct teaching of language. From this time on, the interest of teachers and researchers has focused on what the writers do and think rather than on the linguistic or textual means they use. Recently, several experts have demanded a reconsideration of the role of language in writing (e.g. Feilke 2010, 2012, 2014; Hyland, 2000; Myhill & Fischer, 2010; Steinhoff, 2007) and started to develop theoretical and educational models. However, it is yet to be explored what a linguistically informed writing process might look like and how the formulation process can be supported by knowledge about language. As Feilke (2010, 2012) suggested, a plausible assumption is that writing relies on a high number of routinized textual procedures, which serve rhetorical and structural functions in the construction of meaning.

Corpus linguistics provides several effective approaches at the interface of research in learner language and academic writing, which can be used to identify such routines as phrases, chunks, and collocations. The results of corpus linguistics in the works of Swales (1990, 2004), Hyland (2000), Granger, Hung and Petch-Tyson (2002), Steinhoff (2007), Biber and Conrad (2009), Lüdeling and Walter (2009), Römer and Wulff (2010), Nesi and Gardener (2012), and many others have provided us with insights into the linguistic patterns and resources used by certain communities to solve domain-specific rhetorical problems. By using corpus linguistics, language teaching enters a new technological territory with multiple facets that can be applied and tested: (a) strategies of the CALL framework (cf. Beatty, 2003) or (b) Data-Driven Learning (DDL) (cf. Johns, 1986).

However, technology has scarcely been exploited for interactive tools that support academic writing linguistically (e.g. see Hsieh & Liou, 2009, for a presentation of the POWER and CARE tools). In this study, we will describe several methods of analysis that can be applied to the corpus linguistics results so that they can be used to facilitate academic writing tasks for students writing in English or German (as L1 and/or L2). The methods have been implemented in the interactive academic-writing tool, *Thesis Writer*, designed and constructed jointly by the Department of Applied Linguistics and the Center for Innovative Teaching and Learning of the Zurich University of Applied Sciences in Switzerland. The tool is designed to help students who use either English or German (both as L1 and L2) to write their bachelor or master theses in economics.

2. Method

2.1. Brief description of the academic writing tool

Thesis Writer is primarily a learning platform, but it can also be used as a research tool to collect and analyze data about academic writing. *Thesis Writer* (Figure 1) supports students by (1) structuring the writing process; (2) providing short tutorials for all major steps and actions; (3) offering a "proposal wizard" to guide students through the critical issues of the thesis proposal structure; (4) supporting the transfer of the proposal into the final version of the thesis; and (5) offering help with organizing and revising the thesis.

Figure 1. Road map of *Thesis Writer*

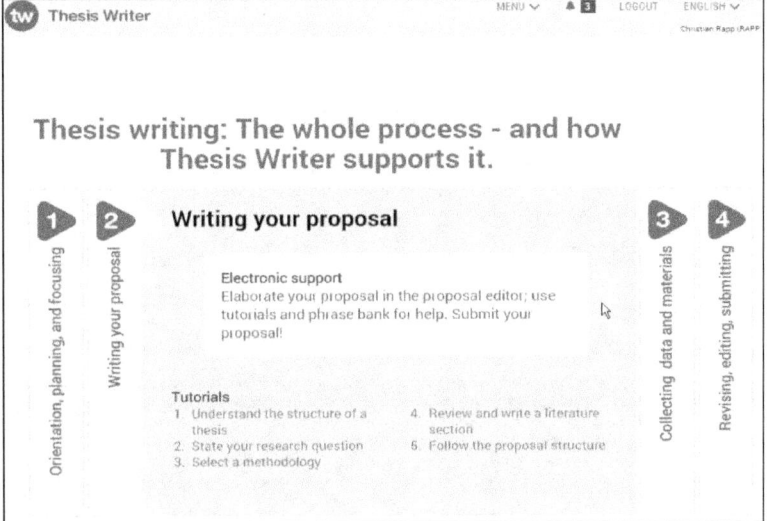

2.2. Technical details

The technical platform for *Thesis Writer* is driven by a LAMP server (Linux, Apache, MySQL, PHP) developed with the PHP-based framework yii1 following strict design patterns for object-oriented programming and the principles of model-view-controller (for more details, see Rapp, Kruse, Erlemann, & Ott, 2015). What happens from a technical perspective when a user seeks language-sensitive linguistic support in *Thesis Writer* by highlighting a word or a passage and clicking the linguistic-support button? The corpus is stored in a database. IMS Open Corpus

Workbench (CWB[4]) enables various queries and actions on the corpus via a number of command line prompts resulting in outputs. To allow the user to perform queries via highlighting and selecting text and using the linguistic support, a Perl script collection and a number of PHP classes mediate between the GUI of *Thesis Writer* and the command line tools of CWB. To improve the quality of suggestions made to the user, we utilize TreeTagger[5] to parse the entire user's text.

2.3. Corpus simple search tool

One of the simplest platform-intermediated corpus methods refers to word-in-context free searches. The IT specialists in the team have helped us design and integrate a user-friendly button, i.e. "linguistic support", so that the linguistic searches are performed directly on the platform by a registered user of *Thesis Writer*, with CWB processing data in the back-end (Figure 2).

Figure 2. Linguistic support tool

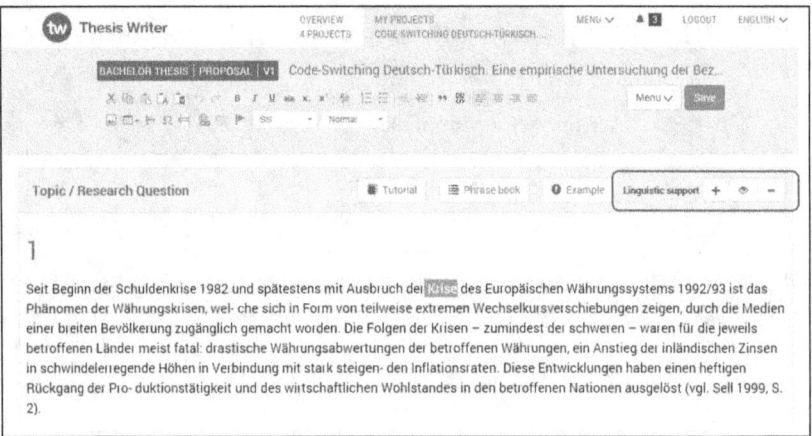

2.4. Corpus syntactic search tool

Still in the testing stage, this tool is intended to offer students the option to look for recurrent syntactic patterns, if research demonstrates that such patterns affect the quality of student writing. We looked at [Adj. + Subst.] patterns and found that the syntactic string is quite prolific. One of the challenges at this stage is

---

4. More information: http://www.ims.uni-stuttgart.de/forschung/projekte/CorpusWorkbench.html

5. More information: Schmid (1994).

also the correct retrieval of the desired POS patterns and the elimination of errors from the list (see the case "schwer -" at the end of the search list in Figure 3). A computational linguist is currently working on solving this matter. The technical solution for the integration in *Thesis Writer* will be implemented by the end of 2015.

Figure 3. Syntactic search in CWB

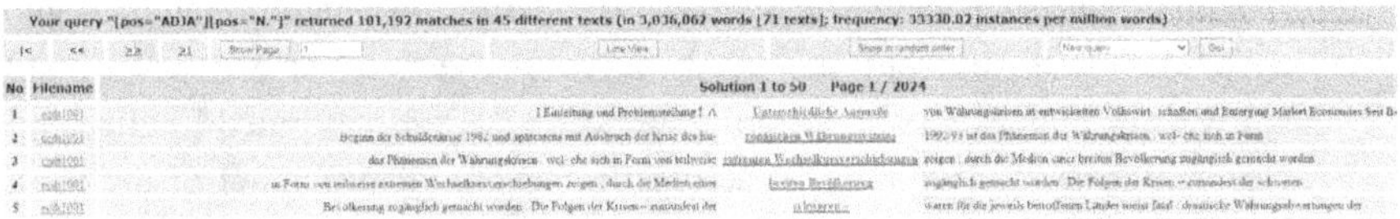

2.5. Construction of an academic phrase book

A more complex linguistic-support method is the list-of-phrases generator that provides useful academic phraseology when users are working on certain sections of their papers. The phrase book is comparable to the Academic Phrasebank of the University of Manchester[6], but it significantly differs from it because the lists of academic phrases compiled for *Thesis Writer* are organised according to the section of the thesis they are generally typical for. The methodology used for the compilation of the academic phrase book implies several analysis steps:

- *Academic phrases in theory*: Given the fact that the self-compiled corpora are not yet content annotated (e.g. annotation of academic phrases), in order to be able to start the identification of the most frequent academic chunks, a pre-selection stage was performed. This involved the collection of information on academic writing phraseology from textbooks[7] or online informative materials[8].

- *Academic phrases within the research cycle*: Afterwards, we conducted another intermediary processing stage in which the lists of phrases extracted from literature were re-arranged in order to match the sections in *Thesis Writer*: (1) Topic/Research Question, (2) Relevance, (3) Research Gap/ Knowledge Gap, (4) State of the Art, (5) Method/Procedure, (6) Discussion,

---

6. More information: http://www.phrasebank.manchester.ac.uk/

7. For instance, Bigler and Bugmann (2007).

8. For instance, for academic writing in German, one source of information was bab.la (Schroeter & Uecker, n.d.).

(7) Results, and (8) Conclusions. Each of the sections included sub-categories of phrases as well (see Table 1 below).

- *Keywords in academic phrase lists*: By analyzing the list of phrases resulting from the re-arrangement within the research-cycle categories, we were able to identify several academic keywords.

- *Academic phrase book construction*: Using corpus linguistics methodology, each identified keyword was analysed with the help of a concordance[9] software, which can make instant searches in the self-compiled English and German corpora. Two main strategies led to the identification of the most relevant academic phrases: (a) the software retrieved the clusters in which the indicated "keyword" was included; (b) the analysis was conducted in such a way that the most frequent collocation patterns at the left and right position (+/- 5 words) could be filtered out. From the compiled lists, the most frequent and/or most typical academic-writing phrases were extracted and compiled into a discipline-specific academic phrase book.

Table 1. Academic phrases within the research cycle

Main category in research cycle	Subcategory in research cycle	Keyword(s)	Phases (e.g.)	Translation EN
Fragestellung/ Forschungsfrage				*Topic / Research Question*
	Einleitung			*Introduction*
		Arbeit/ Kapitel/Studie/ Abschnitt:	- um diese Frage zu beantworten... - Antwort auf diese Frage - zur Beantwortung dieser Frage - die Frage, ob	*Paper/Chapter/Study/Section:* *- in order to answer this question...* *- the answer to this question...* *- to answer this question...* *-the question whether...*
		Frage Beginn	... ...	*Question* *Beginning*
	Thema nennen	... ...	... ...	*Name topic*
...	...	...	...	...

3. Discussion and conclusion

Although the testing of *Thesis Writer* by users (i.e. students) is still in preparation, there are several hypotheses on which the functionality of the linguistic tools has been based:

---

9. For simple queries, WordSmith tools (V. 6) (Scott, 2012) were used.

- *Support during writer's block*: It is anticipated that the simple searches will be useful especially to L2 writers during writer's block stages of thesis writing. We imagine that if students have a more or less definite idea of the argumentation line they want to follow at a certain phase of the thesis, they might sometimes have difficulties in identifying the right words/phrases. They then make use of the discipline-specific corpora in order to find out which possible constructions would fit their needs. We do not intend that the students will use this option as a copy-paste procedure, and we would like to prevent that by programming the searches to be retrieved only at a limited left-right number of words.

- *Rhetoric support*: Students sometimes lack the rhetoric awareness of a specific academic genre. TW can help them identify the right argumentative or academic phrase at the time and place they need it.

- *Support for students' writing linguistic diversity*: Scholars often warn against the use of academic phrase lists since it might prevent creativity and encourage repetitions in student writing. However, we anticipate that the diversity of research-cycle-based academic phrases extracted from the corpus (supplemented with the free search in corpus, where students can take inspiration for creating their own repertoire of academic phrases) will be evaluated positively by users.

References

Beatty, K. (2003). *Teaching and researching computer assisted language learning*. New York: Longman.

Biber, D., & Conrad, S. (2009). *Register, genre, and style*. Cambridge: Cambridge University Press. doi:10.1017/CBO9780511814358

Bigler, C., & Bugmann, H. (2007). *Wissenschaftliches Arbeiten: ein Leitfaden für die Ausarbeitung von Masterarbeiten*. Internal report. ETH Zurich. Retrieved from https://www1.ethz.ch/fe/education/teaching_material_secured/Wissenschaftliches_Arbeiten.pdf (login required).

Feilke, H. (2010). "Aller guten Dinge sind drei" – Überlegungen zu Textroutinen & literalen Prozeduren. In I. Bons, T. Gloning, & D. Kaltwasser (Eds.), *Fest-Platte für Gerd Fritz. Giessen*. Retrieved from http://www.festschrift-gerd-fritz.de/files/feilke_2010_literale-prozeduren-und-textroutinen.pdf

Feilke, H. (2012). Was sind Textroutinen? Zur Theorie und Methodik des Forschungsfeldes. In H. Feilke & K. Lehnen (Eds.), *Schreib- und Textroutinen. Theorie, Erwerb und didaktisch-mediale Modellierung* (pp. 1-31). [Forum Angewandte Linguistik Bd. 52]. Frankfurt a.M.: Peter Lang.

Feilke, H. (2014). Argumente für eine Didaktik der Textprozeduren. In T. Bachmann (Ed.), *Werkzeuge des Schreibens. Beiträge zu einer Didaktik der Textprozeduren* (pp. 11-34). Stuttgart: Fillibach bei Klett.

Granger, S., Hung, J., & Petch-Tyson, S. (Eds.). (2002). *Computer learner corpora, second language acquisition, and foreign language teaching*. Amsterdam: Benjamins. doi:10.1075/lllt.6

Hsieh, W.-M., & Liou, H. C. (2009). A case study of corpus-informed online academic writing for EFL graduate students. *CALICO Journal, 26*(1), 28-47.

Hyland, K. (2000). *Disciplinary discourses: social interactions in academic writing*. Harlow, England: Pearson Education.

Johns, T. (1986). Micro-concord: a language learner's research tool. *System, 4*(2), 151-162. doi:10.1016/0346-251X(86)90004-7

Lüdeling, A., & Walter, M. (2009). Korpuslinguistik für Deutsch als Fremdsprache. Sprachvermittlung und Spracherwerbsforschung. Stark erweiterte Fassung von Lüdeling / Walter Korpuslinguistik. In HSK 19, *Deutsch als Fremdsprache*. Mouton de Gruyter, Berlin. Retrieved from http://www.linguistik.hu-berlin.de/institut/professuren/korpuslinguistik/mitarbeiter innen/anke/pdf/LuedelingWalterDaF.pdf

Myhill, D., & Fisher, R. (2010). Editorial: writing development: cognitive, sociocultural, linguistic perspectives. *Journal of Research in Reading, 33*(1), 1-3. doi:10.1111/j.1467-9817.2009.01428.x

Nesi, H., & Gardner, S. (2012). *Genres across the disciplines: student writing in higher education*. Cambridge: Cambridge University Press.

Rapp, C., Kruse, O., Erlemann, J., & Ott, J. (2015). Thesis Writer–A system for supporting academic writing. In *Proceedings of the 18th ACM Conference Companion on Computer Supported Cooperative Work & Social Computing (CSCW'15 Companion)* (pp. 57-60). ACM, New York, NY, USA. doi:10.1145/2685553.2702687

Römer, U., & Wulff, S. (2010). Applying corpus methods to written academic texts: Explorations of MICUSP. *Journal of Writing research, 2*(2), 99-127. doi:10.17239/jowr-2010.02.02.2

Schroeter, A., & Uecker, P. (n.d.). bab.la Phrasen–Wissenschaftlich [Online software]. Retrieved from http://de.bab.la/phrasen/wissenschaftliches-schreiben/

Schmid, H. (1994). Probabilistic part-of-speech tagging using decision trees. *Proceedings of International Conference on New Methods in Language Processing, Manchester, UK*.

Scott, M. (2012). WordSmith tools (Version 5) [Stroud: Lexical Analysis Software].

Steinhoff, T. (2007). *Wissenschaftliche Textkompetenz*. Tübingen: Niemeyer. doi:10.1515/9783110973389

Swales, J. M. (1990). *Genre analysis: English in academic and research settings*. Cambridge: Cambridge University Press.

Swales, J. M. (2004). *Research genres: explorations and applications*. Cambridge: Cambridge University Press. doi:10.1017/CBO9781139524827

Exploring collaborative writing in wikis: a genre-based approach

Francesca Coccetta[1]

Abstract. While CALL research into collaborative writing in the L2 using wikis has mainly focused on the texts written by learners in terms of their grammatical accuracy (e.g. Mak & Coniam, 2008; Lee, 2010), the purpose of the present study is to draw attention to these texts as instances of a given genre. It reports on a small-scale experiment investigating a collaborative writing assignment using wikis focusing on the narrative genre. Specifically, it explores the extent to which first-year students in the Degree Course in Linguistic and Cultural Mediation at Ca' Foscari University of Venice (Italy) used wikis to include hypermedia objects such as audios, videos, images and hyperlinks when engaging with this genre online. The study draws on Systemic Functional Linguistics (Halliday & Matthiessen, 2004) theory and its extensive research into genre analysis, in particular Hasan's (1984) Generic Structure Potential (henceforth, GSP) and its application to nursery tales.

Keywords: wiki, collaborative writing, genre analysis.

1. Introduction

The use of wiki for collaborative writing in L2 is nothing new. Several studies have focused mainly on the writing process, demonstrating that, *inter alia*, from a pedagogical standpoint, wikis promote peer-to-peer interaction (e.g. Bradley, Lindström, & Rystedt, 2010) and facilitate effective, collaborative language learning (e.g. Oskoz & Elola, 2010), while from a linguistic perspective they enhance learners' attention to lexicogrammatical form (e.g. Lee, 2010). In particular, wiki texts have been analysed in terms of their lexicogrammatical accuracy (e.g. Mak & Coniam, 2008), while their compliance with genre conventions has, in comparison, been rather neglected (but see Alyousef & Picard, 2011; Kuteeva, 2011). Yet the

---

1. Ca' Foscari University of Venice, Italy; francesca.coccetta@unive.it

How to cite this article: Coccetta, F. (2015). Exploring collaborative writing in wikis: a genre-based approach. In F. Helm, L. Bradley, M. Guarda, & S. Thouësny (Eds), *Critical CALL – Proceedings of the 2015 EUROCALL Conference, Padova, Italy* (pp. 133-137). Dublin: Research-publishing.net. http://dx.doi.org/10.14705/rpnet.2015.000322

affordances provided by wikis as regards well-established genres such as those explored in the studies mentioned above (i.e. stories, brochures and reports) ought, perhaps, to arouse interest among linguists, too.

A wiki is a website where those who use it can add, edit and delete contents in terms of written text, hyperlinks, and multimedia objects such as audios, videos, and images; it also has a *page history* that keeps a record of all the changes the page has undergone thus allowing users to understand the page's evolution over time. Providing a thorough account of how wikis can reshape existing genres – a book waiting to be written – falls outside the scope of this paper. Rather, in this study, the goal was to measure compliance with and deviation from Hasan's (1984) model of bedtime stories in collaborative wiki writing.

In theory, the reading pathway in a wiki *vis-à-vis* a book can be affected by the use of hyperlinks: a book's sequential reading convention gives way to multiple readings, as hypertext fiction has shown (Aarseth, 1997). Readers' roles change as they can decide how the story will develop by either clicking or ignoring a link. Moreover, while in children's storybooks illustrations commonly function to "expand, explain, interpret, or decorate a written text" (Bodmer, 1992, p. 72), in wikis they can be used in more creative ways. An example is provided in *Il racconto a disegni* (*The tale in drawings*) in the Italian children's magazine *La Pimpa*[2] where drawings replace carefully-selected nouns (e.g. the noun *pappagallina* (*parrot*) in the noun phrase *la pappagallina Tita* (*Tita the parrot*)). Finally, audio files can be used in lieu of language for direct speech or provide background music to amuse the readers during the reading.

Using Hasan's (1984) model of nursery tales, this paper reports on an experiment to discover whether the hypermedia affordances provided by wikis engendered compliance or deviance with regard to this model.

2. Method

2.1. Participants

The experiment involved 55 first-year students in the Degree Course in Linguistic and Cultural Mediation at Ca' Foscari University of Venice attending a 30-hour course on the English verb phrase. The class was divided into 13 groups of four

---

2. A sample is available at http://www.francopaniniragazzi.it/pimpa/it.fcp.pimpariviste.aprile/disegni.html

students each and one of three. Each group had a wiki page and a forum they were encouraged to use to swap ideas.

2.2. Assignment

The online assignment was designed to foster students' communicative competence (Hymes, 1972) in English, thus complementing the traditional grammar-translation method adopted in class. Each group was asked to write an original bedtime story collaboratively using a wiki. In the instructions, the students were encouraged to use Hasan's (1984) textual model and to add the multimedia resources available through the wiki toolbar (e.g. videos, photos and emoticons) to this language only genre model.

2.3. Data analysis

The 14 bedtime stories that were produced were analysed following Hasan's (1984) GSP model which provides the structural elements present in tales, specifies the obligatory and optional ones, and arranges them in order on the basis of their occurrence. The model is shown in Figure 1.

Figure 1. Hasan's (1984) GSP model of nursery tales

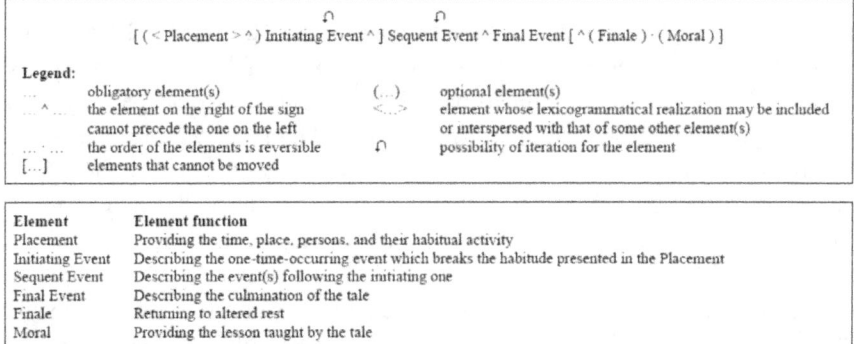

The analysis also took the semiotic resources used in the development of the story and their function into account.

3. Discussion

The themes of the 14 stories are run-of-the-mill. For example, they involve stories about beautiful princesses who succeed in not marrying the old man their father imposed on them, as well as stories about mistreatment of humanised animals in zoos that in the end are freed. The picture emerging from these stories indicates strong compliance with Hasan's (1984) model and limited use of hypermedia resources. None of the groups included hyperlinks with the result that the story follows the top-bottom, left-right reading pathway typical of the printed page. Similarly, no audios were included. However, two groups included a video taken from *YouTube*, specifically a video presenting Brahm's lullaby – a favourite among parents. In one case, the video precedes the start of the story and in the other case it comes after the end as if it were a mere adjunct in terms of Hasan's (1984) model. Both these adjuncts are action-oriented: the first invites the reader to play the song as a warm-up and if they let it play, it will accompany the reading; the second invokes the typical action of singing a lullaby that parents undertake once the story they are reading is finished.

As can be inferred from the posts published in the forum, students were particularly sensitive to images: all the groups made use of images, some even drew their own drawings, while others made use of computer graphic software tools – not in the wiki toolbar – to draw them. From a subjective point of view, the degree of image integration varies: while there is general coherence between the details provided in the text and the drawings, some groups using clip arts do not seem to achieve the desired coherence between text and image.

From a more objective standpoint, there is compliance with Hasan's (1984) model as all the obligatory elements are present. A good example is the animal story mentioned above where the animals decide to do something to help a mistreated lion cub (Initiating Event), go to his cage to comfort him, but when the zookeeper discovers them he realises he has been mean to them (Sequent Events) and frees the animals (Final Event). Additionally, many stories included the optional Moral element. The students' forum discussion about whether this was compulsory indicates their interest in genre coherence. Some pleasing creativity *vis-à-vis* textual structure is evident such as the optional mini-genre (Baldry & Thibault, 2006) we can call *Book Cover* consisting of a picture recalling the content of the story, the story's title and the names of the writers occurring at the top of the page. However, none of the students' story significantly modifies the narrative structure outlined in Hasan's (1984) model.

4. Conclusions

The affordances provided by wikis to reshape the narrative genre have been partly documented. The experiment reported is an attempt to shift the research focus from lexicogrammatical accuracy to students' awareness and mastery of text and genre characteristics. Many aspects of this shift, such as the effects of peer collaboration in the writing process, on the end product warrant further investigation that goes beyond this pilot study.

References

Aarseth, E. (1997). *Cybertext.* Baltimore: JHUP.

Alyousef, H. S., & Picard, M. Y. (2011). Cooperative or collaborative literacy practices: mapping metadiscourse in a business students' wiki group project. *AJET, 27*(3), 463-480.

Baldry, A., & Thibault, P. (2006). *Multimodal transcription and text analysis.* London: Equinox.

Bodmer, G. R. (1992). Approaching the illustrated text. In G.E. Sadler (Ed.), *Teaching children's literature: issues, pedagogy, resources* (pp. 72-79). New York: The Modern Language Association of America.

Bradley, L., Lindström, B., & Rystedt, H. (2010). Rationalities of collaboration for language learning in a wiki. *ReCALL, 22*(2), 247-265. doi:10.1017/S0958344010000108

Halliday, M. A. K, & Matthiessen, C. (2004). *An introduction to functional grammar* (3rd ed.). London: Arnold.

Hasan, R. (1984). The nursery tale as a genre. *Nottingham Linguistic Circular, 13*, 71-102.

Hymes, D. H. (1972). On communicative competence. In J. B. Pride & J. Holmes (Eds.), *Sociolinguistics: selected readings* (pp. 269-293). Harmondsworth: Penguin.

Kuteeva, M. (2011). Wikis and academic writing: changing the writer-reader relationship. *ESP, 30*, 44-57. doi:10.1016/j.esp.2010.04.007

Lee, L. (2010). Exploring wiki-mediated collaborative writing: a case study in an elementary Spanish course. *CALICO Journal, 27*(2), 260-276. doi:10.11139/cj.27.2.260-276

Mak, B., & Coniam, D. (2008). Using wikis to enhance and develop writing skills among secondary school students in Hong Kong. *System, 36*, 437-455. doi:10.1016/j.system.2008.02.004

Oskoz, A., & Elola, I. (2010). Collaborative writing: fostering foreign language and writing conventions development. *Language Learning & Technology, 14*(3), 51-71.

Activities and reflection for influencing beliefs about learning with smartphones

Robert Cochrane[1]

Abstract. English education in Japan faces numerous challenges, including an English as a Foreign Language (EFL) context, mandatory English classes, and an exam-oriented education system. Computer technology and the almost universal possession of smartphones can ease the burden of learning, but only if these tools are used effectively. Japanese university students report having very low computer skills and their smartphones are seen as tools for maintaining social contacts and as gaming devices. Smartphones then become a distraction, keeping students from achieving academic success. What is unclear is whether students are unaware of, or unwilling to use, the educational and productivity functions of their smartphones. This project aimed to examine beliefs about learning with smartphones and what changes in beliefs and behavior occur through the introduction of smartphone apps and online applications utilizing task-based activities requiring the educational and productivity aspects of smartphones. Pre and post intervention surveys were administered measuring beliefs about learning and smartphone usage. Four first-year university classes (N=146) enrolled in a mandatory listening and speaking course participated in this study. This presentation will report the findings of the survey on learning and what changes were observed. The design of the activities and problems that occurred during the term will also be discussed.

Keywords: mobile learning, TBLT, learner beliefs, action research.

---

1. Kyushu Sangyo University, Japan; cochranesensei@gmail.com

How to cite this article: Cochrane, R. (2015). Activities and reflection for influencing beliefs about learning with smartphones. In F. Helm, L. Bradley, M. Guarda, & S. Thouësny (Eds), *Critical CALL – Proceedings of the 2015 EUROCALL Conference, Padova, Italy* (pp. 138-143). Dublin: Research-publishing.net. http://dx.doi.org/10.14705/rpnet.2015.000323

1. Introduction

Technology has now become an ever-present part of our lives and mobile technology has played a very important part in the lives of Japanese youth from the development of the pager to the keitai (cell phone) to now, the smartphone (Boase & Kobayashi, 2008). The presence of these devices in the hands of students can lead one to believe that they are proficient and productive in their use. This is not necessarily the case with students at a mid level Japanese technical university who report poor computer literacy and confidence in their skills with Information and Computer Technology (ICT). Recently it is becoming evident that students are proficient with a limited number of applications (apps), usually social networking, or entertainment in nature, and are not the digital wizards we would expect (Bicen & Kocakoyun, 2013; Margaryan, Littlejohn, & Vojt, 2011; Thompson, 2013; Watanabe, 2012).

In the case of Japanese university students, their end goal of attaining high scores on English tests is influenced by a number of factors. Policy makers propose policy statements setting goals of a society that can use English to communicate. Parents are concerned with their children getting into a good university, which means passing high stakes entrance exams. Secondary school teachers are under pressure to prepare students for these exams and to get through an overwhelming syllabus. Add to this a lack of support for teacher development and training, and the result is a grammar translation driven curriculum with little time for communicative language learning.

Technology plays a small role in Japanese high schools, with little time given to using computers for learning. Mobile devices are used primarily for social or entertainment purposes with some studies reporting that students prefer not to use their mobile devices for educational purposes (Lockley & Promnitz-Hayashi, 2012; Takahashi, 2008) Observations suggest students approach the high stakes testing environment of high school by trying to remember enough to get past the next test. Their focus is on remembering for reproduction as opposed to learning for understanding.

This study aimed to investigate students' beliefs about learning and introduced tasks that exposed learners to the productive aspects of smartphones and computers. The goal was to increase student productivity and academic performance by having students see the ways that their smartphones can improve their university life. The first year of university is a prime point to introduce new ideas, as this is a transitional point for these students.

2. Method

2.1. Participants

Participants were 1st year university students at a mid-level technical university in Japan. They were enrolled in a mandatory English listening and speaking course. The participants were a sample of convenience comprised of four classes instructed by the researcher ($N=146$). English placement is based on the Test of English for International Communication (TOEIC) Bridge test administered by ETS. The scores put these students in the lower end A1 band of the Common European Framework of Reference (CEFR).

2.2. Method

This study is exploratory in nature and was designed following a mixed method approach utilizing survey data that collected both qualitative and quantitative data. The design involved a survey at the beginning of the course setting a baseline for beliefs about learning and technology use. Smartphone apps and multiplatform online applications were introduced using an action research approach. Homework tasks were assigned that required the use of this technology. The tasks were accompanied by a reflection component. At the end of the term a modified version of the survey was administered.

2.3. Survey

The survey was constructed by examining previous surveys involving language-learning beliefs and focused on strategies and metacognitive awareness. Reports on student interaction with homework and technology use, namely computers and smartphones, were also investigated. Items were selected to confirm previous assumptions and observations of student technology use. The final survey included open-ended questions about how students thought their learning or smartphone use had changed since the start of the term.

2.4. Tasks

An action research model was selected for the intervention. The problem being investigated was how to introduce students to the productive and educational aspects of technology. The reasoning is that lack of motivation and academic performance may be due to a lack of awareness of effective study strategies and how to use the tools available to them. Knowledge and practice with the tools available to them may improve their chances of success. The first step was to introduce productivity and educational aspects of smartphones through tasks that were relevant to their university life.

Task types were designed to increase productive use of technology. Task performance was examined and design elements were adjusted in subsequent tasks. The task types involved setting reminders, tracking their time, using the voice recorder, and using Google apps. Different approaches were selected and the outcomes evaluated. These approaches involved giving detailed step-by-step instructions on how to do a task, to a less guided approach where the task is assigned and options for how to complete it are provided but allowing for student independence with how they want to proceed.

3. Discussion

3.1. Initial reports

Students' reports regarding learning beliefs were generally positive. However, the amount of time they reported spending on homework or studying in high school was quite low. Time spent using smartphones was quite high with video, text, music and game apps being the most frequently used apps. Educational or productivity apps were not used at all.

3.2. Final comments

The comments regarding how learning has changed showed that students felt that they increased their studying and were more aware of how they were using their time. Students were unaware of how they could use their phones for academic purposes but now were using them to organize their university time, access dictionaries and record speaking assignments. While many comments reported some kind of insight or improvement, some students did report that there was no change at all.

The results suggest that some students are responsive to the introduction of applications that will assist in their learning. The main problem was trying to reach the students who do not attempt the activities, or do not attend class. Students who are challenged academically may be so due to lack of instruction, not lack of motivation. Some students reported feeling stress at having to figure out how to use the apps by themselves, this could be attributed to the teacher-centered approach they are accustomed to.

3.3. Problems

The first problem was the issue of attrition. Each class contained between 5-10 students who stopped attending classes. Another issue was of the students that did attend, while homework assignments were mandatory, some classes had a number of students who did not attempt or complete the assignments. The total number of responses to the final survey totaled 37, approximately 25% of the initial number of responses.

4. Conclusions

Smartphones take up a large part of university students' time. Unfortunately, this time is mainly social or entertainment related. The use of smartphones for productivity is non-existent. While students have a generally positive attitude towards learning, they seem to lack the knowledge and skills to pursue it effectively. Introducing apps for education or productivity through tasks can have a positive effect on students' academic endeavors. While students felt challenged and stressed, they also were able to notice how knowledge of the productive aspects of their smartphones improved their studies. Integrating new apps into English classes through tasks may be a way to introduce students to the more productive aspects of their technology and lead to a change in their smartphone use for the better.

5. Acknowledgements

We would like to thank Yumiko Cochrane for her invaluable assistance with translating the surveys and forms.

References

Bicen, H., & Kocakoyun, S. (2013). The evaluation of the most used mobile devices applications by students. *Procedia - Social and Behavioral Sciences, 89*, 756-760. doi:10.1016/j.sbspro.2013.08.928

Boase, J., & Kobayashi, T. (2008). Kei-Tying teens: using mobile phone e-mail to bond, bridge, and break with social ties—a study of Japanese adolescents. *International Journal of Human-Computer Studies, 66*(12), 930-943. doi:10.1016/j.ijhcs.2008.07.004

Lockley, T., & Promnitz-Hayashi, L. (2012). Japanese university students' CALL attitudes, aspirations and motivations. *CALL-EJ Online, 13*(1), 1-16. Retrieved from http://www.callej.org/journal/13- 1/Lockley_Promnitz-Hayashi_2012.pdf

Margaryan, A., Littlejohn, A., & Vojt, G. (2011). Are digital natives a myth or reality? University students' use of digital technologies. *Computers & Education, 56*(2), 429-440. doi:10.1016/j.compedu.2010.09.004

Takahashi, T. (2008). Japanese young people, media and everyday life, towards the internationalizing of media studies. In K. Drotner & S. Livingstone (Eds.), *International Handbook of children, media and culture* (pp. 413-430). London: Sage.

Thompson, P. (2013). The digital natives as learners: technology use patterns and approaches to learning. *Computers and Education, 65*, 12-33. doi:10.1016/j.compedu.2012.12.022

Watanabe, Y. (2012). Ready for m-learning? Access to mobile devices by tertiary students studying Japanese. *Future Challenges, Sustainable Futures. Proceedings Ascilite Wellington* (pp. 1030-1038).

High school students' use of digital tools for learning English vocabulary in an EFL context

Diana Cojocnean[1]

Abstract. This study investigated Romanian high school students' use of digital tools for learning vocabulary in English. Although students have a wide range of technological affordances at their disposal, little is known about how they make use of them or the extent to which they are aware of how to use them in their vocabulary learning. The study features a sequential mixed-methods research design combining results from focus group interviews and a self-reported questionnaire which was answered by 1,239 students enrolled in nine high schools across Romania.

Keywords: MALL, CALL, vocabular learning, digital context.

1. Introduction

The current paper reports the results of a large scale study focusing on the way Romanian high school students make use of digital tools in their learning of English as a Foreign Language (EFL) vocabulary. The impact of various technological affordances in the 21st century may have had an impact on the choice and use of vocabulary learning strategies. However, in this cultural context, little is known about learners' motivation and engagement with using technology in language learning, the focus being mostly on teachers' use of technology in teaching.

2. Method

The study used methodological triangulation, a research strategy that can be represented as qual→quan (Dörnyei, 2007). The two methods I combined in

---

1. University of Exeter; UK; diana.cojocnean@gmail.com

How to cite this article: Cojocnean, D. (2015). High school students' use of digital tools for learning English vocabulary in an EFL context. In F. Helm, L. Bradley, M. Guarda, & S. Thouësny (Eds), *Critical CALL – Proceedings of the 2015 EUROCALL Conference, Padova, Italy* (pp. 144-149). Dublin: Research-publishing.net. http://dx.doi.org/10.14705/rpnet.2015.000324

my project are: focus group interviews and the self-reported questionnaire. The questionnaire items were designed on the basis of the results from focus group interviews and on my own apprehension of digital tools, and they showed acceptable reliability. The first phase of data collection consisted in conducting five focus groups in the participant schools. The second phase of data collection involved the parallel administration of the questionnaire, in nine schools, and took place in 2014.

3. Results

Based on the features that characterize technology enhanced tools, the questionnaire items related to students' use of digital tools were grouped into determination, social, metacognitive-cognitive and memory strategies, similar to Schmitt's (1997) grouping of vocabulary learning strategies. The determination digital strategies represent strategies which help one find the meaning of a new word using a digital device.

The social digital strategies are mainly characterized by learning while interacting with others in an online environment. They are associated with social networking and gaming, as, according to the students in the focus groups, it is during these activities that they encounter and learn most of the new words.

The metacognitive-cognitive category includes strategies which focus on the learning or consolidation of new vocabulary using a device, a Computer-Assisted Language Learning (CALL) or Mobile Assisted Language Learning (MALL) app to learn or consolidate new words. I combined the metacognitive-cognitive strategies in one category as strategies may fall into one category or another depending on how the student uses the strategy. For example, using a vocabulary learning app could be either a cognitive or a metacognitive strategy. If the learner uses it only to learn vocabulary, then it is a cognitive strategy, but if the learner uses it independently only to improve the knowledge he/she has of some words, then it is a metacognitive strategy.

The memory digital strategies represent strategies that entail using a device, a program or an app to enable the memorization of new words.

The categorization of digital strategies is determined by how the learners use the device or the app/program, by their learning behavior, which can be directed either towards learning or entertainment. These two purposes often overlap in an online environment as the student can simply start using an app for vocabulary learning as a form of entertainment which also has learning outcomes. Accordingly, there is a limitation behind this categorization as the same strategy may be included in more than one category, depending on how it is used or on the user's learning behavior.

The data indicated that Romanian high school students mostly use determination digital strategies, followed by social digital strategies, memory digital strategies and metacognitive-cognitive digital strategies. Table 1 below shows the types of digital strategies used by Romanian high school students.

Table 1. Types of digital vocabulary learning strategies used by Romanian students

Types of digital tools	M	SD	Min	Max
Social	2.63	0.76	1	5
Determination	2.83	0.62	1	5
Metacognitive-Cognitive	2.05	0.72	1	5
Memory	2.05	0.67	1	5
Total	2.39	1.24	1	5

Table 2 below shows students' preference of individual digital tools. The following reporting scale (Oxford, 1990) was used: 'High Usage' (3.5-5.0), 'Medium Usage' (2.5-3.49), 'Low Usage' (1.0-2.49).

Table 2. Preference of individual digital tools for vocabulary learning

Type of strategy	Item	M	SD
High usage (M=3.5 or above)			
Det	I search new words in an online dictionary on my computer/tablet.	3.56	1.15
Det	I look up for an image on the Internet which could represent the meaning of a word.	3.52	1.09
Medium Usage (M = 2.5–3.49)			
Det	I use a translation app.	3.48	1.21
Det	I learn and figure out the meaning of some words from online games.	3.39	1.16

Det	I search new words in an online dictionary on my phone.	3.31	1.28
Soc	I learn new words in English when using social networking.	3.28	1.26
Det	I learn new words while browsing different webpages on the Internet.	3.27	1.32
Soc	I chat in English when I am online.	3.15	1.29
Mem	I remember words encountered online if I access those pages again.	2.98	1.20
Met-Cog	I watch and listen to tutorials, presentations, talks/podcasts/radio on subjects that I am interested in when I am online.	2.90	1.38
Soc	I ask a friend/classmate who is online about the meaning of a word.	2.62	1.19
Mem	I look up the pronunciation of a word in an online dictionary and I listen to it.	2.57	1.23
Det	I access the link to a new word in an online text which sends me to a definition of the word in the dictionary.	2.55	1.14
Low Usage (M = 2.49 or below)			
Soc	I use new vocabulary through tasks I do on my device (e.g. take photos, record myself, make short videos and present them, role play, group conversations in English on WhatsApp, etc.).	2.47	1.26
Met-Cog	I learn vocabulary through computer assisted tasks at school.	2.47	1.22
Det	I learn new words from apps I'm using.	2.25	1.21
Met-Cog	I play vocabulary games on my smartphone/iPad/computer.	2.25	1.21
Det	I use Thesaurus in Microsoft Word when I need synonyms or antonyms.	2.10	1.13
Det	I download vocabulary learning apps on my smartphone/tablet/iPad.	1.89	1.04
Met-Cog	I test myself on new words by doing online vocabulary quizzes.	1.88	1.06

Met-Cog	I use the spell check in Microsoft Word.	1.87	1.17
Det	I access corpus websites.	1.85	1.04
Soc	I ask questions on various websites/discussion forums related to the meaning of some words/expressions.	1.79	1.00
Met-Cog	I do vocabulary exercises on various webpages on the Internet.	1.77	0.99
Mem	I save new words in a list on my phone.	1.71	1.00
Met-Cog	I use computer assisted vocabulary programs to learn new words.	1.64	0.96
Mem	I put words I want to remember on my computer screen to remind me.	1.50	0.91
Mem	I record myself on my phone/tablet saying the new word.	1.48	0.92

$N=1137$

4. Discussion

Despite the fact that there is a plethora of available computer assisted vocabulary programs and mobile assisted vocabulary learning apps, the data revealed that Romanian high school students have a low usage of computer assisted vocabulary programs and of mobile assisted vocabulary learning apps. Online dictionaries, translation apps, online games, social networking and various online extensive reading and listening activities are the most frequently used resources. According to the data, the respondents learn or practise new words during various online activities, suggesting that students prefer learning while doing something they like.

The students in the focus groups explained their lack of interest in vocabulary learning apps or dedicated Computer Assisted Vocabulary Learning (CAVL) programs by stating a preference for subconscious learning of words while using a digital tool. Also, the data in the focus groups revealed that students' attitudes are partially determined by the fact that students are not aware of any apps or programs which could really have an impact on their language learning and that they do not know how to make a good selection among the numerous available apps.

These outcomes suggest that although students in this context have access to these tools and use them on a regular basis, no CALL or MALL learning culture has been set up in this particular cultural context.

5. Conclusions

There are several features that define learners' digital engagement, respectively: lack of technology-related academic skills, a certain reluctance for using personal handheld devices for educational purposes, the perception of handheld devices and computers as content delivery tools rather than potential metacognitive tools, reluctance to mix formal and informal learning outside the classroom, unawareness as to the existence and use of various digital tools for vocabulary learning. Although Romanian students have a wide range of digital instruments to learn and practise vocabulary at their disposal, they mostly use the least intrusive ones and the ones which do not imply extensive repetition of vocabulary items.

References

Dörnyei, Z. (2007). *Research methods in applied linguistics: quantitative, qualitative and mixed methodologies.* Oxford: Oxford University Press.

Oxford, R. L. (1990). *Language learning strategies. What every teacher should know.* Boston: Heinle & Heinle Publishers.

Schmitt, N. (1997). *Vocabulary learning strategies.* In N. Schmitt & M. McCarthy (Eds.), *Vocabulary: description acquisition and pedagogy* (pp. 199-228). Cambridge: Cambridge University Press.

Design and empirical evaluation of controlled L2 practice through mini-games—moving beyond drill-and-kill?

Frederik Cornillie[1] and Piet Desmet[2]

Abstract. A key design issue for tutorial CALL is that controlled practice activities need to engage learners in meaningful L2 processing, so that any knowledge developed in such practice may transfer to meaningful L2 use in complex skills. Furthermore, activities for controlled practice ideally engender intrinsic motivation, so that learners are willing to practise and remediate problems outside of the classroom. This paper reports on an experimental and design-focused study that tackled these challenges by means of mini-games embedded in a mystery story read in class. Results show that intensive receptive practice helped learners to develop knowledge that was accurate and quickly retrievable on tests of near transfer, and that practice also transferred to more complex written productive tasks, as well as—to a smaller extent—to spoken productive tasks. We make suggestions for future design on the basis of the spoken productive language test used in this study.

Keywords: tutorial CALL, controlled practice, design, L2 grammar learning, mini-games.

---

1. ITEC, KU Leuven & iMinds, Kortrijk, Belgium; Frederik.Cornillie@kuleuven-kulak.be
2. ITEC, KU Leuven & iMinds, Kortrijk, Belgium; Piet.Desmet@kuleuven-kulak.be

How to cite this article: Cornillie, F., & Desmet, P. (2015). Design and empirical evaluation of controlled L2 practice through mini-games—moving beyond drill-and-kill?. In F. Helm, L. Bradley, M. Guarda, & S. Thouësny (Eds), *Critical CALL – Proceedings of the 2015 EUROCALL Conference, Padova, Italy* (pp. 150-157). Dublin: Research-publishing.net. http://dx.doi.org/10.14705/rpnet.2015.000325

This paper was presented at the 2014 EUROCALL Conference, Groningen, The Netherlands, and parts of this research have been published in Cornillie, van den Branden, and Desmet (2015). Reproduced with kind permissions from the organisers of the XVIIth International CALL Research Conference In Tarragona (Spain) and editing authors of the volume of proceedings.

1. Introduction

In current-day L2 pedagogy, the power of some kind of focus on form is undisputed, preferably in complex and meaning-oriented L2 tasks, disrupting the communicative flow to a minimal degree, and focusing on forms that are psycholinguistically relevant and necessary for the communication to succeed (Doughty & Williams, 1998). Yet, there is little scope in language teaching programmes for intensive controlled practice of specific linguistic constructions, accompanied by consistent Corrective Feedback (CF), equally embedded within meaning-oriented L2 use. Such practice may help to automatise knowledge in implicit memory, which could in turn free up attentional resources for higher-order skills during complex learning tasks. The state-of-the-art in second language acquisition theory assumes a dynamic interface between explicit and implicit knowledge (Ellis, 2005), and hence provides support for various attention-raising techniques, including controlled practice with CF. Furthermore, proponents of such practices have argued, from the perspective of skill acquisition theory, that CALL is *the* field that holds promise for the future of practice (DeKeyser, 2007), as it allows for massive and fine-grained data collection in longitudinal experimental designs, potentially in ecologically valid settings. Moreover, tutorial CALL affords the provision of consistent, error-specific, and supportive CF.

However, the implementation of tutorial CALL practice presents at least three serious design challenges. First, explicit focus-on-form practice needs to engage learners in meaningful L2 processing (DeKeyser, 1998; Wong & VanPatten, 2003), which is presumed necessary for realising transfer to complex skills. Secondly, given the little time there usually is for communicative L2 learning, teachers are likely to relegate practice to contexts outside of class. So, the key will be "to design interesting drills that are not demotivating" (Dörnyei, 2009, p. 289) and that—ideally—catalyse intrinsically motivated behaviour, so that learners are willing to practise without regulation from teachers. A third and related challenge is that consistent feedback inherent in practice may harm learners' competence needs (e.g. Robinson, 1991).

This paper reports on the empirical validation of an instructional design hypothesis for tutorial CALL practice that primarily addresses the first challenge (for the other two challenges, see Cornillie & Desmet, 2013), and which is inspired by principles from skill acquisition theory, task-based language teaching, and game design. To this end, we rely on the notion of *mini-games* (Cornillie & Desmet, 2016), i.e. gameful activities that can be completed in brief sessions, are constrained in scope, provide consistent feedback, and thus lend themselves well to focused practice.

We address the following research question: to what extent does controlled L2 practice supported by mini-games and embedded in meaning-focused L2 use help learners to develop knowledge that is useful for their performance on various transfer tasks?

2. Method

The study took place from January to March 2014 in secondary education in Flanders, and used an experimental between-subjects design with one control group (N=61) and two treatment groups (N=125). The treatment groups participated in reading and discussion activities concerning a mystery story based on the early history of Coca-Cola, in which mini-games were embedded which were intended to help the Dutch-speaking learners acquire the constraints on two grammatical features of English (quantifiers and the double object construction). Participants in the treatment groups received rule instruction, and were assigned at random to either a practice condition in which metalinguistic and error-specific CF was available (ML CF), or to a condition which only comprised 'knowledge of results' CF (KR CF), lacking metalinguistic explanation. Practice was receptive, and consisted of performing grammaticality judgments of sentences drawn from the mystery story; first in a 'tutorial' version of the mini-game, lacking time pressure and reward systems and comprising immediate CF for learners in the metalinguistic group (see Figure 1, left); then in a version involving time pressure, rewarding, between-learner competition, and vivid CF (i.e. 'knowledge of results' feedback adapted to the game fantasy) (see Figure 1, right).

Figure 1. Tutorial version of the mini-game, with metalinguistic CF (left); full version of the mini-game (right)

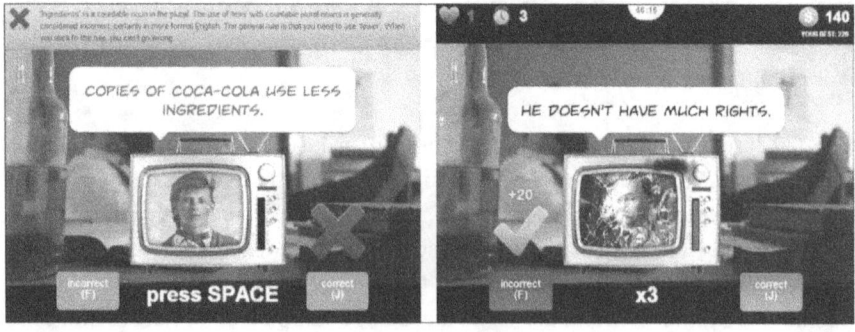

The learners were introduced to the practice activities in class, and had opportunities to practise further at home. Practice behaviour was logged. The instructional procedure (i.e. instruction, text, and practice activities) lasted one month.

Prior to, immediately following, and one month after the procedure, all participants (including the control group) were tested on their knowledge of the target features using two transfer tasks: a Timed Grammaticality Judgment Test (TGJT; Loewen, 2009), and a Written Discourse Completion Test (WDCT). Participants in the treatment groups completed two more tests. First, they filled out a Metalinguistic Knowledge Test (MKT) aimed at measuring their knowledge of the grammar rules. Further, subsequent to the immediate post-tests, 69 learners were selected to participate in an oral production task known in the literature as the Oral Elicited Imitation Test (OEIT; Erlam, 2009). This test took the form of a role-play between the researcher and the participant, and required the learners to attend to both meaning and form. During the OEIT, participants were supported by means of slides to help them formulate their responses (see Figure 2). Learners were selected for this task on the basis of two parameters: the type of CF received during practice, and the amount of time spent on practice.

Figure 2. Visual support for the ungrammatical oral stimulus *Charley revealed Candler the secret recipe of Coca-Cola*, used in the OEIT

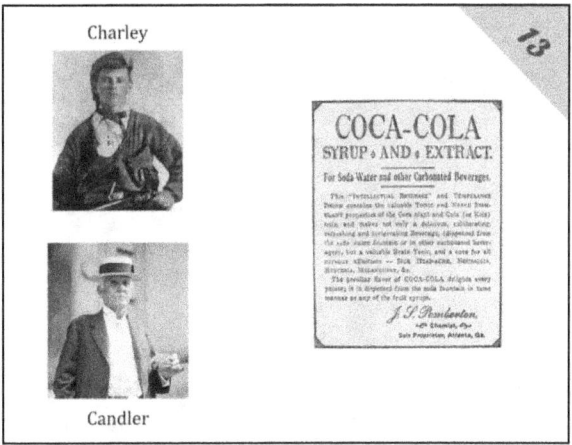

3. Results

The data show that the treatment groups outperformed the control group on the post-tests of the TGJT in terms of accuracy rate and response times (see Figure 3).

Figure 3. Average accuracy rates (left) and response times (right) on the TGJT

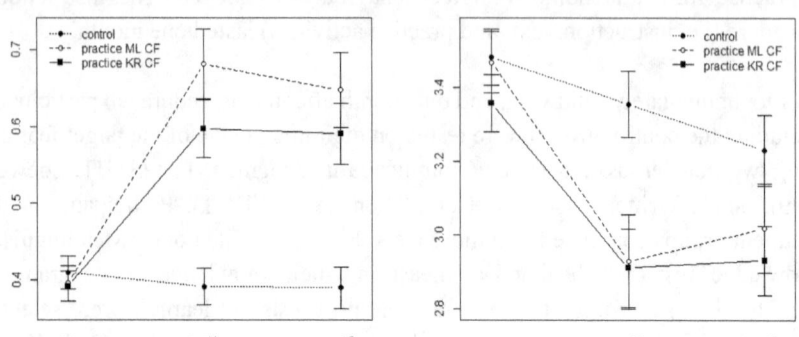

As for the post-tests of the WDCT (Figure 4), the average accuracy rates of the participants in the treatment groups were higher than the average accuracy rate of the control group. Participants responded equally quickly in all groups.

Figure 4. Average accuracy rates (left) and response times (right) on the WDCT

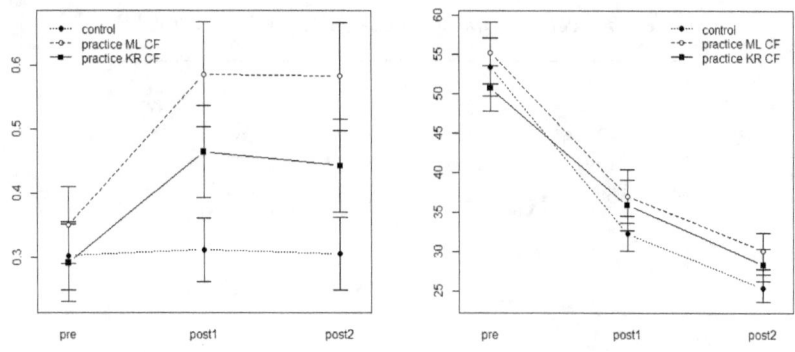

The linguistic accuracy scores on the OEIT were considered separately for the participants who had realised (despite the strong focus on meaning) that they were being tested on grammar ($N=41$) and for the unaware participants ($N=8$); the scores of the other 20 participants were disregarded, because it was unclear whether these learners had been focusing on form. The mean accuracy rates of the OEIT were regressed, for each group separately, onto two main predictors (i.e. feedback type; and time spent on practice, range between 2.9 and 85.7 minutes) and three control variables (accuracy scores on the pre-tests of TGJT and WDCT, and the MKT scores). Two outliers were removed from the aware group, as these learners had misinterpreted the test instructions, affecting their scores negatively. The results of the regression analyses show that the mean accuracy rates of the aware group were positively affected by the time spent on practice ($\beta=.084$, $p<.05$) (see Figure 5) and by performance on the first WDCT ($\beta=.322$, $p<.01$). This regression model explained 32 percent of the variance in the mean accuracy rates (adjusted $R^2=.32$, $F(5, 32)=4.523$, $p<.01$). The same model applied to the unaware group revealed no effects.

Figure 5. Plot for relation between time spent on practice and mean accuracy on the OEIT (aware participants)

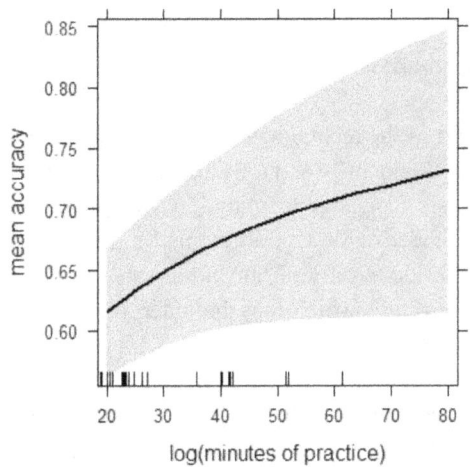

4. Discussion and conclusion

The results show that intensive practice with CF supported by mini-games and a mystery story helped learners to develop L2 grammar knowledge that was useful for their performance on various transfer tasks. There was evidence of transfer of practice to a follow-up task (TGJT) that was highly similar to the fairly simple and mechanical practice tasks (i.e. near transfer), but also to more complex written (WDCT) and spoken (OEIT) follow-up tasks (i.e. far transfer). Moreover, on the near transfer task, the knowledge developed during practice was quickly available.

However, observation of the learners in practice suggests that they were treating the practice tasks rather mechanically. Moreover, on the OEIT, learners were clearly monitoring their spoken production, and the gains in accuracy were small. This may be due to the fact that the practice tasks were not very transfer-appropriate in relation to more complex tasks, and was consistent with skill acquisition theory, which posits that the effects of practice are skill-specific.

Therefore, if tutorial CALL practice aims to support learners in developing automaticity in speaking—which ideally it does—future research needs to find ways of engaging learners in more meaningful and productive, ideally spoken language practice. The OEIT, used in this study as a transfer test, is a primary candidate for such practice, especially if robust automatic speech recognition technologies can be used to elicit, structure, and give feedback on spoken language practice.

5. Acknowledgements

The conceptual design of the technology-based practice environment used in this study, but not its development, was partly realised through interaction with the Games Online for Basic Language learning (GOBL) project (519136-LLP-2011-NL-KA2-KA2MP), funded with support from the European Commission. This publication reflects the views only of the author, and the Commission cannot be held responsible for any use which may be made of the information contained therein.

The practice activity contains a still from the film noir project *The Big Smoke* (copyright 2012 Kenneth Gawne). Icons are from the Coquette icon set.

References

Cornillie, F., & Desmet, P. (2016). Mini-games for language learning. In L. Murray & F. Farr (Eds.), *Routledge Handbook of Language Learning and Technology*. Routledge.
Cornillie, F., & Desmet, P. (2013). Seeking out fun failure: how positive failure feedback could enhance the instructional effectiveness of CALL mini-games. In *Global perspectives on Computer-Assisted Language Learning. Proceedings of WorldCALL 2013* (pp. 64-68). University of Ulster.
Cornillie, F., van den Branden, K., & Desmet, P. (2015). From language play to linguistic form and back again. Lessons from an experimental study for the design of task-based language practice supported by games. In J. Colpaert, A. Aerts, M. Oberhofer, & M. Gutierrez-Colon Plana (Eds.), *Task design and CALL; Proceedings of the Seventeenth International CALL Research Conference, Tarragona, Universitat Rovira i Virgili, 6-8 July 2015*. Antwerp: University of Antwerp.

DeKeyser, R. M. (1998). Beyond focus on form. Cognitive perspectives on learning and practicing second language grammar. In C. Doughty & J. Williams (Eds.), *Focus on form in classroom second language acquisition* (pp. 42-63). Cambridge: Cambridge University Press.

DeKeyser, R. M. (2007). Conclusion: the future of practice. In R. M. DeKeyser (Ed.), *Practice in a second language: perspectives from applied linguistics and cognitive psychology* (pp. 287-304). New York: Cambridge University Press.

Dörnyei, Z. (2009). *The psychology of second language acquisition*. Oxford: Oxford University Press.

Doughty, C., & Williams, J. (Eds.). (1998). *Focus on form in classroom second language acquisition*. Cambridge: Cambridge University Press.

Ellis, N. C. (2005). At the interface: dynamic interactions of explicit and implicit language knowledge. *Studies in Second Language Acquisition, 27*(20), 305-352. doi:10.1017/s027226310505014x

Erlam, R. (2009). The elicited oral imitation test as a measure of implicit knowledge. In R. Ellis, S. Loewen, C. Elder, R. Erlam, J. Philp, & H. Reinders (Eds.), *Implicit and explicit knowledge in second language learning, testing and teaching* (pp. 65-93). Bristol: Multilingual Matters.

Loewen, S. (2009). Grammaticality Judgment Tests and the Measurement of Implicit and Explicit L2 Knowledge. In R. Ellis, S. Loewen, C. Elder, R. Erlam, J. Philp, & H. Reinders (Eds.), *mplicit and explicit knowledge in second language learning, testing and teaching* (pp. 94-112). Bristol: Multilingual Matters.

Robinson, G. L. (1991). Effective feedback strategies in CALL: learning theory and empirical research. In P. A. Dunkel (Ed.), *Computer-assisted language learning and testing: research issues and practice* (pp. 155-167). New Jersey: Newbury House.

Wong, W., & VanPatten, B. (2003). The evidence is IN: drills are OUT. *Foreign Language Annals, 36*(3), 403-423. doi:10.1111/j.1944-9720.2003.tb02123.x

Training ELF teachers to create a blended learning environment: encouraging CMS adoption and implementation

Travis Cote[1] and Brett Milliner[2]

Abstract. E-learning has become a crucial component of most tertiary institution's education initiatives (Park, Lee, & Cheong, 2007) and core to most e-learning strategies is the institution's Content Management System (CMS). A CMS has the potential to enhance language courses by facilitating engagement with class content, providing students with opportunities to communicate, promoting student confidence during virtual interactions, fostering deeper connections between teachers and peers, and creating more personalized learning activities. However, getting faculty to use a CMS proves to be challenging (Black et al., 2007). As part of a study by the authors to learn how they might encourage teachers in a campus-wide English as a Lingua Franca (ELF) program to adopt a CMS, this paper reports on results from a Technology Acceptance Model (TAM) analysis (Alharbi & Drew, 2014).

Keywords: CMS, blended learning, ELF, teacher training.

1. Introduction

Within the large variety of e-learning technologies on the market, universities around the world have invested in electronic CMSs or Learning Management Systems (LMSs) for a range of purposes (Alharbi & Drew, 2014; Toland, White, Millis, & Bolliger, 2014). Defined by McCabe and Meuter (2011) as "an integrated set of web-based tools to help facilitate course administration and delivery" (p. 150), a CMS makes it possible for teachers to manage their courses both electronically

---

1. Tamagawa University, Tokyo, Japan; travis@bus.tamagawa.ac.jp

2. Tamagawa University, Tokyo, Japan; milliner@lit.tamagawa.ac.jp

How to cite this article: Cote, T., Milliner, B. (2015). Training ELF teachers to create a blended learning environment: encouraging CMS adoption and implementation. In F. Helm, L. Bradley, M. Guarda, & S. Thouësny (Eds), *Critical CALL – Proceedings of the 2015 EUROCALL Conference, Padova, Italy* (pp. 158-163). Dublin: Research-publishing. net. http://dx.doi.org/10.14705/rpnet.2015.000326

and remotely, fulfilling such tasks as document sharing, assignment distribution and collection, quizzes, wikis, blogs, discussion boards, exam management, and grading management (Toland et al., 2014). Effective CMS implementation also allows students to engage with class content at times convenient for them and they can utilize a variety of learning tools found within the system.

Using the Technology Acceptance Model (TAM), this study will report on staff perceptions of the established Blackboard CMS in a university-level ELF program, and present some suggestions for augmenting the effective use of the CMS in a language program.

1.1. The technology acceptance model

Introduced by Davis (1989), the Technology Acceptance Model (TAM) remains a favored theory that models how users of information systems come to accept and use a technology. The TAM model's longevity can be attributed to its reliability and flexibility as a measurement device (Fathema & Sutton, 2013). The model considers factors that affect an individual's intention to use computer systems or software applications and explores the interaction between two key variables: Perceived Usefulness (PU) and Perceived Ease Of Use (PEOU). PU was identified by Davis (1989, p. 320) as the extent to which the potential software application augments the user's job performance. PEOU considers whether the performance benefits of a system outweigh the efforts of use.

Recognizing that teachers have crucial roles to play in the application and use of CMS technology, few studies have focused on teachers. This study mirrors the work of Alharbi and Drew (2014) who considered the perceptions of a LMS among university faculty in Saudi Arabia.

1.2. The teaching context

This investigation is being undertaken by a center which manages a campus-wide, university ELF program in Tokyo, Japan. The program is comprised of approximately 2600 students taught by 41 teachers – 29 of whom are part-time. As this program observes a hiring policy that all teachers need not be native English speakers, it has attracted a diverse faculty representing 12 different nationalities. The faculty have different teaching experiences and varying degrees of familiarity with technologies. This diversity and the substantial number of part-time teachers represents a challenge in that CMS adoption, and a willingness to use a CMS, may be influenced by both employment status and previous experiences with technology for educational purposes. As most faculty in this study teach at multiple universities, there may also be a reluctance to invest the time and energy required to implement a CMS effectively.

Among all faculties, ELF teachers are recognized as the heaviest users of the CMS – with 88% of the full-time and 78% of part-time faculty using the system (Milliner & Cote, 2014). In spite of relatively high levels of use, the authors were interested in teachers' perceptions of the CMS to learn how they might leverage adoption and usage rates.

2. Research methods

2.1. Hypothesis testing

The basic assumption of the TAM model is that (a) a teacher's intention to use the CMS is positively affected by their perception of usefulness and their overall attitude towards the CMS, (b) a teacher's attitude towards using the CMS is positively affected by their perceptions of the CMS' usefulness and ease of use, and (c) a teacher's perception of usefulness is directly affected by their perceptions of ease of use. In the context of this study, PU is defined as the degree to which CMS use would support and/or enhance teaching practices, while PEOU is the perceived degree of effort required when learning how to use the CMS. This study investigates eight hypotheses (listed below) concerning relationships between the following variables: PEOU, PU, Attitude Towards Using (ATU), and Intention To Use (ITU) the CMS. Two additional variables were tested: the possible influences Employment Status (ES) and Blackboard Experience (BE) may have on intentions to use the CMS.

2.2. Participants

29 teachers employed as full-time assistant professors (7) or part-time instructors (22) participated in the study.

2.3. Instrumentation

Prior to the 2015 academic year, all teachers were asked to complete an online questionnaire. The first five items focused on teaching and experience using Blackboard, while the remaining questions (20) concerned the TAM analysis. All TAM items used a seven-point Likert scale and a reliability assessment was completed using Cronbach Alpha. Our calculation of Cronbach Alpha produced an overall result of 0.91, which reinforces the reliability claims of the TAM scale and enhances the validity of the following results.

3. Results

3.1. Respondent data

11 of the 29 respondents (38%) reported that they had either never used Blackboard (8), or used it for less than a year (3). The most common response was 1-3 years of Blackboard experience (14/48%). Four teachers (14%) reported that they had been using Blackboard for more than three years.

3.2. Hypothesis testing

For the TAM items, a correlation analysis was implemented to examine the relationship between different variables, and ultimately, to make decisions on whether to accept or reject the eight research hypotheses. Table 1 (below) provides a summary of the statistical results.

Table 1. Summary of Spearman's r correlation statistics ($N=29$)

	PEOU	PU	ATU	ITU	ES	BE
PEOU r_s-value	1.000	.512**	.461*	.364	.058	.260
PU r_s-value	.512**	1.000	.754**	.669**	.164	-.183
ATU r_s-value	.461*	.754**	1.000	.595**	.039	-.194
ITU r_s-value	.364	.669**	.595**	1.000	.030	-.048
ES r_s-value	.058	.164	.039	.030	1.000	
BE r_s-value	.260	-.183	-.194	-.048		1.000

*. p<.05. **. p<.01.

Our analysis enabled us to accept the following hypotheses:

- Perceived ease of use positively affects perceived usefulness of the Blackboard CMS (.512).

- Perceived ease of use positively affects attitudes towards using the CMS (.461).

- Perceived usefulness positively affects attitudes towards using the CMS. This correlation (.754) was the strongest hypothesis tested.

- Perceived usefulness positively affects behavioural intention to use the CMS. This correlation was also notable (.669), suggesting that teachers' perception of usefulness may be the most significant variable influencing their decisions to use the CMS.

- Attitude towards using positively affects intention to use the CMS (.595).

The following hypotheses were rejected:

- Perceived ease of use positively affects intentions to use the Blackboard CMS.

- Employment status positively affects intentions to use the Blackboard CMS.

- Prior Blackboard experience positively affects intentions to use the Blackboard CMS.

4. Conclusion

Similar to previous findings, this investigation has been able to confirm the reliability of the TAM for measuring faculty members' intentions to use new technologies. When teachers face the decision to utilize a new technology or not, it appears that perceptions of its usefulness, and more importantly, the degree to which it could augment teaching practices, is most significant. Nevertheless, perceptions about whether the benefits of a technology outweigh the efforts to use the technology are similarly important because, as our analysis found, perceived ease of use influences teacher attitudes towards using the CMS and their perceptions of its usefulness.

Moving forward, the authors of this study intend to consider the information gathered from this TAM analysis to refine their strategy of increasing CMS adoption among the faculty. Specific plans call for a review of individual course templates and default settings to make them more useful; to provide training sessions that highlight the usefulness of certain functions by demonstrating with examples from our own classes; and, bring attention to the quality of e-learning support at the university.

5. Acknowledgements

We would like to thank Dr. Takanori Sato of the Center for English as a Lingua Franca, Tamagawa University for his invaluable help and advice on our statistical analysis of the TAM data.

References

Alharbi, S., & Drew, S. (2014). Using the technology assessment model in understanding academics behavioral intention to use learning management systems. *International Journal of Advanced Computer Science Applications, 5*(1), 143-154. doi:10.14569/IJACSA.2014.050120

Black, E. W., Beck, D., Dawson, K., Jinks, S., & DiPietro, M. (2007). Considering implementation and use in the adoption of an LMS in online and blended learning environments. *TechTrends, 51*(2), 35-39. doi:10.1007/s11528-007-0024-x

Davis, F. (1989). Perceived usefulness, perceived ease of use, and user acceptance of information technology. *MIS Quarterly, 13*(3), 319-340. doi:10.2307/249008

Fathema, N., & Sutton, K. L. (2013). Factors influencing faculty members' learning management systems adoption behaviour: an analysis using the technology acceptance model. *IJTEMT, 2*(4), 20-28.

McCabe, D. B., & Meuter, M. L. (2011). A student view of technology in the classroom: does it enhance the seven principles of good practice in undergraduate education? *The Journal of Marketing Education, 33*(2), 149-159. doi:10.1177/0273475311410847

Milliner, B., & Cote, T. (2014). Blackboard in the center for English as a lingua franca. *e-Education Newsletter, 2*, 1-6.

Park, N., Lee, K. M., & Cheong, P. H. (2007). University instructors' acceptance of electronic courseware: an application of the technology acceptance model. *Journal of Computer-Mediated Communication, 13*(1), 163-186. doi:10.1111/j.1083-6101.2007.00391.x

Toland, S., White, J., Mills, D., & Bolliger, D. U. (2014). EFL instructors perceptions of usefulness and ease of use of the LMS Manaba. *The JALT CALL Journal, 10*(3), 221-236.

Il Vivit: vivi l'italiano. Un portale per la diffusione della lingua e cultura italiana nel mondo

Elena Maria Duso[1] e Giovanni Cordoni[2]

Abstract. Il Portale *VIVIT Vivi Italiano* (www.viv-it.org) è stato creato attraverso un progetto di ricerca coordinato dall'Accademia della Crusca (con il presidente Francesco Sabatini), che ha coinvolto due centri di ricerca dell'Università di Firenze (il CLIEO "Centro di Linguistica Storica e Teorica. Italiano, Lingue europee, Lingue orientali" e il MICC "Media Integration and Communication Center"); il Dipartimento di Scienze del Linguaggio e della Cultura dell'Università di Modena-Reggio Emilia ed il Dipartimento di Romanistica dell'Università di Padova. Si tratta di un repository informatico di materiali e strumenti rivolti agli italiani all'estero, in particolare di seconda e terza generazione, ma utilissimi anche per quanti vogliano perfezionare la lingua a partire da un livello intermedio, e per gli insegnanti. Offre infatti schede di approfondimento culturale e linguistico, sia sull'italiano che su dialetti e lingue di minoranze, e percorsi didattici interattivi per l'apprendimento della lingua. Mette quindi per la prima volta a disposizione tre archivi digitali sul lessico italiano interrogabili con un unico metamotore di ricerca. Dalla piattaforma sono accessibili anche il Dizionario degli Italianismi nel mondo e le banche dati dell'Accademia. Qual è l'utilità di un portale del genere per chi voglia rafforzare le proprie conoscenze linguistico-culturali sul Paese? Quali vantaggi offre rispetto al materiale preesistente? E quali i suoi limiti? Com'è possibile superarli? Primi esperimenti condotti in classe e a distanza ne illustrano problematiche e soluzioni.

Parole chiave: apprendimento a distanza, corpora, italiano L2, cultura italiana.

---

1. Università di Padova, Italy; elenamaria.duso@unipd.it
2. Accademia della Crusca, Italy; gcordoni@libero.it

How to cite this article: Duso, E. M., & Cordoni, G. (2015). Il Vivit: vivi l'italiano. Un portale per la diffusione della lingua e cultura italiana nel mondo. In F. Helm, L. Bradley, M. Guarda, & S. Thouësny (Eds), *Critical CALL – Proceedings of the 2015 EUROCALL Conference, Padova, Italy* (pp. 164-169). Dublin: Research-publishing.net. http://dx.doi.org/10.14705/rpnet.2015.000327

Il Vivit: vivi l'italiano. Un portale per la diffusione della lingua e cultura italiana nel mondo

1. Presentazione del sito

A differenza dei molti siti ormai disponibili per l'apprendimento delle prime basi della lingua, o che propongono materiali anche più avanzati ma poco strutturati, il Portale Vivit offre una panoramica a tutto tondo della lingua italiana: non è semplicemente una fotografia, ma un ipertesto costruito programmaticamente come un "castello a otto porte" cui accedere tramite le otto domande chiave nella *home page* (si veda Figura 1), quelle che si potrebbe porre "chi, avendo una pur minima conoscenza della lingua italiana, voglia inquadrarne l'origine, la posizione nei confronti dei dialetti, la sua funzionalità nella società attuale, la sua veste scritta rispetto al parlato, il suo percorso evolutivo dall'età di Dante in poi, il suo uso attraverso i media, la sua diffusione nel mondo, l'interesse che suscita negli altri Paesi" (Relazione Scientifica Consuntiva, p. 2).

Figura 1. Home page di Vivit

Ciò che caratterizza il sito è infatti l'attenzione alla lingua nella sua evoluzione e nelle sue diverse varietà: al di là dell'italiano standard, vengono infatti presentati

- attraverso brevi schede e campioni di lingua scritta e parlata – anche l'italiano dell'uso medio, i diversi italiani regionali, i dialetti, ma anche l'italiano degli emigranti e degli immigrati. Una lingua viva e variegata, analizzata nelle sue sfumature, senza però eccesso di tecnicismi, e documentata in modo multimediale attraverso oltre 1000 immagini e circa 250 audio e video, tratti dalle Teche Rai e da molti altri archivi pubblici e privati. La specificità di Vivit sta dunque nell'impronta linguistico-culturale fortemente caratterizzata, che rende affidabile il suo utilizzo, riservato tuttavia ad apprendenti con un certo *background* alle spalle e una conoscenza dell'italiano di livello almeno intermedio, come appunto figli e nipoti di italiani emigrati all'estero.

Vediamo dunque come sia possibile sfruttare il sito come studenti e docenti di italiano come Lingua seconda (L2) e Lingua straniera (Ls).

2. La navigazione autonoma e i percorsi didattici

Figura 2. I percorsi didattici

Una prima forma di navigazione è quella libera a partire dalle otto domande chiave: cliccando su ciascuna di esse si apre una finestra con una sintetica risposta, ma viene incoraggiata poi la ricerca autonoma, attraverso rimandi ad altre sezioni e ai multimedia collegati. Tale modalità si presta particolarmente all'uso individuale, così come adatti all'autoapprendimento sono i *Percorsi didattici* su temi diversi, culturalmente legati all'Italia (mass media, sport, cucina, teatro, letteratura, arte, emigrazione).

Figura 3. Indice del percorso didattico *Merica Merica*

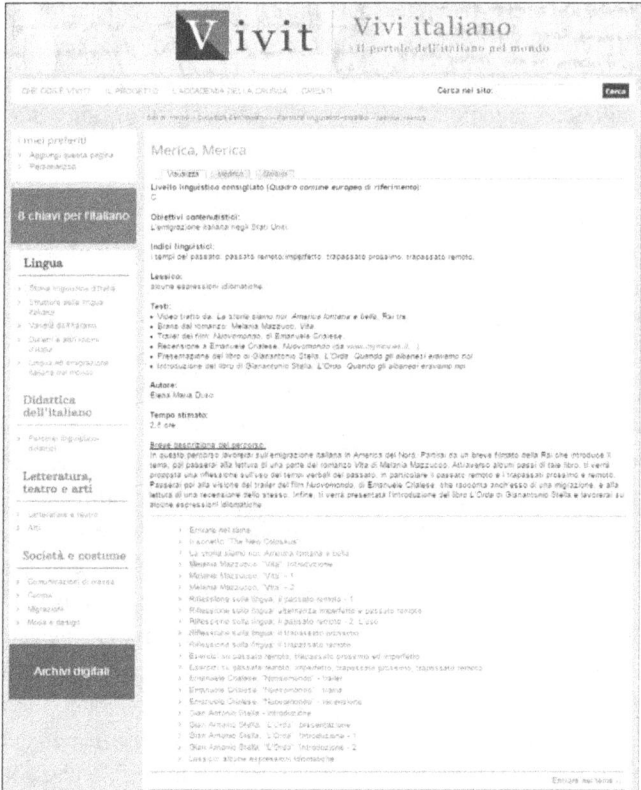

I percorsi, molto strutturati (es. Figura 3), prevedono un'introduzione al tema, la fruizione di audio, video, testi scritti con domande di comprensione a risposta chiusa fornite di *feedback*, cui seguono attività di focalizzazione su indici linguistici del livello scelto (tarati sul sillabo Lo Duca, 2006), con riflessioni sulla lingua corredate da esercizi interattivi e da proposte di approfondimenti attraverso altre sezioni del sito o materiali *online*. I testi offerti, di tipologie e registri linguistici differenziati, offrono anche campioni di italiani regionali (dal siciliano parlato al mercato di Palermo a quello di un liutaio della Foresta trentina di Paneveggio), di dialetti, italiano di stranieri, e lingue derivate dall'italiano, come taliàn e lunfardo.

3. Le sezioni tematiche e gli archivi digitali

È possibile anche navigare sul sito, per approfondire singole tematiche attraverso le sezioni Lingua, Letteratura, teatro ed arti e Società e costume.

Strutture della lingua italiana offre poi una grammatica decisamente innovativa rispetto ai materiali presenti in rete, soprattutto per la sintassi della frase su modello valenziale di Francesco Sabatini, particolarmente indicata per un confronto interlinguistico, sia scaricabile in pdf in italiano ed in altre quattro lingue europee (francese, inglese, spagnolo e tedesco), sia adattata in pagine web con brevi approfondimenti contrastivi.

Soffermiamoci inoltre sulle sezioni *Varietà dell'italiano* e *Dialetti ed altri idiomi*, concepite come schede con brevi descrizioni teoriche e campioni di lingua: in classe, esse si prestano a proporre agli studenti dei percorsi, selezionati dai docenti o dagli stessi apprendenti. In un corso di livello B2 tenuto presso il Centro linguistico di Padova abbiamo ad esempio costruito un itinerario sull'italiano regionale veneto ed il dialetto, partendo dai documenti testuali forniti, di tipologia molto varia: brani teatrali di Paolini e di Goldoni (*Baruffe chiozzotte*), letterari di Meneghello, Rigoni Stern, ed il documentario "Pescatori di Chioggia" di Andrea Segre, attraverso il quale gli studenti hanno potuto osservare il *code-switching*, ossia il frequente passaggio dal dialetto all'italiano regionale che caratterizza il Veneto. Le loro osservazioni spontanee sulle due varietà sono state successivamente rielaborate ad affinate attraverso l'analisi delle schede descrittive. Un giovane brasiliano infine, utilizzando gli approfondimenti sull'immigrazione veneta nel suo paese della sezione *Migrazioni* e sul taliàn, lingua creata dagli emigranti veneti, ha impreziosito il percorso svolto attraverso una sua presentazione *power point* sui veneti in Brasile e la loro lingua, proponendo suoi esempi di taliàn. In questo modo, il sito è stato utilizzato come fonte di reperimento di materiali, che poi però sono stati manipolati ed arricchiti dagli apprendenti. Lavorando in classe ed integrando i materiali del sito con altri strumenti tecnologici, come presentazioni o forum (ad es. in *Moodle* o in *Facebook*) è possibile infatti implementare l'uso di un sito che di per sé è più indicato all'esercizio delle abilità ricettive, sviluppando anche le abilità produttive. Alcuni prodotti finali degli studenti possono essere spediti al Vivit, utilizzando lo strumento *CondiVivit*, ossia uno spazio per la condivisione di esperienze, testi, immagini e altri materiali attinenti, iscrivendosi al quale è possibile inviare contributi personali. Stiamo cercando di utilizzarlo anche per consentire al docente di restare in contatto con gli apprendenti, che, tornati ai loro paesi, possono continuare a studiare l'italiano sul sito, interagendo con esperienze e riflessioni. Si tratta di primi tentativi che andrebbero sviluppati e potenziati: un sito di questo genere, che nasce da un intenso lavoro d'*équipe* di esperti e che ha costi di costruzione notevoli, necessita infatti di continua manutenzione, gestione dei forum ed implementazione di materiali, con inevitabili costi ulteriori.

Utili alla classe di italiano L2 risultano infine gli archivi digitali lessicografici, ampi corpora che offrono uno spaccato dell'italiano contemporaneo, scritto e parlato: si prestano infatti a confronti linguistici sull'uso diamesico di forme e costrutti o all'esame di particolari forme, come i segnali discorsivi, che spesso sono problematici per gli apprendenti. Attraverso il motore di ricerca è possibile non solo visualizzare la frequenza e le stringhe contestuali in cui una certa forma appare, ma anche ricavare una serie di dati su di essa (sesso, età etc) e, nel caso dell'italiano radiofonico e televisivo, accedere ad una più ampia porzione di audio/video e alla trascrizione completa dei passi.

4. Conclusioni

Nel complesso, gli esiti delle prime sperimentazioni, in classe o a distanza (con apprendenti europei e cinesi) risultano molto positivi: dal *feedback* degli studenti, ricavato dai giudizi scritti da loro inviati o attraverso i *Diari* di autoapprendimento *online* durante il corso, emerge infatti che le attività risultano interessanti ed utili ed i percorsi sono in genere ben tarati sul loro livello. È possibile visualizzare alcuni commenti degli apprendenti accedendo direttamente al *CondiVivit*.

5. Ringraziamenti

Ringraziamo il professor Francesco Sabatini, coordinatore generale, e tutta l'*équipe* che ha lavorato al Vivit per averci dato la possibilità di rappresentare il gruppo presentando il sito in questa sede. Nell'impossibilità di nominare tutti i collaboratori, rinviamo alla pagina http://www.viv-it.org/schede/crediti.

Bibliografia

Lo Duca, M. G. (2006). *Sillabo di italiano L2. Per studenti in scambio*. Roma: Carocci.
Relazione Scientifica Consuntiva / Protocollo: RBNE07JTPA. Nel sito http://www.viv-it.org/schede/progetto

What do students learn by playing an online simulation game?

Stephan J. Franciosi[1] and Jeffrey Mehring[2]

Abstract. Studies suggest that simulations and games not only improve target language skills, but they can also support knowledge creation regarding a broader variety of topics. Thus, we wanted to explore how playing an online simulation game affected knowledge of energy supply and its relationship to environmental and economic factors among learners of English as a Foreign Language (EFL) in Japan. This particular topic was selected due to its immediate relevancy in Japan which faces energy supply and environmental issues in the wake of the Fukushima nuclear accident. The presentation will report on a qualitative exploration of debriefing reports produced by Japanese university students after playing Energy City, an online simulation game. The game models various urban scenarios in which the objective is to supply sufficient energy to power a city with electricity while minimizing environmental impacts, addressing stakeholder concerns and balancing a budget. Students used the game in small groups, after which they completed debriefing reports designed to foster reflection on the game playing experience. We performed a content analysis on the reports to identify major trends and themes which could offer insights regarding the learning outcomes. The results indicate the possibility that gameplay may influence attitudes toward nuclear power production and personal behavior with regard to energy consumption. The principal investigator intends to use these results to author a quantitative survey instrument for the purpose of investigating whether attitude and/or behavior change occurs at a statistically significant level.

Keywords: content-based instruction, game-based instruction, learning outcomes.

---

1. Osaka University, Japan; steve.franciosi@gmail.com
2. Ohkagakuen University, Japan; mehring@ohkagakuen-u.ac.jp

How to cite this article: Franciosi, S. J., & Mehring. J. (2015). What do students learn by playing an online simulation game? In F. Helm, L. Bradley, M. Guarda, & S. Thouësny (Eds), *Critical CALL – Proceedings of the 2015 EUROCALL Conference, Padova, Italy* (pp. 170-176). Dublin: Research-publishing.net. http://dx.doi.org/10.14705/rpnet.2015.000328

1. Introduction

This paper presents the content learning outcomes of using a simulation game, *Energy City* (Jason Learning), in four English as a Foreign Language classes taught by the principal investigator in a content-based instructional framework at a Japanese university.

The principal investigator used a simulation game in the courses because a growing body of empirical data strongly suggests that simulations and games can improve knowledge of a variety of educational content (e.g. Clark et al., 2011) as well as foreign language skills (Peterson, 2013). Thus, a game seemed ideal for integrating content and language instruction.

The principal investigator chose the topic presented in *Energy City*—energy generation and conservation strategies in an urban setting—because (1) it is relevant in post-Fukushima Japan (Aldrich, 2013), and (2) simulations and games may be effective tools for educating people on issues related to climate change (Eisenack & Reckien, 2013).

However, we were uncertain what, if anything, the students were learning about the topic from playing the game. We believed this to be problematic, particularly in the case of politically-charged topics such as energy and conservation strategies in Japan. Therefore, we wanted to explore the learning outcomes of playing *Energy City* in terms of information, knowledge and attitudes that may influence their behavior in the broader socio-cultural and political context.

We conducted a qualitative analysis of debriefing reports submitted by students after playing the game. The analysis revealed themes that could provide some indication as to what the students learned about energy and conservation strategies. In this paper we present these findings and outline research goals going forward.

2. Method

2.1. Participants

The target population of the present study was comprised of students in four mandatory English as a Foreign Language courses at a Japanese university ($n=67$). Most of the students were male (84%), first-year students (57%) from the school of science (46%) or engineering (31%).

2.2. Materials

2.2.1. Energy City

We adopted *Energy City* (Jason Learning) as the core lesson material in the present study (Figure 1). The object of this simulation game is to plan and implement a virtual city's energy and conservation strategies in order to maintain an adequate energy supply while not imparting excessive damage to the environment.

Figure 1. Screenshot of *Energy City*; used with permission of *Jason Learning*

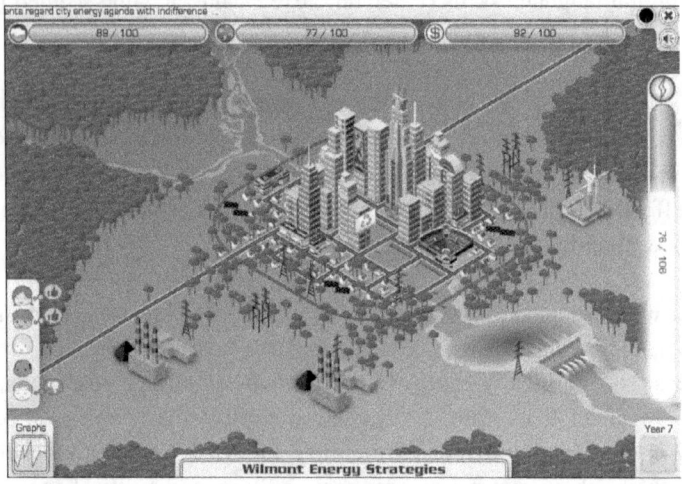

2.2.2. Debriefing report

We used a debriefing report for the game as the data collection medium. The report was authored in a Google Form generally following the guidelines set forth by Kriz (2008). Specifically, the report consisted of four prompts as follows: How did you feel after playing the game? What happened in the game? What did you learn from playing the game? How can you apply what you learned in real life? In all, 92 reports were submitted with a total word count of 6,132 and an average response length of 26 words.

2.3. Coding and results

We performed a qualitative analysis of the debriefing reports using the coding schedule shown in Table 1, which is based on the taxonomy of outcomes proposed by Kraiger, Ford and Salas (1993). We further sub-categorized the text based on emergent themes within the larger taxonomy.

Table 1. Coding schedule

Outcomes	Learning Constructs	Nature of Evidence
Cognitive	Declarative Knowledge	Accurate propositions about game elements
	Mental Models	Interrelating game elements
	Metacognitive Skills	Self-awareness, awareness of nature of material
Affective	Attitude	Direction and/or strength
	Motivation	Self efficacy, goal setting

2.3.1. Cognitive outcomes

We found evidence of each learning construct for this type of outcome, as shown in Table 2. We further found that the emergent themes in the text were well aligned with major concepts introduced in the game, such as strengths and weaknesses of various energy generation technologies.

Table 2. A summary of cognitive learning outcomes and associated emergent themes

Learning Constructs	Theme	Example
Declarative Knowledge	Budgeting	*I learned that it is important how to use money.*
	Technology	*I understood the usefulness of natural energy and the nuclear power*
	Environment	*Environmental quality is important.*
	Public policy	*It's quite hard to listen to stakeholders and make your city better.*
	Communication	*In the game, we learned how important it is to listen to citizens' offers.*
Mental Models	Technology	*I learned that air quality will drop greatly by relying on fossil fuels and that bio fuels have a negative on air quality.*
	Environment	*I learned how to deal with the balance between the economy and environment.*
	Game vs. real world	*In fact, nuclear power plants have various problems, but in the game those are great in energy and air quality!*
Metacognitive Skills	Planning	*We have to endure a few years if you want to gain a good final outcome.*
	Public policy	*I could play this game at the view from a manager not a resident. So I got a new view.*

2.3.2. Affective outcomes

We found evidence of each learning construct for this type of outcome. The results are summarized in Table 3. Notably, several of the students expressed positive attitudes toward the use of nuclear power plants, and even the intention to advocate for their use. This result was unexpected in that we assumed an overall negative attitude toward nuclear power in the general population (Aldrich, 2013).

Table 3. A summary of affective learning outcomes and associated emergent themes

Learning Construct	Theme	Example
Attitudes	Pro-renewable	We need clean energy to make our life better.
	Anti-fossil fuel	We shouldn't use oil power plants very often both in this game and in reality.
	Pro-nuke	Nuclear power plant is great!
	Anti-nuke	I disagree nuclear. That's because it is danger.
	Conditional nuke	If you live in a country which don't have earthquake, nuclear energy will be good help.
	Environment	We should think environment.
Motivation	Public policy	I will vote with careful.
	Nuclear advocacy	I will be critical about abandoning nuclear power plant. It'd better to reconsidering.
	Knowledge sharing	I want to share new knowledge with my friends.
	Conservation	When it is summer, I will not use air conditioner.
	Innovation	I want to create a new energy.

3. Discussion

Overall, we found that the emergent themes collectively accounted for all major elements of the *Energy City* game. The students reported new understanding of planning and implementing an energy strategy, including the crucial role of financial resources, the nature of various energy generation technologies, and the importance of environmental health. Notably, the students were also able to think critically about the game itself, recognizing that it can provide new perspectives while distinguishing it from reality.

Further, the data indicate two affective outcomes in particular that deserve further exploration. First, an apparent support of nuclear energy was notable in a sociocultural context of strong scepticism toward this technology. Second, students expressed motivation to adopt energy-saving consumption behaviors.

We believe results related to attitudes toward nuclear power generation and energy consumption behavior are of primary interest because of the current energy supply situation in post-Fukushima Japan. However, because the present study is qualitative, and because we did not measure attitudes prior to playing *Energy* City, we cannot determine whether playing the game persuades learners to change their perspectives regarding this topic—either negatively or positively—in a manner that is statistically significant. Therefore, the principal investigator intends to design a survey based on the present results to gather quantitative data on perspectives regarding nuclear power generation and conservation behavior.

4. Conclusions

The purpose of the present study was to explore the learning outcomes of playing the *Energy City* simulation game. In particular, we were interested in discovering whether learners using the game gained knowledge of energy and conservation strategies in an urban setting, and whether playing the game influenced attitudes and motivation regarding the topic. We conducted a qualitative analysis of debriefing reports that students completed after playing the game. We found evidence of both cognitive and affective learning outcomes, and that these outcomes were closely related to the main themes represented in the game. Specifically, learners reported a greater understanding of energy generation technologies, and motivation to modify their behavior to address the current energy situation in Japan.

References

Aldrich, D. P. (2013). Rethinking civil society–state relations in Japan after the Fukushima accident. *Polity*, *45*(2), 249-264. doi:10.1057/pol.2013.2

Clark, D. B., Nelson, B. C., Chang, H.-Y., Martinez-Garza, M., Slack, K., & Angelo, C. M. D'. (2011). Exploring Newtonian mechanics in a conceptually-integrated digital game: comparison of learning and affective outcomes for students in Taiwan and the United States. *Computers & Education*, *57*(3), 2178-2195. doi:10.1016/j.compedu.2011.05.007

Eisenack, K., & Reckien, D. (2013). Climate change and simulation/gaming. *Simulation & Gaming*, *44*(2-3), 245-252.

Kraiger, K., Ford, J. K., & Salas, E. (1993). Application of cognitive, skill-based, and affective theories of learning outcomes to new methods of training evaluation. *Journal of Applied Psychology*, *78*(2), 311-328. doi:10.1037//0021-9010.78.2.311

Kriz, W. C. (2008). A systemic-constructivist approach to the facilitation and debriefing of simulations and games. *Simulation & Gaming, 41*(5), 663-680. doi:10.1177/1046878108319867

Peterson, M. (2013). *Computer games and language learning*. New York, NY: Palgrave Macmillan.

Gli apprendenti di italiano L2 all'università e le loro abitudini tecnologiche

Ivana Fratter[1] e Micol Altinier[2]

Abstract. Negli ultimi anni il pubblico del Centro Linguistico di Ateneo dell'Università (CLA) di Padova è cambiato conseguentemente ai processi di internazionalizzazione, messi in atto dalle politiche universitarie, e ai recenti accordi con università non appartenenti alla Comunità Europea. Analogamente, le profonde trasformazioni avvenute nella società della conoscenza, con l'introduzione sia dei dispositivi portatili sia dei nuovi social network, richiedono che sia fatta luce sul nuovo profilo dei destinatari dei corsi di lingua e al contempo sulle loro "abitudini tecnologiche" per poter progettare una offerta formativa il più possibile rispondente alle nuove esigenze. L'articolo illustra i dati di una indagine condotta su 225 studenti stranieri in mobilità internazionale mettendo a fuoco il profilo di tale tipo di studenti e l'uso delle Tecnologie dell'Informazione e della Comunicazione (TIC) per la formazione continua.

Parole chiave: TIC, e-learning, apprendimento formale e informale, self-study.

1. L'indagine: il questionario e gli informanti

Nel II semestre dell'a.a. 2014-2015 presso il CLA dell'Università di Padova è stata condotta una indagine su 225 studenti stranieri in mobilità internazionale volta a osservare i loro comportamenti e le loro abitudini tecnologiche relativamente all'uso delle TIC nella formazione e nella vita quotidiana. Per l'indagine è stato utilizzato un questionario composto da 85 domande volte a raccogliere informazioni sui seguenti punti: biografia linguistica degli apprendenti, esperienze pregresse di studio delle lingue straniere e dell'italiano, utilizzo delle TIC per l'apprendimento

---

1. Università di Padova, Italia; ivana.fratter@unipd.it
2. Università di Padova, Italia; micol.altinier@unipd.it

How to cite this article: Fratter, I., & Altinier, M. (2015). Gli apprendenti di italiano L2 all'università e le loro abitudini tecnologiche. In F. Helm, L. Bradley, M. Guarda, & S. Thouësny (Eds), *Critical CALL – Proceedings of the 2015 EUROCALL Conference, Padova, Italy* (pp. 177-180). Dublin: Research-publishing.net. http://dx.doi.org/10.14705/rpnet.2015.000329

linguistico, esperienze innovative di studio delle lingue con i nuovi dispositivi mobili, utilizzo dei social network e loro integrazione nel percorso di formazione linguistica.

I 225 soggetti coinvolti sono stati in prevalenza femmine (68,8%) e il 31,2% maschi con una età media di 24 anni. Si tratta per lo più di studenti partecipanti a progetti di mobilità Erasmus + (52,4%), per l'8,8% di studenti stranieri iscritti all'università di Padova, per il 7,04% di dottorandi e per il 3% di ricercatori. Gli informanti provengono da 48 nazioni dell'Europa, dell'Africa, dell'America, dell'Oceania e dell'Asia. Le nazionalità più rappresentate del campione raccolto sono: spagnola (20%), tedesca (16%), brasiliana (8%), inglese (5,3%), cinese e polacca (8%) e francese (7%).

2. Esperienze innovative di apprendimento

Relativamente alle esperienze pregresse di studio delle lingue straniere la maggior parte degli apprendenti conosceva 2 (46%) o 3 lingue straniere (31%) e per l'84% aveva avuto esperienze di studio di tipo tradizionale in classe e, solamente, il 16 % aveva avuto esperienze di apprendimento linguistico di tipo online con un grado di soddisfazione abbastanza buono (68%).

L'esperienza di apprendimento linguistico online è vista positivamente in particolare per lo sviluppo delle abilità ricettive (ascolto e lettura) ma anche per la gestione autonoma del tempo. Per coloro che, invece, hanno espresso un giudizio negativo sulle esperienze pregresse di partecipazione a corsi online, la ragione principale addotta riguardava la mancanza di contatto faccia a faccia con l'insegnante.

Tra le esperienze innovative di apprendimento sono state indicate anche quelle di collaborazione online (p.es. e-Tandem) tuttavia il numero di informanti che ha avuto delle esperienze di tale tipo è molto esiguo (18%) sembra dunque una pratica ancora poco diffusa, una delle ragioni sembra essere legata alla lentezza e instabilità dei collegamenti di rete.

3. Gli apprendenti sono *digital learners?*

Contrariamente alle attese, alla domanda "come preferisci imparare una lingua: online, in presenza, in modalità blended?" i dati del questionario mostrano come il 78% degli apprendenti, che pur appartengono alla cosiddetta "era digitale", preferiscono apprendere le lingue frequentando corsi in presenza con l'insegnante. Le ragioni di tale scelta sono principalmente legate alla possibilità di avere un feedback immediato e mirato al proprio apprendimento, al coinvolgimento emotivo derivante dai corsi in presenza, alla socializzazione con altri apprendenti. I corsi in presenza sono visti come la modalità migliore per lo sviluppo delle abilità produttive e interazionali.

Per quanto riguarda invece i corsi *blended,* essi sono visti come un'opportunità per il potenziamento degli aspetti grammaticali della lingua (22,2%). Infine la preferenza dei corsi online è stata data inaspettatamente da un unico informante. Quest'ultimo dato è interessante in quanto anche tra coloro che avevano avuto esperienze pregresse di frequenza di corsi online (48%), tra questi la maggior parte 80% ha dichiarato di preferire i corsi in presenza. In sintesi il fatto che i corsi online non vengano considerati come un valore aggiunto alla formazione linguistica porta a riflettere a livello di progettazione dei corsi e sulla scelta del modello pedagogico offerto (Fratter, 2014) che, con ogni probabilità, nonostante l'utilizzo di piattaforme di apprendimento di matrice costruttivista, i corsi vengono di fatto "confezionati" come corsi con un impianto di matrice comportamentista e che al contempo richiedono una grande capacità di organizzazione del tempo di apprendimento e portano anche all'isolamento dell'apprendente.

4. Materiali e dispositivi preferiti dagli apprendenti

Il digitale, grazie alle politiche di mercato, è entrato in maniera massiccia anche nel settore della produzione di materiali per l'apprendimento linguistico, infatti l'offerta oggi disponibile spazia dalle forme più tradizionali quali il manuale cartaceo di lingua, per passare al libro in formato e-Reader per arrivare persino al libro "liquido" ovvero un libro che si trasforma in colore, caratteri e dimensioni a seconda delle esigenze dell'utente stesso. Tenendo conto delle innovazioni nel settore dell'editoria e al fine di proporre un'offerta formativa aggiornata e adeguata ai bisogni formativi degli stessi utenti, nella presente indagine si è cercato di scoprire quali fossero le preferenze degli apprendenti relativamente agli strumenti per la formazione linguistica; si sono osservati elementi quali la flessibilità dei materiali e le eventuali versioni liquide che riguardano aspetti pedagogici ed elementi legati all'aspetto economico quale il costo dei materiali online e cartacei. I dati offrono il seguente spaccato: il 72% preferisce studiare su materiali in formato cartaceo, il 25% su materiali interattivi online e il restante 3% ha scelto come materiale preferito la fruizione del tipo e-Reader.

Per quanto riguarda l'uso degli hardware di questo tipo di popolazione la maggior parte dispone di 1 o 2 dispositivi personali: l'82% computer portatile, il 48% smartphone, il 20% computer fisso e solo il 4% di un tablet. In sintesi i dati mostrano il profilo di una utenza "indipendente" nel possesso di dispositivi mobili e potenzialmente ricettiva alla modalità *Bring YOur personal Device* (BYOD) (Fratter, in stampa).

5. Conclusioni: il profilo dell'apprendente in mobilità europea

Quello che emerge dalla presente indagine è il profilo di un apprendente straniero femmina, con un'età media di 24 anni che conosce almeno due lingue straniere e ha fatto poche esperienze di apprendimento innovativo in rete ma che nonostante tutto preferisce studiare le lingue in classe con l'insegnante e utilizza la modalità blended come supporto al proprio apprendimento.

In conclusione si tratta di *digital natives* così come delineati da Prensky (2012) in quanto utilizzano la rete, posseggono in genere almeno due dispositivi e hanno almeno un profilo sociale in rete sui più comuni social network (Facebook e Instagram), tuttavia non possiamo definirli degli "apprendenti digitali" (*digital learners*) in quanto preferiscono non solo strumenti di studio tradizionali quali il libro in formato cartaceo ma anche il formato tradizionale di corso in presenza; in particolar modo la lingua orale è una necessità sentita molto fortemente da questa tipologia di apprendenti e tale abilità trova il suo naturale sviluppo in corsi in presenza.

Riferimenti bibliografici

Fratter I. (2014). *Il docente di lingue e le TIC: conoscenze, competenze e abilità*. In I. Fratter & E. Jafrancesco (a cura di), *Guida alla formazione del docente di lingue all'uso delle TIC. Le lingue straniere e l'italiano L2* (pp. 25-56). Roma: Aracne.

Fratter I. (in stampa). *Il mobile learning e le nuove frontiere per la didattica delle lingue*. In D. Troncarelli & M. La Grassa (a cura di).

Prensky, M. (2012). *From digital natives to digital wisdom: hopeful essays for 21st century learning.*. Thousand Oaks, CA: Corwin.

L'evoluzione del test di piazzamento per i corsi di Italiano L2 al Centro Linguistico dell'Università di Padova: utilità e criticità delle TIC

Ivana Fratter[1], Luisa Marigo[2], e Luigi Pescina[3]

Abstract. Negli ultimi dieci anni l'utenza dei corsi di Italiano come Lingua Seconda (L2) presso il Centro Linguistico di Ateneo (CLA) di Padova ha subito numerosi cambiamenti dovuti a diversi fattori, quali i processi di internazionalizzazione operanti nelle università italiane, gli accordi bilaterali stipulati tra diverse università e non da ultimo il nuovo programma di scambio dell'Unione Europea 'Erasmus+'. Tali cambiamenti hanno richiesto continui adattamenti del test di piazzamento – nonché delle modalità di somministrazione dello stesso – necessario per la formazione delle classi. Inoltre, la necessità di una valutazione in entrata in grado di differenziare sei livelli di competenza dell'italiano (A1-C2) per l'inserimento nelle classi ha portato il gruppo degli insegnanti di Italiano L2 del CLA ad elaborare – dal 2001 ad oggi – due diverse proposte di test di piazzamento. Questo contributo si propone di: 1. descrivere i passaggi che hanno condotto all'attuale versione del test di piazzamento e di indicarne i vantaggi e i limiti, nonché le potenzialità da sviluppare grazie alla piattaforma Moodle che lo ospita; 2. condurre a una riflessione su come lo sviluppo delle Tecnologie dell'Informazione e della Comunicazione (TIC) abbia permesso la realizzazione di prove di piazzamento sempre più mirate e flessibili rispondenti alle mutate esigenze dell'utenza; 3. considerare l'eventualità di sostituire il test d'ingresso con l'autovalutazione da parte dello studente.

Parole chiave: testing, Moodle, piazzamento, adattivo.

---

1. Università di Padova, Italia; ivana.fratter@unipd.it
2. Università di Padova, Italia; luisa.marigo@unipd.it
3. Università di Padova, Italia; luigi.pescina@unipd.it

How to cite this article: Fratter, I., Marigo, L., & Pescina, L. (2015). L'evoluzione del test di piazzamento per i corsi di Italiano L2 al Centro Linguistico dell'Università di Padova: utilità e criticità delle TIC. In F. Helm, L. Bradley, M. Guarda, & S. Thouësny (Eds), *Critical CALL – Proceedings of the 2015 EUROCALL Conference, Padova, Italy* (pp. 181-185). Dublin: Research-publishing.net. http://dx.doi.org/10.14705/rpnet.2015.000330

1. Il primo test di ingresso del CLA

A partire dal 2000 presso il CLA di Padova si è progettato un test di ingresso per la discriminazione di sei livelli di competenza linguistica (da A1 a C2 secondo il Quadro Comune Europeo di Riferimento, QCER) necessario alla formazione delle classi di italiano L2. Il test è stato realizzato in formato cartaceo per passare nel 2004 alla somministrazione su supporto informatico. Il test è stato suddiviso in due parti, ciascuna delle quali atta a determinare tre dei sei livelli; sono stati preparati due test, uno denominato "test di fascia uno" che discriminava i livelli A1, A2 e B1 e il secondo, "test di fascia due", per discriminare i livelli B2, C1 e C2. All'inizio gli apprendenti completavano un pre-test selezionando gli indici grammaticali da loro conosciuti e, in base al numero e al tipo di argomenti scelti, essi venivano indirizzati allo svolgimento di una delle due parti. Il test di tipo comunicativo presentava prove di tipo chiuso per misurare la comprensione orale, scritta e la competenza metalinguistica; la prova aperta di produzione scritta veniva necessariamente valutata a parte.

Nel 2005 il test di ingresso è stato trasferito su supporto informatico (*Computer Based Test*) grazie al software *QuestionMark Perception* (Castello, 2006) permettendo così la correzione di un numero consistente di prove in tempi brevissimi in quanto la valutazione di tutte le prove chiuse era automatizzata. Anche se *QuestionMark Perception* offriva la possibilità di somministrare il test online, per ragioni legate alla sicurezza, i tecnici informatici avevano scelto la somministrazione in presenza.

Il mutamento dei progetti di mobilità tuttavia richiedevano con sempre maggiore impellenza alcuni cambiamenti, primi tra i quali la somministrazione a distanza del test di ingresso, la possibilità di somministrazioni non rigide rispetto a delle date prefissate e non da ultimo l'abbattimento dei costi legati alle licenze del software. Per quanto riguarda invece i parametri di validità del test, nel corso degli anni sono stati evidenziati alcuni punti critici legati alla discriminazione dei livelli B1 e B2, in quanto talvolta gli apprendenti di livello intermedio 'sfuggivano' ai parametri fissati da noi nel pre-test discriminante le due fasce. Inoltre il formato del test, in particolare di fascia due, risultava di durata eccessiva non solo per quanto riguarda i fattori cognitivi (soglia di attenzione durante testing) ma anche per ragioni di ordine tecnico e gestionale. Infine ragioni di ordine economico richiedevano la drastica riduzione dei costi per la gestione e somministrazione dei test con il passaggio a piattaforme open source come Moodle. Questi fattori hanno portato all'elaborazione di un nuovo formato di test nella piattaforma Moodle.

2. Il test adattivo al computer

Questo articolo spiega i motivi della realizzazione di un test d'entrata online in Moodle ed illustra la struttura del test di tipo semiadattivo, che comprende cioè prove di abilità di livello e difficoltà variabili in funzione dell'esito di un modulo iniziale adattivo sulle competenze linguistiche; in questo contributo si descrivono poi le tipologie di prove e di item utilizzate oltre che le modifiche operate dal nostro personale tecnico-informatico per elevarne gli standard di validità e affidabilità.

La scelta di usare la piattaforma Moodle presenta indubbiamente diversi vantaggi: consente allo studente straniero di svolgere il test a distanza, dal suo paese, offrendo a noi insegnanti tempo aggiuntivo indispensabile per organizzare al meglio i corsi e le classi in base ai risultati pervenuti. La piattaforma inoltre mette a disposizione validi strumenti di gestione delle informazioni (ad es. lo storico degli studenti) e di analisi dei dati del test (in termini quantitativi e qualitativi).

Uno dei maggiori vantaggi offerti dalla piattaforma Moodle è stata la possibilità di avvalerci della tecnologia adattiva che ne aumenta l'efficienza: il test infatti 'si adatta' allo studente presentandogli prove il più vicino possibile al suo livello reale (evitando quesiti troppo facili o difficili). Questo aspetto è fondamentale per valutare in un arco di tempo ragionevolmente breve e prestabilito le competenze iniziali in italiano L2 di studenti potenzialmente appartenenti a tutti i 6 livelli descritti dal QCER.

Sarebbe interessante approfondire la ricaduta del test adattivo su altri piani. Chalhoub-Deville (2001) sottolinea infatti che i cambiamenti prodotti dal Computer-Based Testing (CBT) e Computer Adaptive Testing (CAT) sono stati esaminati inizialmente soprattutto in termini di maggiore efficienza e usabilità mentre l'aspetto più interessante e ancora da approfondire offerto dal CBT è l'approccio adattivo che porta ad un uso 'disruptive' della tecnologia, un uso cioè che cambia il modo stesso di ideare il costrutto, creare item e compiti, trasformando quindi l'obiettivo del test e modificando di conseguenza le pratiche per la valutazione,

> "[i]n terms of construct representation, it is well documented that the L2 construct is multidimensional and involves a variety of interacting components and processes [...]. Language testers need to utilize technology to design measures that increasingly explore and better measure such critical aspects of the construct. Additionally, researchers have argued that some abilities and processes, which are critical for beginning language learners, become less salient for more proficient learners, for whom yet

other aspects of the construct begin to emerge [...]. Technology provides an excellent capability to trace test takers' language development thus enabling researchers to better understand how aspects of the construct evolve across different ability levels" (Chalhoub-Deville, 2001, p. 96).

3. Un test di autovalutazione. Perché?

All'interno dell'economia della glottodidattica proposta in un ente formativo che opera con grandi numeri di studenti, il test d'entrata – finalizzato a una coerente formazione di gruppi-classe distinti per competenza linguistica (A1, A2, B1...) – rappresenta la fase propedeutica ed imprescindibile del corso di lingua (Freddi, 1994); solo attraverso una certa omogeneità della padronanza della L2/LS tra gli apprendenti è possibile presentare all'attenzione della classe l'"i+1" teorizzato da Krashen (Balboni, 2014).

I 'grandi numeri' sopra accennati impongono che il test sia erogato attraverso una piattaforma informatica che, come noto, assicura sensibili benefici in termini di a. tempo e di b. spazio: a. i risultati di un test computerizzato che contiene prove a risposta chiusa sono immediati, b. il test può essere fornito in qualsiasi parte del globo raggiungibile via Internet.

I benefici temporali e spaziali, tuttavia, si scontrano con le esigenze specifiche legate all'oggetto testato, e cioè la lingua: se le prove di comprensione trovano nel Computer-Assisted Language Learning (CALL) un validissimo aiuto, non si può dire lo stesso al riguardo delle prove di produzione i cui risultati dipendono da un valutatore 'umano' e non – almeno attualmente – dall''intelligenza' del *software*; e pure il fattore spazio trova un *handicap* nella sostanziale impossibilità del controllo (se il test è erogato a distanza il soggetto testato può 'imbrogliare').

Inoltre, riferendoci al CLA di Padova, sono in continuo aumento gli studenti in mobilità che al momento dell'iscrizione al corso di Italiano L2 presentano un attestato di frequenza a un corso pregresso che 'obbliga' – anche moralmente – la Segreteria alla registrazione del soggetto al corso di livello successivo. Infine, motivi legati all'inserimento in un gruppo di un livello giudicato incoerente dallo studente spesso costringono a passaggi di classe e livello.

Questi punti critici – unitamente all'evidenza di un indubbio investimento di lavoro finalizzato alla progettazione, alla realizzazione, all'erogazione e all'aggiornamento di un test online computerizzato – ci hanno portato a prendere in considerazione l'eventualità di lasciare scegliere allo studente il livello del corso che desidera frequentare, tenuto conto anche del fatto che: a. ormai la scansione in sei livelli del qcer è ampiamente conosciuta dentro e fuori l'Europa, b. gli utenti dei corsi di un centro linguistico universitario hanno un alto grado di scolarità e dunque possiedono una buona consapevolezza del loro percorso formativo, c. la responsabilizzazione dello studente rientra tra le mete educative della moderna pedagogia (Secci, 2013).

Al momento dell'iscrizione online, quindi, lo studente indicherà il livello del corso desiderato e in questo – se lo riterrà opportuno – sarà coadiuvato da un link che lo condurrà ai descrittori dei livelli del QCER e ai programmi (divisi per livello) stabiliti dal sillabo adottato al CLA.

Riferimenti bibliografici

Balboni, P. E. (2014). *Didattica dell'italiano come lingua seconda e straniera*. Roma: Bonacci.
Castello E. (2006), The current state of online language testing at the University of Padova Language Centre. In M. G. Lo Duca, F. Dalziel, D. Griggio (a cura di), *il CLA verso l'Europa: e-learning, Testing, Portfolio delle Lingue* (pp. 223-231). Padova: Cleup.
Chalhoub-Deville, M. (2001). Language testing and technology: past and future. *Language Learning & Technology*, 5(2), 95-98. Retrieved from http://llt.msu.edu/vol5num2/pdf/deville.pdf
Freddi, G. (1994). *Glottodidattica. Fondamenti, metodi e tecniche*. Torino: UTET.
Secci, C. (2013). *Apprendimento permanente e educazione. Una lettura pedagogica*. Milano: FrancoAngeli.

Developing and evaluating a multimodal course format: Danish for knowledge workers – labour market-related Danish

Karen-Margrete Frederiksen[1] and Katja Årosin Laursen[1]

Abstract. This paper presents our reflections on developing the Computer-Assisted Language Learning (CALL) course *Danish for knowledge workers – labour market-related Danish*. As defined by Laursen and Frederiksen (2015), knowledge workers are "highly educated people who typically work at universities, at other institutions of higher education and research, or in private companies working with development and research at a level corresponding to that of a university" (p. 62). We base our reflections primarily on a participant survey, which focuses on the integration of Information and Communications Technology (ICT) into the course format. Our point of departure for developing the course is blending online and classroom learning. In order to fully meet the Danish language needs of the knowledge workers, one essential aspect to reflect on is that of authenticity in language learning, for instance authentic input aimed at specific academic purposes. The notion of authenticity in language learning is a many-faceted concept (Gilmore, 2007; Pinner, 2014); depending on what aspects of language learning you focus on, authenticity may relate to the input, the tasks, or the social situation of the classroom. In order to become part of the workplace, investment (Norton & Toohey, 2011) in Danish language learning is an important keyword. The course participants invest time and energy into learning Danish, and the workplace ideally invests time and money in the employees' language learning with the aim of integrating the employees both socially and professionally.

Keywords: needs analyses, user-driven learning, authentic and personalised input, investment, multimodal CALL.

---

1. University of Copenhagen, Denmark; nkd633@hum.ku.dk; pcq855@hum.ku.dk

How to cite this article: Frederiksen, K.-M., & Laursen, K. Å. (2015). Developing and evaluating a multimodal course format: Danish for knowledge workers – labour market-related Danish. In F. Helm, L. Bradley, M. Guarda, & S. Thouësny (Eds), *Critical CALL – Proceedings of the 2015 EUROCALL Conference, Padova, Italy* (pp. 186-191). Dublin: Research-publishing.net. http://dx.doi.org/10.14705/rpnet.2015.000331

1. Introduction

The CALL course *Danish for knowledge workers – labour market-related Danish* was initiated as part of the European Social Fund project: Copenhagen Talent Bridge (CTB[2] 2012-2014). The overall aim of CTB has been to "create a regional platform and regional collaboration in order to attract and retain international talents and their families to the Capital Region of Denmark"[3]. Our part, i.e. the Centre for Internationalisation and Parallel Language Use[4] (CIP), University of Copenhagen, in the project (Work Package 3.1) has been to develop and offer a Danish course for international knowledge workers on the basis of needs analyses. In the project period we have decided a course layout of 250 lessons: 5 modules of 50 lessons.

We have managed to negotiate funding so that the course can continue after the project period. Accordingly, our course has to meet specific requirements from the Ministry of Education regarding the content: general Danish which can be used in everyday life, work-related Danish and matters in relation to work environment, work culture and safety. Likewise we have to meet some administrative requirements, including a final test.

2. Method

The evaluation presented in this paper is part of a bigger needs analysis (Long, 2005), and is based on an online questionnaire distributed by email to all present and former participants of the course in June 2014. Prior to distributing the questionnaire we tested it on a number of informants.

As already discussed in Laursen and Frederiksen (2015),

> "The questionnaire was sent out to 167 participants [...], from which we received 71 replies: 57 completed, and 14 partly answered. We have given each respondent a number, for example R. 33.
>
> The questionnaire consists of four parts. The first three parts consist primarily of closed questions, while part four has open-ended questions.

---

2. Copenhagen Talent Bridge: http://talentcapacity.org/copenhagen-talent-bridge/

3. Retrieved from http://talentcapacity.org/copenhagen-talent-bridge/

4. For more information: http://cip.ku.dk/english/

Part one contains questions regarding personal information: nationality, age, gender and mother tongue. Part two deals with language competences in Danish and other languages. This part includes the self-assessment grid from CEFR and information on the course module the respondents are currently attending. Part three covers Danish language needs and use at the workplace, specifically regarding academic tasks, practical tasks and socialising at work. Furthermore, we ask about the respondents' position at the workplace, duration of their stay, and who they speak Danish with. Part four is focused on the respondents' experience with the course. They evaluate and reflect on the course format and their learning process. The questions regard the combination of face-to-face learning and online lessons, learning outcome from online feedback, learning outcome from submitting revised versions of texts, the usefulness and relevance of the overall input, and finally to what extent their suggestions regarding content and structure of the course are being heard" (p. 63).

3. Discussion

The aspects of the evaluation regarding the course format which we find most interesting are

- relevance and usefulness of the input;
- combining face-to-face learning and online lessons;
- investment in the participants' Danish language learning.

3.1. Relevance and usefulness of the input

In order to develop the course further we asked the following question: do you think the input (material used in face-to-face learning and online lessons) is useful and relevant? Please specify (Figure 1).

Figure 1. Percentage of responses to relevance and usefulness of the input

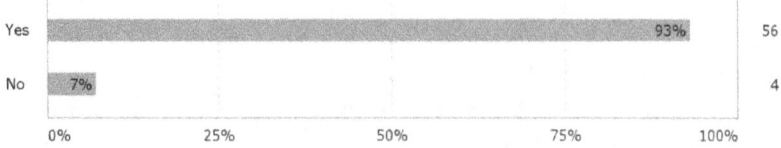

Examples of comments relating to the answer "Yes"

> "most topics are useful in every-day-conservations and at the workplace – I appreciate this very much" (R.13).

> "It is very practical, it refers to situations that you frequently encounter in daily life" (R. 51)

> "but again: I would prefer a textbook" (R. 29).

> "but more structured would be even better" (R. 33).

Figure 1 shows that 93 % of the respondents (N=60) agree that the input is relevant and useful. The comments are very valuable to us because they show where we can develop the input further. The respondents find that the input meets their needs in their everyday lives at the workplace and in other contexts. But their answers also reveal that we have not been clear enough about the course format. Several respondents remark that they would like more structure content wise, e.g. having a textbook.

In response to these findings, we do now give the participants more explicit information about the course format. Furthermore, we are creating a course website on the university's intranet, which allows us to structure the material more clearly and in a more user-friendly form. We need to emphasise that the course is user-driven in that we encourage the participants to bring new words, topics and input such as e-mails and minutes from meetings in order to personalise their Danish language learning. By doing so we hope to create a course, which the participants regard as authentic and useful. Following this learning principle means that the input is more flexible and dynamic than the input in a static textbook. Thus, as well as providing more structure, having a course website also gives the learners and teachers a flexible learning space.

3.2. Combining face-to-face learning and online lessons

We are also interested in knowing the participants' view on the course format, i.e. how we combine face-to-face learning and online lessons because it is what we regard as one of the guiding principles in the course design. Therefore we asked this open-ended question: what do you think of the combination of face-to-face learning and online lessons (including KungFuWriting, Dropbox, websites, audio files, videos, etc.)? Please specify.

Examples of answers to the question:

> "I think the combination is good. Most of us have a lot to do, so the online lessons give the freedom to do the assignments whenever you have time" (R. 29).

> "So far is better than other language learning experiences. It is very positive that this course is tailored to the specific needs and profile of the group" (R.10).

Most of the respondents are satisfied with the combination of face-to-face learning and online lessons. R.10 emphasises the fact that the course is tailor-made to this specific target group. An example is that we make use of authentic texts from the workplace, including video and audio files. However, based on the answers we will work towards integrating more oral interaction activities both in the classroom, in the workplace and online.

3.3. Investment in the participants' Danish language learning

Throughout the answers and comments in the questionnaire it is clear that the respondents would prefer more opportunities to speak and listen to Danish. Besides integrating more oral interaction into the material, we will recommend the workplace to create opportunities for their international employees to speak and listen to Danish in a safe environment. An option could be to allocate time to a Danish speaking employee, for instance, half an hour per week to chat with the international employee.

4. Conclusions

Overall the respondents are very satisfied with the course input and with the combination of face-to-face learning and online lessons. They would like more structured input and more opportunities to speak and listen to Danish. Based on the information gained from the survey, we are now trying to integrate oral interaction into online learning, we have more oral interaction in class, and we discuss how to make all involved parties invest more in the Danish language learning.

References

Gilmore, A. (2007). Authentic materials and authenticity in foreign language learning. *Language Teaching, 40*(2), 97-118. doi:10.1017/S0261444807004144

Laursen, K. Å., & Frederiksen, K.-M. (2015). The notion of authenticity in the context of the course: Danish for knowledge workers. In J. Colpaert (Ed.), *CALL Journal Proceedings from Seventeenth International CALL Conference, Task design and CALL, 6.-8. July 2015.* Retrieved from http://wwwa.fundacio.urv.cat/congressos/public/usr_docs/call_2015_conference_proceedings.pdf

Long, M. H. (2005). *Second language needs analysis.* Cambridge: Cambridge University Press. doi:10.1017/CBO9780511667299

Norton, B., & Toohey, K. (2011). Identity, language learning, and social change (State-of-the-Art Article). *Language Teaching, 44*(4), 412-446. doi:10.1017/S0261444811000309

Pinner, R. (2014). The authenticity continuum: towards a definition incorporating international voices. *English Today, 30*(4), 22-27 doi:10.1017/S0266078414000364

Tracking student retention in open online language courses

Kolbrún Friðriksdóttir[1] and Birna Arnbjörnsdóttir[2]

Abstract. Many scholars call for more diverse data on learners´ behaviour in CALL (Colpaert, 2012; Fischer, 2007, 2012; Stockwell, 2012). Student retention and the inconclusive efficacy of online language courses (Gaebel, 2013) has received increased attention with the proliferation of MOOCs (Koller, Ng, Do & Chen, 2013). In this paper we introduce initial findings of tracking data over an eight year period on forty-three thousand learners' progression through the seven courses of *Icelandic Online*, an open, guided online course in Icelandic as a second/foreign language. Preliminary findings indicate low course completion rates, from 2.4% to 18.2%, that vary across courses and seem to cluster around certain junctures in the course content. Results show that retention varies according to mode of delivery (Harker & Koutsantoni, 2005), with the blended learning mode (self-directed learning on campus with a tutor) as most effective in retaining students, followed by the distance learning mode (self-directed learning outside campus with a tutor). Retention is lowest among self-directed students learning outside the context of formal education. These findings raise questions about factors that motivate retention in online courses, which appear to be not only the modes of delivery but also the course content.

Keywords: tracking data, student retention, different modes of delivery, Icelandic Online.

---

1. The University of Iceland, Reykjavík, Iceland; kolbrunf@hi.is

2. The University of Iceland, Reykjavík, Iceland; birnaarn@hi.is

How to cite this article: Friðriksdóttir, K., & Arnbjörnsdóttir, B. (2015). Tracking student retention in open online language courses. In F. Helm, L. Bradley, M. Guarda, & S. Thouësny (Eds), *Critical CALL – Proceedings of the 2015 EUROCALL Conference, Padova, Italy* (pp. 192-197). Dublin: Research-publishing.net. http://dx.doi.org/10.14705/rpnet.2015.000332

1. Introduction

Icelandic Online (IOL) is a website that offers seven courses in Icelandic as a second/foreign language. The courses are open and free to users. Great effort was taken to design 'plot-driven' courses, that is, created around storylines related to everyday lives of university students, and based on 'relevant' SLA principles (Arnbjörnsdóttir, 2004; Chapelle, 1998). The first courses were launched in 2004 and approximately 140,000 visitors have logged on to the website. Of those, 43,000 have been active learners on one or more of the courses. The website is maintained by the University of Iceland and has had a great impact on access to Icelandic (Friðriksdóttir, 2015; Hafsteinsson et al, 2013).

Since 2006, we have been tracking students' behaviour online. The purpose of the tracking is to establish who is using the website, to map out learner's behaviour as they progress through the courses, and to determine the efficacy of the course materials, whether the pedagogic principles that guided the course development process have led to language acquisition. The study of retention in online courses and the inconclusive results regarding their efficacy (completion rates ranging from 2 to 10 percent) has received attention recently due to the proliferation of Massive Open Online Courses (MOOCs). Koller et al. (2013) have questioned whether retention is the right metric by which to measure success in online courses and argue that retention should be considered within the context of student intent.

The effectiveness of different modes of learning has also been a focal point with findings showing that the blended learning mode is more effective in terms of student retention than the distance learning mode (Harker & Koutsantoni, 2005). Fischer (2007) calls for diverse data on students' actual behaviour while engaged in language learning online. Stockwell (2012) and Colpaert (2012) suggest that the Computer Assisted Language Learning (CALL) knowledge base may be too reliant on 1) researchers studying their own and their students' use of technology and 2) surveys of what learners say they do online. There are fewer studies on what learners actually do while studying language through computers (including mobile devices). This is one such study. This article describes initial findings from an analysis of eight years of collected tracking data from forty-three thousand users of *Icelandic Online*.

2. Method

The main objective in this initial phase of the study was to retrieve demographic information about users, tabulate overall retention rates for all courses, and to examine specifically the effect of different modes of delivery on retention. Available modes were: open courses (without any intervention), distance non-credit bearing courses with a tutor, and blended courses where Icelandic Online serves as part of face to face credit bearing courses.

The demographic information is provided by users as they log in to the website. The retention data is collected through a tracker that is built into the software where the position of a user is tracked in each course by 'page'[3]. Each 'page' may include 3-6 learning objects. If a user takes multiple courses the system tracks user progression through all courses. All the data is stored in a database, and transferred to an SPSS statistics program for analysis.

3. Results

The registration data provide metrics on enrolment, gender ratio, age, educational background and geographic distribution for all visitors on *Icelandic Online* from 2006 to 2014 ($N=139,941$). Of those, 31% are active learners ($N=43,468$), that is to say, learners who went beyond eight activities in a course. In this study we focus exclusively on the active learners. The registration data reveal that 51% of *Icelandic Online's* active learners are female and 49% are male, 69% of the learners are under the age of 31 years, 54% of the learners have received a university's degree, and 63% come from ten countries of origin[4], leaving the rest scattered around the world.

The data reveal that the overall completion rates of the seven courses of Icelandic Online range from 2.4% to 18.2%. As part of an effort to break down retention data and better understand the nature and motivation of the high withdrawal rates, two *Icelandic Online* courses (IOL1 and IOL2) were examined. In the table below we compare the three different modes of delivery for completion of IOL1 and IOL2, showing from 2.9% to 8.3% completion rate in IOL1, and from 4.4% to 14.2% completion rate in IOL2.

In short, the study found significant differences in both courses between the three modalities in terms of student retention, with the blended learning mode proving to be much more effective in retention than the open learning and the distance learning mode. The results are presented in Table 1.

---

3. Page here is a reference to organisation of content and not to an actual page online.

4. The top ten countries are the US, Germany, Poland, the UK, France, Canada, Sweden, Norway, Spain, and Italy.

Table 1. Course completion in three different modes of delivery in *Icelandic Online 1* and *2*

	Icelandic Online 1			Icelandic Online 2		
Mode of Delivery	Open	Distance	Blended	Open	Distance	Blended
Completion %	2.9%	4%	8.3%	4.4%	4.8%	14.2%
N/total	189/6419	4/101	36/434	152/3462	3/62	40/281

Additionally, the tracking data revealed regular attrition patterns across all modes of delivery in both courses. Figure 1 shows the concentrations of drop-outs at certain junctures in the course (IOL2). The concentration of drop-outs at these particular junctures may have several explanations that will be discussed in the next section.

Figure 1. Attrition pattern in three different modes of delivery in *Icelandic Online 2*

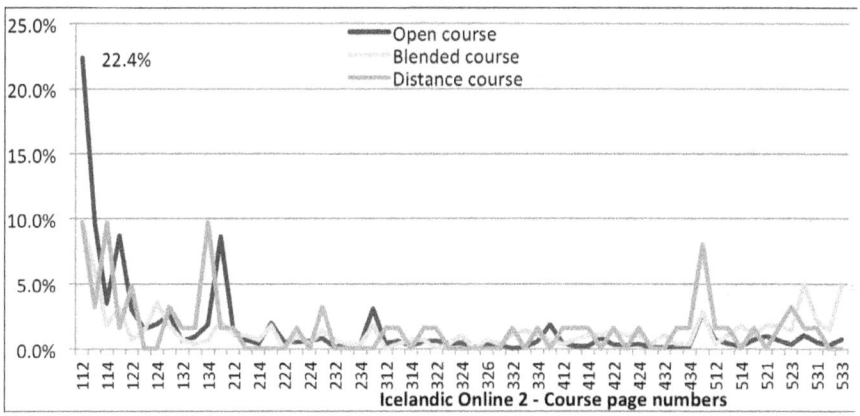

4. Discussion

The results of the tracking data presented above resonate with findings on student retention in MOOCs where overall completion rates are low (Gaebel, 2013), and attrition rates are highest at the very beginning of courses (Reich, 2014). Our data clearly demonstrates that blended learning is most effective in keeping students in courses. As shown in Figure 1, in one of the courses examined specifically in this study (IOL2) all three modes have large drop-out rates at the beginning of the course, on the first three 'pages' (112-114). Bundles of drop-outs are not as consistent as students advance in the course. Furthermore, Figure 1 presents an interesting perspective in that although the drop-out rates appear in bundles at certain junctures, there are also many sections where learners do not leave. This applies across modes of delivery. At this point we do not know whether these bundles of drop-outs (or retentions) are related to course content, types of learning objects/technology, learning objectives, student intent, or other personal reasons.

5. Conclusions

This study raised more questions than it answered. We are in the beginning stages of a mixed method research project. The aim is to gather as much data as possible on whether the pedagogical goals and objectives that guided the development of *Icelandic Online* have led to language acquisition. In the next phase of this research, the factors influencing learners' decisions to withdraw or persist in a course will be explored further. The difference between the blended learning mode and the other two modalities in terms of retention as well as the reasons for the bundles of drop-out and persistence will be investigated further. This will be the focus of the next phase of this study where evidence from students' self-reports in the form of surveys and interviews will be explored.

6. Acknowledgements

We would like to thank Jozef Colpaert for his helpful comments.

References

Arnbjörnsdóttir, B. (2004). Teaching morphologically complex languages online: theoretical questions and practical answers. In P. J. Henrichsen (Ed.), *Call for the Nordic Languages. Tools and Methods for Computer Assisted Language Learning* (pp. 79-94). Copenhagen Studies in Language 30. Copenhagen: Samfundslitteratur.

Chapelle, C. A. (1998). Multimedia CALL: lessons to be learned from research on instructed SLA. *Language Learning and Technology, 2*(1), 22-34.

Colpaert, J. (2012). The "publish and perish" syndrome. *Computer Assisted Language Learning, 25*(5), 383-391. doi:10.1080/09588221.2012.735101

Fischer, R. (2007). How do we know what students are actually doing? Monitoring Students' behavior in CALL. *Computer Assisted Language Learning, 20*(5), 409-442. doi:10.1080/09588220701746013

Fischer, R. (2012). Diversity in learner usage patterns. In G. Stockwell (Ed.), *Computer-assisted language learning: diversity in research and practice* (pp. 14-32). Cambridge: Cambridge University Press.

Friðriksdóttir, K. (2015). Styðjandi námsumhverfi Icelandic Online [e. Icelandic Online – enhancing vocabulary L2 learning and reading comprehension]. *Frændafundur, 8*. Tórshavn: University of the Faroe Islands (in press).

Gaebel, M. (2013). MOOCs – Massive Open Online Courses. *European University Association*. Retrieved from http://www.eua.be/News/130225/Massive_Open_Online_Courses_MOOCs_EUA_to_look_at_development_of_MOOCs_and_trends_in_innovative_learning.aspx

Hafsteinsson, H., Rögnvaldsson, E., Freysteinsdóttir, F., Geirsdóttir, G., Ómarsdóttir, S., Jakobsdóttir, S. et al. (2013). *Skýrsla starfshóps háskólaráðs um vefstudda kennslu og nám* [e. Report commissioned by the University Governing Board for the University of Iceland on Computer Assisted Teaching and Learning]. Reykjavík: University of Iceland. Retrieved from http://www.hi.is/sites/default/files/admin/meginmal/skjol/mooc_skyrsla_endanleg_mai2013_4.pdf

Harker, M., & Koutsantoni, D. (2005). Can it be as effective? Distance versus blended learning in a web-based EAP programme. *ReCALL, 17*(2), 197-216. doi:10.1017/S095834400500042X

Koller, D., Ng, A., Do, C., & Chen, Z. (2013). Retention and intention in massive open online courses: in depth. *EDUCAUSE Review*. Retrieved from http://www.educause.edu/ero/article/retention-and-intention-massive-open-online-courses-depth-0

Reich, J. (2014). MOOC completion and retention in the context of student intent. *EDUCAUSE Review*. Retrieved from http://www.educause.edu/ero/article/mooc-completion-and-retention-context-student-intent

Stockwell, G. (Ed.). (2012). *Computer-assisted language learning: diversity in research and practice*. Cambridge: Cambridge University Press.

Implementing verbal and non-verbal activities in an intercultural collaboration project for English education

Kiyomi Fujii[1] and Maki Hirotani[2]

Abstract. Technological development offers language teachers a myriad of options for collaborative activities. Learners, in turn, benefit from increased opportunities to interact with people who can speak their target language. Research has previously highlighted the importance of developing learners' intercultural competence through such activities. The researchers implemented verbal and non-verbal activities in an intercultural collaboration project for learners of English in Japan and learners of Japanese in the U.S. This paper will detail the project activities and provide a comprehensive summary of the results, especially as they pertain to interaction with native speakers of the target language to develop verbal and non-verbal communication skills.

Keywords: EFL, intercultural competence, verbal and non-verbal.

1. Introduction

With recent developments in Internet technology, many collaborative activities between native and non-native speakers have been conducted in foreign language classrooms (Belz, 2007; Jauregi & Canto, 2012; Jin, 2013; Kitade, 2008; O'Dowd, 2005). Previous studies have examined the effects of such collaborative activities and reported positive effects on the development of language skills (Belz, 2007; Jauregi & Canto, 2012; Jin, 2013; Kitade, 2008; Tudini, 2007). Researchers have also identified the importance of developing learners' intercultural competence

---

1. Kanazawa Institute of Technology, Nonoichi, Japan; kfujii@neptune.kanazawa-it.ac.jp
2. Rose-Hulman Institute of Technology, Terre Haute, Indiana, United States; hirotani@rose-hulman.edu

How to cite this article: Fujii, K., & Hirotani, M. (2015). Implementing verbal and non-verbal activities in an intercultural collaboration project for English education. In F. Helm, L. Bradley, M. Guarda, & S. Thouësny (Eds), *Critical CALL – Proceedings of the 2015 EUROCALL Conference, Padova, Italy* (pp. 198-203). Dublin: Research-publishing.net. http://dx.doi.org/10.14705/rpnet.2015.000333

through such activities. According to the Association of American Colleges and Universities (AACU), intercultural knowledge and competence is "a set of cognitive, affective, and behavioral skills and characteristics that support effective and appropriate interaction in a variety of cultural contexts" (n. p.), which can be classified into two types of cultural knowledge (self-awareness and worldview frameworks), two types of skills (empathy and verbal/non-verbal communication), and two types of attitudes (curiosity and openness). Within the above classification, the skills of verbal and non-verbal communication are what we commonly think pertains to the study of language. It follows, then, that both verbal and non-verbal communication skills be assessed in detail, yet no study to date has investigated the development of both of these skills through collaborative activities.

In an effort to bolster this area of inquiry, the researchers brought together English as a Foreign Language (EFL) learners from a university in Japan, and Japanese as a Foreign Language (JFL) learners from a U.S. university in a collaborative online environment. Rather than a proprietary, locked system, we opted for Facebook as our platform of choice to engage both groups of students in verbal and non-verbal activities. In this paper, we will detail the aforementioned activities using the student-created video skit data from Facebook.

2. Method

2.1. Overview of the project

Twenty students enrolled in an English course at a private college in Japan (KIT) and ten students enrolled in second-year Japanese courses at a private college in the U.S. (RH) were involved in this project. The project was conducted from September, 2014 to February, 2015, lasting over four months during KIT fall semester and RH fall and winter semesters. We created two types of private Facebook pages for the project, where students communicated exclusively in English or Japanese. The students at each institution were divided into four groups (A, B, C, and D) and worked within their group to complete the assignments. The verbal and non-verbal activity was implemented in this Facebook project in two phases: (1) introduction of verbal and non-verbal expressions to students' overseas counterparts in their native language and (2) creation of skits that incorporate the learned expressions.

2.2. Materials

Students were surveyed before and after the project with a set of questionnaires to self-evaluate the development of their verbal and non-verbal communication knowledge and skills, as well as attitudes toward other cultures with reference to the AACU rubric for knowledge and skills (Elola & Oskoz, 2008). A reflection log of students' views of the activities and a vocabulary quiz were compiled to assess their comprehension of the verbal and non-verbal expressions. At the end of the semester, KIT students took the quiz, which consisted of ten verbal expressions ("break a leg", "awesome", etc.), and five non-verbal expressions (e.g. "crossed fingers") that the RH students introduced. In the vocabulary quiz, students were also asked to indicate whether they knew the expressions before their participation in the project. Facebook videos and posted comments were also analyzed to gauge students' verbal and non-verbal communication.

2.3. Verbal and non-verbal activities

A number of video assignments were given on specific topics: (1) self-introduction, (2) school life, (3) introducing verbal and non-verbal communication, (4) skit, and (5) culture survey.

Figure 1. RH student video introducing verbal and non-verbal expressions on Facebook

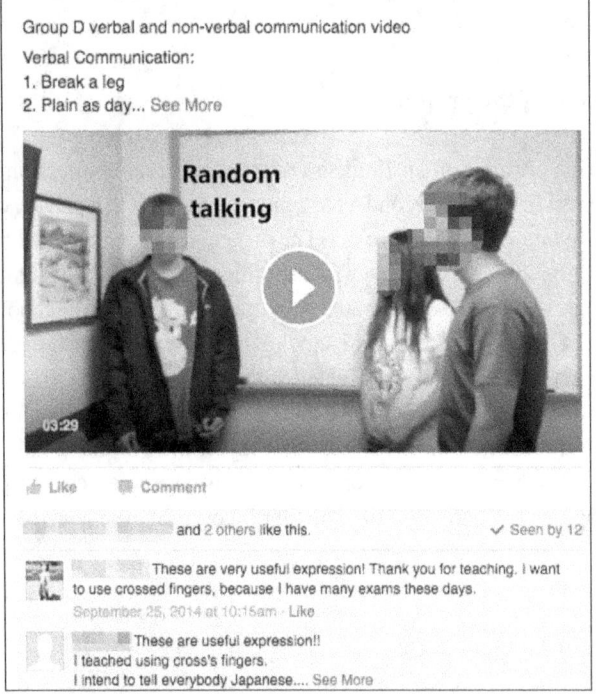

Students then posted the videos created in their groups on Facebook. For verbal and non-verbal activities, RH students in the U.S. introduced verbal expressions to KIT students, commonly used by American college students but not easily found in EFL textbooks, as well as non-verbal expressions, including body language and gestures (Figure 1). Each group member was charged with introducing one expression and one gesture. The general procedure was as follows: one student introduces a verbal communication expression while showing a flashcard of the expression in their first language. After repeating the expression a few times, the student explains the meaning of the expression and how it can be used, the student and his/her group members provide a short skit to demonstrate the use of the verbal expression in natural conversation, the student shows one gesture without speaking. After showing the same gesture a couple of times, the student explains the meaning of the gesture and its use, and the student and his/her group members provide a short skit illustrating the use of the non-verbal expression in natural conversation.

Figure 2. KIT students video skit on Facebook

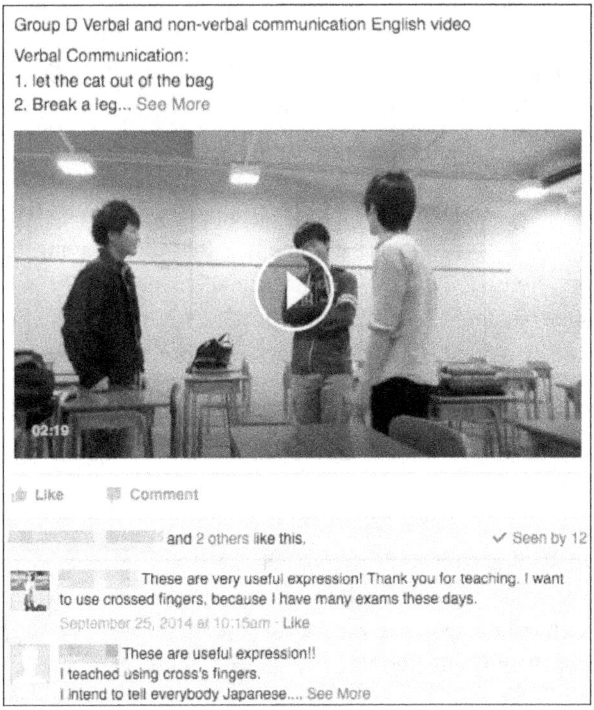

After KIT students watched the videos uploaded by their RH counterparts, we conducted vocabulary activities to reinforce the learners' vocabulary building in class. Handouts of all verbal and non-verbal expressions that were introduced by RH students were provided for the in-class activity, along with slide presentations to practice expressions. Then, students created skits in English using the newly learned verbal and non-verbal expressions. Students were required to incorporate at least five verbal expressions and five non-verbal expressions into their video skits, and post the videos to the English page on Facebook. The students were given the freedom to choose any topic for their skits, but were prohibited from simply reading off a prepared script during the recording. Conversely, the verbal and non-verbal expressions introduced by the KIT students to their U.S. peers were also used in RH students' skits in Japanese for reinforcement (Figure 2).

3. Results and discussion

The questionnaire results indicate that KIT students felt that they gained knowledge and skills for both verbal and non-verbal communication (Hirotani & Fujii, 2015, this volume). The students' comments from the reflection log support this result. It is evident through their self-evaluations that through this project, students grew aware of the differences and similarities between Japanese and American verbal and non-verbal expressions. In the results from the vocabulary quiz, approximately 88% of the items were new words for the students and 61.7% of the non-verbal expressions were previously unknown. Students stated that in English classes or textbooks they learn formal expressions, but this activity allowed them to learn casual expressions that American college students normally use. A few students also commented that after having learned useful everyday expressions, they now want to use them personally and teach them to other Japanese students. Finally, the reflection log reveals that the follow-up vocabulary activity helped students to understand not just the words themselves, but also the context in which they can be used in daily situations. Overall, the response was highly positive.

4. Conclusion

We speculated that a collaborative project that took advantage of a platform familiar to most students, and that focused on verbal and non-verbal activities to improve intercultural competence would pay dividends precisely by putting groups of students from the respective target countries together virtually. To test this supposition, we conducted a project between EFL and JFL learners at colleges in Japan and the U.S., using Facebook. Although it is still early, the results described in the present paper indicate that those who participated in this collaborative project felt that they gained knowledge and skills in verbal and non-verbal communication.

These are partial results and call for more research, but the preliminary findings are encouraging.

References

AACU. *Intercultural knowledge and competence*. Retrieved from https://www.aacu.org/sites/default/files/files/VALUE/InterculturalKnowledge.pdf

Belz, J. A. (2007). The role of computer mediation in the instruction and development of L2 pragmatic competence. *Annual Review of Applied Linguistics, 27*, 45-75. doi:10.1017/s0267190508070037

Elola, I., & Oskoz, A. (2008). Blogging: fostering intercultural competence development in foreign language and study abroad context. *Foreign Language Annals, 41*(3), 454-477.

Hirotani, M., & Fujii, K. (2015). The integration of a three-year-long intercultural collaborative project into a foreign language classroom for the development of intercultural competence. In F. Helm, L. Bradley, M. Guarda, & S. Thouësny (Eds.), *Critical CALL - Proceedings of the 2015 EUROCALL Conference, Padova, Italy* (pp. 235-242). Dublin Ireland: Research-publishing.net. doi:10.14705/rpnet.2015.000339

Jauregi, K., & Canto, S. (2012). Impact of native-nonnative speaker interaction through video-web communication and Second Life on students' intercultural communicative competence. In L. Bradley & S. Thouësny (Eds), *CALL: Using, Learning, Knowing, EUROCALL Conference, Gothenburg, Sweden, 22-25 August 2012, Proceedings* (pp. 151-155). Dublin Ireland: Research-publishing.net. doi:10.14705/rpnet.2012.000043

Jin, L. (2013). Language development and scaffolding in a Sino-American telecollaborative project. *Language learning & Technology, 17*(2), 193-219.

Kitade, K. (2008). The role of offline metalanguage talk in asynchronous computer-mediated communication. *Language learning & Technology, 12*(1), 64-84.

O'Dowd, R. (2005). Negotiating sociocultural and institutional contexts: the case of Spanish-American telecollaboration. *Language and Intercultural Communication, 5*(1), 40-56. doi:10.1080/14708470508668882

Tudini, V. (2007). Negotiation and intercultural learning in Italian native speaker chat rooms. *The Modern Language Journal, 91*(4), 577-601. doi:10.1111/j.1540-4781.2007.00624.x

Graded lexicons: new resources for educational purposes and much more

Núria Gala[1], Mokhtar B. Billami[2], Thomas François[3], and Delphine Bernhard[4]

Abstract. Computational tools and resources play an important role for vocabulary acquisition. Although a large variety of dictionaries and learning games are available, few resources provide information about the complexity of a word, either for learning or for comprehension. The idea here is to use frequency counts combined with intra-lexical variables to account for the difficulty of a word. By using such predictors, we have built a lexical resource for French, ReSyf, where words are available with their word senses and their synonyms according to a complexity level. In this paper, we will present the methodology used to build the resource and we will discuss possible applications, from enhancing vocabulary acquisition to text simplification.

Keywords: iCALL, vocabulary acquisition, graded synonym lexicon, lexical complexity, text simplification.

1. Introduction

Computational tools and resources play an important role for vocabulary acquisition. Encouraged by the extensive use of mobile devices, recent intelligent Computer-Assisted Language Learning (iCALL) applications and platforms propose a large variety of learning games that offer challenging possibilities (see

---

1. Aix Marseille Université & LIF-CNRS, Marseille, France; nuria.gala@lif.univ-mrs.fr
2. Aix Marseille Université & LIF-CNRS, Marseille, France; mokhtar.billami@lif.univ-mrs.fr
3. CENTAL Université Catholique de Louvain, Louvain-la-Neuve, Belgium; thomas.francois@uclouvain.be
4. LiLPa, Université de Strasbourg, Strasbourg, France; dbernhard@unistra.fr

How to cite this article: Gala, N., Billami, M. B., François, T., & Bernhard, D. (2015). Graded lexicons: new resources for educational purposes and much more. In F. Helm, L. Bradley, M. Guarda, & S. Thouësny (Eds), *Critical CALL – Proceedings of the 2015 EUROCALL Conference, Padova, Italy* (pp. 204-209). Dublin: Research-publishing.net.
http://dx.doi.org/10.14705/rpnet.2015.000334

Cornillie, Thorne, & Desmet, 2012) compared to more traditional exercises which emphasize repetition (explicit learning[5]). Recent educational tools are These features were on modern pedagogical criteria, offering among other things hyperlinks to electronic dictionaries or concordancers. The information a student can find is related to word forms (morphology), word meanings (semantics, usage) and word patterns (syntax, collocations). These electronic resources may even offer information concerning the origins of the word, its particular usage (constructions), and typically related words (semantically or thematically, word-families).

However, very few tools provide information about the complexity of a word, either for learning or for comprehension (showing for example that 'monster' is a simpler term than its hyponyms 'phoenix' or 'behemoth', or that 'to walk' is easier than its synonyms 'to stroll' or 'to ramble'). Yet, the idea of using frequency counts as a proxy for word difficulty is not new: frequency word lists were built in the past, see for instance Thorndike (1921) and Gougenheim (1958).

The principle behind these lists is that the frequency of a word affects its recognition, thus its acquisition. Based on that principle, which basically relies on corpus-based features, some resources have been built where words are classified across difficulty levels: the English Profile Wordlists (Capel, 2010), or for French, Manulex (Lété, Sprenger-Charolles, & Colé, 2004) and FLELex (François, Gala, Watrin, & Fairon, 2014).

In this paper we introduce a new graded lexical resource for French synonyms, ReSyf, that relies on a large set of intra-lexical and psycholinguistic features to assign a grade level to each synonym. The resource was first introduced in Gala, François, Bernhard, and Fairon (2013), but the current version has been enhanced, especially as regards the possibility to discriminate between synsets of synonyms.

2. Methodology to build ReSyf

ReSyf[6] is a lexical database with graded word-senses containing 31,141 entries, extracted, filtered and annotated using different resources available for French. A

---

5. Explicit and implicit learning depends on the users' attention paid to the words (Ma & Kelly, 2006); exercises specifically focused on vocabulary (explicit learning) or activities where lexical acquisition rather occurs implicitly, as a side-effect: the student is repeatedly exposed to words, like in reading.

6. Retrieved from http://resyf.lif.univ-mrs.fr

predictive model based on lexical and psycholinguistic features related to lexical complexity (Gala et al., 2014) was used to assign grade levels to the entries and synonyms.

2.1. From words to word-senses

The entries were extracted from the list of concepts[7] in French from BabelNet 2.5.1 (Navigli & Ponzetto, 2012). As defined by Navigli and Ponzetto (2012), a "concept in [BabelNet] is represented as a synonym set (called *synset*)[: a] set of words that share the same meaning. For instance, the concept of play as a dramatic work is expressed by the following synset" *drame, jeu dramatique, pièce (théâtre), pièce de théâtre, texte dramatique, œuvre dramatique* (p. 218). Each concept was extracted with a list of associated weighted synsets. The weight of a synset corresponds to its semantic connections in BabelNet.

The list obtained at this stage was filtered with two French reference resources: Lexique 3 (New, Pallier, Ferrand, & Matos, 2001) and the Trésor de la Langue Française informatisé (TLFi) (Dendien & Pierrel, 2003). While BabelNet provided an important amount of data, the reference resources were used to validate the lexical items and to remove wrong items (words in languages other than French, orthographic errors, rare or domain-specific terms, etc.). The monosemic words without information from BabelNet were enriched with synonyms extracted from JeuxDeMots (Lafourcade, 2007).

All the words obtained were tagged with TreeTagger[8] (Schmid, 1994). As a result of the Part Of Speech (POS) tagging, we removed wrong lemmas and verified that all the synonyms of the synset had the same POS tag as the target word. When the concept appeared as a multiword expression or collocation, we kept the POS tag of the first item (i.e. noun for *texte dramatique*). Finally, when a concept appeared with a hypernym (i.e. *pièce – théâtre*) we verified that the hypernym was included in the domain list of JeuxDeMots[9] and we kept the hypernym as a synonym. The results obtained are reported in Table 1, while Table 2 presents the number of final words containing at least one synonym.

---

7. We are interested in the selection of the concepts without taking into account the presence of the named entities. We consider a concept as being a sense in the lexical network BabelNet (Navigli & Ponzetto, 2012).
8. TreeTagger, morphosyntactic annotation tool, retrieved from http://www.cis.uni-muenchen.de/~schmid/tools/TreeTagger/
9. There are 3,086 different domains in JeuxDeMots, version 05/2015.

Table 1. Number of target words in ReSyf filtered with Lexique 3 and TLFi

POS	One sense	Polysemic	Total
Nouns	15 482	16 825	32 307
Verbs	1 003	1 890	2 893
Adjectives	2 620	2 032	4 652
Adverbs	451	595	1 046
Total	19 556	21 342	40 898

Table 2. Number of target words in ReSyf for which each sense contains at least one synonym

Nouns	Verbs	Adjectives	Adverbs	Total
24 599	2 612	3 094	836	**31 141**

2.2. Word-senses graduation with a level of difficulty

The difficulty of the entries and the synonyms in ReSyf was established as the result of a twofold process. First, we gathered a "gold standard" list of about 19,000 frequent words in French having difficulty level information. This resource was obtained from Manulex by Gala et al. (2014), who transformed the frequency distribution across the three levels in Manulex into a single grade level.

In a second step, we trained a statistical model on this gold standard, using 49 intra-lexical and psycholinguistic features. The set of features is further detailed in Gala et al. (2014) and includes the number of letters, the number of phonemes, the number of syllables, the presence of specific spelling patterns, the syllabic structure, morphemic information, the number of meanings, frequency of the word in Lexique3, etc. These features were combined within a linear Support Vector Machine (SVM) model with L2 regularization[10]. The final model reached an accuracy of 63%, which was 2% better than the baseline relying only on frequency as a predictor, but still was not a satisfactory result for our purpose. As

---
[10]. The only metaparameter of this model is the cost, which was set to 0,5 as the result of a grid search between values of 100 and 0,001.

a consequence, in the building of ReSyf, our model was used only to assign grade level to words absent from Manulex. Otherwise, the level assigned was directly obtained from this resource.

Table 3 presents an example of an entry: the word *jeu* (game) with its POS tag and its grade. The list of graded synonyms has also a weight according to the relevance of the sense.

Table 3. Example of a ReSyf entry with different lists of synonyms

Target word	*Graded synonyms*
jeu_N_1	[partie_N_1, catch_N_3]+1425 [jeu de hasard_N_1, pari_N_1]+918 [drame_N_2, jeu dramatique_N_2, pièce (théâtre)_N_1, pièce de théâtre_N_1, texte dramatique_N_2, œuvre dramatique_N_3]+392 [casse-tête_N_3, puzzle_N_1]+392 [blague_N_1, bouffonnerie_N_1, farce_N_1, plaisanterie_N_1, tour_N_1]+345

3. Conclusion

In this paper, we have presented a graded lexicon for French synonyms where words account for a level of complexity calculated from frequency counts, intra-lexical and psycholinguistic features. While aimed at text simplification, this graded lexicon can also help learners of French to acquire vocabulary and to improve language acquisition. On the one hand, the lexicon itself can be used for explicit learning of French vocabulary guided by the different grades of the synonyms of a word. On the other hand, it can be used to carry out word substitution within an automatic text simplification system aiming at helping learners and children with reading impairments to get through a text, rediscovering the pleasure of reading (as they can better understand what they read), and thus entering a virtuous circle, whereby reading and decoding skills are trained through reading practice.

References

Capel, A. (2010). Insights and issues arising from the English Profile Wordlists project. *Research Notes, 41*, 2-7. Cambridge: Cambridge ESOL.

Cornillie, F., Thorne, S. L., & Desmet, P. (2012). Digital games for language learning: from hype to insight? *ReCALL*, 24(3), 243-256. doi:10.1017/S0958344012000134

Dendien, J., & Pierrel, J.-M. (2003). Le Trésor de la langue française informatisé : un exemple d'informatisation d'un dictionnaire de langue de référence. *Traitement Automatique des Langues, 44*(2), 11-37.

François T., Gala, N., Watrin, P., & Fairon, C. (2014). FLELex: a graded lexical resource for French foreign learners. *International conference on Language Resources and Evaluation (LREC 2014), poster session, Reykjavik, Iceland.*

Gala, N., François T., Bernhard, D., & Fairon, C. (2014). Un modèle pour prédire la complexité lexicale et graduer les mots. *Actes de Traitement Automatique des Langues Naturelles (TALN 2014), Marseille.*

Gougenheim, G. (1958). *Dictionnaire fondamental de la langue française.* Paris: Didier.

Lafourcade, M. (2007). Making people play for lexical acquisition. In *Proc. SNLP 2007, 7th Symposium on Natural Language Processing, Pattaya, Thailande.*

Lété, B., Sprenger-Charolles, L., & Colé, P. (2004). Manulex: a grade-level lexical database from French elementary-school readers. *Behavior Research Methods, Instruments & Computers, 36*(1), 156-166. doi:10.3758/BF03195560

Ma, Q. & Kelly, P. (2006). Computer assisted vocabulary learning: design and evaluation. *Computer Assisted Language Learning, 19*(1), 15-45. doi:10.1080/09588220600803998

Navigli, R., & Ponzetto, S. P. (2012). BabelNet: the automatic construction, evaluation and application of a wide-coverage multilingual semantic network. *Artificial Intelligence, 193,* 217-250. doi:10.1016/j.artint.2012.07.001

New, G. A., Pallier, C., Ferrand, L., & Matos, R. (2001). Une base de données lexicales du français contemporain sur Internet : lexique 3. *L'année psychologique, 101,* 447-462. doi:10.3406/psy.2001.1341

Schmid, H. (1994). Probabilistic part-of-speech tagging using decision trees. *Proceedings of International Conference on New Methods in Language Processing, Manchester, UK.*

Thorndike, E. (1921). *The teacher's word book.* New York: Columbia University.

Podcast-mediated language learning: levels of podcast integration and developing vocabulary knowledge

Mahboubeh Gholami[1] and Mojtaba Mohammadi[2]

Abstract. Podcasting is being exploited incrementally by teachers as a tool for presenting educational content and encouraging language learning outside traditional classrooms. This paper reports on an investigation of three levels of podcast integration sustaining on the Iranian learner's lexical knowledge learning English as a Foreign Language (EFL). The learners were divided into three groups with high, low, and no integration of podcast into their syllabus. Data were collected from vocabulary pre- and post-tests administered to the sample: 90 intermediate students between 20 and 30 years old. The findings of the study indicated that there were statistically significant differences between groups with podcast integration and the one with no integration regarding their lexical knowledge in the way that the former outperformed the latter. The findings revealed that the improvement of the students in the high integration group is more than in the low integration group. On administering an attitude survey before and after the project, we found that they unanimously preferred podcasts as an interesting pedagogical tool.

Keywords: podcast, English vocabulary, integration, attitude.

---

1. English Language Teaching Department, Faculty of Persian Literature and Foreign Languages, Roudehen Branch, Islamic Azad University, Roudehen, Iran; gholami.m2011@yahoo.com

2. English Language Teaching Department, Faculty of Persian Literature and Foreign Languages, Roudehen Branch, Islamic Azad University, Roudehen, Iran; m.mohammadi@riau.ac.ir; mojtabamohammadi@gmail.com

How to cite this article: Gholami, M., & Mohammadi, M. (2015). Podcast-mediated language learning: levels of podcast integration and developing vocabulary knowledge. In F. Helm, L. Bradley, M. Guarda, & S. Thouësny (Eds), *Critical CALL – Proceedings of the 2015 EUROCALL Conference, Padova, Italy* (pp. 210-214). Dublin: Research-publishing.net. http://dx.doi.org/10.14705/rpnet.2015.000335

1. Introduction

Before technology expansion, teachers used to teach vocabularies through methods such as translation, synonym and antonym, memorization, picture exploitation, and definition. But, with the emergence of computer-assisted language learning, there has been a growing interest to integrate technology in the process of language learning.

Podcasts offer "language learners with samples of real language and authentic materials (Thorne & Payne, 2005). [They can be used] as a supplement to their textbook materials (Stanley, 2007)" (Hasan & Hoon, 2013, p. 129). Hasan and Hoon (2013, p. 129) further point out that Warschauer and Healey (1998) underlined the integration of podcasts as providing language learners with real, meaningful, authentic situations. This has also been theoretically supported by the socio-cognitive view of language learning which emphasizes real language use in a meaningful, authentic context.

Podcasting is being exploited incrementally by teachers for presenting educational content and encouraging language learning outside traditional classrooms. As mentioned by Hasan and Hoon (2013),

> "[r]esearch studies on podcasting have already acknowledged its potentiality and have documented much evidence that podcasts can greatly help develop learners' language skills, especially in developing learners' speaking and listening skills (e.g. Ashton-Hay & Brookes, 2011; O'Bryan & Hegelheimer, 2007)" (p. 128).

The results of the study by Evans (2008) indicated

> "that students believe that podcasts are more effective revision tools than their textbooks and they are more efficient than their own notes in helping them to learn. They also indicate that they are more receptive to the learning material in the form of a podcast than a traditional lecture or textbook" (p. 491).

Tan, Lim, and Goh (2013) also showed that the use of podcasts as a learning tool was beneficial and podcast-based learning can be implemented as one of the creative ways to teach or learn a foreign language. Ducate and Lomicka (2009), however, concluded that students' pronunciation through making podcasts did not significantly improve with regards to accentedness or comprehensibility, although the attitudes changed toward pronunciation over the semester.

The major purpose of the study is to find out the impact of three levels of podcast integration on sustaining the Iranian EFL learner's vocabulary knowledge. The learners' attitude toward weekly podcast-based tasks was also investigated.

2. Method

2.1. Participants

To accomplish the purpose of the present research, 120 students who were taking English classes at Shokouh English language institute in Tehran were selected. The age of the participants ranged from 20 to 30 years. After analyzing the data from the proficiency test, 90 participants were equally divided into three groups of 30 students. Simple random sampling was used to put the students in three groups with high, low, and no integration of podcasts into their syllabus.

2.2. Procedure

In order to conduct the research and to fulfill the purpose of the study, the following steps were taken. The Nelson language proficiency test was administered to the subjects to find out the homogeneity of the students regarding their English language proficiency. After data analysis, 60 participants whose scores were at the modified percentile level were selected as two experimental groups and 30 as a control group.

In the high integration group with 30 participants, learners were required to listen to audio files from online podcasts and were expected to do some podcast-based tasks such as recording a dialogue or monologue content using new vocabulary items from the podcast files which were introduced and taught by the teacher. Learners were first required to make their own recorded audio files using the new words. Then, they were supposed to listen to podcasts created by other learners regularly and leave comments for them. On the other hand, the learners of the low integration experimental group were allowed to have access to podcast audio files and listen to them if they wanted. But they were not required to do the recording task or to comment on the podcast audio files.

The third group with 30 learners was considered as the control group (no integration group). In the no integration group, learners only listened to files in the classroom as their listening comprehension task. Their listening process did not deviate from the conventional listening process; that is, they only had access to podcast files as a CD package.

An achievement vocabulary test was designed by the researchers for pre-test and post-test. It consisted of 50 multiple choice items to measure their vocabulary knowledge and was administered before and after the treatment sessions in all three groups.

In both high and low integration groups, an attitude survey was also administered at the beginning and end of the semester in order to find how much students' attitude toward the use of podcast in class changed.

3. Discussion

The main concern of this study was to investigate whether or not the podcast integration had any significant positive effects on EFL learner's vocabulary knowledge. To assure and determine any significant change in the vocabulary knowledge of our subjects, after receiving the treatments, the performance results of each group were analyzed applying one way ANOVA.

The results of the analysis reveal that podcast integration significantly improved the learners' knowledge of vocabulary. Besides, the attitudes of the students toward the use of podcast in class turned out to be more positive. The findings are consistent with Rosell-Aguilar (2007), who stated that podcasts as one of the helpful means of language learning in the class should be encouraged since bringing podcasts and social media into language learning courses can lift learning to a whole new level.

Moreover, the results of this paper concerning the manipulation of podcast in increasing the personal abilities of the language learners is in accordance with the findings of Onsrud (2009), who acknowledged that the exploitation of podcasting as a delivery tool compared to the traditional in-class presentation establishes a learner-centered environment which encourages an active real-life communication.

4. Conclusions

The results revealed a significant increase in the performance of subjects in the integration of podcasting. It is believed that learners who had more contact with mobile learning through podcasting were more motivated to learn the language. The improvements can also be partly due to the fact that students are more attracted by the glamour of the online atmosphere. Also, it suggests that technologies of this type can provide opportunities for the learners to learn at their own pace.

References

Ashton-Hay, S., & Brookes, D. (2011). Here's a story: using student podcasts to raise awareness of language learning strategies. *EA Journal, 26*(2), 15-27.

Ducate, L., & Lomicka, L. (2009). Podcasting: an effective tool for honing language student's pronunciation. *Language Learning and Technology, 13*(3), 66-86.

Evans, E. (2008). The effectiveness of m-learning in the form of podcast revision lectures in higher education. *Computers and Education, 50*(2), 491-498. doi:10.1016/j.compedu.2007.09.016

Hasan, M., & Hoon, T. B. (2013). Podcast applications in language learning: a review of recent studies. *English Language Teaching, 6*(2), 128-135. doi:10.5539/elt.v6n2p128

O'Bryan, A., & Hegelheimer, V. (2007). Integrating CALL into the classroom: the role of podcasting in an ESL listening strategies course. *ReCALL, 19*(2), 162-180. doi:10.1017/S0958344007000523

Onsrud, E. M. (2009). *Podcasting in the foreign language classroom: improving communication.* Unpublished Master's thesis. University of Wisconsin-Stout, Menomonie, Wisconsin.

Rosell-Aguilar, F. (2007). Top of the pods - in search of podcasting "pedagogy" for language learning. *Computer Assisted Language Learning, 20*(5), 471-492. doi:10.1080/09588220701746047

Stanley, G. (2007). Podcasting ELT: a new way to reach students and colleagues. *Electronic Village Online*. Retrieved from http://webpages.csus.edu/~hansonsm/podcasting.html

Tan, T. G., Lim, T. H., & Goh, C. S. (2013). Developing a Mandarin learning podcast for flexible learning. *Journal of Creative Practices in Language Learning and Teaching, 1*(1), 61-76.

Thorne, S., & Payne, J. (2005). Evolutionary trajectories, internet-mediated expression, and language education. *CALICO, 22*(3), 371-397.

Warschauer, M., & Healey, D. (1998). Computers and language learning: an overview. *Language Teaching, 31*(2), 57-71. doi:10.1017/S0261444800012970

Toward implementing computer-assisted foreign language assessment in the official Spanish University Entrance Examination

Ana Gimeno Sanz[1] and Ana Sevilla Pavón[2]

Abstract. In 2008 the Spanish Government announced the inclusion of an oral section in the foreign language exam of the National University Entrance Examination during the year 2012 (Royal Decree 1892/2008, of 14 November 2008, Ministerio de Educación, Gobierno de España, 2008). Still awaiting the implementation of these changes, and in an attempt to offer the Government a cost-effective technological solution, the CAMILLE Research Group at Universidad Politécnica de Valencia set about creating an online language examination platform complying with the official examination parameters based on the *InGenio* Learning Management System. Once the system had been created, the researchers implemented several test exams and conducted a pilot study with 183 high school students. The quantitative analysis of the study shed light on the learners' attitudes toward using such a system in the context of a high stakes examination.

Keywords: oral assessment, Spanish university entrance examination, *InGenio* learning management system.

1. Introduction

Over the last few years, the use of technology in education has brought about changes in teaching and learning materials and methodologies. Assessment too has

---

1. Universitat Politècnica de València, Spain; agimeno@upvnet.upv.es
2. Universitat de València, Spain; ansepa@upvnet.upv.es

How to cite this article: Gimeno Sanz, A., & Sevilla Pavón, A. (2015). Toward implementing computer-assisted foreign language assessment in the official Spanish University Entrance Examination. In F. Helm, L. Bradley, M. Guarda, & S. Thouësny (Eds), *Critical CALL – Proceedings of the 2015 EUROCALL Conference, Padova, Italy* (pp. 215-220). Dublin: Research-publishing.net. http://dx.doi.org/10.14705/rpnet.2015.000336

been affected by these changes, and among the official exams that are currently working on offering a computerised version is the Spanish University Entrance Examination (in Spanish, *Prueba de Acceso a la Universidad - PAU*). It is a high stakes exam that has a considerable impact on the academic and professional future of Spanish students. Consequently, there is also a washback effect that leads students and teachers alike to focus only on what is assessed by the exam (Saif, 2006), that is, grammar, vocabulary, reading comprehension and writing, leaving out listening comprehension and speaking. Therefore, the inclusion of oral assessment in the PAU foreign language exam would be beneficial for pre-university students as more attention would be paid to oral skills which are currently being neglected (e.g. listening comprehension and speaking). The inclusion of these two skills was announced by the Spanish government by means of a Royal Decree (Ministerio de Educación, Gobierno de España, 2008).

As a response to the changes to be introduced in the new PAU and so as to facilitate the simultaneous examination of thousands of Spanish students in a cost-effective way, the CAMILLE Research Group at Universidad Politécnica de Valencia launched a government-funded project aimed at examining the feasibility of a computerised PAU exam. To achieve this goal, an online language examination platform complying with the official examination parameters and based on the *InGenio* learning management system was developed. The system is known as PAULEX. Once the system had been created the researchers implemented several test exams and conducted a pilot study with 183 high school students to test the affordances of the platform in terms of the creation, management, delivery and correction of the PAU foreign language exam.

Some of the changes that the government would like to implement in the oral section of the exam are an opportunity to develop online tools that can optimise the performance of such an exam. A similar thing has already happened to a greater or lesser extent with other high stakes language exams, such as the Test of English as a Foreign Language (TOEFL) and the Cambridge First Certificate in English Examination (FCE). This opportunity could materialise, for example, in the form of virtual interviews to assess oral skills as an alternative to face-to-face interviews so as to grant anonymity. Also, a significant number of computer-based tools can be used to optimise other aspects of the PAU exam, from designing the actual exam to delivering and correcting them. Technology today makes it possible to achieve this without threatening security. Two of the most prominent examples that demonstrate the validity and feasibility of a large-scale computerised or online test, at least as far as official language tests are concerned, are the aforementioned TOEFL and FCE computerised/online tests.

Among the advantages of computerising the PAU exam is the protection of both the annual exams to be taken and the completed ones, as well as the possibility of programming automatic backups. In addition, an electronic format would make it easier for raters and subsequent exam reviewers to immediately, safely and efficiently access student exams, in addition to a record of the changes and modifications made by each user. With regard to the speaking section, which is to become part of the final construct of the PAU foreign language exam once the announced changes are implemented (Ministerio de Educación, Gobierno de España, 2010), the use of an online version would facilitate the simultaneous examination of the approximately 19,000 students who take the PAU exam annually in the Valencian Community in a more efficient and cost-effective way.

2. Method

2.1. Context

Participants consisted of a total of 183 Secondary Education final year students (2nd year of Bachillerato) – 52.46% male and 47.54% female – from 3 public and 3 private high schools in the Valencian Autonomous Region in Spain. Their ages ranged between 16 and 19 and they all intended to take the PAU exam. Of these, 97.3% (178) were Spanish nationals, whereas 2.7% (5) were not. Except for 2 of them (1.1%), the rest owned a personal computer and 100% of them reported using the Internet on a daily basis from 1 to 2 hours.

2.2. Procedure

Participants filled in two questionnaires. The pre-treatment questionnaire was aimed at compiling qualitative data and it included demographic information: age, gender, experience in the use of Information and Communications Technology (ICT), etc. Using the PAULEX platform, students sat an exam in the Virtual Learning Environment (VLE) which was an adaptation of the English paper-based exam of the 2007 official PAU exam in the Valencian Region. The items of this exam were adapted to the online environment and new items were added for the assessment of listening and speaking skills. Once students had submitted all their answers, they filled in a post-treatment questionnaire which comprised 16 close-ended questions, based on a 4-point Likert scale, relating to the usability of PAULEX and the participants' overall level of satisfaction, and 6 open-ended questions relating to the usefulness of such an online exam and their expectations regarding the computerisation of the PAU English language exam.

The exam tasks included watching several video clips and answering multiple-choice listening comprehension questions and "validating" answers before sending final responses to the server for correction. As for the speaking section, this was assessed by means of an activity based on an appealing image concerning a current issue. Students were asked to observe the image for a couple of minutes and then answer a question relating to the topic depicted in the image, giving their opinion and ideas about it. Once they had thought out what they wanted to say, participants recorded a short speech (no longer than 4 minutes) with the platform's built-in media player.

3. Discussion

During the test the vast majority of participants showed an exemplary attitude and expressed their satisfaction toward the new exam format, a fact that came as no surprise bearing in mind that they belong to a generation of digital natives (Prensky, 2001) who are accustomed to working and interacting with electronic resources. On the other hand, several interesting aspects were observed during the experiment. The students were given 60 minutes to complete the simulation instead of the 90 minutes officially allocated. This reduction was necessary so as to avoid interfering with their daily school duties and to limit the experiment to the time allotted to their regular English classes.

In spite of the time reduction, all the students were able to complete the test within the allotted time, completing all the activities which assessed the different skills, including listening comprehension and speaking. Students browsed through the different parts of the exam, wrote or chose their answers and then validated them, section by section. The students' answers were then stored on a server to avoid loss of information in case of system failure or errors during the course of the trial. All in all, the online format was very well received by students, who made numerous positive comments regarding its practicality.

Table 1. Statistical data describing overall satisfaction

	N	Min.	Max.	Mean	Standard dev.
I think it is a good programme.	183	1	4	3.15	.553
It is easy to use.	183	1	4	3.10	.579
The programme is fin to use.	183	1	4	2.77	.712
The programme works just as I expect it to.	183	1	4	2.93	.700
I would recommend a friend to use it.	183	1	4	2.97	.670
The programme fulfils my expectations regarding what an online test should be like.	183	1	4	3.21	.612
N valid responses	183				

Table 1 summarises the overall satisfaction as reported by the students who participated in the survey. As we can see, all of the items enquired about resulted in a favourable attitude.

4. Conclusions

The changes in the new PAU foreign language exam require solutions for the implementation of a cost-effective and feasible way to assess oral skills. The results of the survey and the solutions proposed can be considered a valid alternative for foreign language assessment in the Spanish University Entrance Examination, including the evaluation of oral skills. Moreover, these results pinpointed the fact that it is indeed feasible to implement the assessment of oral skills in the PAU foreign language exam. Moreover, this computerised version can be easily updated and adapted to the specific characteristics and requirements of the new PAU exam in terms of content, usability and security, among others.

As for the students' opinions, they were optimistic and willing to switch to the online format. All of this suggests that the PAULEX platform meets a number of conditions that make it suitable for the preparation and implementation of the new PAU exam and, specifically, its foreign language section. However, for the successful large-scale implementation of this platform, more research is needed and further studies should be conducted with a larger sample which might lead to more conclusive results: the empirical study described in this article was conducted with only 183 students as opposed to the total number of 19,053 students who sat the PAU exam in 2015 in the Valencian Community, according to the data provided by the Valencian Regional Government (2015).

5. Acknowledgements

We would like to thank the Spanish Ministry of Education for funding the PAULEX Project (HUM2007-66479-C02-01/FILO), from which this study stems.

References

Ministerio de Educación, Gobierno de España. (2008). *Real Decreto 1892/2008, de 14 de noviembre, por el que se regulan las condiciones para el acceso a las enseñanzas universitarias oficiales de grado y los procedimientos de admisión a las universidades públicas españolas.*
Ministerio de Educación, Gobierno de España. (2010). *Características específicas de la prueba oral del ejercicio de lengua extranjera de la PAU.* Secretaría de Estado de Educación y Formación Profesional; Dirección General de Evaluación y Cooperación Territorial.

Prensky, M. (2001). Digital natives, digital immigrants part 1. *On the Horizon, 9*(5), 1-6. doi:10.1108/10748120110424816

Saif, S. (2006). Aiming for positive washback: a case study of international teaching assistants. *Language Testing, 23*(1), 1-34. doi:10.1191/0265532206lt322oa

Valencian Regional Government. (2015). *Estadístiques PAU Sistema Universitari Valencià. Juny de 2015*. Retrieved from http://www.cece.gva.es/univ/docs/estadisticas_JUNIO2015.pdf

Open online language courses: the multi-level model of the Spanish N(ottingham)OOC

Cecilia Goria[1] and Manuel Lagares[2]

Abstract. Research into open education has identified a *high number of participants* and *unpredictable mixed abilities* as factors responsible for the relatively weak presence of language Massive Open Online Courses (MOOCs). This contribution presents a model for open online language courses that aims to bridge this gap. The tangible context is a course in Spanish Language and Culture offered by the University of Nottingham: an online course confined within the boundaries of the institution and yet exhibiting several pedagogical features typical of MOOCs. Our Spanish Nottingham Open Online Course combines cultural content and language activities ensuring that language learning is enriched and complemented by informed exchanges on a variety of topics related to the Spanish speaking world. The novelty of our course rests in its design: a highly structured learning environment that facilitates mobility across different language levels and capitalises on community collaboration as a way to support unpredictable mixed abilities and cope with a high number of participants.

Keywords: course design, open online course, OER, language teaching.

1. Introduction

The purpose of this short contribution is to present the course design model of an online language course which will be offered by the University of Nottingham in autumn 2015, under the registered trademark of Nottingham Open Online Course

---

1. University of Nottingham, United Kingdom; cecilia.goria@nottingham.ac.uk
2. University of Nottingham, United Kingdom; manuel.lagares@nottingham.ac.uk

How to cite this article: Goria. C., & Lagares. M. (2015). Open online language courses: the multi-level model of the Spanish N(ottingham)OOC. In F. Helm, L. Bradley, M. Guarda, & S. Thouësny (Eds), *Critical CALL – Proceedings of the 2015 EUROCALL Conference, Padova, Italy* (pp. 221-227). Dublin: Research-publishing.net. http://dx.doi.org/10.14705/rpnet.2015.000337

(NOOC). The present study is one of the many attempts to address some of the issues that have been identified in the literature (Martín-Monje & Bárcena, 2014; and references therein) as the causes for the late appearance of language courses within the MOOCs movement that has revolutionised the educational scene over the last decade.

The NOOC, titled *Spain and Latin America: Transatlantic Crossings* (henceforth SNOOC), offers a cultural perspective to the theme of people's migration inside the Spanish speaking world, juxtaposed with a related language component. The uniqueness of the SNOOC rests in its ambition to cater for three levels of language proficiency, namely:

- Level 1: suitable for complete beginners or participants up to CEFR A2 level;

- Level 2: for participants from CEFR B1 to B2.1;

- Level 3: for those with advanced skills (CEFR B2.2-C1).

The SNOOC, which is hosted in Moodle, is an eight-week course divided into four two-week units. Each unit comprises a cultural and a language tier (2-tier structure), and the language tier of each unit is further divided into the three language ability levels mentioned above (3-level structure).

The pedagogical model of the SNOOC relates to that of MOOCs in a number of ways.

The SNOOC, unlike MOOCs, is not massive but it is expected to exceed by far the participant number of a traditional class. Furthermore, in contrast with MOOCs, the SNOOC is not offered globally – it is restricted to affiliates of University of Nottingham, including the overseas campuses in China and Malaysia. On the other hand, the SNOOC shows several of MOOCs' pedagogical features, as it:

- is open in that it has no application prerequisites;

- is based on open dialogues between all participants, tutors and students alike;

- relies on and generates Open Educational Resources (OERs);

- is delivered entirely online;

- is a course, i.e. it includes a taught structure led by MOOC-like roles of tutors and facilitators.

As mentioned earlier, the present study aims to deal with some features typical of open online learning that appear to be problematic for language learning and teaching. The concerns of the SNOOC are:

1) the high number of participants;

2) the diversity of the community of participants and the difficulty in predicting the participants' skills and abilities; and as by product of 1) and 2):

3) the degree of interaction in the target language required to achieve the learning outcomes.

Thus, this study seeks to provide some answers to the following issues:

- how to cope with a number of participants that is by far superior to that of conventional language classes;

- how to cope with mixed abilities and the related unpredictability factor, considering that language classes tend to target participants with a similar level of language skills;

- how to select language content to cater for different language levels and a heterogeneous audience;

- how to provide the level of interaction in the target language required to ensure language improvement, given the high number of learners and the different levels of language abilities.

In the following section, the structure of the SNOOC is presented – it is by leveraging course structure and activity design that we address the SNOOC's concerns outlined above.

2. Methodology

It was mentioned earlier that the structure of our SNOOC is a 2-tier and 3-level model, as illustrated in the Table 1 below.

Table 1. 2-tier/3-level model

Week 1: Culture All levels		Week 3: Culture All levels		Week 5: Culture All levels		Week 7: Culture All levels	
Week 2: Language	1	Week 4: Language	1	Week 6: Language	1	Week 8: Language	1
	2		2		2		2
	3		3		3		3

A number of considerations guided the design process. Firstly, we identified the main features of our course and, relying on Lane's (2012) tripartite typology of MOOCs, we designed the SNOOC to include:

- features of task-based MOOCs: it relies on the participants to perform pre-defined tasks;

- features of content-based MOOCs: it provides pre-determined content, instructions and automated drill-and-practice activities;

- features of networked-based MOOCs: it relies on the community of participants for generating content, providing language practice and peer-feedback.

Secondly, we delineated the characteristics of the SNOOC's community of participants by ensuring that the our design answered guideline questions as in Table 2. These questions were informed by the Galley, Conole, and Alevizou's (2014) community indicators framework which identifies four key aspects of community experience. These are:

> "participation – the ways in which individuals engage in activity; cohesion – the ties between individuals and the community as a whole; identity – how individuals perceive the community and their place within it; and creative capability – the ability of the community to create shared artefacts, and shared knowledge and understanding" (Galley et al., 2014, p. 379).

Thirdly, we focused on activity design and ensured that: 1) the medium of communication within the cultural component is English; 2) resources from the cultural tier are adapted for language tasks; 3) a given resource is adapted to create learning activities for the three language levels supported by the SNOOC; and 4) each language unit includes linguistic explanations; practice exercises, consolidation and interactive tasks.

Table 2. Community indicator framework guideline questions (adapted from Galley et al., 2014)

Participation	Identity	Cohesion	Creative capability
Does our design encourage participants to take a social and facilitative role? Does our design encourage participants to make repeated contributions? Does our design encourage participants to engage equally with both tiers of the SNOOC?	Does our design encourage participants to connect their existing knowledge and experience to that of others? Does our design encourage people to interact in the target language?	Does our design encourage participants to share ideas and experience? To what extent is our design inclusive for learner with low or no Spanish language skills?	Does our design encourage participants to express multiple points of view? Does our design encourage our participants to make links between concepts and ideas?

The pedagogical significance of these choices is discussed below.

3. Discussion: the power of course design

In this section, we highlight the role of the SNOOC's model in addressing the study questions outlined in section 1.

3.1. 2-tiers

Within the cultural tier all participants are presented with the same resources in English and interact in English as one and the same group. As English is the medium of communication, the language competence of the learners is irrelevant and subsequently the educational outcomes of this tier are not strictly concerned with linguistic achievement. In this way, our model will ensure that 1) the learners engage more deeply with the content, given the absence of the language barrier effect; 2) all participants gain familiarity with the same content; and 3) community cohesion is strengthened.

Points 1) and 2) are significant as deeper engagement and increased familiarity with the content are expected to facilitate learning within the language tier. This is achieved by recycling and adapting content of the cultural tier to create the language learning activities of the language tier of each unit. Point 3) is significant because it is by increasing the sense of community that we encourage our participants to be more readily prepared to engage in student-led activities across language levels. In this way we aim to address the concerns 1) and 3) presented in section 1.

3.2. 3-levels

The three language levels and their related learning outcomes are based on the CEFR descriptors and the language content is adapted from the *Plan Curricular del Instituto Cervantes*' inventory.

Within the language tier, the participants take their own learning path: self-diagnostic tests and self-perception will help the learners to select the language level that best suits their needs. In this way, the model deals with different learners' language abilities (concern 2).

In addition, the language learning resources are shared by all language levels. That is, a given resource is adapted to generate language learning materials for each language level. By doing so, our design model facilitates 1) mobility across the levels, allowing the learners to move up or down a level in accordance with their needs; and 2) peer-collaboration across the levels, especially peer-feedback from the higher levels of language proficiency to the lower ones.

The most significant consequence of 2) is the expected increase in the degree of interaction in the target language, which is no longer provided solely through the tutor-learner exchanges, but also through the additional interaction amongst the learners (concern 3).

4. Conclusion

In this short contribution we have highlighted the significance of course structure and activity design in the context of an open online language course. We have contextualised our study within the MOOCs' scenario, we have raised the concerns that justify the study and we have presented our attempt to deal with these concerns, namely the SNOOC's 2-tier/3-level model by which we address the issues of:

- high number of participants by supporting interaction across levels and facilitating peer feedback, especially from the higher to the lower levels;

- mixed abilities by facilitating mobility across the levels – same resource for all levels;

- providing the participants with the necessary degree of interaction in the target language by strengthening the sense of community and increasing community cohesion.

To conclude, by prioritising the alignment between pedagogical approach, the role of the community and course structure and activities design, the SNOOC attempts to resolve some of the issues that have held the MOOC culture from affecting language teaching with the same speed witnessed in other subject fields.

References

Galley, R., Conole, G., & Alevizou, P. (2014). Community indicators: a framework for observing and supporting community activity on Cloudworks. *Interactive Learning Environments, 22*(3), 373-395. doi:10.1080/10494820.2012.680965

Lane, L. (2012). *Three kinds of MOOCs*. Retrieved from http://lisahistory.net/wordpress/2012/08/three-kinds-ofmoocs/

Martín-Monje, E., & Bárcena, E. (Eds.). (2014). *Language MOOCs: providing learning, transcending boundaries*. Warsaw/Berlin: De Gruyter Open Ltd.

Improving summarizing skills with TED talks: an account of a teaching lesson using explicit instruction

Shin'ichi Hashimoto[1], Eri Fukuda[2], and Hironobu Okazaki[3]

Abstract. This paper reports on a study which investigated the effectiveness of an explicit instruction approach in a Japanese university setting with third-year science and technology students in an English for Specific Purposes (ESP) course. The two aims of this study were: 1) to explore changes in students' attitudes and understanding of summary writing, and 2) to observe changes in the ability of students to incorporate specific ideas of summary writing. First, students were given a short questionnaire about their current knowledge and background related to summary writing to provide a base measure. Next, the instructor presented information about specific features of summary writing. Then, students were introduced to a short TED Talk on a technical topic as the content material. Using this content, students were put into groups to discuss and identify the main points of the talk. For homework, they were assigned to write individual summaries. In the next class, students shared their individual summaries with their group members and produced a second draft to be evaluated. Finally, a post-questionnaire about summary writing was given to students. In the future, the researchers aim to make lessons like the above part of an on-line Learning Management System (LMS) that they are currently developing.

Keywords: summary writing, TED Talk, explicit instruction, ESP, LMS.

---

1. University of Electro-Communications, Tokyo, Japan; shin.hashimoto@uec.ac.jp
2. Chugokugakuen University, Okayama, Japan; erifukuda2014@gmail.com
3. Akita Prefectural University, Yurihonjo, Japan; okazaki@akita-pu.ac.jp

How to cite this article: Hashimoto, S., Fukuda, E., & Okazaki, H. (2015). Improving summarizing skills with TED talks: an account of a teaching lesson using explicit instruction. In F. Helm, L. Bradley, M. Guarda, & S. Thouësny (Eds), *Critical CALL – Proceedings of the 2015 EUROCALL Conference, Padova, Italy* (pp. 228-234). Dublin: Research-publishing.net. http://dx.doi.org/10.14705/rpnet.2015.000338

1. Introduction

In the past decade, the advancement of technology and online services has been remarkable, and language education has benefited from this development. For example, Youtube, MOOCs, and various language learning web applications offer a tremendous amount of authentic learning material and inspire instructors to develop classes utilizing these services, especially in the field of ESP.

Hutchinson (1987) explains, "ESP is [...] an approach to language learning, which is based on learner needs. The foundation of all ESP is this simple question: Why does this learner need to learn a foreign language?" (p. 19). Due to the international nature of current technological cooperation and research, students majoring in science and technology are often required to have aptitude in academic English writing and presentation skills. In order to write academic papers in English, the learning of content in English is essential to acquire the technical knowledge and terminology to communicate effectively. To prepare ESP students for this multi-media reality, teaching methods and materials should support literacy skills. This study is based on the use of a TED Talk (www.ted.com) for such an approach.

TED Talks are one of the aforementioned online services that are now widely available. These talks are of high educational value for many reasons (Carlo, 2014; Denskus & Esser, 2015; Rubenstein, 2012; Sugimoto & Thelwall, 2013; Taibi et al., 2015). One being the availability of linguistic support, another being the innovative and engaging content, and yet another being the clarity of the presentation structure. The full subtitles and transcripts in a multitude of languages which are available in TED Talks enable the incorporation of content into language instruction with ease for both teachers and students. TED Talk presenters share the latest innovations in a variety of fields including science and technology, which makes this website highly suitable for ESP courses. These talks are inherently interesting for students, thereby increasing enthusiasm for study. The clarity of the structure of the presentations lend themselves easily to teaching summary writing skills.

The process of summary writing was chosen as a focus for this study as many English learners find this task highly complex and difficult. One reason for this perception may be the fact that students have not had many opportunities to explicitly learn an approach to summary writing. This study aimed to make the process of summary writing clearer so that students could become more aware of specific points that should and should not be included in a summary, and to provide a chance for them to think about and discuss what summary writing entails

(Baumann, 1984; Guido & Colwell, 1987; Johns & Mayes, 1990; Kim, 2001; Li, 2014).

2. Method

2.1. Criteria for video selection

The following criteria were taken into consideration for selecting an appropriate video. First of all, the topic had to be science-technology related, as the class was an ESP course for engineering majors. Only videos under 8 minutes were considered, as this duration was thought to be optimal to retain students' concentration. Also, considering the students' English proficiency level, Japanese subtitles for L1 support was important, so the availability of Japanese subtitles was another criterion. Furthermore, it was important to select stimulating talks in terms of content, speaker's delivery, and proximity of the topic to students' interests. At the same time, in order not to discourage elementary level students, linguistic difficulty was addressed as well, including speech rate and vocabulary level. Finally, one additional advantage of TED Talks is the varied background of the speakers with regard to sex, age, ethnicity, and first language. Selecting talks delivered by different types of speakers creates a more exciting class and complemented class content by raising students' awareness of World Englishes.

2.2. Current study

The TED video which was chosen for this project was "The Shape-shifting Future of the Mobile Phone" by Fabian Hemmert filmed in Berlin, Germany in 2009[4]. It is a relatively short video – only four minutes in duration. The structure of the talk is laid out fairly clearly, with him talking about three possible new features of future mobile phones.

The first part of the current study involved gathering information about students' current knowledge and experiences with summary writing. A questionnaire was delivered to students via the university's LMS (WebClass UEC) and done as homework. The information gathered provided a base measure of students' concept of what summary writing entails. Generally speaking, it was gleaned from the responses that students did not have many opportunities to learn explicitly about summary writing prior to coming to university – either in Japanese or English.

---

4. http://www.ted.com/talks/fabian_hemmert_the_shape_shifting_future_of_the_mobile_phone

The second part of the current study was conducted in class. After asking students to discuss guiding questions about summarizing, the instructor presented some information about the specifics of summary writing. Next, the TED Talk by Hemmert was shown in class, and the subtitle and transcript functions for English and other languages on the TED website were demonstrated. Handouts of the English transcripts were given to the students.

For homework, students were to download the template for an outline and summary. Then, specifics about the outline format and content were conveyed. One guideline for making the summary was to condense the main idea from one paragraph of the text (transcript) into one sentence of the summary. Following this, the content of the summary sentences was explained in more detail. It was explained that after writing out a draft of the paragraph, sentences were to be reviewed for coherency and logical order. Examples of transition words were provided. Finally, students were asked to be conscious of the word limit (between 100 to 150 words), and the "word count" function on MS Word was demonstrated.

As a wrap up, the instructor reminded the students that a good summary is comprehensive, concise, coherent, shows understanding of the text, and is written in their own words. Students were told not to use more than 3 words in a row from the text in their summary, and that unique expressions from the text should be indicated with quotation marks. Furthermore, students were asked to omit their personal opinions, specific examples and raw data, and sections of the original text in their summaries.

The third part of the current study was also done in-class, requiring students to share their individually written summary outlines and paragraphs with a partner using a checklist to evaluate whether or not all the points were covered correctly. The checklists were used to revise their outline and summary. Face-to-face peer review was used in this part of the lesson to have students participate more actively in giving feedback on their peers' writing and reduce writer apprehension as suggested by Chaudron (1984), and promote greater student-autonomy (Ho & Savignon, 2007; Hu & Lam, 2010; Lundstrom & Baker, 2009; Miao, Badger, & Zhen, 2006). Students were reminded to make their outlines with keywords and short phrases (not sentences), and to use their own words in the summary paragraph. Their second draft of the summary outline and paragraph were submitted in one week, by uploading it to WebClass UEC.

The fourth and last part of the current study was the collection of a post-questionnaire of the students. This questionnaire revealed that students felt more confident about summarizing tasks, as they became more familiar with the specific components of a summary paragraph. They also found the outlining process a good way to focus on key points and to see the structure of a text. Some common difficulties were putting things into their own words, and figuring out the main points of the talk.

3. Discussion

There are so many approaches that could be taken in the presentation and implementation of a summary-writing activity. For example, Baumann (1984) presents data which supports a direct instruction paradigm, Guido and Colwell (1987) model a direct instruction approach of writing summaries, Johns (1988) argues for an approach that helps students recognize underlying text-types, and Strever and Newman (1997) promote writing summaries of student-written dialogue journals. The researchers of this study were most drawn to an explicit approach, as it seemed most practical in terms of ease of implementation.

Some of the positive features of the approach used in the current study is the fact that 1) multi-media content of a field-related topic with L1 support kept the interest-levels of the students high, 2) explicit step by step instructions on how to make a summary made the task manageable, 3) outlining the text helped promote deeper understanding of the structure and content of the material, and 4) the drafting process using a checklist gave students more opportunities to try out and reflect on the necessary elements of writing a summary.

4. Conclusions

Providing more explicit instruction concerning how to write a summary seemed to be very helpful for students, and many students expressed their appreciation for this opportunity. The responses from the questionnaires somewhat surprised the researchers concerning the lack of opportunities students have to learn about summarizing. Especially in a field such as science and technology where there are constantly many new developments, obtaining up-to-date information and sharing that with colleagues is no doubt a valued skill for both researchers and professionals alike. Introducing a more multi-format approach to teaching and teaching materials in English classes is one way to keep expanding skills as a teacher, while at the same time making learning more relevant for students.

As a future project, the researchers hope to incorporate lessons like summarizing as a component of an on-line LMS that is being developed. It is our hope that the

LMS will be a comprehensive program that can be used by teachers and learners to help manage English learning from a myriad of perspectives.

5. Acknowledgements

This research is partially supported by Grant-in-Aid Scientific Research (B) (25282061) by Japan Society for the Promotion of Science (JSPS).

References

Baumann, J. F. (1984). The effectiveness of a direct instruction paradigm for teaching main idea comprehension. *Reading research quarterly, 20*(1), 93-115. doi:10.2307/747654

Carlo, G. S. (2014). The role of proximity in online popularizations: the case of TED talks. *Discourse Studies, 16*(5), 591-606, doi:10.1177/1461445614538565

Chaudron, C. (1984). The effect of feedback on students' composition revisions. *RELC Journal 15*(1), 1-15.

Denskus, T., & Esser, D. E. (2015). TED talks on international development: trans-hegemonic promise and ritualistic constraints. *Communication theory, 25*, 166-187.

Guido, B., & Colwell, C. G. (1987). A rationale for direct instruction to teach summary writing following expository text reading. *Reading research and instruction, 26*(2), 89-98. doi:10.1080/19388078709557900

Ho, M., & Savignon, S. J. (2007). Face-to-face and computer-mediated peer review in EFL writing. CALICO journal, 24(2), 269-290.

Hu, G., & Lam S. T. E. (2010). Issues of cultural appropriateness and pedagogical efficacy: exploring peer review in a second language writing class. *Instructional science, 38*(4), 371-394. doi:10.1007/s11251-008-9086-1

Hutchinson, T. (1987). *English for specific purposes*. Cambridge: Cambridge University Press. doi:10.1017/CBO9780511733031

Johns, A. M. (1988). Reading for summarising: an approach to text orientation and processing. *Reading in a foreign language, 4*(2), 79-90.

Johns, A. M., & Mayes, P. (1990). An analysis of summary protocols of university ESL students. *Applied linguistics, 11*(3), 253-271. doi:10.1093/applin/11.3.253

Kim, S. (2001). Characteristics of EFL reader's summary writing: a study with Korean university students. *Foreign language annals, 34*(6), 569-581. doi:10.1111/j.1944-9720.2001.tb02104.x

Li, J. (2014). The role of reading and writing in summarizing as an integrated task. *Language testing in Asia, 4*(3). doi:10.1186/2229-0443-4-3

Lundstrom, K., & Baker, W. (2009). To give is better than to receive: the benefits of peer review to the reviewer's own writing. *Journal of second language writing 18*, 30-43. doi:10.1016/j.jslw.2008.06.002

Miao, Y., Badger, R., & Zhen, Y. (2006). A comparative study of peer and teacher feedback in a Chinese EFL writing class. *Journal of second language writing, 15*, 179-200. doi:10.1016/j.jslw.2006.09.004

Rubenstein, L. D. (2012). Using TED talks to inspire thoughtful practice. *The teacher educator, 47*(4), 261-267. doi:10.1080/08878730.2012.713303

Strever, J., & Newman, K. (1997). Using electronic peer audience and summary writing with ESL students. *Journal of college reading and learning, 28*(1), 24-33. doi:10.1080/10790195.1997.10850051

Sugimoto, C. R., & Thelwall, M. (2013). Scholars on soap boxes: science communication and dissemination in TED videos. *Journal of the American society for information science and technology, 64*(4), 663-674.

Taibi, D., Chawla, S., Dietze, S., Marenzi, I., & Fetahu, B. (2015). Exploring TED talks as linked data for education. *British journal of educational technology, 46*(5), 1092-1096. doi:10.1111/bjet.12283

The integration of a three-year-long intercultural collaborative project into a foreign language classroom for the development of intercultural competence

Maki Hirotani[1] and Kiyomi Fujii[2]

Abstract. Many studies on intercultural communication introduced how their collaborative projects were conducted. There are also several studies that discuss how intercultural collaborative activities can be integrated into a foreign language curriculum, as well as a big project (the INTENT project) that helps teachers integrate collaborative activities into their language curricula. Nonetheless, intercultural collaborative projects have not yet been mainstreamed for various reasons, such as insufficient pedagogical support from their institutions and a lack of interest in getting involved in projects among colleagues. We need to continuously examine and develop activities that can be relatively easily integrated into language curricula and that are appealing to more teachers to get involved in collaborative projects. Starting in the fall of 2013, we have been conducting a three-year experimental Facebook video project with learners of English in Japan and those of Japanese in the US. This paper will provide a brief overview of the Facebook collaboration projects and present the outcomes.

Keywords: intercultural competence, Facebook, Japanese as a foreign language, English as a foreign language.

1. Introduction

Many researchers of foreign language learning have pointed out the importance of the development of learners' intercultural competence along with their

---

1. Rose-Hulman Institute of Technology, United States; hirotani@rose-hulman.edu

2. Kanazawa Institute of Technology, Japan; kfujii@neptune.kanazawa-it.ac.jp

How to cite this article: Hirotani, M., & Fujii. K. (2015). The integration of a three-year-long intercultural collaborative project into a foreign language classroom for the development of intercultural competence. In F. Helm, L. Bradley, M. Guarda, & S. Thouësny (Eds), *Critical CALL – Proceedings of the 2015 EUROCALL Conference, Padova, Italy* (pp. 235-242). Dublin: Research-publishing.net. http://dx.doi.org/10.14705/rpnet.2015.000339

language competencies. It has been claimed that learners could develop their intercultural communication skills through activities with native speakers, and many collaborative projects have been conducted in foreign language education (e.g. Belz, 2003; Jauregi & Canto, 2012). There are several studies that discuss how intercultural collaborative activities can be integrated into a foreign language curriculum, as well as a big project (the INTENT project) that helps teachers integrate collaborative activities into their language curricula (e.g. Furstenberg & Levet, 2010; O'Dowd, n.d.). Nonetheless, intercultural collaborative projects have not yet been mainstreamed for various reasons, such as insufficient pedagogical support from their institutions and a lack of interest in getting involved in projects among colleagues due to the amount of work for organizing a project (O'Dowd, 2011). We need to continuously examine and develop activities that can be relatively easily integrated into language curricula and that are appealing to more teachers to get involved in collaborative projects.

Starting in the fall of 2013, we have been conducting a three-year experimental Facebook video project using learners of English in Japan and those of Japanese in the US. The purpose of our research is to identify effective procedures and activities to establish guidelines for intercultural collaboration which could be integrated into an actual foreign language curriculum. During the first and the second years of this project, we have reviewed the outcomes of the previous year's project and revised the procedure and activities for the next project. We plan to conduct a more systematic project in the fall and winter of 2015 and 2016. This paper will briefly provide an overview of the Facebook collaboration projects and present part of the outcomes of the projects.

2. Method

2.1. Overview of the project

The students involved in this project have all been enrolled in the same English (general English) and Japanese (second-year Japanese) courses at the same colleges in Japan (KIT) ($N=40$) and the US (RH) ($N=21$), respectively. Each collaborative project lasts from September to February every year, and the students work on many activities both in English and Japanese to develop their intercultural competence as well as their linguistic competencies. The following chart shows a brief overview of the project conducted from 2013 to 2014 and 2014 to 2015.

As shown in Figure 1, each project started and ended with a questionnaire which is a self-evaluation of students' intercultural communication knowledge and skills. The

Facebook project started with a Skype meeting with their partner university. After producing self-introduction videos on Facebook, student groups at both schools worked on several sets of series of activities on particular topics, such as verbal/non-verbal communication, school culture introduction, and culture research survey, and interacted with each other during this phase. Each set of activities included several activities other than Facebook as well, such as reflection logs on the video assignments, in-class conversation activities, using the expressions introduced by the partner school, and in-class PowerPoint group presentations.

Figure 1. Overview of the project

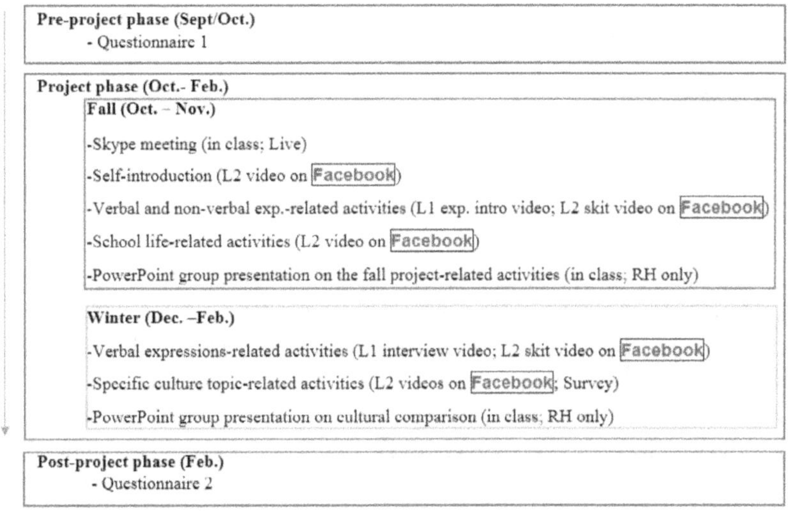

```
Pre-project phase (Sept/Oct.)
  - Questionnaire 1

Project phase (Oct.- Feb.)
  Fall (Oct. – Nov.)
    -Skype meeting (in class; Live)
    -Self-introduction (L2 video on Facebook)
    -Verbal and non-verbal exp.-related activities (L1 exp. intro video; L2 skit video on Facebook)
    -School life-related activities (L2 video on Facebook)
    -PowerPoint group presentation on the fall project-related activities (in class; RH only)

  Winter (Dec. –Feb.)
    -Verbal expressions-related activities (L1 interview video; L2 skit video on Facebook)
    -Specific culture topic-related activities (L2 videos on Facebook; Survey)
    -PowerPoint group presentation on cultural comparison (in class; RH only)

Post-project phase (Feb.)
  - Questionnaire 2
```

For verbal and non-verbal communication activities conducted in the fall, for instance, in case of RH students, each group introduced English verbal and non-verbal expressions and posted their video on the English page on Facebook. KIT students did the same tasks: introducing Japanese expressions and posted videos on the Japanese page. Each RH student then learned the L2 (Japanese) expressions and worked on the self-reflection log. Each group produced a skit video in L2, posted the video on the Japanese page, and interacted with KIT students.

The culture-research survey activities, on the other hand, were research based, though there was less interaction observed on Facebook due to the nature of the activities. Figure 2 shows a series of activities that each group worked on[3].

---

3. Due to the curriculum difference, only RH students worked on the fifth and the six activities.

Figure 2. Culture research survey

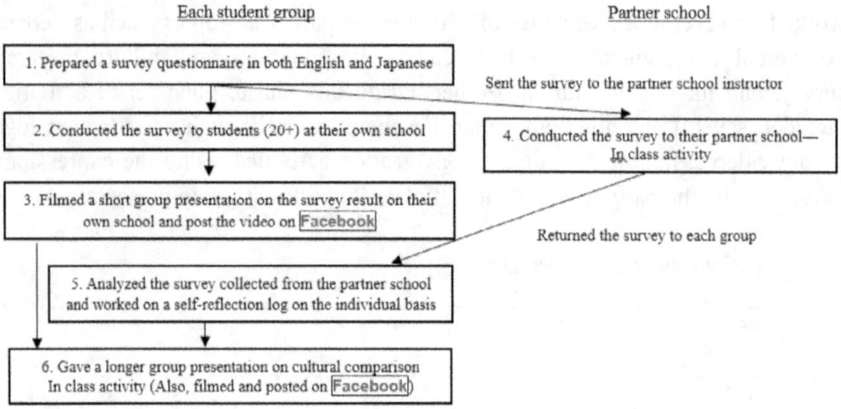

Each student group

1. Prepared a survey questionnaire in both English and Japanese

2. Conducted the survey to students (20+) at their own school

3. Filmed a short group presentation on the survey result on their own school and post the video on Facebook

5. Analyzed the survey collected from the partner school and worked on a self-reflection log on the individual basis

6. Gave a longer group presentation on cultural comparison In class activity (Also, filmed and posted on Facebook)

Partner school

Sent the survey to the partner school instructor

4. Conducted the survey to their partner school— In class activity

Returned the survey to each group

2.2. Materials

We have used a wide range of methods to assess our intercultural collaborative projects with reference to the previous research (Deardorff, 2009), including observation by the instructors, student presentations, student portfolios (several sets of assignments in both written and oral forms), and pre- and post-self-evaluation questionnaires conducted before and after each project. However, we will present the outcomes of the self-assessment questionnaires for the sake of the limited space in this paper.

2.3. Self-assessment questionnaires

As one of the tools to assess learners' intercultural communication knowledge and competence, we prepared self-assessment questionnaires which were used before and after each project in 2013-2014 and 2014-2015.

The questionnaires consisted of self-evaluation items on verbal and non-verbal communication knowledge (section A) and skills (B) as well as attitudes toward other cultures (C). We referred to the intercultural knowledge and competence rubric prepared by The American Association of Colleges and Universities for section A and B items (AACU[4]), Elola and Oskoz (2008) for section C (see Appendix).

---

4. https://www.aacu.org/sites/default/files/files/VALUE/InterculturalKnowledge.pdf

3. Results and conclusion

As shown in Table 1, the results of the Wilcoxon Signed Ranks Test showed a significant difference between the pre- and the post-project in many of the questionnaire items. Overall, students at both colleges tended to feel that they gained more knowledge (A) and skills (B) of verbal and non-verbal communication. The reason that the RH students' results in C1 and C2 did not show significant differences might be related to the initial differences between the two schools. The Mann Whitney test showed that RH students scored significantly higher regarding the relevance between the language and culture (C1) and lower regarding sharing the same values among people in the same society (C2). These results imply that the average RH student had thought that learning the culture was important to learn the target language and that each individual in one society had different values toward money, family, and religions before the project started.

Table 1. Results of the Wilcoxon signed ranks test

	N	A (knowledge)		B (skills)		C (attitudes)		
		A1. Verbal	A2. Non-v	B1. Verbal	B2. Non-v	C1	C2	C3
RH (US)	21	<.01	<.05	<.01	n.s.	n.s.	n.s.	<.05
KIT (Japan)	40	<.01	<.01	<.01	<.01	<.01	n.s.	<.05

Concerning item C3 (learning cultural differences), we observed the opposite results: while RH students thought that they learned cultural differences through the project, KIT students did not. These differences were statistically significant. This might be related to the fact that due to the curriculum difference, KIT students could not work on cultural comparison related tasks (see items 4 and 5 in Figure 2), that their partner schools did. Even though students at both schools completed almost the same tasks throughout the project, explicit tasks on cultural differences and similarities between two schools (i.e. student presentation) might have actually helped students to reflect on them or perhaps have simply affected student perceptions of how much they learned. Further studies in this regard shall be called for.

References

Belz, J. A. (2003). Linguistic perspectives on the development of intercultural competence in telecollaboration. *Language learning & Technology, 7*(2), 68-99.
Deardorff, D. K. (2009). Implementing intercultural competence assessment. In Darla K. Deardorff (Ed.), *The SAGE handbook of intercultural competence* (pp. 477-491). Los Angeles, CA: SAGE.

Elola, I., & Oskoz, A. (2008). Blogging: fostering intercultural competence development in foreign language and study abroad context. *Foreign Language Annals, 41*(3), 454-477. doi:10.1111/j.1944-9720.2008.tb03307.x

Furstenberg, G., & Levet, S. (2010). Integrating telecollaboration into the language classroom: some insights. In S. Guth & F. Helm (Eds.), *Telecollaboration 2.0. Language, literacies and intercultural learning in the 21st century* (pp. 305-336). New York: Peter Lang AG.

Jauregi, K., & Canto, S. (2012). Impact of native-nonnative speaker interaction through video-web communication and Second Life on students' intercultural communicative competence. In L. Bradley & S. Thouësny (Eds.), *CALL: Using, Learning, Knowing, EUROCALL Conference, Gothenburg, Sweden, 22-25 August 2012, Proceedings* (pp. 151-155). Dublin Ireland: Research-publishing.net. doi:10.14705/rpnet.2012.000043

O'Dowd. (n.d.). INTENT project news. *Scoop. It.* Retrieved from http://www.scoop.it/t/intent-project-news

O'Dowd, R. (2011). Online foreign language interaction: moving from the periphery to the core of foreign language education? *Language Teaching, 44*(3), 368-380. doi:10.1017/S0261444810000194

Appendix

Questionnaire

Please answer the following questions. This questionnaire will provide us with information that will help us develop the cultural curriculum for this course. Please, be honest, since this questionnaire will not affect your grade.

A. Knowledge on intercultural communication (verbal: A-1; non-verbal A-2)

Which following statement(s) well describe(s) your knowledge on intercultural communication?

		A-1: In verbal communication (choose one ↓)	A-2: In non-verbal communication (choose one ↓)
1	I have a **minimal** level of understanding of cultural differences in verbal/non-verbal communication.		
2	**I identify some cultural differences** in verbal/non-verbal communication and am **aware** that **misunderstandings** can occur based on those differences.		

3	**I recognize** and **participate** in **cultural differences** in verbal/non-verbal communication.		
4	I articulate a **complex understanding** of cultural differences in verbal/non-verbal communication (e.g. demonstrates understanding of the degree to which people use physical contact while communicating in different cultures or use direct/indirect and explicit/implicit meanings).		

B. Skills on intercultural communication (verbal: B-1; non-verbal: B-2)

Which following statement well describe(s) your skills on intercultural communication?

		B-1: In verbal communication (choose one ↓)	B-2: In non-verbal communication (choose one ↓)
1	I am **unable** to negotiate a shared understanding of cultural differences in verbal/non-verbal communication **in Japanese**.		
2	**I begin** to negotiate a shared understanding based on cultural differences in verbal/non-verbal communication **in Japanese**.		
3	I am **able** to negotiate a shared understanding of cultural differences in verbal/non-verbal communication **in Japanese**.		
4	I am **able** to **skillfully** negotiate a shared understanding based on **various aspects** of cultural differences **in Japanese**.		

C. On a scale from 1 (strongly disagree) to 5 (strongly agree), answer the following statements

1. Given that I am studying Japanese, it is relevant to learn about Japanese culture (from Japan).

        1   2   3   4   5

Explain:

2. I believe that in general people in Japan have the same values towards family, money, education and religion.

        1   2   3   4   5

Explain:

3. I believe that talking to the KIT students will help me see that there are differences between people from your home country and people from Japan.

        1   2   3   4   5

Explain:

Selective teaching of L2 pronunciation

Olaf Husby[1], Jacques Koreman[2], Violeta Martínez-Paricio[3], Jardar E. Abrahamsen[4], Egil Albertsen[5], Keivan Hedayatfar[6], and Øyvind Bech[7]

Abstract. The pronunciation of a second or foreign language is often very challenging for L2 learners. It is difficult to address this topic in the classroom, because learners with different native languages (L1s) can have very different challenges. We have therefore developed a Computer-Assisted Listening and Speaking Tutor (CALST), which selectively offers exercises for listening and pronunciation training tailored in relation to the learner's native language (L1). Based on information given in its connected database L1-L2*map*, CALST offers exercises focused on Norwegian segmentals for speakers of more than 500 languages, and exercises related to phonotactics for 10 languages. Exercises focusing on stress placement in words, word tones, fast speech phenomena and intonation are under development. As there is no spoken standard of Norwegian, the user can choose one of eight dialects as target language. The latter choice is so far valid for segmental exercises only. L1-L2*map* is easily expandable, and single language access is given to expert contributors on request at http://calst.hf.ntnu.no/L1-L2map/. At present, CALST can be used to learn Norwegian pronunciation (www.calst.no). However, it can easily be extended to other languages by adding relevant content into the existing framework.

---

1. Norwegian University of Science and Technology (NTNU), Trondheim, Norway; olaf.husby@ntnu.no
2. NTNU, Trondheim, Norway; jacques.koreman@ntnu.no
3. NTNU, Trondheim, Norway; violeta.martinez-paricio@ntnu.no
4. NTNU, Trondheim, Norway; jardar.abrahamsen@ntnu.no
5. NTNU, Trondheim, Norway; egil.albertsen@ntnu.no
6. NTNU, Trondheim, Norway; keivan.hedayatfar@ntnu.no
7. NTNU, Trondheim, Norway; oyvind.bech@gmail.com

How to cite this article: Husby, O., Koreman, J., Martínez-Paricio, V., Abrahamsen, J. E., Albertsen, E., Hedayatfar, K., & Bech, Ø. (2015). Selective teaching of L2 pronunciation. In F. Helm, L. Bradley, M. Guarda, & S. Thouësny (Eds), *Critical CALL – Proceedings of the 2015 EUROCALL Conference, Padova, Italy* (pp. 243-248). Dublin: Research-publishing.net. http://dx.doi.org/10.14705/rpnet.2015.000340

Keywords: pronunciation training, second or foreign language, contrastive analysis, sound contrasts, phonotactics.

1. Introduction

In Norwegian language courses for foreigners there is generally not much time allocated for individualized pronunciation or listening training, since these activities are considered as going at the expense of more basic and important language learning needs. Adequate pronunciation and listening skills are however of great importance in practical communicative situations and will, if mastered, normally enhance the students' integration process when it comes to academic studies, professional careers or social life.

Even though teaching of Norwegian as a second language has been going on for about 50 years, teaching material aiming at pronunciation and listening skills must be described as scarce. There are several reasons for this. One of them is related to the fact that there is no spoken standard of Norwegian.

The default choice in pronunciation teaching has put a spoken form of *Bokmål*, the most common of the two written forms of Norwegian, as its goal. Both segmental inventory and prosody vary significantly from dialect to dialect. The application of the dialectal variants into spoken Bokmål results in several versions of the target language, and these are the forms that are introduced to learners in the second language classroom.

Spoken Bokmål in its different forms is not used in verbal interaction between Norwegians, who prefer to use their dialect in all kinds of public and private verbal interactions. The second language speaking skills of adults learning Norwegian is thus restricted to a form that Norwegians only use when reading Bokmål aloud, but not when they are speaking. This means that speaking and listening skills taught to foreigners in general will differ more or less from dialects used in Norway.

The pronunciation teaching provided is mostly segmentally orientated and is normally found in the first chapters of introductory books. There is not much material found that is explicitly aiming at a wider scope of pronunciation skills. The teaching material is also general in the sense that is aiming at particularities of Norwegian without taking the learners' mother tongue into consideration.

The project presented here takes both these matters into account. The learner decides what will be the target dialect of Norwegian, and this is connected to information about the speaker's L1. Based on this information a contrastive analysis is performed in the L1-L2*map* database, and from that analysis a set of exercises is picked from the exercise bank of CALST and put into action.

2. Resources

2.1. L1-l2map

This database is created from information made available through the UCLA Phonological Segment Inventory Database (UPSID, Maddieson, 1984), the Lyon-Albuquerque Phonological Systems Database (LAPSyD) and other available sources.

The information is accessible in two ways. In L1-L2*map* (http://calst.hf.ntnu.no/L1-L2map/) phonological information is presented as in the IPA chart (Koreman, Bech, Husby, & Wik, 2011). Other information like phonotactic patterns is in designated tables (Martínez-Paricio et al., 2014). The dialectal perspective of Norwegian is maintained, as phonological information of eight Norwegian dialects is included (two dialects from each of the four dialectal regions).

The database is permanently under construction. On one hand new languages are included; today L1-L2*map* contains more than 500 languages. On the other hand, the language information is being "widened" in the sense that segmental information given in UPSID is supplemented with information related to phonotactics and stress placement. Later other prosodic features like tone and intonation will be included.

L1-L2*map* functions as a wiki, and experts on non-included languages are invited to contribute. There are no priorities for which languages to add, but from a Norwegian point of view, information on immigrant languages is of course important.

2.2. Multilingual tool

The contrastive analysis can be made between any of the languages in the database. In this sense CALST is a multilingual tool that can provide exercises for all languages included in the database given that such exercises are made available. A second version of CALST is currently under construction. Here English is the target language. Any initiative to broaden this perspective is welcomed.

2.3. CALST

The CALST exercise module has two submodules: vocabulary and phonology (Wik, 2011). The first contains 1000 frequent words. It introduces the central vocabulary for language learners at beginners level. The dialectal approach also allows the learner to check the pronunciation of each word in several dialects. In this way the skills in understanding different forms of Norwegian is improved.

The second module consists of phonological oriented exercises based on the linguistic data provided by L1-L2*map*. The linguistic data function as a filter and is fed into the exercise databank of CALST to create language specific exercises related to the spoken form of Norwegian chosen by the user.

The student activities are logged. The information on scores and progress is available to students, teachers and researchers. In addition, CALST is a learning system as exercises that do not present challenges to students will be removed. This is based on analysis of the behaviour of the initial group of students of a certain L1. Exercises where all students get top scores are regarded as not necessary, and will be removed by the program.

2.4. Exercises

The vocabulary exercises are of three kinds:

- *Listen and click*, where students click on illustrations as a response to spoken key words.

- *Listen and speak*, where students repeat spoken key words. The evaluation of the pronunciation is currently done by the user. We are now working to develop speech recognition systems to provide relevant feedback to accented pronunciation.

- *Listen and write*, where students type the keyword.

Speech samples can be provided at slow and normal speech rates, and the user can choose to see English translations of words.

Among the segmental exercises, there are two kinds of *Listen and click* exercises (AXB, Minimal pairs) in addition to *Listen and repeat*, and *Listen and write*.

The same exercises are found for exercises related to phonotactic properties. Since it is impossible to predict the repair strategy/ies which L2-learners use to adapt L2 structures to the restrictions which apply in their L1, CALST offers exercises to learn strategies to overcome these like simplification of clusters, replacement of sounds in clusters and metathesis.

3. Discussion

The construction of CALST has presented us with several challenges. Language data needed for L1-L2*map* is hard to find outside what is found in UPSID or LAPSyD. Descriptions may also be insufficient as information is completely lacking or not complete. The information may also be inconsistent. For levels "above" the segmentals, the problems can be summarized as follows:

- The theoretical foundation of phonological properties may have different approaches. For instance retroflex sounds have different status in phonological descriptions of Swedish, where they are not regarded as phonemes, and Norwegian, where they have phonemic status.

- The phonological properties of one single language may be analysed in several ways. One may ask who is the reliable authority of a given language to be quoted.

- The description of the phonological properties is insufficient. For instance information on diphthongs or phonotactics may be absent.

- There is no theoretical framework that can function as a reliable basis for contrastive analysis of phonological properties. What is the conceptual basis for crosslinguistic comparisons relating tones, intonation or speech rhythm?

For CALST the main challenge is to provide adequate ways of analysing the user's accented L2 Norwegian. Today the student is responsible for deciding whether their pronunciation is adequate.

In order to be able to make more objective evaluations, we have just launched a project with the aim to use automatic speech recognition as a basis to detect insertion, for instance (not to mention duration, stress placement, sound quality, intonation and speech rhythm).

4. Conclusions

CALST is a new multilingual tool that can be adapted to any target language if there is phonological information available. So far CALST contains segmental exercises related to eight Norwegian dialects. Exercises related to English as a second language is under development.

5. Acknowledgements

CALST is developed on the basis of funding from Norgesuniversitetet, the Norwegian Agency for Lifelong Learning (Vox), and Norwegian University of Science and Technology.

References

Koreman, J., Bech, Ø., Husby, O., & Wik, P. (2011). L1-L2*map* : a tool for multilingual contrastive analysis. *Proceedings of the 17th International Congress of Phonetic Sciences (ICPhS2011)*. Hong Kong.

Maddieson, I. (1984). *Patterns of sounds*. Cambridge: Cambridge University Press. doi:10.1017/CBO9780511753459

Martínez-Paricio, V., Koreman, J., Husby, O., Abrahamsen, J., & Bech, Ø. (2014). Expanding CALST: multilingual analysis of L1-L2 phonotactics for language teaching. *Pronunciation in Second Language Learning and Teaching (PSLLT 2014), Santa Barbara, EE. UU., 5-6 September 2014*.

Wik, P. (2011). *The Virtual language teacher: models and applications for language learning using embodied conversational agents*. Ph.D. thesis. KTH Royal Institute of Technology, Stockholm, Sweden.

VISP 2.0: methodological considerations for the design and implementation of an audio-description based app to improve oral skills

Ana Ibáñez Moreno[1] and Anna Vermeulen[2]

Abstract. In this paper the methodological steps taken in the conception of a new mobile application (app) are introduced. This app, called VISP (Videos for Speaking), is easily accessible and manageable, and is aimed at helping students of English as a Foreign Language (EFL) to improve their idiomaticity in their oral production. In order to do so, the app invites the user to make the Audio-Description (AD) of a clip, as part of a communicative task. This paper gives an account of the processes followed after creating and testing VISP, until arriving at the conception of its second version, VISP 2.0. This was accomplished by carrying out several empirical tests to evaluate the app and the learning outcomes it contributes to achieve. The data obtained to date have led to the proposal of some pedagogical guidelines that can be applied to a Mobile-Assisted Language Learning (MALL) app in order to make it enjoyable and, above all, effective.

Keywords: language learning, audio-description, speaking, MALL.

1. Introduction

Keeping in mind the idea of making audiovisual products accessible to visually impaired people, from the 1970s some films began to be audio-described. This means that, taking the gaps between dialogues, visual information is described orally. Interesting studies (Bourne & Jiménez Hurtado, 2007, for instance) have

---

1. Universidad Nacional de Educación a Distancia (UNED), Spain; aibanez@flog.uned.es

2. Ghent University, Belgium; anna.vermeulen@ugent.be

How to cite this article: Ibáñez Moreno, A., & Vermeulen, A. (2015). VISP 2.0: methodological considerations for the design and implementation of an audio-description based app to improve oral skills. In F. Helm, L. Bradley, M. Guarda, & S. Thouësny (Eds), *Critical CALL – Proceedings of the 2015 EUROCALL Conference, Padova, Italy* (pp. 249-253). Dublin: Research-publishing.net. http://dx.doi.org/10.14705/rpnet.2015.000341

shown the pedagogical benefits of this new mode of audiovisual translation, called audio-description (AD).

Additionally, in recent years AD has been applied in the face-to-face foreign language (FL) classroom (Ibáñez Moreno & Vermeulen, 2014), as well as in CALL (Talaván & Lertola, 2013) to improve students' competences, with positive results. In order to contribute to this new line of research, we have implemented AD as a tool to promote oral production skills with mobile devices (android operating systems). We designed a MALL application named VISP (VIdeos for SPeaking), which invites users with a B1 level of English (CEFR, 2001) to audio-describe a short film clip. The main aim of this app is to improve their idiomaticity (fluency, vocabulary, phraseological competence).

In this paper we outline the methodological steps which led to the creation of the second version of VISP, once the first version had been tested with Spanish and Belgian (Dutch speaking) EFL students at Universidad Nacional de Educación a Distancia (UNED) –VISP 1.1 – and at Ghent University (Belgium) –VISP 1.2. Taking into account the data obtained from the pre-questionnaire, the recordings and the post-questionnaire, we address the shortcomings of VISP 1 at different levels, which have been solved in VISP 2.0.

2. Method

2.1. Methodological preliminaries

VISP is conceived as a MALL app to be used ubiquitously in order to enhance the oral competences of EFL students. It has been designed in the framework of the communicative approach to language teaching and learning and follows the CEFR (2001) levels. Even if ubiquitous learning environments have increased and new technologies have been developed to adapt to the new learning styles, we believe that there are fewer chances for the average user, in this context, to practice oral production. In this sense, AD has proved to be a useful tool to promote oral skills in the FL classroom (Ibáñez Moreno, & Vermeulen, 2014), but it had not yet been tested in MALL. Therefore, VISP is the first AD-based MALL-app.

Within the philosophy of the communicative approach there are several methods and techniques. In this application we use the task-based approach, in the sense that VISP consists of communicative tasks whose goal is to achieve a specific learning objective (Ellis, 2003).

2.2. Conception of VISP

VISP has four screens, as seen in Figure 1 below.

Figure 1. Home screen of VISP

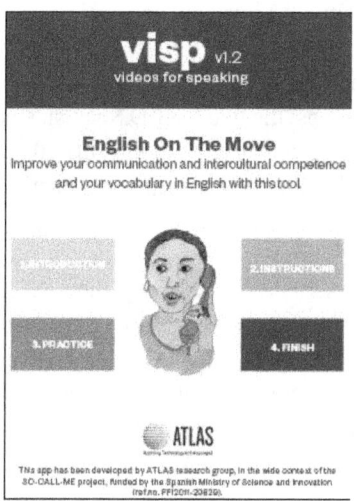

The first button, *Introduction*, includes a five-second sample of an AD, extracted from Memoirs of a Geisha, as a warming-up listening task. At the bottom of the *Introduction* page there is also a link to a pre-questionnaire, where users can complete a short test, which includes language content that will appear on the AD task and therefore on the AD script. The second button is the *Instructions* screen. The next step is the *Practice* screen, where the main task is found. There, users find 30-second-clips that they have to AD. Users can watch the clips as many times as they want, by clicking on Play and Rewind, until they feel ready to record their own AD (by clicking on Record). Once users are satisfied with their AD they go to the Finish screen. There they send their recording to an e-mail account. This screen also includes a self-evaluation section in the form of a post-questionnaire where they can watch the original clip with the oral AD, as well as the written original AD script, and compare their own AD to it.

3. Discussion

By now, a total of 22 students have tried the app: 12 Spanish students and 10 Belgian students. Two of the Spanish students were UNED students following a CALL course on English for Tourism, and the other 10 were on an Erasmus stay at Ghent University (Belgium). All participants had a B1 level of English (in terms of the CEFR). They all performed the main and essential part of the task, that is, the creation of the AD, and sent their recordings. As for the pre-questionnaire and the post-questionnaires, all Spanish students filled them in, whereas only two of the Belgian students took the time to complete them. The Spanish students also left some comments and (positively) rated the app.

The analysis of the transcriptions, in terms of accuracy, illustrated a significant difference between the groups: the two UNED Spanish students and the 10 Belgian students performed slightly more accurately than the 10 Spanish Erasmus students. When it came to self-evaluating their description of actions, however, the Spanish Erasmus students felt remarkably positive about how they had described what the character does. However, there is a discrepancy between these students' perception of what they say they described and the way they described it. In terms of the students' attitudes towards the app, measured through the questionnaires, the results show that all the Spanish students were more open and positive towards VISP than their Belgian counterparts. Also, the Spanish students rated VISP more positively, while the two Belgian students were more critical.

4. Conclusions

In the light of all the results described, in VISP 2 we observed the need to implement several changes. As regards the attitudinal contents, even if thanks to the post-questionnaires users can make the AD task a really effective one and assess whether their learning goals have been achieved, not all users like questionnaires and are so open for them. The Belgian users, who come from a more individualistic society (in pragmatic terms, as in Goethals & Depreitere, 2009), did not complete them. Therefore, our future work is in the line of giving alternative options to those users who do not find questionnaires attractive, and of designing the questionnaires in a different way so that they can also capture the attention of all users. As for procedural contents, in VISP 2.0 the post-questionnaire has been designed so as to more accurately assess the users' performance. That way, they will be able to analyse their own results in a more realistic way.

5. Acknowledgements

We would like to thank the Spanish Ministry of Science and Innovation, because this paper is funded through the Grant FFI2011-29829: Social Ontology-based Cognitively Augmented Language Learning Mobile Environment (SO-CALL-ME).

References

Bourne, J., & Jiménez Hurtado, C. (2007). From the visual to the verbal in two languages: a contrastive analysis of the audio description of The Hours in English and Spanish. In J. Díaz Cintas, P. Orero, & A. Remael (Eds), *Media for All* (pp. 175-187). Amsterdam: Rodopi.

CEFR. (2001). Common European framework of reference for languages: learning, teaching, and assessment. Cambridge: Cambridge University Press and the Council of Europe.

Ellis, R. (2003). *Task based language learning and teaching*. Oxford: Oxford University Press.

Goethals, P., & Depreitere, L. (2009). SpreekTaal: un proyecto didáctico y de investigación acerca de las funciones comunicativas. *Mosaico, 21*,14-18.

Ibáñez Moreno, A., & Vermeulen, A. (2014). La audiodescripción como técnica aplicada a la enseñanza y aprendizaje de lenguas para promover el desarrollo integrado de competencias. In R. Orozco (Ed.), *New directions on Hispanic linguistics* (pp. 263-292). Baton Rouge: Cambridge Scholars Publishing.

Talaván, N., & Lertola, J. (2013). Audiodescription and foreign language education: new approaches. *Paper presented at the 5th International Conference of Media for All association, Audiovisual translation: Expanding Borders, Dubrovnik, Croatia.*

The effects of video SCMC on English proficiency, speaking performance and willingness to communicate

Atsushi Iino[1] and Yukiko Yabuta[2]

Abstract. This paper introduces a case course with videoconferencing as a way of Synchronous Computer Mediated Communication (SCMC) for foreign language education in Japan. Research questions were to see the effects of videoconferencing on the learners' speaking ability and general English language proficiency, and also to see how the learners' international posture changed over time. Eight pairs of Japanese university English as a Foreign Language (EFL) learners experienced two semesters of 9-10 videoconferencing sessions per semester with an English teacher living in the Philippines. The task for the pairs was to discuss a social issue together with the teacher once a week. Their goal was to exchange mutual ideas on the designated topic. To lower the anxiety of speaking English as well as to practice discussion with fellow Japanese students, there was a 90-minute preparation period prior to each videoconferencing session. Pre-tests and post-tests results showed significant improvement in fluency, particularly in the amount of speech, and complexity of their speaking abilities. The learners also demonstrated progress in English proficiency. Their international posture stayed at a high level, but did not change much. However, their increased interest in working or participating in volunteer activities overseas was observed. The results indicated that the instruction based on videoconferencing helped improve learners' language and their global mind as a part of international posture.

Keywords: EFL learners, videoconferencing, speaking, international posture.

---

1. Hosei University, Japan; iino@hosei.ac.jp

2. Seisen Jogakuin College, Japan; yabuta@seisen-jc.ac.jp

How to cite this article: Iino, A., & Yabuta, Y. (2015). The effects of video SCMC on English proficiency, speaking performance and willingness to communicate. In F. Helm, L. Bradley, M. Guarda, & S. Thouësny (Eds), *Critical CALL – Proceedings of the 2015 EUROCALL Conference, Padova, Italy* (pp. 254-260). Dublin: Research-publishing. net. http://dx.doi.org/10.14705/rpnet.2015.000342

1. Introduction

Videoconferencing, an oral and visual mode of SCMC, seems to provide one of the solutions to EFL learners who have less opportunities to use L2 orally for communication. It has been found that such opportunities that include eye-contact, gestures, and taking turns in L2 enhances positive attitudes and motivation to learn L2 (Jauregi, de Graaff, van den Bergh, & Kriz, 2012; Yanguas, 2012). Negotiation of meaning, including clarification requests, modified output and corrective feedback for example, is expected to occur during videoconferencing, which leads to the learners' focus on form and eventually brings about their interlanguage development. Yet, these effects have been mainly based on the modes of text chat and oral SCMC.

It is rare to find research on the effects of audio/video CMC on the development of speaking skills (Wang, 2006) and Willingness To Communication (WTC, Yanguas & Flores, 2014). Thus, we decided to provide the learners videoconferencing experience through Skype with native English speakers regularly during a semester in order to see how their output skill in speaking, input skill proficiency and international posture changed. We particularly focused on international posture in this study, which is claimed to be strongly related to WTC (Yashima, 2002). This psychological concept is defined as the learner's attitude of openness to different cultures, which is indicated, for example, by the willingness to go abroad, readiness to communicate with native speakers, and this in turn is claimed to affect the learner's communication behavior. In order to find the effects of the videoconferencing, we set the following questions:

- What are the effects of videoconferencing on the learners' output in speaking?

- What are the effects of videoconferencing on the learners' input skill proficiency?

- How does the learners' international posture change over time through videoconferencing?

2. Method

2.1. Participants

Sixteen sophomore and junior students at a university in Japan received instruction including videoconferencing for one year. They consisted of 10 males and 6 females. These students had learned English for six years at the secondary level and one year at the university level. The proficiency level of English measured by TOEIC test with listening and reading sections was 539.1 points (SD=165.1), which is a little beyond all the test takers' average in Japan (M=512 points, SD=181), according to the Educational Testing Service (2014).

All the participants agreed to the use of their data for this research.

2.2. Instruction: task-based videoconferencing

The goal of the course was to enhance the ability of using English and to practice cross cultural communication. The classes were held every Tuesday, and the videoconferencing was held at the designated time on the following days in the same week. Eight pairs of learners interacted with an English teacher in the Philippines through Skype once a week and did a role play. The goal for the students in the role play was to persuade the teacher to support their position on a particular issue. For example, one learner took the role of promoting casinos in a small town, the other took the role of stopping it, and the teacher played the role of the mayor of the town. At the end of the task, the teacher, as mayor, judged which side won. Such sessions were held 9 times in the spring semester, and 10 times in the fall semester.

For the task-based videoconferencing to be successful, reading material featuring pros and cons of social issues were assigned to comprehend beforehand. The preparation class on Tuesdays was constructed with the following activities as pre-tasks:

- Step 1. Discussion between learners on an issue.

- Step 2. Sharing expressions that they wanted to say but could not say in the previous step. The learners used L1 and the Japanese teacher of English helped find the proper expressions in English.

- Step3. Presentations on the issue of the week given by three designated pairs and other learners take notes of key concepts.

- Step 4. Practice a role play task in a group of three in which each learner takes one of the three roles: an advantage or positive side, a disadvantage or negative side, and a decision maker.

- Step 5. Role play through videoconferencing with an English teacher in the Philippines who plays the role of a decision maker.

- Step 6. Consolidating essay writing about the videoconferencing discussion with 150 words as an assignment for the next week's class.

2.3. Measurement

To measure speaking skill, a picture narration task was adopted. The learners were required to tell a story from three serial pictures. They took the test at the beginning and at the end of the academic year. The spoken data was recorded and analyzed from the perspectives of complexity, accuracy, and fluency.

To measure overall English proficiency, a TOEIC mock test was conducted at the beginning and the end of the year. The test consisted of 50 points for listening comprehension, and 50 points for vocabulary, grammar, and reading comprehension.

To measure WTC and international posture, a questionnaire based on Yashima (2002) was conducted at the beginning, the middle, and the end of the academic year. Six componential concepts were branched into 32 questions.

3. Results and discussion

Table 1 shows the descriptive statistics of the spoken data analyses. Wilcoxon's sign rank test was adopted for nonparametric statistical analyses due to the limited number of participants.

Regarding fluency, progress was observed in most of the criteria (picture description point, duration of speech, number of words, holistic evaluation) except for Words Per Minute (WPM). In the results of complexity, the number of words per sentence showed positive and statistically significant differences. The repetition of the same task could explain this progress.

Regarding accuracy, no significant difference was found. This could have resulted from a 'trade off effect' between fluency and accuracy (Skehan, 1996). Another factor could be the absence of explicit focus on form instructions.

Regarding the differences in English proficiency, significant positive increase of the mean scores were observed (see Table 2).

Regarding the change in WTC and international posture, the positive change was observed in the group's interest in international vocation or activities. More learners seemed interested in working in a global workplace compared to the pre survey. It could be said that a long-term instruction targeted for videoconferencing fosters a global mind. In other componential concepts, no significant difference was found among the three times of data collection (the beginning, the middle, and the end of the academic year). One possible reason is the fact that the learners demonstrated a fairly positive attitude from the beginning of the year and the videoconferencing might have helped maintain their positive attitude.

Table 1. Descriptive statistics of spoken data and the results of Wilcoxon signed-rank test

		M	SD	Z-value	p-value	Effect Size r
Fluency	Pre: Points to describe	2.87	1.3			
	Post: Points to describe	4.07	0.7	-2.88	.004*	.53
	Pre: Number of words	47.53	17.86			
	Post: Number of words	71.2	12.62	-3.30	.001*	.60
	Pre: Duration of speech	51.33	10.22			
	Post: Duration of speech	67.73	10	-2.79	.005*	.51
	Pre: Holistic Evaluation	2.93	0.96			
	Post: Holistic Evaluation	3.67	0.49	-2.60	.009*	.47
	Pre: WPM	57.18	22.88			
	Post: WPM	64.81	17	-1.59	.112	.29
Complexity	Pre: Number of clauses	4.73	2.46			
	Post: Number of clauses	7.2	1.86	-2.29	.022*	.42
	Pre: Number of words/clause	9.83	1.68			
	Post: Number of words/clause	11.12	0.93	-2.44	.015*	.45
Accuracy	Pre: Number of correct verbs	2.27	2.02			
	Post: Number of correct verbs	3.4	1.59	-1.92	.055	.35
	Pre: % of correct verbs	46%	36%			
	Post: % of correct verbs	45%	21%	-0.18	.861	.03

* $p < .05$

Significant differences were found in all items in English proficiency measured by the mock version of the TOEIC test. The scores in pre- and post-tests in listening and total score were statistically significant at the 1 percent level and showed medium effect size. Those scores in reading were statistically significant at the 5 percent level and showed large effect size.

Table 2. Descriptive statistics of TOEIC mock tests

	M	SD	Z-value	p-value	Effect Size r
Pre: TOEIC LISTENING	33.43	7.97			
Post: TOEIC LISTENING	38.79	5.74	-2.7	.007**	0.49
Pre: TOEIC READING	37.57	7.19			
Post: TOEIC READING	41.14	5.07	-2.58	.010*	0.47
Pre: TOEIC Total	71	14.19			
Post: TOEIC Total	79.93	10.19	-2.9	.004**	0.53

* $p < .05$, ** $p < .01$

4. Conclusion

This research revealed that the effectiveness of videoconferencing was quite evident on speaking skill, overall proficiency, and international posture. The results seem to come from the repetitive and longitudinal involvement with authentic communication through videoconferencing and the impact from the preceding activities. Through the learning cycle, the learners increased their English proficiency and international posture. It was not only the experience of videoconferences, but also the before and after activities that seemed important for the learners' development.

5. Acknowledgements

This research was partially supported by the Ministry of Education, Science, Sports and Culture in Japan, Grant-in-Aid for Scientific Research (C), 2014-2016 (26370675, Atsushi Iino).

The authors appreciate the members of the project for their valuable advice: Professor Hideo Oka (Professor Emeritus of the University of Tokyo), Dr Akiko Fujii (the University of Sacred Heart), Professor Yoichi Nakamura (Seisen Jogakuin College), and Ms Heather Johnson (Hosei University).

References

Educational Testing Service. (2014). *Report on test takers worldwide: the TOEIC® listening and reading test*. Retrieved from https://www.ets.org/s/toeic/pdf/ww_data_report_unlweb.pdf

Jauregi, K., de Graaff, R., van den Bergh, H., & Kriz, M. (2012). Native-non-native speaker interactions through video-web communication: a clue for enhancing motivation? *Computer Assisted Language Learning, 25*(1), 1-19. doi:10.1080/09588221.2011.582587

Skehan, P. (1996). A framework for the implementation of task-based instruction. *Applied Linguistics, 17*(1), 38-62. doi:10.1093/applin/17.1.38

Wang, Y. (2006). Negotiation of meaning in desktop videoconferencing-supported distance language learning. *ReCALL, 18*(1), 122-145. doi:10.1017/S0958344006000814

Yanguas, I. (2012). Vocabulary acquisition in oral computer-mediated interaction. *Calico Journal, 29*(3), 507-531. doi:10.11139/cj.29.3.507-531

Yanguas, I., & Flores, A. (2014). Learners' willingness to communicate in face-to-face versus oral computer mediated communication. *The jaltcalljournal, 10*(2), 83-103.

Yashima, T. (2002). Willingness to communicate in a second language: the Japanese EFL context. *The Modern Language Journal, 86*(1), 54-66. doi:10.1111/1540-4781.00136

An EFL flipped learning course design: utilizing students' mobile online devices

Yasushige Ishikawa[1], Reiko Akahane-Yamada[2], Craig Smith[3], Mutsumi Kondo[4], Yasushi Tsubota[5], and Masatake Dantsuji[6]

Abstract. This paper reports on a research project in a university English as Foreign Language (EFL) program in Japan which explored ways to sustain active participation in e-learning tasks. The tasks were intended to improve students' scores on the Test of English for International Communication (TOEIC), a test used by businesses to make hiring decisions. The research adopted a Flipped Learning (FL) approach to Blended Learning (BL). A web-based courseware, ATR CALL BRIX (http://www.atr-lt.jp/products/brix/index.html), which featured e-learning materials for the TOEIC Test, was used. The students used mobile devices to access the courseware before class in order to prepare for in-class teacher-student analysis of their performance on the learning tasks. The teaching methodology integrated the online and in-class tasks in a single learning environment by means of an e-mentoring system used in conjunction with an in-class student self-evaluation task. The findings of pre- and post-TOEIC testing showed a significant degree of TOEIC score improvement in the experimental group. Post-course evaluations revealed that the combination of e-mentoring and the in-class self-evaluation system had encouraged sustained engagement in outside-of-class learning activities.

Keywords: EFL, blended learning, flipped learning, MALL.

---

1. Kyoto University of Foreign Studies, Japan; yasuishikawa@hotmail.com
2. ATR Intelligent Robotics and Communication Laboratories, Japan; yamada@atr-lt.jp
3. Kyoto University of Foreign Studies, Japan; craigkufs@hotmail.com
4. Tezukayamagakuin University, Japan; kondo@la.tezuka-gu.ac.jp
5. Kyoto Institute of Technology, Japan; tsubota-yasushi@kit.ac.jp
6. Academic Center for Computing and Media Studies, Kyoto University, Japan; www-call@media.kyoto-u.ac.jp

How to cite this article: Ishikawa, Y., Akahane-Yamada, R., Smith, C., Kondo, M., Tsubota, Y., Dantsuji, M. (2015). An EFL flipped learning course design: utilizing students' mobile online devices. In F. Helm, L. Bradley, M. Guarda, & S. Thouësny (Eds), *Critical CALL – Proceedings of the 2015 EUROCALL Conference, Padova, Italy* (pp. 261-267). Dublin: Research-publishing.net. http://dx.doi.org/10.14705/rpnet.2015.000343

1. Introduction: flipped learning for foreign language education

BL is a combination of conventional classroom face-to-face delivery of lesson instruction with online-mediated instruction (Osguthorpe & Graham, 2003). FL is a BL teaching methodology which uses the two BL channels of communication to reverse the conventional patterns of classroom teaching and learning. FL rests on an assumption that students will use learning task materials before class, so that classroom time can be devoted to interaction between students and their teacher that will support the outside-of-class study through mutual problem-solving tasks and analytical examinations of learning materials. This study examined a FL approach to generating, and then sustaining, student motivation that would result in effective long-term use of on-line EFL learning materials.

Until recently, it has been expected that university students would mainly use laptop and desktop computers to access online learning materials at school and elsewhere. However, the use of a variety of mobile devices with online access, such as mobile phones and tablet computers, is now the preferred means of student-to-student online communication in some university communities. For example, 94.9% of students who will graduate in Japan in 2016 have smartphones compared with 16.4% of the 2012 graduates. More than 85% of these students use one Social Network System, LINE, not only to communicate with their friends but also as a source of information. In sharp contrast, only 11.2% of the 2016 graduating class use desk top computers as their main means of information acquisition (Mynavi, 2015). Thus, this research project explored a mobile assisted language learning medium of BL methodology.

2. Course design: the EFL flipped learning course

Figure 1. Procedure of activities in one session

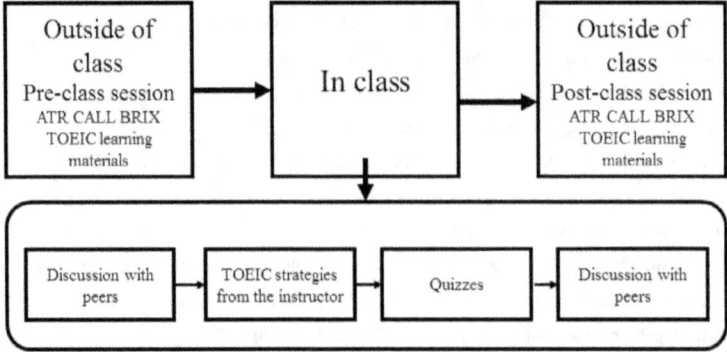

In order to help students improve their TOEIC scores, an original two-semester EFL FL course was implemented from April 2014 to January 2015 at a university in Japan. Each learning unit had three phases: 1) pre-class online completion of TOEIC course materials; 2) individualized problem-solving instruction in class; and 3) post-class online completion of self-assessment and reflection learning tasks (see Figure 1).

2.1. ATR CALL BRIX

Outside of class, a www-based courseware, ATR CALL BRIX (http://www.atr-lt.jp/products/brix/index.html), which included a Learning Management System (LMS), was used. The LMS provided a variety of learning materials designed to prepare students for the TOEIC Test. Seven different functions were featured on the LMS: 1) study logs, 2) feedback on the achievement rates of student-set goals, 3) records of the frequency of the use of the materials, 4) a record of time spent on learning, 5) a continuous update of the average score on the TOEIC learning tasks, 6) an evaluation of students' weak points and advice for further learning, and 7) students' rankings in comparison with other students in the course (Ishikawa et al., 2014).

2.2. A student self-evaluation system

A student self-evaluation system that was intended to contribute to the development of students' self-regulated learning attitudes, skills and behavior, and thus, sustain student use of the learning materials, was integrated in the courseware. The system combined e-mentoring in the LMS outside of class, and weekly in-class self-evaluations as part of the course routine. At the beginning of the first semester, students were placed in three groups – high, mid and low – according to their TOEIC scores. An e-mentoring team of one teacher and a teaching assistant sent different need-based messages of advice and encouragement to the students every week by means of a social networking system called LINE (http://line.me/en/). The messages were varied according to how successfully the students had completed the learning materials (Ishikawa et al., 2015).

3. Validation of the study

3.1. Participants

551 first-year students who enrolled in a TOEIC course participated in this study. 348 students were included in an experimental group and 203 students in a control

group. The students in the experimental group were placed in three groups – high, mid and low (mean ± 0.5SD) – according to their scores of the TOEIC Test which they took at the beginning of the course.

3.2. Methods

For the experimental group, the course design described in section 2, above, was implemented. In the control group, students followed the same course design but they used neither the web-based courseware, ATR CALL BRIX, nor the self-evaluation system. All their learning materials were paper-based.

Pre- and post-TOEIC Tests were conducted before the course started and at the end of the second semester in January 2015. The experimental-group students took the TOEIC Test again at the end of the first semester in July 2014, in addition to the pre- and post-TOEIC Test. The students also completed course evaluations at the end of the second semester.

4. Results and discussion

4.1. TOEIC testing

The increase of TOEIC scores between the mid and low groups in the experimental group and the control group was compared. The high group in the experimental group was excluded because the average scores for the pre-test in both experimental and control groups should be comparable. The increase of the scores in the experimental group was 151.38 and that in the control group was 54.04. The scores of the post-test in the two groups was compared and there was a significant difference ($p<.001$; $d=.56$) as is shown in Table 1.

Table 1. Results of pre- and post-TOEIC testing

	Experimental			Control			t	d
	Mean	SD	n	Mean	SD	n		
Pre-TOEIC (April)	345.97	66.82	243	361.03	89.14	203	2.00 *	0.14
Post-TOEIC (January)	497.35	107.77	243	415.07	107.20	203	8.05 ***	0.56

*$p<.05$, ***$p<.001$

Furthermore, students who took the TOEIC Test in April and July in 2014, and January in 2015 in each of the three groups of the experimental group improved their TOEIC scores by approximately 150 points from April in 2014 to January in 2015 as is shown in Table 2.

Table 2. Results of TOEIC testing of the three groups in the experimental group

	April		July		January		n
	Mean	SD	Mean	SD	Mean	SD	
High	511.95	61.21	603.38	81.75	652.38	86.43	105
Intermediate	393.89	28.71	507.17	71.91	543.44	96.14	122
Low	286.12	43.65	409.58	79.17	443.50	96.35	107

4.2. Post course student evaluation

The course evaluation for the experimental group conducted at the end of the second semester consisted of 20 questions (see Table 3). Four open-ended questions asked about the students' feelings about the course and the in-class activities, the problems that they may have found in using the LMS learning materials, and the messages sent by the e-mentor team. A 4-point Likert scale was used for the responses in order to adequately allow for the expression of a range of participants' feelings about the course. The ratings of 2 and 1 respectively corresponded to disagree, and strongly disagree; and the ratings of 3 and 4 respectively corresponded to agree, and strongly agree. The rate of reliability of the twenty 4-point Likert scale questions was high ($\alpha=.91$).

Table 3. Results of the questions in the participants' course evaluation

Item	Mean	SD
1 The in-class activites helped improve my total TOEIC score.	3.26	0.79
2 The in-class activites helped improve my TOEIC listening score.	3.24	0.81
3 The in-class activites helped improve my TOEIC reading score.	3.17	0.84
4 The in-class activites helped improve my vocabulary.	2.90	0.84
5 The in-class activites helped improve my English listening skills.	3.19	0.82
6 The in-class activites helped improve my English reading skills.	3.00	0.85
7 In the in-class activities, I was able to solve problems that I found in the outside-of-class activities.	2.76	0.84
8 I was interested in the in-class activities.	2.82	0.89
9 I want to continue the in-class activities.	2.80	0.93
10 I used the learning materials in the LMS of the ATR CALL BRIX.	3.38	0.82
11 The learning materials in the LMS of the ATR CALL BRIX helped improve my total TOEIC score.	2.91	0.90
12 The learning materials in the LMS of the ATR CALL BRIX helped improve my TOEIC listening score.	3.05	0.86
13 The learning materials in the LMS of the ATR CALL BRIX helped improve my TOEIC reading score.	2.77	0.93
14 The learning materials in the LMS of the ATR CALL BRIX helped improve my vocabulary.	2.88	0.91
15 The learning materials in the LMS of the ATR CALL BRIX helped improve my English listening skills.	3.00	0.89
16 The learning materials in the LMS of the ATR CALL BRIX helped improve my English reading skills.	2.81	0.94
17 I was interested in using the learning materials in the LMS of the ATR CALL BRIX.	2.50	0.98
18 I want to continue using the learning materials in the LMS of the ATR CALL BRIX.	2.49	1.05
19 I often found some problems using the learning materials in the LMS of the ATR CALL BRIX.	2.51	1.03
20 The flipped learning lessons suited my own learning style.	2.67	0.87

$n = 331$

As for the in-class activities, the participants were convinced that the activities were useful for strengthening their TOEIC listening and reading skills. Typical comments were similar to the following student's response: "I enjoyed the in-class activities. I was able to learn TOEIC test-taking strategies to improve my TOEIC scores". However, some participants did not feel that they were able to solve problems that they had faced while using the LMS learning materials: "I don't know why but I often had problems in using the learning materials". There were other negative reactions to the use of the LMS: looking at the display screen hurt their eyes; and they found problems in using the learning materials at home.

However, the majority of the participants felt that the learning materials in the LMS helped improve their TOEIC scores. Some of the participants believed that the FL approach in the study suited their own learning styles: "The encouragement from the teacher let me continue the outside-of-class activities, I really think so".

5. Conclusion

The results of the pre- and post-TOEIC testing showed that the EFL FL course design for the experimental group was more effective in helping students improve their TOEIC scores than the course design for the control group, and that the students at all TOEIC-score levels in the experimental group improved their TOEIC scores by an average of approximately 150 points. Moreover, the study revealed that the self-evaluation system encouraged students to sustain engagement in outside-of-class e-learning learning activities. Further research should be conducted to investigate the most productive uses of mobile devices for e-learning.

6. Acknowledgements

This study was supported by a Grant-in-Aid for Scientific Research (#23242032) from the Japan Society for the Promotion of Science.

References

Ishikawa, Y., Akahane-Yamada, R., Kondo, M., Smith, C., Tsubota, Y., & Dantsuji, M. (2014). An interoperable ICT educational application for TOEIC preparatory study. In M. Khosrow-Pour (Ed.), *Encyclopedia of information science and technology* (3rd ed.) (pp. 2433-2444). Hershey, PA: Information Science Reference.

Ishikawa, Y., Akahane-Yamada, R., Kitamura, M., Smith, C., Tsubota, Y., & Dantsuji, M. (2015). Student self-evaluation system: sustaining outside-of-class CALL activities in a university EFL blended learning course. In A. Gimeno-Sanz, M. Levy, F. Blin, & D. Barr (Eds.), *WorldCALL: Sustainability and computer-assisted language learning* (pp. 316-353). London, UK: Bloomsbury Publishing.

Mynavi. (2015). *2016 nen sotsu daigakusei no life style report* [Survey report on the life style of university students who will graduate in 2016]. Retrieved from http://saponet.mynavi.jp/enq_gakusei/lifestyle/data/lifestyle_2016.pdf

Osguthorpe, R. T., & Graham, C. R. (2003). Blended learning environments: definitions and directions. *The Quarterly Review of Distance Education, 4*(3), 227-233.

Integrating telecollaboration for intercultural language acquisition at secondary education: lessons learned

Kristi Jauregi[1]

Abstract. The TILA[2] project originated from the need to explore whether and how telecollaboration affects language learning processes for communication, intercultural understanding and motivation of youngsters learning foreign languages at secondary schools and to empower teachers to pioneer meaningful pedagogical innovation in the curriculum of foreign languages at secondary schools. In the 2,5 year project, 837 pupils, 300 student teachers and 48 teachers participated in telecollaboration exchanges. The results show that task-based telecollaboration can be successfully integrated in the foreign language curriculum by blending different pedagogical activities. These exchanges can contribute to enhance pupils' communicative competence, intercultural awareness and motivation.

Keywords: telecollaboration, multimodal interaction, intercultural competence, motivation, teacher training, tasks.

1. Introduction

Much has been written about telecollaboration projects and how they contribute to shape the development of communicative competence (Guth & Helm, 2010; Canto, Jauregi & Bergh, 2013), intercultural awareness (Belz & Thorne, 2006; O'Dowd, 2007; Canto, Graaff, & Jauregi, 2014) and motivation (Jauregi, Graaff, Bergh, & Kriz, 2012) of those engaging in telecollaboration tasks (González-Lloret & Ortega, 2014; Jauregi et al. 2011; O'Dowd & Waire, 2009). But most of these studies report on experiences carried out at tertiary education (Pol, 2013). The question is whether these results are transferable to secondary education where

---

1. Utrecht University & Fontys University of Applied Sciences, Netherlands; k.jauregi@uu.nl

2. TILA: Telecollaboration for Intercultural Language Acquisition (www.tilaproject.eu).

How to cite this article: Jauregi, J. (2015). Integrating telecollaboration for intercultural language acquisition at secondary education: lessons learned. In F. Helm, L. Bradley, M. Guarda, & S. Thouësny (Eds), *Critical CALL – Proceedings of the 2015 EUROCALL Conference, Padova, Italy* (pp. 268-273). Dublin: Research-publishing.net. http://dx.doi.org/10.14705/rpnet.2015.000344

young pupils have to learn foreign languages in quite different circumstances. But very little is known about it.

The TILA project (Jauregi, Melchor-Couto, & Vilar, 2013) originated from this very specific need and aimed at exploring how telecollaboration may affect language learning processes for communication, intercultural understanding and motivation of youngsters at secondary schools. One of the ambitions of TILA has been to design a model for sustainable integration of telecollaboration activities in blended pedagogical approaches at secondary education.

2. Data and methodology

837 learners, 300 student teachers and 48 teachers participated in different pilot experiences using synchronous (chat, videocommunication and 3D virtual worlds) and/or asynchronous (wikis, blogs and discussion forum) communication tools between November 2013 and June 2015. 55 tasks for different target languages, proficiency levels, interaction tools and communication constellations have been developed[3] for telecollaboration exchanges (Jauregi, 2015).

Pupils participated in dyadic or small group interactions either using the target language as *lingua franca* (a foreign language for those pupils collaborating in the exchanges) or in a tandem constellation, with pupils interacting with a native/ expert speaker of the target language, alternating languages (French pupils learning Spanish who communicate in French and in Spanish with Spanish pupils learning French). Although in the first pilot experiences most teachers preferred the tandem communication constellation (60% of all exchanges), in the follow up sessions the *lingua franca* constellation was the favourite one (72%).

In the initial pilot experiences telecollaboration exchanges were organised at school, mostly in the computer lab, but as many technological problems were experienced with the school hardware and internet connections, and because of lack of privacy for pupils when conducting the conversations, in the follow up many of these exchanges were carried out quite successfully ,from home by flipping pedagogies.

Data from surveys, recordings and interviews were gathered for our mixed method research approach to studying the effects of telecollaboration on youngsters at secondary schools.

---

3. Tasks are all available at the project site: www.tilaproject.eu.

3. Findings

In the following, the main findings of the study will be presented focusing on the impact of telecollaboration on pupils' intercultural communicative competence and their motivation.

3.1. The development of intercultural communicative competence

Results on the analysis of chat logs and video communication recordings indicate that telecollaboration exchanges have a positive impact on pupils' intercultural communicative competence as pupils are provided with opportunities for spontaneous and authentic written and spoken communication with real peers. The telecollaboration tasks seemed to enhance intercultural competence and awareness as pupils engaged in conversations, exchanging their opinions on cultural similarities and differences, and reflected upon rich intercultural points that emerged in discourse. In this sense, tasks that are close to pupils' lives, where they can draw on their own experiences and opinions seem to work best in telecollaboration exchanges. Pupils were curious about other ways of organising lives, of doing things; they succeeded in showing openness and interest to know more about the *Other* and resorted to meta discursive conversational devices to clarify intercultural meaning (Kroon, Jauregi, & Thije, 2015). An overall cooperative communication attitude seemed to prevail in the exchanges analysed.

It was observed that the various tools greatly differ in their communication affordances. Chat discourses were found to be quite fragmentary, highly task driven, with few instances where pupils truly engaged in topic co-creation and negotiation of meaning. Communication patterns in BigBlueButton (video communication platform), on the contrary, were far more complex, with pupils being more engaged in elaborating topics, in sharing personal experiences and in negotiating meaning. Because of the speakers' visual presence and the immediacy of spoken language, interactions in BigBlueButton seemed to be more conducive to enhancing intercultural openness curiosity and awareness (Tró Morató, 2015). The favourite interaction tool for telecollaboration exchanges was video communication (the open source BigBlueButton) both in the pilot (64%) and the follow-up activities (83%).

The differences in communication patterns that tools allow for should be seen as an opportunity for complementary pedagogic use. "A multi-modal telecollaboration approach offering tool options from virtual worlds and video communication to chat and forum is ideally suited for providing practice opportunities for all skills relevant in foreign language learning from reading and writing to listening and speaking" (Hoffstaedter & Kohn, 2015, p. 5).

3.2. Impact on motivation

Within the TILA project, a study was carried out to explore the motivational dimension in secondary school pupils. A total of 202 foreign language learners from Spain, France, the Netherlands and the UK took part in this study between September 2013 and June 2015.

All participants completed an average of four foreign language interaction sessions either by written chat or by video communication. They worked in either lingua franca, tandem or mixed constellations. After every session, pupils completed a questionnaire including 21 items to be rated on a 5 point Likert scale. The data collected shows relevant findings that provide new insights to this particular field of research. Pupils that interacted via chat and in tandem constellations tend to show higher self-efficacy beliefs than those engaged in lingua franca exchanges using video communication. With regards to anxiety levels, they seem to decrease significantly as sessions progress. In addition, statistical differences were found according to the communication constellation used, with the lingua franca group presenting systematically the lowest anxiety scores. Similarly, the chat environment turned out to be less anxiety-provoking than the video communication platform. Regarding the use of webcam, participants seem to feel more at ease when their partner cannot see them through the webcam only during the first sessions.

4. Conclusion

TILA has pioneered a pedagogical innovative change in secondary education by looking at sustainable ways to integrate telecollaboration in foreign language curricula, while studying the effects that such exchanges may have on the intercultural communicative competence and motivation of pupils.

A wealth of data has been gathered for analysis. Initial results show that task-driven telecollaboration exchanges do have a positive impact in the development of intercultural communicative competence of pupils and on their motivation. Video communication seems to stimulate more complex discourse production than chat encounters and might be more useful for stimulating richer intercultural exchanges than chat. Yet, chat and *lingua franca* communication constellation seem to trigger less anxiety than video communication. Additional research will be needed to substantiate these findings.

5. Acknowledgements

We would like to thank the pupils and their teachers in the participating schools as well as the whole TILA community for their contribution to the TILA research team.

References

Belz, J., & Thorne, S. (Eds.). (2006). *Internet-mediated intercultural foreign language education.* Boston: Thomson Heinle.

Canto, S., Graaff, de R., & Jauregi, K. (2014). Collaborative tasks for negotiation of intercultural meaning in virtual worlds and video-web communication. In M. González-Lloret & L. Ortega (Eds.), *Technology and tasks: exploring technology-mediated TBLT.* Amsterdam / Philadelphia: John Benjamins.

Canto, S., Jauregi, K., & Bergh, van den H. (2013). Integrating cross-cultural interaction through video-communication and virtual worlds in foreign language teaching programs. Burden or added value? *ReCALL, 25*(1), 105-121. doi:10.1017/s0958344012000274

González-Lloret, M., & Ortega, L. (Eds.). (2014). *Technology-mediated TBLT: researching technology and tasks.* Amsterdam: John Benjamin. doi:10.1075/tblt.6

Guth, S., & Helm, F. (Eds.). (2010). *Telecollaboration 2.0: language literacies and intercultural learning in the 21st century.* Bern: Peter Lang.

Hoffstaedter, K., & Kohn, K. (2015). Telecollaboration for intercultural foreign language conversations in secondary school contexts: task design and pedagogic implementation. In *TILA Research Results on Telecollaboration.* Retrieved from http://www.tilaproject.eu/moodle/mod/page/view.php?id=1495

Jauregi, K. (2015). Task development for telecollaboration among youngsters. In *Proceedings of the ANTWERP CALL 2015 Conference: Task design and CALL, 6-8 July 2015*, Universitat Rovira i Virgili, Tarragona, Spain.

Jauregi, K., Canto, S., de Graaff, R., Koenraad, A., & Moonen, M. (2011). Verbal interaction in Second Life: towards a pedagogic framework for task design. *Computer Assisted Language Learning Journal, 24*(1), 77-101. doi:10.1080/09588221.2010.538699

Jauregi, K., Graaff, de R., Bergh, van den H., & Kriz, M. (2012). Native non-native speaker interactions through video-web communication, a clue for enhancing motivation. *Computer Assisted Language Learning Journal, 25*(1), 1-19. doi:10.1080/09588221.2011.582587

Jauregi, K., Melchor-Couto, S., & Vilar, E. (2013). The European Project TILA. In L. Bradley & S. Thouësny (Eds.), *20 years of Eurocall: learning from the past looking to the future* (pp. 123-129). Dublin: Research-publishing.net.. doi:10.14705/rpnet.2013.000149

Kroon, L. v. d., Jauregi, K., & Thije, J. ten. (2015). Telecollaboration in foreign language curricula: a case study on intercultural understanding during synchronous telecollaboration sessions through video communication. *International Journal of Computer-Assisted Language Learning & Teaching, 5*(3), 20-41.

O'Dowd, R. (Ed.). (2007). *Online intercultural exchange: an introduction for foreign language teachers*. Clevedon: Multilingual Matters.

O'Dowd, R., & Waire, P. (2009). Critical issues in telecollaborative task design. *CALL Journal, 22*(2), 173-188. doi:10.1080/09588220902778369

Pol, L. (2013). *Telecollaboration in secondary education: an added value?* Unpublished Master thesis. Utrecht University.

Tró Morató, T. (2015). *Telecollaboration for intercultural language acquisition. Analysis of secondary education pupils' discourses in chat and videoconference format within the Telecollaboration for Intercultural Language Acquisition (TILA) framework*. Unpublished Master Thesis. University of Girona.

Cross-cultural discussions in a 3D virtual environment and their affordances for learners' motivation and foreign language discussion skills

Kristi Jauregi[1], Leena Kuure[2], Pim Bastian[3], Dennis Reinhardt[4], and Tuomo Koivisto[5]

Abstract. Within the European TILA[6] project a case study was carried out where pupils from schools in Finland and the Netherlands engaged in debating sessions using the 3D virtual world of OpenSim once a week for a period of 5 weeks. The case study had two main objectives: (1) to study the impact that the discussion tasks undertaken in a virtual environment have on the discussion skills and motivations of high school pupils, and (2) to explore how the presence of a peer from a different culture might influence the discussions and pupils' engagement. The discussion tasks in virtual worlds were very much appreciated by the participants. Telecollaboration, or the possibility to interact with pupils across borders, was found to have an additional motivational effect on pupils. Even if participants with varying linguistic resources may successfully work together in many authentic situations, telecollaboration in a Lingua Franca with focus on debates, for example, requires careful matching of the participants according to their proficiency levels. Otherwise the experience might increase anxiety levels of the less proficient pupils.

Keywords: telecollaboration, multimodal interaction, virtual worlds, intercultural communication, discussion skills.

---

1. Utrecht University & Fontys University of Applied Sciences, Netherlands; k.jauregi@uu.nl
2. University of Oulu, Finland; leena.kuure@oulu.fi
3. Utrecht University, Netherlands; p.bastian@students.uu.nl
4. Utrecht University, Netherlands; d.reinhardt@students.uu.nl
5. University of Oulu, Finland; tuomo.koivisto@eduouka.fi
6. Telecollaboration for Intercultural Language Acquisition: www.tilaproject.eu

How to cite this article: Jauregi, K., Kuure, L., Bastian, P., Reinhardt, D., & Koivisto, T. (2015). Cross-cultural discussions in a 3D virtual environment and their affordances for learners' motivation and foreign language discussion skills. In F. Helm, L. Bradley, M. Guarda, & S. Thouësny (Eds), *Critical CALL – Proceedings of the 2015 EUROCALL Conference, Padova, Italy* (pp. 274-280). Dublin: Research-publishing.net. http://dx.doi.org/10.14705/rpnet.2015.000345

1. Introduction

Telecollaboration introduces an important dimension to foreign language learning, as it puts authentic interaction with peers in an intercultural setting at the center of the innovative pedagogical agenda. In this sense, language learning is not just about learning grammar and words and filling in gaps; it is about activating and using language to communicate with real people, in our case, across borders, and come to know who they are, how they live, what they think and undertaking activities together while reflecting about intercultural concerns. Teachers can resort to different internet applications to organise telecollaboration sessions. One of the appealing environments are 3D virtual worlds because of the rich multimodal communication affordances they offer and the actions they allow for in different scenarios.

This paper introduces a case study which focuses on telecollaboration among pupils from Dutch and Finnish schools. The aim was twofold: to shed light on the impact of the discussion tasks undertaken in a virtual environment on the participants' discussion skills and motivations, and to explore how the intercultural aspect might influence the discussions and pupils' engagement.

2. Data and methodology

The 18 participants came from two schools, one in the Netherlands and another in Finland. The pupils were between 15-18 years of age and their English skills were roughly at level B2 (CEFR). The pupils were divided into three groups. The first group of participants consisted of 6 Dutch pupils who carried out the same tasks in the virtual world but with classmates and was used as a control group (Dutch C). The other two groups consisted of 6 pupils each; 3 Finnish and 3 Dutch pupils.

All pupils participated in a specifically designed discussion task series, with 5 tasks in total and a tutorial at the start. Diverse types of data were gathered and analysed: pre- and post- tests on discussion ability, surveys, recorded interactions and interviews. The analysis focused on the impact of the role tasks (González-Lloret & Ortega, 2014; Jauregi et al., 2011) and the presence of peers from another culture on the pupils' discussion skills, engagement and motivation (Geer, 2001; Deutschmann & Panichi, 2009; Jauregi et al., 2011). Furthermore, multimodal aspects of actions and interactions in the virtual environment were examined (Jones, 2005; Norris, 2011). Ethical issues were considered carefully including informed consent and handling of data.

3. Findings

In the following, the main findings of the study will be discussed.

3.1. The development of discussion skills

As we can see in Figure 1 there was a clear difference in the pupils' proficiency level prior to starting the project. Overall the Finnish pupils had a lower oral proficiency mean value (3.7) than the Dutch pupils, both the control group (6.4) and the ICC[7] group (7.7).

Differences between pre- and post-test values show that the three groups of pupils increased their discussion skills. Growth was higher for the Finnish and the Dutch control group (average improvement 0.7) than for the Dutch ICC group (0.3).

Figure 1. Average pre- and post-test results per group (Finnish and Dutch pupils interacting cross-culturally & Dutch Control group)

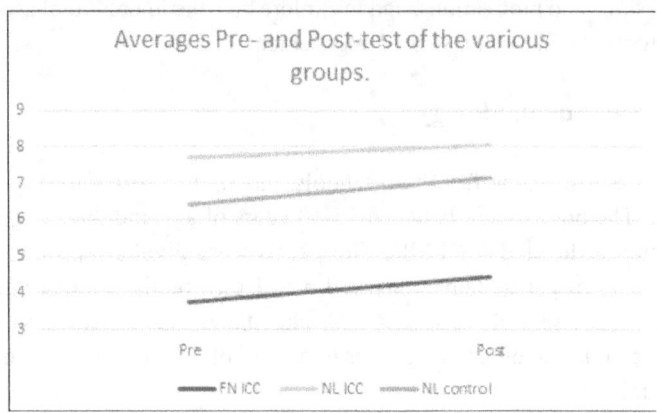

3.2. The pupils' engagement and motivation

Pupils were positive about the 3D virtual environment used during the project, although they reported having experienced technological problems with sound. Interestingly, pupils felt very comfortable and would not have preferred to carry out the discussion tasks face-to-face (see Table 1).

---

7. Dutch ICC group: those interacting with the Finnish pupils.

Table 1. Pupils' reactions to the use of virtual worlds (5 point Likert-scale. 1: strongly disagree; 5 strongly agree). *Dutch C (control group, that carried out the tasks with classmates in the virtual world)

Items	Finnish		Dutch		Dutch (C)*	
	Mean	SDev	Mean	SDev	Mean	SDev
OpenSim is useful as a tool.	3.8	0.4	3.8	0.8	4.0	0.0
OpenSim worked well during the experiment.	3.0	1.1	3.2	1.0	3.2	0.8
The audio worked during all the sessions: I could hear other people well.	2.8	0.8	2.5	1.4	2.6	0.5
I felt comfortable in OpenSim: I could move and act the way I wanted.	3.8	0.8	4.7	0.5	4.2	0.4
If you had had the possibility to carry out the tasks face-to-face, would you have preferred this option to using OpenSim?	1.7	1.8	1.8	0.8	2.8	0.4

As to the anxiety and self-efficacy issues, when comparing pre- and post questionnaires, a difference was detected among the Dutch and the Finnish pupils (Table 2). The Dutch pupils became less anxious and more confident when speaking in English, while the opposite was found for the Finnish pupils. This might well be due to the difference in speaking skills as Dutch pupils had a high B2 proficiency level and the Finnish pupils a B1 – low B2 level.

Table 2. Anxiety and self-efficacy values comparing pre- and post- questionnaires. (FN: Finnish group. NL: Dutch group. *C (control group)

Item	Pre-FN		Post-FN		Pre-NL		Post-NL		Post-NL C*)	
Anxiety/self-efficacy	Mean	SD	Mean	SD	Mean	SD	Mean	SD	Mean	SD
I feel uneasy whenever I have to speak English.	1.5	0.5	2.2	0.8	2.8	1.2	1.5	0.5	1.6	0.5
I am confident about my English speaking skills.	3.5	0.8	3.0	1.1	3.1	1.1	3.7	1.5	3.4	0.5
I am confident about my English discussion skills..	3.7	0.5	3.3	0.8	2.5	1.2	3.5	1.4	3.0	1.0
I feel very uneasy whenever I make a mistake while speaking English.	2.3	0.5	2.5	1.0	3.1	1.3	2.5	1.4	2.6	0.9
I feel very uneasy whenever I do not understand what is being said in English	3.0	0.6	2.8	1.2	2.3	1.3	1.8	1.2	2.2	0.8
I feel more at ease when I cannot be seen (on a webcam) while communicating.	2.3	0.5	3.0	0.9	2.8	1.5	3.7	1.0	3.2	1.1

Pupils enjoyed the discussion tasks (Table 3). They were felt to be useful for language learning and development of discussion skills. Dutch pupils particularly enjoyed the last two tasks (Police station & Courthouse) while the Finnish pupils preferred the first two ones. The Finnish pupils also found these tasks to be more demanding than the tasks they usually carry out in the classroom setting. The Dutch control group also enjoyed the discussion tasks.

Table 3. Pupils' evaluation of tasks

Items	Finnish		Dutch		Dutch (C)	
I **enjoyed** participating in the following tasks:	Mean	SDev	Mean	SDev	Mean	SDev
Task 1: Campsite	3.8	0.4	3.3	1.5	3.4	0.9
Task 2: Church	3.8	0.4	2.7	1.2	3.8	0.4
Task 3: Airport/Vacation	3.7	0.5	3.3	0.8	2.6	0.9
Task 4: Police station	3.3	0.5	4.2	0.4	4.0	0.7
Task 5: Courthouse	3.2	1.2	4.0	0.9	4.6	0.5
The tasks were **harder** than assignments in my English class.	4.0	1.1	2.0	0.6	2.0	1.0

Both Dutch and Finnish pupils felt they had learned about the other culture and found it quite interesting to interact with pupils with a different cultural background (Table 4).

Table 4. Intercultural gains

Items	Finnish		Dutch	
	Mean	SDev	Mean	SDev
I knew a lot about Finnish/Dutch culture before starting the course.	2.5	0.8	1.7	1.2
I know much more about Finnish/Dutch culture now that I finished the course.	3.8	0.4	3.0	1.3
It was interesting for me to communicate with the Finnish/Dutch pupils.	3.3	0.8	3.7	1.5

Finally, pupils would like to continue participating in these kinds of projects or would recommend other peers to do so. The values are noticeably higher by the Dutch pupils (Table 5). It might be due to different reasons: the Finnish pupils being younger, having a slightly lower proficiency level and different interaction patterns in Dutch and Finnish, which could all be influencing the way Finnish and Dutch pupils interact. Dutch pupils were observed to take continuously the floor to discuss task issues, while Finnish pupils adopted a more receptive role. In the Dutch control group discussions were more symmetrical.

Table 5. Overall project evaluation

Items	Finnish		Dutch		Dutch (C)	
How do you value the project?	Mean	SDev	Mean	SDev	Mean	SDev
I would like to participate in a similar project again in the future	3.2	1.0	4.0	0.0	4.6	0.5
I would recommend other pupils to participate in a similar project.	3.2	1.0	4.0	0.0	4.8	0.4

3.3. Multimodal (inter)actions

An initial viewing of the data from a multimodal perspective highlighted the participants' involvement in social actions across multiple timescales and places, characterised as layered simultaneity (Blommaert, 2005). This complexity was orchestrated through attention structures (Jones, 2005; Norris, 2011) afforded by the virtual world and created during the social activities at hand. As in gaming events, time was spent familiarising with the environment, getting organised and sorting out problems, beside the discussion tasks themselves. These "meta events" provide the participants with constant opportunities for learning.

4. Conclusion

Pupils improved their discussion skills and enjoyed the discussion experience in 3D virtual worlds. Even the control group, who did not have the opportunity to collaborate with pupils abroad, was very positive about the experience.

Based on the results of this case study we recommend teachers willing to integrate oral telecollaboration practices in Lingua Franca in their teaching to pair pupils having similar proficiency levels to reduce anxiety of those having lower proficiency levels.

5. Acknowledgements

We thank the pupils and their teachers in the participating schools as well as the support staff from the TILA project for their important contribution to the study.

References

Blommaert, J. (2005). *Discourse: a critical introduction.* Cambridge: Cambridge University Press. doi:10.1017/CBO9780511610295

Deutschmann, M., & Panichi, L. (2009). Designing oral participation in Second Life – a comparative study of two language proficiency courses. *ReCALL, 21*(2), 206-226. doi:10.1017/S0958344009000196

Geer, P. van der (2001). *De Kunst van het Debat* (2nd ed.). Den Haag: Sdu Uitgevers.

González-Lloret, M., & Ortega, L. (Eds.). (2014). *Technology-mediated TBLT: researching technology and tasks*. Amsterdam: John Benjamins. doi:10.1075/tblt.6

Jauregi, K., Canto, S., de Graaff, R., Koenraad, A., & Moonen, M. (2011). Verbal interaction in Second Life: towards a pedagogic framework for task design. *Computer Assisted Language Learning*, 24(1), 77-101. doi:10.1080/09588221.2010.538699

Jones, R. (2005). Sites of engagement as sites of attention: time, space and culture in electronic discourse. In S. Norris & R. Jones (Eds.), *Discourse in action: introducing mediated discourse analysis* (pp. 144-154). London: Routledge.

Norris, S. (2011). *Identity in (inter)action: introducing multimodal (inter)action analysis*. Berlin: deGruyter Mouton. doi:10.1515/9781934078280

Testing an online English course: lessons learned from an analysis of post-course proficiency change scores

Rebecca Y. Jee[1]

Abstract. Voxy, an English-language-learning company, has developed a custom, in-house proficiency exam, the Voxy Proficiency Assessment (VPA), which is given to all learners at the beginning and end of their courses. Using Multinomial Logistic Regression (MLR), the impact of covariates, such as total learning activities completed and total number of resource types, on the likelihood of Voxy users showing a gain, maintenance, or loss in proficiency after twelve weeks of software use, was explored. Relevance of these findings for the design of online language learning activities as well as implications for assessment-related research within the L2 online learning environment will be discussed.

Keywords: blended learning, distance learning, language proficiency, proficiency over time.

1. Introduction

A Department of Education meta-analysis (Means et al., 2010) on blended learning and significant empirical research on the impact of blended language learning on learner gains (Blake, Wilson, Cetto, & Pardo-Ballester, 2008; Jee & O'Connor, 2014; Miyazoe & Anderson, 2010) offer support for using a blended method as an alternative to traditional classrooms. However, and given that it is difficult to have distance learners take pre- and post-course assessments (Nielson, 2014), thus contributing to the dearth of research on proficiency improvements with distance language learning, many online language courses and technological tools for

---

1. Voxy, New York, NY, USA; rebecca@voxy.com

How to cite this article: Jee, R. Y. (2015). Testing an online English course: lessons learned from an analysis of post-course proficiency change scores. In F. Helm, L. Bradley, M. Guarda, & S. Thouësny (Eds), *Critical CALL – Proceedings of the 2015 EUROCALL Conference, Padova, Italy* (pp. 281-287). Dublin: Research-publishing.net. http://dx.doi.org/10.14705/rpnet.2015.000346

distance language learning remain untested (Blake et al., 2008). Since pre- and post-course assessment results would offer valuable insights into the efficacy of a course as well as the test-takers' true abilities and learning needs, an English-language-learning company analyzed the results of its proficiency assessment that is given to learners at the beginning of their courses and again three months later. The data collected from these assessments allow Voxy to evaluate how various covariates impact proficiency change scores and to determine what leads to the greatest gains for English-language learners in their use of the online course.

2. Method

2.1. Learners

Learners in the study included 309 university students and working professionals learning English as a foreign language. All took at least two versions of the VPA, the in-product tool used to measure global English proficiency, discussed in more detail below. The learners currently reside in various countries worldwide and are native speakers of a wide range of languages, but the majority are native speakers of Portuguese and Spanish. Proficiency levels varied across learners as well, with level 1 being the lowest and level 12 being the highest (the highest Voxy proficiency level is 15). All learners used Voxy in conjunction with English courses they attended at a physical location.

2.2. Tools

Voxy is an online English-language-learning product that offers synchronous and autonomous instruction via an integrated, multi-platform system. Learners are able to access Voxy on computers or on mobile devices. Voxy was designed within the Task-Based Language Teaching (TBLT) pedagogic framework (Long & Crooks, 1992) and developed using established principles of instructed Second Language Acquisition (SLA) (Gass & Selinker, 2001) and effective online language learning (Nielson & Gonzalez-Lloret, 2010). In conducting this exploratory study, the VPA, Voxy resources, and VPA activities were focused on specifically.

2.2.1. VPA

Once learners provide information about what their interests and learning goals are, the next step is to take the VPA, a multiple-choice test that assesses grammatical knowledge, reading comprehension, and listening comprehension. Subsequent forms of the VPA are offered every three months, the results of which are used to measure improvements in learner proficiency. All forms of the VPA are parallel so that the content and difficulty level of each of the items is the same across all forms. This way, test-takers' scores do not change over time based on difficulty level of the test item.

2.2.2. Voxy resources and activities

Each Voxy lesson is comprised of one resource and three subsequent activities. A resource could be any piece of authentic, real-world media like photos (Image resource), news articles (Article resource), and recorded conversations (Conversation resource) and videos (Video resource) of native English speakers completing everyday tasks. Activities target skills like vocabulary, reading comprehension, listening comprehension, pronunciation, and writing. It is important to note that depending on the first VPA score, learners will see more or fewer of certain resource types. For example, a more beginner-level learner will see more Image resources, which primarily focus on introducing various lexical items to learners, than a more advanced-level learner who will see more Video resources, which aim to familiarize learners with more authentic, real-life environments.

2.3. Procedures

Existing records on VPA answers, VPA scores, and Voxy usage for each learner were searched to identify learners who had taken at least two VPAs, since this is the only way to determine what kind of proficiency change took place. In order to examine the probability of category membership on more than two dependent variables in which each is nominal, a multinomial logistic regression (MLR) was used for this analysis. What types of Voxy resources would predict the likelihood of proficiency gain (moving up at least one Voxy level, and marked as "1") versus proficiency loss (moving down at least one Voxy level, and marked as "-1"), and the likelihood of proficiency maintenance (staying in the same Voxy level, and marked as "0") versus proficiency loss, were examined. The dependent variables were 1) gain, 2) maintenance, and 3) loss; the predictor variables were 1) total number of activities, 2) total number of image resources, 3) total number of article resources, 4) total number of conversation resources, and 5) total number of video resources. The multi-collinearity statistics showed that none of the predictor variables were highly correlated – if they had been, it would have been impossible to determine which of the variables was truly predicting proficiency change within the regression equation. Since the research is exploratory, the significance threshold was set at 0.1 rather than 0.05 (Cavana, Delahaye, & Sekaran, 2001; Merrill, 2013).

3. Findings and discussion

Figure 1 shows the actual breakdown of starting and ending Voxy proficiency levels for the 309 learners in this study. You can see that the majority of the learners are identified as Level 2. On the Voxy proficiency scale, this means that a learner is of a more beginner level. Table 1 shows the descriptive statistics for the total number of activities and resource types completed by all learners in this study. As aforementioned, the number of resource types varies greatly due to the nature of the breakdown of learner levels (i.e. many more Image resources than Video resources because there are more beginner-level learners than advanced learners).

Figure 1. Breakdown of learners' starting and ending proficiency levels

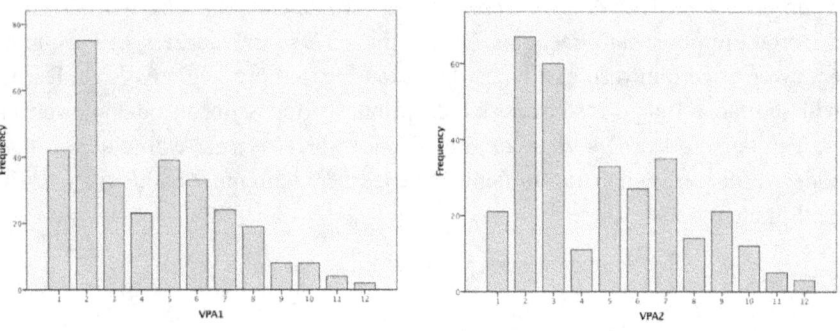

Table 1. Total number of activities and resource types completed

	N	Minimum	Maximum	Mean	Std. Deviation
Activities	309	0	3026	294.60	307.677
Image	309	0	2203	112.61	191.230
Article	309	0	1082	127.39	146.348
Conversation	309	0	197	34.02	33.642
Video	309	0	133	18.99	20.985
Valid N (listwise)	309				

Table 2 shows that for the grammar sub-skill, completing more activities lessened the likelihood of maintenance as opposed to loss, and all resource types increased the likelihood of maintenance. Completing more activities, that is to say, may not necessarily be the key to maintaining grammatical knowledge, but what may suggest maintenance is the type of resources learners complete. None of the predictor variables (i.e. total number of activities, image, article, conversation, and video resources) was significant with respect to the likelihood of gain. This can most likely be attributed to the fact that Voxy lessons, in accordance with TBLT principles, do not focus on providing explicit grammar instruction when not relevant or necessary.

Table 2. Grammar sub-skill results

Parameter Estimates

VPA G[a]		B	Std. Error	Wald	df	Sig.	Exp(B)	90% Confidence Interval for Exp(B)	
								Lower Bound	Upper Bound
0	Intercept	-.027	.307	.008	1	.929			
	Activities	-.242	.127	3.632	1	.057	.785	.637	.967
	Image	.240	.127	3.567	1	.059	1.271	1.031	1.566
	Article	.238	.127	3.503	1	.061	1.268	1.029	1.563
	Conversation	.254	.128	3.957	1	.047	1.289	1.045	1.590
	Video	.231	.129	3.207	1	.073	1.260	1.019	1.559
1	Intercept	.890	.199	20.087	1	.000			
	Activities	-.008	.036	.051	1	.822	.992	.936	1.052
	Image	.007	.036	.042	1	.838	1.007	.950	1.068
	Article	.008	.036	.055	1	.815	1.008	.951	1.069
	Conversation	.019	.036	.272	1	.602	1.019	.960	1.081
	Video	-.013	.039	.112	1	.738	.987	.926	1.052

a. The reference category is: -1.

Table 3 shows that for the reading sub-skill, none of the predictor variables were significant with respect to the likelihood of gain or maintenance compared to loss.

Table 3. Reading sub-skill results

Parameter Estimates

VPA R[a]		B	Std. Error	Wald	df	Sig.	Exp(B)	90% Confidence Interval for Exp(B)	
								Lower Bound	Upper Bound
0	Intercept	2.000	.406	24.323	1	.000			
	Activities	.008	.078	.010	1	.921	1.008	.886	1.147
	Image	-.010	.079	.017	1	.896	.990	.869	1.127
	Article	-.003	.079	.002	1	.969	.997	.876	1.135
	Conversation	.006	.079	.005	1	.944	1.006	.884	1.144
	Video	-.016	.085	.034	1	.853	.984	.855	1.133
1	Intercept	1.336	.417	10.241	1	.001			
	Activities	-.047	.086	.302	1	.583	.954	.828	1.099
	Image	.049	.087	.315	1	.575	1.050	.910	1.210
	Article	.052	.087	.355	1	.551	1.053	.913	1.214
	Conversation	.051	.086	.345	1	.557	1.052	.913	1.212
	Video	.043	.093	.215	1	.643	1.044	.896	1.217

a. The reference category is: -1.

Table 4 shows that for the listening sub-skill, completing more Video resources decreased the likelihood of maintenance compared to loss, meaning that completing more Video resources may not necessarily be the key to maintaining listening comprehension skills. This may seem counter intuitive, given that Video resources should foster listening comprehension skills, since it is crucial for learners to understand the spoken content in these resources to complete the lesson. However, because many of the learners in this study were at proficiency levels that would not enable them to see Video resources in the first place, this finding should be interpreted with caution – it would be more difficult to see proficiency gain or maintenance for this sub-skill if sufficient input was not provided in the first place.

Table 4. Listening sub-skills results

Parameter Estimates

VPA L[a]		B	Std. Error	Wald	df	Sig.	Exp(B)	90% Confidence Interval for Exp(B)	
								Lower Bound	Upper Bound
0	Intercept	.003	.245	.000	1	.990			
	Activities	.067	.051	1.715	1	.190	1.069	.983	1.163
	Image	-.067	.051	1.688	1	.194	.936	.860	1.018
	Article	-.069	.051	1.820	1	.177	.933	.857	1.015
	Conversation	-.053	.052	1.057	1	.304	.948	.871	1.032
	Video	-.092	.055	2.790	1	.095	.912	.833	.999
1	Intercept	.372	.208	3.217	1	.073			
	Activities	.011	.047	.057	1	.811	1.011	.935	1.094
	Image	-.009	.047	.038	1	.844	.991	.916	1.071
	Article	-.013	.048	.072	1	.788	.987	.913	1.068
	Conversation	-.014	.048	.087	1	.768	.986	.911	1.067
	Video	-.001	.050	.001	1	.977	.999	.919	1.085

a. The reference category is: -1.

4. Conclusion

The purpose of this exploratory study was to examine whether certain Voxy resource types or the extent of Voxy usage, as represented by the number of completed activities, would be able to predict a learner's proficiency gain, maintenance, or loss. While finding what would likely lead to proficiency gain was difficult, discovering which resource types would likely lead to maintenance and loss is sufficient in determining what improvements should be made to Voxy lessons to foster proficiency gain. It is also necessary to remember that the VPA is a *proficiency* assessment aiming to assess global proficiency and not an *achievement* test that assesses the learners' knowledge of what was taught in the lessons. Therefore, it would be difficult to determine exactly what learner behaviors when interacting with the Voxy product would most likely lead to proficiency gains. Due to the exploratory nature of the study, no additional information was collected on what learner activity takes place outside of the Voxy product or what happens during their English courses that take place in a physical location.

For future studies, perhaps knowledge of participation, or the lack thereof, in other learner activity, such as watching English language television shows and movies or having a native English-speaking pen pal, would contribute to a more complete picture of global proficiency change for these learners. Overall, the initial findings of this exploratory study show that it is difficult to predict what leads to proficiency gain, but these findings are valuable in determining what steps can be taken to further improve the product.

5. Acknowledgements

I would like to thank Dr Katie Nielson and Mr Cesar Koirala for their support and guidance and Ms Megan Masters for setting the groundwork for this study. And it goes without saying that none of this would have been possible without the providence and support of Voxy.

References

Blake, R., Wilson, N., Cetto, M., & Pardo-Ballester, C. (2008). Measuring oral proficiency in distance, face-to-face, and blended classrooms. *Language Learning and Technology, 12*(3), 114-127.

Cavana, R. Y., Delahaye, B. L., & Sekaran, Y. (2001). *Applied business research: qualitative and quantitative methods.* Australia: John Wiley & Sons Ltd.

Gass, S. M., & Selinker, L. (2001). *Second language acquisition: an introductory course.* London: Lawrence Earlbaum Associates.

Jee, R. Y., & O'Connor, G. (2014). Evaluating the impact of blended learning on performance and engagement of second language learners. *International Journal of Advanced Corporate Learning, 7*(3), 12-16.

Long, M., & Crooks, G. (1992). Three approaches to task-based syllabus design. *TESOL Quarterly, 26*(1), 27-56. doi:10.2307/3587368

Means, B., Toyama, Y., Murphy, R., Bakia, M., & Jones, K. (2010). *Evaluation of evidence-based practices in online learning: a meta-analysis and review of online learning studies.* US Department of Education. Retrieved from http://files.eric.ed.gov/fulltext/ED505824.pdf

Merrill, R. M. (2013). *Fundamentals of epidemiology and biostatistics: combining the basics.* Burlington, MA: Jones & Barlett Learning.

Miyazoe, T., & Anderson, T. (2010). Learning outcomes and students' perceptions of online writing: simultaneous implementation of a forum, blog, and wiki in an EFL blended learning setting. *System, 38*(2), 185-199. doi:10.1016/j.system.2010.03.006

Nielson, K. B. (2014). Evaluation of an online, task-based Chinese course. In M. Gonzalez-Lloret & L. Ortega (Eds.), *Technology-mediated TBLT: researching technology and tasks* (pp. 295-321). Amsterdam/Philadelphia: John Benjamins.

Nielson, K., & González-Lloret, M. (2010). Effective online foreign language courses: theoretical framework and practical applications. *The Eurocall Review, 17,* 27-35.

An investigation of a multimedia language lab project in Turkish state universities

Yasin Karatay[1]

Abstract. This paper reports on a nation-wide study designed to investigate the use of Multimedia Language Labs (MLLs) and the attitudes of students toward MLLs at tertiary level. The study will also explore the factors affecting students' attitudes towards MLLs. In an attempt to catch up with the technology, many institutions have invested in MLLs and included them in their curricula. In the same vein, in 2012, the Council of Higher Education in Turkey equipped all state universities with MLLs. Since they are new in Turkey and they have many differences from traditional labs available in almost all of the schools of foreign languages, a nation-wide study is needed to explore how they are perceived by students. The purpose of this study is to investigate, a) the attitudes of students towards MLLs, and b) the factors affecting students' attitudes towards MLLs. Questionnaires were used as a data collection instrument. Since this is the first research conducted on MLLs in Turkey, it has the potentiality of taking a snapshot of a country in terms of the current use of these labs. This study also reveals suggestions for material designers.

Keywords: multimedia language lab, classroom technologies, TELL, CALL, EFL.

1. Introduction

Technology influences many aspects of our lives, language learning included. It has an undeniable impact on almost all aspects of language education by providing many opportunities to support language teaching and learning. In recent years, computers in particular have been regarded as one of the prominent technological instruments and they have played a crucial role in English language teaching. The twenty-first century has provided Computer-Assisted Language

---

1. Düzce University, Turkey; karatayyasin@gmail.com

How to cite this article: Karatay, Y. (2015). An investigation of a multimedia language lab project in Turkish state universities. In F. Helm, L. Bradley, M. Guarda, & S. Thouësny (Eds), *Critical CALL – Proceedings of the 2015 EUROCALL Conference, Padova, Italy* (pp. 288-293). Dublin: Research-publishing.net. http://dx.doi.org/10.14705/rpnet.2015.000347

Learning (CALL) with many opportunities to benefit from; in other words, CALL has utilized from each technological advance for the delivery of CALL (Beatty, 2010). Many institutions provide their students with the opportunity to make use of language labs, which became popular in secondary schools and other institutions in the late 1960s and early 1970s (Davies, Bangs, Frisby, & Walton, 2005). Thanks to new technological developments, language labs have turned into MLLs designed with special software and have become an aid for the language teacher to enhance teaching and learning. These MLLs enable a teacher to monitor and control student computers in or outside the classroom and differ from older analogue language labs in several key aspects such as in nature and functionality, and also in terms of what they require from the teacher (Vanderplank, 2010). As many institutions see their benefits, also in an attempt to keep up with technological development, they have invested in these up-to-date labs and included them in their curricula. With the same purpose, in 2012, the Council of Higher Education in Turkey equipped all state universities with MLLs.

In these labs, the most common practices are listening comprehension, discussion, model imitation, and subtitling activities. Since these labs are not 'self-access' centers, the teacher should be there to initiate the activities and evaluate the students' performances in addition to giving immediate feedback to them. As these labs are new to Turkey and there is little large-scale research available, it is hoped that this study will contribute to filling the gap in large-scale studies on the use of MLLs, since most published research consists of small-scale studies.

2. Method

2.1. Setting and participants

This study was conducted in fourteen different state universities where MLLs are used throughout Turkey. These fourteen institutions are in five different regions of Turkey. 510 students participated in the study. All of the students who were included in the study were preparatory class students with different proficiency levels of English and studying in the school of foreign languages in these universities (see Table 1). In any one institution, not all classes using MLLs for language teaching purposes were necessarily surveyed. In any institution, if there were more than one class where MLLs were integrated into the weekly schedule, the class in which the MLL had been used most often or for the longest time was surveyed. If the students from different classes had the same degree of MLL experience, one sample class was chosen at random.

Table 1. Background information of students

Regions of Institutions			Level of English Proficiency			MLL Exposure		
	f	%		f	%		f	%
Aegean	65	13	Elementary	45	9	1-2 Hours	387	76
Marmara	73	14	Pre-Intermediate	296	58	3-5 Hours	79	15
Mediterranean	55	11	Intermediate	112	22	6-Above	44	9
Central Anatolian	163	32	Upper-Intermediate	32	6			
Black Sea	154	30	Advanced	25	5			
Total	510	100.00	Total	510	100.00	Total	510	100.00

Note: f: Frequency; %: percentage

2.2. Data collection

A student questionnaire was administered in this study in order to collect data about the attitudes of students towards MLLs at Turkish state universities and to reveal the factors affecting their attitudes towards MLLs (see Appendix). The questionnaire included five-point Likert-scale questions, with responses ranging from "Strongly Agree" (5) to "Strongly Disagree" (1), as well as open ended and multiple choice items. The first part of the student questionnaire aimed to collect data about the students' backgrounds. In the second part, the students were expected to answer 21 items about their attitudes towards MLLs in language learning.

2.3. Data analysis

The researcher analyzed all items, except for the open-ended questions at the end of the questionnaires, using descriptive statistics in the Statistical Package for Social Sciences (SPSS) Version 20. The open-ended responses from the students were categorized as positive or negative statements according to the sections in the analysis of the questionnaire data.

3. Results and discussion

The second section of the questionnaire consists of four parts. In the first part, the items were aimed to explore students' attitudes towards the use of MLLs in terms of their effect on learning. By considering the highest mean score ($M=4.19$) in this section, we can understand that most of the students believe that their learning is promoted by the audio and visual materials in MLLs. Also, four fifths of the students believe that MLLs provide a great variety of resources for them and also think that MLLs have the potentiality of making lessons more interesting and exciting. Also, a large majority (83%) of the participants think that studying in MLLs helps them learn more.

In the second part, items were aimed to explore the students' attitudes towards MLLs in terms of technical issues. The purpose was to explore whether some technical breakdowns (such as broken headphones and microphones) hinder their motivation in the MLLs and to reveal the frequency of technical breakdowns. A large majority of the respondents think that the frequency of the breakdowns in MLLs is high. More than half of the students (65%) agreed that these breakdowns decrease their motivation. Considering this fact, either the teachers should have the capacity to handle these kinds of problems right away, or the project owner should provide the universities with immediate technical support.

In the third part, the items were related to the students' feelings about the use of MLLs in English classes. A large majority (84%) of the respondents like using the computers in MLLs. In parallel with this result, as the second highest mean score ($M=3.94$) elicits, the students' preference is the lessons that are taught in the MLLs rather than in class. For the open-ended questions, 56 of the respondents wrote that thanks to the software installed in the MLLs, they all felt like in the process of learning interactively, which is something they said they did not feel in the classroom. In the light of these results in this section, it can be inferred that the students should be provided with a variety of instruction methods in order to engage them in the class.

In the final part of the questionnaire, there are items aiming to explore students' attitudes towards MLLs in terms of motivational issues. These issues were about the students' concentration level, their participation and their attention spans during the lessons in the MLLs. A majority (77%) of the respondents either agreed or strongly agreed with the idea that MLLs increase their concentration span. Since they feel more concentrated in the MLLs, they (73%) think that they participate in the lessons more as well. In the open-ended section, 23 students stated that they felt like the lessons were always student-centered and they never fell behind the process in the MLLs. From this last statement, we can infer one of the prominent advantages of technology, which is the potentiality that enables students to easily recap the topics that have just been taught in the class.

4. Conclusions

Overall, from these results, it can be inferred that the students, who are digital natives as well, get along with the technology very well. If given the opportunity and provided with the right equipment with the right purposes, the students can take a great step on the path through language proficiency. However, teachers should also be aware of the potentiality of the MLLs and make the most of them in the aim of presenting a variety of instruction to increase their students' motivation.

Almost all of the educational institutions have invested or are finding ways to invest in technological tools and integrate them in their curricula. With the same purpose, the Council of Higher Education in Turkey have made an attempt to meet the expectations of the digital natives studying at universities.

By offering insights about the effective use of MLLs and by revealing more about the attitudes of all the students studying at English classes, this study is expected to contribute to language instruction practices at tertiary level. Also, curriculum designers should be aware of the potential benefits or limitations of MLLs.

5. Acknowledgements

This study is a part of my ongoing thesis at Bilkent University, Turkey. I would like to thank to my thesis advisor, Asst. Prof Dr. Julie Ann Mathews Aydinli, Bilkent Universtiy MA TEFL program.

References

Beatty, K. (2010). *Teaching and researching: computer-assisted language learning* (2nd ed.). Great Britain: Pearson Education Limited.

Davies, G., Bangs, P., Frisby, R., & Walton, E. (2005). *Setting up effective digital language laboratories and multimedia ICT suites for MFL*. CILT, The National Centre for Languages and the Association for Language Learning.

Vanderplank, R. (2010). Déjà vu? A decade of research on language laboratories, television and video in language learning. *Language Teaching, 43*(1), 1-37. doi:10.1017/S0261444809990267

Appendix

Please check the best option you think	Strongly Agree	Agree	No Idea	Disagree	Strongly Disagree
I learn more when we study in MLLs.					

It is easier to understand the lesson when we study in MLLs.					
Computer is not different from the book from the point of my learning English.					
Audio and visual materials we use in MLLs helps me understand the lesson better.					
I find the opportunity to learn from different sources with the help of MLLs.)					
Technical problems (broken headphones and microphones) which I encounter in the LAB decreases my motivation.					
Computers in MLLs often break down.					
I like using the computers in MLLs.					
It seems difficult for me to use the computers in MLLs.					
I prefer lessons that are taught in MLLs.					
It makes me uncomfortable when my work is shown to the whole class with the system in the MLLs.					
I concentrate better when my teacher teach in the MLLs.					
I participate in lessons more when my teacher teach in the MLLs.					
MLLs make learning more interesting and exciting.					
It is easier to keep my attention when we study in MLLs.					
MLLs make it easier for me to be motivated during the lesson.					
When my teacher teaches in MLLs, I cannot keep up with the lesson because the pace of the lesson is much faster.					
The lessons become more organized in MLLs.					
MLLs saves time.					
There is no difference between my teacher's teaching techniques and methods in traditional class and MLLs.					
I think there is not much difference between my learning in MLLs and traditional class.					

Combining online and hybrid teaching environments in German courses

Lucrecia Keim[1]

Abstract. In this article, we briefly offer the main characteristics of a hybrid design for Face-to-Face (FtF) and online German courses in the degree of Translation and Interpreting that combines the textbook with activities moderated with technology. We particularly focus on the activities designed for practicing oral production at level A2.2., where we have included self-evaluation as a component in such a way that each activity is linked to a questionnaire of a reflective nature that enables the teacher to offer feedback on the activity carried out. FtF and online students have been sharing the same classroom and interacting with each other. Students' perception of the classroom design is positive according to the results of the submitted questionnaire. They highly value the structure of the Moodle classroom, the design of the tasks and the possibility to interact with students of the other modality, respectively. However, the analysis of the self-evaluations of oral activities shows unequal awareness of the potential significance of multimodality as well as a low conscious use of interactional strategies.

Keywords: course design, oral tasks, German as a second foreign language.

1. Introduction

In 2008 the Faculty of Translation and Interpretation at the University of Vic started offering the degree in Translation and Interpreting not only for FtF students but also for online students. German is offered in this degree as a second foreign language and most students begin with no previous knowledge of the language. They are expected to achieve a B1 level after having been exposed to 30 ECTS tuition. The virtual classrooms for online students were designed in a Moodle environment, taking into account the characteristics of online learning and teaching, but following

---

1. University of Vic, Uvic-UCC, Spain; lucrecia.keim@uvic.cat

How to cite this article: Keim, L. (2015). Combining online and hybrid teaching environments in German courses. In F. Helm, L. Bradley, M. Guarda, & S. Thouësny (Eds), *Critical CALL – Proceedings of the 2015 EUROCALL Conference, Padova, Italy* (pp. 294-300). Dublin: Research-publishing.net. http://dx.doi.org/10.14705/rpnet.2015.000348

the textbook designed for FtF teaching, *Schritte international* (Hilpert et al., 2006; Niebisch et al., 2006). When we began offering the online modality, each group worked in a separate virtual classroom. However, we have been progressively adapting to a hybrid pedagogic design, both with regard to the materials as well as the teaching itself that is briefly presented in this paper.

2. Teaching concept and methodology

In the design of the online courses the following points were considered:

- Comparing students' needs and our teaching goals with the material presented in the chosen students textbook.

- Selecting and ordering the sequence of activities for the students.

- Seeking alternatives for those activities of the textbook that were designed exclusively for FtF teaching and were significant for learning needs.

- Formulating the work guidelines so that they help students, establishing a bridge between the textbook and the Moodle virtual classroom and choosing the digital tool that best suits the communicative goal or the learning need.

Thanks to the kind collaboration of Hueber publishing house, we set up in a pilot version the virtual classroom complementing the textbook with webpages in which we inserted the textbook audios and images of the textbook aiming to reinforce the orientation of the students. Other learning resources (external links, internal webpages, short videos or PDFs) and our work guidelines monitor students in a way which is coherent with the teaching goals and learning needs (Figure 1).

As for the activities and tasks (Figure 2), we introduced

- Moodle quizzes linked to listening or reading skills or practice of language structures;

- written tasks that can respond to different genres and are mostly individual tasks. Some of them can be adapted to a wiki or a blog format;

- interactive written activities (forum or chat);

- interactive oral activities (asynchronous and synchronous).

Lucrecia Keim

Figure 1. Work guidelines in the virtual classroom of German 1

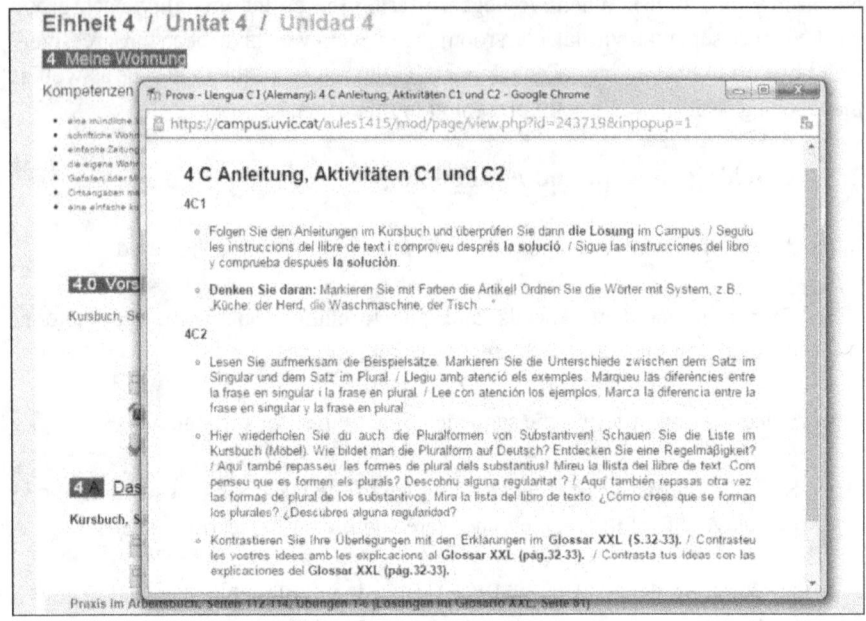

Figure 2. Students working through the Videochat

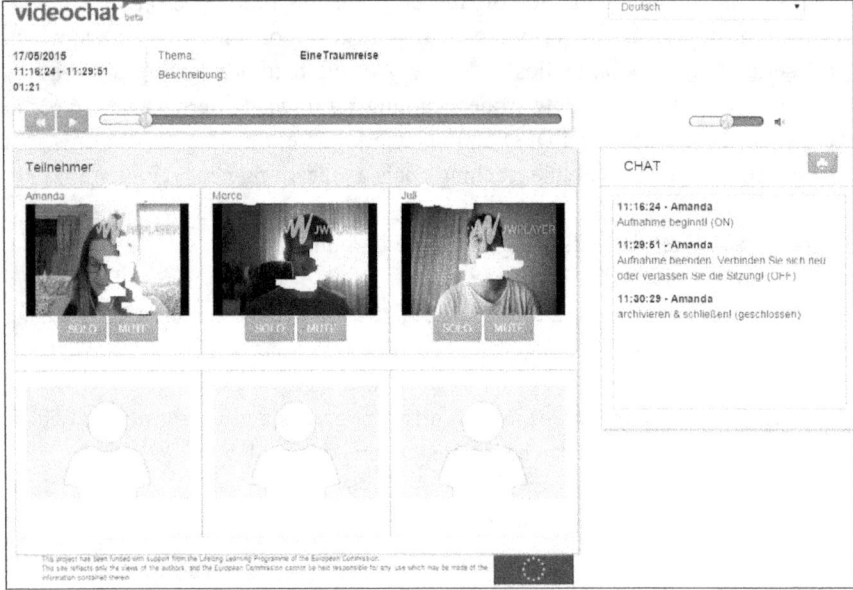

The result is that FtF as well as online students work following Solares (2014) in a technology mediated textbook-bound context. One of the lessons we have learned is that redundancy in this case plays in our favor and offers supplementary learning opportunities. For instance, forum activities can begin in the FtF classroom and can be continued at home by both FtF and online students. This is one way to trigger and guide the forum.

2.1. Oral production activities

The interactive asynchronous and synchronous activities introduced in the German level 4 course (approx. A2.2.) aim to address different levels of complexity of language, of the task and of the technology. In order to promote, as far as possible, focusing on both the content as well as the form and to motivate students to observe their production and to evaluate their progress, the guidelines and the assessment of each activity were linked to the pre-structured reflective questions of a Moodle quiz (Figure 3).

Figure 3. Guide questions for reflection

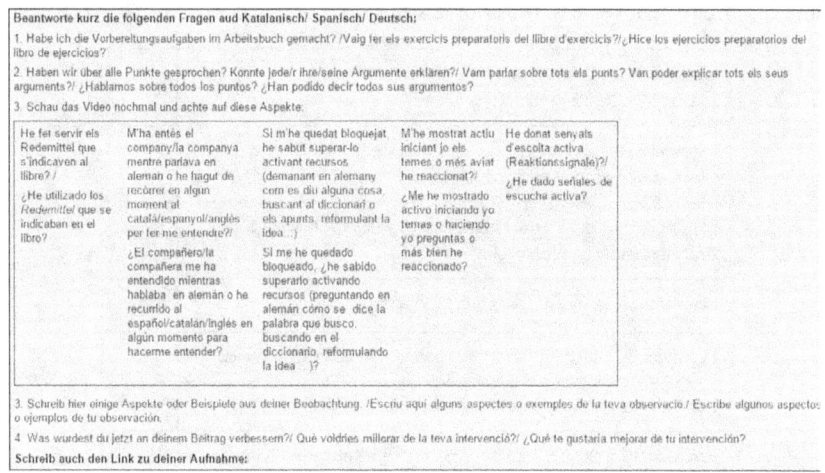

As a pilot project, with this group of students we joined the platform of the Speaks Apps Project (EU-Project, http://www.speakapps.eu/es/) and had access to the tools Langblog (forum + Video) and Videochat (web conference system).

At the beginning of the course the teacher published in the virtual classroom the schedule for all the activities along with an explanation of the aims and the technical aspects (Table 1).

Table 1. Tasks schedule

Main goal	Task type	Social form	Tool
Introducing yourself	Talking about oneself (Video monologue and reaction to others)	Individual	Langblog
Planning an excursion	Reaching a consensus	Pairs chosen by students	Videochat
Describing a beloved object	Talking about oneself (Video monologue and reaction to others)	Individual	Langblog
Apologizing to a friend	Role-play	Pairs chosen by students	Videochat
Planning a journey	Reaching a consensus	Trios chosen by the teacher	Videochat

3. Results and discussion

In the questionnaire submitted by 85 % ($N=32$) of all German students, they agreed (4) or strongly agreed (5) on a 1-5 points Likert Scale with the following items that refer to the course's design (see Table 2).

Table 2. Items that refer to the course's design

I appreciate the boundedness between the text book and the Moodle classroom.	75%
I appreciate the links to resources or webpages with additional explanations inserted in the Moodle classroom.	93%
I appreciate the quiz format in order to practice the language structures and to get feedback.	78%
I consider the design of the forum tasks appropriate.	68%
I consider the design of the written production tasks appropriate.	75%
I consider the design of the oral production tasks appropriate.	53%
I consider that when teachers correct me with correction symbols, this fosters my learning process.	84%
I consider the formative assessment procedures implemented during the course support my learning process.	78%
I would appreciate the introduction of learning games.	62.5%

As for the oral activities in the German level 4 course, we can say that they were well accepted by students if we ignore the complaining about technical inconveniences.

However, FtF students didn't deliver the questionnaires in a consistent way. This could be related to the fact that these students had the possibility to comment on the recordings in the FtF-classroom.

In their self-evaluations students value positively the possibility of hearing and analyzing their outputs as well as the possibility of working with students of the other modality. Some students mention explicitly that the repetition of tasks reduced the self-perception of anxiety.

In their comments they focus more on the speaker role than on the hearer role. Reflections of lower-level students are more superficial than those of higher-level students, who are able to focus also on form and detect errors. Comments on negotiations of meaning are rare, due in part to the task type. One lesson learnt is the necessity of introducing more task type varieties.

Moreover, some students experienced in a negative way the fact of having to search for new words they needed in the online dictionary during interaction. As a matter of fact, they don't activate interaction strategies that would allow them, for instance, to apologize for a short interruption and so looking up for words in the dictionary results in a long silence, which stops interaction. In other cases, low-level students seem to be overloaded by the fact of having to attend to the interaction on the screen and looking up expressions in the book simultaneously.

4. Conclusions

Combining a hybrid and an online teaching environment in a technology mediated textbook-bound context has turned out to offer interesting and motivating learning potential for students. In short, lessons learnt are that the design should be not too open but not too restrictive as well as not too optional but not too compulsory. Tools used should be aligned with learning needs as well as communicative goals. Finally, there is still a way to go in order to motivate students to profit from the full potential of multimodality (Lamy & Flewitt, 2011).

References

Hilpert, S. et al. (2006). Schritte 3 + 4 international. Lehrbuch und Arbeitsbuch. München: Hueber.

Lamy, M. N., & Flewitt, R. (2011). Describing online conversations: insights from a multimodal approach. In C. Develotte, R. Kern, & M. N. Lamy (Eds.), *Décrire la communication en ligne: le face-a-face distanciel* (pp. 71-94). Lyon: ENS Editions.

Niebisch, D. et al. (2006). Schritte 1 + 2 international. Lehrbuch und Arbeitsbuch. München: Hueber.
Solares, M. E. (2014). Textbooks, tasks and technology: an action research study in a textbook-bound EFL-context. In M. González-Lloret & L. Ortega (Eds.), Technology mediated TBLT. Researching technology and tasks (pp. 79-114). Amsterdam: Benjamins. doi:10.1075/tblt.6.04sol

Future language teachers learning to become CALL designers – methodological perspectives in studying complexity

Tiina Keisanen[1] and Leena Kuure[2]

Abstract. Language teachers of the future, our current students, live in an increasingly technology-rich world. However, language students do not necessarily see their own digital practices as having relevance for guiding language learning. Research in the fields of CALL and language education more generally indicates that teaching practices change slowly and the integration of technologies into pedagogic practices needs to be developed. This sets challenges for language teacher education: we should be able to educate language teaching professionals who are agile (but responsible) in adapting their pedagogic practices in response to the changes in society. To meet this challenge, we have been developing an approach for university language students to strengthen their expertise in designing theoretically informed CALL pedagogies. However, these attempts have not been fully successful as the development of pedagogic expertise involves a complex rhizome of factors and issues reaching from the participants' early language histories to current practices in the field. In order to shed light on this complexity, three different research approaches are compared for their suitability to explore developing pedagogic expertise, i.e. nexus analysis, conversation analysis and multimodal (inter)action analysis. The analysis focuses on multiple data from the university course, used as a case example.

Keywords: research methods, professional expertise, language teacher education, change.

---

1. University of Oulu, Finland; tiina.keisanen@oulu.fi

2. University of Oulu, Finland; leena.kuure@oulu.fi

How to cite this article: Keisanen, T., & Kuure, L. (2015). Future language teachers learning to become CALL designers – methodological perspectives in studying complexity. In F. Helm, L. Bradley, M. Guarda, & S. Thouësny (Eds), *Critical CALL – Proceedings of the 2015 EUROCALL Conference, Padova, Italy* (pp. 301-305). Dublin: Research-publishing.net. http://dx.doi.org/10.14705/rpnet.2015.000349

1. Introduction

Our everyday life is increasingly technology-rich and we are constantly urged to take this into account in different fields of society, especially education. However, research indicates that teaching practices change slowly (see Facer & Sanford, 2010). There is also variation in relation to how newly qualified language teachers adapt to changes. Some tend to believe that there are external forces constraining their pedagogic approaches, while others feel empowered as language educators making their own choices (Ruohotie-Lyhty, 2011).

It also seems to be challenging to put objectives into practice: even if the course plan appears to promote professional competence and lifelong learning, the concrete activities performed in the classroom may be very mechanical (Jalkanen, Pitkänen-Huhta, & Taalas, 2012). Diverse attempts have been made for facilitating modern pedagogic design in the fields of learning design (e.g. Conole, 2012), design-based research (see Bergroth-Koskinen & Seppälä, 2012), educational engineering related to conflicting personal and pedagogic goals (Colpaert, 2010) as well as participatory design of language learning with new technologies (Kuure et al., 2015). The current study takes a methodological perspective to the issues involved.

2. Method

The investigation of the development of pedagogic expertise of future language teachers involves a complex rhizome of factors and issues. Three research approaches will be examined as regards their suitability for capturing the complexity of developing pedagogic expertise.

2.1. Three approaches to study complex (inter)actions

This study focuses on the following question: what are the affordances and constraints of nexus analysis, conversation analysis and multimodal interaction analysis in studying the development of professional expertise among future language teachers?

Nexus Analysis (NA) applies diverse tools of discourse and interaction analysis, with an ethnographic emphasis. Social action is seen to arise from the social relationships among participants (interaction order), people's life experiences, memories and learning (historical body) and the physical, semiotic setting (discourses in place) (Scollon & Scollon, 2004). In doing NA, the researcher first engages the nexus of practice by becoming a participant in the activity being examined. S/he then navigates the nexus of practice, at the same time contributing to change as a member of the community.

The interest in **Conversation Analysis** (CA) lies in discovering the orderly practices with which people conduct their everyday lives in social interaction with others. CA views social interaction as organized in sequences of actions where the design and timing of a vocal or embodied action builds on what has occurred immediately before and, in turn, impacts on what comes next (e.g. Sacks, 1992). Interactional practices can thus be examined as they emerge and evolve through participation and collaboration in multiparty interactions on a moment-by-moment basis, in video-recorded data (see, e.g. Goodwin, 2013).

Multimodal (Inter)action Analysis (MIA) (Norris, 2004) is based on mediated discourse theory, as is nexus analysis. Social action is the unit of analysis, produced by social actors with tools, the environment and each other. MIA also pays attention to the more distant discourses traceable in the site of engagement, visible as frozen actions (e.g. design of a traditional classroom). Collaborative identity production, which is considered as an orchestration of identity elements (e.g. being a mother or a wife), is also highlighted (Norris, 2011).

2.2. Data and the research process

The observations are based on four iterations of a university level course that focused on the affordances of new technologies on language learning and teaching. The materials were gathered from face-to-face meetings and online work. Course design drew on a socio-cultural view of language learning, emphasizing the learners' opportunities for participation. A problem-based approach was followed whereby students designed and implemented different kinds of technology-enhanced projects. Cultural probes and diverse action methods were used to facilitate the students' critical examination of current practices and search for new solutions for future CALL.

The engaging perspective involved ethnographic fieldwork on language education with special emphasis on language teacher education. We examined the nature of current practices and future developments of language education together with the students. In so doing we navigated the practices using different kinds of action methods and the approach of participatory design. These were attempts at contributing to the language students' understanding of the requirements of their future profession as language teachers.

3. Discussion

Throughout the annual iterations, we have observed difficulties in how the shared goal is being negotiated among participants. Despite the various efforts to help students detach themselves from the current classroom-based practices of language teaching to envision new kinds of futures for language learning, the students easily returned back to their familiar practices and thinking.

In order to understand these challenges and the complexities of the situation (e.g. multiple participants, interactions, discourses, materialities and temporalities), we have explored the notion of change through theoretical considerations and empirical analysis. Each iteration of the course has produced some insight into the complexity of change, leading to different kinds of experimentations and new interventions for instigating change. However, traditional views and historical bodies change very slowly, and the problems still persist. Our current understanding is that the next step would be to apply nexus analysis in the course for the students' own examination of their historical bodies.

4. Conclusion

Investigating and contributing to change requires long-term commitment. As CALL designers, and in studying the complexity of developing pedagogic expertise, we have found that NA suits our work well as an overall framework: it enables the development of participatory agency through its focus on social action as an intersection of interaction order, discourses in place and especially historical body of all the participants. The sites of engagement where future directions and their links to our past are negotiated, are crucial from the point of view of change. These moments face-to-face or in distributed time-places can be investigated in detail with MIA and CA. MIA enables one to examine communication in its wider socio-historical context, while CA provides a view on social interaction as it is constituted in situ. These approaches provide an interpretative framework for understanding what is going on and where the crucial social actions hindering or advancing change are made visible and hence analyzable. This enables the participants (teachers and students themselves) to research and facilitate change.

In teacher education, the concepts of reflective practitioner and action research are widely acknowledged. The present approach takes this a step further: it provides a participatory research perspective on future language teachers' professional growth and provides tools for social change.

5. Acknowledgements

We would like to thank the language students who have participated in the courses actively and as co-researchers provided important perspectives to interpret language learning and teaching in the technology-rich world.

References

Bergroth-Koskinen, U.M., & Seppälä, R. (2012). Teacher-researchers exploring design-based research to develop learning designs in higher education language teaching. *Apples - Journal of Applied Language Studies, 6*(2), 95-112.

Colpaert, J. (2010). Elicitation of language learners' personal goals as design concepts. *Innovation in Language Learning and Teaching, 4*(3), 259-274. doi:10.1080/17501229.2010.513447

Conole, G. (2012). *Designing for learning in an open world.* New York: Springer.

Facer, K., & Sanford, R. (2010). The next 25 years?: Future scenarios and future directions for education and technology. *Journal of Computer Assisted Learning, 26*(1), 74-93. doi:10.1111/j.1365-2729.2009.00337.x

Goodwin, C. (2013). The co-operative, transformative organization of human action and knowledge. *Journal of Pragmatics, 46*(1). 8-23. doi:10.1016/j.pragma.2012.09.003

Jalkanen, J., Pitkänen-Huhta, A., & Taalas, P. (2012). Changing society – changing language learning and teaching practices? In M. Bendtsen, M. Björklund, L. Forsman, & K. Sjöholm (Eds.), *Global trends meet local needs* (pp. 219-239). Vasa: Åbo Akademi Press.

Kuure, L., Molin-Juustila, T., Keisanen, T., Riekki, M., Iivari, N., & Kinnula, M. (2015). Switching perspectives: from a language teacher to a designer of language learning with new technologies. *Computer Assisted Language Learning.* Manuscript accepted for publication. doi:10.1080/09588221.2015.1068815

Norris, S. (2004). *Analyzing multimodal interaction: a methodological framework.* London: Routledge.

Norris, S. (2011). *Identity in (inter)action: introducing multimodal (inter)action analysis.* Berlin: deGruyter Mouton. doi:10.1515/9781934078280

Ruohotie-Lyhty, M. (2011). Constructing practical knowledge of teaching: eleven newly qualified language teachers' discursive agency. *The Language Learning Journal, 39*(3), 365-379. doi: 10.1080/09571736.2010.544750

Sacks, H. (1992). *Lectures on conversation.* Oxford: Blackwell.

Scollon, R., & Scollon, S.W. (2004). *Nexus analysis: discourse and the emerging Internet.* London: Routledge.

Practical evaluation of a mobile language learning tool in higher education

András Kétyi[1]

Abstract. Following on preliminary research (Kétyi, 2013), in this project we looked for a mobile language learning solution, which combines computers and mobile devices. Our main idea was to explore whether by integrating mobile devices in our language teaching practice, our students at the Budapest Business School would gain valuable additional learning time outside school and whether that would improve their language learning efficiency. The mobile language learning application that was chosen for the project was busuu (https://www.busuu.com/enc/). The participants ($N=94$, $M=20.77$ years) were studying four different foreign languages (German, English, Spanish, Italian). The findings of this exploration show that busuu and other similar language learning apps are still new and unknown to the students, only one of them had used busuu before. The use of busuu was easy and simple, the app worked smoothly on the students' devices; during the study, the experimental group increased their performance (+2.2%) according to the language test results while the control group decreased it (-3.1%) and the difference at the post measurement is statistically significant ($p=.013$). An analysis of the results across gender showed that the female students performed at the post measurement significantly better than the male students ($p=.032$), and according to the students' opinions, busuu provides limited help concerning the language skills.

Keywords: mobile assisted language learning, MALL, second language acquisition, mobile app, busuu.

1. Introduction

Language learning nowadays is essential, especially for students at the Budapest Business School who need to take at least two language exams for their degree. In

---

1. Budapest Business School, Hungary; ketyi.andras@kkk.bgf.hu

How to cite this article: Kétyi, A. (2015). Practical evaluation of a mobile language learning tool in higher education. In F. Helm, L. Bradley, M. Guarda, & S. Thouësny (Eds), *Critical CALL – Proceedings of the 2015 EUROCALL Conference, Padova, Italy* (pp. 306-311). Dublin: Research-publishing.net. http://dx.doi.org/10.14705/rpnet.2015.000350

the last decade, learning a foreign language has involved technology (Technology-Enhanced Language Learning, TELL), in most cases computers (Computer-Assisted Language Learning, CALL), and in the last couple of years mobile devices (Mobile-Assisted Language Learning, MALL). There are a lot of language learning tools available, but we can find only a small amount of research conducted in this field regarding their effectiveness.

Because of the increasing penetration of mobile devices we conducted a pilot project with the aim to transform CALL into MALL (Kétyi, 2013). In the present project we looked for a mobile language learning solution which combines computers and mobile devices. The mobile language learning application that was chosen for the project, busuu, was positively received by our students. Our main idea was that if we integrated the mobile devices in our language teaching practice, our students would gain valuable additional learning time outside school, something that could improve their language learning efficiency.

2. Method

2.1. Research design

The participants in the study were 94 students of the Budapest Business School who volunteered to participate in the study. They were studying four different foreign languages (German, English, Spanish, Italian) and all of them were native speakers of Hungarian.

The study lasted for eight weeks and was conducted between March 2014 and May 2014. The use of the busuu language learning tool was an addition to their language lessons, which generally took place over 90 minutes twice a week.

The main evaluation tool was a language test for all four languages. In addition to the language tests we also performed a short motivation questionnaire. The language test and the motivation questionnaire were made during a pre-measurement stage in the first week of March 2014 and during a post-measurement at the end of May 2014. In May, the experimental group also had to fill out a short questionnaire about the busuu app.

2.2. Sample description

At the beginning of the study we had 122 students, but at the deadline only 94 filled out the placement test and the motivation questionnaire.

We divided the participants into an experimental group and a control group. We asked the students whether they wanted to use busuu immediately in the spring semester or two months later in the summer. Those who chose the immediate access became the members of the experimental group and the others became the members of the control group. The former was composed of 51 students, while the latter has 43 students. One third of the students was male (32.3%), two thirds (67.7%) female. This ratio is typical for the whole college, so none of the genders were over- or underrepresented. The youngest student was 19 years old and the oldest 25, the average age was 20.8.

3. Discussion

3.1. Effectiveness

At the pre-test (placement test), the experimental group (53.7%) performed better than the control group (47.5%), but the difference was not statistically significant (Table 1).

During the research, according to the language test results, the experimental group increased their performance (+2.2%) while the control group decreased it (-3.1 %), and the difference at the post measurement became statistically significant ($p=.013$).

Table 1. Language test results of the control and research group

	Group	N	Mean (%)	Std. Deviation	Std. Error Mean
Pre-Test Result	Control	43	47.5395	16.41598	2.50341
	Research	51	53.7688	21.12746	2.95844
Post-Test Result	Control	35	44.4400	17.07716	2.88657
	Research	45	*55.9111 (p=.013)*	21.91307	3.26661

3.2. Factors of effectiveness (gender, study time, motivation)

Analysing the *gender results* we found significant difference ($p=.032$) in the progress of the experimental group where the female members performed better (54.5%) than the male members (44.2%). The male members of the research group decreased their performance (-4%), whereas the female members increased it (+2.2%).

According to the answers to the post-busuu survey by the research group, the *average study frequency* was once per week and the average study length was between 10 and 15 minutes. It means for the whole research only 120 minutes, 2 hours on average, which is a very low value. This low value cannot explain the significant difference between the two groups.

Despite the statistically significant higher values of the experimental group for the *motivation scores* we did not find any correlation between the test results and motivation.

3.3. User satisfaction

Figure 1. Contribution of busuu

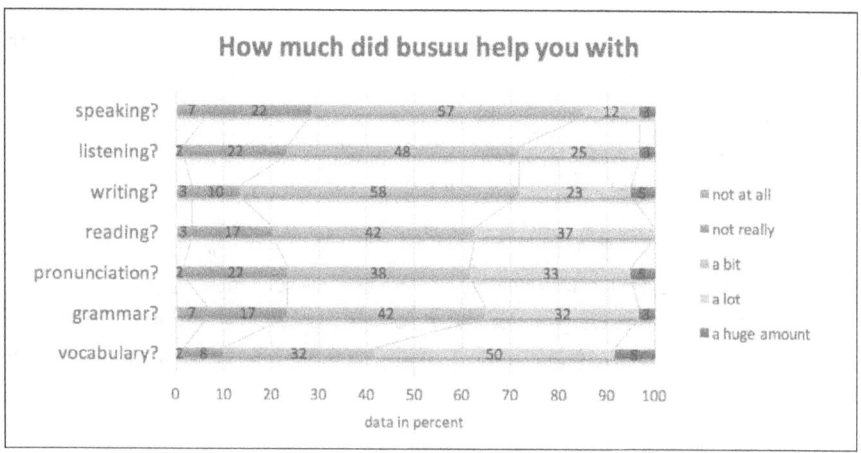

According to our post survey data (see Figure 1), we found that:

- Language learning apps like busuu are still unknown among the majority of students.

- Android is the most popular platform for our students followed by iOS and Blackberry, and Samsung is the most popular smartphone.

- Busuu is a useful learning application especially at vocabulary and writing.

309

- The overwhelming majority of the students (73.3%) think that busuu can help, but is not the ultimate tool for language learning.

- Busuu could not achieve a regular use. The regular users (3-6 times a week) are below 10%. Half of the students used the app less than a week and 40% only once or twice.

- Slightly more than half of the students spent 10 to 20 minutes on busuu. Every fifth student used the app less than 5 minutes and only every tenth student was a heavy user.

4. Conclusions

Despite the ongoing penetration of smart phones, busuu and similar language learning apps are still new and unknown for the students, only one of them had used busuu before and six of them another similar program.

According to students' experience, the use of busuu is easy and simple, the app worked smoothly on the students' devices. The post-busuu questionnaire also gave by and large positive feedback on the app, its strengths dominating clearly over its weaknesses, but unfortunately using the busuu app did not become a regular habit, as the students spent very little time using it.

Despite the sporadic and short use of the app, busuu could contribute remarkably to the learning progression of the students. While the experimental group increased their performance (+2.2%) during the research, the control group decreased it (-3.1%) and the difference at the post measurement was statistically significant ($p=.013$).

We also found that overall, the experimental group was more motivated, the difference of the motivational values was significantly higher in 3 out of 5 sub-categories, but we did not find any correlation between the test results and motivation values.

Analysing the gender results we found that female students performed significantly better at the post measurement than male students ($p=.032$).

Despite the good test results, the students thought that busuu provides limited help with the language skills and the vast majority wouldn't pay for the app after the trial period.

5. Acknowledgements

We would like to thank busuu for their kind support and for the two-month premium access during the project.

Reference

Kétyi, A. (2013). Using Smart Phones in Language Learning – A Pilot Study to Turn CALL into MALL. In L. Bradley & S. Thouësny (Eds.), *20 Years of EUROCALL: Learning from the Past, Looking to the Future. Proceedings of the 2013 EUROCALL Conference, Évora, Portugal* (pp. 129-134). Dublin Ireland: Research-publishing.net. doi:10.14705/rpnet.2013.000150

The provision of feedback types to EFL learners in synchronous voice computer mediated communication

Chao-Jung Ko[1]

Abstract. This study examined the relationship between Synchronous Voice Computer Mediated Communication (SVCMC) interaction and the use of feedback types, especially pronunciation feedback types, in distance tutoring contexts. The participants, divided into two groups (explicit and recast), were twelve beginning/low-intermediate level English as a Foreign Language (EFL) students from different departments of a university in Southern Taiwan. Each group consisted of two sub-groups (SVCMC with and without webcam image). All participants completed spoken tasks with a student tutor who provided each of them with either explicit or recast feedback over four sessions. The data were collected from students' pre- and post-pronunciation performance and the tutor interview transcripts with the students. The findings of the study are presented in this paper.

Keywords: feedback types, SVCMC, visual cues, interaction dyads.

1. Introduction

Many Taiwanese university students do not speak English fluently, in spite of their high scores on English proficiency tests. Limited class time and lack of classroom interactions may hinder their oral proficiency development (Yang & Chang, 2008). Even when such interaction opportunities are provided to learners, they may not receive timely feedback and corrections of their pronunciation errors due to large class sizes.

---

1. National Sun Yat-sen University, Kaohsiung, Taiwan; dophmer@gmail.com

How to cite this article: Ko, C.-J. (2015). The provision of feedback types to EFL learners in synchronous voice computer mediated communication. In F. Helm, L. Bradley, M. Guarda, & S. Thouësny (Eds), *Critical CALL – Proceedings of the 2015 EUROCALL Conference, Padova, Italy* (pp. 312-317). Dublin: Research-publishing.net. http://dx.doi.org/10.14705/rpnet.2015.000351

However, pronunciation is essential to oral communication, especially for beginners since phonetic errors can cause communication breakdown in interactions (Alastuey, 2008). Although pronunciation is vital to oral communication, this subject has not been sufficiently investigated in Computer Assisted Language Learning (CALL). Moreover, there is little research in terms of pronunciation feedback, a crucial factor in learning pronunciation (Neri, Cucchiarini, Strik, & Boves, 2002). Hence, this study aimed to investigate the effective use of pronunciation feedback types in SVCMC. As such, it proposed the following questions:

- Does SVCMC interaction affect EFL learners' pronunciation skills development? If so, how?

- Which feedback type is more beneficial to EFL learners' oral proficiency in SVCMC?

- Do different dyads have any effect on EFL learners' feedback reception? If so, what is the effect?

- Does the provision of image affect EFL learners' feedback reception? If so, how?

2. Method

2.1. Participants

The participants were 12 beginning/low-intermediate level tutees in a university in Southern Taiwan. They were randomly divided into two groups (explicit and recast). Each group consisted of two sub-groups, SVCMC with and without webcam (see Table 1).

Table 1. Tutees' group division situations

Feedback	Explicit						Recast					
Mode	Webcam			Non-webcam			Webcam			Non-webcam		
Tutee	A	B	I	C	D	J	E	F	K	G	H	L
Original TOEIC score	530	365	440	500	630	530	420	310	600	635	470	560
Tutored by Tutor	1	1	2	1	1	2	1	1	2	1	1	2

Two student tutors recruited from the university provided the tutoring sessions of the study. Tutor 1 was a female local senior undergraduate student who has been tutoring in the University English Center for over one year. Tutor 2 was a male Croatian first-year graduate student who had tutored for over six months. They received two-hour teaching and technology training before the study

2.2. Procedures

Each participant took four tutoring sessions (one hour/session) through Skype by using webcam and microphone. Their tutor provided each of them with either explicit or recast feedback in terms of their pronunciation/linguistic errors over four sessions.

2.3. Data collection

Both quantitative and qualitative data were collected for this study. The qualitative data included tutors' and tutees' interview transcripts. The quantitative data included tutees' pre- and post–pronunciation tests, of which the total score was 100. One point would be deducted for one phonetic error. Then, the tutees' scores were transformed into z-scores to see if they had made progress from the study.

3. Discussion

Regarding research question 1, the quantitative data (see Table 2) revealed that SVCMC interaction had positive effects on the learners' pronunciation proficiency development.

A Wilcoxon Singed Rank Test revealed a statistically significant difference after the study, $p=.002$ (<.05). The learners' median scores on the pronunciation tests improved from the pretest ($Md=84.5$) to the posttest ($Md=93$).

The interview data showed that most interviewees (9 out of 12) agreed that the online environment is appropriate for them to develop pronunciation skills. However, some technology problems interrupted their communication. In addition, this online learning made some of them feel not 'real'. Six tutees said they preferred face-to-face learning.

Concerning research question 2, the quantitative data (see Table 3) revealed the two feedback types had similarly positive effects on the tutees' pronunciation proficiency. There were statistically significant differences between the pretest and posttest for both groups ($p=.027$).

Table 2. Comparison of the tutees' pretest and posttest

Feedback mode	Explicit						Recast					
	Webcam			Non-webcam			Webcam			Non-webcam		
Tutee	A	B	I	C	D	J	E	F	K	G	H	L
Scores (pre-)	81	74	82	83	90	91	77	78	94	86	90	96
Z-score (pre-)	-0.59	-1.58	-0.45	-0.31	0.68	0.82	-1.15	-1.01	1.25	0.12	0.68	1.53
Scores (post-)	91	77	86	94	97	94	92	85	97	90	97	98
Z-score (post-)	-0.08	-2.32	-0.88	0.40	0.88	0.40	0.08	-1.04	0.88	-0.24	0.88	1.04
Z-score (post)-(pre)	0.51	-0.74	-0.43	0.70	0.20	-0.43	1.23	-0.03	-0.37	-0.36	0.20	-0.49

(Total original score=100)

Table 3. Effect of the feedback type on the tutees' pronunciation performances

Descriptive Statistics

	N	50th (median)
Explicit (pretest)	6	82.5000
Explicit (posttest)	6	92.5000
Recast (pretest)	6	88.0000
Recast (posttest)	6	94.5000

A close look (see Table 2) at the tutees' performances showed that some tutees' perception of their improvement did not correspond to their real pronunciation learning situation. The intervention program only had positive effects on Participants A, C, D of the explicit group and Participants E, and H of the recast group. It was the most beneficial for Participant E (recast group) and the least to Participant B (explicit group).

The two participants (E and H) in the recast groups who improved their pronunciation skills after the study had higher received rates of the recast compared to the other four participants of the same group (Table 4). They tended to notice the recast better. The participants who received a lower rate of the recast seemed unable to sometimes perceive their error corrections.

In terms of research question 3, the quantitative data showed that the dyad did not seem to influence the tutees' pronunciation improvement (see Table 2) and the tutors had their preferred feedback use during the tutoring regardless of their assigned feedback type. Although both tutors indicated their preferred feedback use (Tutor 1 – recast feedback, Tutor 2 – explicit feedback), Tutor 1 used more explicit feedback, and Tutor 2 used more recast feedback to teach the tutees in both groups.

When asked about their satisfaction with the feedback, only Tutee J, K, and L (tutored by Tutor 2) expressed dissatisfaction. The quantitative data showed that Tutor 2 used more recast feedback, but his tutees did not receive most of the feedback, which might explain why his 3 tutees were dissatisfied with his corrections (Table 4).

Table 4. Numbers of feedback given and received during the tutoring

	Explicit						Recast					
mode	Webcam			Non-webcam			Webcam			Non-webcam		
Tutee	A	B	I	C	D	J	E	F	K	G	H	L
EF	90	302	52	121	86	25	163	156	27	161	176	21
RF	8	2	34	32	14	44	17	48	59	56	22	36
RF not received	2	1	18	19	10	32	3	28	53	34	9	25
RF received %	75	50	47	41	29	27	82	42	10	39	59	31

(*EF=explicit feedback, RF=recast feedback)

Concerning research question 4, both the tutors and all the tutees confirmed the positive effect of the webcam use. However, a Mann-Whitney U test revealed slightly significant differences in the pronunciation improvement for the webcam (Md=88.5, n=6) and non-webcam groups (Md=95.5, n=6), p=.053.

Although all the tutors and tutees agreed that using webcams had some advantages (e.g. availability of the tutor's mouth shape, mutual availability of facial expressions and body language, focus and ease in communication, and perception of 'real' feeling), some tutees said they felt less embarrassed and nervous in non-webcam communication.

4. Conclusions

In sum, SVCMC interaction does affect EFL learners' feedback reception. Despite some disadvantages, most tutees confirmed the positive effect of online learning on pronunciation skills development.

In terms of feedback reception, explicit feedback was more easily perceived by the tutees whose original TOEIC score was lower in SVCMC. However, recast feedback was not necessarily more suitable for those whose original TOEIC score were higher; instead, it was appropriate for those with 'good' ears and high perception abilities.

In addition, different dyads did not seem to affect EFL learners' feedback reception, but the tutor's teaching style did. Both tutors and tutees could find ways to adapt to online teaching and learning.

Finally, the provision of image influenced EFL learners' feedback reception. Regardless of the advantages of webcam use, some participants felt more comfortable and courageous speaking in non-webcam situations.

5. Acknowledgements

This project was funded by the National Science Council, Taiwan.

References

Alastuey, M. C. B. (2008). Synchronous – voice computer-mediated communication: effects on pronunciation. *CALICO Journal, 28*(1), 1-20. doi:10.11139/cj.28.1.1-20

Neri, A, Cucchiarini, C., Strik, H., & Boves, L. (2002). The pedagogy-technology interface in computer assisted pronunciation training. *Computer Assisted Language Learning, 15*(5), 441-467. doi:10.1076/call.15.5.441.13473

Yang, Y. T., & Chang, L. Y. (2008). No improvement – reflection and suggestions on the use of Skype to enhance college students' oral English proficiency. *British Journal of Educational Technology, 39*(4), 721-725. doi:10.1111/j.1467-8535.2007.00769.x

The word frequency effect on second language vocabulary learning

Cesar Koirala[1]

Abstract. This study examines several linguistic factors as possible contributors to perceived word difficulty in second language learners in an experimental setting. The investigated factors include: (1) frequency of word usage in the first language, (2) word length, (3) number of syllables in a word, and (4) number of consonant clusters in a word. Word frequency is often treated as the quantifiable correlate of word familiarity, and word length and number of syllables measure structural complexity of a word. Consonant clusters were introduced as the measure of phonetic complexity. A total of 217 native speakers of Spanish and Portuguese were given a vocabulary identification task in which they had to determine whether the words were 1) *Easy to learn,* 2) *Difficult to learn*, or 3) *Unknown*. The findings showed that there is a correlation between English word frequency and perceived word difficulty of the ESL learners. In contrast, there were no clear effects of the other factors on perceived difficulty when the words were controlled for frequency.

Keywords: word difficulty, word frequency, word length, syllables, consonant clusters.

1. Introduction

Research has shown that some words are relatively harder than others for second language learners to acquire. For instance, it has been reported that English speakers find it difficult to learn Russian words with non-English sound combinations compared to the words with sound combinations that are present in English words (Rodgers, 1969). Hence, estimating the difficulty level of an individual word is important for effective language instruction. In order to do so, it becomes necessary to identify the factors that make words difficult.

---

1. Voxy, New York, NY, USA; cesar@voxy.com

How to cite this article: Koirala, C. (2015). The word frequency effect on second language vocabulary learning. In F. Helm, L. Bradley, M. Guarda, & S. Thouësny (Eds), *Critical CALL – Proceedings of the 2015 EUROCALL Conference, Padova, Italy* (pp. 318-323). Dublin: Research-publishing.net. http://dx.doi.org/10.14705/rpnet.2015.000352

First language research has identified several factors that contribute to perceived word difficulty. One such factor is *word frequency*. For instance, the word 'phone' is less difficult than the word 'floccinaucinihilipilification' because we hear 'phone' more frequently than 'floccinaucinihilipilification'. However, frequency is not the only factor that contributes to word difficulty. 'Phone' is the easier of two words also because it is shorter in length. In fact, several variables collectively contribute to L1 word difficulty. In the same vein, research in second language learning has shown the effects of several variables on L2 vocabulary learning. Words can be difficult because of factors like frequency (c.f. Chen & Truscott, 2010), length (Culligan, 2008), abstractness (Higa, 1965), and many others. Most studies have investigated the effect of individual factors on *L2* word difficulty, and there have been very few studies that examined word difficulty in the context of more than one variable at one time (c.f. Alsaif & Milton, 2012).

The contributions of the study undertaken are twofold. First, it is shown that frequency is also a predictor of L2 word difficulty in the case of ESL Spanish and Portuguese speakers. Second, it is shown that within the same frequency band, the other factors have minimal effect on perceived word difficulty. Hence, we examine the relative contribution of the factors rather than individual contribution.

We investigate four variables: (1) *Frequency* of word usage (2) *Word length* in number of characters (3) *Number of syllables* in a word (4) *Number of consonant clusters* in a word. Word frequency is often treated as the quantifiable correlate of *word familiarity*, and word length and number of syllables measure *structural complexity* of a word. In the current study, we introduce consonant clusters as the measure of *phonetic complexity*. Phonetic complexity is a dimension of word difficulty that concerns perception and oral production of the word. Some languages have no (or very few) words with consonant clusters. As a result, speakers of those languages have difficulty perceiving and producing foreign words with consonant clusters. For example, Japanese prohibits consonant clusters, and as a result Japanese speakers report hearing a vowel [u] in words like [ebzo] in between [b] and [z] (Dupoux et al., 1999).

2. Experiment design and procedure

A set of 140 words, chosen randomly from a corpus of public domain books from Project Gutenberg (https://www.gutenberg.org/), was divided into four subgroups: words with varying frequencies, words with varying word lengths, words with varying counts of syllables, and words with varying numbers of consonant clusters (Table 1). The words in each subgroup were controlled for other variables, with equal number of words per condition within each subgroup. The subgroups and conditions are explained in more detail below.

Table 1. Survey subgroups

Subgroups	Conditions
1. Varying frequency bands	1-5, 5-50, 50-500, 500-5000
2. Varying word length	3, 4, 5, 6, 7, 8, 9, 10, 11, 12, 13, 14
3. Varying number of syllables	1, 2, 3, 4
4. Varying number of consonant clusters	0, 1, 2, 3

Subgroup 1 consisted of 48 words belonging to four different frequency ranges – 1 to 5, 5 to 50, 50 to 500, and 500 to 5000. There were 12 words in each frequency range, and all the words were of length 5. Subgroup 2 consisted of 36 words of length 3 to 14. There were 3 words in each length condition. All the words were in the frequency range 50-500. Subgroup 3 consisted of 32 words with syllable counts 1 to 4. Like subgroup 2, all 32 words belonged to the frequency range 50-500. Subgroup 4 consisted of 24 words divided equally among the four consonant cluster conditions - 0 clusters, 1 cluster, 2 clusters, and 3 clusters. All the words belonged to the frequency range 50-500. The survey consisting of these 140 words was sent to 217 Spanish and Portuguese ESL learners. Their task was to decide whether a word was 1) *Easy to learn,* 2) *Difficult to learn,* or 3) *Unknown word.*

We used a three-point scale (easy, difficult, and unknown) instead of two (easy and difficult) because we wanted to differentiate words that learners find difficult from the ones that they aren't familiar with. This distinction is especially relevant for subgroup 1 (words with varying frequencies). As mentioned above, word frequency is treated as the quantifiable correlate of word familiarity, and it does not make sense to measure familiarity of unknown words. However, for other measures of complexity (structural and phonetic) we treat unknown words as difficult words and report combined results.

3. Results

3.1. Frequency

The results showed a negative correlation between word difficulty and word frequency; as frequency increased, difficulty decreased (Figure 1). This is similar to the relationship between word difficulty and word frequency in the first language. The correlation between word frequency and unknown words is also worth noticing. More words in lower frequency ranges were marked as unknowns than the words in higher frequency ranges.

Figure 1. Effect of frequency

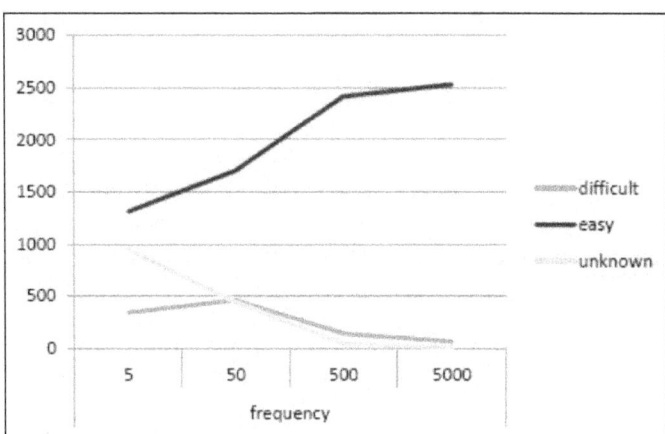

3.2. Word length and number of syllables

Unlike the frequency effect, the results did not show a clear trend for varying word length and varying counts of syllables. Most words in these two subgroups were rated as easy by most participants as shown in Figure 2 and Figure 3, respectively.

Figure 2. Effect of word length

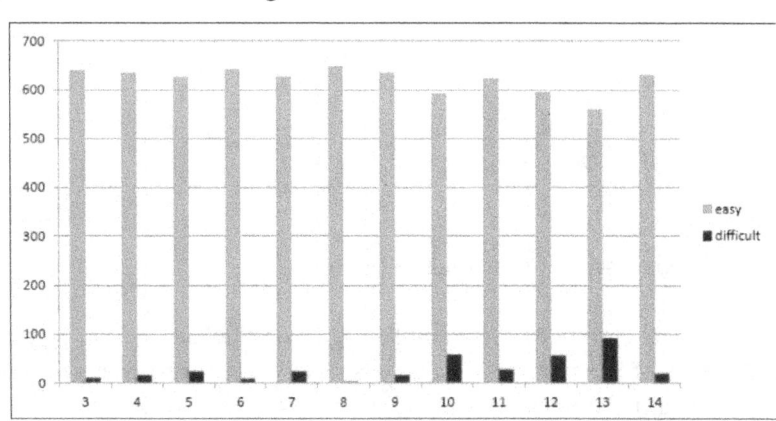

Figure 3. Effect of number of syllables

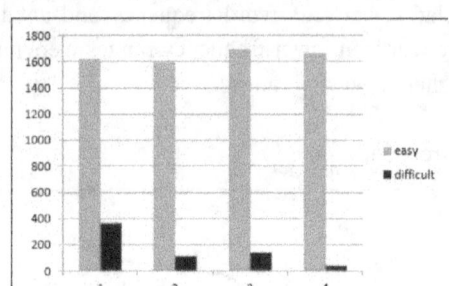

Note that the words in these subgroups were controlled for frequency – they fall in the same frequency range. So, one reason for this result could be that frequency is a better predictor for word difficulty, and as these words fall in the same frequency band, they were rated to be almost equally difficult.

3.3. Consonant clusters

Again, word-frequency seems to dominate participants' responses. As the words were in the same frequency band, they were rated similarly irrespective of varying number of consonant clusters. The second graph in Figure 4 shows that difficulty increases with the increase in number of clusters, but the result is not significant.

Figure 4. Consonant clusters

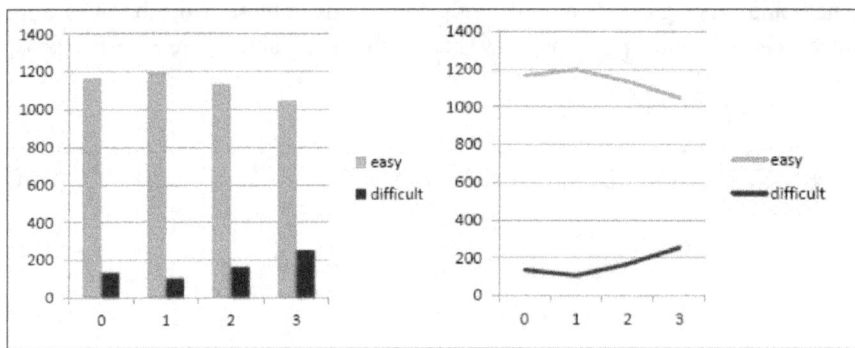

4. Discussion and conclusions

Results show a correlation between English word frequency and perceived word difficulty of Spanish and Portuguese speakers. Most participants rated low frequency words to be either difficult to learn or unknown words.

There were no clear results for other factors besides word frequency. It was found that within the same frequency band, the other factors have minimal effect on perceived word difficulty. Most words in the other subgroups were categorized as easy to learn irrespective of their structural or phonetic complexities.

Hence, while examining the relative contribution of the factors on perceived difficulty, word frequency seems to overshadow the effects of other factors.

In order to examine the aforementioned hypothesis, a follow up experiment shall be conducted. In the follow up experiment, the words in subgroups 2, 3 and 4 will be replaced by (1) words in higher frequency range (500-5000), and (2) words in lower frequency range (1-5). Our hypothesis will be supported if most words in 1 are judged easy and most words in 2 are judged difficult irrespective of their structural and phonetic complexities.

These preliminary results could be suggestive to technology-based language instruction platforms. Estimating word frequency as well as controlling for frequency seems essential for effective second language vocabulary learning.

References

Alsaif, A., & Milton, J. (2012). Vocabulary input from school textbooks as a potential contributor to the small vocabulary uptake gained by English as a foreign language learners in Saudi Arabia. *The Language Learning Journal, 40*(1), 21-33. doi:10.1080/09571736.2012.658221

Chen, C., & Truscott, J. (2010). The effects of repetition and L1 lexicalization on incidental vocabulary acquisition. *Applied Linguistics, 31*(5), 693-713. doi:10.1093/applin/amq031

Culligan, B. (2008). *Estimating word difficulty using yes/no tests in an IRT framework and its application for pedagogical objectives*. Doctoral dissertation. Temple University, Japan.

Dupoux, E., Kakehi, K., Hirose, Y., Pallier, C., & Mehler, J. (1999). Epenthetic vowels in Japanese: a perceptual illusion? *Journal of Experimental Psychology: Human Perception and Performance, 25*(6), 1568-1578. doi:10.1037/0096-1523.25.6.1568

Higa, M. (1965). The psycholinguistic concept of "difficulty" and the teaching of foreign language vocabulary. *Language Learning, 15*(3-4), 167-179. doi:10.1111/j.1467-1770.1965.tb00799.x

Rodgers, S. (1969). Measuring vocabulary difficulty: an analysis of item variables in learning Russian-English vocabulary pairs. *International Review of Applied Linguistics in Language Teaching, 7*, 327-343. doi:10.1515/iral.1969.7.4.327

Experimental analyses of the factors affecting the gradience in sentence difficulty judgments

Cesar Koirala[1] and Rebecca Y. Jee[2]

Abstract. Although a reader's text-level comprehension is affected by the comprehension of individual sentences in a text, little attention has been paid to the difficulty of sentences. This study investigates whether measures (features) of text difficulty affect the *gradience* observed in sentence difficulty judgments. We examine two traditional features (*sentence length* and *number of low-frequency words*) and six nontraditional features (counts of *clauses*, *dependent clauses*, *coordinate phrases*, *t-units*, *complex t-units*, and *Wh nominals*). Five English language instructors participated in a sentence difficulty behavioral experiment. They had to judge how difficult the sentences were on a scale of 1 to 4, where '1' means *very easy*, '2' means *easy*, '3' means *moderately difficult*, and '4' means *difficult*. The scale of 1-4 allowed the subjects to treat perceived difficulty as a relative point on the scale rather than as categorical values ('easy' and 'difficult'). It was found that both traditional and nontraditional measures of text difficulty correlate with participants' perceived difficulty suggesting that both types of features play roles in the perception of sentence difficulty. In addition, a tree-based readability model was implemented using the same sentences and features. The preliminary data suggests that the traditional features are more important while classifying new observations.

Keywords: machine learning, NLP-based features, sentence difficulty, text readability.

---

1. Voxy, New York, NY, USA; cesar@voxy.com

2. Voxy, New York, NY, USA; rebecca@voxy.com

How to cite this article: Koirala, C., & Jee, R. Y. (2015). Experimental analyses of the factors affecting the gradience in sentence difficulty judgments. In F. Helm, L. Bradley, M. Guarda, & S. Thouësny (Eds), *Critical CALL – Proceedings of the 2015 EUROCALL Conference, Padova, Italy* (pp. 324-329). Dublin: Research-publishing.net. http://dx.doi.org/10.14705/rpnet.2015.000353

1. Introduction

It is well known that learning is effective when learners are able to truly engage with the material presented to them. If a piece of material is too difficult, learners will not be able to understand or retain the information. For this reason, we find abundant readability research in both first language (L1) acquisition and second language (L2) acquisition. However, although it is well known that the comprehension of individual sentences in a text affects a reader's text-level comprehension, little attention has been paid to the difficulty of sentences (c.f. Scott, 2009).

As mentioned above, text readability has been the subject of several studies, and traditional formulas for computing text readability like Flesch Reading Ease (Flesch, 1948) and Flesch-Kincaid Grade Level (Kincaid, Fishburne, Rogers, & Chissom, 1975) date decades back. Most traditional formulas developed for assessing text difficulty are based on combinations of simple features like vocabulary *frequency* or sentence *length* (c.f Klare, 1984; DuBay, 2004). With the emergence of efficient Natural Language Processing (NLP) systems, new researchers have been able to use sophisticated features that need more time and resources to compute. Some of these studies have suggested that sophisticated NLP-based features combined with machine learning algorithms perform better than traditional readability formulas in predicting text difficulty (c.f Francois & Miltsakaki, 2012).

In this study, we are interested in the perceived difficulty of individual sentences, and not the entire text. Furthermore, we examine gradient difficulty of sentences (*very easy* to *difficult*) rather than categorical difficulty (*easy* and *difficult*). We ask the following questions in particular:

- How well do the measures of text difficulty predict sentence difficulty? We investigate the effects of two traditional features (*sentence length* and *number of low-frequency words*) and six nontraditional features (counts of *clauses, dependent clauses, coordinate phrases, t-units, complex t-units,* and *Wh nominals*) (Lu, 2010).

- Can these features explain the gradience in sentence difficulty perception?

2. Behavioral experiment

A behavioral experiment was devised to investigate whether the traditional and nontraditional features of text difficulty affect the gradience observed in sentence difficulty judgments. It is shown that both types of features correlate with the subjects' perceived difficulty, suggesting that both types of features play roles in the perception of sentence difficulty. The components of the experiment are described in detail below.

2.1. Subjects

Five English language instructors were recruited from Voxy, an education technology startup in New York. The participants were unaware of the design and purpose of the experiment.

2.2. Stimuli

The stimuli consisted of 499 English sentences. A python script was used to pull the sentences randomly from the Voxy corpus. The corpus consisted of articles from authentic sources such as Oxford University Press, Bloomberg, the Associated Press, and the Financial Times. It also contained teaching materials prepared by the company's own publishing team. The stimuli covered a wide range of topics like sports, technology, entertainment, and politics, as exemplified below:

- Mexican soccer star Rafael Marquez may leave Barcelona.

- Amazon launched the $199 tablet last November.

- Is the world becoming more and more obsessed with covering celebrities?

- Republican attempts to amend the law will continue, he said, but outright repeal is no longer a possibility.

2.3. Procedure

The experiment was implemented using E-prime software (http://www.pstnet.com/eprime.cfm). Subjects saw English sentences on the computer screen and were asked to judge the difficulty of the sentences on a scale of 1 to 4, where '1' means *very easy*, '2' means *easy*, '3' means *moderately difficult*, and '4' means *difficult*. The subjects were instructed to make use of the whole scale as much as possible. In order to avoid the response bias (a general tendency to respond either yes or no), the scale of 1 to 4 was used rather than providing 'yes' or 'no' options to the subjects. This also allowed the subjects to treat perceived difficulty as a relative point on the scale rather than saying the sentences were exactly 'easy' or 'difficult.'

3. Results

Figure 1 shows the average number of words and average number of low-frequency words per sentence for the values on the scale. Perceived difficulty increased with the increase in both traditional features.

Figure 1. Traditional features

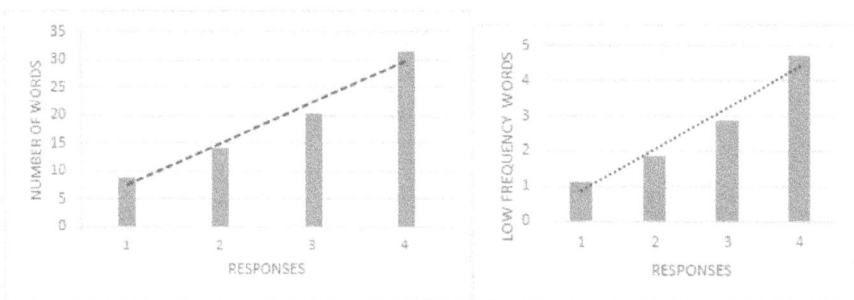

Like traditional features, the perceived difficulty increased with the increase in the counts of nontraditional features, as shown in Figure 2.

Figure 2. Nontraditional features

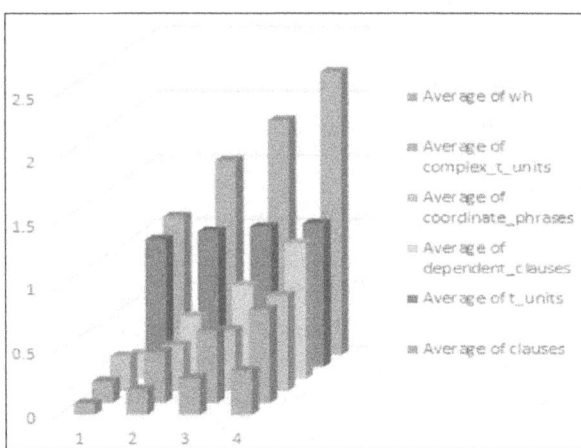

4. Feature importances

Using Scikit-learn (Pedregosa et al., 2011), a *random forest* classifier for sentence difficulty was implemented using the same sentences and features. The random forest algorithm can be used to estimate the importance of variables in a classification task. The feature importances estimated by the random forest model for the data are plotted in Figure 3 below, where '0' is 'number of words,' '1' is 'number of low-frequency words,' and '2' to '7' represent nontraditional features.

Figure 3. Feature importances

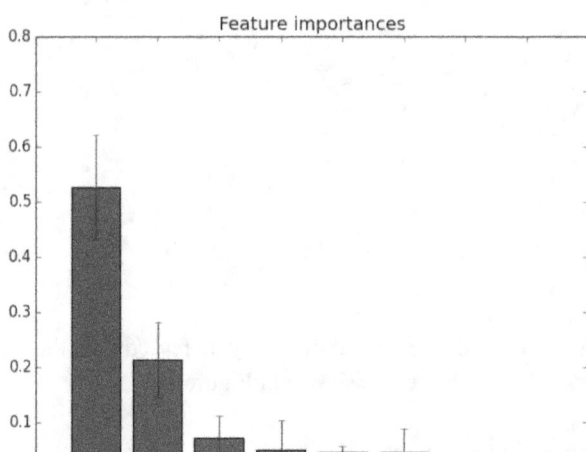

Results show that traditional features outperform the nontraditional features as single predictors of difficulty.

5. Conclusions

We examined whether or not the measures of text difficulty affect the *gradience* observed in sentence difficulty judgments. Results of the behavioral experiment suggested that both traditional and nontraditional measures of text difficulty play roles in determining sentence difficulty. For all features, as the counts of features increased, perceived difficulty increased as well, exhibiting gradience of difficulty. We also implemented a *random forest* classifier for sentence difficulty using the same sentences and features. It was found that traditional features are more important as they are better as single predictors of difficulty. This could be due to overlaps between the two types of features. For instance, *counts of clauses* measures the length of production unit, and *sentence length* does the same, too. In the future, we plan to construct classifiers that use all 14 features in Lu (2010) to test whether these findings still hold.

It is important to note that the language instructors agreed on the perceived difficulty of sentences even without rubrics that help distinguish difficulty scales. As a follow-up experiment, we plan to conduct this same experiment on language learners and compare those findings with these current findings.

References

DuBay, W. H. (Eds.). (2004). *The principles of readability*. California: Impact Information.

Flesch, R. (1948). A new readability yardstick. *Journal of Applied Psychology, 32*, 221-233. doi:10.1037/h0057532

Francois, T., & Miltsakaki, E. (2012). Do NLP and machine learning improve traditional readability formulas? *In Proceedings of the First Workshop on Predicting and Improving Text Readability for Target Reader Population, NAACL*.

Kincaid, J. P., Fishburne, R. P. Jr., Rogers, R. L., & Chissom, B. S. (1975). Derivation of new readability formulas (automated readability index, fog count and flesch reading ease formula) for navy enlisted personnel. *Research Branch Report*, 8-75. US: Naval Air Station, Memphis.

Klare, G. R. (1984). Readability. In P. D. Pearson, R. Barr, M. L. Kamil, & P. Mosenthal (Eds.), *Handbook of Reading Research* (pp. 681-744). New York, NY: Longman.

Lu, X. (2010). Automatic analysis of syntactic complexity in second language writing. *International Journal of Corpus Linguistics, 15*(4), 474-496. doi:10.1075/ijcl.15.4.02lu

Pedregosa, F., Varoquaux, G., Gramfort, A., Michel, V., Thirion, B., Grisel, O., Blondel, M., Prettenhofer, P., Weiss, R., Dubourg, V., Vanderplas, J., Passos, A., Cournapeau, D., Brucher, M., Perrot, M., & Duchesnay, E. (2011). Scikit-learn: machine learning in Python. *Journal of Machine Learning Research, 12*, 2825-2830.

Scott, C. M. (2009). A case for the sentence in reading comprehension. *Language, Speech, and Hearing Services in Schools, 40*, 184-191. doi:10.1044/0161-1461(2008/08-0042)

GenieTutor: a computer assisted second-language learning system based on semantic and grammar correctness evaluations

Oh-Woog Kwon[1], Kiyoung Lee[2], Young-Kil Kim[3], and Yunkeun Lee[4]

Abstract. This paper introduces a Dialog-Based Computer-Assisted second-Language Learning (DB-CALL) system using semantic and grammar correctness evaluations and the results of its experiment. While the system dialogues with English learners about a given topic, it automatically evaluates the grammar and content properness of their English utterances, then gives corrective feedback on grammar and semantics. The system consists of a non-native optimized speech recognition module and a semantic/grammar correctness evaluation based tutoring module. The tutoring module decides to continue the dialogue or asks learners to try again by evaluating semantic correctness of their utterances, and also gives them turn-by-turn semantic and grammatical corrective feedback. The semantic correctness evaluation consists of a 2-classes classifier for the 'pass or try again' and a 6-classes classifier for semantic corrective feedback, using the domain knowledge and language model. The grammatical correctness is evaluated by a hybrid grammatical error correction system composed of four approaches: a rule-based, a machine learning-based, an n-gram based, and an edit distance based approach. In the experiments, in which 30 subjects in a real environment took part, we acknowledged that the 'pass or try again' evaluation has a success rate of 97.5%, the semantic feedback classification has a success rate of 87.8%, and the precision and recall for grammar error correction are 79.2% and 60.9%, respectively.

1. Electronics and Telecommunications Research Institute, Korea; ohwoog@etri.re.kr
2. Electronics and Telecommunications Research Institute, Korea; leeky@etri.re.kr
3. Electronics and Telecommunications Research Institute, Korea; kimyk@etri.re.kr
4. Electronics and Telecommunications Research Institute, Korea; yklee@etri.re.kr

How to cite this article: Kwon, O.-W., Lee, K., Kim, Y.-K., & Lee, Y. (2015). GenieTutor: a computer assisted second-language learning system based on semantic and grammar correctness evaluations. In F. Helm, L. Bradley, M. Guarda, & S. Thouësny (Eds), *Critical CALL – Proceedings of the 2015 EUROCALL Conference, Padova, Italy* (pp. 330-335). Dublin: Research-publishing.net. http://dx.doi.org/10.14705/rpnet.2015.000354

Keywords: computer-assisted second-language learning system, grammar error correction, semantic correctness evaluation, non-native-optimized speech recognition.

1. Introduction

For second language learning, the use of language learning software is recently considered as natural. The software is very important in blended learning environments and individual learning for second language learning. Most second language learning systems mainly focus on vocabulary memorization, pronunciation practice, grammar acquisition, and simple repetition of given conversation. These one-way teaching-learning and simple repetition learning methods cannot attract voluntary participation from learners. To overcome the shortcomings, we have been investigating an interactive system which plays the role of the language tutor and native friends, using spoken dialog processing and natural language processing technologies. We developed a DB-CALL system, called GenieTutor[5], which has a conversation with learners and gives them semantic and grammar corrective feedback. GenieTutor does not currently provide language learning and practices for free conversation which is suitable for learners with high proficiency levels. However, GenieTutor allows learners to freely speak whatever learners think within the fixed scenario and provides corrective feedback. GenieTutor has been developed with the purpose of assisting learners with low and middle levels to achieve higher proficiency levels. Although GenieTutor was developed for English learning, we plan to extend GenieTutor for Korean learning and also improve the technologies of GenieTutor for free conversation.

2. GenieTutor

GenieTutor is a role-play dialogue system for second language learners that uses a spoken dialog understanding technology. GenieTutor promotes dialogue with learners on through two types of English learning stages, called Think & Talk and Look & Talk. In Think & Talk, each topic consists of several fixed role-play dialogues. Learners first select a topic, and then select their favorite scenario among the several scenarios available. GenieTutor and learners have a communication based on the selected role-play scenario. In Look & Talk, learners select a picture and then GenieTutor asks the learner to describe the picture. Figure 1 shows the dialogue exercises in the Think & Talk and the Look & Talk. Although GenieTutor runs according to a fixed scenario of a given topic, it allows learners to freely speak

---

5. Information about GenieTutor can be found at http://genietutor.etri.re.kr/index.asp

with diverse responses to each utterance of GenieTutor, then evaluates semantically and grammatically the response and provides feedback on semantic and grammar correctness.

Figure 1. Examples of dialogue exercises in Think & Talk and Look & Talk

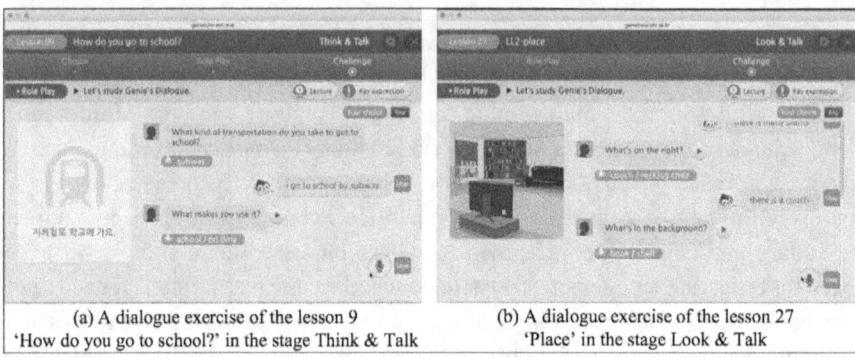

(a) A dialogue exercise of the lesson 9 'How do you go to school?' in the stage Think & Talk

(b) A dialogue exercise of the lesson 27 'Place' in the stage Look & Talk

The schematic diagram of GenieTutor consists of Automatic Speech Recognition (ASR) and tutoring modules. We optimized the ASR module to recognize the English utterances of Korean learners as well as native speakers' utterances (Chung, Lee, & Lee, 2014; Lee, Kang, Chung, & Lee, 2014), and also to recognize grammatically wrong sentences uttered by learners (Kwon et al., 2015). To minimize the effects of ASR errors, GenieTutor forces learners to confirm their utterances recognized by the ASR module. If they are not correct, learners speak again or edit the wrong sentences to correct themselves.

The tutoring module consists of semantic and grammar correctness evaluation, turn-by-turn feedback generation, and overall feedback generation. Semantic and grammar correctness evaluation evaluates the semantic properness of learners' responses which is appropriate to previous utterances of GenieTutor, and detects their grammar errors and finds the corrections. The semantic correctness evaluation classifies learners' responses into 6 classes ("perfect", "too few modifiers", "inflection error", "subject-verb error", "keyword error", and "illegal expression"), using the domain knowledge and language model. The 6 classes are defined as follows:

- "Perfect" class: the utterance is semantically perfect in the dialogue context.

- "Too few modifiers" class: the utterance is semantically good, but has the modifier mistakes.

- "Inflection error" class: the utterance is semantically good, but has the inflection mistakes.

- "Subject-verb error" class: its subject and main verb aren't semantically appropriate as the response of the previous utterance.

- "Keyword error" class: learners omit to speak some important words which are necessary for the response to the previous utterance of GenieTutor.

- "Illegal expression" class: the utterance has some wrong English expressions.

The grammar correctness evaluation is performed by a hybrid grammatical error correction system composed of four approaches: a rule-based, a machine learning-based, an n-gram based, and an edit distance based approach. Because of false alarms in which correct words are detected as errors is critical in second language learning, the hybrid system was aimed to decrease the false alarms by filtering implausible correction candidates using votes of several different methods (Lee, Kwon, Kim, & Lee, 2015).

The turn-by-turn feedback generation generates the corrective feedback in a step-by-step and sequential manner. It firstly shows pass or fail feedback to the learner using the results of semantic correctness evaluation. If the result is "perfect", "too few modifiers", or "inflection error", pass feedback is generated, and otherwise, fail feedback is generated. If the learners' utterance is "perfect", it doesn't generate any feedback, but otherwise, it shows the result of semantic correctness evaluation and grammar error words detected by grammar error correction. The last part is the corrective feedback which consists of some recommendation sentences as semantic corrective feedback and the corrections of grammatical errors described in the second part. Figure 2 (a) shows an example of turn-by-turn corrective feedback when a learner replied "I go to school subway." to the system question "How do you go to school?" in the stage Think & Talk.

Once the dialogue is over, the module provides an overall feedback consisting of 4 assessments for "task proficiency", "grammar accuracy", "vocabulary diversity", and "syntactic complexity" to show which part the learner should focus more on (Kwon et al., 2015). Figure 2 (b) shows an example of overall feedback after a dialogue ended in the lesson 27 'Place'.

GenieTutor provides an authoring tool that enables English teachers and course designers to construct new topics and role-play scenarios for the Think & Talk and the Look & Talk. The authoring tool also provides the customizing semantic and grammar correctness evaluation into the new scenarios. The customization is simply performed by training the domain knowledge and language model from the new scenarios and human annotated keywords for each utterance.

Figure 2. The educational feedback of GenieTutor

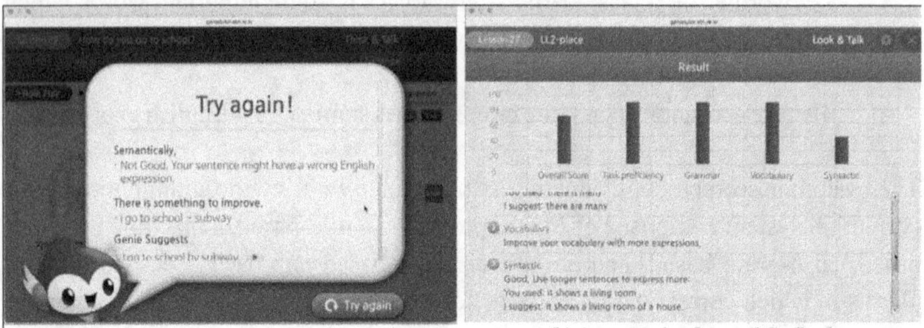

(a) An example of turn-by-turn corrective feedback (b) An example of overall feedback

3. Experiments

To evaluate the semantic and grammar correctness evaluation component of GenieTutor, we made a semantic evaluation set consisting of 3,024 utterances and a grammar error correction evaluation set consisting of 858 sentences which were randomly selected from dialogues produced by about 50 Korean learners using GenieTutor over two months. The students were college students or college graduates.

In the experiments for semantic evaluation, the pass or try again evaluation has a success rate of 94.1% and the semantic feedback (6 categories) classification has a success rate of 85.5%. In the experiments for grammar error correction evaluation, we achieved a precision of 91.3% with a recall of 45.1%.

Experiments in a real environment were also conducted, and 30 subjects were recruited (15 subjects had TOEIC scores lower than 500, while 15 subjects had TOEIC scores between 500 and 900). Each subject had a dialogue with GenieTutor on 30 learning topics of Think & Talk and Look & Talk. Contrary to our expectations, the results were very similar across the two groups. The experiments showed that the pass or try again evaluation has a success rate of 97.5%, the semantic feedback classification had a success rate of 87.8%, and the precision and recall for grammar error correction are 79.2% and 60.9%, respectively.

4. Conclusion

This paper described GenieTutor - a DB-CALL system based on semantic and grammar correctness evaluations and learner performance. GenieTutor has a fixed list dialogue flow given a lesson (topic), so it doesn't generate diverse utterances to respond to the learner. Despite this it allows learners to freely respond to the fixed questions on the given topic. GenieTutor evaluates semantically and grammatically the learners' freely spoken utterances, then decides to continue the conversation or requests the learner to respond again after providing feedback such as semantic evaluation results, grammatical error correction results, and some recommendation sentences. Through the experiments of semantic and grammar correctness evaluation, the evaluation showed good performance to provide educational feedback to second-language learners. However, we did not explore the extent to which the feedback provided by GenieTutor is useful to learn a second language, and whether second language learning using GenieTutor can improve learners' language skills. In the near future we plan to evaluate the effectiveness of English learning using GenieTutor.

5. Acknowledgements

This work was supported by the ICT R&D program of MSIP/IITP [10035252, Development of dialog-based spontaneous speech interface technology on mobile platform].

References

Chung, H., Lee, S. J., & Lee, Y. K. (2014). Weighted finite state transducer-based endpoint detection using probabilistic decision logic. *ETRI Journal, 36*(5), 714-720. doi:10.4218/etrij.14.2214.0030

Kwon, O. W., Lee, K., Roh, Y.-H., Huang, J.-X., Choi, S.-K., Kim, Y.-K., Jeon, H. B., Oh, Y. R., Lee, Y.-K., Kang, B. O., Chung, E., Park, J. G., & Lee, Y. (2015). GenieTutor: a computer assisted second-language learning system based on spoken language understanding. *IWSDS, 2015*. Retrieved from http://www.uni-ulm.de/fileadmin/website_uni_ulm/allgemein/2015_iwsds/iwsds2015_submission_29.pdf

Lee, S. J., Kang, B. O., Chung, H., & Lee, Y. (2014). Intra- and inter-frame features for automatic speech recognition. *ETRI Journal, 36*(3), 514-517. doi:10.4218/etrij.14.0213.0181

Lee, K, Kwon, O.-W., Kim, Y.-K., & Lee, Y. (2015). A hybrid approach for correcting grammatical errors. In F. Helm, L. Bradley, M. Guarda, & S. Thouësny (Eds), *Critical CALL – Proceedings of the 2015 EUROCALL Conference, Padova, Italy* (pp. 362-367). Dublin Ireland: Research-publishing.net. doi:10.14705/rpnet.2015.000359

EFL students' perceptions of corpus-tools as writing references

Shu-Li Lai[1]

Abstract. A number of studies have suggested the potentials of corpus tools in vocabulary learning. However, there are still some concerns. Corpus tools might be too complicated to use; example sentences retrieved from corpus tools might be too difficult to understand; processing large number of sample sentences could be challenging and time-consuming; also, not all English as a Foreign Language (EFL) learners know how to induct and deduct information from the concordance lines. So far, not much is known regarding how EFL writers actually perceive such tools as writing aids. To better understand this question, building on the same data set as the one published in 2015 (Lai & Chen, 2015), this study investigated students' perceptions of corpus tools right after they applied such tools to three writing tasks. Four online corpus tools, including monolingual and bilingual concordancers and collocation retrieval systems were provided along with two online dictionaries. After tool-training sections, students performed three timed-writing tasks online in three consecutive months and received individual recall interviews after each writing task. The interviews served as the major source of data. The analysis of the qualitative interview data revealed how the students perceived (1) the corpus tools as writing references, (2) the roles of the authentic example sentences, (3) the bilingual feature of the corpus tools, (4) the presentation of the corpus results, and (5) the features of the collocation retrieval system. Overall, the 14 students greatly valued corpus tools as writing references. The data also revealed how consulting the corpus helped the students to increase their confidence in writing, particularly in terms of wording. By eliciting students' perceptions and comments right after they integrated these tools into their writing tasks, the results obtained revealed not just writer perceptions but also on-site empirical data regarding how corpus tools contribute to EFL writing.

Keywords: reference tools, concordancers, EFL writing.

---

1. National Taipei University of Business, Taiwan; shulilai@gmail.com

How to cite this article: Lai, S.-L. (2015). EFL students' perceptions of corpus-tools as writing references. In F. Helm, L. Bradley, M. Guarda, & S. Thouësny (Eds), *Critical CALL – Proceedings of the 2015 EUROCALL Conference, Padova, Italy* (pp. 336-341). Dublin: Research-publishing.net. http://dx.doi.org/10.14705/rpnet.2015.000355

1. Introduction

Corpus tools have gained increasing attention in the field of English as a Second Language (ESL)/English as a Foreign Language (EFL) learning in recent years. Their unique characteristics, providing abundant example sentences and presenting keywords in context, are believed to be beneficial in L2 learning, especially in regard to vocabulary learning and L2 writing. It has been argued that such tools have an impact on vocabulary learning and ESL/EFL writing. They draw learners' attention to word patterns, collocation information, and contextual environments. They also increase learners' depth of vocabulary knowledge. Teaching or learning vocabulary using corpora assistance is known as the "corpus-based" approach and is often associated with the "data-driven approach" or "Data-Driven Learning" (DDL), coined by Tim Johns (1991). He established the relationship between corpora and language learning, believing that learners should be guided to detect the underlying rules or patterns in language use and to draw conclusion from clues in the data (Johns, 1994, 2002). Then, students will gradually learn how to discover facts about the language from the concordance lines and eventually become independent learners.

Research findings have suggested some benefits of corpus learning. It increases L2 writers' lexical and contextual awareness (Tribble, 2002); it encourages autonomous learning and improves critical thinking skills (Kirk, 2002). It also helps translation and interdisciplinary language studies (Boulton, 2011, 2012). However, such tools also carry some limitations. Observing the large amount of authentic sample sentences can be time-consuming and may frustrate learners (Granger & Tribble, 1998). Also, although the features of keywords in context facilitate the inference and generalization of rules, not all learners know how to induct information from concordance lines (Gabel, 2001). Some of the concordancing tools are complicated to use and present the concordance outputs in formats that learners may find difficult to interpret or generalize (Yoon & Hirvela, 2004). With the potential contributions and limitations of corpus tools, how EFL writers perceive such tools after they actually use them during the writing process is not clear. This study was conducted to further explore this question.

2. Method

2.1. Research design

The study was conducted in an EFL introductory writing class for non-English majors ($N=14$) over a semester. Participants were all college students, mostly with engineering backgrounds. The students performed three in-class writing tasks in a semester, each followed by a semi-structured interview. The interview notes served as the major data of this study. The writing processes were screen-recorded by a computer program. The video files of the writing process served as stimuli during the interview process.

2.2. Online reference tools

While students composed their writing online, they had access to two online dictionaries and four web-based corpus tools. Of the four corpus tools, two were concordancers and the others were collocation retrieval systems. For each type, a monolingual and a bilingual tool were provided (see Table 1).

Table 1. The four corpus tools

Tools	Features	Corpus
TotalRecall[2]	Bilingual concordancer	Sinorama (1990-2000)
VLC web concordancer[3]	Monolingual concordacner	Brown corpus, LOB, news articles from times on various topics, short stories
Tango V-N collocation[4]	Bilingual collocational retrieval system	Sinorama (1990-2000)
NTNU collocation retrieval system (NTNU CCRS)	Monolingual collocation retrieval system	British National Corpus

In addition to the four corpus tools, and in order to provide students' with a natural writing setting, similar to their previous writing experience, students had access to two online dictionaries as well (see Table 2). Most students rely on the bilingual online dictionary (i.e. the online yahoo dictionary) when they have to write in English. Some students even use the monolingual dictionary, though not many. The researcher thus could find out how students used dictionaries and concordancers differently, and how they perceived the two different kinds of tools as writing aids.

Table 2. The two dictionaries

Tools	Features	Outputs
The Yahoo dictionary	Bilingual	Chinese definitions with English examples
Cambridge advanced learners' online dictionary	Monolingual	English definitions with English examples

3. Results and discussion

Overall, students' perceptions of the corpus tools as writing references were positive. They reported that the corpus tool was a complement to the bilingual dictionary, as has been previously discussed (Lai & Chen, 2015). Very often, bilingual dictionaries do not provide enough sample sentences. Several students commented on the crucial roles of the example sentences in their writing. They provided contextual clues and displayed key words in context. They helped students generate the meaning of the word and differentiate apparent synonyms. Additionally, these sentences provided syntactical information and acted as models for usage of the keywords. Students expressed their happiness about having a sentence to imitate. One even related this experience to the L1 learning experience he had where he practiced writing a sentence by imitating how people wrote. According to Martin-Rutledge (1997), exposure to sufficient contexts explains words better than definitions or explicit information in dictionary entries can. In addition to the linguistic help, students reported that they sometimes got inspired by reading the concordance lines. They enriched their content as well.

In this study, students used the bilingual concordancers much more often than the monolingual concordancers. One student commented that providing both Chinese and English examples, in parallel forms, is very important. He even further noted that whether the tools provided bilingual example sentences was his main concern when deciding the type of tool to use. The bilingual tool, one the one hand, allows bidirectional searches; on the other hand, the Chinese parallel concordances provided clues to help the students quickly find the information they needed. In fact, it also gave those who had limited reading proficiency a chance to make sense of the corpora and to make use of such tools. Clues were found in this study as well. This might explain why students with different proficiency levels all managed to use the corpus tools in some way, and all held a positive view, which contradicts the findings of some similar studies (e.g. Yoon & Hirvela, 2004). It is very likely that the bilingual feature of the corpus tools eased the process and made it easier for EFL writers to retrieve information from concordance lines.

Students also liked the way corpus tools presented their results, especially VLC. When VLC presents its results, the keywords are aligned in the middle, highlighted in red; in addition, the words following the keywords are listed in alphabetical order. Students even encountered some incidental learning regarding word usage during the corpus observation process. In fact, students' perceptions of the presentation of the corpus results by VLC carries a number of theoretical and pedagogical implications. The unique format, different from a dictionary, drew students' attention to the collocation behaviors, grammatical patterns, and related meanings. Thanks to this, students were more likely to notice the patterns. According to Schmidt (2001), SLA is mostly driven by what learners pay attention to, and what learners notice in the target language.

Students' perceptions of the collocation tool, NTNU CCRS, is also positive. It was reported to be helpful and user-friendly. Through several mouse clicks, the student writers could find the collocation behaviors of the target words and the frequency of each collocation. As one student commented, this gave him some clues and helped him to make a better decision about which word to use in his writing. As found in the other study, students need more reference tools in addition to the dictionary, especially tools that allow collocation research (Lai & Chen, 2015). One student mentioned that he just relied on his intuition before he learned about such tools. Although the frequency counts carried information that was important and useful for the EFL writers, one student reported that people should be cautious about these numbers. He commented that the most frequent collocates may not be the right words for the writing context. On the one hand, students saw the strength of such tools, and were able to make good use of the frequency information; on the other hand, they were very cautious when selecting a word to use. They took the frequency into consideration and looked into each instance to evaluate the contexts.

4. Conclusions

In general, students believed that corpus tools provided information that was not likely to be found in a bilingual dictionary. Corpus tools were found to provide more example sentences and give information on collocations. Overall, the students greatly valued them and stated that having access to corpus tools helped them to improve their wording and increase their confidence in their own work.

5. Acknowledgements

I would like to thank the developers of the corpus tools mentioned in the study for designing them and for generously giving all users open access to them.

References

Boulton, A. (2011). Bringing corpora to the masses: free and easy tools for language learning. In N. Kübler (Ed.), *Corpora, language, teaching, and resources: from theory to practice* (pp. 69-96). Bern: Peter Lang.

Boulton, A. (2012). Beyond concordancing: multiple affordances of corpora in university language degrees. *Procedia-Social and behavioural science, 34*, 33-38. doi:10.1016/j.sbspro.2012.02.008

Gabel, S. (2001). Over-indulgence and under-representation in interlanguage: reflections on the utilization of concordancers in self-directed foreign language learning. *Computer Assisted Language Learning, 14*, 269-288. doi:10.1076/call.14.3.269.5792

Granger, S., & Tribble, C. (1998). Learner corpus data in the foreign language classroom: form-focused instruction and data-driven instruction and data-driven learning. In S. Granger (Ed.), *Learner English on computer* (pp. 199-209). New York: Longman.

Johns, T. (1991). Should you be persuaded: two examples of data driven learning. ELR Journal (New Series), 4, 1-16.

Johns, T. (1994). From printout to handout: grammar and vocabulary teaching in the context of data-driven learning. In T. Odlin (Ed.), *Perspectives on pedagogical grammar* (pp. 293-313). Cambridge: Cambridge University Press. doi:10.1017/CBO9781139524605.014

Johns, T. (2002). Data-driven learning: the perpetual challenge. In B. Kettemann & G. Marko (Eds.), *Teaching and learning by doing corpus analysis: proceedings of the Fourth International Conference on Teaching and Language Corpora, Graz, 19-24, July, 2000* (pp. 107-117). Amsterdam: Rodopi.

Kirk, J. (2002). Teaching critical skills in corpus linguistics using BNC. In B. Kettemann & G. Marko (Eds.), *Teaching and learning by doing corpus analysis* (pp.154-164), Amsterdam: Rodopi.

Lai, S. L., & Chen, H. J. (2015). Dictionaries vs concordancers: actual practice of the two different tools in EFL writing. *Computer Assisted language Learning, 28*(4), 341-363. doi:1 0.1080/09588221.2013.839567

Martin-Rutledge, V. (1997). *Use of examples in the bilingual dictionary: an empirical study.* Unpublished master's thesis, University of Ottawa, Canada.

Schmidt, R. (2001). Attention. In P. Robinson (Ed.), *Cognition and second language instruction* (pp. 3-32). Cambridge: Cambridge University Press. doi:10.1017/CBO9781139524780.003

Tribble, C. (2002). Corpora and corpus analysis: new windows on academic writing. In J Flowerdew (Ed.), *Academic discourse* (pp. 131-149), Harlow: Longman.

Yoon, H., & Hirvela, A. (2004). ESL student attitudes toward corpus use in L2 writing. *Journal of Second Language Writing, 13*(4), 257-283. doi:10.1016/j.jslw.2004.06.002

Developing and piloting an app for managing self-directed language learning: an action research approach

Elizabeth Lammons[1], Yuko Momata[2], Jo Mynard[3], Junko Noguchi[4], and Satoko Watkins[5]

Abstract. Paper-based tools such as self-evaluation activities, learning plans, reflective journals and learning logs are commonplace for managing Self-Directed Language Learning (SDLL). Such tools not only promote ownership over learning and provide a sense of achievement to learners, but they also promote reflection and raise awareness of learning processes. Paper-based tools ('modules') for SDLL have been used successfully at a small university in Japan since 2003, but with the gradual introduction of student-owned iPads, the authors explore how technology tools have the potential to enhance the SDLL experience for learners. In this paper, the authors outline the rationale and process of adapting paper-based modules to create an iPad app. The paper then gives an overview of the research approaches that were chosen to systematically gather and analyse ongoing input from users. Finally, the authors share some of the preliminary findings from the pre-pilot and pilot phases of the project.

Keywords: self-directed language learning, app development, action research.

---

1. Kanda University of International Studies, Japan; elizabeth-l@kanda.kuis.ac.jp
2. Kanda University of International Studies, Japan; momata@kanda.kuis.ac.jp
3. Kanda University of International Studies, Japan; jomynard@gmail.com
4. Kanda University of International Studies, Japan; junko-n@kanda.kuis.ac.jp
5. Kanda University of International Studies, Japan; watkins-s@kanda.kuis.ac.jp

How to cite this article: Lammons, E., Momata, Y., Mynard, J., Noguchi, J., Watkins, S. (2015). Developing and piloting an app for managing self-directed language learning: An action research approach. In F. Helm, L. Bradley, M. Guarda, & S. Thouësny (Eds), *Critical CALL – Proceedings of the 2015 EUROCALL Conference, Padova, Italy* (pp. 342-347). Dublin: Research-publishing.net. http://dx.doi.org/10.14705/rpnet.2015.000356

1. Introduction

In this paper we describe the rationale and the research approaches we adopted in order to design, develop, implement and evaluate an iPad app for managing SDLL. By way of background, we work at a private university near Tokyo in Japan where all of the students are majoring in languages.

In addition to attending classes, students are encouraged to make use of the well-resourced Self-Access Learning Centre ('the SALC'). All of us work full time in the SALC whose mission is to promote language learner autonomy through our advising, resources, learning communities and facilities. Four of us are learning advisors and one of us is an assistant manager.

We have been using 'self-directed learning modules' with our students for more than ten years. There are two paper-based modules: Effective Learning Module 1 (ELM 1) and Effective Learning Module 2 (ELM 2), both completely voluntary and lasting 8 weeks. For the first four weeks, ELM 1 introduces the learners to some essential SDLL skills which we had established from a needs analysis and subsequent SDLL curriculum development work (see Thornton, 2013; Takahashi et al., 2013 for more details). For the remaining four weeks, students implement their own plan of self-directed study.

ELM 2 is a follow-up module that begins with a learner designing his or her own eight-week plan and then implementing it with support from a learning advisor. Around 400 students take the modules each year and it could be said that these paper-based modules have been operating effectively for many years, but we wanted to capitalise on the affordances of the available technology to enhance transformative learning. By 'transformative learning', we mean learning which is socially mediated and results in reflection and ultimately shifts in thinking (e.g. Mezirow, 1997).

In order to conceptualise the desired affordances for the app, we drew upon the Framework-for-Action (FFA) developed by Hughes et al. (2011). By using the FFA, we believe that we can build on the strengths of the paper versions of the modules and use the technology to facilitate transformative learning.

Whereas it would be relatively simple to create an app which simply reproduced the current module in digital format, we wanted to go beyond what is known in the FFA model as 'replacement', and further enhance learning through 'amplification' and 'transformation' in the following ways:

Amplification

- Including interactive visual tools which would enable learners to visualise their progress more efficiently.

- Embedding activities where responses could be shared with others.

- Including ways for learners to be able track their own progress easily.

Transformation

- Enabling a smooth communication system between learners and their learning advisors.

- Including material in a variety of modes, e.g. audio, text, video, web links to appeal to different learner preferences.

- Enabling the sharing of ideas and progress between learners.

- Enabling learners to respond to advisors and record their learning in a variety of ways, e.g. audio, video, text, photos.

There were three other reasons why we were developing app versions of the modules. Firstly, new students are all asked to purchase iPads and there is an expectation (from students and parents) and interest in using the devices for all aspects of learning. In addition, the administrative systems could be streamlined and made more efficient to manage. Lastly, the university is transitioning to a paperless curriculum so there is an expectation that the SALC will make effective use of technology for learning.

2. Method

2.1. Action research approach

An action research approach was adopted as the project is likely to continue for some time. We wanted to be able to gather data systematically, and make ongoing observations and changes at staggered intervals, so we drew upon Coghlan and Brannick's (2010) cyclical model of action research to guide our process (Figure 1). Within the model, each cycle informs the next one so the research can be broken down into a series of manageable, mini-research projects. The desired outcome –

which may take longer than three cycles – is a fully functioning app which is easy to use, supports SDLL effectively, and has the transformational qualities described in the introduction to this paper. Versions of the app will be revised to gradually include more features and increase degrees of 'amplification' and 'transformation' affording to the FFA (Hughes et al., 2011).

Figure 1. Cycles of action research (Coghlan & Brannick, 2010, p. 10)[1]

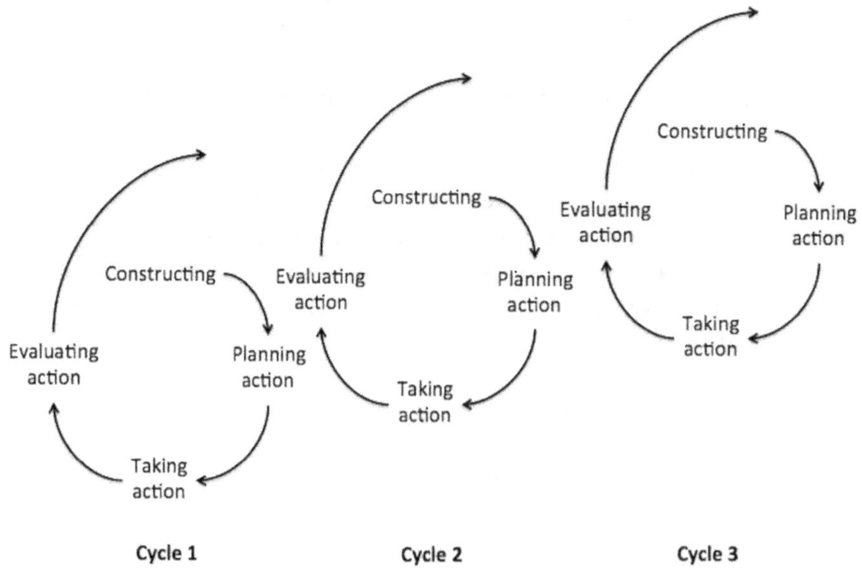

2.2. Cycle 1: pre-pilot and pilot phases (January 2014-March 2015)

The purpose of Cycle 1 was to develop a basic version of the ELM 1 app and pilot it in order to notice issues and gather feedback in order to make the app ready for larger-scale implementation in April 2015. The cycle consisted of working with the developers to create a workable version of the app and piloting it with a limited number of students and learning advisors. The research questions were:

- What are learning advisors' views on using the app?

- What are students' views on using the app?

---

1. Reproduced with kind permission from the author.

- What can be observed from the ways in which the learners and learning advisors used the app?

Methods included open-response questionnaires (students and learning advisors), focus groups (students), and observation field notes. The main findings were that users were excited and motivated to use the app, however technical difficulties hindered usability and overshadowed learning benefits. The main changes that were made were related to ensuring that everything worked as planned. The appearance was also improved to include more colour, photos and a more attractive font.

2.3. Cycle 2: wider introduction of the app (January 2015-March 2016)

The purpose of Cycle 2 was to address the problems identified from the previous cycle, introduce the app to more students, notice how the app was being used, and gather feedback and usage statistics in order to make changes for April 2016 (Cycle 3). An updated version of the app was made available to students and we were involved in promoting the app, training users, and monitoring app usage. The research questions were:

- How successful was the uptake of the module app?

- What are learning advisors' views on using the app?

- What are students' views on using the app?

- What can be observed from the ways in which the learners and learning advisors used the app?

The methods used were descriptive usage statistics, mixed-item type questionnaires (students), interviews (students), observation/field notes, document analyses, and semi-structured discussions (learning advisors).

Data is still being collected, but preliminary observations indicate that (1) users' experiences with using the app tend to be positive, (2) the app allows for more frequent communication between advisors and learners, (3) learners use the app in different ways from the paper version, (4) the management system (for learning advisors) has some features which advisors find annoying and this influences their views on credibility and usability of the app. Once all of the data have been analysed, the research team will draw up a list of priorities and work with the app developers to improve the app for Cycle 3.

3. Discussion

An action research approach was appropriate for this kind of project and it has enabled research team members to manage the data collection, analysis and changes in a staggered and systematic way. Initial findings indicate that the app does seem to have the potential to be an effective tool for managing self-directed learning, however, there is much that can be done to improve the app. We are aware that the current version offers few examples of transformational learning, but we hope to incorporate these over the coming years. This is inevitably subject to budgetary constraints and to a certain extent technical limitations outside our control.

4. Conclusions

In this paper we have shared the rationale and framework for developing, implementing and evaluating an app for managing self-directed learning. Findings from research currently being collected will enable us to continue to develop it over the coming years.

5. Acknowledgements

We are grateful to our students and colleagues for their helpful comments on the app, and the institutional support we are receiving for our research.

References

Coghlan, D., & Brannick, T. (2010). *Doing action research in your own organization* (3rd ed.). London, UK: Sage Publications Ltd.

Hughes, J. E., Guion, J., Bruce, K., Horton, L., & Prescott, A. (2011). A framework for action: intervening to increase adoption of transformative web 2.0 learning resources. *Educational Technology, 51*(2), 53-61.

Mezirow, J. (1997). Transformative learning: theory to practice. *New Directions for Adult and Continuing Education, 74*, 5-12. doi:10.1002/ace.7401

Takahashi, K., Mynard, J., Noguchi, J., Sakai, A., Thornton, K., & Yamaguchi, A. (2013). Needs analysis: investigating students' self-directed learning needs using multiple data sources. *Studies in Self-Access Learning Journal, 4*(3), 208-218.

Thornton, K. (2013). A framework for curriculum reform: re-designing a curriculum for self-directed language learning. *Studies in Self-Access Learning Journal, 4*(2), 142-153.

Assessing the impact of computer-based formative evaluations in a course of English as a foreign language for undergraduate kinesiology students in Chile

Santos Lazzeri[1], Ximena Cabezas[2], Luis Ojeda[3], and Francisca Leiva[4]

Abstract. This study assesses the impact of computer-based formative evaluations in an undergraduate English course for second semester kinesiology students at the Universidad Austral de Chile – Valdivia (UACh). The target of the course is to improve the students' online reading comprehension skills in their field. A preliminary study was carried out in order to select the platform to implement the formative evaluations. Two platforms were available: a Dokeos-based system (Dokeos, 2015), and Questionmark Perception (Questionmark-Corporation, 2015). We performed a technical review of both platforms and an empirical test in a pilot group where students' preferences were analyzed. Perception was selected since it proved to be the best choice in terms of functionality and ease of use. The target kinesiology group was divided into two subgroups, G1, and G2, of the same size and similar composition in terms of gender. Each group had the opportunity to use the computer-based formative evaluations for one half of the semester, while the other group took traditional classroom lessons in the corresponding period of time. Most students using the computer-based approach had better performance than their counterparts in the actual exam, which was taken in a paper and pencil format.

Keywords: formative evaluations, English as a foreign language, online reading comprehension, English for specific purposes.

---

1. Computer Systems Consultant - Universidad Austral de Chile, Chile; sglazzeri@yahoo.com
2. Facultad de Medicina - Instituto de Medicina - Universidad Austral de Chile , Chile; xcabezas@uach.cl
3. Facultad de Ciencias Económico-Administrativas Instituto de Estadística - Universidad Austral de Chile, Chile
4. Facultad de Medicina - Escuela de Enfermería - Universidad Austral de Chile, Chile

How to cite this article: Lazzeri, S., Cabezas, X., Ojeda, L., & Leiva, F. (2015). Assessing the impact of computer-based formative evaluations in a course of English as a foreign language for undergraduate kinesiology students in Chile. In F. Helm, L. Bradley, M. Guarda, & S. Thouësny (Eds), *Critical CALL – Proceedings of the 2015 EUROCALL Conference, Padova, Italy* (pp. 348-354). Dublin: Research-publishing.net. http://dx.doi.org/10.14705/rpnet.2015.000927

1. Introduction

English is the language of choice for business, science, and technology, which requires professionals in these disciplines to develop their English reading comprehension skills. We focus on English online reading comprehension, defined as the ability to read resources on a computer that offers capabilities like hypertext, access to multimedia, and web navigation. These capabilities constitute a fundamentally different medium than printed texts, offering a much richer experience to the reader, but demanding better skills to fully profit from this new media (Henry, 2005). The increase in books and texts available on the Internet has forced students to read more documents online than on paper, for which it is fundamental to develop systems to improve the development and evaluation of online reading comprehension skills.

The Faculty of Medicine (FAME) at UACh receives very heterogeneous student groups in terms of their English proficiency levels. Programs of study at FAME require students to acquire competencies to communicate in their professional area. Furthermore, the need to get accreditation for linguistic communication competencies according to international quality standards makes it necessary for students to get used to the Computer-Based Assessments (CBA) systems used in international foreign language proficiency or English for Specific Purposes (ESP) tests.

Both formative and summative evaluations at FAME are done in paper and pencil format, which involves a most time-consuming grading job for professors, reducing their available time for materials preparation and diversification of teaching strategies, also causing delays in the feedback delivery time. Motivated by these arguments, our study's objective is to determine whether the introduction of formative CBA evaluations in ESP courses have in fact a positive impact on student learning at FAME.

2. Method

2.1. Preliminary study

Objective: to select the software tool to use in our main study.

Study group: 78 graduate students from a technical English course offered to the different Master and PhD programs at UACh were used for the initial survey. 12 volunteers from that group participated in the empirical study.

Candidate platforms to implement formative evaluations:

- SIVEDUC (Sistema Virtual de Educación) based on Dokeos (2015). An evaluation development tool integrated to a Learning Management System (LMS) currently available at UACh;

- Questionmark Perception, considered for several years as one of the most complete authoring systems, which is also integrated to an LMS (Hogan & Smith, 2005; Shulman, 2005).

Table 1. Initial survey results

Characteristic of Students in the pilot group	%
Students owning a mobile computing device	95
Students with previous online computer based evaluation experience	23
Students that prefer taking online tests instead of paper and pencil	62
Students with previous experience that prefer taking online tests	82

Table 2. Technical evaluation comparison

Questionmark's Perception vs SIVEDUC (dokeos based) Comparison Summary		
	Perception	SIVEDUC
# of Question Types	22	8
Question Type	Developer's Preference	End User's Preference
Essay	Equal	Equal
Multiple Choice	Equal	Equal
Ranking	Perception	Perception
Column Match	Perception	Equal
Cloze	SIVEDUC	Equal
True or False	Perception	Perception

An initial survey yielded students' demographics and their attitudes and knowledge regarding the use of computer-based evaluations. This information was presented in Lazzeri, Gallardo, Cabezas & Leiva (2013). Table 1 summarizes these results, which let us conclude that the group had appropriate skills and motivation to take online formative assessments, and thus help us decide the tool to use in the main study. Afterwards, the group completed different exercises using SIVEDUC, and Perception. A final survey showed that over 70% of the students preferred Perception to answer each of the question types used: essay, multiple choice, cloze, ranking, column match, and True/False.

We also performed a technical evaluation of both platforms, comparing primarily the number of types of questions offered, and the ease of use, both from the student/user and the professor/developer's perspectives in terms of the number of actions required to carry out each task. This comparison also favored Perception, since it provided more types of questions, and, in most cases, it required less work for the developer to create and for the user to interact with the types of questions available in both systems. Table 2 summarizes these results, which led us to use Perception.

2.2. Main study

Figure 1. Sample formative evaluation: column match exercise and background material[5]

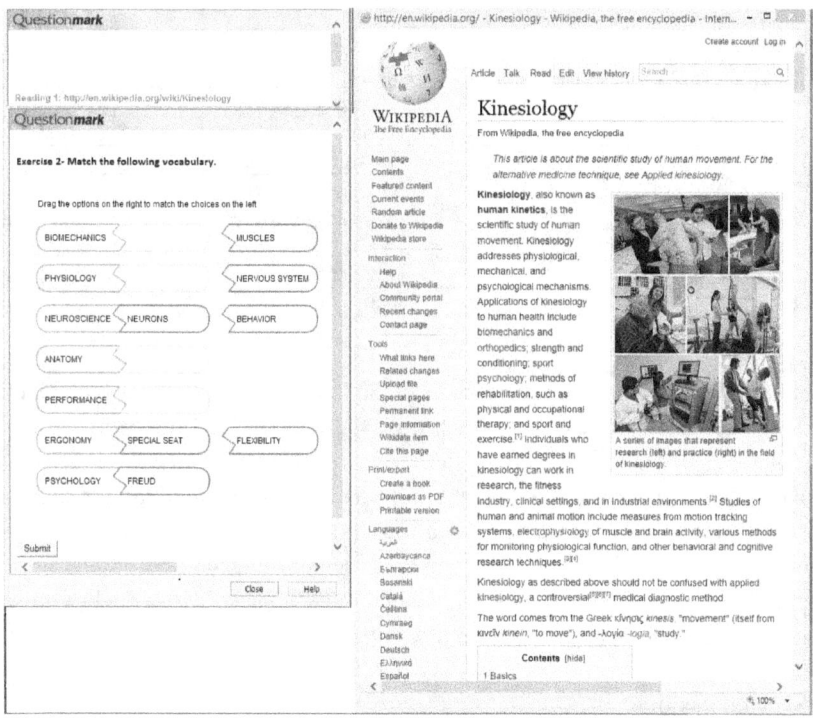

The computer-based formative evaluations were developed using Perception. The course's instructor provided the contents of the evaluations in a word processor format, then the software administrator implemented them in Perception. This

---

5. Screenshot reproduced with kind permission from Questionmark™

implementation was very time consuming since the ability of Perception to import word processor documents or plain text files is very limited. Occasionally, it proved useful to employ a third party software, Respondus (2015), to simplify this task, but there was still a lot of work to be done manually.

Formative evaluations consisted of one or more reading sections along with a set of exercises. Figure 1 shows a sample exercise from the first formative evaluation implemented in Questionmark. Table 3 presents the composition of the second formative evaluation used in the study.

Table 3. Composition of second formative evaluation

EXERCISE TYPE	DESCRIPTION
Technical Kinesiology Paper (pdf)	4 pages, 3047 words
Classification	25 items
Translation	20 items
Multiple Choice (4)	20 items
Cloze	10 items
Essay	10 items
Class Time	90 minute
Off Class Access	Open, Unlimited
Feedback	Correct answers to each question answered were given every time responses were submitted
Submissions allowed	Unlimited

A pilot study to determine the usefulness of the formative evalutions was conducted on the target kinesiology group, which was randomly divided into two subgroups, G1, and G2, of the same size and similar composition in terms of gender. Each group had the opportunity to use the CBA Formative Evaluations for one half of the semester, while the other group took traditional classroom lessons in the corresponding period of time. We compared the performance of the subgroups in the actual exams which took place at the end of each phase. The actual exam was graded in a 1-7 scale, with a minimum passing grade of 4.

3. Discussion

During the first half of the semester (Phase 1), G1, using CBA, obtained better grades than G2, which used a traditional approach to prepare for the corresponding exam. In the second half of the semester (Phase 2), the roles were reversed, and so were the results: G2, using CBA got the better results. In the intragroup comparison, both groups fared better when using CBA. At the individual level, most students got better results using the CBA than attending the traditional lectures. The descriptive statistics in Table 4 show a clear trend favoring the use of CBA formative evaluations. A post-test survey showed that most students liked the CBA approach and found it useful and easy to use.

Table 4. Summary of results obtained by students in both groups

Group	PHASE 1			PHASE 2			Effect of Technology on Performance					
							Better		Worse		Equal	
	n	Mean	Sdev	n	Mean	Sdev	n	%	n	%	n	%
G1	28	5.6	0.97	28	5.29	0.739	19	68	8	28.5	1	3.5
G2	29	5.51	0.76	27	5.76	0.715	13	48	11	41	3	11
	Using CBA											

4. Conclusions

We can conclude that the CBA formative evaluations had a positive effect on learning in this context, since all intergroup and intragroup comparisons favored students using CBA, and the surveys showed that students enjoyed the CBA approach and found it useful. Individual performances show different kinds of learners: most students did better with the CBA approach, but a few got better scores with the traditional approach. A more in-depth statistical analysis of the results and surveys can be found in Lazzeri et al. (2015). Our results are only directly applicable to our particular context.

5. Acknowledgements

We would like to thank the Dirección de Investigación y Desarrollo (DID) of the Universidad Austral de Chile – Valdivia for sponsoring this research in the context of project DID S- 2013-41. We would also like to thank the Centro de Idiomas at Universidad Austral de Chile - Valdivia for their assistance in the development of this work. Finally, we would like to thank Questionmark Corporation for granting permission to use images generated with their software in this paper.

References

Dokeos. (2015). Dokeos™ e-learning suite. Retrieved from www.dokeos.com
Henry, L. A. (2005). Information search strategies on the internet: a critical component of new literacies. *Webology*, 2(1). Retrieved from http://www.webology.org/2005/v2n1/a9.html

Hogan, P. W., & Smith, M. P. (2005). A usability and cost-effectiveness comparison of popular test-creation software. *Journal of Clinical Anesthesia, 17*(8), 677-678. doi:10.1016/j.jclinane.2005.09.052

Lazzeri, S., Gallardo, M., Cabezas, X., & Leiva, F. (2013). Students' attitudes towards the use of computer-based evaluations. In *4th Regional Conference IATEFL Chile, International Association of Teachers of English as a Foreign Language*. Valdivia, Chile.

Lazzeri, S., Cabezas, X., Ojeda, L., & Leiva, F. (2015). Automated formative evaluations for reading comprehension in an English as a foreign language course: benefits on performance, user satisfaction, and monitoring of higher education students in Chile. In F. Helm, L. Bradley, M. Guarda, & S. Thouësny (Eds.), *Critical CALL – Proceedings of the 2015 EUROCALL Conference, Padova, Italy* (pp. 355-361). Dublin Ireland: Research-publishing.net. doi:10.14705/rpnet.2015.000358

Questionmark-Corporation. (2015). *Questionmark™*. Retrieved from https://www.questionmark.com/us/Pages/default.aspx

Respondus. (2015). *Respondus™*. Retrieved from http://www.respondus.com/

Shulman, D. (2005). Perception questionmark. *Internet and Higher Education, 8*(3), 263-267. doi:10.1016/j.iheduc.2005.06.006

Automated formative evaluations for reading comprehension in an English as a foreign language course: benefits on performance, user satisfaction, and monitoring of higher education students in Chile

Santos Lazzeri[1], Ximena Cabezas[2], Luis Ojeda[3], and Francisca Leiva[4]

Abstract. We assess the effect of automated formative evaluations on reading comprehension skills in a course of English for Specific Purposes (ESP) in the area of kinesiology at the Universidad Austral de Chile – Valdivia (UACh). The evaluations were implemented using Questionmark's Perception (QMP) (Questionmark-Corporation, 2015). We investigate: (1) Do formative reading comprehension assessments enhance students' reading comprehension skills? (2) How do students perceive QMP? The experimental design used for this study was pre-test/post-test with control group. The participants were 57 freshmen, kinesiology students from UACh, randomly divided into two groups: G1-experimental, G2-control. After the pre-test, G1 worked on 11 online reading comprehension modules, which included formative evaluations with automated immediate feedback, while G2 did the same work with printed materials. At the end, both groups took the same post-test. The results show that there were no statistically significant differences between the mean grade differences (post-test grade - pre-test grade) of G1 and G2. G1's surveys showed positive attitudes towards the use of automated formative evaluations. Our conclusions are that for our population, the use of computer technology was at least as effective as instruction without technology. Furthermore, QMP was satisfactorily

---

1. Computer Systems Consultant - Universidad Austral de Chile, Chile; sglazzeri@yahoo.com
2. Facultad de Medicina - Instituto de Medicina - Universidad Austral de Chile, Chile; xcabezas@uach.cl
3. Facultad de Ciencias Económico-Administrativas Instituto de Estadística - Universidad Austral de Chile, Chile
4. Facultad de Medicina - Escuela de Enfermería - Universidad Austral de Chile, Chile

How to cite this article: Lazzeri, S., Cabezas, X., Ojeda, L., & Leiva, F. (2015). Automated formative evaluations for reading comprehension in an English as a foreign language course: benefits on performance, user satisfaction, and monitoring of higher education students in Chile. In F. Helm, L. Bradley, M. Guarda, & S. Thouësny (Eds), *Critical CALL – Proceedings of the 2015 EUROCALL Conference, Padova, Italy* (pp. 355-361). Dublin: Research-publishing. net. http://dx.doi.org/10.14705/rpnet.2015.000358

evaluated by the students, and it allowed the professor to monitor and timely detect students with performance problems thanks to the different reports it provides.

Keywords: formative evaluations, English as a foreign language, online reading comprehension, English for specific purposes.

1. Introduction

Formative assessment has long been believed to be effective, as documented in Black and Wiliam (1998). However, recent studies, like Kingston and Nash (2011), challenge that belief. This controversy, along with the introduction of multiple technological tools that implement evaluations, motivated us to test one such tool: QMP (Questionmark-Corporation, 2015), applied to reading comprehension in ESP. From a curricular viewpoint, our institution currently applies a competencies-based model (Jabif, 2007; UACh, 2007), which adopts a holistic, integrating vision, with methodologies that are based more on student learning than on the professor's teaching. Therefore, the use of computer based formative assessments is consistent with UACh's policies.

The process we followed to select QMP and descriptive statistics of the study are presented in Lazzeri et al. (2015). Here we present a more comprehensive analysis of our population composition and a performance comparison considering the entrance skill level of the students. We also study the students' preferences according to their survey answers, and consider other advantages that a Computer Based Assessment (CBA) software, such as QMP, can offer.

Our research questions are: (1) Do formative reading comprehension assessments enhance students' reading comprehension skills? (2) How do students perceive QMP?

2. Method

2.1. Experimental design

Study Type: Pre-test/post-test with control group.

Population: 57 freshmen kinesiology students from UACh; Age: average=19, SD=2.5; Gender: 51% male, 49% female; High-school type: 38% public, 56% subsidized private, 6% private. Only 19% had a CEFR certification at the ALTE

A2 or B1 levels, which are the goal levels specified by the Chilean government for elementary and high-school graduates, respectively.

Our population was randomly divided into two groups: G1-experimental, G2-control. After the pre-test, G1 worked on seven lessons that were implemented as 11 online reading comprehension modules, which included formative evaluations with automated immediate feedback, while G2 did the same work with printed materials. The only difference was the presentation mode of the material and the automated feedback. Data was collected from a pre-test, post-test, and survey application.

2.2. Instruments

The pre-test and post-test were developed and graded by the course's instructor. The students' satisfaction survey was developed by data analysis specialists. The lessons, used as learning measurement instruments, were designed by the course instructor and implemented by the software administrator in QMP automated formative assessment modules with immediate feedback. Each lesson contained a paper/reading in the field of kinesiology and several exercises related to that reading. Table 1 shows the composition of each lesson in terms of length of paper in words and types of exercises used.

Table 1. Lesson composition

Lesson	Paper Word Count	Number of exercises for each type of question								Total
		Essay	Multiple Choice	Column Match	Cloze	Brief Text	Survey Matrix	T/F	Essay with Extra Text	
1	1167		2	17	10			10		39
2	3047		20	10	10	45				85
3	5363	17		20	10	15		10		72
4	4111			10	10	10		10	10	50
5	4480			10		30		10	10	60
6	5116	10	10	10	10	30	10	10	20	110
7	5504	3		10	20	50		20		103
Total	28788	30	32	87	70	180	10	70	40	519

To determine improvement in reading comprehension skills, we used the dependent variable "Academic Performance on Reading Comprehension" as measured by the grade obtained in the exams, given in a 1-7 scale, where 7 is best, which is the standard in the Chilean educational system. More precisely, we used the difference in academic performance between the post-test and the pre-test results. G1 and G2 were compared in terms of this variable using Student's t-test for independent samples, since the preconditions to use this kind of test were satisfied. The independent variable was "use of QMP" (Yes/No). The statistical analysis was carried out with SPSS 11.5.

The students' satisfaction survey contained 8 Likert-style questions directly related to the use of QMP that allowed us to get the students' perceptions about the platform. The internal consistency of this survey was determined by computing the Alpha Cronbach reliability coefficient as .747, which is deemed acceptable.

3. Discussion

Table 2 summarizes the results of both groups in the pre-test and post-test.

Table 2. Pre-test and post-test results

Group		Post-test		Pre-test	
	n	Mean	Sdev	Mean	Sdev
G1	28	5.60	0.97	2.96	0.92
G2	29	5.51	0.76	3.24	0.69

It is important to notice that G1 had on average lower scores in the pre-test than G2, but after completing the lessons using the QMP modules, they got a higher average than G2 (using printed materials) in the post-test. Nevertheless, there were no statistically significant differences between the mean grade differences with 95% confidence ($t=1.41$, $p=0.16>0.05$) as shown in Table 3.

Table 3. Statistical comparison

	Group	N	Media	Standard Deviation	Levene'sTest for Variance Equality		t-test for media equality	
					F	Sig.	t	Sig.
Difference (Post-test – Pre-test)								
	G1	28	2.64	0.95				
	G2	29	2.27	1.00	0.90	0.79	1.41	0.16

The answers to the questions related to the students' perceptions about QMP for G1 are summarized in Table 4.

Table 4. Survey results

Students' Perception about the use of QMP	Strongly Disagree		Disagree		Neutral		Agree		Strongly Agree	
	n	%	n	%	n	%	n	%	n	%
I liked learning using the methodology based on QMP	1	3.6	1	3.6	8	28.6	13	46	5	17.9
Seeing my classmates' progress motivates me to work	0	0	3	10.7	9	32.1	14	50	2	7.1
At the end of each session I feel that I have learned	0	0	3	10.7	14	50	7	25	4	14.3
The automatic feedback from the platform helps my learning	1	3.6	0	0	8	28.6	7	25	12	42.9
Using QMP made me feel more confident about my knowledge	1	3.6	6	21.4	10	35.7	7	25	4	14.3
I like to have the control over my learning process	0	0	0	0	4	14.3	10	36	14	50
I used the trial and error method as a source of learning.	1	3.6	0	0	4	14.3	19	68	4	14.3
The platform QMP met my expectations.	0	0	5	17.9	10	35.7	11	39	2	7.1

We can highlight that 64% liked the QMP-based methodology, 86% enjoyed controlling their learning process, and 82% used trial and error as a learning strategy. These percentages are obtained by adding the "Agree", and "Strongly Agree" answers for each question. Furthermore, in a separate question, 89.3% recommended their peers to volunteer for the QMP evaluation process. Another positive aspect of QMP is its functionalities to generate useful reports, such as the Test Analysis Report, partially shown in Figure 1, which shows diverse test statistics and a reliability analysis.

4. Conclusions

Despite not finding statistically significant performance improvements, we can conclude that, for our population, the use of computer technology was at least as effective as instruction without technology, which coincides with some of the findings in Grgurović, Chapelle, and Shelley (2013). Furthermore, QMP was satisfactorily evaluated by the students. QMP also allowed the professor to monitor and timely detect students with performance problems thanks to the different reports it provides, which offered relevant information such as students' performance for each exercise and formative evaluation, and items that proved to be easiest or most difficult, among others.

Figure 1. QMP's test analysis report[5]

Test Analysis Report

Assessment name	Handout5	Assessment description	HO5
Assessment author	400219	Assessment ID	3948568167720624
Assessment last modified	Apr 22 2014 00:00:00	Report date & time	Sep 22 2014 01:53:22

Filters
All dates
Participants who finished

Table of Test Statistics

Number of examinees	30	Mean	5/30 (16.67%)	Standard error of mean	1.19/30 (3.97%)
Number of items	21	Median	3/30 (10%)	Standard error of measurement	2.79/30 (9.3%)
Maximum possible score	30	Mode	0/30 (0%)	Skew	2.257
Minimum achieved score	0/30 (0%)	Standard deviation	6.5/30 (21.67%)	Kurtosis	5.217
Maximum achieved score	27/30 (90%)	Variance	42.21/30 (140.7%)	Test reliability (Cronbach's Alpha)	0.816

Reliability is most meaningful if all items cover the same subject area.

Reliability (Topic Level)

Topic	Number of items	Mean	Standard deviation	Reliability
	21	5/30 (16.67%)	6.5/30 (21.67%)	0.816
Kinesiology Handout 5	1	2/10 (20%)	3.01/10 (30.1%)	-
Kinesiology Handout 5\TFHO5	10	3.27/10 (32.7%)	1.98/10 (19.8%)	0.813

Since this is the first time that technology in the area of computer based formative evaluation has been introduced in the Faculty of Medicine at UACh in a course of ESP, we present a preliminary evaluation in this area showing that the use of technology contributes to learning in a different way, more compatible with today's demands from the digital world. However, we cannot generalize the results at this point.

5. Acknowledgements

We would like to thank the Dirección de Investigación y Desarrollo (DID) of the Universidad Austral de Chile – Valdivia for sponsoring this research in the context of project DID S- 2013-41. We would also like to thank the Centro de Idiomas at Universidad Austral de Chile – Valdivia for their assistance in the development of

---

5. Screenshot reproduced with kind permission from Questionmark™

this work. Finally, We would like to thank Questionmark Corporation for granting permission to include in this paper images generated with their software.

References

Black, P., & Wiliam, D. (1998). Inside the black box: raising standards through classroom assessment. *Phi Delta Kappan, 80*(2), 139-148.

Grgurović, M., Chapelle, C., & Shelley, M. C. (2013). A meta-analysis of effectiveness studies on computer technology-supported language learning. *ReCALL, 25*(2), 165-198. doi:10.1017/S0958344013000013

Jabif, L. (2007). *La docencia universitaria bajo un enfoque de competencias: orientaciones prácticas para docentes*. Universidad Austral de Chile.

Kingston, N., & Nash, B. (2011). Formative assessment: a meta-analysis and a call for research. *Educational Measurement: Issues and Practice, 30*(4), 28-37. doi:10.1111/j.1745-3992.2011.00220.x

Lazzeri, S., Cabezas, X., Ojeda, L., & Leiva, F. (2015). Assessing the impact of computer based formative evaluations in a course of english as a foreign language for undergraduate kinesiology students in chile. In F. Helm, L. Bradley, M. Guarda, & S. Thouësny (Eds.), *Critical CALL – Proceedings of the 2015 EUROCALL Conference, Padova, Italy* (pp. 348-354). Dublin Ireland: Research-publishing.net. doi:10.14705/rpnet.2015.000357

Questionmark-Corporation. (2015). *Questionmark*. Retrieved from https://www.questionmark.com/us/Pages/default.aspx

UACh. (2007). *Comisión Curricular, Modelo Educacional y Enfoque Curricular de la Universidad Austral de Chile*. Editorial Universidad Austral de Chile.

A hybrid approach for correcting grammatical errors

Kiyoung Lee[1], Oh-Woog Kwon[2], Young-Kil Kim[3], and Yunkeun Lee[4]

Abstract. This paper presents a hybrid approach for correcting grammatical errors in the sentences uttered by Korean learners of English. The error correction system plays an important role in GenieTutor, which is a dialogue-based English learning system designed to teach English to Korean students. During the talk with GenieTutor, grammatical error feedback and better expressions are offered to learners. We surveyed the grammatical mistakes that occurred in the English sentences uttered by Korean learners. These errors involve preposition errors, verb form errors, agreement errors, noun countability errors and determiner errors. The hybrid error correction system consists of 5 components: an error memory based correction system, a machine learning based correction system, an n-gram based correction system, an edit distance based correction system and a selector. The correction performance of each component is different depending on error types. To evaluate the hybrid system, we used a test set comprising of 858 sentences extracted from utterances by Korean learners. The test set includes not only ungrammatical sentences, but also correct sentences. We conducted various experiments and examined the effect of the hybrid approach on grammatical error correction. The experiments show promising results for correcting grammatical errors.

Keywords: grammatical error correction, dialogue-based computer assisted language learning.

1. Electronics and Telecommunications Research Institute, Daejeon, Korea; leeky@etri.re.kr
2. Electronics and Telecommunications Research Institute, Daejeon, Korea; ohwoog@etri.re.kr
3. Electronics and Telecommunications Research Institute, Daejeon, Korea; kimyk@etri.re.kr
4. Electronics and Telecommunications Research Institute, Daejeon, Korea; yklee@etri.re.kr

How to cite this article: Lee, K., Kwon, O.-W., Kim, Y.-K., & Lee, Y. (2015). A hybrid approach for correcting grammatical errors. In F. Helm, L. Bradley, M. Guarda, & S. Thouësny (Eds), *Critical CALL – Proceedings of the 2015 EUROCALL Conference, Padova, Italy* (pp. 362-367). Dublin: Research-publishing.net. http://dx.doi.org/10.14705/rpnet.2015.000359

1. Introduction

Recently, there has been a growing interest in Computer-Assisted Language Learning (CALL). Particularly in Korea, the time and cost to learn English are enormous and have been on the rise every year. We have developed GenieTutor (Kwon et al, 2015), which is a dialogue-based English learning system for Korean learners. The system consists of non-native optimized speech recognition modules and semantic/grammar correctness evaluation based tutoring modules (Kwon, Lee, Kim, & Lee, 2015). A learner has a talk with GenieTutor on various topics of scenarios consisting of 3 to 4 turns. During the talk with GenieTutor, grammatical error feedback and better expressions are offered to learners. These scenarios help learners not to be out of basic flow of dialogue. Learners take lessons on pronunciation, grammar and useful expressions from conversation with the virtual tutor. In this paper, we describe the hybrid grammatical correction system. Section 2 of this paper gives an overview of our system to detect and correct grammatical mistakes. Section 3 illustrates experimental results. In section 4, we sum up the discussion and show the future research direction.

2. Method

2.1. Grammatical error types

The grammatical error correction system plays an important role in GenieTutor, which is a dialogue based English learning system. The task of the grammatical error correction system is to detect and to correct grammatical mistakes made by an English learner. We defined target errors based on the Cambridge Learner Corpus (Nicholls, 2003) and the NUS Corpus (Dahlmeier, Ng, & Wu, 2013). These errors frequently occur in sentences or utterances by Korean learners. Table 1 shows the grammatical error types which we aim to correct.

Table 1. Grammatical error types

Error Tag	Error Category	Error Tag	Error Category
RV	Replacing a verb	TV	Verb tense
FV	Verb form	AGV	Subject-verb agreement
MV	Missing a verb	UV	Unnecessary verb
RT	Replacing a preposition	MT	Missing a preposition
UT	Unnecessary preposition	MD	Missing a determiner
UD	Unnecessary determiner	RD	Replacing a determiner
RN	Replacing a noun	AGN	Noun agreement
FN	Noun form	MN	Missing a noun
UN	Unnecessary noun	CN	Noun countability

2.2. Hybrid grammatical error correction

Grammatical errors have their unique characteristics. The clues to detect and correct mistakes are also different from error types. There are various approaches to detect and correct grammar mistakes. We devised a hybrid correction system that combines four types of correction systems and a selector. Figure 1 shows the configuration of our hybrid grammatical error correction system. Each correction system takes as an input a sentence uttered by a learner and generates correction candidates according to their strategy to detect and correct errors. A selector then decides a final error type and a correction among correction candidates from each system.

Figure 1. The configuration of a hybrid grammatical error correction system

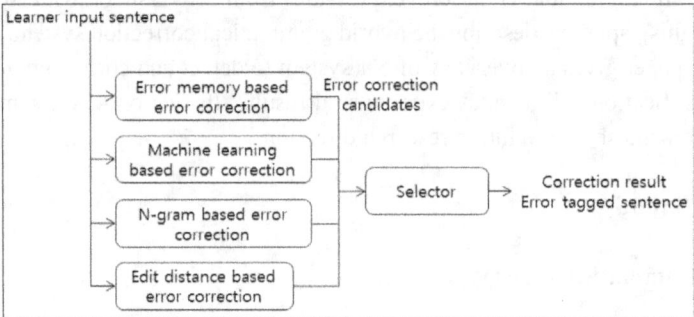

The knowledge for correction used by each component is based on 21,400 learner utterances excluding system's utterances in predefined scenarios.

2.2.1. Error memory based error correction

An error memory is a pattern with context and correction information. An error memory is as follows: *i am interest/interested/FV in music*.

The above error memory is applied to an input sentence "I am interest in music". In this sentence, 'interest' should be replaced by 'interested' and a mistake type is FV (Verb Form). The recall of error memory based correction is low. Its precision, however, is very high.

2.2.2. Machine learning based error correction

A machine learning based error correction system requires a grammatical error tagged training corpus for training classifiers. To build the training corpus we automatically generated erroneous sentences and tagged error codes for the 21,400 sentences mentioned above. At the same time, we collected learner utterances from test service. Then, mistakes were tagged by human using error tags. We used a SVM classifier to detect and correct grammatical errors.

2.2.3. N-gram based error correction

N-gram data is extracted from common 21,400 sentences. In the n-gram correction model, the window size is set to 2 to 5 words. By replacing an input word with a possible form of the word, an n-gram model generates correction candidates and calculates their frequencies.

2.2.4. Edit distance based error correction

Dialogue scenarios consist of system utterances and corresponding correct answers. So, by searching correct answers that are most similar to an input sentence made by a learner, a correction candidate can be generated from the difference. An edit distance based error correction uses this characteristic.

2.2.5. Selector

A selector decides a final error type and correction information using the weight based on the performance of each correction system on error types. We assigned a different weight on each correction method depending on error types and their performance. For example, it is difficult for the error memory based correction system to find the mistakes detected by considering a broad context.

3. Experiments

To evaluate the hybrid grammatical error correction system, 858 sentences were randomly extracted from sentences uttered by Korean learners. The test set includes not only sentences involving words or phrases used ungrammatically, but also correct sentences. Table 2 and Table 3 show the precision and the recall on test.

Table 2. The performance comparison

System	Precision	Recall
Error memory based correction	98.6%	30.5%
Edit distance based correction	90%	15.5%
Machine learning based correction	64.2%	14.6%
N-gram based correction	65.3%	27.5%
Hybrid correction	**91.3%**	**45.1%**

Table 3. The performance of hybrid error correction

Error type	Precision	Recall
AGV	100%	68.8%
CN	60%	27.3%
FV	100%	50%
MD	92.1%	63.6%
MT	88.9%	29.6%
MV	100%	40%
RD	100%	70%
RT	82.4%	58.3%
UD	90%	75%
UT	100%	44.4%
UV	100%	25%
Total	91.3%	45.1%

We surveyed the effect of a hybrid grammatical error correction method. There still remain some problems to be solved:

- How to improve the performance of a hybrid error correction system for more general domains? Our system works well for dialogues similar to given scenarios. However, it is susceptible to correct grammatical errors in sentences which are out of given scenarios. We think that a machine learning based method and an n-gram method will be helpful to solve these coverage problems. So we are consistently collecting and building a training corpus and a n-gram data.

- In our hybrid system, it is very effective to maximize the performance of a selector. Modelling a selector by the performance of each correction system according to error types is needed.

- Because a false alarm is very critical for learning systems, we focused on correction precision for test service. By the same token, we assigned higher weight on the correction candidate of an error memory based system and an edit distance based system. As a future research direction, we consider to improve the recall of our hybrid method.

4. Conclusions

We have described a hybrid grammatical mistake correction system. Our hybrid error correction system consists of five components: an error memory based correction system, a machine learning based correction system, an n-gram based correction system, an edit distance based correction system and a selector. Since grammatical errors are very diverse and have unique characteristics, it is difficult to cover these errors using only one correction system.

We plan to improve recall rate of our system on out of scenario sentences. To do that, the role of a machine learning and an n-gram based error correction approach is very important.

5. Acknowledgements

This work was supported by the ICT R&D program of MSIP/IITP. [R0126-15-1117, Core technology development of the spontaneous speech dialogue processing for the language learning]

References

Kwon, O.-W., Lee, K., Kim, Y.-K, & Lee, Y. (2015). GenieTutor: a computer assisted second-language learning system based on semantic and grammar correctness evaluations In F. Helm, L. Bradley, M. Guarda, & S. Thouësny (Eds.), *Critical CALL – Proceedings of the 2015 EUROCALL Conference, Padova, Italy* (pp. 330-335). Dublin Ireland: Research-publishing.net. doi:10.14705/rpnet.2015.000354

Kwon, , O.-W., Lee, K., Roh, H.-H., Huang, J.-X., Choi, S.-K., Kim, Y.-K, Jeon, H. B., Oh, Y. R., Lee, Y.-K., Kang, B. O., Chung, E., Park, J. G., & Lee, Y. (2015). GenieTutor: a computer assisted second-language learning system based on spoken language understanding, *Proceedings of the International Workshop on Spoken Dialog Systems*. Retrieved from https://www.uni-ulm.de/in/iwsds2015/list-of-accepted-papers.html

Dahlmeier, D., Ng, H. T., & Wu, S. M. (2013). Building a large annotated corpus of learner English: the NUS corpus of learner English. *Proceeding of the Eighth Workshop on Innovative Use of NLP for Building Educational Application* (pp. 22-31).

Nicholls, D. (2003). The Cambridge learner corpus – error coding and analysis for lexicography and ELT. *Proceedings of the Corpus Linguistics* (pp.572-581).

Mi.L.A: multilingual and multifaceted mobile interactive applications for children with autism

Fernando Loizides[1], Iosif Kartapanis[2],
Francesca Sella[3], and Salomi Papadima-Sophocleous[4]

Abstract. In this paper we present the initial stages of a project entitled Minority Language Applications (Mi.L.A) which aims to facilitate material for children with autism in a multilingual setting using interactive multimedia that increase both the awareness as well as the access to information for patients who need it. Pilot testing the applications with three children within the autism spectrum shows favorable initial results. The children would interact with the applications successfully and gain from the sessions in terms of communication skills as well as improved verbal and visual cues.

Keywords: mobile applications, autism, disabilities, multilingual.

1. Introduction

In recent years, there is a growing interest in the area of technology and autism. Researchers have attempted to study many aspects of technology in order to address their potential value in supporting their education. In promoting the independence of the child, the iPod Touch has been used to train Autistic Spectrum Disorder (ASD) children in how to structure their leisure time independently, and without any aid from an adult (Carlile, Reeve, Reeve, & Debar, 2013). Other studies have

---

1. University of Wolverhampton, United Kingdom; Fernando.loizides@wlv.ac.uk
2. Cyprus University of Technology, Cyprus; Iosif.Kartapanis@cut.ac.cy
3. MiLA Solutions; Francesca@mila-solutions.com
4. Cyprus University of Technology, Cyprus; salomi.papadima@cut.ac.cy

How to cite this article: Loizides, F., Kartapanis, I., Sella, F., & Papadima-Sophocleous, S. (2015). Mi.L.A: multilingual and multifaceted mobile interactive applications for children with autism. In F. Helm, L. Bradley, M. Guarda, & S. Thouësny (Eds), *Critical CALL – Proceedings of the 2015 EUROCALL Conference, Padova, Italy* (pp. 368-374). Dublin: Research-publishing.net. http://dx.doi.org/10.14705/rpnet.2015.000360

used computer programs to successfully provide an activity schedule for ASD children (Stromer, Kimball, Kinney, & Taylor, 2006). Although there has been an increase in the use of technology in treating ASD, we recognize that there is lack of applications that cater for children with autism for minority languages (note: we refer to the term 'minority language' in the sense of a language that received little attention in translated applications). A child with autism should not have to (and is often not able to) receive therapy in a second language.

From an extensive search, there are no mobile applications developed for most minority languages for ASD. The population with ASD in minority languages are dealt with as follows: the first option is to use specialized ASD digital tools that are available in common foreign languages; most often English. The second option is to use non-specialized language learning digital tools in the native language. These generic tools are not specialized for individuals with ASD and provide limited assistance or have a reverse effect in that they can damage, frighten or hinder the development process of the individual. A third option is to classify ASD patients as invalids and confining them to be neglected. We present the Mi.L.A initiative. The acronym from the Greek 'μίλα' (pronounced milá) literally means 'speak'. Project Mi.L.A involves creating assistive software (mostly mobile applications) to educate children with disabilities, starting with autism for minority languages with interactive, specialized multimedia content. Specifically, the project aims to:

- create applications targeting minority languages, facilitating parents and therapists with tools required to help children, especially where there are limited resources for therapy: "[a] computer can spend much more time with a patient than a specialist and in a more comfortable, familiar environment" (Edwards, 2014, p. 13);

- give children with autism the chance to experience accessing traditional culture and stories which other children are exposed to through books or storytelling by their parents (Cyprus Interaction Lab, 2014).

The paper continues to present the applications created for patients within the ASD spectrum and presents pilot testing with positive results.

2. Method

In this section, we present the prototypes applications in the Mi.L.A collection. All software developed for the Mi.L.A initiative undergo severe specialized scrutiny before they are released. In order to ensure the quality and suitability of the content of the applications, a User-Centric Design (UCD) process is enforced and every element must pass testing (See Figure 1).

Figure 1. Children with ASD would confuse the two animals; scrutiny uncovered that the animals' whiskers were similar and were subsequently changed

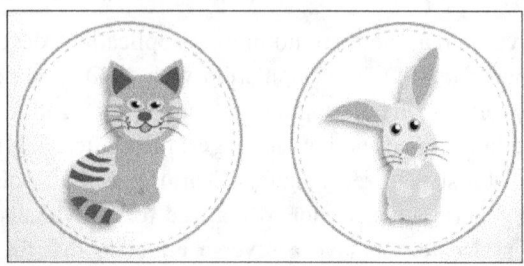

2.1. Object identification

A common exercise for individuals with autism is that of identifying objects they would come across daily (Granpeesheh, Tarbox, & Dixon, 2009). In this part of the software, the child is presented visually with a series of objects and asked (verbally and textually) to identify which of the images the object corresponds to. The child then needs to select by touching the correct object. If the child selects correctly, then a short commendation is given and the next object identification question appears.

2.2. Sound identification

A common exercise for individuals with autism and especially children is identifying sounds they come across on a daily basis (O'Connor, 2012). These include sounds of everyday life. In this part of the software, the child is presented visually with a series of sounds and asked (only verbally) to identify which of the images the sound corresponds to.

2.3. Stories

A part of the culture that children with ASD usually miss is that of traditional children stories. In Mi.L.A, traditional stories are recorded and presented in a sensory friendly way to the children, with animations and audio (See Figure 2).

Figure 2. 'The hare and the tortoise' tale

2.4. Songs

Singing and listening to songs is important in the development of a child. In the field of ASD it is even more important because it aids the development of speech (Gold, Wigram, & Elefant, 2010). Traditional and popular songs are available on the applications with a sensory appropriate visual stimulation in the form of animations to enhance understanding of the songs and increase cognitive attendance.

2.5. Self-care

A very common need of children with ASD is to learn how to take care of themselves (Kern, Wakeford, & Aldridge, 2007). As part of Mi.L.A we developed self-care stories, which will be based on the theory of "Social Stories", a well-documented tool in teaching social behaviors to children with ASD. A narrated story is paired with specially designed animations in order to teach the child these basic daily routines (see Figure 3).

Figure 3. Three stages in self-care video with voice over, teaching the child with ASD the process of brushing his/her teeth

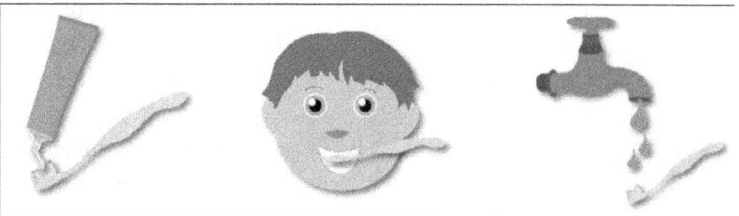

2.6. Expressions

It is well documented that children with ASD have difficulties understanding the emotional cues from people (Shamsuddin & Yussof, 2013). Extensive training can help the child better understand these expressions and thus have a better social interaction. Mi.L.A has a simple game in which the child will learn to discriminate between several expressions (see Figure 4).

Figure 4. Expressions children with Autism may not recognize: crying and laughing

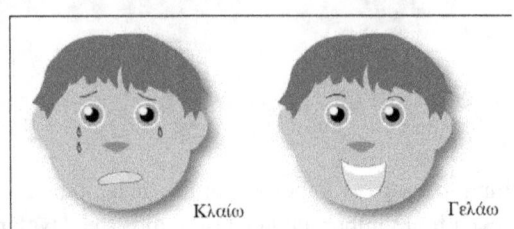

3. Initial testing

We tested the usability and investigated some effects of our application with three children diagnosed with autism by a developmental pediatrician. Each child received a one-hour therapy session weekly for five weeks. The aim of the pilot study was to study the acceptance of the mobile applications to the children with autism and to report early findings on its use and learnability. The test participants' profiles are as follows (names have been changed). Sheryl is an eight-year-old female diagnosed with Rett Syndrome and has limited speech and non-verbal communication skills. Mary is a ten-year-old female with limited communication and presents echolalia and stereotypical behaviors. During therapies and at home she favors playing with tablets. Jay is a 13-year-old male with low developed speech and attention span. There exists hyperactivity and aggression caused by lack of people interactivity skills. A stationary camera in the room recorded interaction both when the child was alone, as well as the session with a therapist. The children initially interacted with the application during the first session with the aid of the therapist, proceeding in future sessions to independently working with the application if able to.

Figure 5. (Left) Sheryl, disgnosed with Rett Syndrome, diverting attention from the tablet; (Right) Mary, with echolalia and stereotypical behavior, selecting the animal on level 2

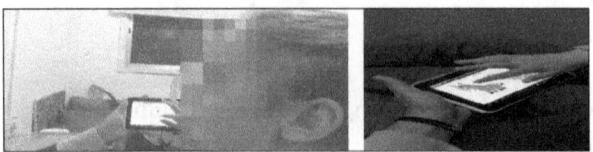

Sheryl has shown an interest in tablets in previous sessions but has severe difficulty in eye-hand coordination. During the first interaction with the game, she avoided eye contact with the tablet several times (see Figure 5) but completed the game with assistance. Even though during the initial contact with the game she lacked interest, on the second session, she walked into the room and situated herself next to the table where the tablet was lying. Her speech was until now limited to a few vowel sounds and saying, "Yes". When interacting with the game, she exclaimed, "where is it?". Mary needed full assistance in keeping attention to the game engaging eye contact with the screen (see Figure 5) and pointing to the animals, during the first two sessions. After 4 sessions, she could engage in short intervals to point to two to three animals. During the game Jay kept engaged with the application for the whole duration of both stage 1 and 2 of the game. In later sessions, the child asked for the game by saying "Pad, Animals". Overall, all of the children participating in the evaluation of the applications showed positive responses interacting to various degrees and showing an interest in the game.

4. Conclusions and future developments

In this paper we presented the Mi.L.A initiative which deals with developing applications to assist people with disabilities in minority languages. All the applications are customized to not only the language of the target audience but also the specific culture. Using visual analysis, different metrics can be introduced from the study in order to be recorded in the longitudinal studies. By expanding the network of users, we will accumulate large data sets to produce user models and a better understanding of ASD.

References

Carlile, K. A., Reeve, S. A., Reeve, K. F., & Debar, R. M. (2013). Using activity schedules on the iPod touch to teach leisure skills to children with autism. *Education and treatment of children, 36*(2), 33-57. doi:10.1353/etc.2013.0015

Cyprus Interaction Lab. (2014). Best social impact award' – Cyprus digital championship 2014. Retrieved from http://cyprusinteractionlab.com/best-social-impact-award-cyprus-digital-championship-2014/?

Edwards, C. 2014. Decoding the language of human movement. *ACM, 57*(12), 12-14. doi:10.1145/2675742

Gold, C., Wigram, T., & Elefant, C. (2010). Music therapy for autistic spectrum disorder. *Editorial Group: Cochrane Developmental, Psychosocial and Learning Problems Group.* doi:10.1002/14651858.CD004381.pub2

Granpeesheh, D., Tarbox, J., & Dixon, D. R. (2009). Applied behavior analytic interventions for children with autism: a description and review of treatment research. *Ann Clin Psychiatry, 21*(3), 162-173.

Kern, P., Wakeford, L., & Aldridge, D. (2007). Improving the performance of a young child with autism during self-care tasks using embedded song interventions: a case study. *Music Therapy Perspectives, 25*(1).

O'Connor, K. (2012). Auditory processing in autism spectrum disorder: a review. *Neuroscience & Biobehavioral Reviews, 36*(2), 836-854.

Shamsuddin, S., & Yussof, H. (2013). Humanoid robot NAO as HRI mediator to teach emotions using game-centered approach for children with autism. *HRI 2013 Workshop on Applications for Emotional Robots*.

Stromer, R., Kimball, J. W., Kinney, E. M., & Taylor, B. A. (2006). Activity schedules, computer technology, and teaching children with autism spectrum disorders. *Focus on Autism and Other Developmental Disabilities, 21*(1), 43-51. doi:10.1177/10883576060210010301

AWE-based corrective feedback on developing EFL learners' writing skill

Zhihong Lu[1], Xiaowei Li[2], and Zhenxiao Li[3]

Abstract. The effective design and use of Automated Writing Evaluation (AWE) tools in developing English as a Foreign Language (EFL) learners' writing skill and learner autonomy have remained great challenges for system designers, developers, and EFL instructors compared with that of the pencil-paper writing in the context of regular teacher-fronted classroom in Chinese higher educational institutions. The function of Corrective Feedback (CF) provided by the *Pigai* system, i.e. a web-based AWE tool in China (http://www.pigai.org/), can be reflected on the students' writing scripts. To measure if AWE-based CF is beneficial to EFL learners in improving their writing skill as well as learner autonomy, a study was carried out based on the *Pigai* system in a web-based college English course which focuses on developing learners' output abilities. The correlated data and feedback showed that the application of AWE-based CF, i.e. 10-minute online writing performance, did have a marked impact on EFL learners' writing skill and learner autonomy. In this paper, the effects of using the AWE system and its CF on students' efficacy in English writing as well as its pedagogical effectiveness will be discussed. Learners' perceptions toward AWE-based CF and the effective use of AWE tools in EFL contexts will also be covered.

Keywords: automated writing evaluation, AWE, corrective feedback, learner autonomy, Pigai system.

---

1. Beijing University of Posts and Telecommunications, China; luzhihong@bupt.edu.cn
2. Beijing University of Posts and Telecommunications, China; lixiaoweisally@bupt.edu.cn
3. Beijing University of Posts and Telecommunications, China; briannalee@163.com

How to cite this article: Lu, Z., Li, X., Li, Z. (2015). AWE-based corrective feedback on developing EFL learners' writing skill. In F. Helm, L. Bradley, M. Guarda, & S. Thouësny (Eds), *Critical CALL – Proceedings of the 2015 EUROCALL Conference, Padova, Italy* (pp. 375-380). Dublin: Research-publishing.net. http://dx.doi.org/10.14705/rpnet.2015.000361

1. Introduction

CF, as defined in Wikipedia (n.d.), is frequently practiced in the field of education as well as learning; "[i]t typically involves a student receiving either formal or informal feedback on his or her performance on various tasks by a teacher or peer(s)" (para. 1). Lightbown and Spada (1999) stated that CF is any indication to the learners that their use of the target language is incorrect. Though the CF in pencil-paper writing class used to have significant effects on improving learners' writing skills, there still exists potential problems that should not be ignored.

Nystrom (1983) discussed teachers' role when giving CF in pencil-paper style and he concluded that "teachers typically are unable to sort through the feedback options available to them and arrive at the most appropriate response" (p. 170). Van Lier (1988) considered that teachers had too much control of students' self-initiated repairs which in turn hampered learners' self-correction ability. Chaudron (1988) and his colleagues found that in traditional classes CFs were, to some extent, biased.

With the rapid development in the fields of information technologies and natural language processing in last few decades, more powerful AWE tools have been developed, making it possible to release instructors' working load while inspiring learners' sense of writing and promoting their awareness of self-correction in writing. This study aims to investigate the effects of the CF function of the *Pigai* system on students' writing scripts, a 10-minute online writing as an embedded task in an integrated college English course and its impact on the learners' writing skill and learner autonomy.

2. Method

2.1. Research questions

The research is driven by the following questions:

- Is AWE-based CF helpful to improve EFL learners' writing skills?

- Is there a significant difference between male and female learners in developing their writing skills by using the AWE tool?

- How do EFL learners perceive AWE-based CF in the process of writing?

2.2. Research design

This study was carried out at one of the first author's college English classes, in which there were 25 non-English majors in a digital lab from September, 2014 to January, 2015. All the students had passed CET-4[4] before taking the course, and 23 students had accomplished all of the ten writing tasks throughout the semester.

Each time in class, students were assigned to a task of four-round productive activities on a controlled topic:

- Round one: 10-minute 3-person group discussion.

- Round two: 5-minute pair-work.

- Round three: 10-minute online writing.

- Round four: 1-minute recorded personal statement.

In round three, students were required to write a passage about 200 words to the same topic on the *Pigai* system within ten minutes. After submission, students could receive their scores immediately with detailed real-time CF and comments. Therefore, students could revise their texts as many times as they wanted within a time period (set by the teacher) and their performance of each time revision could be tracked (see Figure 1 and Figure 2).

Figure 1. A screenshot of the online writing assignments on the *Pigai* system

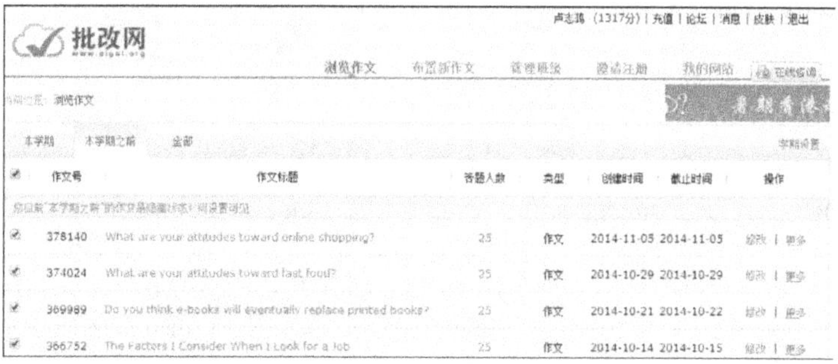

---

4. CET is the abbreviated form of "College English Test". The national College English Test Band Four (CET-4) in China aims to evaluate non-English majors' comprehensive language proficiency. Apart from CET-4, there is also CET-6, which is widely used to evaluate above-average college students' English language proficiency.

Figure 2. A screenshot of the tracking record of a student's writing

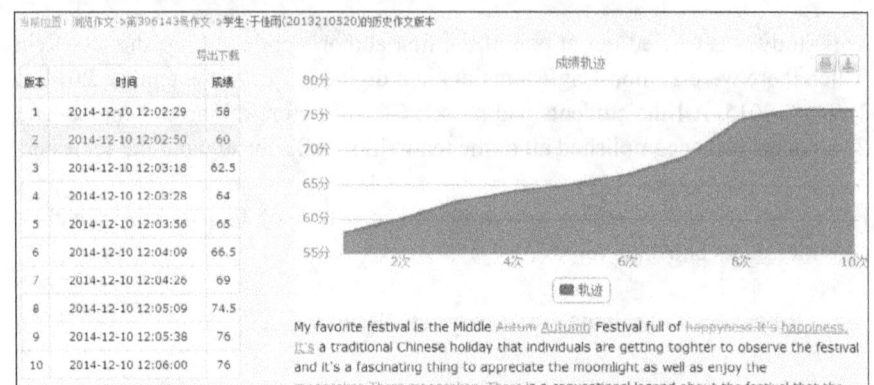

2.3. Instruments

One follow-up questionnaire and a scale of students' perception toward AWE CF (at 5-point Likert) were designed and delivered to the class at the end of the term. A complete set of 10-minute writing tasks including ten writing tasks were required to be completed on the *Pigai* system in class.

2.4. Data collection

All the students' writing scripts were automatically scored and collected through the *Pigai* system.

2.5. Data analysis

Data was processed by using SPSS 22.0.

- Paired sample *t*-tests were used to find out if there were significant differences between the students' improvement in writing and their revision times.

- Paired sample *t*-tests were used to find out if there were significant differences between male and female students in the improvement of their writing and their revision times.

- Descriptive statistics (mean, standard deviation, percentage) were employed to analyze the students' perception of AWE-based CF with respect to the 10-minute online writing task.

3. Discussion

3.1. Analysis of scores

As shown in Table 1, there were significant differences in students' writing scores between their first and last writing tasks, and also between their first and final revisions of the two writing tasks.

Table 1. Paired sample *t*-test for the improvement of scores (201409~201501)

Whole class	Mean	SD	Std. Error Mean	t	df	Sig. (2-tailed)
First revision	-8.087	8.176	1.704	-4.743	22	.000
Final revison	-14.152	9.139	1.905	-7.426	22	.000
Revision times	-8.087	9.361	1.951	-4.143	22	.000
Improvement	-6.065	9.132	1.904	-3.185	22	.004

(N=23)

3.2. Analysis of different genders

The result of a paired sample *t*-test of scores for male and female students showed that there were significant differences across genders in the ten writing tasks. Besides, the revision times were increased significantly throughout the whole term.

The difference was that female students, with a level of significant value of 0.046 ($t=2.252$, $df=11$, $p<0.05$), improved more significantly than male students at level of 0.052 ($t=-2.202$, $df=10$, $p>0.05$).

3.3. Analysis of students' perceptions

With respect to how students perceive AWE-based CF in developing their writing skills in a 10-minute online writing task, nine highly correlated items from the questionnaire (#01, #02, #04, #11, #23~#27) were selected and the mean scores of the items ranged from 4.05 to 4.57, which showed that most students held positive attitude toward AWE-based CF and felt it helpful to improve their writing skills as well as learner autonomy.

4. Conclusions

This study leads to the following conclusions:

- AWE-based CF has positive effects on improving students' writing skills, which can be observed from the following aspects: the scores for the first and final submissions increased; the improvement in the students' writing skills highly correlated with their revision times; the improvement in students' writing after self-revision has been made greatly.

- Both male and female students improved their writing skill significantly in their first and last writing tasks, however, female students' writing skill has improved more significantly than that of male students.

- AWE-based CF, to some extent, may help EFL learners to improve their writing skills as well as learner autonomy.

5. Acknowledgements

This study is part of the humanities and social sciences project "Research on Multidimensional Assessment for a Web-based English Audio-video Speaking Course" (12YJA740052), supported by the Ministry of Education in China. We would like to thank Mr. Zhang Yue and his company for their technical support in the course of the study.

References

Chaudron, C. (1988). *Second language classrooms: research on teaching and learning.* Cambridge: Cambridge University Press. doi:10.1017/CBO9781139524469

Lightbown, P. M., & Spada, N. (1999). *How language are learned.* Oxford: Oxford University Press.

Nystrom, N. (1983). Teacher-student interaction in bilingual classrooms: four approaches to error feedback. In H. W. Seliger & M. H. Long (Eds.), *Classroom oriented research in second language acquisition* (pp.169-188). Newbury House Publishers, Inc.

Van Lier, L. (1988). *The classroom and the language learner: ethnography and second-language classroom research.* Harlow: Longman.

Wikipedia. (n.d.). *Corrective feedback.* Retrieved from https://en.wikipedia.org/wiki/Corrective_feedback?

The flip side of flipped language teaching

Paul A. Lyddon[1]

Abstract. The past decade has seen a growing interest in "flipped teaching", an inversion of traditional teaching methods, whereby instruction formerly taking place in the classroom is made accessible online and lesson time is spent on interaction. Until very recently, flipped learning was largely limited to the Science, Technology, Engineering, and Math (STEM) fields and/or the teaching of blended courses, but some foreign language professionals have also now begun to take notice. At first glance, the approach may appear promising, as it would normalize computers in general instruction and allow teachers to serve more as facilitators and managers rather than purveyors of knowledge. However, reports of its efficacy have so far been mostly anecdotal. Moreover, most flipped teaching as currently practiced assumes top-down presentation that ignores fundamental differences in the nature and purpose of instructional input when content learning is the main, if not sole, objective and language acquisition occurs only incidentally, if at all. As such, without thoughtful adaptation, it is inconsistent with and unsuited for contemporary foreign language pedagogy. This paper discusses potential advantages and disadvantages to consider in the decision of whether to flip the foreign language classroom.

Keywords: flipped learning, inverted classroom, integrated CALL, P-P-P model, SAMR model.

1. Introduction

In 2007, two American high school chemistry teachers began posting video-recorded slide show presentations of their class lectures online with the main intention of assisting students who were absent from their normal lessons (Bergman & Sams, 2012). However, online student access to the course content quickly became so popular that these teachers eventually adopted an entirely different approach to their

---

1. Osaka Jogakuin College, Osaka, Japan; lyddon@wilmina.ac.jp

How to cite this article: Lyddon, P. A. (2015). The flip side of flipped language teaching. In F. Helm, L. Bradley, M. Guarda, & S. Thouësny (Eds), *Critical CALL – Proceedings of the 2015 EUROCALL Conference, Padova, Italy* (pp. 381-385). Dublin: Research-publishing.net. http://dx.doi.org/10.14705/rpnet.2015.000362

pedagogy, now commonly referred to as "flipped teaching", "flipped learning", or the "flipped classroom", an inversion of traditional instructional methods, whereby formerly in-class activities are now completed at home and "homework" activities are done in class. This approach has since spread worldwide, with educators from primary to tertiary level using online videos and podcasts for direct instruction outside of class so as to reserve lesson time for collaborative work and concept mastery exercises.

Although the popularizers of the flipped teaching movement and most of its early adopters taught in the Science, Technology, Engineering, and Math (STEM) fields, some educators and administrators in foreign languages have also now joined the ranks of its advocates. On the surface, flipped teaching appears to announce the dawn of the long-awaited integrated phase of CALL (Bax, 2003), wherein computers will eventually be used as a normal part of everyday instruction and teacher roles will shift to ones of facilitators and managers. Moreover, flipped teaching is often touted for its socio-constructivist approach and its emphasis on active learning as well as its potentially positive effects on learner motivation.

It must be pointed out, however, that most of the evidence to date on the efficacy of flipped teaching has been largely anecdotal. More importantly, key differences between the processes of internalizing subject knowledge and those of acquiring a second language have resulted in correspondingly characteristic pedagogical practices that call for special consideration. Thus, the purpose of this paper is to critically examine some of the potential advantages and disadvantages of flipping foreign language classrooms and to propose a sensible approach to dealing with them.

2. Background

Since the launch of the OpenCourseWare (OCW) initiative by the Massachusetts Institute of Technology (MIT) in 2001, numerous other organizations, such as the Khan Academy, Udacity, and Coursera, have also now established their presence in the world of free, high-quality online learning resources, leading students at brick-and-mortar institutions and their administrators alike to question the value of a traditional university education, the cost of which has only continued to rise in recent years (Bishop & Verleger, 2013). One major response has been a push for more learner-centered instructional approaches to actively engage students in the learning process. These include peer-assisted, problem-based, experiential, collaborative, and cooperative learning, among others. Until recently, however, already overfull curriculums have made the successful implementation of such approaches difficult if not impossible. For this reason, flipped teaching, which frees up valuable lesson time by reassigning class lectures as homework, has garnered increasing attention over the past few years.

By making lectures available in video format online, flipped teaching allows learners to access them whenever and wherever they like and to progress through them at their own pace. Moreover, by permitting teachers to spend their time interacting with individuals and small groups rather than presenting information top-down to the entire class as a whole, flipped classrooms provide important opportunities for better diagnostics and greater differentiation of instruction. Student opinion surveys have shown generally positive attitudes toward video lectures as well as relatively high viewing rates as compared to the completion of traditional assigned readings (Bishop & Verleger, 2013), and while very few empirical studies have been done to assess the impact of flipped teaching on student learning, the early findings suggest improved scores on homework assignments, projects, and written tests, at least in science and mathematics (see Bishop & Verleger, 2013; Fulton, 2012). As such, it should come as no surprise that this novel approach has now caught the attention of educators in other disciplines, including those in foreign languages.

3. Discussion

Schmitt, Herder, and Bhalla (1997) posit that the success of a technological innovation really depends on its ability to abstract and reconstruct the essence of its predecessor, not simply to reproduce its functions. By this standard, however, with respect to language teaching, the flipped classroom fails on both counts. Even following a traditional Presentation-Practice-Production (P-P-P) teaching model, the first two phases should still consist of more than mere transmission, including some degree of interaction to promote intake of the input. According to Puentedura's (2013) bottom-up hierarchy of technological implementations, comprising Substitution, Augmentation, Modification, and Redefinition (SAMR), simple video recordings of class lectures are arguably at the very lowest level. Although the case could be made that video lectures are an augmented form of their live counterparts with the added option to pause and replay them, this additional functionality comes at the expense of another, namely a responsive instructor who can process immediate feedback from learners when a point is unclear, make on-the-spot adjustments, and modify his or her teaching approach before continuing.

Herreid and Schiller (2013) point out that teacher-produced videos in the fields where they now exist are not only often sub-par but also quite time consuming to make. While Tucker (2012) cites a public grade school teacher in the US who considers flipped teaching an opportunity to raise the level of teaching practice and the status of the profession as a whole, that same teacher also admits the formidable challenge of boiling down instruction to its most essential elements, for the recommended video length is as little as four to six minutes, far shorter than the average lecture. One can only imagine the greater time commitment and technological expertise required to create the type of professional quality interactive videos and exercises necessary for effective language instruction. It is possible that the burden of creating an optimal flipped classroom may prove too great for any single instructor, in which case qualified language professionals could even conceivably find themselves in the role of dedicated educational technologists relegated throughout the day to multimedia studios while less expensive teaching assistants take their place as facilitators in the classroom.

Fulton (2012) suggests that in some contexts, teams of teachers might work together to produce a library of videos to share, but even these would need to be frequently re-made to reflect changes in social language use. To avoid this issue altogether, Correa (2015) proposes that teachers might use pre-made videos, just as they routinely use textbooks. However, assigning video lectures for homework, returning to an earlier point, assumes foreknowledge of student needs and interests, for a recorded presenter, unlike a live one, cannot responsively alter his or her message. Moreover, while some knowledge and skills may be prerequisites for others in some fields, there does not appear to be any universal order of language feature acquisition, and in today's highly mobile world, where learners no longer necessarily arrive to the classroom with negligible differences in language background and experience, the issue of sequencing a structure-based syllabus is only so much more complicated.

Although their main concern is authentic intercultural communication, for which they advocate online telecollaboration, the orchestration of which has logistical issues of its own, Kohn and Hoffstaedter (2015) take a broader, and perhaps more suitable view of flipped language pedagogy as "delegating to a virtual learning environment all those tasks and activities that a traditional classroom may not support sufficiently" (p. 2). For instance, in a class of L2 learners all sharing the same L1 and largely interacting in their L2 for the mere sake of practice rather than for real communication and where the interlocutor feedback is, thus, of dubious value, the situation could be remedied by means of online drills. While these types of exercises, similar to valid video lectures, would require both pedagogical knowledge and technical skills to create, they at least do not pretend to substitute for the active learning most seasoned language teachers already try to engender in their face-to-face time with their students and, thus, might more easily be borrowed if necessary.

4. Conclusion

Flipped teaching, if it is to be adopted at all in foreign language classrooms, needs to be considered with great care. First and foremost, we must understand that it is more a matter of pedagogy than of technology and that its interpretation and application in other fields may not be entirely suitable to our own. Thus, in order to decide what to think of it, we must first get at the root of what we are trying to accomplish by our teaching. In other words, we need to clearly identify the factors we believe most effectively promote second language acquisition and determine whether they are better cultivated online or face to face. That said, we should also remain practical, for the greater the time we spend on resource development, not only the more fruitful the potential results will be, but also the more likely we are to find ourselves removed from the classroom altogether. In short, we need to be wise about flipped teaching and approach it with due caution.

References

Bax, S. (2003). CALL—past, present and future. *System, 31*(1), 13-28. doi:10.1016/S0346-251X(02)00071-4

Bergman, J., & Sams, A. (2012). *Flip your classroom: reach every student in every class every day*. Washington, DC: International Society for Technology in Education.

Bishop, J. L., & Verleger, M. A. (2013). The flipped classroom: a survey of the research. In *ASEE National Conference Proceedings, Atlanta, GA*.

Correa, M. (2015). Flipping the foreign language classroom and critical pedagogies: a (new) old trend. *Higher Education for the Future, 2*(2), 114-125. doi:10.1177/2347631115584122

Fulton, K. (2012). Upside down and inside out: flip your classroom to improve student learning. *Learning & Leading with Technology, 39*(8), 12-17.

Herreid, C. F., & Schiller, N. A. (2013). Case studies and the flipped classroom. *Journal of College Science Teaching, 42*(5), 62-66.

Kohn, K., & Hoffstaedter, P. (2015). Flipping intercultural communication practice: opportunities and challenges for the foreign language classroom. Paper presented at *Antwerp CALL 2015: Task design and CALL, Universitat Rovira i Virgili, Tarragona, Spain*.

Puentedura, R. (2013, Jan. 7). *Technology in education: a brief introduction* [Video file]. Retrieved from https://www.youtube.com/watch?v=rMazGEAiZ9c&feature=youtu.be

Schmitt, L.M., Herder, J., & Bhalla, S. (1997). Information retrieval and database architecture for conventional Japanese character dictionaries. In *Proceedings of the Second International Conference on Cognitive Technology, 'Humanizing the Information Age', Aizu-Wakamatsu City, Japan, August 25 – 28, 1997* (pp. 200- 217). IEEE, New York, NY. doi:10.1109/CT.1997.617700

Tucker, B. (2012, Winter). The flipped classroom: online instruction at home frees class time for learning. *Education Next, 12*(1), 82-83.

Layers of CALL hegemonies: an Iranian experience

S. Susan Marandi[1], Khadijeh Karimi Alavijeh[2], and Fatemeh Nami[3]

Abstract. It is a commonly held belief that today's "Read/Write Web" has given voice to previously unheard minorities, and that it has enabled all people with an Internet connection to participate in a new "community-driven, participatory space" (Richardson, 2010). Language teachers, no less than others, are also encouraged to believe that the prevalence of networking on the Internet is increasing the multiculturalism of learning and is breaking down cultural barriers. Such a potential obviously has particular relevance to teaching English as an international language and has led many teachers, ourselves included, to rely on the magic powers of the Internet to ensure that our learners have a real audience, thus motivating them to relate their language learning experience to their real-life concerns. However, our personal experiences have sometimes led us to almost unwillingly empathize with those who express concern that the image of a democratic Internet is in fact merely a mirage, all the more dangerous for creating the illusion of all people being given equal voice, while in fact repressing some voices in the most subtle of ways. In this paper, we would like to offer a somewhat different perspective on the hegemonies of Computer-Assisted Language Learning (CALL), first briefly offering our classification of e-learning/CALL hegemonies which builds on Lamy and Pegrum (2012), and then sharing first-hand experiences of some less-frequently explored layers of such hegemonies. We hope that sharing these experiences might be beneficial in highlighting the need for a more critical view toward CALL.

Keywords: hegemony, inclusion, critical CALL, power relations.

---

1. Alzahra University, Iran; susanmarandi@alzahra.ac.ir
2. Alzahra University, Iran; lg.karimi@yahoo.com
3. Alzahra University, Iran; f.nami22@gmail.com

How to cite this article: Marandi, S. S., Karimi Alavijeh, K., & Nami, F. (2015). Layers of CALL hegemonies: an Iranian experience. In F. Helm, L. Bradley, M. Guarda, & S. Thouësny (Eds), *Critical CALL – Proceedings of the 2015 EUROCALL Conference, Padova, Italy* (pp. 386-391). Dublin: Research-publishing.net. http://dx.doi.org/10.14705/rpnet.2015.000363

1. Introduction

In recent years, there seems to be an increasing goodwill toward e-learning in general and CALL in particular. Even those who believe in the superiority of face-to-face classes generally acknowledge the occasional necessity of online classes. Despite the acknowledged drawbacks of online courses and the continuing controversy over which teaching mode has more merits, certain acclaimed merits of e-learning are widely cited and in fact sometimes almost taken for granted, such as the ubiquity of technology and increased student motivation. Among other claims made with regard to e-learning, there also seems to be a popular belief that online education naturally leads to more openness, democracy, and pluralism. Richardson (2010), for example, claims,

> "[n]o matter how you look at it, we are creating what author Douglas Rushkoff calls a 'society of authorship' where every teacher and every student—every person with access will have the ability to contribute ideas and experiences to the larger body of knowledge that is the Internet. And in doing so, Rushkoff says, we will be writing the human story, in real time, together—a vision that asks each of us to participate" (p. 5).

Similarly, Lehman and Conceição (2010) believe that technology gives us "the opportunity to be present with each other without boundaries" (p. vii). They assert that it has succeeded in "connecting us to diverse people all over the world and bringing us closer together" (Lehman & Conceição, 2010, p. vii). While this is in many ways true, it is equally true that information and communication technologies such as the Internet are "controlled in understated but powerful ways by a myriad of stakeholders" (Marandi, 2014, p. 21), often leading to what may be termed *electronic imperialism*. To look at it from a broader perspective, a variety of *e-learning/CALL hegemonies* may be cited, where an e-learning/CALL element limits the choices available to the relevant stakeholders or exerts undue influence over them. Unfortunately, such hegemonies have received very little attention in the literature until now. An outstanding exception to this is Lamy and Pegrum's (2012) special issue of *Language Learning and Technology*, dealing with "Hegemonies in CALL". In their commentary, they mention technological, pedagogical, educational, social, cultural and intercultural, and sociopolitical hegemonies.

We found this classification to be a very useful starting point, but believe that certain modifications could enhance its usefulness. The e-learning/CALL classification of hegemonies we propose is as follows:

- Linguistic
- Technological
- Economic
- Educational
- Cultural
- Sociopolitical

It must be noted that these categories often overlap, and distinguishing between them is not always possible. *Linguistic hegemonies* refer to the online dominance of an alphabet/language (currently English) over the others, as well as its instrumental use to promote the cultural/ideological domination of its speakers.

Technological hegemonies occur when the hegemonic influence is due to the attributes or predominance of a relevant technology. For example, often popular technologies are limited in the ways they can be used for learning/assessing language skills and subskills, or in the type of skills they favor. Similarly, a technology often addresses certain types of intelligence and not the others. Technological hegemonies also include unwanted investments in expensive technologies, such as being forced to buy or upgrade software/hardware, especially when it interferes with other priorities, such as buying books, paying for a better teacher, etc. Note that this is different from economic hegemonies, which follows.

Economic hegemonies occur when educational and/or technological priorities give way to economic concerns; i.e. when certain necessary educational/technological investments are abandoned/delayed/aborted due to financial concerns. For example, when a fully-equipped computer lab is deemed to be necessary but is not affordable.

Educational hegemonies are when the hegemonic influence is due to predominant educational and institutional policies, principles, practices, and pedagogies; this encompasses the concerns addressed in Lamy and Pegrum's (2012) "pedagogical" and "educational" hegemonies, since we believe that distinguishing between the two is not always feasible or useful. An example of educational hegemonies is the current dominance of web tools which are built based on social constructivist principles.

Cultural hegemonies refer to when the hegemonic influence on e-learning/CALL is due to predominant social and cultural norms; this largely addresses the same concerns as Lamy and Pegrum's (2012) "social hegemonies" and "cultural and intercultural hegemonies". An example is the violence inherent in some games used for learning purposes, or even just the fact that the existing software may encourage beliefs which might not be shared by all the stakeholders. Many scholars insist that technology is by no means neutral, making a critical approach to e-learning crucial (Albirini, 2004; Bowers, 1998; Reinhardt & Isbell, 2002). As Bowers (1998) points out, "thinking within the decision matrix of the software program really involves using the pattern of thinking of the people who designed the software" (p. 54). This relates to the other hegemonies of e-learning/CALL, as well.

Finally, *sociopolitical hegemonies* refer to hegemonies due to "larger social and political structures", or "resistance to these and other hegemonies" (Lamy & Pegrum, 2012, p. 1).

2. Some encounters with less frequently explored hegemonies

As mentioned earlier, one of the frequently-vaunted merits of e-learning is the ubiquity of digital technologies. In fact, a considerable portion of online language learning is achieved using free and open source software. Unfortunately, however, this is not always the case for Iranian learners, who are often subjected to discrimination and are denied access to even the simplest web services that are known throughout the world to be free. An Iranian attempting to download the "free" Adobe Flash Player software or Java Runtime Environment, for example, would be denied access with a message such as, "Forbidden: You are accessing this page from a forbidden country" or "You are not authorized to view this page".

In fact, this discrimination goes far beyond mere access to web services. One of the more subtle hegemonic strategies utilized in certain popular venues for Internet-mediated English education is the inclusion of political news in online educational programs, often resulting in the misrepresentation of periphery countries as a result of bias and distortion. In studies done by two of the authors (Karimi Alavijeh, 2014; Karimi Alavijeh & Marandi, 2014), applying Critical Discourse Analysis to the contents of certain educational English websites, including widely publicized online news services claiming to teach English revealed that the content was orchestrated in such a way so as to misrepresent Iranians as supporters of violence and terrorism. Thematizing the website information through the application of an adaptation of Van Leeuwen's (2008) Social Actor Network revealed that Iranian social actors were associated/dissociated, activated/passivated, and personalized/

impersonalized in such a way so as to link them inextricably to "nuclear programs, sanctions, internal conflicts, espionage, crimes, assassination, terrorist activities, human trafficking, and the like" (Karimi Alavijeh & Marandi, 2014, p. 139).

Similarly, we can point to the turbulences witnessed in Iran after the presidential elections in June 2009. The US government found Twitter to be such an effective tool in support of the Iranian opposition "that it even asked Twitter to postpone its regular maintenance date on June 15, [2010,] saying, 'Iran is in a defining moment, and Twitter is playing such a vital part in it, can you let it just work as usual?'" (English Eastday, 2010, para. 9; see also Markey, 2009; Yang, 2010).

Interestingly, all three authors have had experiences where even their attempts to publish academic articles dealing with the very hegemonies of CALL were denied due to various forms of the same electronic colonialism, calling into question the very foundations of critical CALL education. For example, when two of the authors submitted an academic article on the sociopolitical hegemonies of CALL to a reputable journal dealing with e-learning, we received an email claiming, "As a result of OFAC sanctions, X [journal] is unable to handle submissions with authors who are employed by the Government of Iran. We regret that unfortunately we are unable to handle your manuscript". This is while we had openly declared, "This research received no specific grant from any funding agency in the public, commercial or not-for-profit sectors". In fact, we have no affiliation with the Iranian government except for teaching at a public university. Another journal similarly denied us freedom of speech due to what they called "the sensitive nature of relations between your country and X [country]".

3. Conclusions

The very potentials of the Internet and digital technologies which can lead to new voices being heard may also be abused, resulting in the suppression of other voices and the creation of new "haves" and "have-nots". So far, little has been done to redress this problem. Hopefully, encouraging a truly critical view toward CALL can lead us beyond the mere online learning of a language and toward building a happier and more understanding community.

4. Acknowledgements

We would like to thank our families for their support. We would also like to thank Peppi Taalas, Toni Patton, and Françoise Blin for their kind help, which led to our voices finally being heard.

References

Albirini, A. (2004). *An exploration of the factors associated with the attitudes of high school EFL teachers in Syria toward information and communication technology.* Unpublished doctoral dissertation, Ohio State University, OH. Retrieved from http://etd.ohiolink.edu/view.cgi/Albirini%20Abdulkafi.pdf?acc_num=osu1092688797

Bowers, C. A. (1998). The paradox of technology: what's gained and lost? *Thought & Action, 14*(1), 49-57. Retrieved from http://www.nea.org/assets/img/PubThoughtAndAction/TAA_98Spr_04.pdf

English Eastday. (2010). Comment: Internet - New shot in the arm for US hegemony. English. eastday.com. Retrieved from http://english.eastday.com/e/100123/u1a4972925.html?

Karimi Alavijeh, K. (2014). *The promotion of electronic colonialism in Internet-mediated English education; the representation of Iran in four English educational websites.* Unpublished doctoral dissertation, Alzahra University, Tehran, Iran.

Karimi Alavijeh, K., & Marandi, S. S. (2014). The representation of Iran in EnglishCentral educational website: unfolding the hidden curriculum. *Iranian Journal of Applied Linguistics, 17*(1), 119-146.

Lamy, M-N., & Pegrum, M. (2012). Commentary for special issue of LLT [Theme: Hegemonies in CALL]. *Language Learning & Technology, 14*(2), 111-112. Retrieved from http://llt.msu.edu/issues/june2012/commentary.pdf

Lehman, R. M., & Conceição, S. C. O. (2010). *Creating a sense of presence in online teaching: how to "be there" for distance learners.* San Fransisco, CA: Jossey-Bass.

Marandi, S. S. (2014). Adopting a balanced approach toward CALL. *Roshd FLT, 28*(2), 19-24. Retrieved from http://www.roshdmag.ir/fa/article/9660

Markey, C. (2009). *Attend, watch "Twitter, Iran, and more: Impressions from the front lines of the global media revolution".* Retrieved from http://ndn.org/blog/2009/07/tomorrow-july-15-attend-watch-twitter-iran-and-more-impressions-front-lines-global-media

Reinhardt, J., & Isbell, K. (2002). Building Web literacy skills. *The Reading Matrix, 2*(2). Retrieved from http://www.readingmatrix.com/articles/isbell_reinhardt/index.html

Richardson, W. (2010). *Blogs, wikis, podcasts, and other powerful web tools for classrooms.* (3rd ed.). London: Corwin (SAGE).

Van Leeuwen, T. (2008). *Discourse and practice: new tools for critical discourse analysis.* Oxford: Oxford University Press.

Yang, S. (2010). *Internet: new shot in the arm for US Hegemony.* Retrieved from http://www.chinadaily.com.cn/china/2010-01/22/content_9364327.htm

Integrating CALL into an Iranian EAP course: constraints and affordances

Parisa Mehran[1] and Mehrasa Alizadeh[2]

Abstract. Iranian universities have recently displayed a growing interest in integrating Computer-Assisted Language Learning (CALL) into teaching/learning English. The English for Academic Purposes (EAP) context, however, is not keeping pace with the current changes since EAP courses are strictly text-based and exam-oriented, and little research has thus far been conducted on using computers in EAP classes. Hence, this study was conducted to explore CALL experiences of an EAP class in an Iranian university while focusing upon the participants' attitudes toward CALL, the constraints and affordances of CALL integration in EAP, and its effectiveness in enhancing language skills "in a low-resource setting". To this aim, 25 undergraduate students, their instructor, and a teaching assistant participated in this study. Several instruments were employed to collect data quantitatively and qualitatively. The outcomes of these e-experiences were also analyzed. The findings revealed that the participants generally held positive attitudes toward implementing CALL. They also believed that incorporating CALL into the classroom contributed to the improvement of English language skills. Yet, some challenges emerged in terms of the following barriers in using CALL within EAP courses: infrastructural, institutional, technological, pedagogical, psychological/personal, and sociocultural/political. Finally, several potential solutions were suggested to ameliorate the opportunities and minimize the costs of CALL in the Iranian context.

Keywords: CALL, EAP, affordances, constraints.

---

1. Graduate School of Language and Culture, Osaka University, Japan; u128589a@ecs.osaka-u.ac.jp
2. Graduate School of Language and Culture, Osaka University, Japan; u526392i@ecs.osaka-u.ac.jp

How to cite this article: Mehran, P., & Alizadeh, M. (2015). Integrating CALL into an Iranian EAP course: constraints and affordances. In F. Helm, L. Bradley, M. Guarda, & S. Thouësny (Eds), *Critical CALL – Proceedings of the 2015 EUROCALL Conference, Padova, Italy* (pp. 392-396). Dublin: Research-publishing.net. http://dx.doi.org/10.14705/rpnet.2015.000364

1. Introduction

In recent years, there has been an increasing interest in integrating CALL into English education among Iranian universities. However, as Atai and Dashtestani (2013) remark, the rigidly text-centered and exam-oriented nature of the EAP courses in Iran has not allowed for CALL integration. This research area has thus remained mostly unexplored.

Within the Iranian EAP context, there is a gap in exploring the use of technology in EAP courses and evaluating stakeholders' attitudes toward it. In an attempt to bridge this gap, the present action-research study was carried out to explore CALL experiences of an EAP class in an Iranian university with the focus on the participants' attitudes toward CALL, the constraints and affordances of CALL integration in EAP, and its effectiveness in enhancing language skills "in a low-resource setting".

2. Method

Twenty five female undergraduate students, their instructor, and a teaching assistant participated in this study. Several instruments, including questionnaires, semi-structured interviews, informal discussions, non-participant observations, and diary entries were employed to collect data quantitatively and qualitatively. The outcomes of these e-experiences (e.g. blog entries, peer e-comments, and e-feedback) were also analyzed so as to provide a clearer picture of the interactions which occur when digital technologies are integrated into an EAP program.

A five-part questionnaire was used to explore learners' attitudes toward CALL. The first three parts were developed by Aryadoust, Mehran, and Alizadeh (2015). The last part of the questionnaire was designed by Lee (2010) and translated into Persian (back-translation was done to verify the accuracy of the items).

Content analysis was used to analyze the qualitative data (e.g. research log, interviews, e-comments, open-ended questions in the questionnaire), and SPSS version 21 was utilized for the analysis of the quantitative data (i.e. the questionnaire items).

3. Results and discussion

As Table 1 shows, the findings revealed that the learners generally held positive attitudes toward implementing CALL. They stated that incorporating CALL into the classroom contributed to their improvement of English language skills (particularly in reading and writing). The learners felt motivated and engaged, because they had a broader audience with which they could share their experiences. As students of Theology, they felt that they could propagate their religious ideology throughout the world. The learners also felt self-confident as a result of their active presence in the virtual world. They believed that their e-experiences were geared toward enhancing team work and collaboration, using up-to-date materials, improving computer literacy and skills, augmenting general knowledge, adding further appeal, and offering variety in the classroom. Furthermore, technology integration was found to have created a stress-free environment for the participants.

Table 1. Some questionnaire items measuring learners' attitudes toward the integration of CALL in EAP courses

Item	Strongly disagree %	Disagree %	Agree %	Strongly disagree %
Computer is a useful tool for developing reading skills.	0.0	0.0	48.0	52.0
Computer is a useful tool for developing writing skills.	0.0	8.0	52.0	36.0
I like learning a new language by computer.	4.0	12.0	60.0	24.0
Using computer tools to learn English is a great advantage over traditional methods.	0.0	0.0	48.0	52.0
CALL is a stress-free environment to learn English.	0.0	0.0	56.0	44.0
Using a computer makes language lessons more interesting to me.	0.0	4.0	24.0	72.0
I had a positive experience with the blog project.	0.0	0.0	24.0	72.0
I benefited from writing and reading blog postings.	0.0	0.0	28.0	72.0
Blogging for a broad audience was more appealing than writing for a sole instructor.	0.0	16.0	16.0	68.0
My English has improved as a result of regularly using personal blogs.	0.0	8.0	52.0	40.0

The instructor and the teaching assistant also had positive attitudes toward CALL integration since it promotes more collaboration among the learners, increases the sense of achievement (especially when computer literacy and skills get improved), and enables purposeful English learning.

Yet, from the perspective of both the teacher and the learners, some obstacles emerged in terms of the following barriers in using CALL within EAP courses: *infrastructural* (e.g. lack of formal plans, policies and processes, insufficient funding resources, lack of investment and financial support), *institutional* (e.g. lack of organizational and administrative support, lack of professional development and training), *technological* (e.g. lack of equipment, facilities and resources, lack of IT support, outdated hardware, lack of appropriate software, slow internet connectivity, lack of ubiquitous access to technology, students' low digital literacy, technical difficulties), *pedagogical* (e.g. inauthentic interaction, shortage of time, faculty workloads, curricular restrictions), *psychological/ personal* (e.g. lack of confidence, lack of motivation, technophobia, student anxiety), and *sociocultural/political* (e.g. the Internet filtering, security issues, copyright regulations, hegemonies of CALL).

Based on the findings of this study, it can be concluded that the EAP practitioners, in general, have positive attitudes toward CALL, which indicates promise for the application of technology in EAP courses. This finding is in line with many studies, namely, Atai and Dashtestani (2013) and Dashtestani (2012). Positive attitudes of teachers and learners can lead to a more successful implementation of CALL in the Iranian context. It behoves us to bear in mind that positive attitude is a logically necessary condition yet definitely not sufficient for successful integration of CALL. In accord with the findings of Atai and Dashtestani (2013), Maftoon and Shahini (2012), and Dashtestani (2012), this study also reveals that there are a set of constraints as discussed before which, if not addressed properly, would lead to discouragement and may result in a future change of attitude.

4. Conclusions

To implement CALL successfully in Iran, a fundamental change is called for. This requires the governors and policy makers to provide additional funding since a key barrier to technology integration is the lack of facilities. Moreover, regardless of political reservations, broadband Internet access should be regulated as a utility at least within academic settings. If such constraints and barriers are not eliminated, the positive attitudes of English as a Foreign Language learners and teachers toward CALL might be negatively affected in future. Also, more attention should be directed toward teacher education (for both pre-service and in-service teachers) as well as learner training, since it is not plausible to assume that teachers and learners have the skills required to use and implement technological tools and services most effectively in their teaching and learning processes. In Iran, there is a dearth of CALL teacher education courses. CALL as a mandatory credit course has not yet been established in Teaching English as a Foreign Language programs at Iranian universities. The few existing CALL courses slightly touch upon the issues of technology integration into language education. Yet, they do not teach how to use educational technology through using technology due to the lack of digital facilities. In summary, the participants of this study overall perceived that the application of CALL in EAP created a motivating, collaborative environment which successfully responded to their needs. Such a positive attitude necessitates the improvement of the status quo regarding the use of technology in the Iranian context as "a low-tech setting", and the necessary infrastructures for CALL should be put in place as soon as possible.

References

Aryadoust, V., Mehran, P., & Alizadeh, M. (2015). Validating a computer-assisted language learning attitude instrument used in Iranian EFL context: an evidence-based approach. *Computer Assisted Language Learning*. doi:10.1080/09588221.2014.1000931

Atai, M. R., & Dashtestani, R. (2013). Iranian English for academic purposes (EAP) stakeholders' attitudes toward using the Internet in EAP courses for civil engineering students: promises and challenges. *Computer Assisted Language Learning, 26*(1), 21-38. doi:10.1080/09588221.2011.627872

Dashtestani, R. (2012). Barriers to the implementation of CALL in EFL courses: Iranian EFL teachers' attitudes and perspectives. *The JALT CALL Journal, 8*(2), 55-70.

Lee, L. (2010). Fostering reflective writing and interactive exchange through blogging in an advanced language course. *ReCALL, 22*(2), 212-227. doi:10.1017/S095834401000008X

Maftoon, P., & Shahini, A. (2012). CALL normalization: a survey on inhibitive factors. *The JALT CALL Journal, 8*(1), 17-32.

Exploring the interaction between learners and tools in e-learning environments

Serpil Meri[1]

Abstract. The present research explores the interaction between learners and tools in e-learning environments. In order to explore that issue, this study analyzed and interpreted the findings obtained through observation and interview with 10 international students who wished to improve their learning of English by using the English for Academic Purposes (EAP) toolkit equipped and accessed in Blackboard, where learners can easily use it. Along with data from three-time observations and interviews, an in-depth dataset was provided by means of the think-aloud protocol method, which indicated what the students were doing with and thinking of their experiences in the process of learning in the toolkit. The findings showed that there was a substantial indication of the interaction between learners and tools in e-learning environments and the perceptions about their experience in learning in a self-directed e-learning environment, which might help designers to consider some aspects while they are setting up and improving the tools and online learning resources. In addition, the results provide more issues to discuss in terms of the benefit of promoting interaction in self-directed e-learning environments.

Keywords: e-learning environments, self-directed e-learning environment, interaction, EAP toolkit.

1. Introduction

Learners are supported in different learning environments such as in classrooms, online or blended learning environments. In those environments, they are supposed

---

1. University of Southampton, UK; sm17g10@soton.ac.uk

How to cite this article: Meri, S. (2015). Exploring the interaction between learners and tools in e-learning environments. In F. Helm, L. Bradley, M. Guarda, & S. Thouësny (Eds), *Critical CALL – Proceedings of the 2015 EUROCALL Conference, Padova, Italy* (pp. 397-403). Dublin: Research-publishing.net. http://dx.doi.org/10.14705/rpnet.2015.000365

to interact with their fellows, tutors, media or tools; thus, they can be encouraged to improve their learning. However, there has been a growing interest in providing online learning resources and computers or laptops in educational settings (e.g. Collins & Halversont, 2010; Garrett, 2009; Selwyn, 2003; Yang & Chen, 2007). Therefore, the main interest in research of e-learning environments has been the role of learners in those environments, which is an essential element to be considered by developers (Jarvis, 2012).

Besides, learners have the flexibility to advance in their learning in e-learning environments (Lee & Gibson, 2003; Oladoke, 2006). Together with the flexibility, anytime and anywhere access can be offered to learners, which is the substantial advantage of e-learning environments rather than in classroom-based learning environments (Rhode, 2009).

As illustrated in Laurillard's (2012) conversational framework, learning takes place by means of the interaction between the teacher and learner in blended or classroom-based learning environments. As for learning in self-directed e-learning environments where learners are alone and completely independent (Ghirardini, 2011) and might feel isolated (Zembylas, Theorou, & Pavlakis, 2008), the interaction and communication between learners and tools should be taken into consideration in order to overcome the possibility of their loneliness and isolation. That is, in order to reach the high level of learning in those self-directed e-learning environments, the interaction between them and the tools should be provided, which indicates learners' experiences in using online resources (Hirumi, 2006). In the meantime, designers should be informed about their learning experiences in those environments, as they are the ones to determine and set up the learning design (Hedberg & Sims, 2001).

Although there have been many studies about the interaction between learners and their fellows or instructors in those environments which show that it has a substantial impact on their learning (Angeli, Valanides, & Bonk, 2003; Fung, 2004; Johnson, 2006; Topper, 2005), a few of the studies have been conducted to investigate the interaction between learners and tools which enables learners to improve their learning by themselves (i.e. Jackson, Krajcik,& Soloway, 1998).

Considering the importance of the study, the present research aims to explore the interaction between learners and tools in e-learning environments by looking at their behaviours, experiences, preferences and learning styles in an e-learning environment.

2. Method

2.1. Participants and setting

The participants of the present study were 10 international students who were volunteers to take part in the research from February to the end of May in 2013. In order to further their study for the postgraduate study, the participants came to the UK to improve their skills. Therefore, they attended the English for Academic Studies (EAS) course at the University of Southampton. During their study, they had the opportunity to benefit from the EAP toolkit, which provides "a comprehensive set of interactive learning resources for developing the language and study skills of international students and students whose first language is not English" (eLanguages, 2012, para 1). While learning in the toolkit, they obtained the introduction, information/explanation, instruction and feedback from the activity depending on their use of the learning tasks (see Figure 1). Additionally, they could take the advantage of the section of web links, glossary and dictionary if they needed more help.

Figure 1. A sample of introduction and links in the EAP toolkit

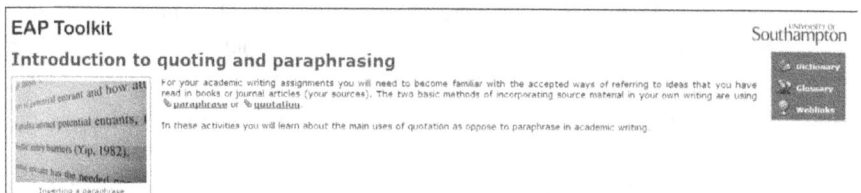

Consequently, a self-directed e-learning environment was provided for participants to develop their skills and academic learning.

2.2. Data collection and analysis procedure

In order to collect data, a qualitative study was conducted. Observations were made for 15 minutes in the beginning, middle and last weeks of the course via Camtasia[2], which recorded both the computer screen and the face of the participants who were performing the activities in the EAP toolkit chosen in the first two observation sessions by the researcher but in the last observation session by the participants. In the process, the think-aloud protocol method was applied to see what they were thinking and how they went through the information or

---

2. https://www.techsmith.com/camtasia.html

conducted the activity. Follow-up and semi-structured interviews were also carried out to let them express their perceptions, feelings and preferences about their experience in an e-learning environment. Data from both observations and interviews were analyzed by creating codes in NVivo[3] and then interpreted and discussed as shown in the next section.

3. Discussion

The findings from observations and interviews shed light on the interaction between learners and tools in e-learning environments. The conduction of the think-aloud protocol method triggered the use of self-talk of approximately all of the participants. Their use of self-talk showed that scaffolds such as introduction, information/explanation, instruction and feedback provided in the toolkit enabled them to instruct, explain, inform and introduce the topic to themselves and reflect on their learning. Furthermore, self-scaffolding was used "through the dialogic self" (Granott, 2005, p. 148) by most of them as if they addressed other people. By this, they improved their confidence by giving themselves motivational scaffolding after looking at the feedback Moreover, the use of 'OK' as self-talk represented their thought, which showed that 'I understand' was not 'unnecessary verbiage' in the present study (Eveland & Dunwoody, 2000). Additionally, they developed their learning strategies including cognitive, metacognitive, affective and meta-affective strategies on their own (Chang & Sun, 2009; Luzón, 2006), which was the result of their interaction with scaffolds in the activities.

Together with the use of self-talk, participants had different experiences in benefiting from learning activities in terms of handling their learning in the toolkit. Although they increased their positive feelings about learning through the toolkit over time, nearly half of them required more audio-visual help and activities in the toolkit or tutor's help because of the lack of support provided in the toolkit. The difference in learning styles can be seen in their preference in following the order of the section in the activities. Most activities were sequential, whereas a few of them were global. As seen, the present research tended to display the interaction between participants and the toolkit via the use of self-talk, the benefit from scaffolders and individual improvement of motivation and learning strategy. However, participants needed more help, despite the improvement in their learning and the increase of their positive perception about their experience in the EAP toolkit.

---

3. http://www.qsrinternational.com/product

4. Conclusions

This study explored the interaction between learners and tools in an e-learning environment. It concluded that learners tended to have a kind of conversation in a self-directed e-learning environment with the help of scaffolding but without any help from tutors. Although their interaction with online resources was in contrast with the indication of the conversational framework for learning with the interaction or conversation with fellows or tutors (Laurillard, 2012), the current research put forward that the tutor might be replaced in e-learning environments if online learning resources are designed according to users' requirements. Above all, that kind of interaction supported learners to have or improve the ability to manage and handle their learning. Considering the importance of enhancing the interaction between learners and online resources in a self-directed e-learning environment, designers should take into account the provision of necessary assistance in order for users to take control over their learning in an e-learning environment. As the main limitation of the current study is that it does not count on a large dataset, further studies should be designed to include more participants and investigate learners' interaction with well-designed online resources.

5. Acknowledgements

I would like to thank the Republic of Turkey to support my research through my PhD study. Also, I appreciate both the help of students by participating in my research and the support of University of Southampton to allow me to conduct this study in their institution. Last but not least, I am very grateful to my supervisor, Professor Vicky Wright for her support and feedback.

References

Angeli, C., Valanides, N., & Bonk, C. J. (2003). Communication in a web-based conferencing system: the quality of computer-mediated interactions. *British Journal of Educational Technology, 34*(1), 31-43.

Chang, W. L., & Sun, Y. C. (2009). Scaffolding and web concordancers as support for language learning. *Computer Assisted Language Learning, 22*(4), 283-302. doi:10.1080/09588220903184518

Collins, A., & Halverson, R. (2010). The second educational revolution: rethinking education in the age of technology. *Journal of Computer Assisted Learning, 26*(1), 18-27. doi: 10.1111/j.1365-2729.2009.00339.x

eLanguages. (2012). The EAP Toolkit. Retrieved from http://www.elanguages.ac.uk/eap_toolkit.php

Eveland Jr, W. P., & Dunwoody, S. (2000). Examining information processing on the World Wide Web using think aloud protocols. *Media Psychology, 2*(3), 219-244. doi:10.1207/S1532785XMEP0203_2

Fung, Y. Y. H. (2004). Collaborative online learning: interaction patterns and limiting factors. *Open Learning, 19*(2), 135-149. doi:10.1080/0268051042000224743

Garrett, N. (2009). Computer-assisted language learning trends and issues revisited: integrating innovation. *The Modern Language Journal, 93*(s1), 719-740. doi:10.1111/j.1540-4781.2009.00969.x

Ghirardini, B. (2011). E-learning methodologies: a guide for designing and developing e-learning courses. *Food and Agriculture Organization of the United Nations*.

Granott, N. (2005) Scaffolding dynamically toward change: previous and new perspectives. *New Ideas in Psychology, 23*(3), 140-151. doi:10.1016/j.newideapsych.2006.07.002

Hedberg, J., & Sims, R. (2001). Speculations on design team interactions. *Journal of Interactive Learning Research, 12*(2), 189-214. Retrieved from http://www.editlib.org/p/8419/

Hirumi, A. (2006). Analysing and designing e-learning interactions. In C. Juwah (Ed.), *Interactions in online education: Implications for theory and practice* (pp. 46-71). New York: Routledge.

Jackson, S. L., Krajcik, J., & Soloway, E. (1998, January). The design of guided learner-adaptable scaffolding in interactive learning environments. In *Proceedings of the SIGCHI conference on Human factors in Computing Systems* (pp. 187-194). ACM Press/Addison-Wesley Publishing Co. doi:10.1145/274644.274672

Jarvis, H. (2012). Computers and learner autonomy: trends and issues. *British Council ELT, 387*. Retrieved from http://englishagenda.britishcouncil.org/sites/ec/files/B208_ELTRP%20Jarvis%20Report_AW.pdf

Johnson, G. M. (2006). Synchronous and asynchronous text-based CMC in educational contexts: a review of recent research. *TechTrends, 50*(4), 46-53. doi:10.1007/s11528-006-0046-9

Laurillard, D. (2012). *Teaching as a design science: building pedagogical patterns for learning and technology*. Oxon, UK: Routledge, Taylor & Francis Group.

Lee, J., & Gibson, C. C. (2003). Developing self-direction in an online course through computer-mediated interaction. *The American Journal of Distance Education, 17*(3), 173-187. doi: 10.1207/S15389286AJDE1703_4

Luzón, M. J. (2006). Providing scaffolding and feedback in online learning environments. *Les Melanges CRAPEL 28 n° spécial: TIC et autonomie dans l'apprentissage des langues*. Retrieved from http://www.atilf.fr/IMG/pdf/melanges/8_LUZON.pdf

Oladoke, A. O. (2006). Measurement of self-directed learning in online learners. *Dissertation Abstracts International, 67*(1), (UMI No. 3206369).

Rhode, J. (2009). Interaction equivalency in self-paced online learning environments: an exploration of learner preferences. *The International Review of Research in Open and Distributed Learning, 10*(1). Retrieved from http://files.eric.ed.gov/fulltext/EJ831712.pdf

Selwyn, N. (2003). Why students do (and do not) make use of ICT in university. *Paper presented to the 'Finding Common Ground: IT Education, Dearing and Democracy in the Information Society' Conference University of Leeds Department of Computing - July 9th 2003*. Retrieved from http://www.leeds.ac.uk/educol/documents/00003130.htm

Topper, A. (2005). Facilitating student interactions through discursive moves: an instructor's experience teaching online graduate courses in educational technology. *The Quarterly Review of Distance Education, 6*(1), 55-67.

Yang, S. C., & Chen, Y. J. (2007). Technology-enhanced language learning: a case study. *Computers in Human Behavior, 23*(1), 860-879. doi:10.1016/j.chb.2006.02.015

Zembylas, M., Theodorou, M., & Pavlakis, A. (2008). The role of emotions in the experience of online learning: challenges and opportunities. *Educational Media International, 45*(2), 107-117. doi:10.1080/09523980802107237

One year of extensive reading on mobile devices: engagement and impressions

Brett Milliner[1] and Travis Cote[2]

Abstract. Extensive Reading (ER) is a popular strategy to improve reading fluency, vocabulary knowledge and reading confidence. The process of ER, traditionally done with paperbacks, is a practice being transformed by smartphone technology. This paper introduces Xreading® (www.xreading.com), an online Graded Reader (GR) library and Learning Management System (LMS) devoted specifically to digital management of extensive reading. For language teaching faculty, Xreading provides a dynamic, ER management system that can negate a range of challenges teachers have faced when implementing an effective ER component. In this one year study at a private Japanese university, students were required to use their smartphone or PC to access the online library of GR's and read extensively on either of these devices. This paper reports on student engagement with this platform and shares feedback from a post-pilot questionnaire and focus group discussion to describe student impressions of this digital approach.

Keywords: extensive reading, MALL, Xreading, e-book reading.

1. Introduction

1.1. Extensive reading

The increasing interest in incorporating extensive reading components into English language programs are representative of the growing body of research advocating the language learning benefits of this approach. Studies (e.g. Beglar, Hunt, & Kite, 2012) have been able to empirically demonstrate the superiority of ER over other

---

1. Tamagawa University, Tokyo, Japan; milliner@lit.tamagawa.ac.jp
2. Tamagawa University, Tokyo, Japan; travis@bus.tamagawa.ac.jp

How to cite this article: Milliner, B., & Cote, T. (2015). One year of extensive reading on mobile devices: engagement and impressions. In F. Helm, L. Bradley, M. Guarda, & S. Thouësny (Eds), *Critical CALL – Proceedings of the 2015 EUROCALL Conference, Padova, Italy* (pp. 404-409). Dublin: Research-publishing.net. http://dx.doi.org/10.14705/rpnet.2015.000366

approaches – such as intensive reading – for developing second language students' reading and linguistic skills. Most extensive reading programs share a common purpose: that learners read large quantities of self-selected, simplified texts in an environment which promotes a liking of the act of reading (Day & Bamford, 1998; Renandya, 2007).

Despite the reported benefits of ER, there is less agreement concerning the best ways to implement ER in the language classroom (Fenton-Smith, 2008). In addition, language teachers have reported a variety of challenges which include: the cost of assembling a library with titles which spread across a variety of genres, while also satisfying the varying levels of student reading proficiencies (Day & Bamford, 1998), how to hold students accountable for their reading (Robb & Kano, 2013) and how teachers can find time to provide adequate reading support.

1.2. The need for an online approach

Successful implementation of an ER component depends equally upon the students and their commitment to the approach. As outlined above, ER can contribute to language learning; however, recent research provides a realistic look at the quantity of reading required for those benefits to be significant (Beglar & Hunt, 2014; Beglar et al., 2012). Beglar and Hunt (2014), and Nation and Wang (1999) noted that students must read 200,000 words or more per year for learning benefits to be observed. Pushing students towards these lofty benchmarks represent a departure from basic ER ideology (e.g. Day & Bamford, 1998) which promotes a self-selected, intrinsic approach. How can teachers effectively exercise their pedagogical powers to motivate students to read in such large quantities?

1.3. E-book ER

The lower costs of e-books, and the ability to share e-books through 24-hour online libraries, has prompted institutions to investigate e-reading and how they can incorporate it into curricula (Gerlich, Browning, & Westermann, 2011). Unlike traditional books, e-books allow readers to customize their reading experience, for example, tailoring font style, size and screen layout. E-books also support access to multimedia features, such as hyperlinks, glossaries, audio narration and links to online dictionaries (Huang, 2013; Lai & Chang, 2011). Additionally, some e-book systems provide the user with a range of feedback on their reading progress (Brown, 2012; Huang, 2013). Online reading systems can chronicle book details and the reading process, including reading speeds, post-reading quiz results, book levels, the total words read and time spent reading. With this feedback, students can track their reading progress and teachers can precisely, and promptly, identify those who might need extra support (Brown, 2012).

The authors of this study hoped that the aforementioned benefits of e-books, and an online GR library, would allow them to overcome a number of the challenges observed during their own implementation of ER. In addition, the ease of access, multimedia functions, and feedback features would enable more students to read the large volumes prescribed by experts in the field (e.g. Beglar & Hunt, 2014; Day & Bamford, 1998; Nation & Wang, 1999).

1.4. Xreading

Launched in April 2014, Xreading is an online GR library and learning management system (LMS) devoted to ER. There are approximately 500 books in the Xreading library, and an individual, one-year license (US $19.40, July 2015 rate) grants access to all books in the library, including post-reading quizzes. Answers to the quizzes are scored and recorded by the LMS. The Xreading site is accessible via mobile device or PC and since it is a virtual library, multiple users can read the same book. Another useful feature is that users can choose to listen to audio of the GR, thereby supporting opportunities to engage in extensive listening. For teachers, administrators and students alike, the LMS functionality allows monitoring of reading progress, including words-per-minute counts, total words read, books read, total reading time, and quiz results.

2. Research

2.1. Research participants

This study was initiated in two English as a lingua franca (ELF) classes taught by one of the authors at a private university in Tokyo, Japan. The average TOEIC score for the participant sample was 512 (CEFR level A2) and the ER component accounted for 10% of the final grade. This percentage was a reflection of the total number of words read (students were expected to read in excess of 50,000 words to receive the full 10%), reading comprehension scores (tallied within the Xreading LMS) and quantity of student engagement as reported by usage log data.

2.2. Student engagement

Table 1 below provides a summary of student engagement with the system during the 2014 academic year. As suggested by the total average words read (13,502), students failed to read the quantities desired by the authors and vastly below the benchmarks prescribed by leading researchers in the field.

Table 1. Summary of student engagement: total words read per class and average number of words read per student over the 2014 academic year

Class number & Semester	Total words read per-class	Average number of words read per-student
1 (n=20) Spring	232,390	15,492
1 (n=20) Fall	185,540	9,277
2 (n=15) Spring	240,210	12,010
2 (n=15) Fall	168,751	11,250

3. Student perceptions

3.1. Post-pilot questionnaire

Participants completed an online questionnaire during the final class of the academic year and a total of 30 students responded. Despite the poor engagement results (see Table 1), 25 students (83%) agreed and three (10%) strongly agreed with the statement, "I like reading in English". When asked how they would like to read a graded reader in the future, 16 (53%) chose on my smartphone and eight (27%) chose on their PC. This response suggests that students are not opposed to reading an e-book and most appear to want to read on their smartphone. Surprisingly, a total of 93% of students were in agreement with the statement "After using Xreading in this class it is more enjoyable to read in English", and an additional 82% were in agreement with the statement, "After using Xreading in this class it is easier to read in English". Students were also asked to list what they liked and disliked about Xreading. The high frequency of responses citing the convenience of the system and an interesting variety of books provide some insight into why students voiced such positive responses to the reading experience.

However, the question remains: if students had such a positive perception of the Xreading system and reading e-books, why did they read so little? This discrepancy pushed the authors to stage a short Focus Group Discussion (FGD) at the end of the course and a more detailed report can be found in Milliner and Cote (2015). Some of the key findings from the FGD included: students need better training in using the system, specifically on how to choose books at the appropriate linguistic level for them; teachers need to establish smaller, incremental word targets throughout the semester; and lastly, teachers need to spend more time raising awareness about the purpose of, and principles behind, ER.

4. Conclusions

The authors of this one year pilot study found that although students appeared to have a positive perception of e-books, reading on their smartphone and using an online library, actual reading engagement suggests a different story. This study has revealed that as teachers, our role in the ER process is still crucial, whether it is done with traditional paperbacks or via an online system. Teachers need to effectively make the case for ER, promote student interest in reading, and call upon their pedagogical strength to motivate students to read consistently. Furthermore, if extensive reading is done electronically, teachers must carefully provide software training and ongoing support.

References

Beglar, D., & Hunt, A. (2014). Pleasure reading and reading rate gains. *Reading in a Foreign Language, 26*(1), 29-48.

Beglar, D., Hunt, A., & Kite, Y. (2012). The effect of pleasure reading on Japanese university EFL learners' reading rates. *Language Learning, 62*(3), 665-703. doi:10.1111/j.1467-9922.2011.00651.x

Brown, D. (2012). Online support systems for extensive reading: managing the tension between autonomy and institutional education. *The Language Teacher, 36*(2), 11-16.

Day, R., & Bamford, J. (1998). *Extensive reading in the second language classroom*. New York: Cambridge University Press.

Fenton-Smith, B. (2008). Accountability and variety in extensive reading. In K. Bradford Watts, T. Muller, & M.Swanson (Eds.), *JALT2007 Conference Proceedings*. Tokyo: JALT.

Gerlich, R. N., Browning, L., & Westermann, L. (2011). E-readers on campus: overcoming product adoption issues with a tech-savvy demographic. *Journal of Higher Education Theory and Practice, 11*(4), 41-52.

Huang, H. (2013). E-reading and e-discussion: EFL learners' perceptions of an e-book reading program. *Computer Assisted Language Learning, 26*(3), 258-281.

Lai, J., & Chang, C. (2011). User attitudes toward dedicated e-book readers for reading: the effects of convenience, compatibility and media richness. *Online Information Review, 35*(4), 558-580. doi:10.1108/14684521111161936

Milliner, B., & Cote, T. (2015). Mobile-based extensive reading: an investigation into reluctant readers. *International Journal of Computer Assisted Language Learning and Teaching, 5*(4), 1-15. doi:10.4018/IJCALLT.2015100101

Nation, P., & Wang, K. (1999). Graded readers and vocabulary. *Reading in a Foreign Language, 12*(2), 355-380.

Renandya, W. A. (2007). The power of extensive reading. *RELC Journal, 38*(2), 133-149. doi:10.1177/0033688207079578

Robb, T., & Kano, M. (2013). Effective extensive reading outside the classroom: a large-scale experiment. *Reading in a Foreign Language, 25*(2), 234-247.

Errors in automatic speech recognition versus difficulties in second language listening

Maryam Sadat Mirzaei[1], Kourosh Meshgi[2], Yuya Akita[2], and Tatsuya Kawahara[2]

Abstract. Automatic Speech Recognition (ASR) technology has become a part of contemporary Computer-Assisted Language Learning (CALL) systems. ASR systems however are being criticized for their erroneous performance especially when utilized as a mean to develop skills in a Second Language (L2) where errors are not tolerated. Nevertheless, these errors can provide useful information and propose further implications. In this study we investigate the relationships between the underlying features causing ASR errors and those that make L2 listening difficult. This research is inspired by the comparable nature of the difficulties both ASR and L2 listeners encounter in recognizing speech. The aim of this study is to enhance Partial and Synchronized Caption (PSC) systems, which we previously developed for fostering L2 listening skill. PSC presents only a selective set of words (those leading to listening difficulties) in order to encourage listening to the audio and read for problematic words only. To enhance PSC's word selection, we strive to detect individual difficult sentences/words in terms of recognition by referring to ASR errors. Our system compares these errors with PSC choices to find the overlaps and seek further enhancement. The results revealed a close relationship between ASR errors and factors leading to L2 listening difficulties. The findings indicated that ASR errors can contribute to word selection in PSC.

Keywords: automatic speech recognition, L2 speech recognition, listening, partial and synchronized caption.

---

1. Kyoto University, Japan; Maryam@ar.media.kyoto-u.ac.jp

2. Kyoto University, Japan; Meshgi-k@sys.i.kyoto-u.ac.jp; Akita@ar.media.kyoto-u.ac.jp; Kawahara@i.kyoto-u.ac.jp

How to cite this article: Mirzaei. M. S., Meshgi, K., Akita, Y., & Kawahara, T. (2015). Errors in automatic speech recognition versus difficulties in second language listening. In F. Helm, L. Bradley, M. Guarda, & S. Thouësny (Eds), *Critical CALL – Proceedings of the 2015 EUROCALL Conference, Padova, Italy* (pp. 410-415). Dublin: Research-publishing.net. http://dx.doi.org/10.14705/rpnet.2015.000367

1. Introduction

There has been increasing interest in the use of ASR technology in the field of second language acquisition. Some possible applications include the pronunciation evaluation in order to improve oral skills and caption generation in order to facilitate listening comprehension (Shimogori, Ikeda, & Tsuboi, 2010; Thomson, 2013).

In spite of their significant advancement, ASR systems are still endeavoring to achieve better accuracy. The limitations of these systems have raised a number of criticisms when they are utilized as a means for L2 development. This is partly because of the particular challenges involved. For instance, the difference between L2 learner's speech (non-native speech) and standard speech used to train ASR systems makes recognition cumbersome and leads to poor ASR performance especially for spontaneous speech (Thomson, 2013). In addition, as regards the ASR-generated caption, the recognition errors in the output often make the captions undesirable for the end-users. In such cases, even captions including less than 5% Word Error Rate (WER) – a significant performance for ASR systems – can cause distraction (Vasilescu, Adda-Decker, & Lamel, 2012).

On the other hand, instead of being constantly seen as the major drawback of ASR systems, some research implications could be considered for ASR errors. This exploratory study conducts a root-cause analysis to investigate the potential of using these errors as an inspiring source to determine difficult speech segment.

The goal of this research is to enhance the PSC[3] system, which we previously developed (Mirzaei, Akita, & Kawahara, 2014). In PSC, with the aim of improving L2 learners' listening skill, we created a smart caption that presents a principled selection of words instead of all words in order to encourage listening to the audio by restricting learners to read only for the selected words (Figure 1).

Word selection in PSC is done by referring to factors that lead to comprehension impairs i.e. by focusing on the words, which are difficult to recognize. In this view, we considered several factors such as the speech rate of the speaker, the difficulty level of the words based on their frequency of occurrence in well-known corpora and also the presence of specific words (e.g. academic terms) in speech.

---

3. Watch videos on http://www.ar.media.kyoto-u.ac.jp/psc/

Figure 1. Screenshot of PSC on a TED talk made from the original transcript "We are evolving to be a more collaborative and hearty species"

In order to enhance word selection in PSC, we need to incorporate more features to enrich the selection criteria. However, the correlation of these features is complicated. As an alternative, in this study we investigate the ASR errors to detect difficult words.

ASR-related studies often compare such systems with native speakers of the target language or with those having no knowledge of that language – Human Speech Recognition (Vasilescu et al., 2012). However, comparative analysis of ASR errors and L2 learner speech recognition would be a more prudent choice, as both parties deal with almost similar difficulties, using available resources and background knowledge. As listed in Table 1, for example, literature emphasizes the important role of high speech rate in deteriorating the performance of ASR systems (Goldwater, Jurafsky, & Manning, 2010) and impairing L2 comprehension (Rost, 2013).

Table 1. ASR errors and L2 listening difficulties

ASR Errors	L2 Listening Difficulties
Pronunciation, co-articulation, speaking style, accent, age, physiology and emotions lead to ASR difficulties (Vasilescu et al., 2012).	Pronunciation, stress, intonation patterns and accent affect L2 listening comprehension (Rost, 2013).
Infrequent words are more likely to be misrecognized (Shinozaki & Furui, 2001).	Infrequent words in speech correlates to complexity (Webb, 2010).
Fast speech / very slow speech increases error rates (Goldwater et al., 2010).	Whether too fast or too slow, speech rate can impair listening (Rost, 2013).
Word length is considered as a useful predictor of high WER (Shinozaki & Furui, 2001).	The length of a word can affect its recognition (Field, 2008).
Open class words have lower error rate compared to closed class (Goldwater et al. 2010).	Learners transcribe the content words significantly better than the function words (Field, 2008).

2. Method

In order to conduct our analysis, we used 64 videos from the TED website (https://www.ted.com/talks). TED provides videos together with human-annotated transcript. This transcript is utilized as a reference to detect ASR errors. Next, the ASR transcripts for these talks are generated by our ASR system based on Julius 4.3.and TED models. The output is then compared with the human-annotated transcript, and the ASR errors together with their confidence measures are stored for the next step. Figure 2 depicts the schematic of this framework.

Figure 2. System schematic

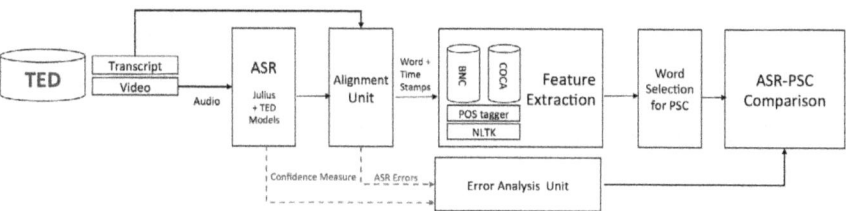

Next, we classify the errors into insertion, deletion or substitution categories and perform a root cause analysis in order to extract profound features such as "speech rate", "word frequency", "word length", etc. As Figure 2 presents, this framework is built on PSC system so that eventually the results can be easily compared with PSC's output.

3. Results and discussion

In total there were 169,402 word tokens, of which 13,755 words were erroneously recognized. WER averaged 8%. These errors are categorized into:

- Substitution errors: ASR output is different from human-annotated transcript (7.0%).

- Deletion errors: ASR omits a word that exists in human-annotated transcript (0.4%).

- Insertion errors: ASR outputs a word that does not exist in human-annotated transcript (0.7%).

We then further analysed these errors to identify the features that led to their occurrences. Findings suggest that for both ASR and L2 learners, the most contributing features to difficulties are following similar trends. Figure 3 illustrates how each feature affects ASR WER. As the figure presents WER increases for too fast/slow speech rates, infrequent words and also words with shorter length.

Figure 3. ASR error trends for different features; vertical axis depicts WER (%)

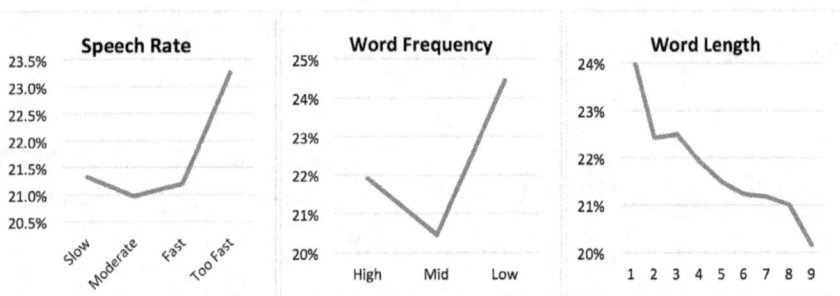

This finding suggests that the errors of the ASR system can be used to predict L2 learners' difficulties in listening. Therefore, in the next phase, we compared these errors with the selected words in the generated PSCs. As Table 2 suggests, around 60% of ASR errors were included in PSC word selection, which indicates that both PSC and ASR found these words difficult to recognize. However, approximately 20% of PSC's selected words were recognized correctly by the ASR system. A part of this mismatch can be explained by the inclusion of proper names and academic words in PSC. However, this finding calls for further investigation to explain the features that induced these errors. Our preliminary analysis indicates that most of these errors are the product of multiple factors such as general ASR processing. Yet, some of them contain useful information such as those related to minimal pairs or proper names. Finally, to verify the difficulty of those ASR errors, which are hidden in PSC, an experiment with L2 listeners is recommended.

Table 2. ASR errors and L2 listening difficulties

	ASR Correct (92%)	ASR Errors (8%)
PSC Shown Words (25%)	20%	5%
PSC Hidden Words (75%)	72%	3%

4. Conclusions

This study made a comparison between ASR errors, L2 listening difficulties and PSC word selection to diagnose the words/phrases, which are hard to recognize. ASR can serve as a simplified model of a language learner. In this view ASR errors can provide useful information and introduce pedagogical implications. The findings of this research suggest that ASR errors can indicate difficult/problematic speech segments and hence can be incorporated into PSC system to better meet L2 listeners' requirements.

References

Field, J. (2008). Bricks or mortar: which parts of the input does a second language listener rely on? *Tesol Quarterly*, *42*(3), 411-432.

Goldwater, S., Jurafsky, D., & Manning, C. D. (2010). Which words are hard to recognize? Prosodic, lexical, and disfluency factors that increase speech recognition error rates. *Speech Communication*, *52*(3), 181-200. doi:10.1016/j.specom.2009.10.001

Mirzaei, M. S., Akita, Y., & Kawahara, T. (2014). Partial and synchronized captioning: a new tool for second language listening development. In S. Jager, L. Bradley, E. J. Meima, & S. Thouësny (Eds), *CALL Design: Principles and Practice - Proceedings of the 2014 EUROCALL Conference, Groningen, The Netherlands* (pp. 230-236). Dublin Ireland: Research-publishing.net. doi:10.14705/rpnet.2014.000223

Rost, M. (2013). *Teaching and researching: listening*. New York: Routledge.

Shimogori, N., Ikeda, T., & Tsuboi, S. (2010). Automatically generated captions: will they help non-native speakers communicate in English? In *ICIC '10 Proceedings of the 3rd international conference on Intercultural collaboration* (pp. 79-86). New York: ACM. doi:10.1145/1841853.1841865

Shinozaki, T., & Furui, S. (2001). Error analysis using decision trees in spontaneous presentation speech recognition. In *ASRU'01*, 198-201. doi:10.1109/asru.2001.1034621

Thomson, R. I. (2013). Computer assisted pronunciation training: targeting second language vowel perception improves pronunciation. *Calico Journal*, *28*(3), 744-765. doi:10.11139/cj.28.3.744-765

Vasilescu, I., Adda-Decker, M., & Lamel, L. (2012). Cross-lingual studies of ASR errors: paradigms for perceptual evaluations. In *LREC* (pp. 3511-3518).

Webb, S. (2010). Using glossaries to increase the lexical coverage of television programs. *Reading in a Foreign Language*, *22*(1), 201-221.

Pedagogical values of mobile-assisted task-based activities to enhance speaking skill

Mojtaba Mohammadi[1] and Nastaran Safdari[2]

Abstract. The purpose of the present study was to examine the impact of online mobile-assisted task-based activities on improving Iranian intermediate English as a Foreign Language (EFL) learners' speaking skills. To achieve the purpose of the study, 90 intermediate language learners were selected ranging between 13 to 16 years old and divided into three interactive, non-interactive, and conventional groups. The interactive and non-interactive groups conducted online task-based speaking activities via WeChat mobile application. In the interactive group, the students were encouraged to interact among themselves on the topics from their course book. The non-interactive group experienced the same condition except that they were only supposed to have learner-teacher interactions with no interaction among peers. The conventional group followed the same task-based speaking activities within the class period but with the absence of technology. Data were collected administering the speaking section of Cambridge Preliminary English Test as pre- and post-tests. The results revealed that learners in the interactive group outperformed those in the face-to-face group regarding their speaking skills.

Keywords: online task-based activities, speaking, m-learning, mobile-assisted language learning, MALL.

---

1. English Language Teaching Department, Faculty of Persian Literature and Foreign Languages, Roudehen Branch, Islamic Azad University, Roudehen, Iran; m.mohammadi@riau.ac.ir; mojtabamohammadi@gmail.com
2. English Language Teaching Department, Faculty of Persian Literature and Foreign Languages, Roudehen Branch, Islamic Azad University, Roudehen, Iran; nastaran_safdari1367@yahoo.com

How to cite this article: Mohammadi, M., & Safdari, N. (2015). Pedagogical values of mobile-assisted task-based activities to enhance speaking skill. In F. Helm, L. Bradley, M. Guarda, & S. Thouësny (Eds), *Critical CALL – Proceedings of the 2015 EUROCALL Conference, Padova, Italy* (pp. 416-420). Dublin: Research-publishing.net. http://dx.doi.org/10.14705/rpnet.2015.000368

1. Introduction

As global cell phone users are spreading like wildfire, the mobile is becoming the integral part of anyone's life. Beyond its purpose as a means of communication, the mobile phone can serve educational purposes, such as developing language learning. Speaking skills, as one of the complex language learning components, can benefit from the pedagogical values of mobile phones. It becomes more vital when we know that "a large percentage of the world's language learners study English in order to develop proficiency in speaking" (Richards & Renandya, 2002, p. 201).

As mentioned by Soureshjani (2013),

> "in this age of communication, [speaking] seems to be playing a major role, and the purpose of teaching the language has shifted from the mastery of structure to the ability to use the language for communicative purposes" (p. 167).

As soon as mobile phones became a crucial part of our lives, more teachers felt the need to use them in language learning tasks. By the advancement of technologies, mobile-assisted language learning caused a new revolution in language teaching and learning.

> "The use of mobile technology is a new gate-way to create more interactive environment in the classroom in an interesting and innovative way by making teaching more and more effective" (Yedla, 2013, p. 92).

Language learning is merely one of the areas that can benefit from the advantages of mobile learning (m-learning). Mobile phones might be used as a medium in different fields of language teaching, i.e. listening, speaking, reading, and writing.

Therefore, on the pillars of the technological supply of mobile phones and the educational demand of improving speaking skills, we have laid the foundations of this article. In the current study, the researcher tried to investigate the way of effective learning through mobile technologies, a shift from teacher-led learning to a student-led one, via m-learning.

The present study aims at answering the following questions:

- Do online task-based speaking activities have any impact on the Iranian EFL learners' speaking ability?

- Are there any statistically significant differences among online task-based speaking and conventional groups regarding Iranian EFL learners' speaking ability?

- Is there any significant difference between male and female students regarding the impact of online task-based speaking activities on Iranian EFL learners' speaking ability?

2. Method

2.1. Participants

In order to accomplish the present study, out of 132 intermediate Persian language learners from English classes in one of the institutes in Tehran, named Simin, 90 were participants of this study. The participants were selected adopting simple random sampling. To ensure that the participants were at the same level of proficiency, a Preliminary English Test was administered. 44 male learners and 46 female learners were selected. Their age ranged from 13 to 16. The 90 students were equally assigned to three classes: interactive, non-interactive, and conventional (face-to-face) groups.

2.2. Instrument and procedure

The instrument that was used in the study is the speaking section of the Cambridge Preliminary English Test 4 (2003) as pre- and post-tests. In order to conduct the present study, the following steps were taken: PET was administered to participants to discover the homogeneity of participants regarding their general proficiency. Therefore, two classes were selected as experimental groups, while one class was the control group. One session was devoted to both experimental groups, in which the teacher taught them how to work with one of the mobile applications (WeChat) prior to the treatment. The participants in the experimental group A received 20-30 minutes treatment for all 20 sessions, including three sessions in a week studying Cambridge English for Students. In every session of experimental group A, the participants connected on WeChat for 20-30 minutes after the class when they were at home. For the online task-based speaking activity, students were expected to follow three stages: pre-task activities, task cycle, and post-task activities.

In the first stage, photos played an important role. Students had to answer a few questions about the photos posted by the teacher. The most important thing in this phase was to focus on the preparation of the main task.

During the task phase, the researcher performed opinion exchange tasks asking students an opinion-based question on the lesson's topic. The students were expected to talk about their ideas and experiences. In addition, the participants were required to ask each other questions and to comment on others orally. During the task phase, the researcher tried to listen to what the participants were saying and also helped them to interact with each other.

In the post-task activities, participants were expected to present what they discovered during the task. It primarily focused on summarizing the outcome of the task.

On the other hand, in experimental group B during the task phase, the students were expected to talk about their ideas and experiences, but they were not required to ask questions and comment on others orally. During the task phase, the researcher only tried to listen to what the participants were telling each other.

During the task phase in the control group, the teacher asked tasks (opinion exchange tasks) and the students were expected to listen and talk about their ideas and experiences within the classroom, but they were not required to ask questions and comment on others orally. The only difference was the absence of technology.

3. Discussion

In order to investigate the effect of mobile-assisted task-based activities on the speaking skills of Iranian students and thus answer the research questions, a post-test was administered to all groups and a quantitative method was applied to compare the results with the ones from the pre-test. The results showed interactive students' speaking ability was significantly improved compared to that among the non interactive students. This finding is consistent with the results of some previous studies which support the significant impact of task-based speaking activities on speaking skill (Levy & Kennedy, 2005; Lu, 2008; Zhang, Song, & Burston, 2011).

Unfortunately, most studies so far involved mobile phones usage in learning vocabularies rather than using mobile phones to interact with a wider Internet audience, although most studies had positive impacts on learning English. According to the results that Levy and Kennedy (2005), Lu (2008), Zhang et al. (2011) found, the researchers tried to develop task-based speaking skills through m-learning.

4. Conclusions

The overall findings of this study suggest the importance of online task-based speaking activities in the instruction of speaking skill to lead students to greater learning opportunities and to make speaking in the second language an autonomous process. In the present study, the results indicated that groups with online task-based speaking activities developed higher speaking ability in English.

All in all, it can be concluded that learners in the interactive group outperformed those in the face-to-face group regarding their speaking skill. Furthermore, the learners' speaking skill showed a greater improvement in the interactive group than that among the other two. Also, there is not any significant difference between male and female students regarding the impact of m-learning on learners' speaking ability.

The findings can be pedagogically advantageous for language teachers, teacher educators, and material developers. However, these conclusions are limited by such factors as the participants' level and the length of the study.

References

Cambridge Preliminary English Test 4 Student's Book: Examination Papers from the University of Cambridge ESOL Examinations. (2003). Cambridge: Cambridge University Press.

Levy, M., & Kennedy, C. (2005). Learning Italian via mobile SMS. In A. Kukulska-Hulme & J. Traxler (Eds.), *Mobile learning: a handbook for educators and trainers* (pp. 76-83). London: Taylor & Francis.

Lu, M. (2008). Effectiveness of vocabulary learning via mobile phone. *Journal of Computer Assisted Language Learning, 24*(6), 515-525.

Richards, J. C., & Renandya, W. A. (2002). *Methodology in language teaching: An anthology of current practice*. Cambridge: Cambridge University Press. doi:10.1017/CBO9780511667190

Soureshjani, K. H. (2013). A study on the effect of self-regulation and the degree of willingness to communicate on oral presentation performance of EFL learners. *International Journal of Language Learning and Applied Linguistics World, 4*(4), 166-177.

Yedla, S. (2013). MALL (mobile assisted language learning): a paradise for English language learners. *IJ-ELTS: International Journal of English Language and Translation Studies, 1*(2), 1-9.

Zhang, H., Song, W., & Burston, J. (2011). Re-examining the effectiveness of vocabulary learning via mobile phones. *TOJET, 10*(3), 203-214.

Using language corpora to develop a virtual resource center for business English

Thi Phuong Le Ngo[1]

Abstract. A Virtual Resource Center (VRC) has been brought into use since 2008 as an integral part of a task-based language teaching and learning program for Business English courses at Nantes University, France. The objective of the center is to enable students to work autonomously and individually on their language problems so as to improve their language skills. We are currently developing the center by applying the theory of Data-Driven Learning, (DDL, Johns, 1991), with the hope to encourage more students' engagement in the center. This paper will describe how micro-tasks have been designed based on DDL theory and integrated to the VRC in order to help learners overcome their grammar problems. The researcher will follow the activities on the VRC of a group of 30 students over six weeks in order to raise students' awareness about the VRC and encourage them to work on their grammar problems on the center. The expected outcome is that students will engage more in the VRC and through a series of processing stages, i.e. thinking and reasoning, solving problems and making decisions, and regular practice, information can be transferred to the long-term memory to be retrieved in the future (Ellis, 2008).

Keywords: corpus linguistics, data-driven learning, Virtual Resource Center, grammar acquisition.

1. Introduction

The VRC was developed as part of a task-based, blended language learning and teaching program for Business English courses at the University of Nantes which

---

1. Nantes University, France; thi-phuong-le.ngo@etu.univ-nantes.fr

How to cite this article: Ngo, T. P. L. (2015). Using language corpora to develop a virtual resource center for business English. In F. Helm, L. Bradley, M. Guarda, & S. Thouësny (Eds), *Critical CALL – Proceedings of the 2015 EUROCALL Conference, Padova, Italy* (pp. 421-426). Dublin: Research-publishing.net. http://dx.doi.org/10.14705/rpnet.2015.000369

was implemented in 2008 to deal with overcrowded and mixed-ability classes as well as to reduce student drop-out rates. The VRC is a self-access training space that currently provides micro-tasks supporting individual meta-linguistic reflection and contextualized language practice (Bertin & Narcy-Combes, 2012). The VRC allows teachers to draw students' attention to particular language problems that they may have. As they give feedback on the students' written productions, they can send them to the VRC to find solutions to their grammar problems. The VRC has recently been developed in order to encourage more students' engagement.

2. Development

2.1. The context

Languages and International Trade at the University of Nantes is a three-year undergraduate program that combines the learning of up to 2 or 3 languages, of which Business English is compulsory. Although the number of students' enrollment increased by 29% between 2008 and 2010, the drop-out rate is at the end of the first year is relatively high, at more than 40%. Another problem of the Business English courses is that teachers have to deal with large size classes of from 45 to 60 students per class and students' language levels are heterogeneous. The large size, heterogeneous class is believed to be a contributing factor that leads to increasing drop-out rates, because individual feedback, student interaction and practice are not adequate in these conditions.

To deal with these problems, a team of teachers and researchers had worked towards a task-based blended language learning and teaching program which was then started in 2008. A VRC, which is aimed at motivating students to work for their individual problems autonomously to improve their language skill, is a constitutive part of this program. However, a recent survey showed only under half of students invested sufficient time for the connection to the center, although a majority of students positively perceived the language resources on VRC useful, (Starkey-Perret, McAllister, Ngo, & Belan, under revision). Therefore, we are currently developing the center by applying the theory of DDL (Johns, 1991), with the hope to encourage more student engagement in the center.

2.2. The development of the VRC

The rationale for choosing this approach is threefold: the DDL approach helps learners to acquire a language by discovering patterns of language use through multiple samples of the same items in the center of sentences (Key Word in Context, KWIC), which helps learners to identify the patterns, and analyze them so as to generalize the language use. This approach also allows learners to be confronted with authentic resources of language input so they can observe what is written in a given circumstance (Bennet, 2010), which has proved to be one of the advantages over non-authentic/invented examples (Aston, 2000). Moreover, it is believed that as learners learn to observe and make generalizations, they develop more autonomy, and this process promotes noticing and grammar consciousness raising (Boulton, 2010).

New micro-tasks of the virtual resource center are designed under the light of the corpus-based approach and data-driven learning method. Each grammar module contains two main parts: grammar explanations and practice exercises. For the first part, the data-driven learning approach is applied to design consciousness-raising tasks. Instead of providing grammatical rules directly to learners, a set of examples are shown and followed with a number of guiding questions, which would lead learners to notice patterns (Figure 1 and Figure 2). For the latter part, a number of exercises are provided so that students can practice with the grammatical forms that they've learned in the previous part (Figure 3).

The input for examples is collected from the Contemporary Corpora of American English (COCA, http://corpus.byu.edu/coca/), while the input for exercises is from the Google news corpora where large quantities of authentic text are updated hourly. The practice exercises are designed as a self-test so that students can see how far their grammar knowledge has gone. It is hoped that through a series of processing stages and practice, information can be maintained in the short-term memory or transferred to the long-term memory to be retrieved in the future (Ellis, 2008).

Figure 1. Example of a grammar consciousness-raising task – sets of examples

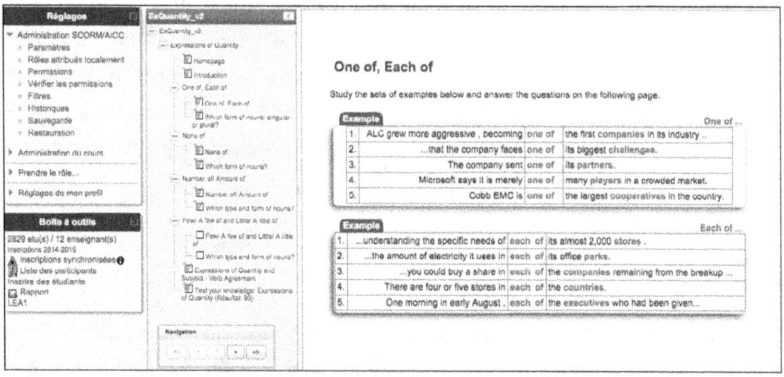

Figure 2. Example of a grammar consciousness-raising task – guiding questions following sets of examples

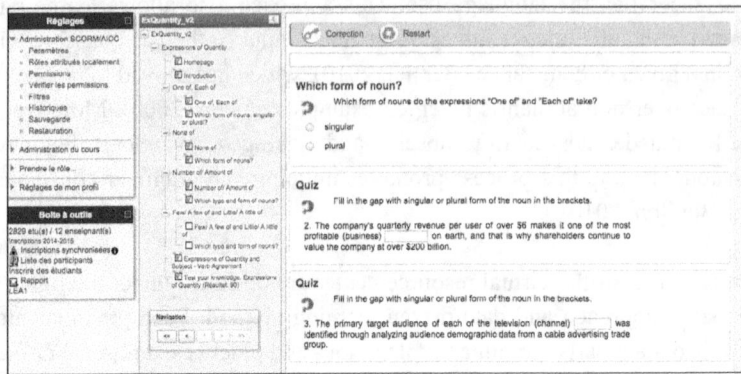

Figure 3. Example of a practice task

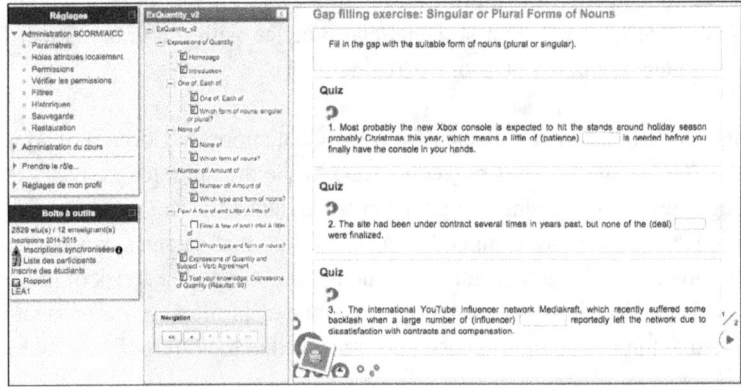

Before launching the newly developed version of the virtual resource center, a pilot survey questionnaire was conducted to investigate students' perceptions of the design of the grammatical modules. The survey questionnaire deals with the clarification of task instructions and explanations, and the level of task difficulty. A group of 32 students were asked to work with a grammatical module in 20 minutes and complete the survey questionnaire.

2.3. Students' awareness raising activities

In order to raise students' awareness about the VRC and how it would help them to find solutions to their grammar problems, the researcher worked with a group of 30 first-year students and the class teacher over six weeks in the second semester. She helped the class teacher to revise students' written productions each week and sent feedback via email to each student. While pointing out students' grammar errors, the researcher also linked them with grammar modules or exercises available on the VRC so that students could easily find what they needed. The researcher also went through some of the grammar modules with students in the multimedia rooms.

3. Discussions

For the survey questionnaire, the responses were very positive. As regards task instructions and questions, 84.38% of respondents agreed that they were clear and easy to understand. 87.5 % of students claimed that grammatical explanations that follow task questions were also clear and easy to understand. 93.75 % of them thought that the tasks were at the appropriate level of difficulty. A small number of students claimed that they would have felt quite nervous if they had been in a test with these types of tasks/questions and that they would need around 1 hour to complete the given module.

The work with the students in order to raise their awareness about the center and encourage them to engage on it is rather challenging, given the fact that the VRC is a supplementary learning resource and students are not obliged to go there to practice. Even though students were provided with links to related grammatical modules on the virtual resource center to find solutions to their grammar problems, not many of them spent time on the center to review. However, when working on some of the grammar modules with the researcher at the multimedia room, the students were very interested and worked effectively. In general, self-test results of the grammar modules of students at the Common European Framework of Reference (CEFR, 2001) A1-A2 level range from 45 – 55%; for B1 students, the results range from 80 – 85% while B2-C1 students have from 90 to 95 %. To conclude, over 6 weeks, the researcher has seen 30% of students autonomously engaged onto the center in comparison with 0% prior to that moment.

4. Conclusions

In the present study, the researcher has showed how she has been using language corpora to develop grammar modules on the VRC as a source of supplementary learning, which is aimed at helping students with their grammar problems. Although the effectiveness of these grammar modules cannot be statistically analyzed because students' engagement on the VRC is low in activities and the number of participants, the possibility of better understanding grammatical rules was observed, especially among B1-B2 students during learning sessions in the multimedia room. In the next phase of the research, the grammar modules will be integrated into the Business Learning courses as post-task activities. Teachers are expected to use the Moodle platform more effectively to make contact with their students as well as to give them task instructions and feedback. With the participation of the faculty of teachers, the number of students engaging on the center is expected to increase and they will also be encouraged to work on more tasks in the center.

5. Acknowledgements

I would like to thank Prof. Marie-Françoise Narcy-Combes, Dr Sophie Belan and Dr Rebecca Starkey-Perret for their continuous support.

References

Aston, G. (2000). Corpora and language teaching. In L. Burnard & T. McEnery (Eds.), *Rethinking language pedagogy from a corpus perspective: papers from the third international conference on teaching and language corpora* (pp. 7-17). Hamburg: Peter Lang.

Bennet, G. R. (2010). *Using corpora in the language learning classroom: corpus linguistics for teachers*. Michigan: University of Michigan Press.

Bertin, J-C., & Narcy-Combes, J.-P. (2012). Tutoring at a distance: modeling as a tool. *Computer Assisted Language Learning, 25*(2), 111–127.

Boulton, A. (2010). Data-driven learning: taking the computer out of the equation. *Language Learning, 60*(3), 534-572. doi:10.1111/j.1467-9922.2010.00566.x

CEFR. (2001). *Common European framework of reference for languages: learning, teaching, assessment*. Council of Europe. Retreived from http://www.coe.int/t/dg4/linguistic/source/framework_en.pdf

Ellis, R. (2008). *The study of second language acquisition*. Oxford: Oxford University Press.

Johns, T. (1991). From printout to handout: grammar and vocabulary teaching in the context of data-driven learning. In: T. Johns (Ed.), *Classroom concordancing (ELR Journal)* (pp. 27-45). University of Birmingham.

Starkey-Perret, R., McAllister J., Ngo, T. P. L., & Belan, S. (under revision). Assessing undergraduate student engagement in a virtual resource center: links between engagement, language learning and academic success. *Recherche et pratiques pédagogiques en langues de spécialité – Cahiers de l'APLIUT*.

The TATL framework for CALL development

Neasa Ní Chiaráin[1] and Ailbhe Ní Chasaide[2]

Abstract. The Theory Actions Techonology Learner context (TATL) framework provides an initial analysis tool to guide Computer-Assisted Language Learning (CALL) development. It entails joint consideration of four key factors that need to be considered prior and during development activities: (1) the underlying pedagogical theory; (2) the learning tasks arising from the theory; (3) the technological provision available for a given language; (4) the cultural context and cognitive style of the learner. The background to this proposal is based in the research and development of speech technology and CALL applications in the ABAIR initiative for Irish (*An Sintéiseoir Gaeilge,* www.abair.ie). Extensive evaluations of three multimodal interactive platforms have led directly to the formulation of the TATL framework.

Keywords: interdisciplinarity, personalised learning, future CALL environment, localisation, TTS synthesis, Irish, Gaelic.

1. Introduction

A framework is proposed, TATL, which aims to provide a 'master environment' for CALL development. It consists of four key factors which we propose should ideally be considered together at the planning and development stages in order to optimise the effectiveness of CALL applications. While much of the CALL literature in the past has been dominated by discussions of its history, its scope and of terminology issues (Davies, Walker, Rendall, & Hewer, 2012), we focus here rather on evolving a framework which can allow CALL development to proceed in a way that takes account of the theoretical and practical context.

---

1. Trinity College Dublin, Ireland; nichiarn@tcd.ie

2. Trinity College Dublin, Ireland; anichsid@tcd.ie

How to cite this article: Ní Chiaráin, N., & Ní Chasaide, A. (2015). The TATL framework for CALL development. In F. Helm, L. Bradley, M. Guarda, & S. Thouësny (Eds), *Critical CALL – Proceedings of the 2015 EUROCALL Conference, Padova, Italy* (pp. 427-432). Dublin: Research-publishing.net. http://dx.doi.org/10.14705/rpnet.2015.000370

Underwood's (1984) characterisation of CALL as "letting computer whizzes first explore how the computer can do something particularly well and then design the program to take advantage of that" (p. 83) still rings true more than thirty years later. In the real world, CALL development, just like other educational development, occurs in a complex context which needs to be explicitly taken into account and the TATL framework is intended as a guideline that encourages this wider level of consideration for practitioners and developers. Clearly, technological innovation should come, not as a response to technical innovation as such, but rather as a response to pedagogical need, and be informed by pedagogical theory and by that branch of cognitive science which explores language learning/language acquisition. This puts the emphasis back on the learning, or on the cognitive modification experienced by the learner, as the central focus of the CALL endeavour. Furthermore, it is crucial that this be done in a way that takes account of the learner's context, level of language skill and outlook. From this perspective, the computer provides a means of delivering the desired content in exciting ways, rather than being the central focus.

2. Developing multimodal synthesis-based platforms for Irish

The present proposal draws on experience gained from research on the development and evaluation of interactive language learning CALL platforms which exploit Text-To-Speech synthesis (TTS) for Irish (Gaelic), a minority language (Ní Chasaide et al., 2011; Ní Chiaráin, 2014; Ní Chiaráin & Ní Chasaide, 2014, 2015). The ABAIR initiative has been developing speech technology resources for Irish, an endangered language (Moseley, 2010) which nonetheless as the first national language is taught to all schoolgoers throughout the Republic of Ireland.

Text-To-Speech facilities have been developed for the three major dialects of the Irish language. A major concern is to ensure that these are exploited for language learning purposes. To this end, a number of interactive synthesis-based platforms have been developed (Ní Chiaráin, 2014). The first, an interactive game, *Digichaint*, involves the learner in solving the mystery of a lost lottery ticket and this is done by interrogating a range of characters in a virtual reality setting. The dialogue is predetermined and at each turn there are a select number of conversational interactions from which the learner can choose. The second platform, *Fáilte go TCD*, is geared towards listening comprehension and the learner navigates a virtual reality scene, eavesdropping on groups of conversants. In the third platform, the learner converses with a conversational agent, a talking monkey, *Taidhgín*. Here, the learner is free to create the language input. However, as we do not yet have speech recognition for Irish, the input is necessarily in text form, while the monkey speaks back.

These platforms were extensively evaluated in many schools by pupils and teachers. One of the major points to emerge from the exercise was the need for CALL developments to be embedded in a considered framework which explicitly recognises the intersection of requirements needed for effective educational resources.

3. The TATL framework

The complex environment which needs to be considered for the development of CALL applications can be summed up in terms of the following four key elements.

- **Theory:** the prevailing theory or theories of language acquisition.

- **Actions:** learning activities prompted by the theory.

- **Technology:** the current state of technological development, especially its capacity to deliver content appropriate to these actions.

- **Learner context:** this covers a multiplicity of factors, such as: the learners' engagement with the technology and its likely influence on their motivation to acquire the target language; learners' language level; cognitive style; sociocultural background and overall motivation.

3.1. Theory

The important point in our view is that developers of CALL applications be theoretically aware, so that at least the assumptions being made are explicit and open to scrutiny. This meta-awareness is all the more important because theory evolves and at present we have no unitary or incontrovertible theory of language acquisition. The dominant theoretical approach to language learning for many years now has been the communicative approach where the emphasis is on the functional use of the target language to communicate in a meaningful way. With the rapid growth in neuroscience there will undoubtedly be a constantly evolving understanding of the learning process.

3.2. Actions

The communicative approach emphasises the need for task-based learning, preferably involving a real-life or simulated real-life engagement between the learner and the system. Two of our platforms involved interactive tasks. The scripted game, *Digichaint*, allowed the learner to control the direction of the game, but the language content was predetermined (even if there were many choices at each turn). The second platform allowed open-ended input (though in text only), and users were tickled by the fact that the monkey appeared to understand and respond to them. This latter game turned out to be the most popular, perhaps not surprisingly as it comes closer to a real-life engagement, even if one does not habitually talk to a monkey.

3.3. Technology

As for Irish, the available technologies often impose limits on what can be provided in CALL. For endangered languages there is a vicious circle. Endangered languages have fewer technology resources available. The consequent lack of attractive teaching resources results in greater difficulties engaging and motivating learners.

Nonetheless, technological deficits, such as the lack of recognition facilities for the *Taidhgín* conversing monkey platform can at least be partly overcome. In this case by using text input, the illusion of a 'conversation' was maintained. The fact that learners found the game to be highly entertaining is encouraging and will empower the evolving cycle of technological developments (here recognition) that will provide the possibility for true simulated dialogue partners.

3.4. Learner context

Within the TATL framework, personalisation of content, localising and adapting it to the needs of learners from a variety of socio-cultural backgrounds, levels and cognitive styles, is paramount. The circumstances in which the learning is taking place is critical. For example, a major challenge for Irish is that many learners have limited access to native speaker models and can often be poorly motivated.

In this context, high quality synthesis-based educational games can play a particularly crucial role: the former deficit is remedied at least partially by the fact that students are exposed to native level speech and the fun aspect of the interactive game has a positive impact on motivation.

Figure 1. Blueprint for a future CALL environment

4. Discussion and conclusion

Initial TATL analysis is intended to raise consciousness from the outset of what the limiting features of a particular CALL application are likely to be and thus, one can adjust one's goals, methods, etc. to take account of them, ensuring that they are, in so far as possible, 'fit for purpose'. The TATL analysis is also useful for those who, like our ABAIR group, are developing the underlying speech and language technologies that are likely to be used in downstream CALL applications, in order to provide useful guidelines as to where the deficits are most keenly felt and where the priorities should be. This goes hand in hand with involving educationalists and end users. The earlier this is done, the greater the potential educational value of the technological development. To this end, the ABAIR group, who are developing speech resources for Irish, use not only the TATL framework but also extensive collaboration and testing with end users.

TATL, at a high-level, underscores the need for interdisciplinary development, ideally involving the cooperation of linguists, pedagogues, engineers, graphics and design experts. Ultimately, to ensure that the broader context guides CALL development, such an interdisciplinary approach should help ensure theory and technology take full account of the learner and the learner's context.

5. Acknowledgements

The authors are grateful for the support of An Roinn Ealaíon, Oidhreachta agus Gaeltachta (ABAIR project) and An Chomhairle um Oideachas Gaeltachta & Gaelscolaíochta (CabairE project).

References

ABAIR. *An Sintéiseoir Gaeilge* [Online]. Retrieved from www.abair.ie

Davies, G., Walker, R., Rendall, H., & Hewer, S. (2012). Introduction to computer assisted language learning (CALL); Module 1.4. In G. Davies (Ed.), *Information and communications technology for language teachers (ICT4LT)*. Slough, Thames Valley University. Retrieved from http://www.ict4lt.org/en/en_mod1-4.htm

Moseley, C. (Ed.). (2010). *Atlas of the world's languages in danger* (3rd ed.). Paris: UNESCO Publishing. Retrieved from http://www.unesco.org/culture/en/endangeredlanguages/atlas

Ní Chasaide, A., Ní Chiaráin, N., Wendler, C., Berthelsen, H., Kelly, A., Gilmartin, E., Ní Dhonnchadha, E., & Gobl, C. (2011). Towards personalised, synthesis-based content in Irish (Gaelic) language education. In *Proceedings of the ISCA Special Interest Group link (SIG) on Speech and Language Technology in Education (SLaTE)* (pp. 29-32). Venice, Italy.

Ní Chiaráin, N. (2014). *Text-to-speech synthesis in computer-assisted language learning for Irish: development and evaluation*. Doctoral thesis, CLCS, Trinity College, Dublin.

Ní Chiaráin, N., & Ní Chasaide, A. (2014). Evaluating text-to-speech synthesis for CALL platforms. *In Antwerp CALL 2014: International CALL Research Conference* (pp. 104-110). Antwerp: University of Antwerp

Ní Chiaráin, N., & Ní Chasaide, A. (2015). Evaluating synthetic speech in an Irish CALL application: influences of predisposition and of the holistic environment. In *SLaTE 2015: 6th Workshop on Speech and Language Technologies for Education* (p. forthcoming). Leipzig, Germany.

Underwood, J. (1984). *Linguistics, computers and the language teacher: a communicative approach*. Rowley, MA: Newbury House.

Successful EFL teaching using mobile technologies in a flipped classroom

Hiroyuki Obari[1] and Stephen Lambacher[2]

Abstract. Two case studies evaluating the effectiveness of a flipped classroom compared to a traditional classroom were performed. The studies were conducted from April 2014 to January 2015 at a private university in Tokyo, targeting 60 first-year and 25 third-year undergraduates, respectively. In the first study, an assessment of pre- and post-treatment Test of English for International Communication (TOEIC) scores revealed students exposed to the flipped lessons improved from a mean of 474 (SD 111) to 649 (SD 96), which was greater than that of the control students who improved from 484 (SD 123) to 617 (SD 115). In the second study, students were exposed to flipped lessons for 24 weeks using a variety of materials such as the 'Lecture Ready II' digital text with iPad, COOORI e-learning software for learning words and phrases related to the digital text, ATR CALL Brix e-Learning, Newton e-Learning, and TED Talks. An assessment of pre- and post-treatment TOEIC scores and Oral Proficiency Interview by computer-based (OPIc) speaking test results showed students improved from a mean of 577 (SD 132) to 758 (SD 105), an improvement of 24% in just the speaking test. Surveys administered after exposure to the flipped lesson activities indicated students were satisfied with their flipped classroom lessons and motivated by the Blended Learning (BL) environment that incorporated mobile learning.

Keywords: flipped classroom, mobile technologies, OPIc assessment, blended learning.

---

1. Aoyama Gakuin University, Tokyo, Japan; obari119@gmail.com
2. Aoyama Gakuin University, Tokyo, Japan; steve.lambacher@gmail.com

How to cite this article: Obari, H., & Lambacher, S. (2015). Successful EFL teaching using mobile technologies in a flipped classroom. In F. Helm, L. Bradley, M. Guarda, & S. Thouësny (Eds), *Critical CALL – Proceedings of the 2015 EUROCALL Conference, Padova, Italy* (pp. 433-438). Dublin: Research-publishing.net. http://dx.doi.org/10.14705/rpnet.2015.000371

1. Introduction

In a reversal to traditional learning, the flipped classroom is a unique educational environment which is quickly gaining in popularity among educators worldwide. In a flipped classroom, students learn the course lectures (i.e. through online videos, course materials, etc.) before they come to class, and spend the bulk of classroom time asking questions and being engaged in interactive discussions. Mobile learning (M-learning) technologies, such as the iPhone, iPad, podcasting, and video-casting, and others, are also rapidly gaining popularity as an effective means to improve foreign language skills around the world. As mentioned by Obari and Lambacher (2014), m-learning is "highly motivating to learners, as it offers them a rich, informal, contextual, and ubiquitous learning environment" (p. 267). Users can control the time, pace, and speed of their own learning which is motivating and liberating for many learners. M-learning is also more personalized than other methods of computerized instruction, as mobile devices can be more easily customized, resulting in the creation of an emotional bond between the user and machine.

M-learning has indeed emerged as the next generation of e-learning. One reason is the high availability of mobile devices in industrialized countries. For example, nearly 100% of Japanese own a mobile phone, with the number of smartphone users in Japan rapidly increasing (Obari, Kojima, & Itahashi, 2010). The smaller screen size and touch interface of smartphones and tablets also leads to more focused learning, as the learner typically has just a single program running at any given time, as opposed to the more common multitasking operations found on desktop and notebook PCs (Gualtieri, 2011). The use of mobile technologies for the purpose of language learning has numerous advantages over other methods, for example, the countless number of English news programs, language learning apps, podcasting, and video-casting that are easily accessible and reasonably priced or for free.

In our study, web-based resources using Web 2.0 tools and mobile computing technologies were integrated to promote collaborative learning activities. Lecture Ready 2 digital text, Newton m-Learning, ATR CALL Brix program are very useful online "learning resources available and [are] very conducive to mobile [(m-)] learning, whereby learning takes place at any time and at any place due to the swift development of mobile technologies" (Obari, 2013, p. 195; see also Obari et al., 2013).

The goal of the present paper is to examine the effectiveness of BL and flipped learning activities integrating m-learning for the purpose of improving the

TOEIC scores and the overall English language proficiency of native Japanese undergraduates, including oral communication and presentation skills. We were particularly interested in seeing if the use of a BL and flipped classroom would be more motivating to students and effective than a traditional classroom setting in improving their overall learning experience and improving their language skills.

2. Methods and evaluation

2.1. Case study 1

Case study 1 was carried out from April 2014 to January 2015 at a private university in Tokyo, and targeted 60 first-year Japanese undergraduates. An experimental group was exposed to flipped classroom lessons for 24 weeks using the textbook 'Lecture Ready I'. Students watched course video lectures and online English learning materials using a mobile device before coming to each class, and then created classroom presentations using PowerPoint for interaction and discussion in small groups during the regular classes. In contrast, a control group of students were taught using traditional methods with the same textbook and no flipped lessons. The control group watched the video lectures and answered the textbook questions but only during the regular classroom periods.

An assessment of pre- and post-treatment TOEIC scores showed that students exposed to the flipped lessons improved from a mean score of 474 (*SD* 111) to 649 (*SD* 96), which was greater than the control students who improved from 484 (*SD* 123) to 617 (*SD* 115). At the end of the eight-month training period, the experimental group had completed nearly 80% of the course content and substantially improved their overall reading, listening and oral communication skills through the online English lectures with flipped lessons.

2.2. Case study 2

Case study 2 was conducted during the same period as study 1 (April 2014 to January 2015) and targeted 25 third-year Japanese undergraduates. The purpose was to ascertain the effectiveness of flipped lessons and independent studies using iPads. This group was exposed to flipped lessons for 24 weeks using a variety of materials such as the 'Lecture Ready II' digital text with iPad, COOORI e-learning software for learning words and phrases related to the digital text, ATR CALL Brix e-Learning, Newton e-Learning, and TED Talks. Students were required to watch the video lectures of 'Lecture Ready II' and then create PowerPoint slides in preparation for classroom presentations and discussions with their iPads before each class. Students shared their presentations and interacted with each other during the regular classes in small groups using their iPads. In addition to 'Lecture Ready II', the students studied the online course materials independently with their iPads.

Figure 1. Results of OPIc speaking assessment

Improvements of Each Level (Pre vs. Post Speaking Test)

	UP and DOWN			
	−1	±0	+1	+2
Advanced Low	1	—	—	
Intermediate High		3		—
Intermediate Mid(3)		1		
Intermediate Mid(2)		4		3
Intermediate Mid(1)	1			
Intermediate Low	1	7	1	
Novice High		1	2	

	Number	UP/DN		UP%
My students	25	+9/−3	+6	+24.0%
Other Univ.	19	+3/−4	−1	−5.3%
Junior Colleges	14	+5/−4	+1	+7.1%

An assessment of pre-treatment and post-treatment TOEIC scores and OPIc computer-based speaking test results showed that students improved from a mean score of 577 (*SD* 132) to 758 (*SD* 105), an improvement of 24% in the speaking test (see Figure 1). Also, the surveys administered after their exposure to the flipped lesson activities to evaluate their effectiveness indicated students were more satisfied with the flipped lessons and motivated by the BL-learning environment incorporating m-learning.

3. Discussion

Two case studies examining the effectiveness of flipped lessons incorporating blended learning were carried out. The results of both studies showed the flipped lessons were more effective in improving students' TOEIC scores and English oral proficiency. An assessment of pre- and post-training TOEIC and OPIc scores revealed that the aforementioned target activities had a positive effect on the students' overall English skills. In addition, the students' listening and oral communication skills improved as a result of integrating blending and flipped learning activities. Students delivered presentations based on their digital and paper textbook, and they also created several digital stories. The survey administered after their exposure to the BL and flipped lesson activities indicated students were satisfied with the variety of online course materials and motivated by the BL environment incorporating m-learning. The students' English oral summary skills also improved after their exposure to the online Lecture Ready II and Globalvoice CALL software.

In examining why the flipped lessons incorporating BL and m-learning were so effective, it could be that the activities, which enabled students to work both in and out of the classroom and to actively explore their learning environment, succeeded in motivating students in wanting to study harder than they would have otherwise. Additionally, Japanese university students seem to have a preference for using mobile devices when learning English, and the m-learning component made it easier for students to regulate their own language learning, thus making their overall experience much more fun and enjoyable.

4. Conclusions

Taken as a whole, these results would seem to indicate that BL and flipped learning activities using mobile technologies can effectively be integrated into the language learning curriculum and play a positive role in improving the language proficiency of second language learners. Additionally, instructor observations of the BL and flipped activities revealed the students were excited by using a variety of emerging new technologies, which enabled them to effectively learn English by accessing a variety of learning materials from their mobile devices. M-learning helped to increase the amount of comprehensible English input with the aid of revolutionary education/learning applications. It was also highly motivating to the students by offering them a rich, informal, contextual, and ubiquitous learning environment in which it was possible for students to control their learning time, environment, and speed.

5. Acknowledgements

We would like to extend our sincere appreciation to the Japanese Ministry of Education for supporting this research fund through a Kakenhi grant.

This work was supported by JSPS KAKENHI, Grant in Aid for Scientific Research (C), 2015-2018. Grant Number: 15K02727.

References

Gualtieri, M. (April, 2011). Mobile app design best practices: when it comes to designing the mobile user experience (UX), context is kingonline article: http://www.forrester.com/rb/Research/mobile_app_design_best_practices/q/id/59132/t/2

Obari, H. (2013). The Impact of Employing Mobile Technologies and PCs for Learning Coursera Online Lectures and TOEIC Practice Kit. In L. Bradley & S. Thouësny (Eds.), *20 Years of EUROCALL: Learning from the Past, Looking to the Future* (pp. 194-199). Dublin Ireland: Research-publishing.net. doi:10.14705/rpnet.2013.000160

Obari, H., Kojima, H., & Itahashi, S. (2010). Empowering EFL learners to interact effectively in a blended learning environment. In *Proceedings of World Conference on Educational Multimedia, Hypermedia and Telecommunications* (pp. 3438-3447). Chesapeake, VA: AACE.

Obari, H., & Lambacher, S. (2014). Impact of a blended environment with m-learning on EFL skills. In S. Jager, L. Bradley, E. J. Meima, & S. Thouësny (Eds.), *CALL Design: Principles and Practice - Proceedings of the 2014 EUROCALL Conference, Groningen, The Netherlands* (pp. 267-272). Dublin Ireland: Research-publishing.net. doi:10.14705/rpnet.2014.000229

Obari, H. Suto, A. Kobayashi, Y., Ogihara, T., & Lambacher, S. (2013). The effects of CALL software in teaching English pronunciation and TOEIC, Courseware showcase. *WorldCALL 2013* (p. 197).

TLC Pack unpacked

Margret Oberhofer[1] and Jozef Colpaert[2]

Abstract. TLC Pack stands for Teaching Languages to Caregivers and is a course designed to support migrants working or hoping to work in the caregiving sector. The TLC Pack resources range from A2 to B2 level of the Common European Framework of Reference for Languages (CEFR), and will be made available online in the six project languages: Dutch, English, German, Greek, Italian and Spanish. TLC Pack will also be available as paper-based materials (PDF) and on a specially designed language learning platform (http://language-for-caregivers.eu). In this paper, we touch upon three challenges we faced during the development of the materials.

Keywords: language for specific purposes, less commonly taught languages, course design, TLC Pack.

1. Introduction

The EU has an ageing population, a situation which will deteriorate markedly in the coming years and beyond. In the EU, life expectancy at birth for males is expected to increase by 7.2 years over the projection period, from 77.6 in 2013 to 84.7 in 2060. For females, life expectancy at birth is projected to increase by 6.0 years, from 83.1 in 2013 to 89.1 in 2060. These figures also indicate that male and female life expectancies will eventually converge (European Commission, 2014). According to data from Eurostat (2015), those aged 65 years or over will account for 28.7% of the EU-28 population by 2080, compared to 18.5% in 2014.

The implications of Europe's ageing population are manifest. First, there could be labour shortages with regard to particular sectors and skills needs. Secondly, ageing

---

1. University of Antwerp, Belgium; margret.oberhofer@uantwerp.be

2. University of Antwerp, Belgium; jozef.colpaert@uantwerp.be

How to cite this article: Oberhofer, M., & Colpaert, J. (2015). TLC Pack unpacked. In F. Helm, L. Bradley, M. Guarda, & S. Thouësny (Eds), *Critical CALL – Proceedings of the 2015 EUROCALL Conference, Padova, Italy* (pp. 439-443). Dublin: Research-publishing.net. http://dx.doi.org/10.14705/rpnet.2015.000372

could have a significant financial impact, for example on social assistance and pension systems, and this will necessitate high levels of employment. Combining immigration from third world countries with increasing participation rates among migrants and minorities within the EU may help mitigate the impact of ageing societies (OECD, 2011).

In recent years, care organisations have increasingly begun hiring staff from other countries. In Belgium, for example, 5000 people from EU countries and 7100 non-EU residents started working in the social sector between 2009 and 2013. These are increases of 44.6% and 63.3% respectively, while the number of Belgian citizens starting work in the care sector increased by only 11.5% (Vlaams ministerie van Welzijn, Volksgezondheid en Gezin, 2015). The main problems experienced by newcomers on the Belgian labour market are cultural differences and a lack of language skills (Wets & de Bruyn, 2011).

2. Method

A European team consisting of six partners aimed to tackle these issues by developing a language course, i.e. the TLC Pack, specifically designed to support the growing number of migrant caregivers working or hoping to work in the caregiving sector. The TLC Pack course not only supports the acquisition of caregiver vocabulary, but also recognises the importance of developing intercultural knowledge and insights. As a result, both aspects are included in the final resource package aimed at migrant caregivers, language teachers and senior professionals in the caregiving sector.

The TLC Pack resources range from A2 to B2 level of the CEFR and will be made available online in the six project languages: Dutch, English, German, Greek, Italian and Spanish. The University of Antwerp was responsible for designing the test unit and developing the Dutch language materials.

The TLC Pack consists of six units, each containing five chapters, which means there are a total of 30 chapters per language. The topics covered in each chapter were defined after a needs analysis conducted in the six partner countries. The topics are:

- Unit 1: Communication (e.g. with residents and their families, colleagues)

- Unit 2: Daily tasks (e.g. briefing during shift changeover)

- Unit 3: Nutrition/Feeding (e.g. assisted feeding, dietary restrictions)
- Unit 4: Mediation and health care (e.g. wound care, insulin administration)
- Unit 5: Post-hospital care (e.g. physical therapy, checking blood pressure)
- Unit 6: Free-time activities (e.g. physical exercises, personal history)

At the heart of each unit is a video of 3-8 minutes in length showing realistic tasks and situations between caregivers and residents, family members and colleagues. Using the videos, learners can complete exercises to practise the four communicative skills (reading, writing, listening and speaking) as well as grammar and vocabulary. At the end of each unit there is a word list and a test.

The course not only supports the acquisition of caregiver vocabulary, but also recognises the importance of developing intercultural knowledge and insights. The intercultural unit centres around topics that were identified as challenging for migrant caregivers during the needs analysis. In Belgium, for example, these include the use of dialect versus standard Dutch and the use of the correct register and style with residents and their family members.

The TLC Pack materials will be available in two forms: a) offline, as a paper-based course (PDF) for language teachers who want to provide specific language materials in class; and b) online, on a specially designed platform for students who want to study independently – anytime and anywhere.

3. Discussion

While developing the materials we faced three key challenges:

- Maintaining a balance between the European approach to the course and country-specific expectations about caregivers' tasks. During the needs analysis at the beginning of the project it became apparent that caregivers' responsibilities differ from country to country. The tasks range from personal hygiene and grooming to support with taking medication. The requirements for entering the job market also differ from country to country. In order to make the materials relevant enough for the sector, we had to consider these differences when developing the materials. As a result, the topics are the same in all language versions of the TLC Pack, but the dialogues have been adapted to suit national circumstances. This was done in close cooperation with experts from the care sector.

- Shooting 30 videos with appropriate actors in authentic locations on a limited budget. In Belgium we cooperated with the Antwerp International Academy for Film and Television (IAFT) in order to achieve this goal. The students filmed and edited the dialogues as part of their training, coached by professionals from the film academy. The actors in the videos were mostly residents in care centres, often aged over 75, who volunteered to help with the dialogues. This cooperation between the generations turned out to be positive for both the project and the participants. Gaining access to an authentic location for the videos was also a challenge. We cooperated with the Zorgbedrijf, the biggest care centre in the region with 16 000 residents and 3700 staff members. This organisation allowed us to film the videos on their premises free of charge.

- Developing exercises to suit the classroom and online learning. The focus in this project was to develop paper-based materials for classroom learning and to transfer these materials to the TLC Pack platform. The exercises in the paper-based version reflect the principles of the communicative language learning approach, with authentic real-life tasks that lead to interactive classroom activities. The challenge was to transfer this wide range of communicative exercise types to a platform which only allows for a limited number of exercise types, such as drag and drop, match, gap fill and ordering exercises. Transferring the materials to a CALL platform inevitably led to certain pedagogical constraints and concessions.

4. Conclusions

The TLC Pack is a language course specifically designed for caregivers who work or want to work in the care sector. The completed materials will become available free of charge at the beginning of 2016 as paper-based materials (PDF) and on the TLC Pack platform. Both the online and offline resources can be accessed via the project website: http://language-for-caregivers.eu.

5. Acknowledgements

The TLC Pack is a European project funded by the European Commission under the Lifelong Learning Programme (Key Activity 2).

References

Eurostat. (2015). Population structure and ageing. Web. 17 July 2015. Retrieved from http://ec.europa.eu/eurostat/statistics-explained/index.php/Population_structure_and_ageing

European Commission. (2014). The 2015 ageing report. Underlying assumptions and projection methodologies. Retrieved from http://ec.europa.eu/economy_finance/publications/european_economy/2014/pdf/ee8_en.pdf

Wets, J., & de Bruyn, T. (2011). Migratie: de oplossing voor het personeelstekort in de zorg- en gezondheidssector. Koning Boudewijnstichting. Retrieved from http://www.kbs-frb.be/publication.aspx?id=295153&langtype=2067

OECD. (2011). Help wanted? Providing and paying for long-term care. Retrieved from http://www.oecd.org/els/health-systems/47836116.pdf

Vlaams ministerie van Welzijn, Volksgezondheid en Gezin. (2015). Actieplan 3.0 Werk maken van werk in de zorg- en welzijnssector. Retrieved from http://jovandeurzen.be/sites/jvandeurzen/files/actieplan%20werk%20maken%20van%20werk%203%200_0.pdf

Dynamic lesson planning in EFL reading classes through a new e-learning system

Takeshi Okada[1] and Yasunobu Sakamoto[2]

Abstract. This paper illustrates how lesson plans, teaching styles and assessment can be dynamically adapted on a real-time basis during an English as a Foreign Language (EFL) reading classroom session by using a new e-learning system named iBELLEs (interactive Blended English Language Learning Enhancement system). iBELLEs plays a crucial role in filling the gaps between the teacher's expectations and students' needs. iBELLEs is used as a feasible tool to help teachers in upper-intermediate level Japanese EFL reading classes gauge students' comprehension of current reading materials, choose appropriate teaching styles and make dynamic assessments to pursue particular sub-goals before reaching the final goal of a given classroom session. iBELLEs is built on a database technology and is used as an electronic textbook equipped with a bidirectional communication facility in face-to-face EFL reading classrooms that are supported by a robust Language Management System (LMS) called WebOCMnext. By obtaining immediate feedback from the students, the teacher can determine an appropriate level of mediation that should be carefully, but quickly adjusted to satisfy individual student's needs. The current study tries to explore how simultaneous feedback from the students can help teachers make dynamic lesson planning and assessment during a single EFL reading classroom.

Keywords: EFL reading, e-learning system, dynamic assessment, immediate feedback.

---

1. Tohoku University, Japan; takeshi.okada.a8@tohoku.ac.jp

2. Tohoku Gakuin University, Japan; yasube.sakamoto@icloud.com

How to cite this article: Okada, T., & Sakamoto, Y. (2015). Dynamic lesson planning in EFL reading classes through a new e-learning system. In F. Helm, L. Bradley, M. Guarda, & S. Thouësny (Eds), *Critical CALL – Proceedings of the 2015 EUROCALL Conference, Padova, Italy* (pp. 444-449). Dublin: Research-publishing.net. http://dx.doi.org/10.14705/rpnet.2015.000373

1. Introduction

1.1. Basic conception of the development of iBELLEs

The fundamental conception of the new e-learning system named iBELLEs is a flexible corpus annotation (Okada & Sakamoto, 2010) which is based on database management technology. The authors have been working on the development of a corpus annotation system that allows system users to design their own tagset and assign any tags as attributions to a given corpus. In corpus annotation, as pointed out in Sinclair (1991), to adopt a certain tagset would mean to accept it a priori and consequently reject other tagging framework. In iBELLEs, every part of a specific EFL reading comprehension passage can be assigned any attribution by its users, i.e. EFL teachers and their students. When using iBELLEs, teachers can 'highlight' particular parts of a given reading passage together with annotations (explanations or hints about the text); the students can also 'highlight' particular parts with three distinctive colours. Additionally, in the database, each constituent of a passage is assigned attributions that mean it is 'highlighted' or 'given annotation'. The teachers define and design their tagsets in the teaching materials making process, whereas the students select the type of the highlight following their teacher's instruction.

As Kissau and Algozzine (2015) point out, in some teaching situations the face-to-face (F2F) mode of instruction is more advantageous than its online counterpart. Based on an idea that these two modes should be blended and arranged in a complementary fashion, iBELLEs is designed to perform best in an F2F classroom in which EFL reading materials and comprehension questions are transmitted online. During an F2F classroom session, a teacher can observe what the students are doing, highlight a target passage and then mediate appropriately their learning activity by giving brief explanations or suggestions. To overcome a mismatch of teaching and learning styles, the teacher determines how to run a class and manage lesson plans and instructional time based on an immediate decision made by visual observation of the students' activity. In order to support the teacher's dynamic decision and management of the EFL reading lesson, it is indispensable for the new system to be equipped with the functionality to allow the teacher to grasp and gauge students' needs immediately and intuitively.

1.2. LMS and a new e-learning system

As can be seen in Figure 1, iBELLEs is developed and placed in an overall blended EFL reading e-learning program. The entire course is supported by a robust LMS named WebOCMnext that manages all activities of both the teacher and students

(Okada & Sakamoto, 2014). The teacher can (1) give quizzes and tests, (2) transmit reading materials, (3) receive different sorts of feedback utilizing e-portfolios or bulletin boards, (4) obtain immediate feedback and give appropriate mediation through iBELLEs and (5) dynamically alter the lesson plan in an actual F2F classroom. On the other hand, the students (1) interact with their teacher and teaching assistant on a real-time basis through iBELLEs, and (2) send their requests or messages on their learning difficulties through e-portfolios, chatting or bulletin boards and (3) are supported in their out-of-classroom (OOC) learning activities.

Figure 1. iBELLEs in an overall EFL e-learning program

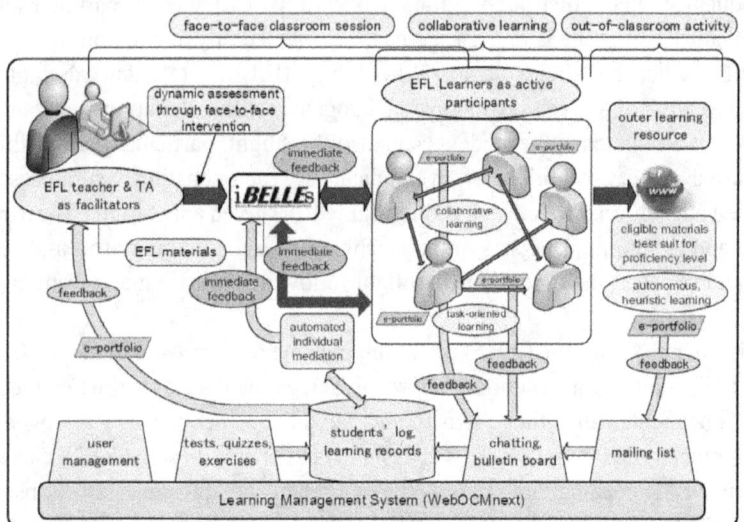

Though iBELLEs is designed for maximum efficacy in the F2F instruction mode, it provides the EFL teacher with opportunities to select the most efficient lesson plans and instruction modes that can be adopted both inside and outside of the classroom. The different sorts of feedback come from not just F2F classroom sessions, but also OOC activities stored and managed by the LMS.

2. iBELLEs, a new e-learning system

2.1. Visual interaction to bridge the gaps between teacher and students

Through the sophisticated interface of iBELLEs, the teacher can observe what the students are actually doing, and can give appropriate instruction in an F2F mode.

Moreover, the teacher can dynamically alter the duration of any lesson prepared beforehand, such as vocabulary, grammar, discourse structure and reading strategy. In every lesson, the teacher can select the most appropriate instruction mode. In a vocabulary lesson, for example, when the teacher observes a wide divergence of vocabulary knowledge among the students, s/he alters the instruction mode from F2F to the individual learning mode; when the teacher notices that the students should work collaboratively on a common reading material to acquire deeper comprehension skills, s/he may change the instruction to the collaborative learning (CL) mode (Davies, 2015).

2.2. Teacher mode

Figure 2 is a screen shot of iBELLEs in its teacher's mode running on the LMS platform. The teacher can instantly and visually grasp what the students are doing on the screen, where highlighted parts indicate their reading difficulties (in Figure 2 different colours show unknown words and half-familiar words of the entire class). Moreover, iBELLEs is equipped with a unique function of selecting different threshold numbers by which the teacher can intuitively observe the general inclination of the class. In addition, the teacher is able to select a particular group of students as well as an individual student by checking the name(s) on the list (the lower right corner). The teacher may intervene and stop individual learning activities and encourage the students to work in a collaborative manner or, conversely, instruct student groups to stop CL and get into individual learning style.

Figure 2. iBELLEs and LMS

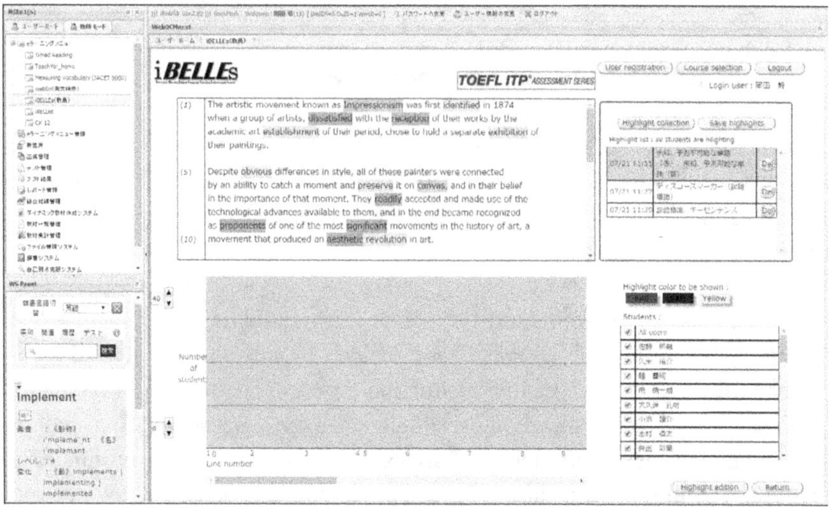

2.3. Student mode

In this mode, each student is prompted to highlight specific parts of the target passage using three pens with distinctive colours. Figure 3 shows a particular student's screen where s/he highlights discourse markers in light blue and key sentences in yellow. At the same time, the student can see the highlighted parts by the teacher, which are displayed in coloured rectangles with corresponding colours. A red rectangle window for hints and explanations pops up when a student left clicks a given part of a passage.

Figure 3. Highlights by student and teacher

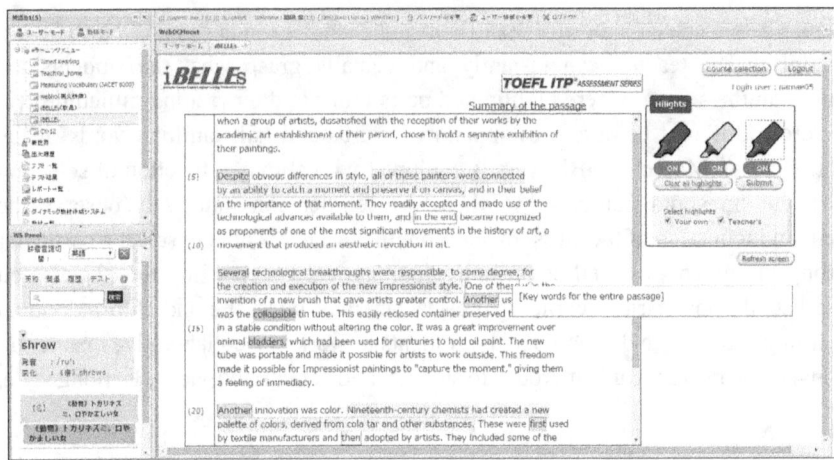

3. Conclusion and further potential uses

Through iBELLEs, the teacher can instantaneously grasp students' expectations and intervene in their learning activity with efficient individual mediation. Based on observations through immediate feedback, the teacher may adapt lesson plans or alter the duration of each lesson.

One of the most important features of iBELLEs' highlighting functionality is the definition of a given highlight: it is not decided in advance but defined by the teacher in the actual EFL reading instruction process. The teacher is required to design the highlight set that is most efficient for the current teaching material, and dynamically decide the teaching styles or lesson plans based on immediate feedback. The unlimited pedagogical potentials of iBELLEs, a handy electronic textbook with bidirectional communication facilities, are an attractive topic for future research.

4. Acknowledgements

This research has been partially supported by the JSPS Grant-in-Aid for Scientific Research (B) (Research No. 26284075). Also, we would like to thank ETS for contracting and granting permission to use genuine TOEFL ITP® test reading materials.

References

Davies, G. (2015). Developing collaborative learning when teaching TOEFL iBT classes. *The Language Teacher,39*(1), 22-25.
Kissau, S., & Algozzine, B. (2015). The impact of mode of instructional delivery on second language teacher self-efficacy. *ReCALL, 27*(2), 239-256. doi:10.1017/S0958344014000391
Okada, T., & Sakamoto, Y. (2010). A new RDBMS and flexible POS tagging for EFL learners and researchers: Designing a corpus analysis system based on the three-tier model. *CAHE Journal of Higher Education, 5,* 43-52, Tohoku University.
Okada, T., & Sakamoto, Y. (2014). The LMS development for a blended EFL e-learning. In S. Jager, L. Bradley, E. J. Meima, & S. Thouesny (Eds.), *CALL design: principles and practice; proceedings of the 2014 EUROCALL conference, Groningen, the Netherlands* (pp. 273-277). Dublin: Research-publishing.net. doi:10.14705/rpnet.2014.000230
Sinclair, J. (1991). *Corpus, concordance, collocation.* Oxford: Oxford University Press.

Learning about language learning on a MOOC: how Massive, Open, Online and "Course"?

Marina Orsini-Jones[1], Laura Pibworth-Dolinski[2], Mike Cribb[2], Billy Brick[3], Zoe Gazeley-Eke[3], Hannah Leinster[4], and Elwyn Lloyd[4]

Abstract. This paper reports on an exploratory research project on the evaluation of the engagement with a Massive Open Online Course (MOOC) carried out by six members of staff and two 'expert students' involved in the MA in English Language Teaching (ELT) in the Department of English and Languages at Coventry University (CU), United Kingdom, between November and December 2014. Its main aim was to investigate how both expert and trainee English teachers and teacher trainers would find the experience of engaging with a FutureLearn MOOC on this subject created by the University of Southampton in collaboration with the British Council – *Understanding Language: Learning and Teaching*. The participants involved agreed to record their thoughts while they were taking part in the MOOC and then met once per week for four weeks at the end of each MOOC unit to carry out a collaborative staff/student reflective evaluation of their experience. The paper will discuss the way in which the participants engaged with this project, which became a blended learning community of professional development practice linked to the global community of practice on the MOOC, and present their perspectives on the pros and cons of integrating a MOOC as an Open Educational Resource (OER) into an existing curriculum.

Keywords: MOOC, language learning/teaching, exploratory research, blended learning.

---

1. Coventry University, United Kingdom; m.orsini@coventry.ac.uk
2. Coventry University, United Kingdom; aa2907@uni.coventry.ac.uk; m.cribb@coventry.ac.uk
3. Coventry University, United Kingdom; b.brick@coventry.ac.uk; ab2931@coventry.ac.uk
4. Coventry University, United Kingdom; leinsterh@uni.coventry.ac.uk; e.lloyd@coventry.ac.uk

How to cite this article: Orsini-Jones, M., Pibworth-Dolinski, L., Cribb, M., Brick, B., Gazeley-Eke, Z., Leinster, H., & Lloyd, E. (2015). Learning about language learning on a MOOC: how Massive, Open, Online and "Course"? In F. Helm, L. Bradley, M. Guarda, & S. Thouësny (Eds), *Critical CALL – Proceedings of the 2015 EUROCALL Conference, Padova, Italy* (pp. 450-457). Dublin: Research-publishing.net. http://dx.doi.org/10.14705/rpnet.2015.000374

1. Introduction

This paper discusses the experience of engaging with a MOOC in a project jointly carried out by six members of staff and two 'expert' students involved in the MA in English Language Teaching at CU in semester one of academic year 2014-2015. Participants agreed to enrol on the FutureLearn MOOC *Understanding language: Learning and Teaching* throughout its four-week duration. The MOOC had been designed as a 'taster' for the online MA in English Language Teaching[5] run by the University of Southampton in collaboration with the British Council (2014). Around 58,000 people enrolled on the MOOC from all over the world (Borthwick, personal correspondence, July 27, 2015).

The staff involved in this project had been investigating novel ways of enhancing their students' experience through blended learning curricular interventions for a number of years, linking the development of autonomous language learning and teaching to the acquisition of critical digital literacies and exploring how OERs can be integrated into existing curricula (e.g. Orsini-Jones, 2010; Orsini-Jones, Brick, & Pibworth, 2013).

Figure 1. Screen-shot from T&MoLL&T(CU Moodle website 2014) with the link to the MOOC

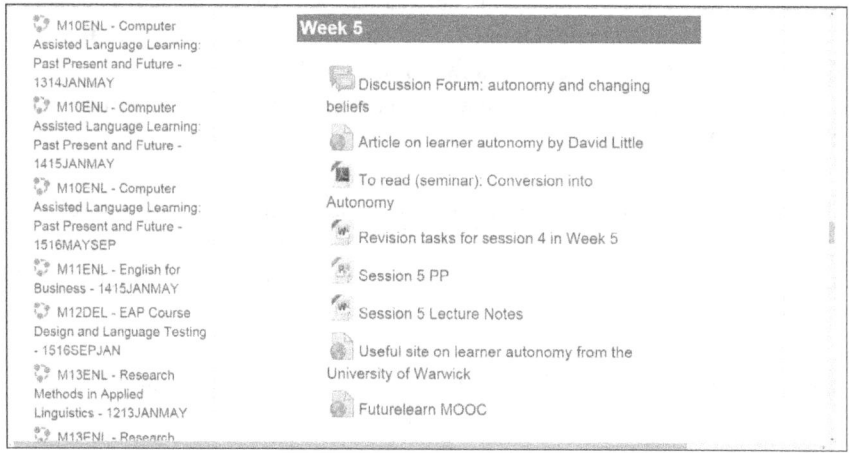

This project ran in parallel with another MOOC evaluation project involving all the students on the MA in ELT, as the MOOC had been embedded as an open

---

5. https://www.teachingenglish.org.uk/article/southampton-universitybritish-council-ma-english-language-teaching-online

educational 'extra line of support' into the curriculum of the compulsory module: Theories and Methods of Language Learning and Teaching (T&MoLL&T), see Figure 1. The focus of this paper will however be on the experience of the eight participants involved in the reflective weekly focus groups to discuss their engagement with the MOOC and the lessons learnt from it.

2. Method

This is a small-scale project that mainly draws on qualitative, exploratory data, but also includes some quantitative results obtained via a survey. The data were collected in three ways:

- participants' logs while engaging with the MOOC;

- weekly 'post-MOOC-unit' focus groups that were recorded;

- online survey.

This study is auto-ethnographical in nature, as participants recorded their reflections during each week throughout the four-week duration of the MOOC and shared them in the weekly focus groups. The study includes quantitative results yielded from a survey administered after the MOOC finished. The survey was created with the Bristol Online Survey tool, which complies with the Data Protection Act and included a mixture of Likert-scale type statements and open-ended questions based on recommendations on survey design provided by Dörnyei (2003).

The project is based upon the evaluation of engaging with the FutureLearn 'Understanding Language' MOOC occurrence that ran between 17th of November and 14th of December 2014 and obtained CU ethical clearance in October 2014. Participants agreed to:

- engage with the MOOC for 3 hours per week (the time recommended in the MOOC instructions to complete each unit);

- carry out the set activities on it for the 4 weeks of its duration;

- record their thoughts relating to the activities and their 'metareflections' on how their learning experience was affected by the platform and its global social collaborative features while engaging with them;

- share the recorded material with the principal investigator (PI) and the research assistant attached to the project;

- engage in a one-hour weekly focus group recorded by the PI using the 'Voice Memos' tool on her iPhone;

- write up the findings collaboratively and participate in their dissemination (self-selected participants with the PI);

- fill in the post-MOOC survey (one designed for staff and one for students).

All participants were asked to answer the 'orienteering' questions attached in the Appendix before the project started and to reflect on the post-MOOC questions (also in Appendix) during the focus groups. The participating tutors were three female lecturers and three male lecturers. The two students – both female – were studying on the MA in ELT at CU. One of them was hired as research assistant for the project.

3. Discussion

As discussed by Mulder (2015), MOOCs can polarise views in academia. The PI for this project agrees with Kim (2015) that MOOCs are opening new educational horizons and they are an "innovation with the potential to have large impact" (p. 3), but there were differing views amongst the participants of this project on this point. As the PI had integrated it into her mandatory module, she was a bit surprised that the survey revealed that her peers thought her curricular actions to be rather risky. However, all participants agreed that there was enough valuable content in the MOOC to make it a useful open educational addition to an existing course.

Also, in the survey answers, all staff agreed that they would recommend studying on a MOOC to their students. Both staff and students enjoyed having access to different perspectives on the topics they were covering on the MA, within an environment that had the added value of a very professional-looking layout, easy navigation and interesting tasks. Most staff commented positively on some innovative activities encountered on the MOOC, like using *Padlet* to share classroom settings from across the world. On the other hand, most of them saw it as a drawback that the MOOC appeared to have been created for specific marketing purposes: to promote the online MA in ELT offered by the University of Southampton with the British Council.

There was one aspect of the MOOC that all staff found disappointing, possibly because they had had high prior expectations of the social-collaborative opportunities offered by the MOOC: that is to say the discussion forums attached to each unit. Here are two comments reported in the open ended section of the survey. Question: "How did you find the communication on the MOOC forums?":

"There were too many comments to follow a thread".

"Impossible. I am not sure how you are supposed to have a meaningful discussion with over 50,000 people. I just read a few comments and moved on. I felt that it was too time-consuming to try to respond to comments that on the whole lacked any substance. It seemed to be people just stating how they were enjoying the course and not really engaging with the topics/subject".

The question of how best to facilitate and structure online discussions on MOOCs to maximise social co-construction of knowledge has been discussed in the literature in various ways. For example, Coetzee et al. (2015) and Towndrow, Aranguiz, Purser, and Pradhan (2013) explore the use of small peer groups to support MOOC participants in their learning of content and reflection on their progress. Perhaps it would have been better to have smaller groupings for the discussions, but this might be impossible to set up in a MOOC that has over 50,000 participants.

The student research assistant commented that engaging with the MOOC had complemented her study on the MA course in that similar topics were covered and her learning was consolidated by having the material presented in a variety of ways and from various different perspectives.

4. Conclusions

Staff and students found that there were learning benefits in engaging with a MOOC and that it was advantageous to be able to study on the MOOC anywhere and at any time after enrolment. Despite the difficulties encountered on the forums, they felt they were part of a global community of practice that also gave them exposure to global perspectives on the topics covered on the MA in English Language Teaching at CU. The MOOC also appeared to offer a different approach to learning, while at the same time supporting the consolidation of the MA content matter, albeit at a somewhat superficial, 'taster' level in some parts.

As for the discussion regarding the acronym, it was agreed that the MOOC was definitely 'Massive' in terms of capacity as its infrastructure appeared to manage to handle thousands of participants engaging at the same time from all over the world. This created some communication issues though, as numbers need to be limited to have a meaningful discussion online. 'Open' applied to many aspects of the MOOC, mainly the fact that it was free (this was seen as a big advantage by all); normally, in MOOC literature, it also refers to ease of accessibility and the delivery of open curricula (Klobas, MacIntosh, & Murphy, 2015). However, some participants commented that it is not really open to all, due to the digital divide: accessibility requires the Internet and powerful computers/tablets/phones. All participants agreed that the MOOC exemplified the 'Online' concept well, in a distance and mainly asynchronous learning mode – but there were live sessions available too – that could be accompanied by classroom-based 'analogues'. Many of the activities on the MOOC could be used (and were used) as a useful springboard for face-to-face discussions. As for 'C' for Course, Klobas et al. (2015) define a course as a "systematic sequence of learning activities" (p. 7). In this sense the FutureLearn MOOC was a course, but one participant thought it resembled more a module than a course. This is possibly just a matter of semantics, as "course" means different things in different countries (e.g. sometimes a UK module is a US course). At a deeper level, a MOOC is not a course because it lacks the scaffolding presence (in Bruner's 1983 terms) of experienced teachers supporting the learners at each step they take.

Despite their reservations on MOOCs in general, all participants agreed that engaging with the FutureLearn *Understanding Language* one had been a worthwhile and stimulating experience even if they came to the conclusion that MOOCs are not as transformational and/or as "disruptive" as some claim them to be.

5. Acknowledgements

We would like to thank Kate Borthwick at the University of Southampton for providing us with information on the number of enrolled participants on the MOOC discussed here and Sreevidya Midanamura, Noof Alhamed, Shoug Altanimi and Marwa Alnajjar, students on the MA in ELT, for their insights into their MOOC experience.

References

British Council. (2014). *Southampton University/British Council MA English language teaching: online*. Retrieved from https://www.teachingenglish.org.uk/article/southampton-universitybritish-council-ma-english-language-teaching-online

Bruner, J. (1983). Child's talk: learning to use language. London and NY: WW Norton and Co.

Coetzee, D., Lim, S., Fox, A., Hartmann, B., & Hearst, M.A. (2015). Structuring interactions for large-scale synchronous peer learning. In *Proceedings of the Collaboration in the Open Classroom Conference, 14-18 March 2015, CSCW* (pp. 1139-1152). Vancouver: CSCW. Retrieved from: http://www.cs.berkeley.edu/~bjoern/papers/coetzee-peerlearning-cscw2015.pdf

Dörnyei, Z. (2003). *Questionnaires in second language research.* London: Routledge.

Kim, P. (Ed.). (2015). *Massive open online courses: the MOOC revolution.* Abingdon: Routledge.

Klobas, J. E., MacIntosh, B., & Murphy, J. (2015). The anatomy of MOOCs. In P. Kim (Ed.), *Massive open online courses: the MOOC revolution.* Abingdon: Routledge/Taylor & Francis.

Mulder, F. (2015). Open(ing up) education for all... Boosted by MOOCs? In C. J. Bonk, M. M. Lee, T. C. Reeves, T. C., & T.H. Reynolds (Eds.), *MOOCs and open education around the world* (pp. xviii-xxvii). New York: Routledge.

Orsini-Jones, M. (2010). Task-based development of languages students' critical digital multiliteracies and cybergenre awareness. In M. J. Luzon, N. Ruiz, & L.Villanueva (Eds.), *Digital genres, new literacies and autonomy in language learning* (pp. 197-224). Cambridge: Cambridge Scholar.

Orsini-Jones, M., Brick, B., & Pibworth, L. (2013). Practising language interaction via social networking sites: the "expert student's" perspective on personalized language learning. In B. Zou (Ed.), *Computer-assisted foreign language teaching and learning: technological advances* (pp. 40-53). Hershey: IGI Global. doi:10.4018/978-1-4666-2821-2.ch003

Towndrow, A., Aranguiz, A., Purser, E., & Pradhan, M. (2013). Quad-blogging: promoting peer-to-peer learning in a MOOC. *eLearning Papers, 33*, 1-4. Retrieved from http://openeducationeuropa.eu/en/download/file/fid/27045

Appendix

Pre-MOOC orienteering questions

- Do you know what a MOOC (Massive Open Online Course) is?

- What are your expectations of studying on a MOOC (students/staff who have not completed/done one yet only)?

- Have you ever completed an online course for CPD (Continuous Professional Development) before? What was your experience of it?

- Have you ever engaged in 'Think Aloud Protocol' for research purposes before? If yes, how did you find it, if not what do you think it entails?

- What are in your opinion the 'troublesome' areas in language learning and teaching?

- Which ones do you expect to be covered by the MOOC on language learning and teaching?

Questions for weeks 1-4 of the MOOC

- How does learning language learning and teaching theories on the MOOC compare with your previous modes of study of the same topic?

- What value-added (if any) do you think there is in taking a MOOC?

- Did the content of the first (or second or third or fourth, depending on the week of study) week meet your expectations in terms of what you had predicted before you started?

- Would you recommend studying on a MOOC to your students? If so, would you take an integrated approach or keep it separate from what you do?

- How does interaction with peers on the MOOC differ from interaction with peers in other settings (e.g. face-to-face CPD, VLE)?

- How are you finding the process of recording your thoughts while engaging on the MOOC?

- Are there any aspects of the MOOC you are not happy with?

- Would you consider writing a MOOC for English Language Teaching? If so, what topic(s) would you like to cover?

- How are you finding the experience of taking part in this reflective project for the purpose of your CPD? And in general?

- Any other thoughts you would like to share?

Instructors' attitudes towards CALL and MALL in L2 classrooms

James W. Pagel[1], Stephen Lambacher[2], and David W. Reedy[3]

Abstract. As part of an ongoing study on learners' and instructors' attitudes toward the use of computers and mobile devices in second-language (L2) learning situations, our purpose here is to identify how language instructors value the use of computers and mobile devices in their teaching. We compare the responses of a survey administered during the past four years to instructors within two faculties of a private university in Tokyo, Japan, with the responses collected from a similar survey administered in 2014 to instructors solicited through various Computer-Assisted Language Learning (CALL) organizations. The response rate for the in-house survey during the first three years was low; however, in 2015 the response rate was much higher, with responses from both full-time and part-time staff totaling 34. The survey responses from the CALL organizations totaled 121. The respondents' places of employment ranged from Europe to the Asia Pacific Rim. In addition to offering an interpretation of a sampling of the Likert scale items found on the surveys, the authors concentrate on comparing the comments offered by instructors regarding which skills they focus on in the CALL classroom, as well as what applications they encourage their students to use on their mobile devices.

Keywords: survey analyses, recommended mobile applications, intrinsic motivation, adoption of mobile technology.

---

1. Aoyama Gakuin University, Japan; jwpagel@yahoo.com

2. Aoyama Gakuin University, Japan; steve.lambacher@gmail.com

3. Aoyama Gakuin University, Japan; dwr615@gmail.com

How to cite this article: Pagel, J. W., Lambacher, S., & Reedy, D. W. (2015). Instructors' attitudes towards CALL and MALL in L2 classrooms. In F. Helm, L. Bradley, M. Guarda, & S. Thouësny (Eds), *Critical CALL – Proceedings of the 2015 EUROCALL Conference, Padova, Italy* (pp. 458-463). Dublin: Research-publishing.net. http://dx.doi.org/10.14705/rpnet.2015.000375

1. Introduction

The incorporation of CALL and Mobile-Assisted Language Learning (MALL) technologies by foreign language educators worldwide has significantly altered the role of the teacher, leading to a validation of Kurzweil's (2000) prediction that "education will advance from 2009, with students using computers nearly exclusively for learning, with teachers available as motivators" (p. 192). However, as language education surges forward, does the incorporation of these technologies benefit the learner or simply satisfy the instructor's need to be innovative? Also, why are some teachers still hesitant to incorporate these potentially powerful technologies? The main goal of this study is to try to answer these questions as a way to help gain a better understanding of current and future states of information and communications technologies and methodologies, and how they can be more effectively utilized to improve foreign language education. We attempt to achieve this goal, in part, by targeting two surveys: the international survey was administered to CALL practitioners around the world, particularly living in and working at universities in Europe and the Pacific Rim region, and the in-house survey was administered to English language instructors currently employed at a private university in Tokyo (Aoyama Gakuin University). Our main goal is to gauge the attitudes of instructors regarding their use of CALL and MALL technologies in teaching English as a second/foreign language. We also attempt to determine what the most commonly used programs and applications being used by instructors are and whether they are having a positive impact both in and out of the language classroom. Additionally, we focus on ascertaining what the main obstacles are that prevent foreign language educators from embracing these rapidly advancing technologies.

2. Method

2.1. International survey

Both surveys were created using SurveyMonkey®[4]. The international survey was comprised of 42 questions based on the Likert scale five-item response type (1 "Strongly Disagree" to 5 "Strongly Agree"). The target audience was organizations comprised of CALL practitioners. The survey was distributed in 2014 to volunteers solicited through the LinkedIn™ CALL page (targeting EUROCALL members) and direct solicitations were made to the members of the CALL section of the Japan Association for Language Teaching (JALTCALL) and to the Asia-

---

4. https://www.surveymonkey.com/

Pacific Association for CALL (APACALL) through their respective organizations. The survey responses from the CALL organizations totaled 121. The respondents' employment locations, as could be expected given the sources tapped, ranged from Europe to Asia, including Japan and other Asia Pacific Rim countries, with a few exceptions. In terms of age, the respondents were equally distributed in the 30s, 40s, and 50s. Male respondents outnumbered females 57% to 43%. Additionally, 80.9% of the respondents were employed as full-time instructors engaged in second language (L2) teaching.

2.2. In-house survey

The in-house survey was comprised of 32 questions of the Likert scale five-item response type (1 "Strongly Disagree" to 5 "Strongly Agree"). The survey was administered four times over a four-year period (2011-2015). To ensure anonymity, all questions regarding personal information, such as age and nationality, were eliminated. The number of English teaching staff of the two faculties currently totals 34. While the total number of respondents participating in the study during the first three years averaged only 16, this number rose in 2015 due to an increase in the number of instructors employed within both faculties as a result of an expanded English curriculum.

3. Results

3.1. Survey (CALL)

Table 1 shows the mean response ratings of a select number of survey items related to CALL. We were interested in gauging both groups' attitudes toward their use of CALL in the classroom. As mentioned earlier, a five-point Likert Scale was used. Overall, both groups responded that CALL technology was readily available at their respective universities, with the in-house group responding slightly higher than the international group (4.4 vs. 3.7). Conversely, the international group was more confident than the in-house group in their comfort level using CALL (4.3 vs. 3.5). In response to "Using CALL is not worth the trouble", the in-house group agreed slightly more than the international group (2.3 vs. 1.9). As shown above, both groups' mean ratings were somewhat high for the following three items related to using CALL for English language learning: "I require my students to use CALL for learning English during class", "Using CALL technology has improved my students' English skills", and "My students enjoy using CALL technology to learn English compared to traditional methods".

Table 1. CALL-related survey items

CALL technology is readily available at my university.	
	In-house: 4.4
	International: 3.7
I feel comfortable using CALL.	
	In-house: 3.5
	International: 4.3
Using CALL is not worth the trouble.	
	In-house: 2.3
	International: 1.9
Using CALL technology has improved my students' English skills.	
	In-house: 3.5
	International: 3.9
My students enjoy using CALL technology to learn English compared with traditional methods	
	In-house: 3.5
	International: 3.7
I require my students to use CALL for learning English during class.	
	In-house: 3.9
	International: 3.9

3.2. Survey (MALL)

Table 2 shows both groups' responses to a select number of MALL-related items. As shown in the table, the international group was predictably more confident in using MALL than the in-house group (4.8 vs. 3.4). In response to "Using MALL is not worth the trouble" both groups were equally divided (2.5 vs. 2.4). In response to the two items "Using MALL technology has improved my students' English skills" and "My students enjoy using MALL technology to learn English", the international group was substantially higher than the in-house group (4.4 and 4.7 vs. 3.3 and 3.4, respectively).

Another area of concern with this paper is the type of applications instructors recommend and the ones the students actually use. Answers were very disparate and non-specific – dictionary and social networking were common responses. This indicates that the respondents may have misinterpreted the questions, "what applications do you recommend" and "which do you observe your students using". Despite the ambiguity of the responses, the applications commonly recommended can be categorized as "vocabulary", "dictionary", "testing", "comprehensive" (inclusive), "management", and "social networking" in descending order. The applications instructors observed their students using are similar, with the inclusion of "radio". In future surveys the authors will rephrase the questions so as to elicit more targeted responses to further this study. However, the authors want to emphasize that the instructor's role in guiding the students to worthwhile applications is crucial. Students may have mastered technology, but they are apt to use the easiest, most common applications available.

Table 2. MALL-related survey items

I feel comfortable using MALL technology.	In-house: 3.4 International: 4.8
Using MALL is not worth the trouble.	In-house: 2.5 International: 2.4
Using MALL technology has improved my students' English skills.	In-house: 3.3 International: 4.4
My students enjoy using MALL technology to learn English.	In-house: 3.4 International: 4.7

3.3. Skills

The final area of inquiry sought to ascertain the skills that instructors focus on with their students when using mobile devices and computers. The overall pattern of responses for both groups (shown below in percentages averaged across both groups) were similar concerning mobile devices, with the following skills preferred: *vocabulary* (82%), *listening* (77%), and *reading* (67%), with *pronunciation* (44%), *writing* (36%), *speaking* (28%) and *grammar* (26%) receiving substantially fewer responses. In contrast, the response patterns for skills when using computers were less congruent. For instance, the international group favored *listening* (80%), *reading* (76%), and *vocabulary* (71%), followed by *writing* (67%) and *speaking* (60%), while the in-house group preferred *listening* (85%), *writing* (69%), *reading* (65%), and *vocabulary* (58%). Overall, both groups emphasized receptive over productive skills when using mobile devices, although with computers the tendency was to focus on both receptive and productive skills.

4. Discussion and conclusions

The results revealed that both groups' attitudes towards CALL and MALL were varied. The international group felt more comfortable and positive in using CALL and MALL in the classroom compared to the in-house group. Similarly, the international group was more in agreement that MALL can be effectively utilized to improve students' English language skills and that their students enjoyed using mobile devices to study English. These results come as no surprise, since a majority of international group participants were CALL specialists, while in-house respondents included a large number of non-CALL practitioners. Moreover, a majority of the in-house respondents lacked experience in using MALL with their students. A somewhat unexpected result was that both groups responded similarly to questions related to CALL technology and English language learning, with both being positive about its impact on their students' English acquisition and student satisfaction and preference for it compared to traditional methods (see Stockwell, 2012 for further analysis in how CALL stacks up with traditional classroom approaches). We are hard-pressed to provide a sensible explanation for this particular response by the in-house group. One possible reason could be that since all in-house instructors are required to conduct their English classes in a CALL classroom and strongly encouraged to use the available technology, some may have felt inclined to respond more positively than they would have otherwise. The results also showed that vocabulary, dictionary, and testing apps were the most commonly recommended category of mobile apps. Additionally, both groups emphasized receptive over productive skills with students, at least when utilizing mobile devices.

5. Acknowledgements

We want to express our sincere appreciation to all the members of EUROCALL, APACALL, JALTCALL, as well as the instructors at Aoyama Gakuin University who participated in our survey.

References

Kurzweil, R. (2000). *The age of spiritual machines: when computers exceed human intelligence*. New York: Penguin.
Stockwell, G. (Ed.). (2012). *Computer-assisted language learning: diversity in research and practice*. Cambridge: Cambridge University Press. doi:10.1017/CBO9781139060981

A critical analysis of learner participation in virtual worlds: how can virtual worlds inform our pedagogy?

Luisa Panichi[1]

Abstract. This paper reports on an exploratory case study of learner participation within the context of online language learning in virtual world platforms. Data for this investigation was collected through a case study of a Business English course within a qualitative Case-Study Research framework. This study examines learner activity in virtual worlds in relation to three main features of the platform: avatars, artefacts and spaces. The study makes use of *Reflexivity* and *Exploratory Practice* as its core methodological approach to the building of the case. The virtual world data is analysed from a multimodal perspective and makes use of *visualisation* as the primary analytical tool. In an attempt to broach the Eurocall 2015 conference topic of Critical Computer-Assisted Language Learning (CALL), this paper will present and discuss three findings: a broadening of our understanding of learner participation in virtual worlds, the critical role played by course designers and teachers in the shaping of learner participation in virtual worlds, and the potential of virtual worlds as a tool for reflective practice and practitioner research.

Keywords: virtual worlds, learner participation, multimodal research, telecollaboration.

1. Introduction

The discussion of this paper draws on data collected by the author under a recently awarded PhD on learner participation in virtual world platforms (Panichi, 2015). The focus of this paper will be on those research findings that are relevant to a discussion of *Critical Call*. With the term "critical", the author intends to discuss to what extent the virtual world platform can inform us about our practice as

---

1. Centro Linguistico Interdipartimentale, University of Pisa, Italy; panichi@cli.unipi.it

How to cite this article: Panichi, L. (2015). A critical analysis of learner participation in virtual worlds: how can virtual worlds inform our pedagogy? In F. Helm, L. Bradley, M. Guarda, & S. Thouësny (Eds), *Critical CALL – Proceedings of the 2015 EUROCALL Conference, Padova, Italy* (pp. 464-469). Dublin: Research-publishing.net. http://dx.doi.org/10.14705/rpnet.2015.000376

CALL practitioners and act as a tool for teacher reflectivity. It is argued that the characteristics of virtual world platforms are such as to allow for a particularly powerful critical evaluation both of what we do as teachers and course designers (our practice) and of our pedagogic rationale (why we do what we do).

1.1. Virtual worlds and language education

Virtual world platforms are generally understood as computer generated environments where users can interact online in real time with other users and the environment via an avatar (Figure 1). An avatar is a graphic representation of the user which is visible within the environment. Without doubt, the most significant characteristic of 3D virtual worlds for language learning and teaching, compared to other online learning platforms, is their "immersiveness" (e.g. Deutschmann & Panichi, 2009a; Jauregi et al., 2011). This immersive nature of the platforms has implications in terms of language learner activity and participation (e.g. Deutschmann & Panichi, 2009a; Jauregi et al., 2011). Role-play activities are considered to be particularly enhanced by virtual world platforms (e.g. Dalgarno et al., 2013; Deutschmann & Panichi, 2009a; 2013), as are action-based learning activities (e.g. Molka-Danielsen & Deutschmann, 2009), and problem-based learning approaches (Brown, Gordon, & Hobbs, 2008). The immersiveness of the platform also has implications in language education in relation to intercultural learning (e.g. Jauregi et al., 2011; Panichi, Deutschmann, & Molka-Danielsen, 2010) and learner identity construction (Wigham, 2012).

Figure 1. Snapshot of a virtual world language class

1.2. Learner participation in virtual worlds

One of the main challenges in Web-based education is to understand and encourage student participation (Bento & Schuster, 2003, p. 157). Initially, virtual world research in Computer-Mediated Communication (CMC) within CALL was limited to an investigation primarily of learner interaction and participation as a linguistic activity (Deutschmann & Panichi, 2009b). However, at the outset of her research project, it seemed to the author of this paper that the focus of the virtual world research literature on learner participation as a linguistic activity was providing a limited understanding of the phenomenon and of the context within which it was being discussed. Thus, the aim of the study was to go beyond the existing understandings of participation at the time and to take a closer look at the specific affordances of the platform in particular.

2. Method

It can be argued that virtual world platforms, with their visual and graphic dimension, demand a methodological approach which is able to take into consideration the visual data generated by the platform as well as the linguistic data. Indeed, in line with a call for a more multimodal approach to research into learner interaction in CALL (e.g. Lamy, 2004; Lamy & Hampel, 2007), the study also aimed to provide for an *exploratory research framework* which would allow for the development of a broader analytical approach to learner participation in context than previous research.

2.1. Research framework

The study reported on in this paper makes use of *Reflexivity* (Alvesson & Sköldberg, 2009; Mason, 2002) and the practitioner research framework of *Exploratory Practice* (Allwright, 2005) as its core methodological approach to the building of an exploratory Case Study (Yin, 2009) within the qualitative Case Study Research tradition (Hood, 2009).

At the heart of the case study research project was the *Talkademy Business English Course*. The course was made up of a total of 10 2-hour lessons which took place in both the virtual world of Second Life® and in Skype®. The course was the result of a telecollaboration project under the umbrella of the EU funded Euroversity Network (www.euroversity.eu) which ended in November, 2014. The partners involved in the running of the course were Hull University, UK, Bielefeld University, Germany and the Talkademy online educational charity, Austria. A total of 16 people were involved in the course (teaching and support staff, and learners). Informed consent was obtained from all participants and the virtual world data was anonymised.

2.2. Data collection and analysis

The research project considered as data all of the information that was produced as part of the researcher's direct engagement with the teaching and design of the *Talkademy Business English Course* described above. In this sense, the Case Study frames and captures data that was generated during the design and implementation of the course and it includes both primary and secondary data as defined by Lamy and Hampel (2007). Recordings, screenshots and snapshots of teacher and learner activity in the virtual world platform were considered primary data. The virtual world data collected under the study was analysed from a multimodal perspective (Lamy, 2004) and made use of *visualisation* as the primary analytical tool (Mason, 2002). The data was analysed in relation to what had been identified during the data classification stage as the three main relevant features of the platform: avatars, artefacts and spaces.

3. Results and discussion

Through a systematic analysis of the case-study data in relation to the features of the virtual world and the definitions and understandings of learner participation from the literature, the following understandings of learner participation emerged.

As far as learner and teacher avatars are concerned, learner participation emerged as being characterised by a *representational* and *performative* dimension. The first dimension refers to the visual impact of the platform on users and is determined by how learner-teacher avatars appear to other avatars and themselves. The latter refers to the nature of learner interactions as avatars within the platform. Within this framework, the data indicated that avatar interaction within the context of language teaching and learning is determined by avatar proximity and positioning, avatar contextualised movement, the scope of avatar interactions and avatar-learner agency.

If we examine avatar use of virtual world artefacts and spaces through the same template, learner participation manifests itself as the sharing of information and experience, learner linguistic contributions to the environment and through the visualisation of learner-avatar intentions, understanding and learning.

In addition, the case-study data clearly indicates that there are three fundamental issues that come into play in relation to learner participation in virtual worlds. They are the learners' motivation and willingness to participate, the features of the platform and the quality of learners' interaction with these features and, last but not least, the role played by the teachers as designers of virtual world tasks and environments for learner interaction.

Finally, as video-recordings capture the interactions of language learning classrooms, current technology enables us to capture the interactions of the virtual world classroom. However, I would like to argue that the representational and performative dimensions of virtual world interactions afforded by the visual nature of the platform provide us with an additional interpretative tool. Indeed, I would argue that it is within this heightened immersive dimension that our practices and our assumptions about language education become more critically "tangible".

4. Conclusions

This paper has made use of data from an EU telecollaboration project to inform a discussion of language-learner participation in virtual worlds. Virtual world platforms have been presented both as a site for the collection of relevant data and as an analytical tool. Through the use of visualisation and the inclusion of non-verbal data as part of a multimodal approach, the study has attempted to address bias towards verbal data in the research literature. The findings are considered to be relevant to research into learner participation in general, course and task design for language learning in virtual worlds and language teacher reflectivity.

References

Allwright, D. (2005). Developing principles for practitioner research: the case of exploratory practice. *The Modern Language Journal, 89*(3), 353-366. doi:10.1111/j.1540-4781.2005.00310.x

Alvesson, M., & Sköldberg, K. (2009). *Reflexive methodology. New vistas for qualitative research* (2nd ed.). London: Sage.

Bento, R., & Schuster, C. (2003). Participation: the online challenge. In A. Aggarwal (Ed.), *Web-based education: learning from experience* (pp. 156-164). Hershey, PA: IRM Press. doi:10.4018/978-1-59140-102-5.ch010

Brown, E., Gordon, M., & Hobbs, M. (2008). Second Life as a holistic learning environment for problem-based learning and transferable skills. In A. Peachey (Ed.), *ReLIVE08: Proceedings of researching learning in virtual environment* (pp. 39-48). Milton Keynes: The Open University. Retrieved from http://www.open.ac.uk/relive08/documents/ReLIVE08_conference_proceedings_Lo.pdf

Dalgarno, B., Gregory, S., Carlson, L., Lee, M. J. W., & Tynan, B. (2013). *A systematic review and environmental analysis of the use of 3D immersive virtual worlds in Australian and New Zealand higher education institutions. Final Report 2013.* dehub Report Series 2013. Armidale NSW, Australia: University of New England and dehub. Retrieved from http://www.dehub.edu.au/downloads/VWSSP_Report_V2_TD_200613_dehub.pdf

Deutschmann, M., & Panichi, L. (2009a). Instructional design, learner modeling, and teacher practice in Second Life. In J. Molka-Danielsen & M. Deutschmann (Eds), *Learning and teaching in the virtual world of Second Life* (pp. 27-44). Trondheim: Tapir Academic Press.

Deutschmann, M., & Panichi, L. (2009b). Talking into empty space? – Signalling involvement in a virtual language classroom in Second Life. *Language Awareness, 18*(3-4), 310-328. doi:10.1080/09658410903197306

Deutschmann, M., & Panichi, L. (2013). Towards models for designing language learning in virtual worlds. *International Journal of Virtual and Personal Learning Environments, 4*(2), 65-84. doi:10.4018/jvple.2013040104

Hood, M. (2009). Case study. In J. Heigham & R. A. Croker (Eds), *Qualitative research in applied linguistics. A practical introduction* (pp. 66-90). Basingstoke: Palgrave Macmillan.

Jauregi, K., Canto, S., de Graaff, R., Koenraad, A., & Moonen, M. (2011). Verbal interaction in Second Life: towards a pedagogic framework for task design. *Computer Assisted Language Learning, 24*(1), 77-101. doi:10.1080/09588221.2010.538699

Lamy, M.-N. (2004). Oral conversations online: redefining oral competence in synchronous environments. *ReCALL, 16*(2), 520-538. doi:10.1017/S095834400400182X

Lamy, M.-N., & Hampel, R. (2007). *Online communication in language learning and teaching*. Basingstoke: Palgrave Macmillan. doi:10.1057/9780230592681

Mason, J. (2002). *Qualitative researching* (2nd ed.). London: Sage.

Molka-Danielsen, J., & Deutschmann, M. (Eds). (2009). *Learning and teaching in the virtual world of Second Life*. Trondheim: Tapir Academic Press.

Panichi, L. (2015). *Participation in language learning in virtual worlds. An exploratory case-study of a Business English Course*. PhD Thesis. School of Languages, Linguistics and Cultures, University of Hull, UK.

Panichi, L., Deutschmann, M., & Molka-Danielsen, J. (2010). Virtual worlds for language learning and intercultural exchange – Is it for real? In S. Guth and F. Helm (Eds), *Telecollaboration 2.0: languages, literacies and intercultural learning in the 21st century* (pp. 165-195). Bern: Peter Lang.

Wigham, C. R. (2012). *The interplay between nonverbal and verbal interaction in synthetic worlds which supports verbal participation and production in a foreign language*. PhD Thesis. Université Blaise Pascal, Clermont 2.

Yin, R. K. (2009). *Case study research. Design and methods* (4th ed.). Thousand Oaks, CA: Sage.

The FARE software

Adriana Pitarello[1]

Abstract. This article highlights the importance of immediate corrective feedback in tutorial software for language teaching in an academic learning environment. We aim to demonstrate that, rather than simply reporting on the performance of the foreign language learner, this feedback can act as a mediator of students' cognitive and metacognitive activity. At the theoretical level, we describe the Computer-Assisted Language Learning (CALL) environment in which this technology should be used, as well as the concept of the cognitive correction mode. This, in particular, deals with students' errors by predicting their possible responses, which can be recorded in the computer system, and by creating messages that are specific to the error and the issue. Such a correction mode aims at assisting students in resolving the proposed activities. On a practical level, this concept was translated into the FARE software, which is distinguished by its recording of messages for hits or for focusing on student errors (Focus Message), for analyzing the issue (Analyze Message), addressing the issue by means of an example (Resolve Message), and for explaining the correct answer in didactic discourse (Execute Message). We will illustrate the FARE software with the first unit of an Italian course for foreign students.

Keywords: online foreign language teaching, automatic corrective feedback, cognitive methodology.

1. Introduction

The tutorial programs of linguistic education have been becoming more and more intuitive and attractive to learners in several technical and educational respects, such as the interactive interface, multimedia content, hypertextual structure, vocal recognition program integration, online dictionary link, etc. However, the asynchronous modality of learning still lacks methodological resources that help

---

1. Universidade de São Paulo, Brasil; adrianapitarello@gmail.com

How to cite this article: Pitarello, A. (2015). The FARE software. In F. Helm, L. Bradley, M. Guarda, & S. Thouësny (Eds), *Critical CALL – Proceedings of the 2015 EUROCALL Conference, Padova, Italy* (pp. 470-474). Dublin: Research-publishing.net. http://dx.doi.org/10.14705/rpnet.2015.000377

learners to undertake the proposed linguistic competence activities successfully and, consequently, to learn the content they convey.

In this article, we propose a new learning methodology to be configured in foreign language teaching-learning tutorials that works the progression of the content presented by means of feedback provided while working on questions. In other words, our proposal is to enhance the educational efficacy of feedback from activities for promoting learning in the foreign language.

We believe it is possible to combine the value of the teacher–student interaction with the automatic feedback based on the prediction of students' answers for each question, so as to match the corrections to the individual errors. Our effort will be to act on the students' metacognition, leading them to reflect on their performance, to analyze the questions and try to solve them based on the cognitive elements of the formal learning of the language itself.

While working on a question, as well as locating any error contained in his or her answer, the student will also have access to analysis messages for the question, tips for resolution on the basis of recasts and examples, and, if still having difficulty in arriving at the solution of the question, the correct answer followed by an explanation. Such extrinsic feedback, which makes the correction steps explicit, gains relevance in setting up a tutorial program for teaching in a foreign language.

> "If extrinsic feedback is used it should always be clear what kind of mistake has been made, and the feedback should provide not only awareness as to where the mistake lies, but also how to improve the learner's performance. Wherever possible, one should avoid abrupt statements such as 'No', 'Incorrect, try again', but instead provide constructive criticism and try to anticipate and predict our learners' behaviour when completing an activity. This may be achieved by carrying out – prior to the design stage – an error analysis based, for instance, on L1 interference" (Gimeno-Sanz & Davies, 2012, section 3.12).

2. Method

The FARE software is designed to teach a foreign language to students with an academic learning style, therefore, school-educated young people or adults who have a basic grasp of the target language in question, when this does not belong to the same family as their native tongue.

The units are introduced progressively from level A1 to level C2. Each level includes approximately 30 units. Each unit is comprised of an initial input, presented in the forms of audio and transcripts, and at least one activity related to linguistic competence. The activities are primarily of the "gap completion" type, with a sequence of FARE messages available for each gap, as can be seen in the Figure 1 below.

Figure 1. FARE software activity model

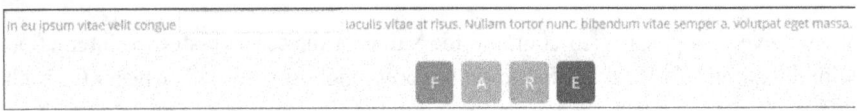

When an answer is entered in the gap, the computer system compares it with answers stored in the program database and provides the relevant message for "Focus" (F). Upon clicking that button, the student will know whether or not his or her answer is correct and, in the case of an error, will learn what the error was. If the answer has not been foreseen, the program informs the user that it was impossible to check the answer, and it invites the student to make sure they did not make any typing errors or click other buttons to obtain more information about the question to be solved.

The other buttons are always active and can be triggered at any moment while working on the activity (even before the insertion of the answer), and in the order that the student wishes to use them. The content available in "Analyze" (A) refers to the concept, to the characteristics or peculiarities of the object of the study. The content available in "Resolve" (R) is a hint on how to solve the question, with an example or an elicitation recast, such as a synonym, or the initial letters of the answer. Finally, the content available in "Execute" (E) gives the required answer followed by its justification.

3. Discussion

By means of the (meta)cognitive methodology of the FARE software, learners have the opportunity to learn the language consciously, obtaining objective answers for hypotheses that arise while working on activities and forthright information about the object of study. The anguish caused by uncertainties will give way to a feeling of encouragement to discover and face challenges that knowledge provides. Our intention is to train a critical speaker, capable of really understanding the content. The detailed feedback for each question, broken down into a freely accessible sequence, gives students the chance to build their own linguistic knowledge, testing their hypotheses and gaining control over their learning. For Howatt (1991),

> "if learning proceeds by a process of hypothesis-testing or 'trial-and-error', the response of the teacher in providing appropriate feedback is clearly crucial in promoting the development of the learner's internalized linguistic system" (p. 286).

As such, mistakes should not perplex, but should be seen as an opportunity for learning to occur. It is exactly in this sense that the proposed methodology differs from the methodology of tutorials that are well established in the market, such as Rosetta Stone and Duolingo, both of which have a methodology[2] that tends toward the behaviorist, merely testing knowledge of the language in an asynchronous manner.

Some tests were performed on the pilot FARE program in 2013, with students of Italian at the University of São Paulo (Pitarello, 2014). The results were very promising, as we found that, when they had doubts, they became visibly pensive at their computers, using cognitive strategies to arrive at the solutions of the questions without needing to press the "Execute" button (E).

4. Conclusion

We believe that the FARE software, besides acting on the intrinsic motivation of effective knowledge and of understanding the training, functioning and features of the foreign language, also acts by training critical students, who are not content just to receive information ready to be learned by heart, but, on the contrary are inspired to infer, reflect, and think.

The program has the same layout for all users, but the content it conveys is not "canned". Depending on each student's answer to a question, the program issues different messages – because the hypotheses proposed, when they do not correspond to the correct answer, are rarely the same – that lead to effective actions, going beyond the idea of working just with trial and error.

---

2. "[T]he rosetta stone/duolingo method tried to mirror how you learn your first language as a child: by showing you pictures and telling you the words for what's in the picture, etc"; retrieved from http://www.econjobrumors.com/topic/learning-a-language-the-rosetta-stoneduolingo-method-vs-the-traditional-one.

Thus, within the sphere of Critical CALL, our aim is to teach languages by means of well-planned and pedagogically sound feedback, imagining that this may be the resource that will facilitate "individualized and learner-centered learning" (Bäbler, 2006, p. 278).

5. Acknowledgments

To the University of São Paulo, where I was able to conduct my studies from graduation to doctorate; to CAPES, for the scholarships granted; to EUROCALL, for the opportunity to publish this article; to all those who believe in the potential of the FARE software; and, especially, to Humberto Fontanezi and Rafael Fernandes, software programmers for FARE.

References

Bäbler, A. (2006). Creating interactive web-based Arabic teaching material with authoring system. In K. M. Wahba, Z. A. Taha, & L. England (Eds.), *Handbook for Arabic language teaching professionals in the 21st century* (pp. 275-293). New-Jersey: Laurence Erlbaum Associates Publishers.

Gimeno-Sanz A., & Davies, G. (2012). *ICT4LT module 3.2: CALL software design and implementation*. Retrieved from http://www.ict4lt.org/en/en_mod3-2.htm

Howatt, A. P. R. A. (1991). *History of English language teaching*. Oxford: Oxford University Press.

Pitarello, A. O. (2014). *O computador nas aulas de língua estrangeira: o recurso fare em atividades de correção automática*. Doctoral thesis. São Paulo: University of São Paulo.

Learners' perceptions of online elements in a beginners' language blended course – implications for CALL design

Hélène Pulker[1] and Elodie Vialleton[2]

Abstract. Much research has been done on blended learning and the design of tasks most appropriate for online environments and computer-mediated communication. Increasingly, language teachers and Second Language Acquisition (SLA) practitioners recognise the different nature of communications in online settings and in face-to-face settings; teachers do not simply attempt to replicate face-to-face interactions in online synchronous tutorials, but combine their pedagogical expertise with the affordances of the computer-mediated system they use to produce the conditions for effective language learning. However, there is less evidence that the role and importance of the interplay between pedagogy and technology in online language teaching has been taken into consideration in the learning design of blended courses, where the emphasis is increasingly on the online elements. There is also scant evidence on students' perceptions of the online components in blended language courses. This paper reflects upon the experience of the delivery of a beginners' language course using blended learning in an open and distance learning context.

Keywords: blended learning, distance learning, CALL design.

1. Introduction

Over the years, course developers of open and distance learning materials have traditionally been using instructional design theory combining three theories

---

1. The Open University, United Kingdom; Helene.pulker@open.ac.uk
2. The Open University, United Kingdom; Elodie.vialleton@open.ac.uk

How to cite this article: Pulker, H., & Vialleton, E. (2015). Learners' perceptions of online elements in a beginners' language blended course – implications for CALL design. In F. Helm, L. Bradley, M. Guarda, & S. Thouësny (Eds), *Critical CALL – Proceedings of the 2015 EUROCALL Conference, Padova, Italy* (pp. 475-479). Dublin: Research-publishing.net. http://dx.doi.org/10.14705/rpnet.2015.000378

applicable to adult education – behaviourist, cognitivist and constructionist – to create materials that would replicate what a teacher does in the classroom. Language course developers at the Open University, UK have been following this model, designing language learning courses blending different media and different methods of delivery, thus blending learning theories according to specific learning situations. However, in the last eight years or so, course developers have been gradually integrating a fourth dimension – a connectivist approach – by increasing asynchronous online elements in their blend, replacing some of the face-to-face and instructor-led elements with online and collaborative learning elements. Research shows that blended learning is a successful method of delivery in traditional universities where asynchronous online activities complement the learning taking place in the classroom. However, there is scant literature on blended learning in the context of distance learning, and especially on the perceptions of students of the online elements within a distance learning course.

This paper reports on the second phase of a longitudinal study carried out at the Open University, UK. A three year investigation was set up to identify learners' behaviours and perceptions of the online elements of a French beginners' blended learning course designed for adults studying at a distance. The first phase of the investigation (2012-13) consisted in examining learning analytics data of learners' usage of the Virtual Learning Environment (VLE) and online elements of the course. It revealed that learners' engagement with a number of online elements, such as asynchronous interactive revision activities for example, was limited. A qualitative study was carried out in the second phase of the investigation (2013-14) to further examine learners' perceptions of the online elements of the blended course and in order to identify potential problematic areas of the blend.

2. Method

2.1. Context of study

Adult learners studying at the Open University constitute a very diverse student body with varied cultural, social and educational backgrounds. The majority is in full-time or part-time employment or taking a career break. The medium age is over 45 and 66% are female. Most importantly, students have different goals, aspirations and motivations for studies, and they do exercise some autonomy when engaging with the course (Coleman & Furnborough, 2010). Most students registered on the French beginners' module are new to language learning, and for the majority it is the first module they have studied at the Open University and in distance-learning mode.

The Open University model of blended learning for beginners language courses combines the five key ingredients of the Agilant Learning Model (Carman, 2005), including: live tutorials in the classroom and online through a web-conferencing system, online content (activities, tools and resources in the VLE), collaboration (face-to-face and in online discussions through forums), assessment (four tutor-marked assignments, four interactive computer-marked assignments and one end-of-module assignment, all submitted electronically), and reference learning materials (course books, study guides, feedback, study resources in the VLE, etc.). Every ingredient of the blend incorporates the factors listed by Pankin, Roberts, and Savio (2012), i.e. schedule (synchronous and asynchronous), participation (individual and in the community), technology (online and offline), and guidance (instructor-led and self-paced activities). Learners had approximately 20 hours of a mix of synchronous and asynchronous contact with their teacher and general support. They studied from October 2013 to September 2014.

2.2. Data collection and analysis

We conducted the second phase of the study throughout the 2013-14 academic year. We contacted the 27 students who had failed to submit their second assignment in March and the 51 students who had failed to submit their third assignment in May. Four students volunteered to participate in a qualitative survey: three were new to the Open University, one was continuing their studies, three were registered on a degree programme and one was studying the French beginners' course as a stand alone module. We conducted a one-hour telephone interview with each participant. Each interview was recorded and transcribed verbatim. The qualitative data was analysed following a thematic analysis approach and a coding system based on the dimensions of Carman's (2005) Agilant Learning model of blended learning.

3. Discussion

Blended learning provides new opportunities of interaction with peers and teachers for the language learners. It can develop communication and digital literacy skills, and foster independent and collaborative learning as asynchronous discussions allow time and mental space for reflection, and therefore students have the opportunity to be part of a community of learners and be responsible for constructing their own learning. Blended learning is even seen as a possible way to overcome the challenges of distance education, isolation and self-motivation, and potentially transform education through critical reflection (Garrison & Archer, 2000; Mezirow, 1991). However, the findings of phase two of our study show that an increased amount of asynchronous support and activities has not addressed the lack of social interaction which is a critical aspect of distance learning. Despite the richness and quality of interactions in online forums between students themselves and between teachers and students, the participation is only limited to a minority of students whose learning styles suit this mode of communication. Students expressed a preference for conventional methods of learning (books and face-to-face tutorials) for practical, technical and also pedagogical reasons.

Participants also reported a lack of clarity about the purpose of some of the online activities and of some of the resources and tools (for example, the pronunciation guide). The first phase of the study, using learning analytics, revealed general low usage of online forums and online materials, as well as a general preference for a structured and linear sequence of activities. The phase two interviews revealed a clear sense of confusion, suggesting that a certain type of learners on beginners' language distance courses may respond better to formal rather than informal approaches to language learning.

4. Conclusions

Collis (2003) points out that online learning components often require a large amount of self-discipline on the part of the learners and Simpson (2013) argues that the most important individual success criterion is the student's motivation to learn, and that universities should redirect their efforts on reaching out to students and maintaining their initial motivation levels "rather than focusing entirely on teaching" (p. 112). We may therefore ask how blended learning in distance education can foster self-regulation and autonomy. Do we encourage our learners to reflect sufficiently on their own learning and are we explicit enough about the purpose of the materials and about how they can find their own pathways to meet their personal goals? Should we expect students to design and agree on personal learning plans? Moreover, our study further suggests that evidence should be sought about whether or how asynchronous elements of a blended course facilitate language learning, and that more enquiries would be required to investigate aspects of informal learning in language acquisition in the context of blended language learning.

5. Acknowledgements

We would like to thank Linda Murphy for her encouragement and support in our preparation for this paper.

References

Carman, J. (2005). *Blended learning design: five key ingredients*. Retrieved from http://www.agilantlearning.com/instructionaldesign.html

Coleman, J., & Furnborough, C. (2010). Learner characteristics and learning outcomes on a distance Spanish course for beginners. *System, 38*(1), 14-29. doi:10.1016/j.system.2009.12.002

Collis, B. (2003). Putting blended learning. In C. Bonk & C. Graham, C. (Eds), *Handbook of blended learning: global perspectives, local designs*. San Fransisco, CA: Pfeiffer Publishing.

Garrison, D., & Archer, W. (2000). *A transactional perspective on teaching-learning: a framework for adult and higher education*. Oxford, UK: Pergamon.

Mezirow, J. (1991). *Transformative dimensions of adult learning*. San Francisco, CA: Jossey-Bass.

Pankin, J., Roberts, J., & Savio, M. (2012). *Blended learning at MIT*. Retrieved from http://web.mit.edu/training/trainers/resources/blended_learning_at_mit.pdf

Simpson, O. (2013). Student retention in distance education: are we failing our students? *Open Learning, 28*(2), 105-119. doi:10.1080/02680513.2013.847363

A TELL English course to meet the needs of a multilevel BA in ELT group: what was wrong?

María del Carmen Reyes Fierro[1] and Natanael Delgado Alvarado[2]

Abstract. A Technology Enhanced Language Learning (TELL) course was designed to meet the needs of a multilevel first-semester group of students of the BA in English Language Teaching (ELT) taught at the School of Languages of the Juarez University of the State of Durango (ELE-UJED), Mexico. Amongst the relevant needs, students were to reach a CEFR B1.1 level of English (out of two CEFR B1 sub-levels), notwithstanding their very different overall skill level of English. They also had to be immersed in active, student-centred learning approaches in spite of the wide diversity of language teaching approaches used in their 5-7 previous curricular English courses, or possible additional study in Mexico or abroad. After the results of diagnostic tests and self-assessment checklists, teams were integrated according to similar levels of command. Empirical research carried out throughout the course and a post-study survey demonstrated that the integration of collaborative learning and technology-enhanced language learning, including computer-based assessment and video clip outcomes, were very useful elements for reaching the course goals. However, it was also found out that the designed checklists for self-monitoring of progress were not used by students on a regular basis, even though the survey reported that only a quarter of them considered checklists as not useful/not very useful for raising awareness of their lacks, weaknesses, and strengths.

Keywords: task-based language teaching, course design, technology enhanced language learning, TELL, self-regulated learning strategies.

---

1. Juarez University of the State of Durango (UJED), Mexico, a PhD student at the University of Southampton, UK; mreyes@ujed.mx
2. Juarez University of the State of Durango (UJED), Mexico, a PhD student at the University of Southampton, UK; ndelgado@ujed.mx

How to cite this article: Reyes Fierro, M. d. C., Delgado Alvarado, N. (2015). A TELL English course to meet the needs of a multilevel BA in ELT group: what was wrong?. In F. Helm, L. Bradley, M. Guarda, & S. Thouësny (Eds), *Critical CALL – Proceedings of the 2015 EUROCALL Conference, Padova, Italy* (pp. 480-485). Dublin: Research-publishing.net. http://dx.doi.org/10.14705/rpnet.2015.000379

1. Introduction

After the first cohort of graduates, a study was carried out to identify the real levels of English of selected groups. Among the most relevant findings from the application of the online Dialang exam, a complete heterogeneity of both overall average levels and each of the skills and language system components was found. To find out alternatives to this problem, a protocol for a PhD by research was designed: "how technology-enhanced learning could be designed for English courses taught to a BA in ELT multilevel group in a Mexican university" (Reyes Fierro, in progress).

After the international policies for higher education related to innovation in the knowledge society through the use of information and communication technologies, our 21st century students use technology for almost every aspect of their lives. Therefore, any innovation in language teaching (as promotion of learning) must fall into the TELL arena. Accordingly, this research is aimed at finding out a TELL design pattern for solving out the complex problem of poor learner development into a bilingual communicator, as a result of studying only under standardised contents higher or lower than the students' possibilities or achievement potential.

The TELL course under design is underpinned by current language learning approaches and curriculum-syllabus-course literature acknowledged as a domain for discussing "the concerns of language teaching" (White, 1988, p. 21). In the general technology enhanced learning, also identified as e-learning or educational technology, there is a current trend equivalent to the language course design: "Learning Design" (LD), defined by Conole (2013) as "a methodology for enabling teachers/designers to make more informed decisions in how they go about designing learning activities and interventions, which is pedagogically informed and makes effective use of appropriate resources and technologies" (Kindle location: 724-726). Thus, the richness of LD could be an excellent source of knowledge and technological advances transferable to the TELL arena.

The current design is intended to meet the requirements of the Competence-Based Approach (CBA) under which the ELE-UJED and the whole university must redesign their curricula for all careers. In ELT, the Common European Framework of Reference for Languages (CEFR) offers a well-organised range of competences in terms of can-do descriptors and theoretical background for designing language courses. In addition to the CBA, Task-Based Language Teaching (TBLT), the Lexical Approach, and Cooperative Language Learning, considered under the umbrella of Communicative Language Teaching, are taken into account by the study.

2. Method

The first part of the study starts with an empirical research on the implementation of a course under the task-based teaching with technology approach, with a group of 28 first-semester students attending the English Language Development I course. A diagnosis of level of English, overall and per strand, was carried out, along with an oral exam and self-assessment of technological skills. After the results were obtained, five teacher assistants were identified on the basis of their above-average level of English. Teams were integrated with learners with similar levels under an assistant-teacher as the leader. A C1-level student was in charge of coordinating the team of assistant-teachers. At the end, it was found out that there were only two dropouts for reasons not related to achievement, as opposed to the usual average of six.

Apart from the teacher's records and results of assessment and evaluation, a survey was carried out to identify the learners' perceptions of the course.

3. Discussion

In the survey, learners acknowledged most of the benefits of the course, such as the usefulness of Dialang, Moodle, computer driven assessments, the use of Internet resources, peer and team collaborative learning, and individual development of generic competences selected for the course. These include knowledge and use of digital technologies, self-responsibility for own learning (both rated the highest), peer assessing classmates' work and performance, and self-assessing of own work and performance (both rated as the lowest).

Three main results within the survey and the teacher's record are worth mentioning. From the learners' perceptions in the survey, which were wrong, the most relevant were: (1) an overuse of the computer and/or platform; (2) having too much independent work which "stressed them and distracted them from learning"; and (3) it was found out, as reported in the teacher's records, that most of the learners did not use the checklists on a regular basis.

As these results show, learners are not used to reflect on their/others' learning and appear not to be aware of their learning gains nor the process they need to go through in order to reach them. Accordingly, main changes must be made to systematically incorporate self-regulated learning strategies and a whole redesign to prevent students' dependence on assistant-teachers, carrying out only activities prescribed in tasks.

4. Discussion and conclusions

Since the second stage of the research is the re-design of model and abstraction of pattern after which another course will be designed as a means of piloting, the following changes are proposed on the basis of the problems identified in the first design and implementation.

Concerning the lack of awareness of learners' learning gains and the learning process itself, it is proposed a systematic incorporation of self-regulated learning strategies, cognitive, metacognitive and resource-based, by means of the learning ePortfolio fostering self-regulated learning in three cyclical phases: Forethought, Performance, and Self-Reflection (Zimmerman, 2000). In the forethought phase, when learners set their own goals and design their own plans, they will be offered the opportunity of selecting and adapting critical thinking along with metacognitive and resource-oriented strategies (including exchange with other learners and help seeking). Then, in the performance phase, learners implement their plans in a first attempt to complete the task and publish it as a draft. Finally, in the self-reflection phase, learners reflect on feedback and improve their drafts in order to produce and publish a final version of the task in question.

Figure 1. The final, medium, or initial position of the outcomes determines the type of design as forward, central, or backward (based on Richards & Rodgers, 2014, p. 365)

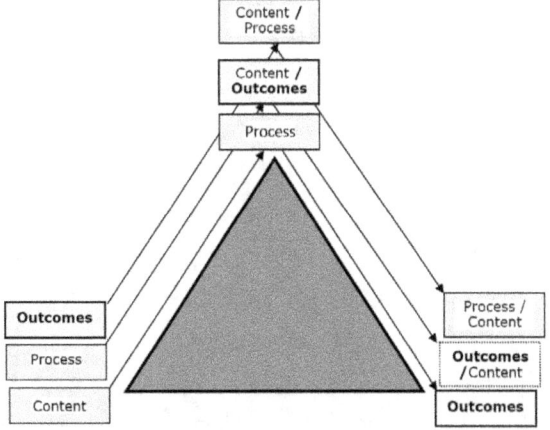

From Richards and Rodgers's (2014) classification of curriculum into forward, central and backward, based on the relationship among its elements and "the process by which they are arrived at" (p. 363), the proposed course can be designed as a backward one, that is, it will start with the outcome instead of the input (Figure 1). In doing so, learners first reflect on their previous knowledge and skills and design outcomes accordingly.

Instead of the TELL with technology tasks, a task-like project blended-learning course will be considered with the tasks designed by learners in teams of learners from the different learning levels resulting from the diagnostic exams. Four cycles instead of three will integrate the design: the Planning Cycle, exemplified in Figure 2, to develop a sense of learning, and the Pre-task, Task, and Post-task cycles, also designed by learners.

There will be two different groups of six tasks each: the core tasks aimed at developing the competences of the B1.1 course and complementary tasks to be carried out by teams or pairs with similar interests and/or needs in connection with can-does (CEFR descriptors of foreign language performance) they lack and need to study, can-does at upper levels, special learning interests such as songs, movies, conversations, etc. Both types of tasks will be developed in 16-hour classes and 16-hour independent study, as stated by the course (Figure 2).

Figure 2. Domains of language use that the learners need to acquire (Reyes Fierro, in progress)

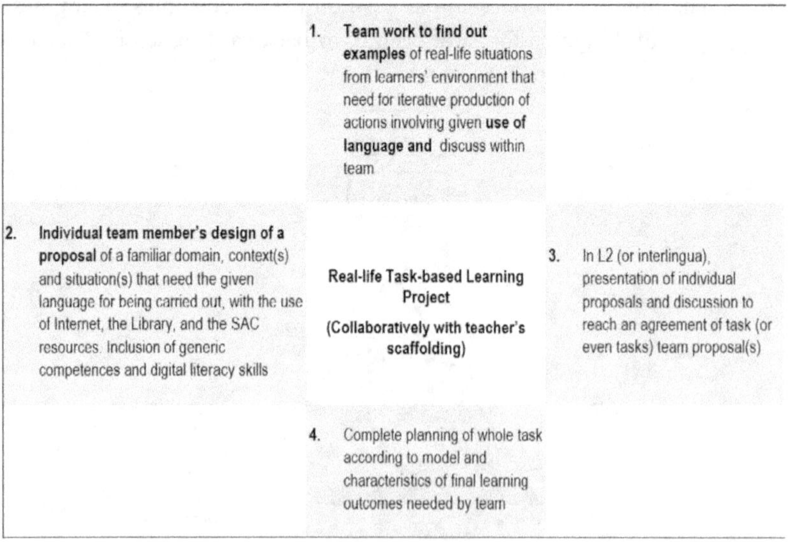

	1. Team work to find out **examples** of real-life situations from learners' environment that need for iterative production of actions involving given **use of language and** discuss within team	
2. Individual team member's design of a **proposal** of a familiar domain, context(s) and situation(s) that need the given language for being carried out, with the use of Internet, the Library, and the SAC resources. Inclusion of generic competences and digital literacy skills	**Real-life Task-based Learning Project** (Collaboratively with teacher's scaffolding)	3. In L2 (or interlingua), presentation of individual proposals and discussion to reach an agreement of task (or even tasks) team proposal(s)
	4. Complete planning of whole task according to model and characteristics of final learning outcomes needed by team	

5. Acknowledgements

Authors would like to thank their supervisors PhD Alasdair Archibald and MA(Ed) Vicky Wright, their common advisor SFHEA Julie Watson as well as the authorities at the University of Southampton, UK and the Juarez University of the State of Durango (UJED), Mexico.

References

Conole, G. (2013). *Designing for learning in an open world: 4 (Explorations in the Learning Sciences, Instructional Systems and Performance Technologies)* [Kindle Edition]. New York: Springer. doi:10.1007/978-1-4419-8517-0

Reyes Fierro, M. d. C. (in progress). *How technology-enhanced learning could be designed for English courses taught to a BA in ELT multilevel group in a Mexican university.* Doctoral thesis. United Kingdom: University of Southampton.

Richards, J. C., & Rodgers, T. S. (2014). *Approaches and methods in language teaching* (3rd ed.). Cambridge, UK: Cambridge University Press.

White, R. V. (1988). *The ELT curriculum: design, innovation and management.* Oxford, U.K. and Cambridge, MA, USA: Blackwell Publishers.

Zimmerman, B. J. (2000). Attaining self-regulation: a social cognitive perspective. In M. Boekaerts, P. R. Pintrich, & M. Zeidner (Eds.), *Handbook of self-regulation* (pp. 13-40). San Diego, California: Academic Press. doi:10.1016/B978-012109890-2/50031-7

Implementing an online vocabulary training program

Charles E. Robertson[1]

Abstract. Although vocabulary acquisition research has shed much light on practical methods for increasing lexical knowledge (Nation, 1994), many foreign language teachers hesitate to implement focused vocabulary-training programs in their classrooms. The reasons most often cited for this hesitation are associated with the difficult tasks of creating, managing and disseminating vocabulary sets. Luckily, an online-based solution has emerged, i.e. Quizlet® (https://quizlet.com/). Quizlet® is a free online flashcard program that supports various vocabulary training approaches. Originally created by a high school student as a means to learn French vocabulary items, Quizlet® has grown to become the most popular online flashcard system in the world with over 20 million registered users. Moreover, Quizlet® continues to add functionality to the website and its excellent mobile applications. According to quantcast.com, more than 20 percent of Quizlet® page views originate from mobile device browsers. Of particular interest to foreign language instructors is Quizlet®'s capability to support vocabulary terms in multiple languages (through its audio and auto-define functions) and create class and individual student progress reports. The author has successfully integrated Quizlet® into a variety of university-level English courses in Japan and hopes to introduce this powerful teaching and learning resource to other foreign language instructors.

Keywords: vocabulary flashcards, intentional vocabulary instruction, word knowledge, mobile learning.

1. Introduction

In 2012, the author taught a science-themed reading course which emphasized the acquisition of science and technology vocabulary. The students, second and third-year university science and engineering majors at a private Japanese university,

---

1. Aoyama Gakuin University, Tokyo, Japan; pacificenglishteacher@gmail.com

How to cite this article: Robertson, C. E. (2015). Implementing an online vocabulary training program. In F. Helm, L. Bradley, M. Guarda, & S. Thouësny (Eds), *Critical CALL – Proceedings of the 2015 EUROCALL Conference, Padova, Italy* (pp. 486-489). Dublin: Research-publishing.net. http://dx.doi.org/10.14705/rpnet.2015.000380

were eager to read articles related to emerging technologies; however, their lack of general vocabulary (let alone knowledge of English for Science and Technology) often caused frustration. This class was large (48 students) and English proficiency levels varied greatly with TOEIC scores ranging from the low 300s to the high 600s. Equally problematic was the inability of most students to organize new vocabulary terms in any meaningful way. The course textbook included a bilingual glossary at the end of each reading passage with sample sentences of "difficult" and/or "technical" terms, yet few students produced their own vocabulary notes. As the author understood the prevailing theories of second-language vocabulary acquisition and was aware of some methods for increasing students' lexical knowledge, he knew that he needed to actively engage his students in targeted-vocabulary training. Specifically, the author wanted his students to be able to effectively create personalized vocabulary sets, study these sets through flashcard-type activities and track their own performance. In other words, it was important to the author that students could manage their own learning. Additionally, as the course instructor, the author wanted to be able to manage and track their performance from within a single program (if possible) and at no cost to students. Finally, an ideal flashcard program would support mobile-based learning through a well-designed mobile application. And while various flashcard systems existed at this time, the author was frustrated at the prospect of being forced to use several web-based solutions in order to realize his ideal vocabulary training program. In the end, after investigating a variety of free web-based flashcard sites and content management system-based programs, the author decided to integrate Quizlet® into his classroom instruction.

2. Experience

Teachers will appreciate the versatility and simplicity of Quizlet®. The process to establish an account, create a bilingual vocabulary set and house this set can be accomplished in minutes. Additionally, teachers can easily guide students through the registration process to activate their free user accounts and download the mobile application. It has been the author's experience that following the initial registration procedure and a 15-minute teacher-led orientation, students soon develop the confidence necessary to utilize Quizlet® outside of the classroom.

Beyond its ease of use, Quizlet® offers several key features which make it a particularly powerful resource from both a learner and instructor perspective. With Quizlet®, students can create and edit vocabulary sets from a PC and/or mobile device, which gives them greater control and responsibility over their own learning. Students can then self-study through various games and quizzes based on these vocabulary sets as well as measure their performance against themselves and other classmates. With the latest PC version of Quizlet®, there are six "study modes and games", available to help users memorize content, and three "study modes and games" through its mobile application. The participants of one study, which compared the effectiveness of three flashcard websites (Chien, 2015), reported that they had "positive attitudes" toward learning vocabulary through these type of web-based activities. Furthermore, these participants mentioned the Quizlet® Speller activity as their favorite, followed by the Test, Scatter, and Space Race activities. As mentioned earlier, students can also improve their listening and pronunciation skills as vocabulary items can be heard in 18 languages (through text-to-speech audio with native-speaker quality) and recorded by users.

With a Quizlet® Teacher account (annual subscription rate: US$24.99), teachers can take advantage of several useful tools to help them manage individual and class performance. In particular, the Class Progress function (which resides within each vocabulary set) groups vocabulary items according to the percentage of time that students correctly identify terms. As a result, "difficult" or unknown vocabulary will appear at the top of the report under the *Students get these terms right 0%-10% of the time* header, whereas, "easier" and/or mastered vocabulary will appear at the bottom of the page under the *Students get these terms right 90%-100% of the time* banner. After students have had a chance to study and practice a given set, the Class Progress report breaks down class proficiency in terms of what a class (as a whole) has scored correctly *0%-10%, 10%-25%, 25%-50%, 50%-75%, 75%-90%, 90%-100%* of the time. Also included in this report is a "study activity" log for each student. This data displays the type of study activity which a student has engaged in, and this information can be selected to reflect the activities completed within the past day, week, month, and year. Taken together, these reports assisted the author to prioritize vocabulary items for review and testing purposes and gauge individual student effort.

Quizlet® allows students and teachers to create customized vocabulary sets in two powerful ways: first, users can copy and edit content from the over 87 million user-generated study sets which are publicly shared; and second, users can copy and edit content from within non-shared study sets. The first benefit means that Quizlet® users do not have to recreate existing vocabulary sets, saving them significant amounts of time. Moreover, this encourages collaboration among teachers who can divide the task of creating large bilingual vocabulary sets which often require a native-speaker to double-check definitions and/or sample sentences. The second benefit of the Quizlet® editing function enables teachers to choose who can edit a particular set of terms. When editing rights are given to students, they can work together to efficiently create vocabulary sets of unknown terms, thus reducing wasted time spent on reviewing mastered items.

3. Conclusions

There is growing research which suggests that the incorporation of multimedia and technology in English learning has become the preferred manner of instruction among students (Hu & Deng, 2007). Additionally, it has been reported that students who have engaged in intentional vocabulary learning via online vocabulary websites have reported increased motivation, which has led, in turn, to improved vocabulary and increased vocabulary knowledge (Chien, 2015). Milliner (2013), for example, has measured the positive effects on student receptive vocabulary knowledge and standardized test performance through the use of Quizlet®. Online flashcard websites enable learners to acquire receptive and productive vocabulary skills through interactive and engaging activities. Moreover, these websites assist students to broaden their vocabulary knowledge to include information related to the form, use and meaning of vocabulary items.

4. Acknowledgements

I would like to thank Brett Milliner at Tamagawa University for introducing me to Quizlet®.

References

Chien, C.-W. (2015). Analysis the effectiveness of three online vocabulary flashcard websites on L2 learners' level of lexical knowledge. *English Language Teaching, 8*(5),111-121. doi:10.5539/elt.v8n5p111

Hu, H.-P., & Deng, L.-J. (2007). Vocabulary acquisition in multimedia environment. *US-China Foreign Language, 5*(8), 55-59.

Milliner, B. (2013). Using online flashcard software to raise business students' TOEIC scores. *Annual Report of JACET SIG on ESP, 15*, 51-60.

Nation, I. S. P. (Ed.). (1994). *New ways in teaching vocabulary*. Alexandria, Virginia: TESOL, Inc.

La sfida dell'ambiente Web 2.0 nella didattica delle lingue minori

Edit Rózsavölgyi[1]

Abstract. Nell'ultimo ventennio lo sviluppo tecnologico, le istanze della crescente globalizzazione e le nuove esigenze della società nei confronti dell'istruzione, in particolare dell'insegnamento delle lingue straniere, oltre che i risultati degli studi sul processo dell'acquisizione nei campi della psicologia cognitiva, della sociologia e della linguistica teorica ed applicata, hanno sollecitato le ricerche nell'ambito della glottodidattica. Gli obiettivi e le modalità dell'apprendimento sono cambiati. Molti lavori hanno evidenziato il fatto che le nuove tecnologie, in particolare gli strumenti dell'ambiente Web 2.0, si prestano ad essere adoperati anche nell'insegnamento delle lingue straniere. Il contesto delle lingue minori offre la possibilità di mettere in atto indagini qualitative nella sfera dell'apprendimento tele-collaborativo contribuendo alle nostre conoscenze in maniera diversa rispetto alle analisi di indirizzo prevalentemente quantitativo che costituiscono la grande maggioranza degli apporti in questo settore di ricerca. In base alle nostre esperienze nell'ambito di un progetto eTandem italo-ungherese, in questo contributo ribadiamo l'utilità di esplorare le specificità individuali degli apprendenti per poter predisporre ambiti di studio sempre più stimolanti e personalizzati nell'ottica di crescere l'autonomia degli studenti.

Parole chiave: glottodidattica, *eTandem*, lingue minori.

1. Introduzione

Oggi la comunicazione ha carattere sempre più interculturale, perciò la competenza comunicativa interculturale deve essere sviluppata negli allievi di una L2. Per attuare tale proposito può essere utile adottare nella didattica gli strumenti del *Web 2.0* che hanno rivoluzionato il mondo della comunicazione, della condivisione e

---

1. Università degli Studi di Padova, Italia; edit.r@unipd.it

How to cite this article: Rózsavölgyi, E. (2015). La sfida dell'ambiente Web 2.0 nella didattica delle lingue minori. In F. Helm, L. Bradley, M. Guarda, & S. Thouësny (Eds), *Critical CALL – Proceedings of the 2015 EUROCALL Conference, Padova, Italy* (pp. 490-494). Dublin: Research-publishing.net. http://dx.doi.org/10.14705/rpnet.2015.000381

della collaborazione tra persone geograficamente distanti. Promuovere pratiche telecollaborative favorisce la cooperazione didattica con costi contenuti e con il coinvolgimento di un numero maggiore di studenti in scambi interculturali dove gli ambienti virtuali sostituiscono quelli reali.

La letteratura di riferimento è basata in larga misura su lavori svolti nel contesto della lingua inglese. E'stato riconosciuto però che il panorama socio-culturale può influenzare i risultati delle indagini (Ushioda & Dörnyei, 2012). Questo contributo si pone l'obiettivo di indagare, in base a una sperimentazione pilota *eTandem* italo-ungherese, su che cosa di positivo l'uso delle nuove tecnologie nel curriculum universitario può aggiungere alla metodologia dell'insegnamento delle lingue straniere mettendo in evidenza gli aspetti specifici delle lingue minori. Riporteremo i punti di forza e di criticità della nostra esperienza come risultati di una microanalisi intensiva delle interazioni, dei dialoghi collaborativi e delle dinamiche sociali, culturali e psicologiche dei partecipanti al progetto.

2. Background teorico

La principale innovazione nella glottodidattica e in particolare nelle ricerche sull'apprendimento di una L2 degli ultimi anni è stata quella di porre al centro dell'attenzione l'apprendente e la sua autonomia. Quest'ultima viene vista come uno degli obiettivi dell'apprendimento stesso. La sua realizzazione condiziona fortemente la pratica didattica e porta inevitabilmente alla trasformazione dei ruoli di ambedue i protagonisti, docenti e studenti, dell'acquisizione linguistica.

Il quadro di riferimento teorico delle nostre ricerche si colloca nell'ambito del cognitivismo. La teoria socio-cognitiva definisce l'apprendimento come acquisizione di conoscenze attraverso l'elaborazione cognitiva di informazioni. Viene enfatizzato il ruolo dell'agentività umana (*agency*), intesa come la capacità di agire attivamente nel contesto in cui si è inseriti, per fare scelte, per progettare e generare azioni mirate a determinati obiettivi e per motivarne e disciplinarne l'esecuzione. Essa comprende anche la facoltà metacognitiva di contemplare se stessi e di riflettere sulle proprie azioni e sui propri ragionamenti (Bandura, 2006). L'idea di una partecipazione attiva della persona nel proprio processo di apprendimento, sotto forma di autoregolazione (*selfregulation*), è parte integrante anche dell'approccio socio-culturale contemporaneo di impronta vygotskyana (Dörnyei, 2005, p. 191).

L'agentività/autoregolazione e la personalità sono i concetti chiave di collegamento delle teorie socio-cognitiva e socio-culturale da una parte e di quella dell'autonomia dall'altra, le prime rappresentando il punto di partenza dello sviluppo dell'autonomia, la seconda costituendone uno dei risultati più significativi. Non si può prescindere inoltre del ruolo fondamentale che la motivazione gioca nell'innesco dei processi di autonomia e dell'apprendimento in generale. La relazione tra motivazione, autonomia e agentività/autoregolazione è data dal fatto che tutte richiedono il coinvolgimento attivo da parte dell'apprendente.

Nell'ottica delineata sopra l'autonomia significa dunque capacità di avere il controllo sulle proprie azioni, di mantenere e aumentare la propria motivazione di fronte a fattori di distrazione ed esperienze emotivamente negative, di avere la facoltà di riflettere in maniera produttiva sul proprio processo di apprendimento, di mettersi in una posizione di partecipante attivo nell'apprendimento.

3. L'eTandem italo-ungherese *Danubadria*

La sperimentazione che costituisce la base empirica della nostra ricerca è rappresentata dal progetto *eTandem* chiamato *Danubadria* in virtù del fatto che coinvolge l'ungherese e l'italiano, due lingue parlate lungo due vie di comunicazione europee importantissime: il Danubio e il Mar Adriatico. Il programma è stato realizzato nel 2011. In questa sede per mancanza di spazio non ci è concesso fornire una descrizione dettagliata della nostra esperienza per la quale si rimanda a Rózsavölgyi e Guglielmi (2011) e Rózsavölgyi (2014). Riporteremo qui i risultati della nostra indagine soffermandoci sugli aspetti positivi di *Danubadria* che superano di gran lunga le aree di criticità, ridotte di fatto ad alcuni contesti della pratica quotidiana come difficoltà nel trovarsi con scadenza regolare prestabilita per le sessioni *eTandem* dovuta al calendario accademico differente delle università di provenienza, divario nei tempi di realizzazione dei compiti, mancanza di variazione dei canali di comunicazione e simili.

La nostra ricerca ha evidenziato che la spinta motivazionale iniziale dello studente di ungherese è alta e di tipo integrativo, legata alla sfera affettiva. Abbiamo riscontrato nello stesso tempo una scarsa autostima negli apprendenti e difficoltà nel 'mettersi in gioco'. Questo quadro ci ha dato un'indicazione precisa sul fatto che tra le finalità del progetto doveva essere contemplato il potenziamento dell'agentività degli studenti a pari passo con la capacità comunicativa interculturale. A questo proposito sono stati messi in opera diversi stratagemmi tra i quali elenchiamo qui di seguito i più significativi.

In fase progettuale l'elaborazione dei dati di un questionario compilato dai partecipanti ha reso possibile una formazione 'sapiente' delle coppie. E' stato scelto un protocollo con autogestione mediata da docenti-*tutor* con valenza curricolare per creare un ambiente personalizzato e flessibile. Per garantire una cornice minima di lavoro comune e per regolare le interazioni si è istituito un protocollo di intesa condiviso con gli studenti.

La piattaforma di lavoro (*Wiki PBworks* con accesso riservato ai partecipanti) è stata percepita come uno spazio diviso in due corsie: la prima è un forum di informazione e di assistenza di carattere generale e uno spazio di socializzazione per l'intero gruppo di *eTandem*, la seconda uno spazio didattico personalizzato per ogni singola coppia con forum, archiviazione dei materiali e tutoraggio. Si è creato così un doppio livello di *scaffolding* ('impalcatura'), uno interno specifico di ogni coppia con sostegno tra pari e da parte dei *tutor* e uno esterno 'perimetrale' ad uso di tutto il gruppo. Questo tipo di costruzione ha sollecitato un alto grado di intensità dialogica e di vicinanza tra tutti i partecipanti, docenti-*tutor* compresi e ha reso possibile percorsi personalizzati.

Il programma *task-based*, organizzato seguendo anche i suggerimenti degli apprendenti, ha ridotto la potenziale dispersione delle informazioni grazie alla possibilità di archiviare e condividere i materiali e agli interventi sul forum. Ha richiesto processi di negoziazione e mediazione impegnativi tra i pari e i *tutor* rafforzando l'identificazione in un progetto formativo comune, oltre che l'interdipendenza positiva tra i partner e l'efficacia dell'azione attiva di tutoraggio sostenendo alla base le istanze motivazionali e di autonomia.

Nel campo delle competenze linguistiche abbiamo lasciato libertà per ogni coppia di decidere quali aspetti della lingua dovessero essere rafforzati durante la creazione dei materiali di consegna e di trovare un equilibrio tra la correttezza grammaticale e la scioltezza discorsiva privilegiando così obiettivi pragmalinguistici ('imparare a fare con la lingua").

4. Conclusioni

I vantaggi della tele-collaborazione integrata e di sostegno all'apprendimento in *eTandem Danubadria* possono essere ricondotti a due principali filoni di dinamiche formative:

- costruzione collaborativa dei contenuti e del programma di lavoro:

- doppio circuito di tutoraggio personalizzato dove condividere i processi di apprendimento.

La personalizzazione nell'*eTandem* ha significato per gli studenti l'adattamento dei propri approcci, bisogni e aspettative all'ambiente tecnologico negoziando con il partner e l'incremento della consapevolezza sul proprio apprendimento e agentività; per i *tutor* il coinvolgimento cognitivo, sociale ed emotivo degli studenti nel processo dell'apprendimento interpretando e stimolando le loro motivazioni, creando delle sfide potenzialmente raggiungibili, assecondando le caratteristiche specifiche delle singole persone nella strutturazione dei *task* e stimolando riflessioni metacognitive.

Questo tipo di lavoro 'fino' ha naturalmente ricadute di diversi esiti sulle persone coinvolte, ma può essere realizzato senz'altro con più facilità nell'ambito delle lingue 'di nicchia' che a loro volta possono contribuire con indagini di matrice qualitativa come quella che abbiamo riportato qui agli studi sul CALL in generale.

Riferimenti bibliografici

Bandura, A. (2006). Toward a psychology of human agency. *Perspectives on Psychological Science, 1*(2), 164-180. doi:10.1111/j.1745-6916.2006.00011.x

Dörnyei, Z. (2005). *The psychology of the language learner: individual differences in second language acquisition*. London: Lawrence Erlbaum.

Rózsavölgyi, E. (2014). Motivare gli studenti in ambiente Web 2.0. In C. Cervini & A. C. Valdiviezo V. (a cura di), *Dispositivi formativi e modalità ibride per l'apprendimento linguistico* (p. 16). Bologna: CLUEB, Collana Contesti Linguistici. Retrieved from http://clueb.it/libreria/contesti-linguistici/dispositivi-formativi-e-modalita-ibride-per-lapprendimento-linguistico/

Rózsavölgyi, E., & Guglielmi, L. (2011). Peer correction and learner's self perception of motivation and autonomy in an Italian-Hungarian eTandem. In G. Raţă (Ed.), *Academic days of Timişoara: language education today* (pp. 450-465). Newcastle upon Tyne: Cambridge Scholars Publishing.

Ushioda, E., & Dörnyei, Z. (2012). Motivation. In S. Gass & A. Mackey (Eds.), *The Routledge handbook of second language acquisition* (pp. 396-409). New York: Routledge. doi:10.1057/9781137032829.0009

Is mobile-assisted language learning really useful? An examination of recall automatization and learner autonomy

Takeshi Sato[1], Fumiko Murase[2], and Tyler Burden[3]

Abstract. The aim of this study is to examine the advantages of Mobile-Assisted Language Learning (MALL), especially vocabulary learning of English as a foreign or second language (L2) in terms of the two strands: automatization and learner autonomy. Previous studies articulate that technology-enhanced L2 learning could bring about some positive effects. The use of technological functions in a mobile device, for example, might activate learning processes, resulting in the easier recall of the target vocabulary. In addition to this, mobile-assisted L2 learning could also facilitate learners' agency or autonomous learning in that successful MALL should rely largely on the agency (Pachler, Bachmair, & Cook, 2010) as an autonomous learner. While engaging in L2 learning with mobile devices, L2 learners should be expected to be autonomous agents not only by receiving knowledge and messages from peers and teachers but also by responding to them. These processes differ from those such as passively listening to the teacher and receiving knowledge from the teacher. From this standpoint, empirical and questionnaire studies are conducted to verify that MALL could enhance the recall of the target phrases for L2 writing and also learners' autonomy, in comparison with paper-based vocabulary learning.

Keywords: mobile assisted language learning, vocabulary recall, writing, learner autonomy.

---

1. Tokyo University of Agriculture and Technology, Japan; tsato@cc.tuat.ac.jp
2. Tokyo University of Agriculture and Technology, Japan; fmurase@cc.tuat.ac.jp
3. Meisei University, Japan; burden.tyler@meisei-u.ac.jp

How to cite this article: Sato, T., Murase, F., & Burden, T. (2015). Is mobile-assisted language learning really useful? An examination of recall automatization and learner autonomy. In F. Helm, L. Bradley, M. Guarda, & S. Thouësny (Eds), *Critical CALL – Proceedings of the 2015 EUROCALL Conference, Padova, Italy* (pp. 495-501). Dublin: Research-publishing.net. http://dx.doi.org/10.14705/rpnet.2015.000382

1. Introduction

A previous study (Sato, Matsunuma, & Suzuki, 2013) revealed that using mobile devices to learn L2 vocabulary could enhance the automatization of vocabulary recall, which can save on cognitive resources, allowing them to be reapplied toward reading activities and thus successful L2 reading comprehension. Those findings supported the assertion of the efficacy of L2 learning using multimodal functions, like many other previous studies that argue that the convergence of technologies in learning resources will improve L2 learners' performance (e.g. Sato & Suzuki 2010, 2012; Yeh & Wang, 2003). Along with the findings in computer-assisted L2 learning, studies on mobile-assisted language learning seem to focus mainly on the benefits of specific technological advances in discussing the advantage of MALL.

However, in order to make more robust claims about the advantages of mobile-assisted L2 learning, the agency (Pachler et al., 2010) or autonomy (Holec, 1981) of learners should also be considered. L2 learning with a mobile device might involve carrying out tasks by receiving learning resources online, as well as sending information such as texts, sounds, photos or movies via one's devices, no matter when and no matter where one may be. To carry out such activities, L2 learners are expected to be autonomous agents, not like those who passively listen to their teachers and receive knowledge from them. Furthermore, the use of a mobile device would allow wider access to authentic L2 resources and enable learners to actively search for resources for the purpose of their own learning, which can be seen as an important quality of autonomous learners who take control over learning content (Benson, 2001).

This study, therefore, hypothesizes that successful mobile-assisted L2 vocabulary learning through the technologically advanced representation of knowledge would enhance learner autonomy, as well as the automatization of vocabulary recall. Based on this hypothesis, this study verifies the effectiveness of MALL in a setting that differs from the one described in Sato et al. (2013), focusing on phrases for academic writing. While developing mobile-based material to learn the phrases that are required to write an academic essay consisting of several paragraphs, empirical research was conducted to examine the following two research questions:

- Does learning the phrases with an application available on mobile devices facilitate the recall of target vocabulary before and during a writing activity?

- Do L2 learners get motivated enough to function as autonomous agents by using a mobile application as a learning tool?

In addition to the experimental research, a questionnaire survey was conducted before and after the implementation of the mobile learning practice. In the following section, the details of this experimental and questionnaire research are described.

2. Method

2.1. Participants

Ninety-seven undergraduate students participated in this research, almost all of which were sophomores from the faculty of engineering in a Japanese university, where some of the authors of this paper are teaching English as a foreign language. Students' majors, which include life science, chemical science, physics and electrical engineering, are not related to English studies, yet their English language skills are sufficient to compose several English sentences by themselves. Participants were divided into two groups: a control group and an experimental group. As the groups were divided according to their English writing classes within their respective departments, the level of their language skills was expected to be equivalent, although no test was conducted to corroborate this assumption.

2.2. Target vocabulary

The participants were asked to learn one hundred phrases frequently used in academic writing. The phrases were extracted from several textbooks and reference books for L2 learners. They consisted mainly of expressions that clarify the logic flow of an essay such as "in the first place" or "provided that". To confirm the difficulty level of the phrases for the participants, a questionnaire survey was conducted prior to the research; the participants were asked to answer whether or not they already knew each phrase.

2.3. Treatment

The control group was asked to memorize the aforementioned phrases with their corresponding Japanese translations in a paper-based vocabulary list. The experimental group, on the other hand, was asked to learn the phrases on their smartphone. To do so, learning materials were developed using Quizlet, a free online learning tool to generate vocabulary learning resources, which are then available on mobile devices such as iPhone and Android. As shown in Figure 1 and Figure 2, the online resource provides different kinds of quizzes for the phrases, for instance matching, and fill in the blanks. These quizzes are available anytime and anywhere as long as students can access the Internet with their smartphone. After being provided with instructions on how to install, register and use the resource on their own mobile device, the experimental group was asked to learn the phrases outside the classroom. To encourage learning in each treatment, the instructors announced that the test for the phrases would be held three weeks after, and the scores would count towards one of their grades for the writing class.

Figure 1. An example of the quizzes developed by Quizlet (matching)

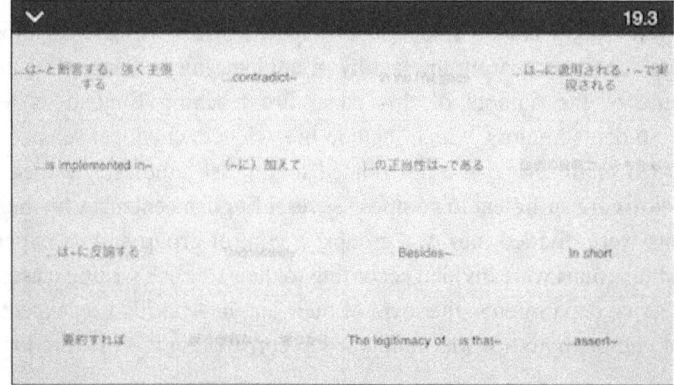

Figure 2. Another example of the quizzes developed by Quizlet (fill in the blanks)

2.4. Procedure

Just after the introduction of the learning materials, all participants were asked to answer an Internet-based questionnaire about their attitudes and views toward learning English, which is designed to measure the technical and psychological dimensions of learner autonomy (Murase, 2015). Students accessed the website and answered the questionnaire items outside the classroom via their mobile devices or PCs.

The test and an essay writing task were conducted three weeks after the introduction of the materials, for a duration of ninety minutes in total. Within the first ten minutes, the participants were asked to answer twenty fill-in-the-blank questions created from the phrases. The questions were selected from the results of the questionnaire carried out before the introduction of the materials. They were selected on the basis of being the phrases that the participants had the least prior knowledge of. They were also asked to write the time they had finished answering at on their answer sheet. After the test, a timed essay writing task was given. The participants were asked to pick out one of the four topics which were given by the instructors and to then write an essay consisting of at least three paragraphs with their opinions. Although they were not allowed to refer to any dictionaries, several key words of the topics were given by the instructors.

After finishing the writing task, they were asked to answer the Internet-based questionnaire again within a few days.

3. Results and discussion

The data collected in this research were analysed to find out the differences between the control and experimental groups. First of all, the score and termination time of the fill-in-the-blank test were compared. In the control group ($N=45$), the average score of the test was 6.18 ($SD=6.02$), and its average termination time was 539 seconds ($SD=119$). The average score and termination time of the experimental group ($N=52$) were 9.14 ($SD=6.43$) and 532 seconds ($SD=110$), respectively. A t-test showed significant differences between groups with respect to average score ($t(95)=-2.33$, $p<.05$), but no significant differences with regard to termination time between the groups ($t(95)=0.28$, $p>.05$).

The results of the Internet-based questionnaire about learner autonomy, which were administered before the treatment (pre-test) and after the treatment (post-test), were also compared. As for the pre-test, no significant difference was observed between the control group (N=33) and the experimental group (N=33). In the post-test, there was no significant difference between the control group (N=46) and the experimental group (N=30), except for two items concerning taking notes while learning, for which the control group marked higher scores. On the other hand, when comparing the results of the pre-test and the post-test, both groups marked higher scores (suggesting a higher autonomy) in the post-test. However, there was no significant difference between the scores in the two tests.

Another section with questions about vocabulary learning experiences was added in the post-test. A t-test was performed and, while no significant difference was found between the control group (N=46) and the experimental group (N=30) in the frequency of their learning during the three weeks ($t(74)$=-.702, p>.05), there was a significant difference concerning their motivation towards vocabulary learning ($t(74)$=-2.01, p<.05). This indicates that students in the experimental group (M=2.93, SD=.640) felt higher motivation towards vocabulary learning on mobile devices than those who used the traditional paper-based list (M=2.63, SD=.645).

4. Conclusions

This study has discussed the advantage of MALL from two perspectives: automatization and autonomy, and set out to explore whether the utilization of mobile devices in L2 learning would not only facilitate the recall of the target vocabulary, but also stimulate learner autonomy. To this end, an experimental study was conducted, whereby students were assigned to two different groups (control vs. experimental) and tested after learning the target vocabulary with the help of paper-based vocabulary lists vs. MALL-based learning materials. In addition, the students participating in the study were asked to compile a questionnaire on learner autonomy. The findings of the study show that the advantage of MALL can be found in enhancing the recall of the target language. Meanwhile, although the questionnaire study did not show any statistically significant effects of MALL on the development of learner autonomy, the data indicated that students in both groups showed a slightly higher level of learner autonomy after the study and also that MALL seemed to contribute to higher motivation towards L2 vocabulary learning. These findings appear to imply that L2 learning with advanced technology should be examined not merely in terms of L2 learning gains, but also motivational effect, which would make the use of mobile devices for L2 learning more effective. Nevertheless, a longer-term study would be necessary to see more meaningful changes in learner autonomy.

References

Benson, P. (2001). *Teaching and researching autonomy in language learning* (1st ed.). Harlow, UK: Pearson Education.

Holec, H. (1981). *Autonomy and foreign language learning*. Oxford, UK: Pergamon Press for Council of Europe.

Murase, F. (2015). Measuring language learner autonomy: problems and possibilities. In C. J. Everhard & L. Murphy (Eds.), *Assessment and autonomy in language learning* (pp. 35-63). Basingstoke, UK: Palgrave Macmillan. doi:10.1057/9781137414380.0008

Pachler, N., Bachmair, B., & Cook, J. (2010). *Mobile learning: structures, agency, practices*. New York: Springer. doi:10.1007/978-1-4419-0585-7

Sato, T., Matsunuma, M., & Suzuki, A. (2013). Enhancement of automatization through vocabulary learning using CALL: can prompt language processing lead to better comprehension in L2 reading? *ReCALL, 25*(1), 143-158. doi:10.1017/S0958344012000328

Sato, T., & Suzuki, A. (2010). Do multimedia-oriented visual glosses really facilitate EFL vocabulary learning? A comparison of planar images with three-dimensional images. *Asian EFL Journal, 12*(4), 160-172.

Sato, T., & Suzuki, A. (2012). From a gloss to a learning tool: does visual aids enhance better sentence comprehension? In L. Bradley & S. Thouësny (Eds.), *CALL: Using, Learning, Knowing, EUROCALL Conference, Gothenburg, Sweden, 22-25 August 2012, Proceedings* (pp. 264-268). Dublin Ireland: Research-publishing.net. doi:10.14705/rpnet.2012.000064.

Yeh, Y., & Wang, C.-W. (2003). Effects of multimedia vocabulary annotations and learning styles on vocabulary learning. *CALICO Journal, 21*(1), 131-144.

Creativity and collaboration: using CALL to facilitate international collaboration for online journalism at a Model United Nations event

Mark D. Sheehan[1], Todd Thorpe[2], and Robert Dunn[3]

Abstract. Much has been gained over the years in various educational fields that have taken advantage of CALL. In many cases, CALL has facilitated learning and provided teachers and students access to materials and tools that would have remained out of reach were it not for technology. Nonetheless, there are still cases where a lack of funding or access to CALL tools prevents teachers and students from reaping the benefits of CALL. Furthermore, in countries inundated by technology, opportunities for students to create and collaborate using CALL may get lost amid the noise of the latest program, or the trendiest learning tools. The project described in this article involves students in a different way to use CALL for learning; it has them work together using technology, troubleshooting problems, and creating online news stories. This article describes a digital journalism simulation called JUEMUN Journalism. JUEMUN, the Japan English University Model United Nations, is an annual event that brings together students from around the globe to participate in a Model United Nations (MUN). A component of this event includes teams of journalists who cover the events at the MUN, and report on them in four formats: podcasts, video broadcasts, a written chronicle, and editorial cartoons.

Keywords: online journalism, Model United Nations, collaboration, troubleshooting.

---

1. Hannan University, Osaka, Japan; mark@hannan-u.ac.jp

2. Kinki University, Osaka, Japan; toddthorpe@hotmail.com

3. Kinki University, Osaka, Japan; robertopithecus@gmail.com

How to cite this article: Sheehan, M. D., Thorpe, T., & Dunn, R. (2015). Creativity and collaboration: using CALL to facilitate international collaboration for online journalism at a Model United Nations event. In F. Helm, L. Bradley, M. Guarda, & S. Thouësny (Eds), *Critical CALL – Proceedings of the 2015 EUROCALL Conference, Padova, Italy* (pp. 502-506). Dublin: Research-publishing.net. http://dx.doi.org/10.14705/rpnet.2015.000383

1. Introduction

The teams that participate in JUEMUN Journalism are comprised of Japanese students and international students. The primary language for reporting is English, and has been expanded to include Chinese, Japanese, and Korean at the 2015 JUEMUN conference.

The benefits of this project are multifarious. The journalists come from a variety of cultures and academic backgrounds; these journalists collaborate on a common goal of reporting news from the MUN. Students are responsible for enlisting technology to help them create, write, and edit their podcasts, news videos, chronicles, and draw editorial cartoons. The journalists' mission is to make a plan, gather information and subsequently report on this three-day event in real time; the 2015 event had 276 students (199 Japanese and 77 international) from 47 universities with participants from over 30 different countries.

Rather than placing the emphasis on tools, students focus on content and ways to communicate that content to the world outside. Technology is an instrument used to reach a goal and remains in the background. The contents of the stories included issues related to fostering global leadership, peace, gender, the empowerment of women, poverty and inequality, reproductive health and rights, education, and climate change. The stories are uploaded to a website that allows others to engage with these important topics; these stories also help promote JUEMUN to future participants and interested educators.

Pairing students with different first languages and backgrounds and exposing them to global issues helps foster a culture of learning and inclusiveness that will serve students when they move out into the world after their studies. Furthermore, students are able to learn a number of technical and interpersonal skills by taking part in this project. This article gives one illustration of ways to get students to collaborate using CALL, and should be of interest to educators who explore ways to engage students in projects in which they create powerful content using technology.

2. Method

2.1. JUEMUN Journalism 2013 and 2014

JUEMUN was founded in 2010. By 2013, it became obvious that there were many other educational opportunities that could be incorporated into JUEMUN to promote learning on a larger scale. In particular, students who may not be suited to be MUN delegates, but who were eager to do something else needed an outlet. As a result, one of the founders of JUEMUN, Associate Professor Todd Thorpe, organized a group of students to report on the events at JUEMUN 2013. The first foray into JUEMUN Journalism had a big learning curve for both students and teachers. Equipment was sparse and students where not familiar with the software that was to be used to create the stories. Nonetheless, the students were able to produce a number of videos, podcasts and newspaper stories to create a record of the event. As the popularity of JUEMUN Journalism grew, international students joined the teams. This inclusion of students from abroad meant that problems with English language skills would be mitigated and the team dynamic would change to include broader perspectives and cross-cultural communication. JUEMUN Journalism 2014 saw a number of upgrades in equipment and students' technical skills. Each team was given cameras, IC recorders, and computers that had audio and video editing software installed on them. The volume of student output increased and the quality of the stories was raised.

2.2. JUEMUN Journalism 2015

JUEMUN Journalism 2015 saw an even greater leap. In 2015, additional formats were added to make JUEMUN Journalism more culturally diverse and to include different types of learners. The languages that stories were created in were increased and went from English only, to Korean and English, Japanese and English, and Chinese and English. Furthermore, to include students who learn and express themselves differently, and who may not have the technical or language skills to be video, podcast, or newspaper reporters, editorial cartoonists joined the team.

3. Discussion

From a CALL perspective, JUEMUN Journalism provided students with a number of opportunities to develop skills and use technology to create stories that could be shared with conference participants and the public at large. Nonetheless, as educators, the project faced a number of challenges, not the least of these was obsolescence in technology.

Educators must be aware of rapid obsolescence in technology. This comes in several forms, but the most common is functional obsolescence, where hardware requirements, or software changes obsolete the functionality of the software, and includes hardware obsolescence caused by software obsolescence; and software that obsoletes software. Less frequently encountered is logistical obsolescence, where parts are no longer available. There is also technological obsolescence, where functional machinery is superseded by more advanced hardware (Sandborn, 2007). The JUEMUN journalists encountered all three of these situations.

Functionally, one of the advisors uses Pages word processing software on an older version of Apple's Mac mini. Although he exported his documents to Word format, they were unreadable by Windows PCs or newer Macs, causing a temporary bottleneck in the editing and uploading process.

Logistically, card reader adapters were needed for modern micro flash memory cards, and lightning-to-USB adapters were also needed.

Finally, technological obsolescence was encountered with the journalists' equipment. Each team was equipped with a high quality digital camera, and digital voice recorder for interviews. In practice the journalists preferred using their smartphones for photography and voice recording.

Educators need to ensure that their hardware and software are up to date, that the peripherals are fully integrated into the network, and that the tools are appropriate for the users.

4. Conclusions

As mentioned above, there were a number of learning opportunities, as well as challenges, in the JUEMUN Journalism project. The greatest achievement that students saw was the ability to use technology to create high-quality multimedia reports in a variety of languages. The greatest challenge that students and teachers faced, despite careful planning, was in troubleshooting technical problems.

While JUEMUN Journalism is a simulation of online journalism, the technical problems were anything but simulated. Students and advisors working in a number of formats had to find ways to remedy compatibility issues and find workarounds so the journalists' assignments could be completed and published online and on time.

Limited budgets and time constraints often prevent people in educational settings from keeping up with the latest technology. However, this does not mean that students and teachers should be prevented from harnessing the power of CALL for learning. Rather, these obstacles allow teachers to rethink how CALL can be used; now more than ever, CALL can encourage educators to innovate. CALL, as an educational methodology, has seen a number of changes and has reached a level of maturity that should position teachers to reflect on, and revise, certain educational practices and goals. JUEMUN Journalism should serve as an example of how changes in technology and pedagogy can be embraced to provide meaningful educational opportunities to learners. Materials created by the student journalists can be viewed on the JUEMUN Journalism website: http://juemun.weebly.com/juemun-journalism.html.

5. Acknowledgements

We would like to thank the founders of JUEMUN for starting and building an amazing educational event. We would also like to thank all the students who have taken part in JUEMUN as delegates, Chairs, journalists, and volunteers. We would like to express our deepest gratitude to the universities that have hosted JUEMUN and have given so much support to make those events possible.

References

Sandborn, P. (2007). Software obsolescence: complicating the part and technology obsolescence management problem. *IEEE Trans on Components and Packaging Technologies, 30*(4), 886-888. doi:10.1109/TCAPT.2007.910918

Feedback on feedback – does it work?

Oranna Speicher[1] and Sascha Stollhans[2]

Abstract. It is well documented that providing assessment feedback through the medium of screencasts is favourably received by students and encourages deeper engagement with the feedback given by the language teacher (inter alia Abdous & Yoshimura, 2010; Brick & Holmes, 2008; Cann, 2007; Stannard, 2007). In this short paper we will report the results of a case study where students moved from passively receiving feedback to actively entering into a feedback dialogue with their language teachers: screencasts were used not only by the teachers to provide audio and visual feedback to students on their written work, but also by the students themselves to comment in depth on the feedback they had received. Participants in the case study were surveyed at the end of the semester, and we will report on the survey findings as well as discuss the limitations and implications of the case study. The paper will reflect on the potential role of technology in providing feedback, the effectiveness of elicitation feedback in the context of this case study and the students' perception of the usefulness of creating their own screencasts in response to the feedback they have received.

Keywords: feedback, screencasts, computer-mediated communication, CMC, student engagement.

1. Introduction

In 2005 the Higher Education Funding Council for England (HEFCE) launched the now annual National Student Survey (NSS) to gauge the level of overall satisfaction amongst final year students regarding their degree courses in the UK. The survey questions cover various aspects of the students' university experience,

---

1. University of Nottingham, United Kingdom; oranna.speicher@nottingham.ac.uk

2. University of Nottingham, United Kingdom; sascha.stollhans@nottingham.ac.uk

How to cite this article: Speicher, O., & Stollhans, S. (2015). Feedback on feedback – does it work?. In F. Helm, L. Bradley, M. Guarda, & S. Thouësny (Eds), *Critical CALL – Proceedings of the 2015 EUROCALL Conference, Padova, Italy* (pp. 507-511). Dublin: Research-publishing.net. http://dx.doi.org/10.14705/rpnet.2015.000384

from the organisation and management of their study programmes and the teaching they experienced, to feedback on their assessments and availability and quality of learning resources. Whilst student satisfaction with assessment and feedback has risen since the start of the survey, last year's figures suggest that it is still the category where, relatively speaking, students express least satisfaction regarding their university experience.

In 2012 HEFCE itself produced guidelines for Higher Education Institutions aimed at increasing students' engagement with the feedback they receive.

If students continue to see feedback as the area of their degree experience that they are least satisfied with, the question arises as to what staff can do in order to improve the way(s) in which feedback is presented to the students. The following study report details the results of a case study where students moved from passively receiving feedback to actively entering into a feedback dialogue with their language teachers.

2. Method

2.1. Participants

Our small scale study took place in the spring semester of the academic session 2014/2015 and involved two distinct groups of students from the School of Cultures, Languages and Area Studies at the University of Nottingham: one second-year group studying German as a degree subject consisting of 10 students (group 1), and one mixed-year group, consisting of 12 students, studying German as a subsidiary module alongside their main degree course through the institution-wide language programme (group 2). The language competence of the participants was approximately in line with level B2 (group 1) or B1 (group 2) of the European Framework of Reference for Languages. All students were undergraduate students at the time the study took place.

2.2. Data collection

In the first instance, both groups of students were given a formative written task: an essay (group 1) and a summary in German (group 2). Both teachers then provided the students with a screencast, using the freely available software screencast-o-matic[3]. In the case of group 1, the screencast showed the students' piece of written

---
3. http://www.screencast-o-matic.com/

work and contained an audio recording of the teachers' elicitation feedback, i.e. the audio feedback consisted of metalinguistic explanations and prompts to encourage the students to work out for themselves how to improve their work (e.g. Lyster & Ranta, 1997). This was done in the target language. In the case of group 2, the non-specialist group, the screencast was in English and it had also written elicitation comments as an additional feedback element.

It is at this point in the feedback process that the innovative element of our study is found: after reworking their essays, the students themselves produced a screencast video, using the same software, in order to explain how they had incorporated the elicitation feedback into their second essay/summary submission.

Finally, students were asked to fill in an online questionnaire created with surveymonkey[4] in order to gauge their perception on the feedback they had received, and how they evaluated its usefulness and the role technology played in both receiving and creating feedback.

3. Discussion

All students in both groups submitted the draft version of their written assignment and received a screencast with audio elicitation feedback. Out of a total number of 22 students, eight created a screencast themselves of their final version of the assignment. Roughly 40% of the total number of the participating students completed the questionnaire with the following results.

The majority of the students had watched the video several times, 50% had watched it three times or more. All participants had then used the feedback to rework their essays accordingly. Open comments like the following suggest that students used the feedback to analyse and work on their linguistic weaknesses, not only for this specific assignment but also beyond:

> "I did use the feedback to identify my main areas of weakness and focus heavily on these aspects on revising for the exam, hopefully significantly improving my marks and the standard of my German".

We asked students to evaluate the following general statements about the activity (Table 1), using a five-point Likert scale (1 = Strongly disagree, 2 = Disagree, 3 = Neither disagree or agree, 4 = Agree, 5 = Strongly agree).

---
4. https://www.surveymonkey.com/

Table 1. Likert-scale type questions of the final questionnaire

Statement	Average response
I found the video feedback useful.	4.63
I found it easy to understand the feedback.	4.63
I think video feedback is more effective than written feedback.	4.25
I would have liked to receive written feedback in addition to the video feedback.	3.38
The video feedback helped me understand my mistakes.	4.00
I think this kind of feedback could help me improve my language skills.	4.38
I think it is important to actively work with the feedback you receive.	4.63
Making my own screencast explaining how I have used the feedback has increased my learning.	3.50

The results suggest that students perceived the exercise as very useful and beneficial to their learning experience, and that working actively with the feedback they had received helped them improve their language skills.

Several open comments suggest that students perceive screencast feedback to be more personal and that it encourages students to work more actively with the feedback. However, students were divided over the idea of creating a screencast themselves, the average score of 3.50 as well as open comments show that some students found it useful, whereas others were not convinced that it had benefitted their learning process.

Regarding the question of whether students would prefer the feedback to be in English or in the target language, 50% opted for the target language, 25% for English, and the remaining 25% did not express a preference.

4. Conclusions

Our aim in running this case study was to see if we could effect a deeper engagement of our students with the feedback they receive on written work. Our findings support the view that audio/video feedback is seen by the students as highly effective and more effective than written feedback alone. It is encouraging to see that the majority of the students surveyed, over 80%, watched the feedback video at least twice, half of them at least three times. We believe the difference in student's opinion about which language the feedback should be given in can be attributed to the students' main study discipline – those studying German as a degree subject prefer the feedback to be in German, those studying German as a subsidiary prefer the language to be English. Our small scale study did not find that students are convinced about the learning benefits of creating a screencast and explaining their revised essays to their teacher.

References

Abdous, M. H., & Yoshimura, M. (2010). Learner outcomes and satisfaction: a comparison of live video-streamed instruction, satellite broadcast instruction, and face-to-face instruction. *Computers & Education, 55*(2), 733-741. doi:10.1016/j.compedu.2010.03.006

Brick, B., & Holmes, J. (2008). Using screen capture software for student feedback: towards a methodology. *In IADIS International Conference on Cognition and Exploratory Learning in the Digital Age.*

Cann, A. J. (2007). Podcasting is dead. Long live video! *Bioscience Education, 10.* doi:10.3108/beej.10.c1

Lyster, R., & Ranta, L. (1997). Corrective feedback and learner uptake. *Studies in second language acquisition, 19*(1), 37-66. doi:10.1017/S0272263197001034

Stannard, R. (2007). *Using screen capture software in student feedback*. Project Report. Higher Education Academy.

A comparative study of the effect of CALL on gifted and non-gifted adolescents' English proficiency

Sophie Tai[1] and Hao-Jan Chen[2]

Abstract. Computer-Assisted Language Learning (CALL) has gained increasing acceptance since it provides learners with abundant resources. Most researches confirm the beneficial effect of CALL on English as a Foreign Language (EFL) learners' cognitive, metacognitive, and affective developments. However, the diversity of students' intelligence is associated with different language learning needs. The study aimed to compare the effect of CALL on gifted and non-gifted EFL adolescents' English proficiency and their perceptions of CALL. The study included 20 EFL seventh graders with similar English proficiencies. Six were recognized as gifted and fourteen were non-gifted with reference to their IQ score in the Wechsler Intelligence Scale for Children- Fourth Edition (WISC-IV). Participants received 8-weeks of the VoiceTube online learning programme. A mixed method was employed to analyze the data obtained from General English Proficiency Test (GEPT) scores, learning logs, questionnaires, and interviews. The result revealed the gifted students' English reading and listening proficiency outperformed the non-gifted ones in the post-test. They were motivated and enthusiastic in challenging themselves with $i+1$ online learning material. By contrast, most non-gifted students held passive attitude toward CALL and doubted its effectiveness for their exams. Some felt anxious about the miscellaneous online learning materials. CALL should be an enhancement, not a replacement, in balance with conventional instruction.

Keywords: CALL, gifted adolescents, English proficiency.

---

1. National Taiwan Normal University, Taipei City, Taiwan; a0937546693@gmail.com
2. National Taiwan Normal University, Taipei City, Taiwan; hjchen@ntnu.edu.tw

How to cite this article: Tai, S., & Chen, H.-J. (2015). A comparative study of the effect of CALL on gifted and non-gifted adolescents' English proficiency. In F. Helm, L. Bradley, M. Guarda, & S. Thouësny (Eds), *Critical CALL – Proceedings of the 2015 EUROCALL Conference, Padova, Italy* (pp. 512-517). Dublin: Research-publishing.net. http://dx.doi.org/10.14705/rpnet.2015.000385

1. Introduction

CALL is deemed as a vital objective of modern education since it provides abundant resources for EFL learners' self-directed learning (Reilly, 2012). Most previous researches confirm the beneficial effect of CALL on EFL learners' cognitive, metacognitive, and affective developments (Golonka et al., 2014). While facing a wide range of abilities in heterogeneous classrooms, teachers desire to meet all students' needs, and believe CALL would help them reach this goal. However, a "one size fits all" approach to promote language proficiency might not work well. Few studies investigate the effect of CALL on promoting the language proficiency of EFL adolescents with different IQs and needs.

Moreover, CALL studies have fallen into the trap of attributing learning gains to the technology itself rather than to the way the technology is manipulated by learners to influence achievement. Therefore, it is essential to conduct an empirical study to gauge the effect of CALL on promoting the English proficiency of EFL learners with different intelligences. The aim of this study was three-fold. The first was to outline a course that put CALL at the center of the curriculum with the aim of increasing EFL learners' reading and listening proficiency, the second was to compare how effective CALL enhanced the gifted and non-gifted EFL learners' English proficiency, and the third was to investigate their attitudes towards CALL.

2. Method

2.1. Participants

The study included twenty EFL 7th graders with similar English proficiencies. Six of them were identified as gifted based on their achievement tests and IQ scores measured by WISC-IV, which included five cognitive domains: verbal comprehension, visual spatial, fluid reasoning, working memory, and processing speed.

The giftedness assessment was administered by qualified psychologists and school teachers. These gifted students acquired and memorized knowledge rapidly. They liked self-directed learning and extensive reading in special interest areas. However, they were not gifted in all areas of academics. They had one or two subjects that they were best in and passionate about. Half of them usually got bored and daydreamed in regular English classes owing to mechanical drills and unengaging content. As for the non-gifted students, they liked teacher-centred instruction and repetitive practice.

2.2. Instruments

The learning materials utilized in the CALL project were the online resources provided by VoiceTube, which is an open and free English learning website. It offered users dynamic language learning experiences and contents of over 15,000 videos, including TED talks, news, movie segments, comics, and games. The other instruments were the GEPT, official documents, learning logs, pre- and post-project questionnaires, and semi-structured interviews.

2.3. Procedures

The study was conducted by means of a pre-survey, treatment programme, and post-test design. Participants had GEPT as the pre-test and post-test. The CALL project took 8 weeks, two hours a week, from September to October in 2014.

Both the gifted and non-gifted groups received 8-weeks of the VoiceTube online learning programme, involving a variety of topics with tailor-made activities. They had to complete questionnaires at the end of the programme. Lastly, semi-structured interviews were conducted with four participants.

2.4. Data analysis

A mixed method was employed to analyze the data obtained from GEPT scores, learning logs, questionnaires, and semi-structure interviews. An independent t-test and paired-samples t-test was conducted to see if there were any intergroup and intragroup differences on the pre-test and post-test separately. Participants' responses on the questionnaires were coded and categorized. The semi-structured interview was analyzed for triangulation.

3. Discussion

3.1. The effect of the CALL project

In Table 1, the results showed that the GEPT scores of the gifted and non-gifted groups were not significantly different in the pre-test ($t=-.30, p=.77$) but they were in the post-test ($t=2.35, p=.03$). Gifted students performed much better than the non-gifted ones in the post-test. Table 2 revealed the results of the paired-samples t-test for the gifted and non-gifted groups. It indicated a strong statistical significance ($t=-11.61; p=.00$) for the gifted group in the variation over time. The increased mean difference indicated the CALL project positively impacted gifted students'

English proficiency. No significant differences were found between pre-test and post-test for the non-gifted group ($t=1.31$; $p=.21$).

Table 1. Results of independent t-test of gifted and non-gifted students' GEPT scores in pre- and post-test

Source		No.	Mean	SD	df	t	p
Pre-test	Gifted	6	119.16	31.02	18	-.30	.77
	Non-gifted	14	125.61	47.81			
Post-test	Gifted	6	159.36	26.93	18	2.35*	.03
	Non-gifted	14	122.30	42.32			

*$p<.05$

Table 2. Results of paired-samples t-test of pre- and post-test of gifted and non-gifted groups

Source		No.	Mean	SD	df	t	p
Gifted	Pretest	6	119.16	31.02	5	-11.61***	.00
	Post-test	6	159.36	26.93			
Non-gifted	Pretest	14	125.61	47.81	13	1.31	.21
	Post-test	14	122.31	42.32			

***$p<.001$

3.2. Participants' reflection on the CALL project

The results revealed all the 6 gifted students expressed a positive attitude but the non-gifted students held different views toward the CALL project.

3.2.1. Motivation

Most gifted students were intrinsically motivated, enthusiastic, and engaged in learning English through VoiceTube, which provided adequate challenges, individualized learning experiences, and maximized opportunities for self-fulfillment. Although the non-gifted students thought the videos and animation were interesting, half of them watched them for fun, not for learning's sake. When VoiceTube was treated as a compulsory learning task, it became an unwanted burden because they had no intention of doing additional exercises.

3.2.2. Multi-media and authentic input

The varied authentic English learning materials of VoiceTube allowed the gifted students to process information in a parallel way. Repetitive practice was skipped.

It reduced boredom and freed up time for them to work on more challenging learning materials at their own pace. It was a challenge, but gifted students did feel they could learn from it.

From Krashen's (1998) perspective, language acquisition takes place when the learner is exposed to input that is just beyond their current stage ($i+1$). In contrast, some non-gifted students were overwhelmed by the abundance of information and felt tense with the various authentic stimuli. Some complained it was time-consuming to find what they needed.

3.2.3. Learner autonomy

The learner-centred English practice provided by VoiceTube best fit the gifted students who liked to work independently. They were active participants in the learning process rather than passive recipients of knowledge. They delved deeply into the learning materials on VoiceTube that interested them. They learned more from self-directed discovery. By contrast, most non-gifted students

> "were bewildered by the idea of accepting responsibility for their learning. [... They felt frustrated] when they found the explanations from the computer unclear or hard to understand" (Lu, 2010, pp. 353-354).

4. Conclusions

The CALL project made the classroom increasingly dynamic and adequately challenging for gifted students. It created a natural and exciting learning environment which helped them to move at an accelerated pace with new materials. Options for self-selected online materials led to their deeper engagement.

On the contrary, some non-gifted students held passive attitudes toward CALL and were limited in their gains in self-directed learning. Most doubted its effectiveness for their exams. The absence of face-to-face professional guidance caused their dissatisfaction and anxiety. Therefore, CALL is suggested to be an optional, voluntary, and complementary means of learning.

5. Acknowledgements

This work was supported by grants from the Office of Research and Development, National Taiwan Normal University, Taipei, Taiwan.

References

Golonka, E. M., Bowles, A. R., Frank, V. M., Richardson, D. L., & Freynik, S. (2014). Technologies for foreign language learning: a review of technology types and their effectiveness. *Computer Assisted Language Learning, 27*(1), 70-105.

Krashen, S. (1998). Comprehensible output? *System, 26*(2), 175-182. doi:10.1016/s0346-251X(98)00002-5

Lu, D. (2010). A salutary lesson from a computer-based self-access language learning project. *Computer Assisted Language Learning, 23*(4), 343-359. doi:10.1080/09588221.2010.511588

Reilly, P. (2012). Understanding and teaching generation Y. *English Teaching Forum, 1*, 1-6. Retrieved from http://files.eric.ed.gov/fulltext/EJ971235.pdf

Are teachers test-oriented? A comparative corpus-based analysis of the English entrance exam and junior high school English textbooks

Sophie Tai[1] and Hao-Jan Chen[2]

Abstract. The communicative language teaching approach has dominated English teaching and learning since the 1970s. In Taiwan, standardized and high-stakes English tests also put focus on the assessment of learners' communicative competence. While the test contents change, the modifications teachers made are superficial rather than substantial. A comparative corpus-based analysis of the English test items in Senior High School Entrance Exams (SHSEE) and curriculum-based English textbooks was conducted to provide more valid information for syllabus design, language instruction, and materials development. Two major corpora were compiled: an exam corpus, consisting of English test items in SHSEE from 2001 to 2014 and a junior high school English textbook corpus. AntConc and Readability Test Tool were employed to analyze the frequency of occurrence of the marked structures (relative, adverbial, and passive clauses) in the two corpora. The results showed rare occurrence of the marked structures in SHSEE but much higher frequency in textbooks. Teachers might be textbook-oriented, rather than test-oriented. It was suggested, based on the corpus-based analysis of the native speakers' use, that a grammar list with finer guidelines for the national curriculum and textbook writers should be built. It could provide teachers easily accessible reference in selecting grammatical patterns for teaching.

Keywords: corpus-analysis, test-oriented, backwash, marked structure.

---

1. National Taiwan Normal University, Taipei City, Taiwan; a0937546693@gmail.com
2. National Taiwan Normal University, Taipei City, Taiwan; hjchen@ntnu.edu.tw

How to cite this article: Tai, S., & Chen, H.-J.. (2015). Are teachers test-oriented? A comparative corpus-based analysis of the English entrance exam and junior high school English textbooks. In F. Helm, L. Bradley, M. Guarda, & S. Thouësny (Eds), *Critical CALL – Proceedings of the 2015 EUROCALL Conference, Padova, Italy* (pp. 518-522). Dublin: Research-publishing.net. http://dx.doi.org/10.14705/rpnet.2015.000386

1. Introduction

Since the 1970s, the communicative language teaching approach has dominated the English language teaching and learning in all contexts. Test writers for SHSEE have intended to bring about the positive changes by testing learners' English communicative competence in Taiwan. However, teachers still devote a substantial amount of class time to traditional activities such as textbook explanation or exercises on grammar (Pan, 2011). They also have a propensity to prepare learners for English tests through abundant test-preparation instruction. Although most studies indicate that teachers tend to teach for the test, several studies state that tests do not significantly influence teaching (e.g. Green, 2007); the modifications teachers have made seem to be superficial rather than substantial. Therefore, in this study, we carried out a comparative corpus-based analysis of the English test in SHSEE and curriculum-based English textbooks. This research aimed to examine whether there was a mismatch between what is being taught and tested. The study was designed to address two research questions. First, what is the frequency of occurrence of marked structures in the English exam in SHSEE and the curriculum-based English textbooks? Second, what is the backwash effect of the English exam in SHSEE on teachers' instruction?

2. Method

2.1. Corpus selection

Two main corpora were compiled for the current study. One was CAP corpus, which consisted of all the English test items in SHSEE from 2001 to 2014. The other one is textbook corpora, including Kang-Xiuan Corpus and Han-Lin Corpus, two major versions of junior high school English textbooks in Taiwan. The marked structures (relative, adverbial, and passive clauses) were chosen for the study because they were difficult for Taiwanese learning English as a foreign language (EFL) (Chang, 2008). Moreover, teachers firmly believed learners had to master these structures to get higher scores in the entrance exam.

2.2. Data analysis

The corpora were analyzed by using AntConc 3.4.3 (Anthony, 2014) and the Readability Test Tool (Simpson, 2014). The frequency of occurrence of the marked structures in the CAP, Kang-Xiuan, and Han-Lin Corpora was counted. Then, a comparative corpus-based analysis of the collected data was conducted.

3. Discussion

Table 1 showed that the total number of the relative clauses occurring in the CAP corpus is 249. About 98% of them were designed for recognition (reading) and only 2% were for production (writing). The adverbial clauses occurred 106 times but only 1.88% of them were tested for production. The passive clauses appeared 87 times but only 13 occurrences were tested for production. Most of the marked structures were tested for recognition (97%), not for production (3%). The rare occurrence of these complex structures in the English exam was in line with Ellis's (2012) proposition that frequent and unmarked structures should be acquired first in L2 acquisition.

Table 1. Frequency of the relative, adverbial, and passive clauses in the CAP corpus

Grammatical Patterns	CAP Corpus		
	Tokens for Recognition	Tokens for Production	Total Tokens
A. Relative			
1. that	126	3	129
2. who	65	2	67
3. which	10	1	11
4. whose	1	0	1
5. where	18	0	18
6. how	6	0	6
7. why	17	0	17
B. Adverb			
1. if	87	1	88
2. although	8	1	9
3. though	8	8	9
C. Passive			
1. by	79	8	87
Total	410	16	426

Teachers in Taiwan invested lots of class time to teach these infrequent marked structures, which was believed to help students get higher test scores (Chang, 2008). However, the results revealed the English exam in SHSEE contained a very low proportion of the marked structures. Test takers were rarely required to produce these marked structures, except for recognition. Teaching for the test, at most, means teachers adhered to the test format, rather than the test construct. Such conflict might be attributed to teachers' incomplete understanding of the nature of the exam, inadequate training, or lack of professional background.

Examining the English textbooks provided another explanation for teachers' overemphasis on marked structure instruction. Table 2 showed the result of the frequency occurrence of the marked structures in the two most popular versions of junior high school English textbooks. The frequency of the complex sentence patterns in Kang-Xuan and Han-Lin corpora were 13.63% and 31.77%, respectively. There was an overemphasis on rarely used marked structures in the English textbooks. The results implied teachers might be textbook-oriented, rather than test-oriented. The findings showed the backwash effect, i.e the effect of the examination on classroom methodology and selection of teaching materials, to be limited, although the test construct of the English exam in SHSEE showed marked changes over the past 14 years in Taiwan.

Table 2. Frequency of the relative, adverbial, and passive clauses in the textbook corpora

Grammatical Patterns	CAP Tokens	CAP Non-tested tokens	CAP Tested tokens	Kang-Xuan Tokens	Han-Lin Tokens
A. Relative					
1. that	129	126	3	89	212
2. who	67	65	2	24	65
3. which	11	10	1	11	31
4. whose	1	1	0	1	3
5. where	18	18	0	7	13
6. how	6	6	0	6	18
7. why	17	17	0	5	7
B. Adverb					
1. if	88	88	0	61	99
2. although	9	8	1	10	19
3. though	9	8	1	1	4
C. Passive					
1. by	87	79	8	51	118
Total	426	410	16	266	589
Total word tokens	55440		.	49050	48072
Total sentence numbers	6551			7104	7362

4. Conclusion

The results indicated a rare occurrence of the marked structures in the English exam in SHSEE; there was, however, an overemphasis placed on them in the surveyed textbooks. Such information can be vital in designing curriculum, and teachers should use this information to effectively direct their pedagogical focus, since it is not sufficient to change exams. As Cheng (2005) mentioned, an exam on its own cannot bring about change if the educational system has not adequately prepared the teacher. Teachers and language testers should try to make a match between what is tested and what is taught. Chang (2008) contends that positive test effects usually occur when there is a match between test content and curricula. To facilitate EFL learners' acquisition, teachers should avoid overloading learners with infrequent and marked structures. Moreover, teachers should not "blindly" follow the textbooks. Two pedagogical implications were suggested. First, there is a need to develop a grammar list with clear guidelines for the national curriculum and textbook writers. Second, a distinction should be made between production and recognition structures in the junior high school English textbook. This would provide an easily accessible reference to guide teachers in selecting grammatical patterns for teaching.

References

Anthony, L. (2014). *AntConc (Version 3.4.3)* [Computer Software]. Tokyo, Japan: Waseda University. Retrieved from http://www.laurenceanthony.net/

Chang, W.-C. (2008). Examining English grammar instruction in Taiwan's senior high schools: a discourse/pragmatic perspective. *English teaching & learning, 32*(2), 123-155.

Cheng, L. (2005). *Changing language teaching through language testing: a washback study.* Cambridge: Cambridge University Press.

Ellis, R. (2012). *The study of second language acquisition* (2nd ed.). Oxford: Oxford University Press.

Green, X. (2007). *Positive or negative—An empirical study of CET washback.* Chongqing: Chongqing University Press.

Pan, Y. C. (2011). Teacher washback from English certification exit requirements in Taiwan. *Asian journal of English language teaching, 21*, 23-42.

Simpson, D. (2014). *The readability test tool* [Computer Software]. Retrieved from http://readable.com/

Use of mobile testing system PeLe for developing language skills

Svetlana Titova[1]

Abstract. One of the objectives of this paper is to investigate the pedagogical impact of both the mobile testing system PeLe (Norway, HiST) and the enquiry-based learning approach on language skills development in the context of mobile-assisted learning. The research aims to work out a methodological framework of PeLe implementation into the language classroom through formative assessment, immediate feedback and interactive post-test activities. The framework was developed and pilot tested in a joint research project (MobiLL) by English as a foreign language (EFL) teachers at Lomonosov Moscow State University (LMSU, Russia) and University College HiST (Norway) during two semesters of the 2013-2014 academic year. Students enrolled in a preparatory English course at LMSU were randomly assigned to 2 experimental groups and 2 control groups. Students in the experimental groups took a series of PeLe supported grammar and vocabulary tests as volunteers using handheld devices. The control groups were tested by the traditional testing method – pen and paper. The analysis based on quantitative research data demonstrated that PeLe supported language classes resulted in language skill gains. Qualitative data analysis highlighted the positive effect of mobile formative assessment and of post-test activities on learner motivation and collaboration skills. This study suggests that the use of technology was effective in engaging students in enquiry-based tasks, to produce more output in the target language.

Keywords: MALL, immediate feedback, enquiry-based learning, formative assessment.

---

1. Lomonosov Moscow State University, Russia; stitova3@gmail.com

How to cite this article: Titova, S. (2015). Use of mobile testing system PeLe for developing language skills. In F. Helm, L. Bradley, M. Guarda, & S. Thouësny (Eds), *Critical CALL – Proceedings of the 2015 EUROCALL Conference, Padova, Italy* (pp. 523-528). Dublin: Research-publishing.net. http://dx.doi.org/10.14705/rpnet.2015.000387

1. Introduction

Mobile devices have become "pivotal in students' everyday life and mobile technologies are expected to play a bridging role between informal and formal practices of learning" (Mobile Education, 2011, p. 12). In spite of the plethora of research in the area of mobile learning, it challenges instructors to examine how mobility relates to their teaching aims, methods and subject matter, because there is not yet consistent Mobile Assisted Language Learning (MALL) methodologies. On the other hand, there is also a need in the new educational framework for mobile testing tools implementation aimed at developing learner skills rather than just assessing learner knowledge and proficiency (Arnesen, Korpås, Hennissen, & Stav, 2013). Hypothesis to guide the framework of our research includes collaborative enquiry-based learning and peer learning approaches and educational opportunities provided by handheld devices such as immediate feedback, interactivity and flexibility. This paper, supported by both current m-learning theory and enquiry-based learning theory, focuses on working out a methodological framework of mobile testing system implementation into the language classroom.

2. Method

2.1. Research objectives

Mobile Language Learning (MOBILL, http://histproject.no/node/859) is an international project involving two institutions: Sør-Trøndelag University College (HiST, Trondheim, Norway), Department of Technology, and Lomonosov Moscow State University (LMSU, Moscow Russia), Department of Foreign Languages and Area Studies. The project was conducted during two periods from September 2013 to May 2014. The data discussed in this paper are related only to the first period of the project. The key objective of this international research project was to work out sound pedagogical strategies on how to implement the mobile testing system PeLe into the traditional language classroom (pedagogical perspective), thus introducing some improvements to the piloting tool (technological perspective).

The project target group consisted of Norwegian and Russian learners of English, all at the same language level (B1). For the first period of experimentation, several classes of learners at LMSU participated, namely: students (n=35) enrolled in a preparatory English course at LMSU were randomly assigned to 3 experimental and 1 control groups. The control group was tested by the traditional testing method, i.e pen and paper. In this paper, data collected only from the LMSU groups will be discussed and analyzed.

The methodological framework of the MALL model based on PeLe implementation includes both enquiry-based methods such as collaborative and peer learning post-test activities, brainstorming, problem solving activities, group discussions and mobile learning opportunities such as immediate feedback, formative assessment, interactivity and flexibility. The project implementation and research design is illustrated in Figure 1.

Figure 1. Methodology of PeLe implementation

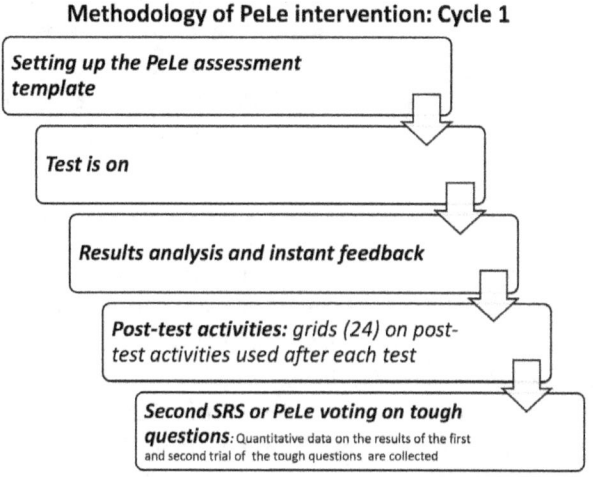

2.2. Data collection

Data collection was done in three cycles:

1. Intervention of PeLe tests (8 tests) as formative assessment tools from September to December 2013. The grids (24) on post-test activities used after each test were completed by the teachers of the experimental groups. Quantitative data were analyzed by mean (M) and standard deviation.

2. Quantitative data of the final tests were gathered in control and experimental groups at the end of the semester, the data were analyzed by mean (M) and standard deviation.

3. In January 2014, the post-intervention questionnaire asked students to reflect on their experience and attitude to the MALL model. Qualitative data were then gathered to help explain quantitative findings.

In the first cycle, students of the three experimental groups took a series of PeLe grammar and vocabulary tests (8). PeLe tests in the experimental groups were used for formative assessment and were provided in the form of in-class grammar tests. Students responded with their smartphones or tablets. They had access to PeLe tests by using Wi-Fi in class.

As previously mentioned in Titova (2014), average scores were included to compare the overall performance of the control and experimental groups after the implementation of the intervention. The intervention data were supplemented by student feedback gained from a post-study Google questionnaire. The post-study questionnaire contains 11 questions in the format of Likert four-level scale aiming to get student views on the strengths and weaknesses of PeLe integration. The questionnaire was completed by 28 students of the experimental groups.

3. Discussion

The data collected on the overall scores of summative tests in two groups during the fall semester of 2013-2014 – control and experimental ones – strengthen Titova's (2014) results that introduction of PeLe supported approach helped improve academic performance of the experimental groups in overall results of the final test, whereas the control group demonstrated decrease in overall scores. The likely interpretation of this improvement could not be attributed specifically to PeLe-assisted testing. As found by Beal, Walles, Arroyo, and Woolf (2007), "[a]n alternate possibility is that students' performance might improve [also] as the result of a general effect of interacting with [mobile devices], for example, by increasing students' attention to the material; prior work suggests that interaction alone may enhance learning" (p. 44; see also Titova & Talmo, 2014). In addition, students might improve because of taking tests regularly, immediate feedback and enquiry-based strategies used by the instructors. Student answers in the post-study Google questionnaire indicated that they had an overall positive outlook regarding the MALL model. Some participants commented on the challenging nature of weekly tests and post-test activities. However, they claim that this approach improved their overall satisfaction because it helped them get prepared for their entrance exams.

4. Conclusions

Since our conclusions are based on subjective and objective data , the study has some limitations that need to be highlighted. Firstly, the number of participants was small ($N=35$), so their reflections may not be equally applicable to all mobile learner perceptions. Another limitation is that PeLe enables the instructor to diagnose not only group performance but also results of each student because each individual's responses are also stored. As a result, an individual student's performance can be tracked across multiple sessions. Further research needs to probe the effect of PeLe implementation on individual performance of the learner. Thirdly, although mobile testing system PeLe holds promise, more research is needed to determine its effects upon developing not only grammar skills but also some other skills such as speaking, writing and listening.

This research suggests that PeLe integration into language learning could be efficient, especially if combined with collaborative enquiry-based learning and peer learning approaches and the pedagogical potential provided by mobile testing systems such as immediate feedback, interactivity and flexibility. The experimental results suggest that the MALL approach, combining current m-learning theory and enquiry-based learning theory and formative assessment, is most advisable. We hope that our approach will provide some constructs for pedagogical thinking about enhancing MALL with new mobile-assisted assessment methodology.

5. Acknowledgements

We would like to thank our Norwegian colleagues – Professor John Stav, Ekaterina Zourou, Arild Smolan, Ketil Arnesen and Even Einum – for making this research happen.

References

Arnesen, K., Korpås, G. S., Hennissen, J., & Stav, J. B. (2013). Experiences with use of various pedagogical methods utilizing a student response system – Motivation and learning outcome. *The Electronic Journal of E-Learning, 11*(3), 169-181. Retrieved from http://www.ejel.org/volume11/issue3

Beal, C. R., Walles, R., Arroyo, I., & Woolf, B. P. (2007). On-line tutoring for math achievement testing: a controlled evaluation. *Journal of Interactive Online Learning, 6*(1), 43-55.

Mobile Education. (2011). *Mobile Education Landscape Report*. London: GSMA. Retrieved from http://gsma.com/connectedliving/wp-content/uploads/2012/03/landscape110811interactive.pdf?

Titova, S. (2014). Mobile voting tools for creating collaboration environment and a new educational design of the university lecture. In Sake Jager, Linda Bradley, Estelle J. Meima, Sylvie Thouësny. (Eds), *CALL Design: Principles and Practice - Proceedings of the 2014 EUROCALL Conference, Groningen, The Netherlands* (pp. 374-378). Dublin Ireland: Research-publishing.net. doi:10.14705/rpnet.2014.000248

Titova, S., & Talmo, T. (2014). Mobile voting systems for creating collaboration environment and getting immediate feedback: a new curriculum model of the university lecture. *International Journal of Mobile and Blended Learning, 6*(3), 18-34. doi:10.4018/ijmbl.2014070102

Mandarin students' perceptions of multimodal interaction in a web conferencing environment: a satisfaction survey

Jun-Jie Tseng[1]

Abstract. A major indicator of whether online courses have been effective and successful is student satisfaction. Copious research points to lack of interaction as the most cited reason for student dissatisfaction. To improve this problem, new Computer-Mediated Communication (CMC) technology could be considered as an option to enhance the online learning platform because it can provide much more varied multimodal communication channels such as audio, video, text chat, images, graphic tools, and pre-programmed emoticons. To understand the quality of interaction in such an online learning environment, a 40-item questionnaire survey of student satisfaction was undertaken to gauge distance students' perceptions of the ways they interacted online with their teachers through multimodal communication channels. It was subsequently found that interactions through modal resources such as voice, video, image-enhanced texts, and graphics were perceived as important; and this aspect of online learning was also rated as satisfactory. Thus the present study should be seen as adding to the understanding of which communication channels are perceived to contribute to multimodal interaction in terms of student satisfaction, thereby making it a worthwhile contribution to research knowledge about student satisfaction of multimodal interaction in a web conferencing environment.

Keywords: student satisfaction, multimodal interaction, web conferencing technology, online language teaching and learning.

---

1. National Taiwan Normal University, Taipei, Taiwan; jjtseng@ntnu.edu.tw

How to cite this article: Tseng, J.-J. (2015). Mandarin students' perceptions of multimodal interaction in a web conferencing environment: a satisfaction survey. In F. Helm, L. Bradley, M. Guarda, & S. Thouësny (Eds), *Critical CALL – Proceedings of the 2015 EUROCALL Conference, Padova, Italy* (pp. 529-535). Dublin: Research-publishing. net. http://dx.doi.org/10.14705/rpnet.2015.000388

1. Introduction

Student satisfaction with online learning is a complex and multidimensional construct. Research has suggested that lack of interaction is the most cited reason for student dissatisfaction (Bolliger & Halupa, 2012; Sun, 2014). This problem could be improved with the advancement of Computer-Mediated Communication (CMC) technology. Compared to asynchronous CMC technology, synchronous CMC technology such as web conferencing technology can foster spontaneous communication and interaction because it essentially provides a number of multimodal functionalities, e.g. audio, video, visuals, text, and emoticons (Guo, 2014; Kear, Chetwynd, Williams, & Donelan, 2012), and these multiple modes can contribute positively to communicative language learning (Wang, 2008).

The issue of course satisfaction of foreign language learners in online courses or programs is not well documented. In particular, not much attention has been paid to their satisfaction with multimodal interaction in CMC environments. The purpose of this study was to determine the level of distance students' satisfaction with the ways in which they interacted with their online teachers through multimodal communication channels afforded by a web conferencing platform in the context of learning Mandarin as a foreign language. It is hoped that new insights could be provided into how students rate multimodal resources and tools in online language teaching and learning in terms of student satisfaction.

This exploratory study attempts to open up a field of enquiry into the following questions:

- How did the distance students perceive multimodal interaction in web conferencing learning environments in terms of satisfaction rating as opposed to importance rating?

- How satisfied were the distance students with the ways they interacted with their teachers through multimodal communication channels?

2. Method

2.1. Research setting

The present study was carried out at a national university in Taiwan, which has run a Mandarin training online program since 2013. Web conferencing technology, i.e. Adobe Connect, was adopted as the online learning platform for the Mandarin training online program. The method in which online courses were conducted was generally in the form of 1:1 tuition. Figure 1 presents a screenshot illustrating the variety of communication channels available on the web conferencing platform: (1) the microphone, (2) the webcam, (3) text chat, (4) pre-programmed emoticons, (5) the shared screen (PowerPoint, images, and MP3 audios), and (6) whiteboard tools (pointer, pencil, and highlighter).

Figure 1. The Adobe Connect interface

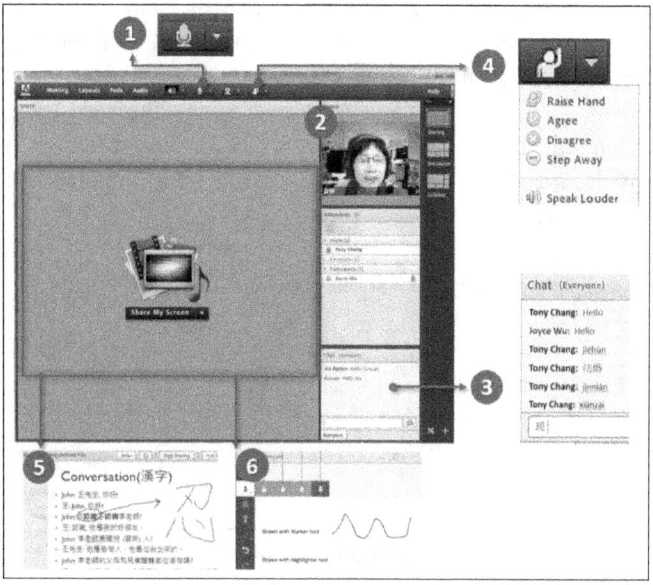

2.2. Data collection and analysis

For the purpose of this study, the researcher designed a questionnaire comprising 40 items in total: (1) six items seeking background information, (2) 12 items seeking the comparison between importance rating and satisfaction rating, (3) 18 items seeking the level of student satisfaction with multimodal interaction, and (4) four items seeking overall ratings. The questionnaire was created using Google Forms and made accessible on the Internet from April 24th, 2015 through to June 18th, 2015. An e-mail message was delivered to all registered distance students who had minimally completed a 20-hour online course, i.e. 95 students. They were invited to voluntarily fill in the web-based questionnaire.

The collected data was then analysed and the following information was compiled:

- importance-satisfaction analysis;

- descriptive statistics for satisfaction level.

3. Results and discussion

Of the overall population of 95 students enrolled in the Mandarin training online program, survey responses were received from 31 students, a response rate of 32.6%. The survey asked respondents to rate the importance of, and their satisfaction with, the ways they interacted with their teachers through multimodal communication channels, namely the microphone, the webcam, text chat, pre-programmed emoticons, PowerPoint materials, and whiteboard tools. While a rating of 1 represented low importance, a rating of 7 represented high importance. Table 1 provides a summary of the mean responses for importance ratings and satisfaction ratings respectively.

Table 1. Mean (and standard deviation) scores of importance-satisfaction ratings

Questionnaire item	Satisfaction (Mean 0-7)	Importance (Mean 0-7)
The way my teacher interacts with me through the microphone.	6.55(1.31)	6.58(1.31)
The way my teacher interacts with me through the webcam.	6.58(1.31)	6.45(1.41)
The way my teacher interacts with me through text chat.	6.16(1.55)	5.32(2.24)
The way my teacher interacts with me through pre-programmed emoticons.	4.13(3.24)	3.39(3.06)
The way my teacher interacts with me through PowerPoint materials on the shared screen.	6.03(2.12)	6.52(1.36)
The way my teacher interacts with me through drawing tools in the whiteboard.	6.32(1.58)	6.45(1.36)

One way to examine importance-satisfaction data, as mentioned by Palmer and Holt (2009), is "the importance-satisfaction grid (Aigbedo & Parameswaran, 2004) – where the importance rating is plotted on the vertical axis and the satisfaction rating is plotted on the horizontal axis" (p. 105). Figure 2 shows the survey data visualized in an importance-satisfaction grid, which is "divided into quadrants using the grand mean for all importance ratings [(5.75)] as a vertical divider and the grand mean of satisfaction ratings [(5.95)] as a horizontal divider" (Palmer & Holt, 2009, p. 105). As further pointed out by Palmer and Holt (2009, p. 105), the quadrants are generally interpreted as follows:

- Quadrant A: high importance and low satisfaction

- Quadrant B: high importance and high satisfaction

- Quadrant C: low importance and high satisfaction

- Quadrant D: low importance and low satisfaction

Figure 2. Importance-satisfaction grid

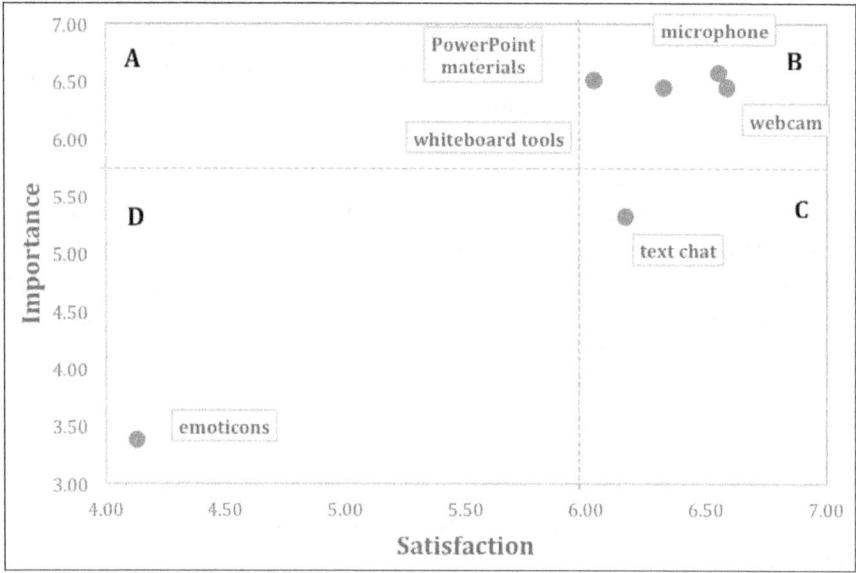

The ways of multimodal interaction that the respondents were satisfied with and rated highly included their interactions via the microphone, the webcam, PowerPoint materials, and whiteboard tools. This meant that the online teachers provided consistently good work because the students thought their interactions through the multimodal communication channels of audio, video, imaged-enhanced texts, and graphics were rewarding. This finding offers additional support for Cummingham, Fägersten, and Holmsten's (2010) study, in which teachers and students were able to find successful ways to communicate through channels such as voice, video, and whiteboard tools. Furthermore the present study confirmed that these aspects of multimodal interaction were recognised and appreciated by the students.

It was seen that lower value was given to the communication channels of text chat and pre-programmed emoticons in student-teacher interactions in web conferencing environments. The finding regarding the insignificant use of text chat contradicts

Kear et al.'s (2012) study, in which students preferred to use text chat instead of voice channel because they could make little verbal contributions. In addition, the result related to the unnecessary use of pre-programmed emoticons is inconsistent with Kozar's (2015) study, which found that emoticons were particularly useful when complementing speaking in online tutoring of English as a foreign language.

The survey also contained questionnaire items that sought the level of student satisfaction on a scale of 0-7. Overall, the respondents rated their satisfaction highly, with mean values mostly between 5 and 7. They were generally satisfied with the ways they interacted with their teachers through practically all multimodal communication channels except for emoticons. This finding reinforces the results of the importance-satisfaction ratings shown above. Of the 18 satisfaction items, 10 items received high ratings between 6-7. These items were constructed to deal with student satisfaction in relation to pedagogical scenarios via the use of multimodal communication channels such as the microphone, the webcam, PowerPoint materials, and whiteboard tools. In contrast, the items with lower mean ratings involved the use of emoticons, reinforcing the result stated above that the respondents perceived interactions through pre-programmed emoticons as not necessarily helpful.

4. Conclusion

The present study provides an early snapshot of how distance students perceive their satisfaction with multimodal interaction in a web conferencing environment, pointing towards interesting questions for future research, such as a survey completed by a large sample pool over an extended period and a survey supplemented by way of open-ended questions or interviews. Nevertheless, the present study makes a worthwhile contribution to research knowledge about student satisfaction of multimodal interaction in a web conferencing environment. The present study adds to the understanding of which communication channels are perceived to contribute to multimodal interaction in terms of student satisfaction. This research offers the foreign language profession some sense that integrating web conferencing technology into the foreign-language curriculum is perhaps a satisfactory and promising option with palpable benefits for multimodal interaction.

5. Acknowledgements

Many thanks go to Mandarin Training Center of National Taiwan Normal University for its administrative support.

References

Aigbedo, H., & Parameswaran, R. (2004). Importance-performance analysis for improving quality of campus food service. *International Journal of Quality & Reliability Management, 21*, 876-896. doi:10.1108/02656710410551755

Bolliger, D. U., & Halupa, C. (2012). Student perceptions of satisfaction and anxiety in an online doctoral program. *Distance Education, 33*(1), 81-98. doi:10.1080/01587919.2012.667961

Cunningham, U., Fägersten, K. B., & Holmsten, E. (2010). "Can you hear me, Hanoi?" Compensatory mechanisms employed in synchronous net-based English language learning. *International Review of Research in Open and Distance Learning, 11*(1), 161-177.

Guo, S. (2014). Evaluation of a web conferencing tool and collaborative tasks in an online Chinese course. In Sake Jager, Linda Bradley, Estelle J. Meima, Sylvie Thouësny. (Eds), *CALL Design: Principles and Practice - Proceedings of the 2014 EUROCALL Conference, Groningen, The Netherlands* (pp. 119-126). Dublin Ireland: Research-publishing.net. doi:10.14705/rpnet.2014.000205.

Kear, K., Chetwynd, F., Williams, J., & Donelan, H. (2012). Web conferencing for synchronous online tutorials: perspectives of tutors using a new medium. *Computers & Education, 58*, 953-963. doi:10.1016/j.compedu.2011.10.015

Kozar, O. (2015). Language education via audio/videoconferencing (LEVAC): a discursive investigation. *Linguistics and Education, 31*, 86-100. doi:10.1016/j.linged.2015.05.007

Palmer, S. R., & Holt, D. M. (2009). Examining student satisfaction with wholly online learning. *Journal of Computer Assisted Learning, 25*(2), 101-113. doi:10.1111/j.1365-2729.2008.00294.x

Sun, S. Y. H. (2014). Learner perspectives on fully online language learning. *Distance Education, 35*(1), 18-42. doi:10.1080/01587919.2014.891428

Wang, Y. (2008). *Distance language learning and desktop videoconferencing: a Chinese language case study*. Saarbrucken, Germany: VDM Verlag.

Computer-mediated synchronous and asynchronous corrective feedback provided by trainee teachers to learners of French: a preliminary study

Julie Vidal[1] and Sylvie Thouësny[2]

Abstract. In this paper, we investigate whether trainee teachers' practices, with respect to multimodal feedback, differ from current research, and to what extent it may affect students' language development. More specifically, the goal of the present study is threefold: (1) it observes how trainee teachers responded, whether synchronously, asynchronously, or a combination of both, to their students' incorrect language while or after interacting orally with them in French via a videoconference platform, (2) it considers the trainee teachers' beliefs regarding the efficacy of their feedback in light of semi-structured interviews, and (3) it explores the students' responses to corrective feedback received in synchronous and asynchronous settings through recorded videoconferencing sessions and interviews. The data set used for this preliminary study is drawn from a multimodal learning and teaching corpus, the InteractionS and Multimodality in lAnguagE Learning (ISMAEL) Project, a large collection of multimodal interactions and productions occurring between French trainee teachers in France and learners of French at university level in Ireland. Results show that asynchronous written feedback might strengthen the reception of oral synchronous feedback, thus leading to internalisation.

Keywords: corrective feedback, multimodality, synchronous, asynchronous, trainee teacher.

---

1. Université Lumière Lyon2, Lyon, France; julievidal.doc@gmail.com
2. Independent researcher, Dublin, Ireland; sylvie.thouesny@icall-research.net

How to cite this article: Vidal, J., & Thouësny, S. (2015). Computer-mediated synchronous and asynchronous corrective feedback provided by trainee teachers to learners of French: a preliminary study. In F. Helm, L. Bradley, M. Guarda, & S. Thouësny (Eds), *Critical CALL – Proceedings of the 2015 EUROCALL Conference, Padova, Italy* (pp. 536-542). Dublin: Research-publishing.net. http://dx.doi.org/10.14705/rpnet.2015.000389

1. Introduction

Corrective feedback, defined as "any indication to a learner that his or her use of the target language is incorrect" (Lightbown & Spada, 1999, p. 172), may be provided to students synchronously or asynchronously, where the main contrast "lies in the timing of the feedback – namely, whether it is immediate or delayed", respectively (Shintani, 2015, p. 17). Corrective feedback may also be implicit or explicit. As specified by Ellis, Loewen, and Erlam (2006), "[i]n the case of implicit feedback, there is no overt indicator that an error has been committed, whereas in explicit feedback types, there is" (pp. 340-341).

Advanced technology nowadays enables teachers to provide corrective feedback in several modes. Multimodality is defined by Siegel (2012) as "the social practice of making meaning by combining multiple semiotic resources" (p. 671). Multimodal corrective feedback, in the context of this preliminary study, implies feedback provided to students both orally during interactive sessions and in writing in an end-of-session report, in which each feedback items could be accompanied with video excerpts from the sessions and audio recordings.

After briefly presenting the data, this paper focuses on how feedback emitted by French trainee teachers either synchronously or asynchronously was received by learners of French.

2. Methodology

2.1. Participants and context

The ISMAEL corpus includes multimodal interactions and productions of 19 first-year university students in Ireland learning French as a foreign language (Blin, Guichon, Thouësny, & Wigham, 2014). They participated once a week during 6 weeks in 45-minute videoconferences with 12 French trainee teachers based in France. Of relevance to the present study are the recordings of 8 videoconferencing sessions involving 4 trainee teachers and 7 students, for which we have the former's immediate and delayed feedback, as well as most post semi-structured interviews for both.

2.2. Data coding and analysis

The data was coded in terms of feedback emission and reception. Our classification with respect to emission of synchronous and asynchronous corrective feedback

(Table 1) is arranged from implicit to explicit and is adapted from the work of Ellis (2009), Lyster and Ranta (1997), and Zourou (2012). The grid of feedback reception is built from our own data observation (Table 2).

Table 1. Feedback emission

Emission	Synchronous	Asynchronous
E0	inconspicuous markers[3]	n/a
E1	facial mimics and/or visible markers	n/a
E2	recast, clarification requests, elicitation, repetition	recast (orally) emphasis (in written)
E3	incorrect form pointed out without further explanations	equivalent
E4	incorrect form pointed out and a link to help students correct the incorrect form provided	equivalent
E5	incorrect form pointed out and metalinguistic explanations provided	equivalent
E6	correct form provided without explanations	equivalent
E7	correct form provided with explanations	equivalent

Table 2. Feedback reception

Reception	Synchronous
R0	students do not show any evidence feedback is received
R1	students do not show intentional evidence feedback is received
R2	students show intentional evidence feedback is received
R3	students show feedback is received with a simple "yes" or "ok"
R4	students ask for clarifications
R5	students use feedback to correct themselves, but inappropriately
R6	students use feedback to correct themselves appropriately

3. Results and discussion

3.1. Trainee teachers' responses to students' incorrect forms

Table 3 shows that trainee teacher Adèle, for instance, identified 29 + 13 errors while interacting with her students, thus providing 42 synchronous opportunities for learners to notice their incorrect forms, from which 29 incorrect forms were further detailed in her written report. In addition, Adèle described 3 errors in her written report, for which she did not provide any synchronous explanations. In general terms, trainee teachers provided more synchronous – or a combination of synchronous and asynchronous – corrective feedback rather than asynchronous only.

---

3. See Guichon, Betrancourt, and Prié (2012).

Table 3. Incorrect forms identified by trainee teachers

Trainee teachers	Errors in sequences for which the trainee teacher provided feedback as:							
	asynchronous feedback only		asynchronous + synchronous feedback		synchronous feedback only		Total	
Adèle	3	6.67%	29	64.44%	13	28.89%	45	100.00%
Melissa	16	38.10%	20	47.62%	6	14.29%	42	100.00%
Samia	6	26.09%	8	34.78%	9	39.13%	23	100.00%
Victor	5	16.66%	8	26.67%	17	56.67%	30	100.00%
Total	30	21.43%	65	46.43%	45	32.14%	140	100.00%

3.2. Trainee teachers' beliefs regarding feedback strategies

The interviews with the trainee teachers reveal that their beliefs with respect to feedback strategies are not always in alignment with their actual practices. For instance, Victor claimed that he deliberately chose not to offer any synchronous feedback while interacting with his student. Yet, we count as much as 83.24% of synchronous feedback compared to 16.66% of exclusive asynchronous feedback. This statement is in line with numerous studies which have found that teachers' beliefs with respect to corrective feedback in educational settings and their actual practices were not always aligned (e.g. Junqueira & Payant, 2015; Roothooft, 2014). For instance, Roothooft (2014) observes that while teachers trust it is important not to disrupt the students' flow of conversation and prefer to leave an error uncorrected, they are convinced that providing oral corrective feedback is an essential stage in language learning; they seem to be unaware of the amount of feedback they actually provide to students while interacting with them.

3.3. Students' responses to corrective feedback

Table 4 displays the tendency of how feedback was received while emitted synchronously. For instance, trainee teachers placed 17 markers (E0) – indicating their intention of asynchronous feedback –, which naturally were not perceived by students (R0). Although it is worth mentioning that no feedback was provided at levels E3, E4, and E5, and that almost half of the feedback was provided at level E2 with only 20.83% of feedback received and properly re-employed (R6), our intention is not to infer that to ensure feedback is received 100 percent of the time (R6), they must be emitted at level E7. As Lantolf and Poehner (2011) argue, "if the instructional aim is simply to help learners arrive at a correct response, then explicit feedback is certainly an efficient means. However, [...] if the intention is to promote development then process must be foregrounded, as in the [zone of proximal development]" (p. 17).

Table 4. Synchronous feedback emission/reception

	R0	R1	R2	R3	R4	R5	R6
E0 (n=17)	100.00%						
E1 (n=5)	80.00%						20.00%
E2 (n=48)	14.58%	8.33%	6.25%	16.67%	6.25%	27.08%	20.83%
E3 (n=0)							
E4 (n=0)							
E5 (n=0)							
E6 (n=37)	2.70%	2.70%		18.92%		10.81%	64.86%
E7 (n=3)							100.00%

In line with sociocultural perspectives, we noted that some corrective feedback (25 in total) was provided as a discussion, where meaning was negotiated, rather than as standalone pieces of information on one particular linguistic aspect. One discussion, for instance, evolved around the word bailler (to yawn). Mélissa, a trainee teacher, asked Ana (student #1) for clarification as she did not understand the student's request. Ana, understanding the trainee teacher's recast, repeated herself (E2/R6). Mélissa asked this time for clarification in writing using the chat modality. Ana understood the task but requested help with respect to spelling (E2/R4). The trainee teacher further requested clarification before seeing what the student meant and proposing the correct form, whose suggestion was straight away accepted by Ana and successfully re-employed (E6/R6). At this stage, Alejandra (student #2) seemed to grasp the meaning of the word with a smile and a timid "yes" (E6/R3). The trainee teacher then went on with Alejandra and offered her the opportunity to repeat and use the word, though this did not happen, as the student only confirmed she understood (E2/R3). While in general, and more particularly in this example, feedback emission (when provided as a set of interactions) tends to go from implicit to explicit, our certitude that the feedback is actually received and at what level is, however, not predictable.

With respect to asynchronous feedback, our dataset shows that more than half of the feedback provided were at level E2, the rest being mostly offered at level E6/E7 (E2=65.55%; E6=15.2%; E7=7.6%; positive feedback related to negative synchronous feedback=1.9%). From Ana's post interview (student #1), we know that the verb bailler (to yawn), further explained in her end-of-session written report, is now fully internalised, thus confirming her reception at level R6 while interacting synchronously. However, the level of reception for Alejandra (student #2) could not be further investigated as this linguistic point was not part of her report.

4. Conclusion

It is worth recalling that the findings of this preliminary study are drawn from the data of a small sample, thus implying that further research is necessary to shed a clearer light on the relation between emission and reception of synchronous and asynchronous feedback.

Although trainee teachers' beliefs with respect to feedback and their actual practices were not always aligned, they tried to make the most of the situation to help students notice their incorrect forms. They all provided synchronous oral corrective feedback during the sessions and gave a more detailed account to some of the errors in their end-of-session written reports.

Either provided synchronously or asynchronously, feedback was mostly emitted at a very implicit or explicit level. Only 1 in 5 implicit feedback was re-employed at the time of the interactions. However, it is worth mentioning that a feedback labeled with a lower reception level does not infer that it was not received, it just indicates that we do not know whether or not it was noticed for later re-use, for instance, in the same or subsequent sessions; this would need further investigation.

Finally, students in general – Ana in particular – were pleased with the additional explanations provided in the end-of-session written reports. While being post interviewed, students talked about their incorrect forms occurring in their reports, which clearly shows that the correct forms for most of them are now fully internalised.

References

Blin, F., Guichon, N., Thouësny, S., & Wigham, C.R. (2014). Creating and sharing a language learning and teaching corpus of multimodal interactions: ethical challenges and methodological implications. *XVIth International CALL Research Conference, 7-9 June, Antwerp, Belgium.*

Ellis, R. (2009). A typology of written corrective feedback types. *ELT Journal, 63*(2), 97-107. doi:10.1093/elt/ccn023

Ellis, R., Loewen, S., Erlam, R. (2006). Implicit and explicit corrective feedback and the acquisition of L2 grammar. *Studies of Second Language Acquisition, 28*(2), 339-368. doi:10.1017/S0272263106060141

Guichon, N., Betrancourt, M., & Prié, Y. (2012). Managing written and oral negative feedback in a synchronous online teaching situation. *Computer Assisted Language Learning, 25*(2), 181-197. doi:10.1080/09588221.2011.636054

Junqueira, L., & Payant, C. (2015). "I just want to do it right, but it's so hard": a novice teacher's written feedback beliefs and practices. *Journal of Second Language Writing, 27*(March), 19–36. doi:10.1016/j.jslw.2014.11.001

Lantolf, J. P., & Poehner, M. E. (2011). Dynamic assessment in the classroom: Vygotskian praxis for second language development. *Language Teaching Research, 15*(1), 11-33. doi:10.1177/1362168810383328

Lightbown, P. M., & Spada, N. (1999). *How languages are learned*. Oxford: Oxford University Press.

Lyster, R., & Ranta, L. (1997). Corrective feedback and learner uptake. *Studies in Second Language Acquisition, 19*(1), 37-66. doi:10.1017/S0272263197001034

Shintani, N. (2015). The effects of computer-mediated synchronous and asynchronous direct corrective feedback on writing: a case study. *Computer Assisted Language Learning, early publication*, 1–22. doi:10.1080/09588221.2014.993400

Siegel, M. (2012). New time for multimodality? Confronting the accountability culture. *Journal of Adolescent and Adult Literacy, 55*(8), 671-680. doi:10.1002/JAAL.00082

Roothooft, A. (2014). The relationship between adult EFL teachers' oral feedback practices and their beliefs. *System, 46*(October), pp. 65-79. doi:10.1016/j.system.2014.07.012

Zourou, K. (2012). Towards a typology of corrective feedback moves in an asynchronous distance language learning environment. In W. M. Chan, K. N. Chin, M. Nagami, & T. Suthiwan (Eds.), *Media in foreign language teaching and learning* (pp. 217-242). Singapore: National University of Singapore.

Examining and supporting online writing – a qualitative pre-study for an analytic learning environment

Ikumi Waragai[1], Tatsuy Ohta[2], Marco Raindl[3], Shuichi Kurabayashi[4], Yasushi Kiyoki[5], and Hideyuki Tokuda[6]

Abstract. The authors present a project that aims at understanding the way language learners write in social media in their every day lives using the target language. How do our students proceed when writing a Social Network Site (SNS) post? What resources do they use for references on word, sentences and text level? By answering these and related questions through extensive collection of empirical data in an analytic learning environment, the design of which is the next step of this project, the authors aim at creating a comprehensive resource that supports different approaches to writing in social media. In the projects' first step, which the authors will lay out in this paper, writing processes of a small number of informants were closely analyzed using experiments, interviews and self-reports. The findings showed considerable differences of resource management between students with different backgrounds in formal learning and revealed a differentiation into 'public' and 'private' space of informal writing in social media, that influenced students' choices regarding the degree of formal elaboration (with respect to correctness) of their texts.

Keywords: writing process, informal learning, SNS, resource management.

---

1. Keio University, Japan; ikumi@sfc.keio.ac.jp
2. Nanzan University, Japan; FZE00305@nifty.ne.jp
3. Dokkyo University, Japan; raindl@dokkyo.ac.jp
4. Keio University, Japan; kurabaya@sfc.keio.ac.jp
5. Keio University, Japan; kiyoki@sfc.keio.ac.jp
6. Keio University, Japan; hxt@sfc.keio.ac.jp

How to cite this article: Waragai, I., Ohta, T., Raindl, M., Kurabayashi, S., Kiyoki, Y., & Tokuda, H. (2015). Examining and supporting online writing – a qualitative pre-study for an analytic learning environment. In F. Helm, L. Bradley, M. Guarda, & S. Thouësny (Eds), *Critical CALL – Proceedings of the 2015 EUROCALL Conference, Padova, Italy* (pp. 543-548). Dublin: Research-publishing.net. http://dx.doi.org/10.14705/rpnet.2015.000390

Ikumi Waragai, Tatsuy Ohta, Marco Raindl, Shuichi Kurabayashi, Yasushi Kiyoki, and Hideyuki Tokuda

1. Introduction

In recent years, learning scenarios using social media have been explored from a multitude of angles (cf. Wang & Vasquèz, 2012; Zourou, 2012 for an overview). Most of the research examines formal educational/learning contexts of use, whereas studies inquiring about the potential of social media in informal learning contexts often center on SNS spaces set-up as an addition to institutionally framed scenarios, either by the instructors (e.g. Peeters, 2015) or by learners themselves (e.g. Liaw & English, 2012). Little is known though about how learners use social media in a completely informal context, i.e. when they communicate with other learners or speakers of the target language by their own initiative in their free time. But informal learning opportunities on social media can be considered of high relevance for learners' competence development: especially in contexts where contact time with the target language is limited, as in the case of learners of German in Japan, informal learning through social media might have the potential to expand learning opportunities considerably.

The vast majority of learners of German in Japan start learning the language on entering university. Motivated learners normally reach a level of around B1 of the Common European Framework of Reference for Languages (CEFR) after about two years of learning. As it might be assumed, learners will only become more willing to use the target language in social media actively as their competence grows and they feel more self-assured about their production. Thus the authors of this paper have been researching how to provide writing support to encourage learners to use social media at an earlier stage, mainly by offering context-aware help linking informal learning opportunities to formal learning experiences through specially designed learning environments (Waragai et al., 2014).

In a new project, the authors set out to analyze learners' resource management for problem solving while writing on SNS by their own initiative – with the long term perspective to describe prerogatives of a resource that would support learners at earlier stages of learning more substantially. In order to gain a first insight into learners' writing processes in informal contexts, the authors took a close look at writing behaviors of a small group of students from two Japanese universities. The findings of this pre-study are presented here.

2. Method

The authors chose a multi-angular qualitative approach to understand learners' writing and problem solving behavior and their attitudes towards target language use on SNS (e.g. concerning formal adequacy). We decided to focus on learners who already had a level between B1 and B2 (CEFR) and used German regularly on SNS. In order to include learners who were experiencing different learning environments in formal education, we selected eight participants from two universities, four from University X, which fosters learning activities online ('group X', with participants X1, X2, X3 and X4), and four from University Z, where the use of computers in language teaching is limited ('group Z', with participants Z1, Z2, Z3 and Z4). The following research questions were formulated: which online (online dictionaries, search engines, translating engines, reference sites etc.) and offline resources do learners use when encountering problems while writing? Which strategies do learners use to extract help from these resources? How much importance do learners attach to their texts being formally correct?

Data were collected in three ways to gain a comprehensive insight into the participants' writing behaviors on SNS: (1) *Writing experiment*: Participants were asked to write an SNS post on a PC the same way they usually did, using the same resources for help. They were asked to think aloud during the writing process. Screen data were captured with a screen capturing software, the utterances of the students were audiographed. When participants used resources other than through PC (e.g. dictionaries or smartphones), their use of these devices was videographed. (2) *Follow-up interviews*: Participants were interviewed about their writing experiences in (1) with a focus on problems they experienced when writing. Apart from these retrospective elements they were asked about their habitual writing behavior in German on SNS. (3) *Self reports*: Participants were asked to fill in a questionnaire about problems experienced when writing immediately after having written an SNS post during their free time (3-5 times over a month). The data of (2) were transcribed and coded. Observations made in (1) and participants' utterances in (2) and (3) were grouped into categories describing tendencies of writing behavior.

3. Findings and discussion

One tendency observed was that the use of resources of participants from group X was very diversified, whereas that of students from group Z tended to be more uniform. While participants X1, X2, X3 and X4 used resources as different as online dictionaries, search engine search by explicit questions (How do you say '...' in German?), search engine search for chunks, Q&A-sites, translation engines – X4 English-German, X1 German-Japanese – and direct help from friends (via Facebook messages), participants Z1, Z2, and Z4 mainly used their portable electronic dictionaries; Z3 referred to a dictionary on her smartphone. Only Z1 and Z2 made use of a web browser on one occasion each, using a search engine to confirm a chunk. An unexpected resource identified during the interviews was the recourse to community help: help of an anonymous community such as on an SNS for language learning (Z1), help from individuals such as native speakers amongst their friends (X1, X2), or from advanced peers (Z2).

Concerning the extraction of information from resources, all participants of group Z skillfully handled their dictionaries, using different approaches to one problem (trying out different Japanese words, counter-checking by entering a German word they had found, shifting the resource) and skimming through translations of example phrases to decide which finding was the most appropriate in a context. Group X showed less unified results with resource use. Overall participants of group X tended to move on with writing more readily, even if they were not quite sure to have found appropriate results or even if their search did not bring any results (Z3 sometimes showed the same tendency to give up on her search).

Inquired about the importance attached to formal correctness, all participants stated that they took care to write as adequately as possible as long as writing for a multitude of readers (i.e. when publishing texts in 'timeline' on Facebook). To the contrary, when using instant messaging (on Facebook or on line) in one-to-one communication, they tended to care less about formal adequacy and to focus on content. Thus, it seems, all participants made a clear distinction between 'public' spaces of writing ('timeline' on Facebook or blogs) and 'private' spaces. Participants gave diverse reasons for this: X1 stated that she, being a teaching assistant for German, had the responsibility to write correctly; others, like for example Z1, expressed that they would feel awkward if they 'made public' a text with many mistakes. Therefore Z1 tends to first publish texts on an SNS for language learning (in her case: Lang-8), where she uses a profile that does not give her clear name, to have it checked by native speakers, before publishing it on Facebook. X2 directly asks a native speaker among her friends to have her writings corrected before publishing them on her 'timeline'. Furthermore, some participants from group Z (Z1, Z2) uttered that they tended to write about topics they felt they could handle easily, using familiar words and structures.

As far as the engagement with publishing on SNS in the target language is concerned, participants reported very different degrees of activity. Especially X1 and X3 said that they posted in 'timeline' regularly, while most of the others said that their main target language activity was reading other posts and that they only sporadically wrote posts themselves. Furthermore many participants identified a stay in a German speaking country as a point of departure for communicating on SNS in German – even though with many of them the activity tapered out after a few months.

4. Conclusions

It might be assumed that the differences observed between group X and Z in choice and usage of resources might be a result of the different formal learning environments that the participants learn in. Further research about these probably environment fostered preferences could address the question if both groups could maybe benefit from an expansion of their strategies for resource management: group Z might benefit from expanding their resource repertory, accessing more online resources (e.g. translation engines, chunk searches, 'social' resources), while for group X training about how to handle resources systematically and effectively might be helpful.

Another outcome of this study is the insight into the division into perceived 'public' and 'private' spaces of writing in social media. Whereas participants reported to have extensive exchange in the target language over instant messages in 'private' (and thus probably a considerable surplus of contact time and opportunity for output), their production in the 'public' space of SNS seems – due to their concerns about formal adequacy – much more limited. Further studies with Japanese learners about social media use in informal contexts should take this aspect into consideration and get a deeper insight in to the 'private' spaces as well.

Finally, looking at the (im)balance between input and output on SNS observed with most participants in this study, further research should take a look at SNS as a space not only for writing, but maybe even more as a reading space. At the same time, though, students who extensively publish on SNS might be interesting subjects for a closer examination in case studies too.

References

Liaw, M.-L., & English, K. (2012). Online and offsite. Student driven development of the Taiwan-France telecollaborative project *Beyond these walls*. In M.-N. Lamy & K. Zourou (Eds.), *Social networking for language education*. Basingstoke, UK: Palgrave Macmillan, 158-176.

Peeters, W. (2015). Tapping into the educational potential of Facebook: encouraging out-of-class peer collaboration in foreign language learning. *Studies in Self-Access Learning Journal*, 6(2), 176-190.

Wang, S., & Vasquèz, C. (2012). Web 2.0 and second language learning: what does the research tell us? *CALICO Journal, 29*(3), 412-429. doi:10.11139/cj.29.3.412-430

Waragai, I., Kurabayashi, S., Ohta, T., Raindl, M., Kiyoki, Y., & Tokuda, H. (2014). Context-aware writing support for SNS: connecting formal and informal learning. In L. Bradley & S. Thouësny (Eds.), *CALL design: principles and practice. 2014 EUROCALL Conference in Groningen Proceedings* (pp. 403-407). doi:10.14705/rpnet.2014.000253

Zourou, K. (2012). On the attractiveness of social media for language learning: a look at the state of the art. *Alsic,15*(1). doi:10.4000/alsic.2436

CALL and less commonly taught languages: challenges and opportunities

Monica Ward[1]

Abstract. Computer-Assisted Language Learning (CALL) researchers face many challenges in developing effective, high-quality CALL. CALL research has a very strong focus on the Most Commonly Taught Languages (MCLTs), particularly English. CALL researchers working with Less Commonly Taught Languages (LCTLs) face further constraints. LCTLs can range from languages with a large speaker and online presence to those with fewer speakers and less online resources. Suitable and effective pedagogical approaches may not be available for LCTLs and the learner needs may also be different. In the case of Endangered Languages (ELs) there are further constraints which include the lack of printed and online resources in the language, dialectal issues, lack of societal support, lack of quality language documentation, lack of an active speaker community or native speakers, competent linguists and teachers. This paper reviews general CALL constraints for MCTLs, the further constraints that particularly apply in the LCTL context and the additional constraints that exist for ELs. It suggests some strategies for dealing with these challenges, including leveraging prior research, reusing existing resources where possible, adopting a pragmatic approach and aiming to be smart with limited resources. CALL for LCTLs and ELs can look at what works for the MCLTs and try to leverage that.

Keywords: CALL challenges, CALL opportunities, less commonly taught languages, endangered languages.

1. Introduction

CALL researchers face many challenges in developing effective, high-quality CALL resources. The challenges include lack of real institutional support, difficulties in

---

1. Dublin City University, Ireland; mward@computing.dcu.ie

How to cite this article: Ward, M. (2015). CALL and less commonly taught languages: challenges and opportunities. In F. Helm, L. Bradley, M. Guarda, & S. Thouësny (Eds), *Critical CALL – Proceedings of the 2015 EUROCALL Conference, Padova, Italy* (pp. 549-552). Dublin: Research-publishing.net. http://dx.doi.org/10.14705/rpnet.2015.000391

ascertaining real learner needs, problems assembling a multidisciplinary team, financial limitations and time issues. Ideally the CALL multidisciplinary team would include language teachers, linguists, pedagogical specialists, learners, software engineers, programmers, and user interface designers, amongst others. Most CALL researchers do not have access to all of these people when designing and developing CALL resources. Language pedagogy is constantly evolving, as is CALL, and there is no 'silver bullet' or magic formula for developing the 'best' CALL resources. This makes the CALL process difficult, regardless of how many resources are available in the language.

2. Method

CALL research has a very strong focus on the MCLTs, particularly English. This is not surprising, given the global dominance of English as a major language of international business and communication. Although CALL researchers working with the MCTLs face challenges, CALL researchers working with LCTLs and ELs face further constraints.

2.1. CALL for less commonly taught languages

LCTL can range from Arabic, Japanese and Polish (who have a large speaker and online presence) to languages such as Bosnian and Bulgarian. While pedagogical strategies have developed over many years for the MCTLs, suitable and effective pedagogical approaches may not be available for LCTLs. Also, for CALL to be successful, it must address learner needs, but questions as to who are the learners, what is their motivation and previous language learning experiences, what their learning needs and goals are may not be clear and this can hamper CALL for LCTLs. It is easy to understand why many people study English. Apart from its global position, it may be compulsory in the education system. However, for LCTLs, there are often different motivations for learning the language, some of which are quite different from those studying English. Some language learners may wish to read literature in the original language, learn a language for heritage reasons, for a holiday visit or for military intelligence reasons. Clearly what they want to learn and how they want to learn will vary. It is also important to consider the age and context of the learners: are they children learning it because it is compulsory or adults learning it for intrinsic reasons? What previous language learning experience do they already have? Are they familiar with the writing system or the sound system? In CALL for Japanese, is it better to teach romaji first (i.e. use the roman alphabet) or use hiragana, katakana and kanji from the start? What CALL strategies should be adopted for teaching Basque? In general, there are also less researchers working in CALL for these languages, so the pool of expertise may be limited. For these reasons, it is more challenging for CALL researchers working with LCTLs to design, develop and deploy CALL resources.

2.2. CALL for endangered languages

ELs, as the name suggests, are languages that are in danger of disappearing. There is a language endangerment scale from not endangered through to severely endangered and extinct. For example, in Italy, Venetian and Sicilian are classified as 'vulnerable', while Gardiol and Griko are both 'severely endangered' (Moseley, 2010). In the case of languages that are threatened or endangered there are further constraints which include the lack of printed and online resources in the language, dialectal issues, lack of societal support and in some cases lack of quality language documentation. For example, the language may not have a writing system or may never have been documented. There may be several dialects and choosing which one to teach can be socially and culturally problematic. Some EL communities may want to restrict access to who can learn the language. The issue of an active speaker community or indeed, access to native speakers and competent linguists and teachers can be a real problem for ELs. For example, for severely endangered languages, the few remaining speakers may be older adults with health difficulties who may live in a remote area and may not be willing or able to help. Obviously, these constraints make CALL for ELs very difficult.

3. Discussion

However, it is important to look for possible solutions to these constraints. In many situations, researchers are not aware of what has worked (and what has not worked) in the past. It is important that they have access to this information so that they can use their limited resources more effectively. For example, while CALL effectiveness research has room for improvement, there appears to be certain areas in which CALL can have a positive impact on learning; e.g. MALL (Burston, 2015) and computer assisted pronunciation training and chat (Golonka et al., 2014). CALL for LCTLs and ELs can look at what works for the MCLTs and try to leverage that. For CALL researchers working with ELs, it is informative to learn what has worked for other EL communities in different parts of the world. Although the context will vary, some of the lessons learnt could be useful for other (relatively less well resourced) communities in other parts of the world. For both EL and LCTL CALL researchers, a useful strategy is to reuse existing resources where possible. For example, Hot Potatoes authoring software provides a tool to enable the development of language learning exercises. While some may have pedagogical doubts about such exercises, they do have a role to play in the language learning process, especially in situations where the learners do not have easy access to target language materials or speakers. Reusing an existing tool allows for more efficient use of CALL researchers' time so they can work on other aspects of the CALL environment. Another important strategy is to adopt a pragmatic approach. Perhaps the CALL resources are not the best or most beautiful and may not adhere to the latest 'correct' way to teach a language, but it is better that they exist than to wait until the 'perfect' CALL resource for the language can be developed. This is especially true in the case of ELs, where time is of the essence and ability to access the remaining speakers may disappear in the near future. Overall, the aim should be to be smart with the limited resources available.

4.   Conclusions

CALL development is difficult regardless of the target language. CALL provides an opportunity for learners of LCTLs and ELs to access learning resources and interact with other learners and speakers – something that otherwise would not be possible. Without CALL, it would be very difficult for learners of LCTLs and ELs to have access to learning materials, as it is often easier, cheaper and quicker to provide them electronically. In some/many cases, it may not be possible to print the relevant resources. Without CALL, it would be very difficult for learners of LCTLs and ELs to hear the language being spoken. For many of these learners, there may be no native speakers near them, or in the case of ELs, there may be very few speakers left in the world. While CALL can help learners of English and the other major world languages to learn the language and can foster social change, arguably CALL can have a bigger impact on LCTLs and ELs. It is more difficult for these languages, but CALL can help learners and the language communities more in these contexts than in the mainstream CALL situation. It is definitely worth the effort.

References

Burston, J. (2015). Twenty years of MALL project implementation: a meta-analysis of learning outcomes. *ReCALL*, 27(1), 4-20.

Golonka, E. M., Bowles, A. R., Frank, V. M., Richardson, D. L., & Freynik, S. (2014). Technologies for foreign language learning: a review of technology types and their effectiveness. *Computer Assisted Language Learning*, 27(1), 70-105. doi:10.1080/09588221.2012.700315

Moseley, C. (Ed.). (2010). *Atlas of the world's languages in danger* (3rd ed.). Paris, UNESCO Publishing. Retrieved from http://www.unesco.org/culture/en/endangeredlanguages/atlas

I'm a useful NLP tool – get me out of here

Monica Ward[1]

Abstract. Irish is a compulsory subject in Irish schools. However, there are several pedagogical issues with teaching and learning the language. Computer-Assisted Language Learning (CALL) is under-utilised in schools in Ireland and even more so in the case of Irish, as there are very few CALL resources for the language. This paper looks at the lessons learnt from other Natural Language Processing (NLP)/CALL projects, and tries to apply them to build Intelligent CALL (ICALL) resources for Irish. It shows that a focus on the learner needs and smart use of existing resources can produce useful NLP/CALL resources for language learners. Close collaboration between NLP specialists, CALL researchers, linguists, pedagogical specialists and learners is important in order for a project of this type to be successful. Abair is a useful text-to-speech (TTS) synthesiser for Irish that is relatively unknown outside the TTS/Irish language community. This is a pity as it is a high-quality NLP resource with potential to enhance CALL resources. This paper reports on the integration of Abair into a CALL resource for Irish orthography and pronunciation. While it was developed specifically for Irish, the system is modular in design, and could be adopted for other languages. Furthermore, the lessons learnt are applicable to other languages, not just Irish.

Keywords: NLP, ICALL, Irish, Abair.

1. Introduction

In Ireland, Irish is a compulsory subject in primary and secondary schools and there are complex socio-cultural issues surrounding the language. Irish orthography is an area of difficulty for learners, which causes problems for spelling and reading Irish words. There are pronunciation rules but they are not fully documented. Furthermore, not many teachers are aware of them and therefore cannot point them

---

1. Dublin City University, Ireland; mward@computing.dcu.ie

How to cite this article: Ward, M. (2015). I'm a useful NLP tool – get me out of here. In F. Helm, L. Bradley, M. Guarda, & S. Thouësny (Eds), *Critical CALL – Proceedings of the 2015 EUROCALL Conference, Padova, Italy* (pp. 553-557). Dublin: Research-publishing.net. http://dx.doi.org/10.14705/rpnet.2015.000392

out to their students (Hickey & Stenson, 2011). This makes it difficult for students to read and spell in Irish.

There are many reasons why NLP is not used in CALL, including lack of knowledge and lack of suitability of application to CALL. Abair (2015) is an Irish language synthesiser. It is a high quality NLP tool that allows the user to type in a word, phrase or sentence in Irish and to listen to a spoken version of the text. It provides text to speech synthesis in two dialects and in five different speed settings. Abair is an example of an NLP resource that overcomes some of the NLP/CALL integration problems. It is a high quality resource that is based on a theoretically sound design plan with a long-term perspective. It has continued to develop over a period of years and has a long-term vision. An NLP resource such as Abair would be difficult and expensive to build from scratch – but it exists and can be used in ICALL resources. To date, Abair is not well-known outside the inner core of Irish language NLP researchers and has a focus on text to speech synthesis rather than language learning.

There is a need for CALL resources for Irish. Several CALL resources exist, but they are sometimes developed by language enthusiasts (with limited pedagogical experience) or may be technically correct (but not appealing to non-linguistic language learners). The majority of Irish language learners are primary and secondary school children who learn it as part of the core curriculum. In general, they are not taught the pronunciation and orthography rules of the language. Often, their teachers are not aware of the rules themselves. Often, the parents are similarly unaware of the rules. Currently, there are no quality CALL resources for Irish pronunciation and orthography – but there is a definite need for them.

2. Method

2.1. Approach

Rather than starting from scratch with the development of a CALL resource for Irish pronunciation, it made sense to look at what research and resources were already available and to try to utilise them where possible. In this regard, there were three main contributions to consider. Firstly, Hickey and Stenson (2011) provide a suggestion as to how the rules of Irish orthography and pronunciation could be taught to learners. They stress that the analysis of the rules was still under development, but the most basic rules were fairly well-established and could be explained to learners. Hickey is an educational psychologist and is an expert on the teaching and learning of Irish as both a first and a second language. Stenson is an expert Irish language linguist and they have worked together in recent years on Irish orthography. Secondly, there is the Abair project. Abair is a high-quality TTS synthesiser for Irish, which currently provides TTS for the Donegal and Connemara dialects of Irish. Thirdly, there was the body of research on why NLP was not more widely used in CALL. Researchers over the years have noted that there have been several NLP resources developed that could potentially be useful in CALL resources, but never made the transition from the NLP world to the CALL world. It is easy to see why this might be the case. For example, Kraif et al. (2004) identified three reasons for this: NLP techniques may not be reliable, NLP resources are difficult and expensive to implement, and end-users may not be aware of NLP possibilities. Granger et al. (2006) note that the lack of communication between NLP specialists, CALL researchers and language teachers is a major challenge to NLP/CALL integration. Many ICALL projects disappear due to lack of funding, lack of long-term perspective, and lack of understanding of pedagogical issues (Tschichold, 2014).

Learning from this research, it seemed logical to use Hickey and Stenson's (2011) work, combined with Abair, to produce a CALL resource for Irish orthography and pronunciation. This combination overcomes some of the NLP/CALL integration difficulties outlined above. Developing a CALL resource that utilised Abair would make its technology available to end-users (without them having to be aware of the technicalities). Pedagogical and linguistic input from Irish language specialists would help to overcome some of the ICALL/pedagogical issues that often arise.

2.2. CALLIPSO system

The CALLIPSO (**CALL** for **I**rish for **P**arents, **S**tudents and **O**thers) system was designed and developed as a CALL resource for Irish orthography and pronunciation. It was based on Hickey and Stenson's (2011) work and uses TTS outputs from the Abair system. The initial version was designed with parents in mind, but it is a modular system and is designed to be customisable to the learning needs of the end-user. This is an overlooked group in terms of CALL resources for Irish. Many parents want to be able to help their children with homework, particularly in primary school. However, they have often forgotten their Irish or may not have a particularly good understanding of the language. Furthermore, in recent years, Ireland has seen an increase in immigrant parents who have no previous Irish language experience and there are no accessible resources for them. In most cases, the parents just want to be able to check their children's spelling and reading, without actually having to learn the language. Their language needs are different from the traditional language learner.

The CALLIPSO system provides information on Irish consonants and vowels, along with sample sounds and words (provided by Abair). It provides some pronunciation exercises for learners so they can check their understanding. It is currently aimed at (false) beginner learners and more detailed information will be provided for more advanced learners (e.g. trainee or current teachers) in future versions. The CALLIPSO system is designed to be L1 and target language independent, although obviously, the target language is Irish in this case. It is planned to provide a version with Polish as the L1, as this is one of the major immigrant languages in Ireland at this time.

3. Discussion and conclusions

It would not have been possible to design and develop the CALLIPSO without reusing existing NLP and research resources. Abair is an example of a high-quality NLP resource that could and should be used more outside its current environs. The initial version of the CALLIPSO system did not have access to the Abair application program interface (API), but it will use the API in future versions. By focusing on learner needs (i.e. the need to be able to understand Irish orthography and pronunciation), it was possible to develop a CALL resource that would be useful to the target learner group. Feedback from parents has been positive and there are plans for further improvements to the system.

As a final remark, combining research with an NLP tool (Abair) made it possible to build a CALL resource that was based on pedagogical guidelines and that was of benefit to the target learner group. The useful NLP tool was able to escape into the wild.

4. Acknowledgements

We would like to thank the abair.ie team in Trinity College Dublin for access to the Abair system. Also thanks to the Centre for Digital Content Platform Research (ADAPT), the global centre of excellence for digital content and media innovation, for its support.

References

Abair. (2015). *Abair.ie – The Irish Language Synthesiser*. Retrieved from http://www.abair.tcd.ie/
Granger, S., Antoniadis, G., Fairon, C., Medori, J., & Zampa, V. (2006). *Report on NLP-based CALL workshop*. Research report - Report number D39.3.1. 2006. Retrieved from https://telearn.archives-ouvertes.fr/hal-00190372/document

Hickey, T., & Stenson, N. (2011). Irish orthography: what do teachers and learners need to know about it, and why? *Language, Culture and Curriculum, 24*(1), 23-46. doi:10.1080/0790831 8.2010.527347

Kraif, O., Antoniadis, G., Echinard, S., Loiseau, M., Lebarbé, T., & Ponton, C. (2004). *NLP tools for CALL: the simpler, the better*. In InSTIL/ICALL Symposium 2004. Retrieved from http://www.cs.columbia.edu/~amaxwell/candidacy/l2learning/iic4_009.pdf

Tschichold, C. (2014). *Challenges for ICALL*. Keynote speech, 2nd workshop on NLP for computer-assisted language learning NoDaLiDa workshop, May 22, 2013, Oslo, Norway. Retrieved from http://spraakbanken.gu.se/sites/spraakbanken.gu.se/files/ICALL_handout_invited_talk.pdf

Learners' agency in a Facebook-mediated community

Greg Chung-Hsien Wu[1] and Yu-Chuan Joni Chao[2]

Abstract. Agency, defined by Gao (2013) as learners' "dynamic strategic behavior" (p. 29) in response to contextual realities, has been central to educational undertakings. While the affordances of social networking sites like Facebook have been extensively examined in a number of educational studies, there has been a scarcity of research on critically appraising language learners' agency in the Facebook community. By exploring learners' agency, this study aims to unveil language learners' self-regulation, autonomous action, and decision-making. Five Taiwanese third-year English majors were recruited as case subjects for the qualitative inquiry. They participated in an extracurricular project for vocabulary learning in Facebook. Data triangulation comprised a set of pre- and post-vocabulary tests to investigate their progress in acquiring academic words, an open-ended questionnaire for their perceptions of the online learning experience, and the data of their postings and interactions in this Facebook community. Results from the in-depth interview reveal that learner agency in vocabulary learning via Facebook depends on their strategically selecting (1) academic words to post, (2) Google images to illustrate the referred words, and (3) online dictionary definitions. In addition, interactiveness and responsiveness among the Facebook community members support the creation of an "affinity space" (Gee, 2003) for the learners that stimulates a critical awareness of their self-regulation and learner autonomy. The pedagogical implication is that the Facebook-mediated community can enhance the interactive learning activity.

Keywords: Facebook, learner agency, learning community.

---

1. National Chengchi University, Taipei, Taiwan; dearcutiepie@gmail.com

2. Providence University, Taichung, Taiwan; joninz@gmail.com

How to cite this article: Wu, G. C.-H., & Chao, Y.-C. J. (2015). Learners' agency in a Facebook-mediated community. In F. Helm, L. Bradley, M. Guarda, & S. Thouësny (Eds), *Critical CALL – Proceedings of the 2015 EUROCALL Conference, Padova, Italy* (pp. 558-563). Dublin: Research-publishing.net. http://dx.doi.org/10.14705/rpnet.2015.000393

1. Introduction

Social media provide the users with synchronous applications to enhance multilateral interaction, facilitate community-building and make meaning through multi-modal content. With the surge in Web 2.0 applications over the recent years, each virtual platform boosts a wide range of attributes such as distinct user agency, reciprocal interactivity, collaborative participation, or polyfocal attention structure (Ang & Zaphiris, 2005; Golonka et al., 2014; Scollon & Scollon, 2004; Wesch, 2007).

Facebook, among all the contending social networking sites, has established itself as the most distributed platform, where visual/textual presentations, aural/verbal communications and synchronous/asynchronous interactions all become reality. Research related to language education through the medium of Facebook has thus proliferated globe-wide (see, e.g. Blattner & Fiori, 2009; Blattner & Lomicka, 2012; Çoklar, 2012; Jones & Hafner, 2012; Wu, Marek, & Huang, 2012). Nevertheless, there has been scarcity of research on critically appraising language learners' agency in the Facebook community.

Agency, defined by Warschauer (2005), is "the power to take meaningful action and see the results of one's decisions and choices" (p. 45). Taking the contextual and structural realities into account, Gao (2013) further contends that agency refers to learners' strategic behaviors in coping with the world and entails each individual's "self-consciousness, reflexivity, intentionality, cognition, and emotionality" (p. 227). Drawing on the concepts of learner agency and aiming to unveil language learners' self-regulation, autonomous action, and decision-making, this research focused on five third-year undergraduates who voluntarily participated in an extracurricular vocabulary learning project on Facebook.

All of these five participants, three males and two females, were English majors. One male participant was Japanese whereas the rest were all Taiwanese. Within this project that lasted for three weeks, each participant was required to accomplish their own learning task by joining a Facebook community and serving dual roles in their own community: as a teacher to select and post vocabulary words along with their corresponding images and definitions for other participants and also as a learner to respond to others' postings. Each Facebook community consisted of five members in conjunction with five weekdays when each member was expected to post at least one academic word a day. Two of the female participants were partners to each other within the same community while each of the male participants participated in three different communities.

2. Method

This qualitative study was conducted in an attempt to explore learners' agency within three weeks of online vocabulary learning in a Facebook community. Data triangulation comprised a set of pre- and post- vocabulary tests to trace their progress in acquiring academic words, an open-ended questionnaire for their perceptions of this online learning experience, and the artifacts inclusive of their postings and interactions in this Facebook community.

Upon completion of this project, a semi-structured interview was also conducted as the primary research instrument. This entire spectrum of data was collected and verified against each other to assure trustworthiness (Lincoln & Guba, 1985; Patton, 1990) of the study. The researchers adopted content analysis (Patton, 1990) and constant comparative methods to analyze and present the findings grounded in the data and to "elaborate on emergent themes and consider theoretical implications" (Duff, 2008, p. 55).

The semi-structured interview protocol, classified into two major domains, is shown below.

Table 1. Topic domain I: vocabulary learning process

Lead-off Question		Follow-up Questions	
1.	How did you decide a word in the list to post?	1	Out of personal interest? Personal amount of need? Easier accessibility? Recent learning encounter?
2.	How and how much time did you find information to write for the chosen word?	2.	How to find the chosen word, the image and the sentence?
3.	How and what did you expect from your vocabulary learning efforts?	3.	What has been acquired? In what way have you acquired them?
4.	Did you have any special experience during this learning process?	4.	Any new cognition about learning a language? Any particular affective episode during the process?

Table 2. Topic domain II: social presence

Lead-off Question		Follow-up Questions	
1.	How relevant is online social constructivist learning to your vocabulary practices in the SDVL project?	1	Why do you believe so?
2.	Does on-line social constructivist learning stimulate your reflective thinking?	2.	Any other constructivist learning experience?
3.	To what extent do you engage in interactive sharing and responding?	3.	The extent of engagement in other FB groups?
4.	Does the peers' responding support you to post more words?	4.	If so, are you motivated to read peer-directed vocabulary? If not, how do you evaluate their online responding?

3. Results and discussion

The results derived from the in-depth semi-structured interview revealed that, to acquire academic vocabulary via the Facebook community, the participants adopted various strategies in selecting (1) academic words to post, (2) Google images to illustrate the referred words, and (3) online dictionary definitions to explain to other members. Behind these strategic behaviors was the fundamental finding that successful vocabulary acquisition relied heavily on the initiative of the learner per se and the learner's own reflexivity, intentionality and emotionality. Before they embarked on learning, they had been conscious of their own weaknesses or preferences, thereby determining to employ an optimal strategy to learn.

In addition, peer-to-peer interactiveness and consistent responsiveness among the Facebook community members proved prophetic to the success of an online learning community. Each community formed an "affinity space" (Gee, 2003; cited by Jones & Hafner, 2012, p. 71) to meet a shared common goal: vocabulary learning, and that stimulated a critical awareness of their own self-regulation and learner autonomy among the participants. The posting and responding regularly recurred, afterwards facilitating the learners' cognitive perception and retention of each newly-acquired word. Pedagogically, the implication of this study was that the Facebook-mediated community did enhance distinct learner agency as well as e-learning interactivity.

4. Conclusions

The encompassing goal of this study was to examine learners' agency as it emerged through his/her social presence in a Facebook community. The roadmap for the future integration of Facebook into students' learning is forthright. On the macro level, while using the Facebook community as a learning medium, the learning partners within the same community are advised to transcend beyond acquaintance level so that meaningful action can be taken and reciprocal collaboration can be ensured (Warschauer, 2005). This is also reiterated by Jones and Hafner (2012), "[s]uccessful communication depends not only on common shared understanding of the culture of the affinity space, but also on more general awareness of the kinds of cultural assumptions that people from diverse backgrounds might bring to the interaction" (p. 115). At the micro level, then, all participants exert a more empowering agency by playing a constructive role as a teacher in his or her community. Instead of being a passive recipient of academic vocabulary, they enjoy taking the initiative for their own learning. Accordingly, as technologies continue to evolve, learners should be given responsibility to maintain their agency.

5. Acknowledgements

Authors are grateful to the Ministry of Science and Technology of Taiwan for financially supporting this project under Contract Number MOST 103-2410-H-126-022.

References

Ang, C. S., & Zaphiris, P. (2005). Developing enjoyable second language learning software tools: a computer game paradigm. In P. Zaphiris & G. Zacharia (Eds.), *User-centered computer aided language learning* (pp. 1-21). Hershey, PA: Idea Group Inc.

Blattner, G., & Fiori, M. (2009). Facebook in the language classroom: promises and possibilities. *International Journal of Instructional Technology and Distance Learning, 6*(1), 17-28. Retrieved from http://www.itdl.org/journal/jan_09/article02.htm

Blattner, G., & Lomicka, L. (2012). Facebook-ing and the social generation: a new era of language learning. *ALSIC, 15*(1). Retrieved from http://alsic.revues.org/2413

Çoklar, A. N. (2012). Evaluations of students on Facebook as an educational environment. *Turkish Online Journal of Qualitative Inquiry, 3*(2), 42-53.

Duff, P. A. (2008). *Case study research in applied linguistics.* New York, NY: Lawrence Erlbaum Associates.

Gao, X. (2013). Reflexive and reflective thinking: a crucial link between agency and autonomy. *Innovation in Language Learning and Teaching, 7*(3), 226-237. doi:10.1080/17501229.2013.836204

Gee, J. P. (2003). *What video games have to teach us about learning and literacy.* New York: Palgrave/Macmillan.

Golonka, E. M., Bowles, A. R., Frank, V. M., Richardson, D. L., & Freynik, S. (2014). Technologies for foreign language learning: a review of technology types and their effectiveness. *Computer Assisted Language Learning, 27*(1), 70-105. doi:10.1080/09588221.2012.700315

Jones, R. H., & Hafner, C. A. (2012). *Understanding digital literacies: a practical introduction.* New York: Routledge.

Lincoln, Y. S., & Guba, E. G. (1985). Establishing trustworthiness. In Y. S. Lincoln & E. G. Guba (Eds.), *Naturalistic inquiry* (pp. 289-331). Beverly Hills, CA: Sage.

Patton, M. Q. (1990). Qualitative evaluation and research methods (2nd ed.). Newbury Park, CA: Sage Publications.

Scollon, R., & Scollon, S. W. (2004). Nexus analysis: discourse and the emergent Internet. London, U.K.: Routledge.

Warschauer, M. (2005). Sociocultural perspectives on CALL. In J. Egbert & G. M. Petrie (Eds.), CALL research perspectives (pp. 41-51). Mahwah, NJ: Lawrence Erlbaum.

Wesch, M. (2007). The machine is us/ing us. Retrieved from http://www.youtube.com/watch?v=NLlGopyXT_g

Wu, W. C., Marek, M., & Huang, H. W. (2012). Using Skype and Facebook as social media to enhance learner communicative competency and cultural awareness in an EFL advanced conversation class. *Proceedings of the 15th International CALL Research Conference* (pp. 681-684). Taiwan: Providence University.

Exploring mobile apps for English language teaching and learning

Bin Zou[1] and Jiaying Li[2]

Abstract. Many recent studies have shown that mobile learning can provide potential possibilities for foreign language learners to practice language skills on their smart mobile phones and tablet PCs (e.g. Chang & Hsu, 2011; Egbert, Akasha, Huff, & Lee, 2011; Hoven & Palalas, 2011; Stockwell, 2010). A number of apps have been created and used for English as a Foreign Language (EFL) learning. However, few studies have given effective examples of tasks for mobile learning. The majority of the existing apps have not yet been very pedagogically useful, due to the possible knowledge gap between the app developers and language teachers (Sweeney & Moore, 2012). Therefore, this study aimed to investigate how mobile apps can be integrated into English language teaching and learning and what sorts of tasks can be employed to enhance learners' EFL learning. A class app was created by the researchers and integrated into English teaching and learning in and out of class. Questionnaires and interviews were conducted so as to explore students' perceptions about the app. The results indicated that mobile learning can be adopted in English lessons and students' self-study. The app which provided sources related to lessons offered extra support to students to practice English in and after class. Participating students expressed positive attitude towards mobile learning.

Keywords: mobile learning, apps, English language teaching and learning.

1. Introduction

Mobile devices, which can be in the form of iPods, mobile phones and tablet PCs, have been an integral part of English learning. During the past decades, technology

---

1. Xi'an Jiaotong-Liverpool University, Suzhou, China; bin.zou@xjtlu.edu.cn

2. Jiaying Li, Xi'an Jiaotong-Liverpool University, Suzhou, China; Jiaying.Li12@student.xjtlu.edu.cn

How to cite this article: Zou, B., & Li, J. (2015). Exploring mobile apps for English language teaching and learning. In F. Helm, L. Bradley, M. Guarda, & S. Thouësny (Eds), *Critical CALL – Proceedings of the 2015 EUROCALL Conference, Padova, Italy* (pp. 564-568). Dublin: Research-publishing.net. http://dx.doi.org/10.14705/rpnet.2015.000394

has developed at an impressive rate, making portable devices equipped with WIFI access, and enabling the third/fourth generation (3G/4G) service to pave the way for the technology-oriented teaching model as well. Mobile learning has been a key issue in the investigation of e-learning (Jeng et al, 2010). It can be seen that enhancement in the mobility and connectivity of mobile devices helps to create a new way for students across different cultures to learn English (Kim, Rueckert, Kim, & Seo, 2013).

Students at Xi'an jiaotong-Liverpool University (XJTLU) normally obtain English sources from Moodle-based internal virtual learning environments during their study. The rapid evolution of handheld devices is changing this via the use of 3G and even 4G. A substantial amount of apps for English learning is also being designed to follow the tendency. Although learning by portable devices has tremendous potential, developing new teaching and learning methods could still be a barrier for educators to put this into practice (Kim et al, 2013). Meanwhile, students' ability of self-control could be another obstruction for mobile learning. For most students, mobile devices are mainly used for entertainment and communication. This study reports on an attempt to design an app to help students access class materials conveniently at anytime and anywhere and investigate students' perceptions about the app. It aims to explore the user experience of the designed app and whether the app is beneficial for academic English learning inside and outside the class. Our research questions included:

- What are students' motivations in mobile-learning tasks on apps?

- What are students' perceptions of features in the English for Academic Purpose (EAP) apps?

2. Method

There were two stages in this study: phase 1 and phase 2. All participants were sophomores majoring in economics or marketing at XJTLU, China, and the age ranged from 18 to 21. All the respondents were from mainland China and were taking an EAP class at the Language Centre at XJTLU, and volunteered to participate in this study.

2.1. Phase 1

40 students from two classes participated in phase 1. The data sources included a questionnaire, interviews and observations. All 40 students completed the

questionnaire and 18 students were randomly involved in interviews. One of the researchers, the English tutor, assigned tasks for mobile learning in class and observed students' usage of apps for English learning. At this stage, the tutor provided some existing apps for English learning including listening, reading, speaking and vocabulary practice both in and outside the class. The tutor adopted blended learning strategies in class, i.e. reading on mobile devices and doing exercises on paper or searching for relevant sources online on mobile devices in class for pair and group discussions. In addition, a class forum on a communication app used on mobile devices (QQ or Wechat) was set up for interaction after class.

2.2. Phase 2

44 students participated in the second phase. Data were gathered through a questionnaire and interviews. All 44 students completed the questionnaire and 19 students were randomly interviewed. Unlike the first stage, the tutor created an EAP app and uploaded some class materials in this app. Apart from resources related to the class, general resources which can help students practice general language skills were also provided in the app including reading, listening, writing and speaking.

3. Discussion

3.1. Students' motivation in various learning tasks on apps

In the first phase, students were asked to complete four types of English learning tasks on suggested apps including listening, reading, speaking and vocabulary practice both within and outside of the class. The results show that participants had high motivation to practice English on these apps. 70 percent of the respondents perceived that they regularly did vocabulary activities outside of the classroom. All students reported that they did reading tasks both in and after class. Despite the fact that some of the respondents prefer reading on paper, the average reading tasks they did via mobile devices rose considerably from seldom to twice a day. Regarding listening practice, more than 70% of the participants felt apps such as BBC, TED Speech and VOA as beneficial for developing their listening skills. The majority of the students practiced listening on those apps several times a day due to their easy access. With respect to speaking tasks, 70 percent of the students stated they were useful, particularly for improving pronunciation. In terms of the communication tool QQ/WeChat (similar to The Line or ICQ), the students contended that it was easy and comfortable for them to communicate in class through the forum on the app with the teacher and the other students. Students felt more confident to discuss lessons in the class forum on their mobile devices. This indicates that it could be one of the good ways/channels for EFL learners to practice English.

3.2. Students' perceptions of features in the EAP app

In the second phase, the results demonstrated students' positive perceptions of features in the EAP app. 80 percent of the students strongly agreed that they enjoyed using the app, which proved that using mobile devices as a learning tool can motivate students' enthusiasm. Furthermore, 87 percent of the respondents valued time-saving and convenient features via the mobiles. Convenience and high-quality contents were considered as the top two significant features for a good app. The majority of the students revealed that learning via handheld devices had become an indispensable part of their lives. Moreover, resources for general English are believed to be beneficial to academic study by the majority of the subjects. For a successful EAP app, therefore, it is important to enhance its convenience and its function to save time, and to ensure high-quality and relevant resources for the learning context.

4. Conclusions

This research aimed to investigate the impact of mobile technologies on college students' English learning activities, in order to understand the current and future situation of mobile learning in general, and the design criteria for good English learning apps in particular. The findings suggested that the majority of the participants held a positive attitude towards mobile learning, and many of them frequently conducted a variety of learning practices on their mobile devices. Then, we explored the efficiency of those existing English learning apps, so as to distinguish the elementary frame of creating our own app. The results indicated that the majority of the subjects enjoyed mobile learning, which can be revealed by their significantly high motivation in carrying out the relevant activities on the apps.

5. Acknowledgements

We would like to thank Xi'an Jiaotong-Liverpool University's TDF (12/13-R6-039) for this study.

References

Chang, C.-K., & Hsu, C.-K. (2011). A mobile-assisted synchronously collaborative translation–annotation system for English as a foreign language (EFL) reading comprehension. *Computer Assisted Language Learning, 24*(2), 155-180. doi:10.1080/09588221.2010.536952

Egbert, J., Akasha, O., Huff, L., & Lee, H. (2011). Moving forward: anecdotes and evidence guiding the next generation of CALL. *International Journal of Computer-Assisted Language Learning and Teaching, 1*(1), 1-15. doi:10.4018/ijcallt.2011010101

Jeng, Y. L., Wu, T. T., Huang,Y. M.,Tan,Q., Yang, S. J. H. (2010). The added-on impact of mobile application on learning strategies: a review study. *Educational technology & Society, 13*(3), 3-11.

Hoven, D., & Palalas, A. (2011). (Re)conceptualizing design approaches for mobile language learning. *CALICO Journal, 28*(3), 699-720. doi:10.11139/cj.28.3.699-720

Kim, D., Rueckert, D., Kim, D.-J., & Seo, D. (2013). Students' perceptions and experiences of mobile learning. *Language Learning & Technology, 17*(3), 52-73.

Stockwell, G. (2010). Using mobile phones for vocabulary activities: examining the effect of the platform. *Language Learning and Teaching, 14*(2), 95-110.

Sweeney, P., & Moore, C. (2012) Mobile apps for learning vocabulary: categories, evaluation and design criteria for teachers and developers. *International Journal of Computer-Assisted Language Learning and Teaching, 2*(4), 1-16. doi:10.4018/ijcallt.2012100101

The use of monolingual mobile dictionaries in the context of reading by intermediate Cantonese EFL learners in Hong Kong

Di Zou[1], Haoran Xie[2], and Fu Lee Wang[3]

Abstract. Previous studies on dictionary consultation investigated mainly online dictionaries or simple pocket electronic dictionaries as they were commonly used among learners back then, yet the more updated mobile dictionaries were superficially investigated though they have already replaced the pocket electronic dictionaries. These studies are also limited in that they concentrated generally on intentional learning and have not much inspected the significance of dictionary consultation for incidental learning. Moreover, most of them selected monosemous words as target lexical items, yet the learning of polysemous words has not been examined in depth. Therefore, in response to the call for research on the effectiveness of mobile dictionary consultation in promoting incidental learning of polysemy, we conducted an experiment among 82 intermediate Cantonese English as a Foreign Language (EFL) learners in Hong Kong, attempting to figure out what challenges these learners encountered while learning target words in the context of reading through consulting mobile dictionaries. These subjects were asked to comprehend a reading text with ten underlined target words, 32 of whom inferred meanings of these words and 50 looked them up using mobile dictionaries. The results of the study showed that mobile dictionaries facilitate word learning significantly, yet the format of these dictionaries is significant, and dictionary training is indispensable.

Keywords: vocabulary acquisition, mobile dictionary, incidental learning, mobile-assisted language learning.

1. The Hong Kong Polytechnic University, Hong Kong; daisy.zou@polyu.edu.hk
2. Caritas Institute of Higher Education, Hong Kong; hrxie2@gmail.com
3. Caritas Institute of Higher Education, Hong Kong; pwang@cihe.edu.hk

How to cite this article: Zou, D., Xie, H., & Wang, F. L. (2015). The use of monolingual mobile dictionaries in the context of reading by intermediate Cantonese EFL learners in Hong Kong. In F. Helm, L. Bradley, M. Guarda, & S. Thouësny (Eds), *Critical CALL – Proceedings of the 2015 EUROCALL Conference, Padova, Italy* (pp. 569-574). Dublin: Research-publishing.net. http://dx.doi.org/10.14705/rpnet.2015.000395

1. Introduction

Playing a significant role in vocabulary acquisition, dictionary use has been the focus of researchers for nearly one hundred years (Lew, 2011). Numerous studies have been conducted and various topics have been explored. With the development of electronic dictionaries, research in their use is abundant. However, previous studies, which were mostly done in the last decade, examined mainly simple pocket electronic dictionaries as they were commonly used among learners then, yet not much research has been conducted to investigate the use of the more updated mobile dictionaries, although they have already replaced the outdated pocket electronic dictionaries. Previous studies are also limited in that they concentrated generally on intentional learning and did not explore the significance of dictionary consultation in the field of incidental learning. Moreover, few studies inspected the facilitative effects of mobile dictionaries for learners' identification of meanings of polysemy in certain contexts. Therefore, in response to the call for research on the effectiveness of mobile dictionary consultation in promoting incidental learning of polysemous words, we conducted a research among Cantonese English learners in Hong Kong.

2. Method

2.1. Research questions

Three questions were raised in this research: (1) does the task of reading and consulting polysemous words in mobile dictionaries and the task of reading and inferencing the meanings of these words significantly promote initial learning and retention of the target words? (2) Are these two tasks similarly effective? (3) From what aspects are they similar or different?

2.2. Participants

82 intermediate Cantonese EFL learners in Hong Kong were involved, 39 females and 43 males. Their ages ranged from 18 to 20, and they had learned English for approximately 10 years.

2.3. The reading text and target words

The text "Coping with Procrastination" from Arlov's (2000) book was adapted. Based on its context, a total of ten polysemous words were selected as the target words. These words (*agitate*, *bromide*, *camouflage*, *catastrophe*, *eclipse*, *lapse*, *perpetual, persecute, ticklish,* and *sterile*) were chosen because they have more than one meaning and all convey familiar concepts to the participants.

2.4. Procedure

All participants were pre-tested to ensure that they had little pre-knowledge of the meanings of the target words in the contexts given by this research. In the experiment, these subjects were asked to comprehend a reading text in which the ten target words were underlined. 32 students inferred the meanings of these words and 50 looked them up using mobile dictionaries. Three dictionary apps were most frequently used, namely: LDOCE 5 (the mobile app of the Longman Dictionary of Contemporary English), Dictionary (the mobile app of dictionary.com) and Oxford Dictionary Quick Search.

To tap into how learners identify the exact meanings of target words using mobile dictionaries, 12 subjects among those who consulted dictionaries were asked to report their thinking processes using different self-reporting protocols. Six of them were trained and asked to do think-aloud while completing the assigned reading and dictionary consultation tasks. The other six were interviewed after their task completion. The remaining 38 subjects were tested immediately after their task completion to measure their initial learning of the target words, and unexpectedly tested again using the same assessment to measure their retention one week later. These two post-tests, which asked the subjects to provide meanings of the target words in given contexts, utilized the same assessment tool. Ten sentences in which the target words have the same meanings as in the reading text were given to the subjects. Two of the researchers graded the answers, giving a score of "1" to a correct answer and a score of "0" to an incorrect one.

3. Results

The scores of the 70 subjects in the immediate and delayed post-tests are shown in Table 1. The mean score of subjects who read and inferred meanings of target polysemous words based on their contexts was 3.48 in the immediate post-test and 2.45 in the delayed post-test. The mean score for those who read and consulted the target words in mobile dictionaries was 4.12 in the immediate post-test and 2.93 in the delayed post-test. The differences in scores of subjects doing different tasks in the pre-test, immediate and delayed post-test are shown in Figure 1.

To investigate whether these two tasks promoted significantly effective initial learning and retention of the target words, four paired samples t-tests were conducted. These four t-tests had the pre-test scores of subjects doing Task 1 and Task 2 and their performances in the immediate and delayed post-tests as the paired variables respectively. Their results showed significant gains of knowledge about the target words, as the sig. values were all smaller than .05.

Table 1. Descriptive statistics of the subjects' scores

	N	Pretest	Immediate posttest		Delayed posttest	
			Mean	Std. dev	Mean	Std. dev
Reading and inferencing	32	0	3.48	4.67	2.45	4.96
Reading and consulting mobile dictionaries	38	0	4.12	4.81	2.93	5.07

To further examine whether significant differences existed between the post-test scores of subjects doing Task 1 and Task 2, two independent samples t-tests were conducted. The first independent samples t-test had the immediate post-test scores of subjects doing Task 1 and those of subjects doing Task 2 as the variables. Its results demonstrated a significant difference between these two sets of scores, as the value of the sig. (2-tailed) was smaller than the significance level of .05. It indicated, therefore, that T1 (paper dictionary) was significantly more effective than T2 (mobile dictionary) in promoting the initial learning of the target words.

The second independent samples t-test was similar to the first one in that it also compared the scores of subjects from these two groups, yet it was different in that the subjects' scores in the delayed post-test were compared. The two variables here were the delayed post-test scores of subjects doing Task 1 and Task 2. Significant difference was shown, as the value of the sig. (2-tailed) was smaller than .05, indicating that T1 (paper dictionary) was significantly more effective than T2 (mobile dictionary) in promoting the retention of the target words.

Figure 1. Subject scores in the immediate and delayed post-tests

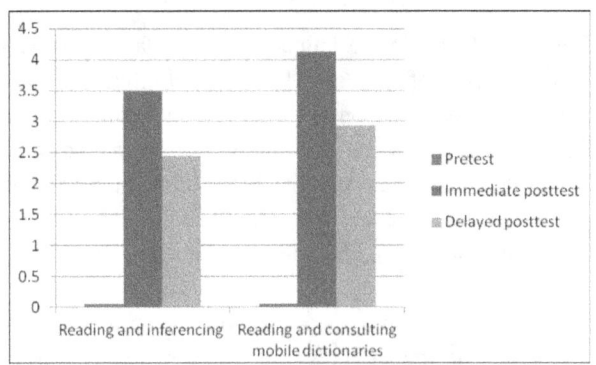

4. Discussion

The results of the study show significant effectiveness of mobile dictionaries in facilitating incidental learning and retention of polysemous words, as the test scores of subjects using mobile dictionaries were significantly higher than those of subjects inferring meanings.

However, the facilitative effects are limited in that the screens of mobile phones are too small to show all the information at once, and users find it difficult to have a brief view of all listed meanings of the target words. Such inconvenience, together with the restriction of learners' language processing capabilities, results in the difficulty of storing several pieces of information in short-term memory, thus further hindering learners from making full use of the rich information provided by mobile dictionaries.

We also observed that some subjects wrote down candidate meanings to solve such problems and assist meaning determination. Our qualitative data collected through self-reporting protocols highlight the importance of dictionary format as learners revealed that they benefited more when dictionaries use diverse colors, fonts, sizes and categories to present different types of information.

Moreover, many learners acknowledge that they were not good at making use of the information provided by mobile dictionaries; dictionary training is therefore necessary. Also, the format is very important. It's important to use different colors, fonts, sizes, space and zones to highlight different parts of speech, meanings and collocations. These make it a lot easier for learners to categorize different information and should help them process it more efficiently.

5. Conclusions

Drawing on a literature review on vocabulary acquisition and dictionary consultation, the present paper noted limitations of previous studies in this field and reported on a corresponding research on monolingual mobile dictionaries in promoting incidental learning of polysemous words. The results, on the one hand, showed significant facilitative effects of mobile dictionaries in promoting word learning; on the other hand, they revealed limitations of mobile dictionaries. Nevertheless, this study is inherently limited in respect to possible influence of experimental conditions and scope of experiment. Future research is therefore suggested to take account of these factors and offer more insights into this issue.

6. Acknowledgments

The work described in this paper was fully supported by a grant from Research Grants Council of Hong Kong Special Administrative Region, China (UGC/FDS11/E06/14).

References

Arlov, P. (2000). *Wordsmith: a guide to college writing.* Upper Saddler River, New Jersey: Prentice Hall.

Lew, R. (2011). Studies in dictionary use: recent developments. *International Journal of Lexicography, 24*(1), 1-4. doi:10.1093/ijl/ecq044

Author index

A
Abrahamsen, Jardar E. 243
Akahane-Yamada, Reiko 261
Akita, Yuya 410
Albadry, Haifa 1
Albertsen, Egil 243
Alizadeh, Mehrasa 392
Allen, Christopher 9, 77
Alonso Ramos, Margarita 16
Altinier, Micol 177
Arnbjörnsdóttir, Birna 192
Artese, Marina 24
Arús-Hita, Jorge 36
Averianova, Irina 30
Ávila-Cabrera, José 36

B
Bárcena, Elena 36
Bastian, Pim 274
Bateson, Gordon 91
Bauer, Ciarán 44
Bech, Øyvind 243
Bernhard, Delphine 204
Berns, Anke 51
Bibauw, Serge 57
Billami, Mokhtar B. 204
Bohát, Róbert 65, 71
Bolona Lopez, Maria del Carmen 77
Brick, Billy 450
Brine, John 91
Bruncak, Radovan 120
Bunting, Leona 97
Burden, Tyler 495

C
Cabezas, Ximena 348, 355
Calderón Márquez, Andrea 51
Calle, Cristina 36
Cardoso, Walcir 102, 108
Carlini, Roberto 16
Castello, Erik 114
Castrillo, María Dolores 36
Chao, Yu-Chuan Joni 558
Chen, Hao-Jan 512, 518
Chen, Yu-Hua 120
Chitez, Madalina 125
Coccetta, Francesca 133
Cochrane, Robert 138
Codina-Filbà, Joan 16
Cojocnean, Diana 36, 144
Colpaert, Jozef 439
Cordoni, Giovanni 164
Cornillie, Frederik 150
Cote, Travis 158, 404
Cribb, Mike 450

D
Dantsuji, Masatake 261
Delgado Alvarado, Natanael 480
Desmet, Piet 57, 150
Devitt, Ann 44
Dodero, Juan Manuel 51
Dunn, Robert 502
Duso, Elena Maria 164

F
Franciosi, Stephan J. 170
François, Thomas 57, 204
Fratter, Ivana 177, 181
Frederiksen, Karen-Margrete 186
Friðriksdóttir, Kolbrún 192
Fujii, Kiyomi 198, 235
Fukuda, Eri 228

G
Gala, Núria 204

Garcia Fuentes, Cesar 108
Gaved, Mark 36
Gazeley-Eke, Zoe 450
Gholami, Mahboubeh 210
Gimeno Sanz, Ana 215
Goria, Cecilia 221
Grimshaw, Jennica 102

H
Hashimoto, Shin'ichi 228
Hedayatfar, Keivan 243
Heo, Younghyon 91
Hirotani, Maki 198, 235
Horáková, Nina 65, 71
Husby, Olaf 243

I
Ibañez, Ana 36
Ibáñez Moreno, Ana 249
Iino, Atsushi 254
Ishikawa, Yasushige 261

J
Jauregi, Kristi 268, 274
Jee, Rebecca Y. 281, 324
Jordano, María 36

K
Kaneko, Emiko 91
Karatay, Yasin 288
Karimi Alavijeh, Khadijeh 386
Kartapanis, Iosif 368
Kawahara, Tatsuya 410
Keim, Lucrecia 294
Keisanen, Tiina 301
Kétyi, Andras 36
Kétyi, András 306
Kim, Young-Kil 330, 362
Kiyoki, Yasushi 543
Ko, Chao-Jung 312
Koirala, Cesar 318, 324

Koivisto, Tuomo 274
Kondo, Mutsumi 261
Koreman, Jacques 243
Koyama, Toshiko 36
Kruse, Otto 125
Kukulska-Hulme, Agnes 36
Kurabayashi, Shuichi 543
Kuure, Leena 274, 301
Kwon, Oh-Woog 330, 362

L
Lagares, Manuel 221
Lai, Shu-Li 336
Lambacher, Stephen 433, 458
Lammons, Elizabeth 342
Laursen, Katja Årosin 186
Lazzeri, Santos 348, 355
Lee, Kiyoung 330, 362
Lee, Yunkeun 330, 362
Leinster, Hannah 450
Leiva, Francisca 348, 355
Li, Jiaying 564
Li, Xiaowei 375
Li, Zhenxiao 375
Lloyd, Elwyn 450
Loizides, Fernando 368
Lu, Zhihong 375
Lyddon, Paul A. 381

M
Marandi, S. Susan 386
Marigo, Luisa 181
Martínez-Paricio, Violeta 243
Mehran, Parisa 392
Mehring, Jeffrey 170
Meri, Serpil 397
Meshgi, Kourosh 410
Milliner, Brett 158, 404
Mirzaei, Maryam S. 410
Mohammadi, Mojtaba 210, 416
Momata, Yuko 342

Murase, Fumiko 495
Mynard, Jo 342

N
Nami, Fatemeh 386
Ngo, Thi Phuong Le 421
Ní Chasaide, Ailbhe 427
Ní Chiaráin, Neasa 427
Noguchi, Junko 342

O
Obari, Hiroyuki 36, 433
Oberhofer, Margret 439
Ohta, Tatsuy 543
Ojeda, Luis 348, 355
Okada, Takeshi 444
Okazaki, Hironobu 228
Orol, Ana 16
Orsini-Jones, Marina 450
Ortiz, Margarita Elizabeth 77

P
Pagel, James W. 458
Palomo-Duarte, Manuel 51
Panichi, Luisa 464
Papadima-Sophocleous, Salomi 368
Pareja-Lora, Antonio 36
Pescina, Luigi 181
Pibworth-Dolinski, Laura 450
Pitarello, Adriana 470
Pomposo, Lourdes 36
Pulker, Hélène 475

R
Raindl, Marco 543
Rapp, Christian 125
Read, Timothy 36
Reedy, David W. 458
Reinhardt, Dennis 274
Reyes Fierro, María del Carmen 480
Robertson, Charles E. 486

Rödlingová, Beata 65, 71
Rodríguez, Pilar 36
Rózsavölgyi, Edit 490
Ruiz-Ladrón, Juan Miguel 51

S
Safdari, Nastaran 416
Sakamoto, Yasunobu 444
Sato, Takeshi 495
Sella, Francesca 368
Selwood, Jaime 36
Sevilla Pavón, Ana 215
Sheehan, Mark D. 502
Smith, Craig 261
Smith, George 108
Speicher, Oranna 507
Stollhans, Sascha 507

T
Tai, Sophie 512, 518
Talaván, Noa 36
Tangney, Brendan 44
Thorpe, Todd 502
Thouësny, Sylvie 536
Titova, Svetlana 523
Tokuda, Hideyuki 543
Tseng, Jun-Jie 529
Tsubota, Yasushi 261

U
Underwood, Joshua 36

V
Vazhenin, Alexander 91
Vermeulen, Anna 36, 249
Vialleton, Elodie 475
Vidal, Julie 536
Vincze, Orsolya 16

W
Waddington, David 102

Author index

Wang, Fu Lee 569
Wanner, Leo 16
Waragai, Ikumi 543
Ward, Monica 549, 553
Watkins, Satoko 342
Wu, Greg Chung-Hsien 558

X
Xie, Haoran 569

Y
Yabuta, Yukiko 254

Z
Zou, Bin 564
Zou, Di 569

www.ingramcontent.com/pod-product-compliance
Lightning Source LLC
Chambersburg PA
CBHW052042290426
44111CB00011B/1592